DS

SO-ATF-168

9

1994

FIELDING'S
SOUTHEAST ASIA

Colorado Christian University
Library
180 S. Garrison
Lakewood, Colorado 80226

Fielding Titles

Fielding's Amazon
Fielding's Australia
Fielding's Bahamas
Fielding's Belgium
Fielding's Bermuda
Fielding's Borneo
Fielding's Brazil
Fielding's Britain
Fielding's Budget Europe
Fielding's Caribbean
Fielding's Europe
Fielding's Far East
Fielding's France
Fielding's Guide to the World's Most Dangerous Places
Fielding's Guide to the World's Great Voyages
Fielding's Guide to Kenya's Best Hotels, Lodges & Homestays
Fielding's Guide to the World's Most Romantic Places
Fielding's Hawaii
Fielding's Holland
Fielding's Italy
Fielding's London Agenda
Fielding's Los Angeles Agenda
Fielding's Malaysia and Singapore
Fielding's Mexico
Fielding's New York Agenda
Fielding's New Zealand
Fielding's Paris Agenda
Fielding's Portugal
Fielding's Scandinavia
Fielding's Seychelles
Fielding's Southeast Asia
Fielding's Spain
Fielding's Vacation Places Rated
Fielding's Vietnam
Fielding's Worldwide Cruises

FIELDING'S SOUTHEAST ASIA

The Adventurous and Up-to-the-Minute Guide to the World's Most Exotic Regions

by
Wink Dulles
Robert Young Pelton

Fielding Worldwide, Inc.
308 South Catalina Avenue
Redondo Beach, California 90277 U.S.A.

Fielding's Southeast Asia
Published by Fielding Worldwide, Inc.
Text Copyright ©1994 Fielding Worldwide Inc.
Icons & Illustrations Copyright ©1994 FWI
Photo Copyrights ©1994 to Individual Photographers

All rights reserved. No part of this book may be reproduced, transmitted or utilized in any form or by any means, electronic or mechanical, including photocopying, recording, or by any information storage and retrieval system, without permission in writing from the publisher. Brief extracts for review purposes for inclusion in critical reviews or articles are permitted.

FIELDING WORLDWIDE INC.

PUBLISHER AND CEO	**Robert Young Pelton**
DIRECTOR OF PUBLISHING	**Paul T. Snapp**
PUBLISHING DIRECTOR	**Larry E. Hart**
PROJECT DIRECTOR	**Tony E. Hulette**
ACCOUNT EXECUTIVE	**Beverly Riess**
ACCOUNT SERVICES MANAGER	**Christy Harp**

EDITORS

Linda Charlton   **Kathy Knoles**

PRODUCTION

Tina Gentile   **Gini Martin**
Chris Snyder   **Craig South**

COVER DESIGNED BY	**Digital Artists**
COVER PHOTOGRAPHERS — Front Cover	**Hiroji Kubota/Magnum Photos Inc.**
Background Photo, Front Cover	**Craig Aurness/Westlight**
Back Cover	**Paul Chesley/Tony Stone Images**
INSIDE PHOTOS	**Werner Funk, Michael S. Yamashita, Nik Wheeler, Josef Beck and Robert Young Pelton/Westlight**

Although every effort has been made to ensure the correctness of the information in this book, the publisher and authors do not assume, and hereby disclaim, any liability to any party for any loss or damage caused by errors, omissions, misleading information or any potential travel problem caused by information in this guide, even if such errors or omission are a result of negligence, accident or any other cause.

Inquiries should be addressed to: Fielding Worldwide, Inc., 308 South Catalina Ave., Redondo Beach, California 90277 U.S.A., ☎ *(310) 372-4474*, Facsimile *(310) 376-8064*, 8:30 a.m.–5:30 p.m. Pacific Standard Time.

ISBN 1-56952-051-8

Library of Congress Catalog Card Number

94-068357

Printed in the United States of America

Dedication

In memory of Antoinette DeLand

ABOUT THE AUTHORS

Wink Dulles

Wink Dulles, 36, is the Southeast Asia correspondent for Fielding Worldwide. His articles have appeared in numerous national publications and his travel writings on Southeast Asia have been published in newspapers across the U.S. including *New York Newsday*, the *Salt Lake Tribune* and the *Santa Barbara News-Press*. Additionally, Dulles is a contributing writer for *AAA World* magazine, *Escape* magazine and Asia editor for *UFM* magazine. His travels through Cambodia, Thailand and Vietnam will continue to provide Fielding with an invaluable prospective on this burgeoning region of the world.

Dulles likes to think he lives in Bangkok, Thailand but he's usually somewhere in Vietnam or Camboida faced with the grueling job of keeping Fielding's *Southeast Asia* the most up-to-date guide on the market.

Robert Young Pelton F.R.G.S.

Robert Young Pelton, 39, as well as being the publisher at Fielding Worldwide, Inc., is known for his various expeditions across, into and out of Malaysia over the last six years. Having driven, hiked, climbed, caved, trekked, crawled and crashed through East and West Malaysia, he has picked up enough travel tips to fill three books. Coincidentally he is the author of the upcoming Fielding's *Borneo*, co-author of Fielding's *Malaysia* and *The World's Most Dangerous Places*. Pelton lives in Hermosa Beach and Bonsall, California with his wife and twin daughters. When he isn't *ulu*, he raises avocados and black swans.

Letter from the Publisher

In 1946, Temple Fielding began the first of what would be a remarkable new series of well-written, highly personalized guide books for independent travelers. Temple's opinionated, witty, and oft-imitated books have now guided travelers for almost a half-century. More important to some was Fielding's humorous and direct method of steering travelers away from the dull and the insipid. Today, Fielding Travel Guides are still written by experienced travelers for experienced travelers. Our authors carry on Fielding's reputation for creating travel experiences that deliver insight with a sense of discovery and style.

Southeast Asia is rapidly growing and changing. Fielding is keeping on top of the dynamism which is the heart and soul of this very special, exotic and largely untamed region of the world. We've researched this year's edition to include remote and fascinating Indochina, as well as reveal and update other rarely frequented corners and outposts. From visits to hilltribes in northern Thailand and excruciating jungle treks on mystical Borneo to lavish five-star wining and dining in Singapore and Thailand, Fielding's *Southeast Asia* will dazzle you as never before.

Today, the concept of independent travel has never been bigger. Our policy of *brutal honesty* and a highly personal point of view has never changed; it just seems the travel world has caught up with us.

Enjoy your adventure.

R Y P

Robert Young Pelton
Publisher and CEO
Fielding Worldwide, Inc.

Fielding Rating Icons

The Fielding Rating Icons are highly personal and awarded to help the besieged traveler choose from among the dizzying array of activities, attractions, hotels, restaurants and sights. The awarding of an icon denotes unusual or exceptional qualities in the relevant category.

RATINGS
Fielding Award · Author Selection · Money Saver · Expensive · Quality · Warning · Danger · Inexpensive · Mild Disapproval · Spacious · Cramped

CULTURAL
Museum/Art · Interesting Architecture · History · Book Reference · Artistically Important · Musically Interesting · Cultural Archeology · Crafts · Theatre

SIGHTS
Picturesque · Great Scenery · Market · Beaches/Resorts · Cultural · Fortress · Castles · Church

WHERE TO STAY
Simple · Luxurious · Cottage · Bed & Breakfast · Scenic · Business · Honeymoon · Chateau

TRAVEL TIPS
Arrival/Departure · By Air · By Water · By Train · By Car · Bus/Local Transit · Barge · River Boat · Calendar · Itinerary · Compass · Kids

ACTIVITIES
Downhill Skiing · X–country Skiing · General Sports · Water Sports · Sailing · Scuba Diving · Snorkeling/Diving · Deep-sea Fishing · Freshwater Fishing · Swimming · Hiking · Walking · Relaxing · Golf · Tennis · Horseback Riding · Cycling · Workout

SPECIAL INTEREST
Mystery · Singles · Romantic · Nude Beaches · Lecture · Spectacular Cuisine · Wine Tasting · Shopping · Nightlife · Cafe Stops · Gardening · Pro Sports

TABLE OF CONTENTS

LIST OF MAPS

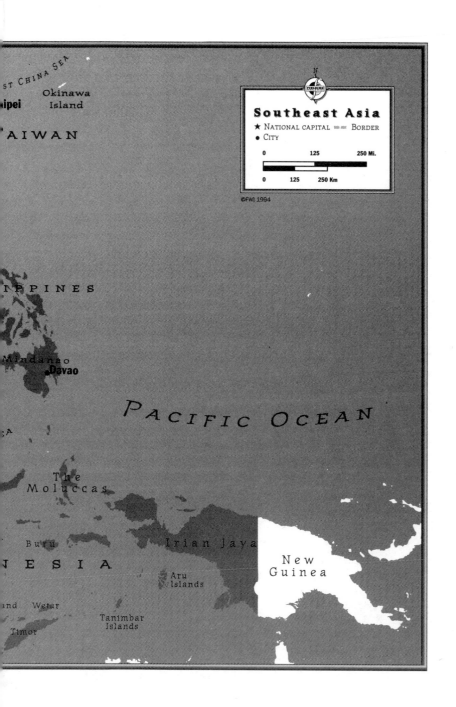

ST CHINA SEA

Okinawa
Island

ipei

TAIWAN

Southeast Asia

★ NATIONAL CAPITAL ▬ ▬ BORDER
● CITY

| 0 | 125 | 250 MI. |

| 0 | 125 | 250 Km |

©FWI 1994

IPPINES

Mindanao
Davao

PACIFIC OCEAN

The
Moluccas

Buru

Irian Jaya

New
Guinea

NESIA

Aru
Islands

nd   Wetar

Tanimbar
Islands

Timor

INTRODUCTION

Welcome to Tomorrowland, where life is both a day in front of you and centuries behind you.

This is a brand new edition of Fielding's *Southeast Asia* and if any book in the series requires constant updating, it is this one. Explore the exotic, mysterious region of East Asia called Indochina including Vietnam, Cambodia and Laos as well as the wild island of Borneo.

Southeast Asia is the world's fastest changing region. From Myanmar to Mindanao this region is exploding. Economic prosperity is transforming the face of the region as Asian Pacific Rim countries make the transition from agrarian-based economies to manufacturing-based ones. Whereas the United States is oozing along at about a three percent per annum growth rate, Thailand enjoys nearly 10 percent annual growth. Malaysia is cruising at an eight percent per annum rate. Vietnam, a 30-year nemesis of the United States is undergoing unparalleled growth, its economy enjoying an astronomical near double-digit growth rate.

Why the boom in Southeast Asia?

Manufacturing accounted for 13 percent of Malaysia's gross domestic product in 1970. The figure grew to nearly 30 percent by 1990. Indonesia's 13,000-plus islands are sitting atop more than eight billion barrels of oil and 85 trillion cubic feet of gas. We could go on.

So it is with some trepidation that we prepare this intro to Fielding's *Southeast Asia*, because as these words are committed to paper, they become out of date. Southest Asia has a maddeningly invigorating habit of doing exactly what you expect the least. Gentle people stage bloody uprisings. Nations hurl themselves from capitalism to religious fanaticism overnight—and vice versa. If one thing is the same in Southeast Asia, it is change.

For 47 years, Fielding has been renowned for its expertise in the globe's more "civilized regions"—such as Europe, Hawaii and the Caribbean. But now, our pioneering books also explore the remote cultures of Borneo and Africa, Mexico and Brazil. And, of course, Southeast Asia.

WHO IS THIS GUIDE FOR?

Fielding's *Southeast Asia* is designed to be more fun than the penurious tomes and dull squeaking of the backpacking guides, with less air-conditioned sterility of the business guides. It's more exciting than the white bread guides and more opinionated than all of them combined. Fielding's *Southeast Asia* is for the person with a lust for the foreign but with a healthy fear of the unknown. You're college educated, have traveled before and really want to get into Southeast Asia, not just surf. This is the guide to lean on when you get confused, tired or hurried—and the one to ignore when you're on a roll.

A WORD ABOUT GUIDEBOOKS

Guidebooks, even this one, aren't the end-all for managing your Southeast Asian adventure. Southeast Asia is a highly dynamic and constantly changing environment. Although Fielding's *Southeast Asia* listings are up-to-date right to press time, businesses, eateries, hotels and tour companies both in and pertaining to Indochina and Southeast Asia are in a constant state of flux. Phone numbers change. Faxes are installed. Businesses boom and bust. Tour companies come and go on the scene as fast as Vanilla Ice. In fact, two calls to Asian tour companies based in the U.S. that are listed in one shoestring traveler's 1994 guide to Vietnam were greeted with disconnection announcements and a third was answered by a bubbly but bemused receptionist at a carpet store in Fountain Valley, CA.

WHERE THE HECK IS SOUTHEAST ASIA?

For most Westerners it's on the other side of the world. Twenty four hours aboard a plane or two or three and you're there. Sure it's a haul. But while Aunt Tess and Uncle Bill are getting toured to death on a bus in Belgium, you're checking out shrines built before there *was* a Europe—cultures and monuments so old they predate written history.

To see just how large this region is, get out the Rand McNally. The Indonesian archipelago, above Australia, is the start of the long southern East Asian arc. It runs north through Malaysia, Thailand and Myanmar—flanked on the east in the South China Sea by Borneo and the Philippines. It curves east through Laos, Cambodia and Vietnam and runs up the China coast.

WHAT'S IT LIKE?

Southeast Asia offers some of the world's most mysterious and exotic attractions. It possesses a beautiful topography. Rain forests here are unmatched in their beauty but unparalleled in the speed of their demise as profit-thirsty industrialists tap into the paydirt of Asia's economic motherload. If the region has had its fill of Western colonialism and domination, it is still very much the virgin for economic exploitation.

The region's new riches have made more evident an astoundingly impoverished societal undercarriage, which really can only be called such because there are now other hugely-rich stratas for comparison. Indonesia's annual per capita income is about $435. The average Vietnamese makes a little over US$200 a year. Laotians average about $180 a year. Any trip to this strange land will open your eyes to extremes you have never before encountered, from economic to religious.

The ballooning cities reveal Asia's remarkable paradoxes. Jakarta, Bangkok and Manila are smog-choked urban sprawls; their people and cars and motorbikes and toxic-cloud-spewing buses packed into rail-thin boulevards like sardines. The noise levels of these cities are not to be believed. And whereas visibility conditions are conventionally discussed among airline pilots and scuba divers, they are of equal importance to sidewalk pedestrians, who traverse metropolitan Southeast Asian arteries in surgical masks to prevent absorbing the thick copper toxic haze that blankets these cities as if in punishment for such a dearth of central planning.

But there are diamonds in the bowels of these urban mines—magnificent ancient temples and museums whose collections date back millennia. There are spectacular hotels and resorts. There are festivals and definitively exotic native dances. And there is the genuine warmth of the Southeast Asian people, whose hospitality belies the jaded neuroses these urban conditions would undoubtedly inflict upon the average Westerner who had to endure them for any length of time.

But these very cities have also become the destinations for the 1990s. In a word, Southeast Asia is hot. For instance, travel is Thailand's single biggest earner of foreign exchange. During the late 80s, these revenues tripled. More than 264,000 Americans passed through this exotic land in 1994. Even the Philippines is being "rediscovered" by Westerners after years of political upheaval, with most visitors saying "I shall return." And if any two countries are truly indicative of the surge in interest in the Far East, Vietnam and Cambodia would have to be riding in the rostrum. In Cambodia, for instance, tourism has enjoyed a whopping 4500 *percent* increase in the past six years. (However, in an ominous turn of events, it's worth noting that tourism to Cambodia has plunged in recent months due to a deteriorating political situation and the resurgence of the Maoist Khmer Rouge, who have recently gained decisive military victories in the battlefield against Cambodian Royal Government soldiers.) In Vietnam, Americans and others are descending upon this paradisiacal nation in droves.

Whereas Europe has served as the traditional target of foreign jaunts by North Americans, travelers these days are tossing around names like Kuala Lumpur, Phnom Penh and Phuket like they once spoke of Amsterdam and Paris.

And, of course the real Southeast Asia lies beyond the cities. It's found on the rice terraces of Bali, around the spectacular volcanos of Indonesia, and in the smoky temples of Bagan. It's found along the banks of the bountiful Mekong in Laos and in the mountain villages of Taiwan and Thailand. It's found in longhouses in the deepest jungles of Borneo. It's chronicled in the works of Maugham, Hesse and Conrad. It is the darkness of Southeast Asia that is its true beacon.

Southeast Asia, for all its part proud, part shameful—and certainly lengthy—heritage, is just being born in many ways and is most assuredly an embryonic host to the seasoned traveler. In its race to beat the West at its own game, much of its heart is now ensconced by Windsor knots and stock tape; but don't let that fool you. It just takes looking a little harder to discover Southeast Asia's soul.

SOUTHEAST ASIA AT A GLANCE

COUNTRY	AREA (SQ. MI.)	POPULATION	LANGUAGES	RELIGIONS
Brunei	2227	250,000	Malay, English, Chinese, Iban	Islam
Cambodia	69,900	8 million	Khmer, Vietnamese, Chinese, English, French	Theravada Buddhism
Indonesia	736,000	175 million	Indonesian (dialects)	Muslim, Protestant, Catholic
Laos	91,430	4 million	Lao, French	Buddhism
Malaysia	127,316	18 million	Malay, Chinese, English, Tamil	Muslim, Hindu, Buddhism, Taoism, Christianity
Myanmar	262,000	38 million	Burmese, English	Buddhism
Philippines	117,187	59 million	Pilippino, English	Catholicism, Protestantism, Muslim
Singapore	239	2.6 million	English, Chinese, Malay, Tamil	Buddhism, Taoism, Christianity, Muslim, Hindu
Thailand	198,114	57 million	Thai, English	Buddhism
Vietnam	127,330	71 million	Vietnamese, French, Chinese, Khmer English	Buddhism, Hao Hao, Cao Dai, Christianity, Islam

DON'T THEY HAVE
A LOT OF WARS THERE?

Yep, they sure do. There are rebel factions in the Philippines, Timor, Myanmar, Cambodia and the Moluccas. But these groups, with the exception of Cambodia's Khmer Rouge, rarely target tourists and clashes typically occur in highly remote areas. Rebel insurgents of Southeast Asia are not typically of the nasty "off 'em all" predisposition of the IRA or the Muslim fundamentalists who bomb shoppers and skyscrapers in New York City.

Tourists could take relative comfort in the presence of more than 22,000 peacekeepers in Cambodia during 1992 and 1993 in avoiding nasty encounters with Khmer Rouge guerrillas, who today still control a full 20 percent of Cambodian soil, much of it the provinces of Siem Reap, Battambang and Banteay Meanchey. There's no evidence at press time that the Khmer Rouge have stepped up their activities with the departure of UNTAC troops. But we wouldn't count on these guys to start working rice paddies anytime soon.

Tioman Island off the east coast of peninsular Malaysia

Additionally, there are an estimated six million land mines buried in Cambodian soil and tonnes of unexploded ordnance lying about. Never, never stray from roads and marked paths.

If the growth of the Philippine Armed Forces from 60,000 troops in 1972 to more than 150,000 in the late 1980s doesn't reveal enough heed to the country's communist insurgents, little else will. Communist rebels, namely members of the New People's Army were active all across the country in the 1980s and even initiated urban sorties during the latter part of the decade. There is calm presently, however. It's still best to take at least some degree of caution when traveling anywhere through the rural Philippines. In the southern region, armed Muslim rebels belonging to the Moro National Liberation Front are engaged in a semi-effort to secure independence for the nation's Muslim population. It shouldn't pose any danger for tourists, however.

In South Korea, the level of urban anti-Americanism rises and falls like a thermometer on a Pennsylvania back porch. Violent clashes between students and police are common, although foreigners are rarely targeted.

Finally, independent travel through the Golden Triangle area is discouraged due to the proliferation and abundance of men with guns. Beware.

For up-to-the-minute recorded information on these and other hot spots call the U.S. State Department's travel advisory line, ☎ *(202) 647-5225.*

The Countries of Southeast Asia

Brunei

SUMMARY

Brunei neither wants nor attracts tourists. It's small, boring, expensive and easy to miss. The best places to see—the government won't let you. So spend some time in Sabah and Sarawak instead. Strictly for country counters and expats.

HIGHLIGHTS

The palace, the palace and the palace and most of all, **leaving**.

Cambodia

SUMMARY

Untamed and entirely exotic. **Angkor** temple complex perhaps the most spectacular in the world. Millions of land mines sprinkled about. Don't play in any softball games.

HIGHLIGHTS

In Phnom Penh: **The Royal Palace** and the **Silver Pagoda**. Also the horrifying **Tuoi Sieng Museum**. The **Hotel Cambodiana** is worth seeing, but not staying at unless you're loaded. Just outside the city are the killing fields of **Choeung Ek**. *Near Siem Reap:* The astounding temples at Angkor, particularly **Angkor Wat, The Bayon** and **Ta Prohm**. Cambodians are a wonderful and friendly people. You'll not want to leave, except maybe to get a decent shower.

Indonesia

SUMMARY

The world's largest Muslim nation is a seething powerhouse of diversity. To describe it as a country is a mistake. If anyone could visit all 13,605 islands there'd still be plenty to see. Best known for the Aussie and German tourist mecca of **Bali**. Indonesia can be a remote jungle trek in **Kalamantan**, or an intense cultural lesson on the island of **Java**. It's an acquired addiction of seasoned travelers. Also for a 1-2 week visit for seekers of the exotic.

HIGHLIGHTS

Bali, of course, but it's overrun compared with the other islands. In Jakarta: the **Central Museum** and the **Presidential Palace**. Also **Krakatoa**. Beautiful areas on **Java**, **Sumatra**, **Sulawesi** and **Irian Jaya**. **Sumba** is pristine. **Flores** offers great diving. *Borneo is wild.*

Laos

SUMMARY

Scenic country of remote hilltribes and ancient temples. So is Thailand and there's less of a chance you'll get your butt shot off in the latter. If you're doing northern Thailand, Vietnam or Cambodia, Laos makes a good stop. Not as enchanted as Myanmar and more backward than Cambodia.

HIGHLIGHTS

Plain of Jars. The **Morning Market** in Vientiane and the **Royal Palace** in Luang Pranbang. The **Bolevens Plateau** and the **Mekong Islands**. Want to find a nice cozy hotel? Build it.

Malaysia

SUMMARY

For the genteel or the adventurous. Malaysia's split personality makes it the adventure destination with training wheels. No Kalishnakovs, no cheap Soviet-made uniforms—just the well-oiled machinery of a country hitting the big time. Even the flag looks like ours. Take your pick of the mainland (for fun or adventure) or Borneo (for outdoor adventurers).

HIGHLIGHTS

Kuala Lumpur with its beautiful **mosques** and dazzling architecture. The **train station** and the **National Mosque**. **Chinatown** and the **Central Market**. Elsewhere there are the **Cameron Highlands, Penang** and **Malacca**. The east coast is unspoiled. **Langkawi** is a nice resort south of the Thai border. Treks into the jungle to meet the Dyaks and Ibans. Sabah and Sarawak are an extreme adventure. Don't miss **Kinabalu National Park**. Beautiful country.

Myanmar

SUMMARY

The Land of the Pagodas. Very controlled tourist access permits trips to the must-see city of **Yangon** (Rangoon). The remarkable **temple of Shwedagon** and the temple plains of **Bagan** make the maximum 15-day stay well worth it.

HIGHLIGHTS

We just mentioned them. Also the **National Museum** in Yangon and the **Mandalay Palace** in Mandalay. Numerous temples in Bagan. Of note are **Gawdawpalin, Mahabodhi** and **Shwezigon** pagodas.

Philippines

SUMMARY

Off the usual Asian itinerary; a largely undiscovered paradise. Travel is safe. A diverse people living on jewels for islands. A beautiful, mountainous land, but a little worn around the edges. See it for a week or a month.

HIGHLIGHTS

In the **Luzon Islands** there's **Baguio** at 5000 feet. In Manila, there's **Chinatown** and **Malacanang Palace**. **Mindanao** is dramatic and beautiful and home to some obscure tribes. In the **Visayas**, see **Bohol** with its chocolate hills.

Singapore

SUMMARY

Dallas East or Chinatown on steroids. Mercifully this crossroads of Asia needs only about two days to see its tacky tourist attractions and shopping malls. Squeaky clean. This town needs an edge.

HIGHLIGHTS

Raffles Hotel and **Raffles Plaza** and anything else called **Raffles**. Bugis Street is gone and the attempt to recreate the old "red light" zone is pink. Also **Underwater World** on Sentosa. There is some Asia left in **Chinatown**. **Orchard Road** for shopping.

Thailand

SUMMARY

The ideal introduction to exotic Asia. Colorful temples, smiling people. **Bangkok** is where you can break all the rules you were taught as a kid. Up north, **Chiang Mai** yuppies create elephant traffic jams visiting "authentic" hill villages. Great beaches in the south and just about everything else you came to Southeast Asia for.

HIGHLIGHTS

Bangkok's **Grand Palace**, **Jim Thompson's House** and the **National Museum**. Also **Wat Phra Keo**. Have a drink at the **Oriental Hotel**. Also catch the **floating markets**. **Hill tribes** in the north and beautiful beaches at **Phuket**, **Ko Phi Phi** and **Ko Samui** in the south. **Ko Samet** off Rayong is open again. **Mae Hae Song** in the northeast is a popular place with two new resorts.

Vietnam

SUMMARY

Plugged as the next big tourist destination. The south welcomes Americans with open arms; the north is a bit more reticent. It'll take a while, but with a developed infrastructure, Vietnam will take on the trappings of Thailand.

HIGHLIGHTS

Vietnam's natural beauty is unmatched—the best reason to come here followed closely by the people. Man-made attractions pale in comparison. If you must, there's **Ho Chi Minh's Mausoleum** in Hanoi. Also the **Fine Arts Museum**. In the south, the **War Museum** and the **Reunification Palace**. Also the **Chu Chi tunnels**. The **Rex Hotel** is a good place to have a drink and watch the sunset.

THE SOUTHEAST ASIA PSYCHOGRAPH

Or East Asia made easy. You're about to travel 10,000 miles or more. Why? Where do you want to go? Not sure? Hey, join the club. If you're a Methodist preacher you're not coming to Southeast Asia to hit the club scene on Bangkok's Patpong streets (at least that your flock is aware of). And you sure as heck shouldn't come to Laos for the beaches. Are you coming for the karma, the shopping or the sin? Let the following help you decide your intinerary.

Credit card heaven	Singapore ★★★ Malaysia ★★
Where you better have a lot of money, honey	Singapore ★
Historian's Nirvana	Cambodia ★★★ Myanmar ★★★ Indonesia ★★ Malaysia ★★ Vietnam ★★
The Orang Puteh (Malay for White Man) route	Thailand ★★★ Malaysia ★★ Indonesia ★
Seeking enlightenment	Myanmar ★★★ Laos ★
The why are you here and when are you leaving tour. For people who think observation by unsmiling people with over-sized sunglasses is part of the adventure	Cambodia ★★★ Myanmar ★★ Brunei ★ Laos ★
The let's eat tour. For people who travel with their stomachs	Singapore ★★★ Malaysia ★★ Thailand ★ Vietnam ★
Marge, stand next to the funny man with the orange bedsheet tour. A cultural feast or for gentle culture shock	Malaysia ★★★ Thailand ★★★ Vietnam ★★★
I love the smell of napalm in the morning. Adrenaline freaks and Nam buffs	Cambodia ★★★ Vietnam ★★★ Laos ★★ Myanmar ★

THE SOUTHEAST ASIA PSYCHOGRAPH

Handicraft heaven. Do you think we should charter a cargo jet to take it all home?	**Malaysia ★ ★ ★** **Thailand ★ ★ ★** **Cambodia★ ★** **Myanmar ★ ★** **Laos ★**
For people from Fargo who hate humidity and giant bugs	**Everywhere from Capricorn to Cancer★ ★ ★**
For people from Fargo who hate humidity and giant bugs but can deal with it for a couple of days while they make a lot of money	**Singapore ★ ★** **Vietnam★ ★** **Thailand★**
Six-foot waves	**Indonesia ★ ★** **Vietnam ★**

BEFORE YOU LEAVE

Travel Documents

Before you even schedule your trip, you'll need to get a passport. Check to find the closest passport agency in your area. Passport agencies are located in most large cities and selected post offices across the country. Passports cost $65 ($55 to renew). You'll need two passport photos (most photo shops can shoot them for you) and an original birth certificate. No copies. Allow about 30 days for processing. You'll need visas to visit some countries in Southeast Asia, although many nations will stamp U.S. and Canadian passports with stays from two weeks (Thailand) up to 90 days (Malaysia) free of charge. Visas, where they're necessary, can be had by contacting the consulates of the countries you'll be visiting. Obtain your visa before entering the country. But relax, they all don't need to be had in the U.S. You can also get them on the road.

FOR U.S. CITIZENS: GETTING VISAS

COUNTRY	WHERE TO OBTAIN	GOOD FOR
Brunei	On arrival	*1 week*
Cambodia	On arrival	*2 weeks*
Indonesia	On arrival	*2 months*
Laos	From embassy	*15 days*

FOR U.S. CITIZENS: GETTING VISAS		
COUNTRY	**WHERE TO OBTAIN**	**GOOD FOR**
Malaysia	On arrival	*3 months*
Myanmar	From embassy	*2 weeks*
Philippines	On arrival	*21 days*
Singapore	On arrival	*1 week*
Thailand	On arrival	*15 days*
Vietnam	From embassy	*30 days*

Solo and Group Travel

Solo wandering is probably the purest form of adventure travel, while group or paired travel offers its own rewards. Wandering alone in faraway places takes on a romantic and nomadic aura. Getting from point A to B can become like a pilgrimage. This type of travel courts disaster but is also the most rewarding. It's exploration at its purest, with little to curb adventure except physical stamina and funds. In only a month or two, you will meet more people, do more things and experience more of life's pitches than in a year's worth of group or paired travel. If you travel in remote regions of Southeast Asia, prepare to be arrested, detained, celebrated, attacked, seduced and tricked. It's all part of the experience. But, remember, if you are a woman traveling alone, you're setting yourself up for thieves, thugs and worse. Men certainly aren't immune but are less likely targets.

The next best scenario is traveling with a single friend. The big drawback is the unintended barrier you'll create between yourselves and the locals. You will use the language less, be invited into fewer homes. But this is a better way for women to travel from a security standpoint. Additionally, you won't get as lonely traveling in a pair—and you *will* get lonely traveling solo. A good way is to split up for portions of the trip, arranging to meet at a preset time and place.

Group travel has its rewards if you've only got a week. But that's about it. Essentially, group travel is like relying on the weakest link in a chain. You can never travel faster than the slowest person; accommodations are always full; tables are too small; the prices are always higher—you name it. Group travel turns a simple pleasure into a military exercise.

Packing

The countries discussed in this guidebook lie in tropical latitudes. This doesn't mean a prescription of Bain de Soleil and thongs. In the highlands of countries such as Laos, Vietnam and Malaysia, temperatures can easily reach freezing at night. And in jungle areas so hot your brain turns to jerky, you'll want as much skin area covered as possible to ward off leeches, malarial mosquitos and the fatal bites of scared, hungry, pissed off or playful cobras, vipers, hanumans and kraits. (Lions and tigers and bears, oh my!) And, ladies, remember where you're going. The peoples of Southeast Asia are a tolerant lot, but a show of skin is taboo. Female lib hasn't reached Mindoro yet. And neither has Madonna's book. Longer dresses, pants and bras are *de rigueur* in most places other than the beach and other heavily touristed areas. And especially in religious temples.

Both sexes should bring along light cotton clothing and not a lot of it. You'll probably—and should—get a lot of what you need where you're going. For starters, a few pairs of trousers and a couple of pairs of shorts will do. Two or three short-sleeved shirts max and a single dress shirt. You determine the underwear. Sandals are a good way of getting around; the Asians seem to think so. Walking or hiking boots are a must for the jungle and the mountains. Sneakers are the best all-around bet. Slip-ons will be good if you'll be seeing a lot of temples; laced shoes are not a good idea if you've got a lot of pagodas on your itinerary. A small towel will also come in handy. Another good idea is a day pack; also a fanny pack. Don't bring things you probably won't need: sleeping bag, heavy outerwear, air mattress and such. Unless, of course, the nature of your journey requires this kind of bulk.

AVERAGE TEMPS IN SOUTHEAST ASIA											
CITY	Jan.	Feb.	Mar.	Apr.	May	Jun.	Jul.	Aug.	Sep.	Oct.	Nov.	Dec.
Bangkok	81	83	85	88	85	83	82	82	81	80	79	79
Jakarta	78	78	79	80	80	79	79	79	80	80	79	79
Manila	78	80	83	85	85	83	80	79	79	80	79	78
Penang, Malaysia	81	82	83	83	82	82	82	81	81	81	81	81
Singapore	78	79	80	81	81	80	80	79	79	79	79	79
Yangon, Myanmar	79	81	84	87	85	82	81	81	82	83	82	80

Take along a sewing kit, electrical current adapters and a good Swiss Army knife. Bring contraceptives and condoms. Yeah, condoms. You can get them there, but Asian condoms break like soap bubbles in a pine forest. A *great* insect repellent is essential. Like DEET. Some folks swear by preparations such as Skin So Soft to keep the little buggers away. Keep a marginal supply of duty-free liquor and American cigarettes handy to pay off officials and impress your friends. Johnnie Walker Red Label whiskey is generally the East Asian poison of choice, as are 555 or Marlboro cigarettes. In-country, carry a roll or two of toilet paper. In a lot of places, you won't find it; just a bucket of water. It's why there's not a lot of social grace in the left hand.

Medical

Also essential is a good first-aid kit with all the trimmings. And add to your booty when you get to Asia. A lot of the drugs you need a prescription for in North America you can get over the counter in Southeast Asia. And if you're going remote, painkillers are a great idea. You'll be thankful if you take a fall. We don't know too many docs stateside who will write a downer "scrip" simply because you've said you'll be running in a road rally in Borneo for a month. But bring with you anti-diarrheal drugs such as codeine, Imodium or Lomotil. Also antiseptic and a laxative.

You should receive inoculations against **yellow fever**, **hepatitis B**, **tetanus**, **typhoid**, **cholera** and **tuberculosis**. An **influenza** shot couldn't hurt either. Ask your doctor about malaria pills.

Health Certificates

Some countries will require that you have, under International Health Regulations adopted by the World Health Organization, an International Certificate of Vaccination against yellow fever. Travelers arriving from infected areas will be required to show proof of vaccination against yellow fever. The certificate will also be stamped with the other inoculations that you have received. Any general practice will be able to provide this service.

International Drivers License

These can be obtained at your state's department of motor vehicles offices or through AAA and other automobile associations. The fee is approximately $7. If you're planning on driving in Asia, get one.

International Student Identity Card

The ISIC card can help with discounts on airline tickets and lodging. There's been a surge in bogus cards, which have been readily available in Thailand and Malaysia.To get a real one, contact the Council on International Educational Exchange (CIEE) at *205 E. 42nd Street, New York, NY 10017-5706;* ☎ *(212) 661-1414.*

International Youth Hostel Card

This will help you in the expensive places such as Japan but may be totally unrecognized in Indochina. You can get this card through any youth hostel office. Or write *733 15th Street N.W., Suite 840, Washington, DC 20005;* ☎ *(202) 783-6161.*

Air Travel

There are now myriad airlines that call on the Pacific Rim from the U.S. Keep in mind that some of them are better than others. It's a long way around to the other side of the globe so you might want to pay the extra bucks for more comfort and better service. Not in terms of upgrading your class, but in choosing an airline. For overall service, comfort, friendliness of the flight crew, food and all the amenities, our hats are tipped to Singapore Airlines. For the feeling of entering Asia the moment you step aboard, these are the folks to fly. Not far behind is Thai Airways. Cathay Pacific and British Airways are in the next league, followed by also-rans Northwest, Korean, Air New Zealand, MAS, Garuda Indonesia, JAL and Philippines. Delta and United also call on the Far East. But most Asia flights on these carriers are like a 24-hour trip from Des Moines to Dallas. Ugh!

When choosing an airline, comfort may be as high a priority as price. Some Asian airlines, such as Singapore, Thai and Cathay Pacific realize this and take extra pains to make the 15-25 hour flights enjoyable. Others, such as MAS and Garuda Indonesia, employ seat configurations and meal strategies designed for a maximum number of Asian travelers.

Flights to Southeast Asia in economy class with advance purchase cost between $800 and $1300 return. The cheapest flights involve layovers in places like Tokyo, Seoul, Taipei and Hong Kong. The more isolated the destination, the more expensive. But tickets to Southeast Asia can be had a lot cheaper through the proliferation of ticket brokers in major cities. Flights that typically cost in the $900 to $1000 range at airline ticket counters and through travel agents can be had for as low as $725 through some brokers upon last inspection at the end of 1994. But beware of these guys. Some of them are as fly-by-night as a red-eye to Seoul. Don't give them your credit card number over the phone. Instead, try to pick up your ticket and render payment simultaneously at their offices. Many a traveler has made telephone arrangements only to watch their departure date come and go without having received their ticket in the mail. Look in the Sunday travel sections of big papers, such as the *Los Angeles Times* or the *New York Times*.

You can also obtain discounted multi-destination airline tickets for about twice the usual return fare to a single destination. These tickets may permit you three or four additional destinations but, of course, restrict you to the cities where the carrier flies. Advance Purchase Excursion tickets are also discounted, but you'll be as equally limited in your choice of destinations. Cancellation penalties can also be enormous.

Another cheap source of airline tickets is in Southeast Asia itself. One-way fares, for instance, from Bangkok–Phnom Penh or Kuala Lumpur–Jakarta are much cheaper when the tickets are purchased in Bangkok or Kuala Lumpur rather than in the U.S. Even aboard the same carrier. There are hundreds of travel agancies in most Southeast Asian cities and, if you're looking for the cheapest fares, shop around. Once in Kuala Lumpur, I was comparing one-way fares from Singapore to Bangkok and, after having called at least a dozen KL travel agents, I couldn't find anything better than Korean's U.S.$225 offering. Finally a last call I almost didn't make gave me an agent who put me on an almost empty Air New Zealand flight for a hundred bucks. It pays to shop around.

DISCOUNT TICKET BROKERS	
American Travel Ventures	☎ *(310) 274-7061*
Angels International Travel	☎ *(800) 400-4150*
Bi-Coastal Travel	☎ *(800) 9-COASTAL*
Discover Wholesale Travel	☎ *(800) 576-7770*
Eros Travel	☎ *(213) 955-9695*
Falcon Wings Travel	☎ *(310) 417-3590*
Moon Travel & Tours	☎ *(800) 352-2899*
Sky Service Travel	☎ *(800) 700-1222*
Silver Wings Travel	☎ *(800) 488-9002*
Supertrip Travel	☎ *(800) 338-1898*
Travel Mate	☎ *(818) 507-6283*

Tours

Taking a tour isn't the cop-out you might think it is. Tours can actually be a better alternative to independent travel if you have only a week or two. You won't experience the delays, language problems or other time-consuming idiosyncracies inherent in the culture you're visiting. Of course you won't be truly experiencing the culture with a few of the tours. Others, though, give you a surprising amount of freedom.

Experienced travelers will tell you that bigger things come in small packages. If you've only got a couple of weeks, it doesn't make sense to bounce around Southeast Asia like a good pinball shot. Limit your destinations so you can get more out of them.

There are a lot of tour operators out there and a lot of new ones trying to cash in on Southeast Asia's growing popularity. Get to know as much as possible about a firm before selecting it. Ideally, talk to some other people who've employed the company before. And remember, there are as many different types of tour companies as there are genres of travel. Some folks travel to Thailand to experience extraordinary bas-reliefs—others for an entirely different kind of relief.

SELECTED TOUR OPERATORS	
Abercrombie and Kent	☎ (800) 323-7308
Absolute Asia	☎ (800) 736-8187
East Quest	☎ (800) 638-3449
Globus Gateway	☎ (800) 221-0090
Here Today, There Tomorrow	☎ (800) 368-5965
InnerAsia Expeditions	☎ (800) 777-8183
IPI	☎ (800) 221-3594
Maupintour	☎ (800) 255-4266
Olson Travelworld	☎ (800) 421-2255
Pacific Delights	☎ (800) 221-7179
Sino American Tours	☎ (800) 221-7982
Trans China Holidays	☎ (800) 969-1339

Books

You'll want some reading material for the trip over. Refer to the "Background Material" headings within each chapter for recommended reading on the countries covered in Fielding's *Southeast Asia*.

WHEN YOU ARRIVE

Bug-eyed in an alien environment, exhausted after nearly 20 hours of nighttime, you'll trudge down the concourse toward customs like you would toward the bathroom after a night with a bad lover.

Keep enough wits to change some money. You can do so before getting to customs or after. On the plane you will have filled out a customs declaration form. Those items you have declared will in all likelihood be inspected. And even though the idea of having your belongings displayed is unappealing (and downright frightening if you've got on your person anything marginally to highly suspicious, such as gems, figurines, poached animal parts, Chinese elixirs or heroin paste), it's invariably no big deal unless you've got something to hide. Know what you can take into and bring out of a country before you enter or exit the country.

Language and Culture

There are a lot of nuances that differ among the peoples of Southeast Asia. But for every contrast, there are 10 commonalities. Asians, as tolerant as they are, will expect you to behave in ways and speak with a body language that will fluster you at first. You'll be tempted to be amused by gestures and customs that seem everything from banal to compulsive. But don't be.

Knowing how to dress, present and compose yourself will dispel a ton of potential problems. Remember, it's better to blend in in Asia than to stand out. Dress coolly but conservatively. Shorts, but not short ones, are okay in informal environments. Ladies should cover as much of their bodies as reasonably possible. You don't have to look like a nun, but it wouldn't hurt. No short dresses, except perhaps at resort beaches. Anything you consider sexy will be taken as offensive by your Asian hosts.

Displays of emotion—from affection to anger—are considered crass and rude. Never show anger, regardless of the situation. Asians abhor conflict. Smile even to the man you'd rather kick than converse with. Equally as offensive, in most places, are public displays of sexual affection. Kissing and even holding hands are discouraged in most Asian communities. Save it for the hotel.

When entering an individual's home, remove your shoes; you may, depending upon where you are, need to remove your socks as well. This is always the case at people's homes, although rarely so at hotels and public structures other than religious temples.

Don't pat anyone on the head, including children. It's a sign of disrespect. And what you do with your hands, do with both hands or your right hand only. The left hand is considered unclean. This includes for eating and passing objects to other people. It's a pain in the rear if you're left-handed, but try and follow the rule at least when it's most appropriate, as in ceremonial occasions, toasts in your honor, etc.

The feet are considered unclean as well. When seated, don't point them in anyone's direction.

If eating with chopsticks, place them horizontally across your bowl when finished. Finally, be especially careful of the gestures you make. Symbols that are considered innocent or even complimentary in the U.S. may be misconstrued abroad. For instance, if a Japanese host in any country asks you how your meal is at a restaurant, don't give him the "okay" sign with your thumb and forefinger pressed. It means money, and you may end up being presented the bill at the end of the evening, which for a typical Japanese meal anywhere can be akin to some other countries' gross national products. Flipping someone the bird in the U.S. is an extreme insult. However, at a drunken party in a longhouse in Sarawak, you may have just bought someone's daughter. Careful.

Behaving in Temples

Always remove your shoes before entering an Asian temple of worship. And if seated before a Buddha, sit on your knees, thigh and hip, with your feet extending behind you. Do not sit in the lotus position (cross-legged). No shorts in temples, although some guides will tell you that it's okay. (They just don't want to offend you.) Cameras may or may not be permitted. Usually they're not, but inquire first.

A Word About Language

We'll admit it; the tongues of Southeast Asia make the languages of Europe seem like dialects of English. Learning Mandarin Chinese, Thai, Malay and Vietnamese virtually requires surgery. But a little effort on your part to pick up some rudimentary phrases will go a long way. Unlike huffy Parisians, Asians are honored when you make an attempt to speak their language, as futile and unintelligible as the resulting utterance may be.

It's an old phrase, but not without relevance. When overseas, you are an ambassador of your country. How you treat your Southeast Asian hosts is how the rest of us will be regarded in your footsteps.

BRUNEI DARUSSALAM

Worshippers at Bandar Seri Begawan's Saifudden Mosque

BRUNEI IN A CAPSULE

2226 square miles of an autonomous sultanate...smallest, richest and youngest sovereign nation in the Far East...240,000 population–70% Malay, sizable Chinese and tribal communities...capital is Bandar Seri Begawan (BSB) on bank of Brunei River...Muara major port...oil and gas rich...per capita income over US$20,000...Malay is national language... English second...hot and humid tropical climate...interesting blend of traditional and modern.

The postage-stamp-size country of Brunei Darussalam became the world's 169th sovereign nation on January 1, 1984, ending nearly a century as a willing and loyal protectorate of the British. About the area of Delaware (some 2,226 square miles), little Brunei Darussalam is a 500-year-old sultanate carved from virgin rainforests in Northern Borneo like a succulent filet mignon sandwiched between the East Malaysian states of Sabah and Sarawak off the China Sea.

Although tiny, the world pays considerable attention to Brunei Darussalam because of its oil and gas riches. The nation is very wealthy, indeed. Per capita income is over $20,000, placing it among the world's wealthiest nations. To be sure, the $2 billion or so in exports earned annually from oil and gas is far more than the government can possibly spend, even though all food is imported and beef arrives from the country's own cattle ranch in Northern Australia. (The ranch is reputed to be larger than Brunei Darussalam itself!)

Brunei Darussalam is governed by the sultan, Haji Hassanal Bolkiah Muizzaddin Waddaulah, who calls home the Istana Nurul Iman Royal Palace located on some 350 acres overlooking his capital, Bandar Seri Begawan (formerly called Brunei Town). *The $300 million royal residence, considered the largest and most expensive in the world,* was designed by Filipino architect Leandro Locsin (also known as "Lucky" Locsin because of his lucrative commissions).

The palace is Moorish-Islamic in design and flavor and features a private helipad, underground parking for 800 cars (of which the sultan owns 40 of the sports car variety) and his personal mosque, appropriately gold-domed. There are approximately 900 rooms in the family quarters for the sultan, his two wives and seven children, three brothers and their families. Landscaping is Japanese, the hardwoods are from the Philippines, the tiles from Italy and the furniture American-bought.

History of Brunei

An autonomous sultanate for centuries, Brunei's history is synonymous with that of Borneo. When Magellan's fleet dropped anchor off the port of Brunei Town in 1521, returning from the Philippines sans Magellan, this was the center of a sea-dominant empire stretching from Sarawak to Manila. Brunei's power declined, however, during the 19th century until it was propped up by the first of the white British rajahs to arrive in North Borneo—James Brooke. The discovery of oil in the early 1900s brought quick prosperity. Today, the nation shares only the jungle climate and terrain of its neighbors—

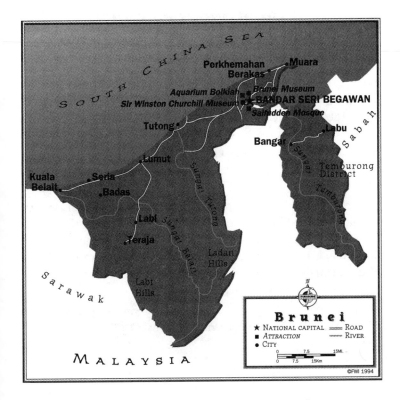

none of its 220,000 inhabitants know anything of poverty or internal political strife.

An Abode of Peace

Completely Islamic, Brunei Darussalam means "Abode of Peace." Its people preserve traditional culture and tradition while enjoying every modern material convenience. It is defended by a military supplemented with some 1,000 Gurkha troops, who helped squash an attempted revolt in 1962, presumably instigated from the outside. All is quiet now and whatever designs the neighbors considered are no longer viable.

Although tourism is certainly not a priority—the country hardly needs the hard currency—Brunei Darussalam is the newest, youngest and richest of the Association of Southeast Asian Nations (ASEAN), which join together to promote economic and social progress as well as cultural development in the region. This joint cooperation is especially seen in the promotion of tourism. The other states in the association are Thailand, Malaysia, Indonesia, Singapore and the Philippines.

A Benevolent Monarch

The 29th sultan is an absolute and benevolent monarch, who is said to have an easy sense-of-humor approach to life and his country. Educated at Sandhurst, the British military academy, he loves fast cars, polo and piloting his own helicopters. He shares the state's oil wealth with his subjects, in the form of electric, water, fuel, and basic staple subsidies. Medical care and schooling are free and the state picks up the tab for university study abroad, pilgrimages to Mecca and junkets to England for many civil servants. There is no such thing as a personal income tax and interest rates are less than one percent!

Although the oil wells are presumed to run dry early next century, no one is worried because the sultan has invested wisely abroad and has some $20 billion in currency reserves—more than Britain or Switzerland. Hence, he can easily present $1 million to the United Nations Children's Fund on the occasion of his country's becoming the 159th member of that world body.

The sultan can also listen to his religious wise men, who picked February 23rd as his country's new National Day.

PLANNING AHEAD

BRUNEI INFORMATION BUREAU

Economic Development Board, Ministry of Finance Bandar Seri Begawan, Brunei (☎ *31794*) is unfortunately the only official tourist information center. Check plans also with local consulates in New York and Washington, as well as the Permanent Mission to the United Nations, *866 United Nations Plaza, Room 248, New York, NY 10017* (☎ *212-838-1600)*, and airlines serving the country. Also ask for Mr. Abdula at the Embassy (☎ *202-342-0159)*.

VISAS

U.S. citizens do not require visas for stays of up to 90 days, provided they are in possession of valid passports and onward or round-trip tickets—but always double check with your carrier for the latest in this regard. If visas are required for just a short tourist stay, go elsewhere.

INOCULATIONS

They're not required for entry and local health officials claim the country is cholera free; however, Americans are advised to have a valid cholera certificate upon arrival.

ENTRY

Entry is through Bandar Seri Begawan's international airport via Royal Brunei Airlines from Singapore, Hong Kong, Bangkok, Manila and neighboring East Malaysian states. Other Far East/Asian airlines also serve the area. A coastal highway links Brunei to the Malaysian state of Sarawak. Taxis to and from the capital cost about $12.50 to $19, depending on your destination, and airport buses start at about $1, but take the Sheraton Utama car service if you are staying at the only international hotel in the country.

DEPARTURE

Departure is via BSB International Airport, which can become congested during Haji, the annual period of pilgrimages to Mecca. There is a duty-free shop at the airport, but liquor is not sold, as this is a strict Muslim country. (Drinks are available to visitors in the restaurant here, however, except during Haji.) There is a departure tax of $B12 to all destinations, except Malaysia and Singapore, where the tax is $B5.

DUTY FREE

Applies only to personal effects, including 200 cigarettes, 1/2 pound of tobacco and 1 quart of liquor (frowned upon). Customs officials are strict on imported items like small electrical appliances and cameras, so declare equipment at airport.

CURRENCY

The Brunei dollar ($B) consists of 100 cents. Brunei notes are in denominations of 1, 5, 10, 50, 100, 500 and 1000 dollars. Coins are in 5, 10, 20 and 50 cent pieces. The exchange rate is approximately $B1.60 to U.S. $1.00. The Singapore dollar is on a par and circulates freely; the Malaysian rianggit has a slightly lower rate. There is no limit on foreign or local currency imported or exported.

LOCAL TIME

Local time in Brunei is Greenwich Mean Time plus 8 hours (13 hours in advance of Eastern Standard Time). Brunei is in the same time zone as Manila, Singapore, Bangkok and Kuala Lumpur.

ELECTRICITY

Local current is 220-240 volts/50 cycles. The populace has all types of fancy, modern equipment and electrical power is good. The PAL system is used by the local television network.

LOCAL WATER

Water is not potable from the tap in most cases. Drink bottled liquids or request boiled water.

OFFICIAL LANGUAGES

Languages in Brunei are Malay, with English widely utilized and understood in business circles. Do not expect to carry on long conversations upriver, however.

BUSINESS HOURS

Business hours in Brunei are 7-8 a.m. to 4 p.m. Monday through Thursday, with a half day on Saturday. Friday is the official Muslim holiday and offices are closed on Sunday. Banks have slightly reduced hours, with lunchtime closing from noon to 2 p.m. Local markets are open from dawn and small shops stay open in the evening.

TIPPING

Tipping varies from person to person, place to place, in this prosperous nation. Tip according to services rendered and the circumstances. Hotels add a 10% service charge.

TELEPHONE, TELEX AND FAX

Services are good if you are in Brunei on business and stay within the confines of BSB. Radio and Television Brunei transmit locally produced programs and programs made elsewhere eight hours daily weekdays, 12 hours on Fridays and 15 hours on Sundays. News broadcasts are in Malay and English. Brunei does have its own color television station, and even longhouse dwellers in the jungle have their own TVs (and personal generators) provided by the government. There is a limited amount of reading matter on the country, but the weekly English-language Bulletin attempts to keep visitors informed about the outside world.

WHAT TO WEAR

Dress in comfortable clothes in this hot and humid climate. Unless you are invited to the palace, you will not need dressy or smart attire. Safari suits for men are fine throughout the day; women should not wear shorts or anything too revealing in respect of Muslim tradition.

LOCAL TRANSPORTATION

Transit by taxis, buses and boats is excellent. There are some self-drive cars available, but traffic is British style (left-hand drive) and can be confusing. An International License is required and minimum age is 23. Hotels will arrange airport transportation with prior notice. Surprisingly, one of the best ways of getting around is with your thumb, especially if you're headed out of BSB. Not that the locals are trying to speed your departure out of town; it's just that they like to chat.

FESTIVALS AND HOLIDAYS

Primarily Muslim but Chinese, Hindu and Christian holidays are also observed.

January 1	*New Year's Day.*
January/February	*Chinese New Year celebrations.*
Variable	*Hari Raya Haji. Celebrated by Muslims to commemorate sacrifice of Prophet Abraham.*
Variable	*First day of Hijrah (Muslim New Year).*
Variable	*Maulud (tenth day of New Year).*
February 23	*National Day.*
May 31	*Anniversary of Royal Brunei Malay Regiment.*
July 15	*The sultan's birthday.*
Variable	*First day of Ramadan (fasting month).*
Variable	*Anniversary of Revelation of the Koran.*
Variable	*Hari Raya Aidilfiltri, a month's feast following the end of Ramadan.*
December 25	*Christmas holiday.*

Bandar Seri
Begawan

Bandar Seri Begawan

BSB IN A CAPSULE

Formerly called Brunei Town, but renamed in 1970 in honor of the sultan's father...a small city with only 80,000 inhabitants...the wealth of Brunei reflected throughout the city...the city was built on the Brunei River...features some memorable museums and mosques.

This is a place you can call Bandar, or even BSB. It's the capital of Brunei and irrefutably the cleanest and most modern city on Borneo.

There is a surprising amount to do in such a relatively small area, situated on an inlet of Brunei Bay—from viewing items of Southeast Asian culture at the Brunei Museum to marveling at the city's mosques. Because Brunei is so rich, it is reflected everywhere in BSB; lawns and grounds all around this compact city are beautifully landscaped. Thoroughly modern architecture marks government and other buildings. You can pretty much walk to all the attractions in BSB and others in outlying areas are quite accessible by taxi.

You won't see a lot of the sights that are commonplace in other Asian cities, namely traffic congestion, garbage, roadside food stalls and beggars. Everything is very tidy in this capital of 80,000 residents.

BSB is split into three areas: the **Old Area**, built in the 1950s; the industrial area called **Gadong**; and the **Seri Complex**, found close to the Sultan's palace.

WHAT TO SEE AND DO IN BANDAR SERI BEGAWAN

Brunei History Centre

The centre was established in 1982. Here visitors can trace the genealogy of the Sultans of Brunei and history of the Sultanate.

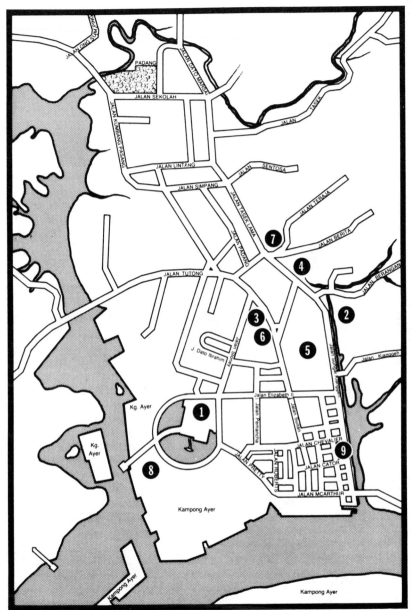

BANDAR SERI BEGAWAN

Key

1) Omar Ali Saifuddin Mosque
2) **Pusat Belia (Youth Center)**
3) Sir Winston Churchill Memorial Museum
4) Sheraton-Utoma Hotel
5) Dewan Majlis (State Council)

6) Aquarium Hassanal Bolkiah
7) Ang's Best Western Hotel
8) Kampong Ayer
9) Brunei Hotel

Brunei Museum

An attractive structure four miles from the center of BSB, it was opened by the sultan and Queen Elizabeth II in 1972. It features spectacular views of Brunei River and houses a fine collection of bronzes, Chinese porcelains, Malay kris (inlaid swords), artifacts of Borneo life and antique Brunei brass, for which the sultanate was famous.

Aquarium Hossanal Bolkiah

Next door to the Churchill Museum. Small but memorable.

Government Buildings

See these magnificent buildings just because they're there: The Language and Literature Bureau Office with its mosaic mural, the Youth Center and Parliament House. All are attractive and beautifully landscaped.

Kampong Ayer

Brunei's water village. A city within the city. Home to some 30,000 people. Actually a series of connecting villages where people live together in houses on stilts (each with its own TV antennae) and sometimes commute to the more modern metropolis. Reached by small motor launches. A fascinating view of how people have lived for centuries. These folks just have a few more modern conveniences than others. Ask about the antiques shops and the last of Brunei's brass workers.

Omar Ali Saifuddin Mosque

Focal point of Brunei. Named after the late sultan. Built with imported materials on reclaimed land beside the Brunei River. Exemplifies the fierce tradition of Muslim worship in an elegant atmosphere made possible only by petro dollars. Don't miss the lagoon in which floats the Mahligai (stone boat).

Royal Tomb and Royal Palace

Pleasant sighting while boating on the river. The royal tomb is less than a mile to the west. The royal palace can be viewed in the distance. Inquire discreetly if palace tours are actually on.

Sir Winston Churchill Memorial Museum

In the city center. The late Sultan Sir Omar Ali Saifuddin was a great admirer of Sir Winston—hence, this fine collection of memorabilia on the last days of the empire. Also pay a visit to the Constitutional Museum, although the Churchill Museum is the gem in town.

Upriver

Upriver is found the lush jungle. It is possible to hire boats for excursions to the longhouse people, the Ibans from Sarawak. Dusun, Muruts, and Settled-Punan also live in villages upriver from BSB, but don't expect too much exotica. They also enjoy the material prosperity of Brunei.

Ardent religious practices and the influx of petro dollars created the elegant atmosphere of the Saifudden Mosque.

Downriver

Downriver features some beautiful beaches along the South China Sea coastline. Good swimming while watching the offshore oil rigs. There are few organized tours available, so be creative.

Bandar Seri Begawan Environs

Kuala Belait

Twenty thousand people live in this small port city on the bank of the Belait estuary. There are shops and a central business district but not much else.

Muara

Although you'll occasionally find a lot of windsurfers at nearby **Serasa Beach**, the beach itself leaves a lot to be desired. A better bet is **Muara Beach**.

Seria

Seria is large by Brunei standards; about 25,000 people live in this oil town. It's the second largest "city" in Brunei. Like other Brunei towns, it was built on the familiar grid pattern. There's a golf course near here, but unless you're an oilman, forget it.

Temburong District

This is the mountainous area of Brunei and you can get to it via plane or boat. The district center is called Bangar; it's a sleepy little town with barely a thousand residents. Longhouses can be found here. Typical for Brunei, expensive cars and television antennas make this a simply bizarre scene.

If you continue up the Temburong River, you'll come upon Batang Duri. Also check out the Kuala Belalong Forestry Center, seeing as you're going upriver anyhow.

WHERE TO STAY IN BRUNEI

Ang's Best Western Hotel   ★★★

Jalan Tasek Lama. ☎ *243553. FAX: 23702.* • *84 rooms.* Simple but comfortable air-conditioned rooms. Friendly service. Restaurant serving Chinese and Western specialties. Bar, swimming pool, hairdresser/barber, meeting room. **Reservations: Best Western Hotels.**

Brunei Hotel   ★★★

Jalan Pemancha. ☎ *242372. FAX: 226196.* • *73 rooms.* Completely renovated in the early 1990s. Restaurant/coffee shop with Western and Chinese dishes. **Reservations: Direct.**

Sheraton-Utama Hotel   ★★★★

P.O. Box 2203, Jalan Bendahara, Bandar Seri Begawan. ☎ *244272. FAX: 221579.* • *170 rooms including 14 suites.* Located opposite Parliament buildings, Churchill Memorial and Park. Transportation arranged from airport, just four miles away. Coffee shop, the Heritage continental restaurant, cocktail lounge. Outdoor pool, meeting facilities, parking, air conditioning, color TV and refrigerator in all rooms. 24-hour service, gourmet shop, beauty salon, gift shop and florist. In short, the only recommended hotel in BSB.

Reservations: Sheraton Int'l.

SAMPLING LOCAL FARE IN BRUNEI

Don't expect much entertainment in BSB, other than a friendly chat with other tourists at the Sheraton or the Royal Brunei Yacht Club—if you happen to know a member. And forget drinking. As this is a strict Muslim country, liquor is served only at designated places and strictly to tourists. The oilfield set have their own private clubs and entertainment, but these are hardly for the casual visitor.

There is plenty of good and interesting food in Brunei, including that succulent beef from Australia! Local dishes run the gamut from Malay curries and rice to Chinese noodles, excellent steaks and local seafood. There are also open-air stalls along the Brunei River opposite Kampong Ayer, which offer a tantalizing array of satay sticks and such, but these are not advised for most delicate American stomachs. Exercise judgment at these and other stalls throughout Asia—or have your Lomotil handy!

Aside from the coffee shop, bar and Heritage continental restaurant at the Sheraton, visitors should inquire of the hotel concierge about good local places to try. There are several, like the **Chayo Phaya** in Klasse Department Store (Thai Muslim dishes) and the **Rasa Sayang** for reasonable Chinese (next to the Chinese Temple).

If you plan to spend a day at one of the lovely beaches, a short drive from BSB, be sure to take along your own food and drink. The Sheraton can pack a lunch and it also has a nice gourmet shop for snack items. (Be sure to include sunscreen and some insect repellent as well, for obvious reasons.)

There are also several private sporting clubs that serve meals, some of which welcome visitors by invitation. They are the **Brunei Tennis Club**, the **Royal Brunei Yacht Club** and the **Pantai Mentiri Golf Club**—all located in the environs of Bandar Seri Begawan. Brunei Shell Petroleum has two clubs in Seria—the **Panaga Club** and the **Shell Recreation Club**—that extend a welcome to visitors who have an introduction. Membership in the posh Jerudong Park Polo Club is by invitation only. Polo happens to be a passion of this sultan.

SHOPPING IN BRUNEI

Locally made handicrafts include **brass cannons** and ornamental **kris** (the Malay knife)—and **rattan furniture** is also tempting if you can figure out how to get it home! Muslims are terrific gold dealers and **24-carat jewelry** is a good buy here, especially in gold bangles. Dealers are honest, as they sell it by weight according to the world market price.

The main shopping area is in the **Seri complex** in BSB with its department stores, supermarkets and boutiques, which accept all major credit cards. Do pay a visit first to the **Brunei Arts and Handicrafts Training Centre** in BSB, where weaving, silver and bronze work, kris and kain songket (handwoven cloth) can be viewed and purchased.

The Tamu Kianggeh open-air market on the bank of the Kianggeh River, open daily from morning to late evening, offers some good buys in arts and handicrafts.

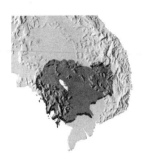

CAMBODIA

Cambodia's Angkor Wat was constructed in the 12th century.

CAMBODIA IN A CAPSULE

Also known as Kampuchea...home to the spectacular Angkor Wat temple complex...trying to crawl out of more than 30 years of civil war...carpet-bombed during the Nixon administration of the Vietnam War...1 million people were killed here by the dreaded Khmer Rouge in the late 1970s...Paris Peace Agreement in 1991 brought more than 22,000 UN peacekeepers here for nearly 2 years...first free elections held in May 1993...still considered the Wild West of East Asia.

Perhaps no country on earth has so brutally suffered from as many forms of conflict over the past 30 years as has Cambodia. Civil wars, border wars, massive bombardment via a superpower's B-52s, a deforestation rate considered unparalleled anywhere in the world and an autogenicide unprecedented in its savagery—effectively eliminating a full seventh of the country's population—have ravaged this once proud and culturally influential empire.

With the help of the United Nations, Cambodia is crawling back into the world on its knees, literally, as so many of the country's citizens are missing limbs after accidental encounters with one of the perhaps six million land mines still buried just beneath the surface of the countryside's rich topsoil. And those not missing arms or legs are most assuredly missing relatives, victims of Pol Pot's murderous Khmer Rouge regime of the mid- and late-1970s.

The Khmer Rouge were responsible for more than a million deaths between 1975 and 1979 alone. Their 82mm mortars are still felt today—by Cambodians, but mainly by the hundreds of thousands of ethnic-Vietnamese who have called Cambodia home for generations. It is not uncommon, even today, for entire villages to be wiped out overnight by Khmer Rouge guerrillas launching rocket-propelled grenades at frightened townspeople from the backs of motorbikes. Even the spectacular and relatively highly touristed ruins at Angkor are not entirely safe from sporadic attacks by Khmer Rouge guerrillas who, despite UN-supervised elections in May of 1993, still control fully 20 percent of Cambodia's landscape. Shortly before the polls that spring, armed guerrillas attacked a UN garrison at Siem Reap and injured a Portuguese tourist. A Japanese tourist fled the area on a motorcycle and streaked all the way to the Thai border, nearly 100 miles away.

In many areas across this lush countryside, bones spring from the earth like desert cactus, still shrouded with the tattered garments their owners were clothed in on the day they were slaughtered. Human teeth can be found among the rocks and grass like pebbles in an old parking lot. And many of these locations are not named, not enshrined by glass and concrete and tour guides and ticket booths. They're just there, baking in the same sun as the resin harvesters dotting the rutted, muddy roads nearby, toting Chinese-made AK-47 rifles and readying to enter the fog-thick encasement of dark green jungle for another day's toil.

Red signs depicting skulls and crossbones are tacked to trees, sharing the bark with bullet holes, warning of land mines. Occasionally,

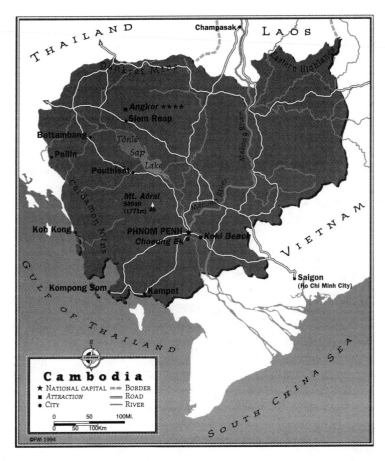

at night, a visitor to this exotic land can witness an exchange of artillery fire between Khmer Rouge forces and soldiers of the Cambodian People's Armed Forces (CPAF). To the uninitiated, the orange tracers streaking in a large arc across the Asian twilight appear to be a display of grand fireworks that simply aren't functioning properly, some sort of defused celebration—which is in fact what Cambodia is.

Cambodia's most significant offering to the world in 1995 is not its art, its dancing, nor its culture; it is its own testament to the country's horrific past. Cambodia's most popular attractions, apart from its magnificent ancient wats, are museums and fields that depict the mass genocide of its people so vividly that many simply don't have the stomach to visit the blood-stained walls of schoolrooms-turned-torture chambers, or of longan fields-turned-open graves.

Many of Pol Pot's victims unlucky enough to have survived the genocide today roam Phnom Penh's trash-laden boulevards like zombies out of a George Romero film. Some are hideously disfigured; nearly all are penniless and they follow around western tourists like gulls behind a shrimper, begging for handouts

Then why would anyone want to come to this land?

Quite simply, Cambodia belies itself; it's perhaps the greatest paradox on the planet in its contrast of human warmth and vile indignity. Its people are arguably the gentlest on the globe, sentenced by circumstance to an environment that's utterly raw and entirely untamed. They are struggling to enter the modern world by investing salaries that average as little as $4 a month on English lessons along Phnom Penh's English Street. (It's English now—not French. The majority of people who were versed in French either fled the country or were executed by the Khmer Rouge.)

To adventure tourists, Cambodia is one of the last frontiers, the Wild West of East Asia where one can hitchhike from Phnom Penh to Angkor Wat with a relatively safe chance of being stopped and detained at rifle point by Maoist guerrillas. Where one can share a ferry ride in a raging storm across the Great Lake of Tonlé Sap on a dilapidated, rusted barge with a dozen sows, cockroaches the size of plums and a few soldiers and joke about the ferry that sank over the same reef last night during a monsoon, killing 50. Where one can sneak across the border from Thailand aboard a speed boat manned by smugglers bound for Kompong Som, harboring a cache of Singaporean VCRs.

Cambodia is all these things and much more. The temples at Angkor may well be the most spectacular ruins in the world. Phnom Penh, the capital, is booming, thanks to the presence of more than 20,000 UNTAC (United Nations Transitional Authority in Cambodia) troops who, during the UN's most ambitious peacekeeping operation to that date, shared the country with the indigents for nearly two years while orchestrating a painful and delicate transition to relative democracy.

Tourism is taking off. Whereas only 2,000 tourists visited Cambodia in 1988, 1991 saw 25,000 foreign visitors to the country. And that figure more than tripled in 1992—to 87,000!

Cambodia's more than 200 miles of pristine coastline, from Krong Koh Kong to Kampot, are mainly virgin (if you can get there), save for the periodic intrusion of a few Chinese-made shell casings that sprout from the sand like snail shells.

Is Cambodia safe? Entirely, if you want it to be. A little less so if you don't. Get a guide. They can come cheap—for as little as $5 a day in the capital and about $20 a day at Angkor and other temple sites visited by tourists. Just the fact that he's alive is a pretty good indication he'll know how to keep you alive.

Cambodia's Interior Ministry is completing plans to introduce tourist police units in Phnom Penh, Siem Reap and the seaside resort, Sihanoukville. Secretary of State for Tourism, Veng Sereyvuth, says the units will be on call 24 hours a day and trained to help tourists in situations ranging from emergencies and crime to simple requests for information.

History of Cambodia

Funan is what much of modern-day Cambodia was called back in the first six centuries A.D. Presiding along the Mekong River, the kingdom of Funan was in an ideal location to take advantage of the trade traffic between India and Java and even between India and China, although China's influence on the kingdom, because of its remoteness, was far less than that of India's. It was mainly Indian culture which formed the mores and institutions of early Funan society. It was a society that contained both Hinduism and Mahayana Buddhism in relative harmony.

Ties were established between Funan and the Khmers in the 6th century and by the middle of that century, the Kambujans (the term for the predecessors of the Khmers), who lived along the Mekong in what is now Laos, split off from Funan. Chenla, as the new society was called, grew quite powerful and absorbed Funan probably near the end of the 6th century. Quarrels forced the kingdom to be split into Land Chenla and Water Chenla around the 8th century. Land Chenla, in the north, prospered, but Water Chenla, in the south, was constantly plagued with internal strife and power struggles.

The Birth of Angkor

In 802, a Khmer prince named Jayavarman II declared independence from Java and began the Angkor kingdom. Declaring himself a god-king, he began to build temples in his own honor and that of the symbol of Siva around the area of the Tonlé Sap. His successor, Indravarman I, built the vast irrigation systems that permitted the Khmers to live so densely. And it was Indravarman who first started constructing the temples of Angkor.

Yasovarman, next in line, chose Angkor as the site for his new capital and it was here, sometime in the late 9th century, that the first of the great temples of Angkor was finally built. But it wasn't until 1107, when Suryavarman II took the throne, that Angkor reached its zenith with the construction of Angkor Wat. He also constructed a road network that connected his vast kingdom, which included much of the Malay peninsula, Thailand, southern Vietnam and all of Laos.

Angkor was sacked in 1177, but Jayavarman VII rebuilt and expanded the kingdom, creating hospitals and even more roads, complete with rest houses. Construction on Angkor Thom was started in 1200 by Jayavarman VII, including the Bayon, the last and—next to Angkor Wat—the most imposing structure built at Angkor. The Bayon was supposed to have taken 21 years to complete, draining the labor force, which had kept the vast irrigation system yielding up to four crops per year. Jayavarman VII was also responsible for the shift from Hinduism to Buddhism. This is evident in the construction of the Bayon, where a third level was added to the structure to reflect increasing Buddhist influence on the Khmers. The shift toward Hinayana Buddhism was also responsible for diminishing the god-like reverence Khmers had for the leaders.

Attacks from the West

It was then centuries before Angkor was finally abandoned, a process that was aggravated by increasing attacks by the Khmers' neighbors the Siamese (modern-day Thais). When the irrigation system that the society was so dependent on could no longer be maintained and following an incursion by the Thais that resulted in the takeover of Angkor, the Khmers fled their capital and established a new base near Phnom Penh.

The next few centuries were marked by continual fighting with the Thais, which also included a request by the Cambodian King Satha for the Spaniards to intervene on the Khmers' behalf in 1594. Instead of helping the Cambodians, the arriving Spaniards and accompanying Portuguese found that Satha had been deposed and replaced by Chung Prei, who had no real affinity for the Europeans. After a number of disputes, the Spaniards raided the palace and eventually placed one of Satha's sons on the throne.

But Cambodia's real worries continued to rest with the Thais. Between the 17th and 19th centuries, Thailand in effect annexed huge parcels of Khmer real estate, including the provinces of Siem Reap and Battambang. The only reason Cambodia continued to exist was due to preoccupations Thailand had with Burma, while Vietnam continued to battle its own problems on the home front.

The French Era

Foreign incursions continued for embattled Cambodia, with the French taking control over the nation in 1863 after King Norodom signed a treaty making Cambodia a protectorate of France. This would mark the beginning of nearly a century of French domination over the Khmers. From the Cambodian point of view, this may have been seen as a blessing, as the French were able to keep both Thailand and Vietnam away from any designs they may have had on further interference with Norodom.

In 1884, Norodom signed another treaty, this time permitting France far greater powers and essentially making Cambodia a French colony. For two years, Cambodians opposed to the treaty harassed and fought with the French, to no avail. This would amount to the only real resistance the French would meet from the Cambodian people until World War II.

In 1941, the French made Prince Sihanouk king of Cambodia, believing they had installed another loyal puppet on the throne who'd do anything the French asked for the price of a lavish existence.

Cambodian Independence

Instead, King Sihanouk moved in the direction of Cambodian independence. In 1953, he declared martial law and dissolved the parliament. On November 9, he proclaimed Cambodia an independent state. But internal divisions continued to hamper the solidarity among the nation's leaders. In 1955, Sihanouk abdicated the throne in favor of politics. His People's Socialist Community party was hugely successful and, in fact, captured every seat in parliament in elections held in 1955. His father, who had gained ascendency to the throne after Nordom stepped down five years earlier, died in 1960. Sihanouk simply assumed both roles, bannered under the title of chief-of-state.

Sihanouk's traits as a politician began to become evident. First, he slowly began drifting Cambodia toward the clutches of China and North Vietnam in the early 1960s in the fear that Cambodia's biggest problems would come from the U.S., Thailand and South Vietnam, even so far as cutting ties with the U.S. and permitting North Vietnamese and Viet Cong to use Cambodia for bases of operation during the Vietnam War.

Then, when a conservative and peasant backlash erupted internally, Sihanouk began aligning Cambodia with U.S. efforts to dispose of the communists in Vietnam, an effort that was backed by the army. Then, in 1969, the U.S. inititiated the first of what would become four years of merciless B-52 bombing strikes of eastern Cambodia, thoroughly decimating vast areas of land and killing thousands of people.

In 1970, an apparently U.S.-backed coup deposed Sihanouk and made Prince Sisowath Matak and Army General Lon Nol leaders of Cambodia. Sihanouk himself fled to Beijing, where he still maintains his primary residence today. It was in Beijing where Sihanouk, acting as a leader in exile, nominally held the strings of the newly formed Khmer Rouge.

Lon Nol's troubles, in the meantime, were just beginning. The U.S. invaded Cambodia in 1970, driving North Vietnamese forces further inside Cambodia. Peasants fled en masse to Phnom Penh to escape the fighting. Civil war raged in the countryside. Cambodia's troubles were further compounded by mainly substantiated charges of deep corruption within the government. Hundreds of thousands of people died in the senseless fighting of the early 1970s.

It was this anarchy that played such a formidable role in the ascendancy of the Khmer Rouge. The Maoist guerrillas, amply supplied by the Chinese, were too formidable a force for Lon to suitably suppress, despite heavy U.S. aid. The Khmer Rouge rolled into Phnom Penh on April 17, 1975. Two weeks later, Saigon fell to the communists.

On that day in April in Cambodia, everything changed. It was the start of Year Zero.

The Year Zero

Pol Pot evacuated the capital; the entire urban populace was force-marched into the countryside where individuals were assigned to state-run collective farms. Phnom Penh became a ghost town overnight. It was Pol's objective to reinvent Cambodia, to transform the society into a single vast agrarian collective. Between 1975 and the end of 1978, these efforts had reduced to rubble cities and towns and ancient pagodas. But even more ghastly, more than a million Cambodians had lost their lives at the hands of the Khmer Rouge. Many hundreds of thousands were tortured and executed. Others simply collapsed and died in the fields from exhaustion and malnourishment. All travel was prohibited—currency abolished. Citizens were executed for merely having the ability to speak a foreign language.

The savagery continued for nearly four years. Although Sihanouk returned to Cambodia in 1975 as chief of state, he was kept in

Phnom Penh under house-arrest until 1978—the year Vietnam invaded Cambodia.

The Vietnamese ousted Pol in just two short weeks and took control of the capital on January 7, 1979—installing Hun Sen and Heng Samrin as leaders. The Khmer Rouge fled into the jungles of western Cambodia, to areas near and beyond the Thai border, leaving behind hectares of burning rice fields in their wake. The ensuing famine forced hundreds of thousands of Cambodians to take refuge in camps across the border in Thailand, camps they have only recently returned from.

Meanwhile, Sihanouk, with China's backing, formed a loose opposition coalition dominated by the Khmer Rouge. Although Pol Pot reportedly handed down the reins of his leadership in 1985, he still remains the group's leader, basing his operations over the border in Thailand's Trat Province.

From 1980 through 1989, government forces engaged in frequent and fierce battles with Khmer Rouge units which, operating out of their base in Pailin, continued to terrorize the Cambodian countryside, using civilians as human shields and planting millions of land mines across the country. And not to discriminate, Hun Sen's troops were equally guilty of turning the countryside into one big jar of nitro-glycerine, by double- and even triple-booby-trapping their own mines.

Although China ceased its quasi-official support of the guerrillas, the Khmer Rouge continued to finance themselves though hardwood logging and gem concessions to Thai businessmen, concessions that have netted the Khmer Rouge more than $100 million to date. The resultant damage to the environment has been catastrophic; only about seven million of the country's 16 million hectares of tropical forests remain today. The Thai military, which controls all the checkpoints along the 500 mile border, had—and still has, many charge—a finger in the Khmer Rouge pie. Thailand's historical tacit support of the guerrillas has stemmed mainly from its traditional hatred of the Vietnamese.

The Paris Peace Agreement

Finally, in Paris in October of 1991, after years of intractable negotiations, an agreement was reached to end the civil war in Cambodia, an accord that also called for free elections to be held in May 1993.

More than 22,000 troops and civilian officials descended upon Cambodia, from Japanese policemen and Australian land mine disposal experts, to crack Indonesian and Malaysian combat units.

More than $2.6 billion was spent. Phnom Penh, as it was transformed so suddenly in 1975, was reborn again. But this time with discos and video stores and hamburger joints and international soldiers with $100 a day allowances, an amount inconceivable to the vast majority of Cambodians—in a year much less a day.

But, despite the massive presence, the fighting continued. At first, it was still contained between the Khmer Rouge and CPAF troops. But by the beginning of 1993, UNTAC soldiers themselves had become the targets of Khmer Rouge ordnance, including the first Japanese to have been killed on a foreign military mission since World War II. A Bulgarian peacekeeping unit was gunned down by Khmer Rouge guerrillas they had invited to lunch. UNTAC helicopters were being shot out of the sky regularly, their passengers being "detained" by Khmer Rouge units. Pol Pot's soldiers attacked Siem Reap, near the site of Angkor Wat. The Khmer Rouge refused to disarm, as the Paris accord required them to do, or to participate in the political process at all.

It seemed that the peace process was doomed, that the elections wouldn't be held at all. The *Los Angeles Times* reported that the "celebratory clinking of champagne glasses in Paris is being mocked by events on the ground."

But, surprisingly, the Khmer Rouge did not follow through on their threats to disrupt the elections, perhaps because of UNTAC's overestimation of their numbers and military capabilities. Polling stations remained relatively violence-free as nearly 90 percent of the Cambodians registered to vote by UNTAC registration teams cast their ballots. The big winner was Norodum Ranariddh, Sihanouk's son and leader of the FUNCINPEC (Cambodian National Front for an Independent, Neutral, Peaceful and Cooperative Cambodia) party. He overcame what at first were heavy odds in favor of incumbent Cambodian Premier Hun Sen to win the May elections. Hun Sen seemed a shoo-in for many months, but Cambodians became disillusioned as more reports surfaced implicating the government in political violence.

But the margin of victory was narrow enough that Sihanouk, still considered by most Cambodians as the nation's leader and battling health problems, flew to Phnom Penh from Beijing, where he announced that a coalition between FUNCEINPEC and Hun Sen would rule Cambodia.

In October, 1993 the U.S., satisfied the UN had accomplished its objective in Cambodia, formally recognized the new Phnom Penh government and established full diplomatic relations with Cambodia. Today the country is referred to as Cambodia or Cambodia.

The Dove is Fragile

In January of 1992, Cambodia cautiously opened its doors to tourists. At first, they came in trickles. If peace becomes a reality, they will come in waves. Today, there are nearly 50 flights a week to Phnom Penh from Bangkok. And soon, there will be direct service to Siem Reap. Cambodia is becoming increasingly requested on Asian itineraries. As a sign that someone's taking peace in Cambodia seriously, the Japanese government has pledged $10 million toward restoration of the temples at Angkor, to be spent over the next two years.

Cambodians are reminded of peace by their visitors. For most, the only barometer they have of peace is the number of Westerners scooting by their hootches on the backs of motorbikes. If there are many, there is peace.

Every transit ticket into this land is an invitation for it to join the world. And with enough invitations, Cambodia is bound to join the party. So hurry.

PLANNING AHEAD

VISAS

One can visit Cambodia as part of a group or as an individual. Some officials say that travel is restricted to Phnom Penh and Angkor, although I've known a few individuals who've strayed well off the beaten path without incident, namely to the beaches near Kampot. This is highly risky, however, as is independent travel in most of the country, particularly in Kompong Thom, Siem Reap and Battambang provinces. **Khmer Rouge guerrillas** control much of the countryside and vast areas of these provinces; your safety is far from assured should you be detained. Officially, travel in Khmer Rouge-controlled areas is restricted.

You can apply to the **General Direction of Tourism**, Chief of Tour Service Office, *3 Achar Mean Boulevard, Phnom Penh,* ☎ *855-2-4607* or *2-3607* or FAX: *855-23-2-6164* or *23-2-6140.*

You will need to send the following: full name, passport number, photocopy of the front section of your passport, date and place of birth, arrival and departure dates and itinerary. They will confirm receipt of application. Visas will then be issued on arrival at Pochentong Airport. You will need 2 passport-sized photos. Visas are good for stays up to 15 days.

That's the official line. But try and get to Bangkok first for the latest dope on getting over the border. Most travel agents there will say you've got to cough up anything from $80 to $120 and wait three days for your visa. But you can also try simply getting on a plane, as I have done and pay $20 U.S. cash money at Pochentong for a 15-day visa.

Visa extensions can be applied for, but not neccesarily granted, in Phnom Penh at the **Foreign Ministry**, *240 St. and Quai Karl Marx;* ☎ *2-4641* or *2-4441.* Or try the **General Direction of Tourism**, *3 Achar Mean Boulevard, Phnom Penh;* ☎ *855-2-4607* or *2-3607;* FAX: *855-23-26164* or *23-26140.* Or try the very friendly folks over at **Phnom Penh Tourism**, *313 Quai Karl Marx;* ☎ *2-3949, 2-5349,* or *2-4059;* FAX: *885-23-26043.* Mr. Yo Sakhan is especially helpful. You can also arrange for visas in Vietnam. Allow 3-5 days for issue.

ARRIVAL/DEPARTURE

If you do it legally, you'll pay about $250 round trip from Bangkok and enter by air at Pochentong Airport on an **SK Air** (Cambodia Airlines) Soviet-made Tupolev 134 jet, or on a Canadian DASH 8 via **Bangkok Airlines**. Thai Airlines also now flies into the capital, as does Silk Air from Singapore. You can also enter from Hanoi twice a week on Vietnam Airlines; Vientiane or Pakse twice a week; Saigon four times a week; Bombay, or even from London on Thai.

The **airport** is a bouncy 4-mile ride from Phnom Penh. You can get to the city by either **taxi** or **motorbike**, whose driver will most likely attempt to convince you to hire him for a day or more as your guide. There is an airport tax of $5 for international flights.

Cambodia's officials do not presently allow visitors to arrive or leave by sea or land from Thailand and Laos, although it's possible (but expensive) to arrive from Saigon by hired car. Additionally, there is now modern bus service between Saigon and Phnom Penh. Buses for Saigon leave daily from the corner of 211 St. and 182 St. At last check, the one-way trip was extraordinarily cheap

—about 300r. The journey takes about 10 hours. Also doable, but risky, is a land crossing from Thailand. But it will be without the correct paperwork. And you'll have to get out the same way. If you are caught, Thai Army units manning the border posts have been known to detain Westerners entering Thailand illegally for up to four days. But even then, you'll still most likely get your passport stamped with a transit visa after you've been "punished."

Entering Cambodia, you are allowed 200 cigarettes and 1 bottle of liquor.

MONEY

The **riel (r)** is the currency of Cambodia. The current rate is about 900 riels to the dollar. And this is changing. Just 1 year ago, the rate was 2,500 riels to the dollar. The arrival of UNTAC troops in Cambodia in 1992 brought with it a new perception for Cambodians of the concept of currency. With some soldiers luxuriating on $100-a-day allowances or more, prices throughout Phnom Penh and elsewhere are skyrocketing, making the already nearly-worthless riel even more so. Exchange dollars into riels, but not a lot of them. Beware: twenty dollars in riels will fill a JanSport. **U.S. dollars** are heartily welcomed and have become Cambodia's real currency. But there still remains strict currency control. You must declare all currency on arrival. You can use smaller U.S. bills in-country. Travelers checks can be cashed at the **Banque du Commerce Extérieur du Cambodge** (26 Soeung Ngoc Ming St.; ☎ 2-4863) or at the **Bangkok Bank** in Phnom Penh. Visa is accepted at both these banks but with a $30 use charge.

You can exchange money at the airport. Thai baht and Vietnamese dong can be changed as readily as dollars.

There is a slight difference in the rate on the black market. Street changers can be found on quai sidewalks throughout Phnom Penh and in apothecaries and at the Grand Hotel d'Angkor in Siem Reap; they offer better rates than the banks.

MEDICAL

Update all your shots and take the usual precautions for **malaria** and other tropical diseases. There are many virulent strains of malaria that are resistant to all phrophylaxis. Inoculations are not required unless you're arriving from an endemic area.

There is no truly modern hospital facility in the country. You will need to buy your own drugs (usually expired). Best to stock up in Bangkok, where many useful preparations can be had over-the-counter. Carry a first-aid kit and medication. **Dangerous snakes** include vipers, cobras and king cobras, hanumans and banded kraits.

CLIMATE

November to March is the northeastern monsoon season, which brings little rain and temperatures between 25-32 C. April through October are the months of the southwestern monsoon. Typically, they're hot, humid and wet—with temperatures above 33 C.

HOURS OF BUSINESS

Government offices are open 7:30 a.m.-12:00 noon and 2:00 p.m.-6:00 p.m., Monday through Saturday. Banks are open from 7:30 a.m.-10:30 a.m. and reopen at 12:00-4:00 p.m., Saturdays 7:30 a.m.-10:30 a.m. Some close Saturday and Sunday. Many attractions keep same hours as banks. Food stalls throughout Phnom Penh open very early in the morning and close at varying times at or after dark. A number of "portable cafes" open around noontime everyday on the banks of the Tonlé Sap River next to the Phnom Penh Tourism building on Quai Karl Marx.

ELECTRICITY

220V/50 cycles in Phnom Penh and 220V/50 and sometimes 110V/50 in the outlying areas. Electricity in areas other than Phnom Penh and provincial capitals is mainly provided by portable generators. In Phnom Penh itself, power outages occur daily, which explains the ever-present blanket of diesel fumes spewed by portable generators. Electricity in Siem Reap is provided centrally but only available on a limited basis, usually only during the early evening hours.

TELEPHONE, FAX & MAIL

You can try to send mail, but don't expect it to arrive any time soon. 150 riels for a postcard to the USA. Mail into Cambodia can take up to three or four months to be delivered. The main post office in Phnom Penh has a telegram, telex, fax and telephone service. With arrival of UNTAC came widespread fax service. Many businesses now have fax service, although it is extremely expensive. In an emergency, you might try the offices of *The Cambodia Times*, one of Phnom Penh's two English-language newspapers, at *252 Achar Mean Boulevard;* ☎ *2-6647* (IDD) or *2.4405* (local); FAX: *2-6647*. I can't guarantee it, but they seem to be the people who might help in a squeeze.

LOCAL TRANSPORTATION

Car rentals are expensive, as high as US$50 a day at the time of this writing. But taxis have become more commonplace, especially in the capital. The easiest way, though, to get around is on the back of a motorbike. Phnom Penh traffic is a mish-mash of trishaws (or cyclos), cars, trucks, bicycles and motorbikes traversing boulevards without stop lights or traffic signs while marginally adhering to Cambodia's right-side-drive hypothesis. Roads outside the capital are rutted and cratered by war. It seems every citizen with at least two wheels in Cambodia has a de facto taxi license—and a **motorbike**. Along with its $5-$10-a-day guide/driver, it's the cheapest, easiest and fastest way to get around the country, although your derrière will pay dearly on longer journeys.

As of this writing, it isn't permitted for foreigners to travel in Cambodia by **local buses**, but this may change soon. The place to find out is at the bus station, next to the central market in Phnom Penh.

Cambodia's highways, although easy enough to understand, are marginally passable at best. National Route 1 to the east and the country's primary link to Vietnam, is in the best shape, namely because the government controls most of this area. I've known a number of foreigners who have **hitchhiked** within Cambodia, mostly along National Route 6 to Siem Reap and National Route 3 to the Gulf of Thailand. It's ballsy and the going is slow, slow, slow.

On the airline scene, SK Air flies its Russian-made Antonov An-24s to Siem Reap daily for about $45 one-way. And that's about the only place you can get to in Cambodia by air. I suggest going one way by air and taking the ferry the other. It can be a harrowing 24-hour ride across the Great Lake and down the Tonlé Sap River when the monsoons hit. It leaves twice a week from both the Psar Cha Municipal Ferry Landing in Phnom Penh and from the lake just south of Siem Reap.

LOCAL TIME

Local time throughout Cambodia is Greenwich Mean Time plus 7 hours, the same time as in Bangkok, Vientiane, Saigon and Hanoi.

FOOD

With UNTAC in town, restaurants have been opening in Phnom Penh and other cities like daffodils after an April shower, featuring cuisines from around the world. **Food stalls**, truly a bargain at usually around US$1 a full meal, are located throughout cities and villages. In Phnom Penh, the big clusters of food stalls can be found at and around the central market, as well as along the Tonlé Sap river near the ferry landing and the Phnom Penh Tourism building.

LOCAL WATER & BEVERAGES

Do not drink tap water anywhere in Cambodia. Many physicians suggest even brushing your teeth with bottled water only, although I both showered and brushed my teeth with tap water without consequences. **Bottled water** is cheap and available everywhere. Avoid drinking the local fruity-looking "soda pop" that's sold by roadside vendors. The liquid may come in a Fanta bottle but, I assure you, this stuff isn't Fanta. You'll get sick.

There are plenty of **soft drinks**, **beers** and **liquors** both in Phnom Penh and throughout the provinces. Coke is everywhere. The most popular beer swilled in Cambodia is Tiger beer, brewed in Singapore. It has a refreshing, light taste but is relatively strong. Don't confuse the Mekong whiskey sold in Cambodia with that of the same moniker found in Bangkok. The Cambodia version tastes like lighter fluid; like it was scooped out of the bilges of a Panamanian freighter on one of the mouths of the Mekong—not that the Thai variety is any Dewars itself.

SHOPPING

Your best bargains will be the beautifully crafted **gold** and **silver jewelry** found throughout Cambodia but, in particular, in Phnom Penh's massive, domed Central Market *(where Achar Hemcheay Blvd. and 118 St. collide, literally)* and a couple of smaller outdoor markets on the way to the airport. Most of the other stuff is an assortment of fake Izods, Levis and Rolexes. And there are mounds and mounds of counterfeit clothing and other products. But if you're looking for fakes, more authentic-looking forgeries can be found on the streets of Bangkok (although there's been a recent police crackdown there) and Kuala Lumpur in Malaysia.

However, the **gold jewelry** is the real thing and it can be had for approximately its price on the world market, despite the untold hours of toil Cambodia's artisans have invested in creating its filigree.

NEWSPAPERS

Cambodians, eager to use their newly-learned English skills, are newspaper hungry. There are now two **English-language newspapers** in Cambodia, both in Phnom Penh—the weekly *Cambodia Times* and the twice-monthly *Phnom Penh Post*. The *Post* is owned by an American, a former philanthropist based in Bangkok, who started the paper on his own savings without any previous journalistic experience. The *Cambodia Times* is Hong Kong-owned, Malay-edited and much better capitalized than its competitor, but sometimes is accused of being too pro-government.

The press in Cambodia is remarkably open, with editors getting away with much more than they could in countries such as Malaysia, Vietnam and even Singapore. Nearly 60% of the *Times* readers are English-speaking Cambodians, a percentage that will increase significantly with the departure of UNTAC troops.

INFORMATION

The General Direction of Tourism, *3 Achar Mean Boulevard, Phnom Penh,* ☎ *855-2-4607* or *2.3607*; FAX: *855-23-2-6164* or *23-2-6140*. I've found Phnom Penh Tourism much more than helpful on frequent occasions. The simple gift of a counterfeit Izod shirt to a staffer will work wonders. Employees here will go well out of their way to help Western tourists, from providing low-cost government hotel rooms, to taxiing them around on the backs of their motorbikes to airline offices, banks, hotels, ferry landings, etc.—at no charge! Etat du Cambodge, *313 Quai Karl Marx;* ☎ *2-3949, 2-5349* or *2-4059*; FAX *855-23-26043*. They can also help with information, car rentals and trips to Angkor.

TIPPING

Tipping is traditionally generally not practiced, although it's become more evident in the last couple of years. Small gifts to Cambodians for special favors are recommended.

SAFETY

Phnom Penh is plagued with **petty theft** so make sure your luggage is locked and/or transported in a canvas cover. Frequent power outages mean you should carry a flashlight when you go out at night. You should not get in the habit of wandering aimlessly at night in the city or the country. Don't wander off the roads or paths due to **land mines** which, believe me, are everywhere. Warning signs are posted on trees in some areas, including areas in

and around Angkor. You won't see a baseball game played in Cambodia this century. Don't pick up or go near any metallic objects. There is a lot of unexploded material lying around all over the country—much of it quite recent—just waiting for the slightest touch to set it off. This may be overly cautious but you only need to screw up once.

It's said in-country that if a Cambodian doesn't return a Westerner's smile, he's a Khmer Rouge. This may or may not be true. The vast majority are perhaps the friendliest people on earth. But it's a known fact that the Khmer Rouge and their sympathizers despise Americans. In Cambodia, especially out in the provinces, you'll be quite tempted to flaunt your peculiarity to the Cambodian people, as many have never seen Westerners. Put simply, you'll get the urge to show off. This makes you even more contemptable in the eyes of the Khmer Rouge, many of whom don't wear uniform fatigues but, instead, civilian clothing—so you won't recognize them. Don't make yourself a target. **Dress** inconspicuously and behave as modestly as possible.

Lastly, refuse all offers of **drugs**. I've seen marijuana smoked openly by Americans in Cambodia, even in astonishingly close proximity to soldiers. But if you get your butt dragged-in, in this part of the world, forget it. You may as well smoke your airline ticket.

PEOPLE & CULTURE

Ninety percent ethnic Khmers. The balance split between ethnic Chinese and ethnic Vietnamese. **Art** in Cambodia is largely a monument to the country's glorious past, rather than a progressive attempt to break new ground. This is most typified by the reemergence of the nearly extinct art form of classical Cambodian dance—which was banned and virtually ruined by Pol Pot. Today, dancers who fled the Khmer Rouge to places such as California, Minnesota and Virginia are returning to Phnom Penh and rearing a new generation of dancers.

Like their Buddhist neighbors in surrounding countries, Cambodians are very gentle, unassuming people. Never display anger when dealing with them. Respect their religious customs by taking off your shoes before entering a pagoda. Never sit in the lotus, or cross-legged, position while facing a Buddha. Instead, sit with your feet facing behind you. Never point your feet at someone and don't pat individuals on the top of the head; it's an insult. And no shorts in religious temples. Ladies, cover up as much as possible. Cambodia isn't Cancun. Elders are addressed as *ta* and elder ladies as *yeay*.

SOME USEFUL INFORMATION

As mentioned earlier, independent travel through Khmer Rouge-controlled territory in Cambodia is highly discouraged. However, should you be the type of individual magnetically attracted to the highly discouraged, take warning. If you are "detained" by Khmer Rouge soldiers, be prepared to surrender your earthly belongings, at the very least—and be prepared to do it with a smile on your face. Complimenting the guerrillas' good taste in the selection of your possessions may not save your belongings from being confiscated, but it may save your life. Phrases such as, "I'm delighted, sir, that you find my wallet of such high quality (*Kayom sabaicet neak kheing kraboup hnyom saart neng la-oh.*)," or, "I'm glad my motorbike will make your travels swifter (*Kayom sabaicet kongmoto kayom aui neak baek lar-hah*)," will go

a long way in making your own travels swifter.

UNITED STATES MISSION

The U.S. Mission in Phnom Penh is located at *27 EO Street, 240, Phnom Penh;* ☎ *85-23-26436;* FAX: *855-232-6437.* The U.S. established full diplomatic relations with Cambodia in October, 1993. However, at press time, the official U.S. presence in Cambodia is still considered a mission. Officials at the State Department haven't yet determined whether a new embassy will be at a different site than the mission.

FESTIVALS AND HOLIDAYS

Cambodians commemorate a number of days important to their past, in particular, their recent past.

January 7	National Day	*Celebrates the overthrow of Pol Pot and the Khmer Rouge by the Vietnamese in 1979.*
January (late) February (early)	Tet New Year	*Cambodia's ethnic Vietnamese and Chinese celebrate Tet, the Chinese and Vietnamese new year.*
February 18	Vietnam Friendship Treaty Day	*Celebrates the Cambodia and Vietnam Friendship Treaty signing (1979).*
April 17	Victory Day	*Anniversary of the fall of Lon Nol's government to the Khmer Rouge in 1975.*
April	Chaul Chnam	*The celebration of the Cambodia new year.*
April	Visak Bauchea	*Celebrates the birth of Buddha.*
May 1	May Day	
May 9	Genocide Day	*Memorial for the victims of the Khmer Rouge genocide of the mid 1970s.*
May	Chrat Prea Angkal	*The start of the sowing season.*
June 19		*Celebration of the founding of the Revolutionary Armed Forces of Kampuchea (1951).*
June 28		*Celebration of the founding of the People's Revolutionary Party of Cambodia (1951).*
September (late)	Prachum Ben	*Offerings are made to the spirits of Cambodians' ancestors.*
October (late)	Water Festival	*Celebrates when the Tonlé Sap River, feeding the Great Lake with the waters of the swollen Mekong since July, reverses its flow back toward the Mekong.*
December 2		*Anniversary of the founding of the Front for National Reconstruction (1978).*

Background Material

Sideshow: Kissinger, Nixon and the Destruction of Cambodia by William Shawcross (Simon & Schuster, 1979) is a brilliant documentation of Cambodia's role in the Vietnam War and events leading up to Pol Pot's takeover in 1975. Perhaps the quintessential story of modern Cambodia.

Also by Shawcross, *The Quality of Mercy: Cambodia, Holocaust and Modern Conscience* (1984), examines the famine in 1979-80 and international efforts to end it.

The Stones Cry Out: A Cambodian Childhood, 1975-1980 by Molyda Szymusiak (Hill & Wang, 1986) is a tear-jerking account of childhood in the Khmer Rouge era.

The Ancient Khmer Empire by L.P. Briggs is perhaps the most highly regarded work concerning early Khmer history.

I also highly recommend:

"On the Front Line: With Asian Troops in Cambodia" (*Asia Week*, March 17, 1993) and "On the Front Line: Guarding Cambodia's Life" (*Asia Week*, March 24, 1993), both articles by Geoffrey Klaverkamp. This is a great 2-part series documenting the journalist's travels with UNTAC peacekeepers and the Khmer Rouge all across Cambodia during UNTAC's deployment in 1992-93.

Phnom Penh

A new generation reaches for peace.

PHNOM PENH IN A CAPSULE

Capital of Cambodia since the mid-15th century...Gateway to the spectacular temple ruins at Angkor...The base for more than 22,000 UN peacekeepers in 1992-93...Evacuated entirely in 1975 by Pol Pot, who force-marched residents to farm collectives in the country...Located where the Tonlé Sap and Mekong rivers join...Evidence of 30 years of civil war is everywhere.

This is the city you'll most likely use as a base camp to begin your travels, if for no other reason than it's the only city in which you are legally allowed to begin your travels in Cambodia.

Phnom Penh has about a million inhabitants, give or take a million or so depending on who's running the government. During peace (moments of which are few and far between), the population tends to decrease, as Cambodians move back into the countryside to till the soil. But during eruptions of violence and civil war, the population of Phnom Penh swells with refugees from the countryside seeking the relative safety of the big city. As a case in point, Phnom Penh's population more than quadrupled back in the mid-1970s, from 500,000 to more than 2 million, as Lon Nol's troops battled with the Khmer Rouge in the countryside.

Today, Phnom Penh is safe. Relatively so. Only during the latter stages of the UN-sponsored peace process before the May, 1993 elections did the Khmer Rouge attempt any forays within the city itself—and these were little more than inconsequential hit-and-run sorties at video stores. And even these were designed to intimidate the UN command and strike fear into Phnom Penhois more than to accomplish any military gain. At the time of this writing, the UN objectives in Cambodia—namely conducting the country's first multi-party, freely-held elections; removing all Vietnamese forces from Cambodia and supervising the repatriation of nearly 360,000 Cambodian refugees living in Thai border camps—have been achieved. With the withdrawal of UNTAC troops, it's anyone's guess what will happen to Phnom Penh and all of Cambodia, should the Khmer Rouge rekindle their malevolent activities. But, for now, the city is peaceful.

Phnom Penh, which sits on the banks of the Tonlé Sap River where it joins the Mekong in its flow to the South China Sea, retains a great deal of its early colonial charm, despite years of war. The wrought iron balconies and French architecture give the city the appearance of New Orleans' French Quarter after, say, a hurricane's gone through it. The streets are rutted and garbage-strewn. And they're also home to thousands of Phnom Penhois, who sleep on the crumbled sidewalks by night, cut hair or serve kuy teav in food stalls by day. The smell of diesel fuel is incessant, as nearly daily, the portable generators of businesses and hotels are cranked up to inject power back into the veins of a city that just can't seem to keep itself lit at night.

Pedestrians, motorists and others swarm across its confusing street system like a massive colony of ants in a maze. Beggars and horribly maimed people are everywhere, frequenting primarily the haunts of the monied Westerners. Outside some of the city's more expensive restaurants at night, poor Phnom Penhois gather in front of the eateries in large groups, their eyes and shirts dimly bathed by the incandescence inside—and in a macabre display—peer into the windows, considering the satiated and rotund foreigners as they might a scene in a movie in a dark theater.

Since the arrival of the first UN troops at the end of 1991, Phnom Penh has been undergoing a radical physical, economic and cultural transformation. Each day, the capital's skyline seems to change, towering farther into the sky as yet another hotel is erected. Foreign investment has started and the people of Phnom Penh are tasting material advantages for the first time ever. Young men are now driving cars; the women apply makeup before mirrors in the Central Market. "Essential English" schools line Tou Samouth Boulevard and English Street like Bangkok girlie bars.

Phnom Penh may well be the phoenix of Asia and now's the time to see it, before its wings are fully spread and it's just another Kentucky Fried Chicken.

WHAT TO SEE AND DO IN PHNOM PENH

The Royal Palace

The Royal Palace (*Lenin Boulevard*), built in the mid-19th century by the French, was the lavish home to King Norodom and was, in effect, France's means of purchasing Cambodia. It is the official residence to Prince Sihanouk. However, the current leader and figurehead is rarely on its grounds, instead making his primary residence in Beijing, due at least in part to medical reasons. Today, sections of the sprawling complex are opened to tourists—but not the residential quarters itself—for a few hours in the morning and a few in the afternoon. When recently checked, the hours were 8 a.m. to 11 a.m. and between 2 and 5 in the afternoon. There is approximately a $2 charge to bring in a still camera, $5 for a video camera and pictures are not allowed inside any of the buildings on the grounds.

An area to visit is the Throne Room, with its Bayon-inspired tower that reaches to nearly 200 feet. Here, foreign dignitaries were received. The Khmer Rouge destroyed much of what was displayed here. Cameras aren't permitted.

The Silver Pagoda

This is a beautiful pagoda, also called *Wat Preah Kaeo*, that truly lives up to its name. The pagoda's floor is constructed from 6 tons of silver blocks—over 5,000 in all. This is one of the few pagodas that wasn't entirely trashed by the marauding Khmer Rouge, who used the wat as testament to their supposed efforts at preserving the Khmer glory of Cambodia's cultural past. In the center of the pagoda is a 17th-century Buddha, made entirely of Baccarat crystal. Additionally, another 198-lb. gold Buddha is encrusted with 9,584 diamonds! There is an admission charge. Permits once issued only by the tourist office for gaining entry are no longer required, at least as of this writing. Again, same story—no picture-taking inside. And remember to leave your shoes outside.

The National Museum

On 184 Street and 13 Street, across from the Royal Palace, is the National Museum built in 1920. Colored a deep brick red, the museum houses Cambodia's largest collection of ancient Khmer art dating all the way back to the Funan period (1st-6th centuries). Additionally, many exhibits date from the Angkor period. This is a must stop if your only destination in Cambodia is Phnom Penh. Although a highly worthwhile stop if you've got plans to visit Angkor, the museum is only a pale substitute for the trip west. If you're doing both, do the museum first. It'll be a letdown if you've seen the temples first. There is a shop that sells reproductions of Cambodian art from Angkor, so keep your receipt in case you get hassled by an obstinate customs officer on your return. There is an admission fee and cameras aren't permitted inside the museum.

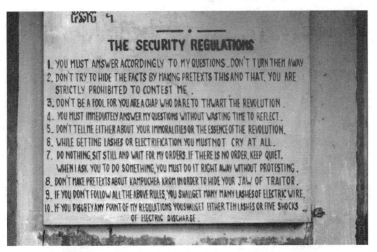

The rules at Phnom Penh's Khmer Rouge horror house, Security Prison 21.

Tuoi Sieng Museum

Here we leave the vibrant, mystical history of the Khmers for the bloody, terrifying realities of their present. This place, the former Tuol Svay Prey High School, is nothing short of shocking. Pol Pot converted these sprawling (by Phnom Penh standards) two-story buildings into a blood-spattered, horrific campus of terror called Security Prison 21. The large classrooms were transformed into crude brick 2-by-4-foot cells which reach to the ceiling. Here, tens of thousands of innocent Cambodians were forced to live out their final days in unimaginable circumstances while preparing for their deaths in the interrogation rooms on the first floor.

After the Khmer Rouge fled during the first days of 1979, the newly-installed regime of Hun Sen did absolutely nothing to the premises to lead any subsequent visitors to the school to believe the place was anything short of the slaughterhouse it was. Inside each of these rooms of torture is a single rusted steel cot. An enlarged black-and-white photograph above each gruesomely depicts the bodies the liberating Vietnamese soldiers discovered on the cots the day they entered the compound. Blood still covers the walls and tile floors of the rooms. The walls of another room are covered with head shot photos of Pol's victims at Security Prison 21. Chillingly, some prisoners smile shyly for the executioner's lens, despite being bloodied and obviously in or near varying states of torture.

Tuoi Sieng is not an attraction for the squeamish.

Chrouy Changvar Bridge

One of the dominant features of Phnom Penh's physical layout is the ruined Chrouy Changvar bridge that once spanned the Tonlé Sap river, *just off Achar Mean Blvd. north of the city center.* The bridge was blown up by the Khmer Rouge in 1975. It's an eery but compelling sight. You can walk along the bridge about a quarter of the way across before it drops off about a hundred feet to the murky brown waters of the Tonlé Sap below. From its summit, you have a good view of the city, the dilapidated foreign-registered freighters at anchor below, the imposing Oz-like Hotel Cambodiana on the bank of the snaking Tonlé Sap looking south and the Mekong River in the distance. Food stalls open in the late morning along its span, some precariously close to the bridge's unfenced abyss.

Wat Phnom

Wat Phnom is situated on the only real hill in Phnom Penh *next to UNTAC headquarters*, the former French colonial Wat Phnom Hotel. The pagoda itself, built in 1373, is reached by a long staircase on the east side of the structure. Carvings of wild-looking lions greet you at the base of the staircase, and ascending the stairs, you'll see smaller pavilions and offerings to Buddha of chickens and other fowl.

On Sundays, the area around the pagoda, a serene wooded park, can become quite crowded. I'd suggest another day to bring a camera, which I successfully used in the pagoda, without flash and without being banished from the country.

Wat Phnom Hotel

The massive Wat Phnom Hotel is not actually a hotel, but was a guesthouse for visiting heads of state before the UN made the compound headquarters for its military, political and transitional operations in Cambodia. As of this writing, the building is a beehive of military and civilian traffic. The white Toyota Land Cruisers of the UNTAC forces fill the streets in the vicinity of the structure like a car dealership. It's difficult to enter the compound without official business—Pakistani and Bangladeshi soldiers guard the gates with automatic rifles—but there are not a lot of foreigners in Phnom Penh who aren't there on official business. I found entry into the headquarters relatively easy.

Inside, with soldiers and civilians from dozens of nations scurrying about, you really get the feeling of being part of the pulse of modern Cambodia. You feel the kineticism and urgency of the moment. If you can get in, do it. It's not known how long UNTAC will maintain a presence here.

Wat Lang Ka

This wat used to be one of the most beautiful in Phnom Penh before it was ruined by the Khmer Rouge in the mid 1970s. Today, it has been mostly rebuilt and houses some beautiful depictions of Buddha's life on its walls. Located at *274 Street and Samouth Boulevard.*

Central Market

At the *intersection of Achar Hemcheay Boulevard, 118 Street and about a dozen other quais,* is the yellow-domed Central Market. Here can be found some of the finest gold- and silver-crafted jewelry in all of Indochina and at incredibly cheap prices, which explains why it was so thickly frequented by UNTAC personnel when they were in the city in force. About everything conceivable can be had at this perpetually crowded market center, from Thai silk to bogus Rolexes. Food stalls abound. One dark wing, covered by a sagging cloth canopy, has so many eateries they appear to be one. The aisles couldn't be any tighter, the canopy of colorful garments and rattan making passage through them an adventure in itself.

English Street

Take a stroll down English Street (*near the corner of Tou Samouth Boulevard and 184 Street*) after sunset and hear classroom after classroom filled with young Cambodians learning "Essential English." The small one-story bungalows are crammed next to each other, lit softly inside by kerosene or candles, as the choruses of children in differing stages of syntax make for a cacophony floating across the humid Phnom Penh night. It's a scene unimaginable 15 years ago.

The Former French Embassy Building

People like to say this building, *on Achar Mean Blvd.*, was made famous by the film *The Killing Fields.* It wasn't made famous by the film *The Killing Fields.* Rather it was made infamous by the 800 or so foreigners and 600 Cambodians who sweated out their fates within its gates while the Khmer Rouge figured out what to do with them after the capital fell to Pol Pot's merry henchmen in April 1975. The foreigners were trucked out and the Cambodians were taken away and killed.

The Former United States Embassy Building

Although it isn't much to behold now, the former U.S. embassy (*near the corner of Tou Samouth Blvd. and Quai Karl Marx*) was the scene of utter chaos as the Khmer Rouge entered Phnom Penh in April 1975. On April 12, five days before the Phnom Penh government would capitulate to Pol Pot, U.S. helicopters—in a frantic rush to get Americans, their dependents and selected Cambodians to safety—dropped hundreds of Marines to secure the embassy zone while the mass evacuation took place. Hundreds of other Cambodians, seeking to be evacuated with the Americans, congregated in panic outside the embassy's gate, only to be turned away to meet their fates at the hands of Pol Pot's approaching soldiers.

Phnom Penh Environs

More than 17,000 Cambodians were slaughtered at Choeung Ek.

Choeung Ek

The Killing Fields. There are no words to quite describe the horror that awaits visitors here, about eight miles south of the capital. On approach, it's hard to imagine the human butchery that occurred in these sunny, peaceful fields in the late 1970s. More than 17,000 Cambodians—men, women and children—were killed here by the Khmer Rouge and buried in shallow mass graves. Bones sprout from the earth, many still clothed in the frayed, burlap-like garments their owners were attired in the day they died.

Most killed here had been tortured at Security Prison 21 in downtown Phnom Penh first, then brought to these fields to be bludgeoned to death. (Bullets were saved by the Khmer Rouge to fight other armed factions.) The Memorial Stupa, a 20-foot-tall glass monolith, stands near the shallow bone craters. It houses hundreds, perhaps thousands, of human skulls that have been exhumed in recent years—although only a fraction of the remains buried here have been recovered. The skulls grotesquely line the shelves of the memorial. Most have been tagged: "Asian, Male, 15-20 years old," "Asian, Female, 5-10 years old." They all bear gaping holes in their sides, marking where they had been struck by axes. Many have two chasms.

Clothes have been recovered and are stuffed into a separate shelf. Human teeth are everywhere. You'll be asked by the guide to sign a guestbook and leave a message for the future of Cambodia. Quite understandably, you'll be too numb to devise anything appropriate.

Koki Beach

On Sundays, it seems as if half of Phnom Penh is here, vying for tiny parcels of real estate near the river in which to relax, eat, socialize and sleep. You can get here by motorbike or taxi by taking National Route 1 eight miles past the Monivong bridge; hang a left.

WHERE TO STAY IN PHNOM PENH

Phnom Penh is crawling with journalists, technicians and aid workers. At press time, it was still overflowing with UNTAC soldiers. Since the arrival of the soldiers, prices—and new hotels—have shot up dramatically. We've done our best to keep up with these changes. Keep in mind that many lodgings raise and lower their prices with the demand.

Hotel Cambodiana ★ ★ ★
313 Quai Karl Marx; ☎ *23-2-6139* • This is one of the few places where you might forget you're in Cambodia. Air conditioned chalet-style rooms with views of the Tonlé Sap and Mekong Rivers. Business center, TV, tennis courts, 2 restaurants, pool, health center, travel center, shops. It's the best hotel in Cambodia and is always full, though it may be easier to stay here as UNTAC withdraws. Great place to get the latest info from UN people. Expensive. *Reservations: Direct.*

Motel Cambodiana
313 Quai Karl Marx; ☎ *23-2.6139* • Don't get this confused with the Hotel Cambodiana, although it's nearly as comfortable. Air conditioned bungalows with a restaurant and a view of the river. You can also eat next door at the Cambodina. Moderate.*Reservations: Direct.*

Hotel Monorom
89 Achar Mean Blvd; ☎ *2-6149* • You're back in Cambodia. Air conditioned rooms without the style or elegance of the above two hotels. If you book your lodgings stateside, chances are you'll probably end up in one of these three hotels. Run by Phnom Penh Tourism. Moderate. *Reservations: Direct.*

Paradis Hotel
Achar Mean Blvd., south of Achar Hemcheay Blvd.; ☎ *2-2951* • Good location. Amid the hustle and bustle of Achar Mean Blvd. Relatively new establishment. But aren't they all. Moderate.
Reservations: Direct.

Renakse

On Lenin Blvd. across from the Royal Palace; ☎ *23-2-6036* • This is a charming old French colonial hotel that had previously been an office until 1991. Inexpensive for the amenities. Fax, air conditioned, restaurant. Attracts tourists and UN-related business people. Moderate.

Reservations: Direct.

Royal (formerly Hotel Le Phnom)

92 St. and Achar Mean Blvd.; ☎ *2-3051* • French colonial hotel popular with journalists during the war(s). Can be booked with or without a tour. Cool place if you like 'em seedy and nostalgic. Moderate.

Reservations: Direct.

Capitol Hotel

No 14 AEo Road 182 • The basic essentials. Room with bath. No hot water. Highly popular with the backpack set. Open-air cafe downstairs serves good Cambodian fare and is a great place to meet other travelers and plot Angkor strategy. Cycle and motorbike drivers wait on the street four or five deep, vying for work and generally taking in the oddities called Western tourists. Good place to get a guide to the Killing Fields.

Reservations: Direct.

WHERE TO EAT IN PHNOM PENH

Like hotels, restaurants have started to proliferate in Phnom Penh in the last couple of years. Most are quite inexpensive. Others, though, won't look a gift horse in the mouth when they see it. The gift horse being, of course, those outrageous allowances UNTAC soldiers can spend on gold, Viet hookers and French food.

Food stalls are a great way to eat well and shamefully inexpensively. Food stalls are located throughout the city, but in concentration in and around the Central Market, the Psar Cha Municipal Ferry Landing and across Quai Karl Marx from the Phnom Penh Tourism building on the banks of the Tonlé Sap River.

Rock Hard Cafe

Quai Karl Marx (next door to the Phnom Penh Tourism building) • This is a blatant miniature rip-off of the real thing. Logo's the same and everything. But what lawyer in his right mind's gonna come to Cambodia and do anything about it? Hamburgers, beer and rock 'n roll here. Started by a couple of Western expats mainly to make money off homesick UNTACers—and, boy, do they. Prices for a burger and a brew were outrageous at last check.

Cafe No Problem

Next to the National Museum on 178th Street • Memorable continental restaurant in a restored colonial mansion. This is where a number of Western expats hang out.

Restaurant Tonlé Sap

Quai Karl Marx & 106th Street • They actually have dancing here when they're open and not the Cambodian variety either.

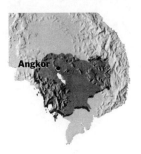

Angkor

An arched gateway to Cambodia's ancient city of Angkor Thom

ANGKOR IN A CAPSULE

Spectacular ancient city...the kingdom once ruled almost all of present-day Indochina and much of Thailand...more than 1 million people lived here at the empire's height in the 11th and 12th centuries...after Khmers fled to Phnom Penh in the 15th century, they became lost...discovered in 1860 by French naturalist Henri Mouhot...site of continued fighting between the Khmer Rouge and government troops through mid-1993...is reachable by independent travelers.

There are four reasons for foreigners being in Cambodia: to supervise elections, repair Russian aircraft, commit suicide and marvel at the vast spectacle of Angkor.

The temples at the lost civilization of Angkor may very well be the most spectacular architectural ruins found on earth. What French naturalist Henri Mouhot discovered in 1860, an endless complex of hundreds of overgrown carved stone temples and structures, was a lost city that reflected the zenith of Khmer history.

In its prime, Angkor stretched 15 miles east to west and six miles north to south. Constructed between the 9th and the 13th centuries, the temples were built around the Khmer interpretation of Indian religious and political beliefs that ultimately evolved from Hinduism to Buddhism. The complex architectural grandeur of Angkor Wat itself, with its remarkable bas reliefs, towers and pools, is arguably unmatched among ancient temples anywhere in the world. In fact, there really isn't anything on earth like Angkor Wat, the most magnificent of all the Khmer temples. The Acropolis in Athens and the Colosseum in Rome come to mind, but can't compare in sheer vastness.

For the last few years, visitors to Angkor have reported having to pay upwards of $100 or more to visit the temples. The money, the government said, was to help pay for the restoration of the temples. This system seemed to self-destruct after UNTAC came to town, though and I never encountered authorities at Angkor asking for an admission payment.

You should put aside at least two days for viewing the temples. Three does the visit more justice. Neighboring Siem Reap has comfortable and cheap accommodations.

And get a guide. They are easily available throughout Siem Reap. Even if you've brought along a map and a guidebook, bring along the human kind with you, as well—if for no other reason than to give yourself a favorable chance of avoiding the many land mines buried in the area. During my last stay, I visited perhaps 80 percent of the sites and felt completely safe. But the relatively new Chinese-made shell casings that litter the area and occasional reports of temple passages being booby-trapped, are grim reminders that ignorance is indeed not the bliss it's made out to be. And these guides, like their Phnom Penh counterparts, are remarkably accomplished in English. Although some areas in the ruins are marked with signs cautioning about mines in the vicinity, many others are not. Just as you'd no more walk around the Grand Canyon at night, you don't move many places in the Siem Reap Province without a guide.

The going rate for Angkor guides is between $15 and $20 a day. If you're like me, you'll become surprisingly close to your new friends in Siem Reap in a short time. And it's not unheard of for guides to provide such favors as doing your laundry if you're in town for a few days.

INSIDER TIP

Most guidebooks say that visits to Angkor are controlled by the govern-ment, that you must be part of a package tour to see the temples and that there is a "fee" of approximately US$100. This is ca ca. You can show up by boat, plane or car, where the splendor of Angkor awaits you abso-lutely free.

WHAT TO SEE AND DO IN ANGKOR

Angkor Wat   ★ ★ ★

With its phenomenally preserved **bas reliefs**, Angkor Wat may well be the most spectacular ancient temple in the world. Constructed some-time between 1112 and 1152 on a low flat alluvial delta surrounded by the most elaborate irrigation system of any ancient city in the world, Angkor Wat was erected to honor the god-king Vishnu. When the Khmers relocated their capital to Phnom Penh during the 15th century, Buddhist monks occupied the structure and protected it from both invaders and the natural elements. Its walls tell of dozens of Khmer legends and depict ancient invasions by monkeys and men alike. In fact, the temple features the largest bas relief carving found in the world.

Angkor Wat is surrounded by an enormous network of **canals** and **moats**, once teeming with crocodiles, that served to irrigate the then-thriving capital city. Most of the crocs, as well as the gibbons in the trees, are gone now from this jungle. Many of the finer statues in the complex were removed and taken to France by archeologist Louis Delaporte in 1873. Restoration on the temple began in earnest in 1898 and the resulting 2-volume book, *Les Monuments du Combodge*, is still acknowledged as the most comprehensive depiction of the site. The book also served to intrigue a variety of visitors, treasure hunters, robbers and vandals (mostly European) who began the tradition of looting and defacing the sculpted city.

The wholesale destruction of Angkor Wat didn't start until 1971 when the Khmer Rouge used the temple complex as a headquarters. To generate income and to simply kill time, the guerrillas began methodically dismantling statues and carvings and removing Buddha statue heads—which were then sold to art dealers in Bangkok. They also heavily mined the jungle and fields surrounding the temples. These mines and others buried by government troops, are numerous and widespread and very, very operable. Stay only on marked paths.

After a disastrous period of clumsy restoration, with workers using acid, cement and abrasive tools on the temple, UNESCO has imple-mented a plan to begin a comprehensive and enduring restoration of Angkor Wat. The temple, though, remains one of the best preserved structures at Angkor. The most plausible explanation is that the sandstone used to construct Angkor Wat was imported from many miles away, as opposed to the predominant use of local stone in the construction of other temples at the complex.

Angkor Wat is one of the few temples facing west and, consequently, the best time for viewing it is during the afternoon.

The Bayon ★★

The Bayon is perhaps the next most spectacular structure in Angkor. A few kilometers north of Angkor Wat, this spooky, ambiguous temple was built directly in the center of the ancient city of Angkor Thom. After its construction, the temple was partially rebuilt, with a third level added to reflect the growing influence of Mahayana Buddhism on the Khmers. The outer wall on the first level features extraordinary bas reliefs depicting Cham soldiers battling Khmer troops.

The Bayon was built during the Khmer transition from Hinduism to Buddhism; its spooky architecture reflects the influences of both faiths.

Ta Prohm ★

If Angkor Wat is spectacular for how well it is preserved, then Ta Prohm is known for how well it isn't. The jungle has literally grown up right through this Buddhist temple constructed during the 12th century. Massive trees are attached to dismembered parts of the structure like molasses, roots oozing through the stone of the courtyards to the jungle floor. Bas reliefs are choked by moss and thick, spiraling vines in this unique osmosis between jungle and stone.

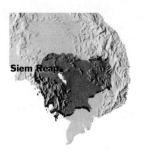

Siem Reap

SIEM REAP IN A CAPSULE

This is your gateway to the temples at Angkor...a quaint little village with a few raggedy remnants of French colonialism...villagers bathe in the Siem Reap River...it's the best place to find a guide to the temples...there's only one hotel, but a small number of friendly guesthouses ...has been the scene of sporadic battles between Khmer Rouge guerrillas and both government and UNTAC troops...the airport briefly fell to the guerrillas early in 1993.

This quaint little village will be your base while you visit the temples at Angkor. It was also a provincial base for UNTAC, which made the town an occasional target for Khmer Rouge rocket attacks during 1993. So don't let its apparent cheerfulness fool you—Siem Reap is the definition of sanguinity. One night early in the year, 40 guerrillas astride motorbikes and brandishing rocket-propelled grenade launchers attacked the town and its airport in relative earnest, battling UNTAC troops at both the airport and at their garrison and injuring a Portuguese tourist visiting the ruins.

For the most part, though, the village—it's the provincial capital—is pretty quiet, its inhabitants lazily working in the surrounding jungle collecting resin from the gum trees. The town center itself is a little dilapidated, but there are a few minor attractions here other then the temples at Angkor.

Because everyone knows each other here, festivals are fun to be around for. A number of bands get together in a large field behind the Grand Hotel d'Angkor and play Cambodian and Thai popular dance tunes during the celebration that marks the end of the rainy season (Festival of the Reversing Current) in October. During the night around Siem Reap, it's not unusual to see the tracers of artillery rounds being exchanged by warring factions in the countryside.

GETTING THERE

The two primary ways of getting to Siem Reap and Angkor are via daily flights from Phnom Penh aboard a Russian-built Cambodia Airlines Antonov An-24, or by the twice-weeky ferry out of Psar Cha Ferry Landing. If you take the ferry, stock up on provisions for this interesting and occasionally bizarre 24-hour journey across the Tonlé Sap Lake and down the Tonlé Sap River. And get a hammock. They can be had at the Central Markets both in Phnom Penh and Siem Reap for about $3. It'll be your only means to get some z's.

The flight's about 45 minutes and goes for about $50 one way; the ferry's only a couple of bucks. Hope you don't mind a few cockroaches.

Adventure tourists regulary hitchhike National Route 6 between Phnom Penh and Siem Reap.

INSIDER TIP

Most adventure tourists opt to get to Siem Reap by means other than aircraft these days, now that it's relatively safe to do so. Hitchhiking is still a little risky. The other option is going by ferry from Phnom Penh's Psar Cha Ferry landing. The ferry leaves twice a week, from both Phnom Penh and Phnom Krom (about 6 miles south of Siem Reap). The ride along the Tonlé Sap River and across the Tonlé Sap Lake is usually a 24-hour affair. But these boats are dilapidated and it's not unusual for one to go down every now and then in a monsoon. First, buy a hammock. They're cheap. Then stock up on enough provisions for two days. Bring a lot of fruit, bread, water and toilet paper.

WHAT TO SEE AND DO IN SIEM REAP

Central Market

The busy Central Market in Siem Reap (about a mile east of the Siem Reap River) is a muddy, bustling marketplace best for stocking up on fresh fruit and local delicacies. Both the pineapple and the durian were the sweetest I've ever tasted. Here, you can also watch artisans creating magnificently-filligreed gold jewelry. But wear boots during the southwestern monsoon season. Although marginally covered, this place never dries out.

Siem Reap Zoo

The zoo, located on the road to Phnom Krom, is really not much more than what's outside the zoo, but with a fence around it. However, there's a bunch of large crocs lounging about that make the stop worth it. Also, don't screw around with the monkeys, who roam the grounds freely. If you get between a mama gibbon and her kid, she may end up on your back. It hurts. Across from the zoo is where a number of townspeople bathe in the sometimes raging Siem Reap River.

WHERE TO STAY IN SIEM REAP

Grand Hotel d'Angkor

Located on the road to Angkor, about a hundred yards north of National Route 6; ☎ *15* • The only real hotel in Siem Reap. French colonial. 60 rooms at last check. Air conditioning in most of the rooms. Restaurant, bar. The restaurant's expensive. Colonial feel, but dark. Closest lodging to the temples. Moderate.   ***Reservations: Direct.***

Dr. Ith Kim Phan's Guesthouse

0129 Achar Hem Chiev • This is my recommendation when coming to Siem Reap. Dr. Ith and his wife are the warmest people this side of tomorrowland. They're popular with the villagers, so staying here is a great way to get to know your new neighbors. The rooms are cozy, clean and comfortable. The stilt home has an airy, woodsy feel. And it's cheap, about $10 a night. There's a cafe out back that was big with the UNTAC crowd. Inexpensive.   ***Reservations: No such thing.***

WHERE TO EAT IN SIEM REAP

Food stalls can be found throughout Siem Reap. The road running north along the east side of the Siem Reap River has a number of the largest ones. Like Phnom Penh, full meals can usually be had for under $1. Additionally, food stalls and refreshment stands can be found in and around the temple sites.

The Outer Limits

Along the Coast

Cambodia isn't known for its beaches and that's what perhaps makes them such a treat when you reach them. The country has more than 200 miles of coastline, most of it totally unspoiled. What's kept people away from these areas has been the Khmer Rouge, who ruined entire towns and villages in the late 1970s in their maniacal upheaval, including the once popular resort of Kep. In fact, by the time Pol Pot fled Phnom Penh, not a single structure was left standing in this town.

Kampot also suffered at the hands of the Khmer Rouge. And if the new FUNCINPEC government starts tapping its coasts for resort development, Kampot is one area expected to be targeted.

Kompong Som, Cambodia's only seaport, is another area that may experience relatively significant growth over the next few years.

Koh Kong is a small island in the Gulf of Thailand, only about 20 miles from the Thai border. It's surrounded by calm, azure waters—a diver's paradise. This area, too, has reportedly been targeted for tourism.

Eastern, Central & Western Cambodia

Other than Siem Reap, these areas of Cambodia remain largely inaccessible, both for political and infrastructure reasons. The U.S. State Department, as of this writing, is still urging Americans to avoid any form of travel in central and western Cambodia. The Khmer Rouge still controls approximately 20 percent of the country, with most of the area located in the west. Pailin, near the Thai border, for instance, has been entirely under Khmer Rouge control since 1975. The guerrillas make Pailin their principle base.

Battambang, with a population estimated at 90,000, is the country's second largest city. It's also along Cambodia's main rail route. But the city continues to be shelled regularly, although rarely accurately, by Khmer Rouge units and is, again, not a place most tourists would consider a destination.

Cambodia's northeastern region is sparsely populated and extremely inaccessible. Population centers in the east are found primarily along or near National Route 1, the route to Saigon.

Take extreme caution when traveling anywhere in Cambodia. It'll be a long time before this place is tamed. If it ever is.

INDONESIA

Sittin' on the dock of the bay, Kalimantan. Young Dayaks are leaving their villages in the interior for jobs in Kalimantan's coastal boom towns.

INDONESIA IN A CAPSULE

World's largest archipelago with 13,677 islands reaching from Pacific to Indian Ocean...more than half uninhabited...estimated population is 190,000...Java is home to more than half the population...Bali is the most visited destination...official language is Bahasa Indonesian...variety of natural wonders from volcanoes to lush rainforests and coral reefs...famous for headhunter Dayak tribe, Komodo dragons and handmade batik...produces world's most sought-after spices...fifth largest producer of oil in the world and leading exporter of natural gas.

It's no wonder that Indonesia's motto translates to "Unity in Diversity." Indonesia offers more contrasts than perhaps any nation on the globe, both in terms of its natural geographic wonders and its people. From modern, cosmopolitan Jakarta to Stone Age tribes whose customs and mores remain unchanged for millennia, Indonesia is a microcosm of the history of the earth.

Its estimated population of 190,000 people—from Asmats to Balinese to Dayaks—speak hundreds of different languages and live in an area twice the size of Britain that would stretch well past the span of the United States. The islands reach from the Pacific to the Indian Ocean. And more than half of them are uninhabited! In fact, the island of Java itself is home to more than half the population.

The islands are beautiful, offering astounding vistas and a variety of natural wonders—from active volcanoes (perhaps 200 of them) towering above lush tropical rainforests and terraced rice fields, to crystal clear waters, clean white beaches and beautiful coral reefs. There are glaciers in the Central Highlands and tropical swamps in Sumatra.

Indonesia has found its place on the tourist map, although you'll find true amenities only in areas that have been targeted for tourism. The rest of the nation retains its fertile, unspoiled nature.

The island of Bali is the most visited destination in the archipelago and although you might be tempted to bypass it because of how heavily touristed it is, you'd be making a mistake—as its spectacular volcanoes and ancient temples perched on cliffs offer both history and unmatched panoramas.

Java is a lush tropical paradise and home to one of man's earliest ancestors. Huge black sand dunes and the rugged landscape of Mount Bromo alone make a stop here worth it. Java is the economic, political and cultural backbone of the country. Some of Indonesia's most highly acclaimed art is created on Java.

Sumatra is the fifth largest island on the planet and is the third most touristed island in Indonesia. It offers incredible trekking opportunities as well as challenging rafting trips. The Batak people on the island live in colorful, intricately carved houses that sit on poles. And there's a popular lake resort at Lake Toba.

The infamous headhunter Dayaks inhabit Kalimantan on the island of Borneo. They've mellowed out a bit in recent years, so don't reach for your neck if these guys invite you over for a party. They're some of the friendliest people in Indonesia and they do like to party.

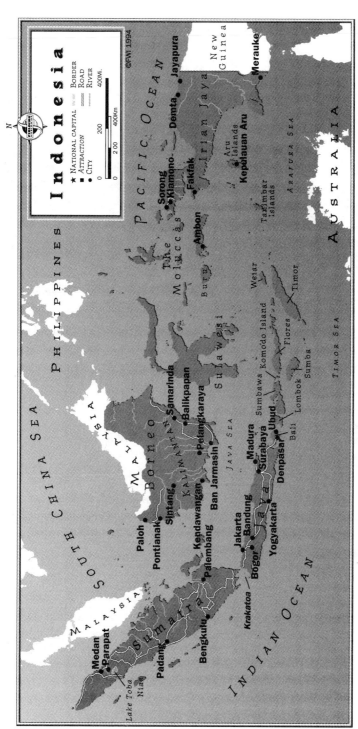

Waiting for customers, Kalimantan. Under Indonesia's transmigration program, thousands of Balinese and Javanese have been brought in to inhabit Kalimantan's interior.

The Maluku archipelago is a vast chain of more than 1,000 islands, featuring volcanoes and dazzling coral reefs. These islands are also home to some of the world's most sought-after spices, including cloves, mace and nutmeg.

Indonesia today is OPEC's fifth largest producer of oil and the world's leading exporter of natural gas. The government is stable and the country is remarkably easy to get around—especially by air.

History of Indonesia

Traders from China and India, who assimilated into the local animistic beliefs of religions from the East—such as Hinduism, Brahmanism, Vishnuism and Mahayana Buddhism—were among the earliest outside influences on the Indonesian archipelago. This process of peaceful assimilation lasted for some six centuries and eventually engulfed this entire vast group of islands. For example, the Mahayana Buddhist kingdom of Shri-Vijaya in Sumatra came to power around A.D. 672 and reigned throughout the 13th century. During this period, the largest and most renowned monument extant to Buddha was erected—the vast stupa of Borobudur, which dates from the 9th century under Shri-Vijaya's Shailendra Dynasty. Other historic monuments that represent ambitious examples of the Hindu-Buddhist influence in the archipelago at this time are the temples at Prambanan, Pawon, Mendut and Kelasan.

The Arrival of Islam

While trade was burgeoning during the 13th century (indeed, Marco Polo is said to have stopped by the Moluccas in 1292 and immediately called them the "spice islands"), yet another religion was introduced. This was Islam, which arrived in Sumatra as early as the 13th century and spread gradually through the archipelago for the next 200 years. As more and more Islamic "kingdoms" arose in Sumatra, Java, Sulawesi, Kalimantan and the Moluccas, the Hindu era came to an end. Hence, many Hindu followers fled to Bali where they continued their religion in isolation. To this day, Bali is the only island in the chain where the greater part of the population embraces Hinduism.

That the Indonesian people can be considered among the most tolerant and peace-loving on this earth is understandable from their location between Asia and Australia and their fascinating history. Furthermore, they can rightfully boast the discovery in 1891 of the "Java Man" (*Pithaecanthropus erectus*) of the Pleistocene Era, proving that some sort of civilization occurred here on what was most likely still part of the Asian mainland (about 500,000 years ago), while sheets of ice still covered Europe and the Western Hemisphere. "Solo Man" was unearthed in the 1930s, not far from Trinil and thought to be between 60,000 and 100,000 years old—of a Stone Age culture.

Colonial Rule

The Portuguese conquest of Malacca brought Europeans into the region. These Portuguese were especially interested in the Moluccas, because they wanted their spices at the lowest prices possible! By the end of the 17th century, the Portuguese were being challenged by the Dutch and the British. The rivalry of the three powers culminated in the triumph of the Dutch East India Company, which had already established itself in Java in 1619 and renamed the principal port city Batavia. Except for a few brief years during the Napoleonic Wars (1811-1815), when the English were in control and Sir Thomas Stamford Raffles was the much respected governor (and wrote the still worthy *History of Java*), the Dutch ruled Indonesia with an iron hand for about three centuries.

During colonial rule, a number of popular heroes challenged the unsympathetic policies that emanated from The Netherlands. Among them were Trunajaya, Surapati, Iman Bonjol (plenty of streets named after this one), Teuku Umar and Prince Diponegoro. Leading the resistance prior to the Second World War were Mohammed Hatta and Achmed Sukarno, later considered "father of the country" and its first president. These two men were symbols of the struggle against Dutch repression of the native Indonesian language, education for all and work opportunities. Both were often jailed and even exiled. The Dutch were dispersed in 1942 as the Japanese arrived, bringing yet another occupation. But the Indonesians soon realized that this subjugation was only temporal; to ensure as much cooperation as possible, the Japanese espoused eventual independence from colonial rule.

The Move Toward Independence

Indonesian nationalism received a hefty boost between 1942 and 1945. The Japanese military regime relied heavily on local administrative and political support, reinstated the Indonesian language in schools and renamed Batavia "Jakarta." The regime also recognized the ideals of both Sukarno and Hatta who, on the very day of the Japanese surrender to the Allies, issued their famous Proclamation of Independence. It was August 17, 1945 and it was one of the postwar shots "heard 'round the world."

Four long and arduous years followed as Indonesians fought a revolution to regain their land from the foreign devils who had occupied it for so long. It took world opinion and some discussion in the United Nations before the Dutch bowed and returned the sovereign rights of The Netherlands East Indies back to the new Republic of Indonesia. Queen Juliana finally signed the official document on December 27, 1949.

Achmed Sukarno became the new nation's first president, a post he held until deposed in 1965. He was a brilliant and charismatic man, whom his fellow countrymen called "Bung" (brother) Karno. Some said his manner was so mesmerizing that he could persuade and cajole just about anyone. However, in his later years of power he seemed to "run amok" and misuse the trust bestowed upon him by the people. He married a Japanese call girl, who called herself Dewi (goddess), and lavished jewels and furs upon her while most of the country lived in poverty. He elected himself president "for life" and put forward a "guided democracy," against all that was written in the Constitution. He erected costly monuments to his glory and entered into an unnecessary confrontation with neighboring Malaysia. He withdrew membership of the Republic from the United Nations and espoused "Nasakom," an acronym for nationalism, religion and Communism.

The Foiled Communist Takeover

An attempted Communist coup in September 1965 failed but instigated more than a year of intense bloodshed, as Indonesians turned on each other in an attempt to rid the country of inside and outside Communist influences. Almost half a million lives were estimated lost—sometimes whole villages—before the Sukarno regime was deposed. The "father of the country" died a broken man, under house arrest. He was succeeded by Major General Suharto, who was installed as president of the Republic in 1968.

Under Suharto's leadership, the bankrupt and bereft country has reclaimed its place in the world. There are enviable natural resources (including plenty of gas and oil) and healthy foreign investments. However, there are still plenty of problems: immense poverty, too great a distinction between the classes, high illiteracy and infant mortality, factions between certain ethnic groups and a rampant bureaucracy. Yet, visitors never fail to be overwhelmed by the beauty of the land and the people.

The Advent of Tourism

Tourist facilities are developing slowly but steadily (though in Bali, in the past few years, development has been too rapid for some), as the government understands how important this industry is. Travelers not only bring in much needed "hard currency," they also offer an appreciation of the diverse cultures of the archipelago and the indigenous artistry inherent here. Worldwide concern for the restoration of Borobudur prompted IBM to offer computer technology, saving years of work and millions of dollars. At the same time, this concern brought focus to Yogyakarta—cultural capital of the country—and the preservation of such arts as batik, wayang plays, the ramayana ballet, silver-working and other manifestations of the archipelago's colorful history.

Sexual Equality

Perhaps it is the women of Indonesia who make the country so vibrant in the eyes of Westerners, for they have never been anything but "liberated." Proud, beautiful and forthright, they fought alongside their men in the struggle for independence and then took their well-earned place in the social and economic world. In addition to their beauty and feminism, Indonesian women are equal partners with the men in any business, profession, or trade they may wish to pursue. They also have the rare distinction of pointing proudly to a period in their history when a kingdom ruled by women flourished. (Even today among the Bataks of Sumatra, a multilineal society still prevails where inheritance and lineage are traced from the maternal line and local issues are settled by a village council in consultation with women.) So, it comes as no surprise that one of modern Indonesia's greatest heroes is Ibu (Mother) Kartini, the little princess who advocated freedom and emancipation for all during the late 19th century.

PLANNING AHEAD

INDONESIAN TOURIST PROMOTION OFFICE

The tourist office for North America is located at *3457 Wilshire Blvd., Los Angeles, CA 90010* (☎ *213-387-2078).* Since the tourist office is sometimes slow in responding to requests, a good alternative for assistance is Garuda Orient Holidays, the tour operator affiliate of Garuda Indonesia, the country's national airline. Garuda Orient has two offices in the U.S.—one in Los Angeles *(☎ 213-389-4600),* in the same building as the tourist office and one at *51 E. 42 St., New York, NY 10017* (☎ *212-983-6288).* Tourist information and visas are available at the Indonesian Embassy in Washington, DC and Ottawa, Ontario, Canada; the Indonesian Consulate General in New York City, San Francisco and Houston; and the Indonesian Consulate in Los Angeles and Vancouver. There is also an Honorary Consul for Indonesia in Hawaii (c/o Pacific Resources Inc. in Honolulu). A **Visitor Information Center** is located in the Jakarta Theatre Bldg. at *9 Jalan M. Husni Thamrin,* not far from the Hotel Indonesia (☎ *354094).* Other local information can be obtained from **NITOUR**, the National and International Tourist Bureau at *2 Jalan Majapahit* and at offices throughout the country.

VISAS

Visas are not required of bona fide tourists holding valid U.S. and Canadian passports for a stay of up to two months for entry at Denpasar (Bali), Jakarta, Medan, Biak and Manado. An onward ticket is necessary and passport must be valid for at least six months after date of arrival.

INOCULATIONS

Inoculations for smallpox and cholera are required for entry and must be validated in an International Health Certificate if arriving from an infected area. Yellow fever inoculation may also be required if arriving from an infected area. Depending upon length of stay and itinerary, other inoculations you should discuss with your doctor are typhoid, paratyphoid and gammaglobulin (for hepatitis). Ask about malaria pills.

ENTRY BY AIR

Getting in by air is through the Cengkareng (Soekarno-Hatta) International Airport in Jakarta, Halim Hlp International Airport, Ngurah Rai International Airport at Denpasar on Bali, or Polonia International Airport in Medan (Sumatra), Batubesar (Batam), Simpang Tiga (Pekanbaru), Sam Ratulangi (Manado), Pattimura (Ambon) and Bitung (North Sulawesi). A new terminal that opened at the **Soekarno-Hatta Airport in 1992** has helped alleviate congestion. Cengkareng is about 19 miles from Jakarta but the trip takes one hour. A **taxi** from the airport into Jakarta costs about rupiah (Rp) 15,000; the airport bus costs Rp 3,000. If you are not part of a tour and being taken care of, opt for a hotel limousine into the city. Taxis add a surcharge plus road toll so you need a fistful of rupiahs even before the door is closed. There are banks for changing currency and porterage service at all the airports. Be sure to save plenty of time for baggage handling, immigration and customs. Speed is not a virtue here!

EXIT BY AIR

Leaving is a normal procedure, provided you have not overstayed your welcome, your onward passage is confirmed and you are not exporting Indonesian currency and/or valuable artifacts. **Departure tax** is Rp 15,000 for international flights. The tax for domestic flights varies, but averages about Rp 3,500.

ARRIVAL BY SEA

Entering Indonesia by sea is possible through the international ports of Belawan (Sumatra), Denpasar (Bali), Jakarta (Java), Padang Bay (Bali), Surabaya (Java) and Padang (Sumatra). If you are planning to disembark your luxury cruise vessel or cargo ship in one of these ports, be sure to enlist the aid of the line's local agent to clear immigration and customs.

The cruise lines sailing the Indonesian archipelago, or calling at Indonesian ports, include Princess, Renaissance, Seabourn, Cunard, Seven Seas, Classical, Crystal, Royal, Holland America and Pearl Cruises.

DUTY FREE

Duty free is not the byword here and the importation of consumer goods, other than personal effects, is carefully noted. Bona fide visitors may bring in the usual amount of alcoholic beverages (2 liters per adult), cigarettes (200), 50 cigars or 100 grams of tobacco and a reasonable amount of perfume. Photographic equipment, typewriters, radios, and other accoutrements must be recorded and the serial numbers may be entered right into your passport. Since this is the usual practice in most controlled countries, travelers should not be offended but rather save time by entering the serial numbers themselves (the last page is best).

On the customs declaration, visitors will also be required to state the exact amount of foreign currency in their possession as well as the amount of film (specify exposed or not). And avoid carrying pets, plants, or fruit.

CURRENCY

The currency of Indonesia is the Rupiah (Rp). The approximate rate of exchange is about 1773 Rp. to U.S.$1.00. Coins in denominations of Rp 5, 10, 25, 50 and 100 are circulated, and notes are Rp 100, 500, 1000, 5000 and 10,000. Stick to the lower denominations outside major hotels, as change may not be available. Use the coins for tips and the many unfortunate ones you may encounter on the streets, who always have their hands out.

The best rate of exchange is through major banks, although it is more convenient in hotels. Rupiahs can be reconverted at the airport, provided you have receipts to prove the transaction. It is prohibited to carry Indonesian currency in or out of the country.

LOCAL TIME

The time in most of Indonesia is Greenwich Mean Time plus 7 hours. Jakarta is exactly 12 hours in advance of Eastern Standard Time and in the same zone as Bangkok, Java, Bali, Sumatra and Madura. It is 1 hour behind Hong Kong, Manila and Taipei and 2 hours behind Tokyo and Seoul. Since the Indonesian Archipelago is so vast, the islands of Kalimantan, Sulawesi and Nusa Tenggara (not Bali) are on GMT plus 8 hours; and the islands of Maluku and Irian Jaya are on GMT plus 9 hours.

LOCAL CURRENT

The current is 220 volts, 50 cycles, so travelers should pack converters and extension cords.

LOCAL WATER

Water should be avoided. Only bottled or boiled water should be used (supplied in major hotels). Ice in top tourist hotels is made with boiled water (or so they say), so use your discretion according to the sensitivity of your intestines.

This is a country in which belly problems can be frequent.

OFFICIAL LANGUAGE

The official language in Indonesia is Bahasa Indonesia, although regional languages like Javanese, Balinese and Chinese often take over in the outlying areas. English is widely spoken in major tourist centers and old-timers will remember the Dutch they were forced to learn in school. Bahasa Indonesia is based on Malay and contains many words of Sanskrit and Arabic origin. It was introduced as a national language in 1928, while the country was still under Dutch colonial rule and spread rapidly as a matter of nationalist pride. The grammar is quite simple and it is rather easy to learn a few words during your stay.

There are some 25 major daily publications on Java, with two in English, the *Indonesia Times* and *Indonesian Observor*. They are available along with overseas publications (sometimes censored) in major hotels. There are almost 50 radio stations and one government-owned television station in the country. Some of the television programs broadcast in the evening will be familiar to Americans. Whoever would have dreamed that Indonesian was spoken in the Wild West!

Maps and small area guides in English are available from the Directorate General of Tourism in Jakarta as well as in hotel shops.

BUSINESS HOURS

Businesses are generally open from 8 a.m.-3 p.m. Mon. through Thurs.; until 11:30 a.m. on Fri. only; and from 8 a.m.-2 p.m. on Sat. Some firms close at 4 p.m. weekdays, with an hour off for lunch. Banks are often only open from 9 a.m. until noon weekdays; from 9-10:30 a.m. on Sat.; so always make

your transactions early to be assured of service.

NOTE: *It is best not to accept someone else's word for hours of business; find out for yourself.*

There are plenty of local trade associations and multinational companies in Jakarta, especially for those in the business of oil, cement, or banking. The **American Chamber of Commerce** in Indonesia is located in the Citibank Bldg. *(8th floor), 55 Jalan M. H. Thamrin* (☎ *354993;* Telex: *44368).* The president is H.V. Ward. The **Investment Coordinating Board** is located at *6 Jalan Jen. Gatot Subroto, Selatan, Jakarta* (☎ *512008; Telex: 44368).* Anwar Nawawi is the promotion chief.

The **U.S. Embassy** in Jakarta is located at *5 Jalan Medan Merdeka, Selatan* (☎ *3400019).* The **Canadian Embassy** can be found at *29 Jalan J. Sudirman Kav* (☎ *584030).*

TIPPING

It's becoming a practice in Indonesia, but it is still mainly in the Rp 500 range for small services (taxi drivers, porters, bellboys and barbers). If your luggage is especially cumbersome, another Rp 100 is in order, per bag. Major hotels and restaurants add a straight 10% service charge to accommodation, bar and restaurant chits but another 5% (equivalent) here and there doesn't hurt. (Be prepared for the 11% government tax on top of everything else, however.)

TELEPHONE, TELEX AND FAX

These services in Indonesia have improved somewhat in the past 15 years but never expect miracles. Always use the telex in your hotel so you can scream about payment when it gets messed up (some businessmen book hotels according to the integrity of the telex operators). Overseas telephone calls should also be made from your hotel and it is always better to call out than to receive (hotel operators in Indonesia are notorious for saying, "Sorry, he or she is not registered" when indeed you are sitting upstairs waiting). The local telephone system is not much better and usually out of order. Rely on the good services of your hotel for local calls to avoid unnecessary frustration.

Major hotels are also helpful in mailing letters and packages back home, but be sure to insist upon actually feeling the stamps (once bought and paid for) and attaching them yourself. Don't play the "all out" game; waiting another day for stamps will ensure delivery of your mail.

WHAT TO WEAR

Wear what the Indonesians wear, the loveliest cotton batik in the world. As the archipelago actually straddles the equator, you can assume that the climate is exceptionally hot and sticky. It also rains frequently and fast, but the nights are blissfully cool. Synthetic fibers and pantsuits should be left at home. Here, you will need natural cottons that do not confine the body. Sport shirts and slacks are fine for the men, dresses and loose-flowing garments for the ladies. Life in Indonesia is casual and although local businessmen do don Western-style suits and ties, they need "dress up" only in the major hotels at dinnertime. Then, it becomes almost a necessity because the air conditioning is so cold.

Comfortable shoes are also a necessity here, because walking around in the heat will probably make your feet swell. Sunhats or parasols and plenty of sunscreen are also advisable because the rays are extra strong at this latitude. If your touring includes a stop at a tea plantation or a sacred mountain, the air will be quite cool so slacks and sweaters are in order. For beach and pool time, many visitors buy a length of batik and wear it as a sarong while walking through hotel lobbies and the like. In fact, the batiks are so irresistible that you may find a new wardrobe following you home!

LOCAL TRANSPORTATION

Transit throughout Indonesia varies from two- to four-wheeled vehicles to trains and an extensive domestic air service. **Taxis** are plentiful in the large metropolitan areas. In Jakarta, it is best to use the Bluebird taxi company fleet which has meters that work. In Denpasar (Bali), taxis often set fixed rates between town and the hotels. There are also pick-up taxis between Jakarta and resort areas and each passenger pays according to the length of the ride. Major hotels have their own taxis, which are air-conditioned and comfortable but more expensive. But passengers pay for the convenience of a driver who has been properly instructed and maneuvers carefully through the usually clogged city traffic. These cars can also be hired for the day, for visitors and/or business executives with a tight schedule.

Local **buses** are best left to the natives; they are uncomfortable and hopelessly overcrowded and language is a problem. There are express buses linking major towns if you don't mind a bouncy ride. Cities linked by bus service in Java are Jakarta, Yogyakarta, Surabaya, Bogor, Cirebon, Semarang, Surakarta, Tegal, Purwokerto, Magelang, Malang and Bandung. In Sumatra, bus service links Banda Aceh, Medan, Parapat, Sibolga, Padang, Bukittinggi, Pekan Baru, Jambi, Palembang, Bengkulu and Tanjungkarang.

One of the most widely used routes is between Surabaya and Bali.

For traveling short distances around the town, you can choose among the **oplet, bemo, becak, ojek**, or **tonga**.

The **oplet** (actually opelette) is Jakarta's answer to the Philippine jeepney but lacks the colorful exterior. Cheap and handy, they ply regular routes like buses and even go as far as Bogor. The **bemo** is considered the poor man's taxi; a three-wheeled motorized pedicab, it also runs regular routes although it can also be hired for individual purposes. The bemo seats one passenger in front and six in the back compartment. In Bali the bemo is a converted pick-up truck and seats about 10 passengers on wooden benches. The **becak** is a three-wheeled pedicab and only operates in Jakarta between the hours of 10 p.m. and 6 a.m. by law, although they operate freely in Yogyakarta. Fares for the oplet and bemo, as well as the **ojek**—a kind of bicycle taxi (often motorized), and the **tonga**, a horsecart, should be negotiated and agreed upon before the ride. The tonga is called a **dokar, delman**, or **sado** in Indonesia. It seats one passenger next to the driver and about three behind for a minimum fare of Rp 200. They are most frequently found in the outlying areas, not in towns or cities.

Railway buffs may wish to try either the **bima** or **mutiara** train between Jakarta's Kota Railway Station and Surabaya via Yogyakarta. The bima is the better, with berths and a dining car. The mutiara has only reclining seats for the trip that takes from 15-1/2 to 18 hours but passes some interesting countryside (although mainly in the dark). There are other trains in Java and Sumatra, but be prepared for primitive travel.

Domestic **air** service is frequent and inexpensive and the most recommended way to travel within Indonesia. Garuda Indonesia offers Americans and other passengers who use its flights internationally money-saving Indonesia Air Passes on its domestic services (☎ 800-3-GARUDA). Garuda Indonesia Airways links Jakarta with 30 domestic destinations using DC9 jets. Merpati Nusantara Airlines covers the smaller areas with smaller planes. Bouraq Indonesian Airlines has a large fleet for charter service only.

There is also **ferry** service available between Merak, Java and Padang, Sumatra, with six departures daily. Ferries between Ujungganyar (Java) and Kamal (Madura) depart every 30 minutes; those between Ketapang (Java) and Gillimanuk (Bali) depart approximately every 2-1/2 hours. Fares are incredibly cheap to match the lack of luxury.

Finally, for do-it-yourself touring, there are plenty of **rental cars** available from international companies (Avis, Hertz, National) but prices are high for chauffered-vehicles. Expect to pay more than U.S.$100 per day. Actually, the **motorcycle** is the favored beast of burden in Bali and Yogyakarta. Motorcycles can be rented for about $5.50 per day. Beachniks hire them by the day or week. They are practical, easy to manage and totally ruin what is left of the atmosphere.

LOCAL CUSTOMS

Customs in Indonesia vary among the islands in the archipelago because so many ethnic groups inhabit this vast area. Despite a turbulent history and considerable bloodshed in the 20th century, the people are courteous and gentle. Westerners who dress immodestly, speak in loud voices and use rude gestures are not appreciated. The Indonesians are very hospitable and visitors are expected to at least taste food and drink when offered. As in all Moslem countries (only Bali is Hindu), the left hand is considered unclean and should not be used to pass or eat food.

When visiting religious monuments and places considered sacred, proper dress should be worn and polite respect observed. *Photographers should always ask permission before "shooting,"* especially in outlying areas where the imprint of one's image may be contrary to tradition and belief.

The Javanese seem to engage in rule by consensus and dislike outward signs of disagreement, so consider anything but a firm "YES" to be a silent "NO"—a word that will not pass their lips. And take along an extra supply of patience, for it takes a long, long time to accomplish anything in this country. Time means nothing here, despite the influx of digital watches from Japan and Hong Kong and the waiting period for appointments is often lengthy. Of course, a little *baksheesh* (tip) will always pave the way and is the usual practice in this country.

FESTIVALS AND HOLIDAYS

Festivals and holidays occur in Indonesia almost daily and are part of the charm of this country. In Bali, expect some type of temple celebration wherever you go (details available locally). The Ramayana Ballet Festival is held between May and October during the full moon at the Prambanan Temple near Yogyakarta. Wayang kulit (Indonesian shadow plays) are performed all year round in Yogyakarta at the Gedung Kiwo and the Ambarrukmo Palace Hotel. Public holidays are marked with an asterisk(*).

*January 1	New Year's Day	
January 11	Sekaten	*Week-long Moslem fair in Yogyakarta and Surakarta that precedes the prophet Mohammed's birthday.*
January 14	Galungan	*Most important event in the Balinese year. It symbolizes victory of good over evil with decorations, offerings, gamelan music and dancing.*
January 18	Grebeg Maulud	*Ceremonies in Yogyakarta and Surakarta commemorate the birth of the prophet Mohammed. Music plays at midnight.*
January	Kunigan	*Offerings and religious ceremonies throughout Bali to honor ancestral spirits.*
January/ February	Chinese New Year	*Noisy celebrations among Jakarta's Chinese population.*
*March	Idul Fitri	*End of Ramadan, the traditional month of fasting for Moslems. Two full days of holiday and feasting. The date of this holiday changes from year to year as it is based on the 10-month Moslem calendar cycle.*
March	Nyepi	*A Hindu day of silence, celebrated in Bali.*
March/April	Wafat isa Aimasih	*Christian Good Friday.*
May	Sedang Sono Pilgrimage	*Javanese Catholics make pilgrimage to Sendang Sono, a shrine dedicated to Holy Virgin.*
May	Waicak	*Commemorates Lord Buddha's birth...country's few Buddhists attend ceremonies at Borobudur.*
May 30	Sarawati	*Commemorates the God of Knowledge in Bali with religious ceremonies at temples and reading the Veda book in homes.*

FESTIVALS AND HOLIDAYS

June 3	Pagerwesi	*Religious rituals throughout Bali honor Sang Hyang Pramesti Guru, creator of universe and offerings are made to ward off evil forces.*
***June 22**	National Founding Day	
July 17	Balimu	*This ritual of purification falls prior to the month of fasting, especially at Negeri Pau and Durian Tinggi in West Sumatra, where you can see processions and a show of martial arts by young men of both villages.*
August 13	Galungan	*Repeat of January's festivities on Bali.*
***August 17**	Independence Day	*Parades, official ceremonies and carnival atmosphere, plus decorated buildings in Jakarta.*
August 23	Kuningan	*Same observances as January holiday, repeated throughout Bali.*
September 23	North Sulawesi Anniversary	*Cultural performances, horse and bull racing events in Manado.*
***October 8**	Idul Adha	*Eve of Haj is marked by an annual pilgrimage to Mecca for Moslems. Cattle are slaughtered and offered to the poor.*
December 23	Batara Turun Kabeh	*Temple ceremonies at Panataran Agung, Besakih in Bali.*
***December 25**	Christmas	*Celebrated throughout Indonesia.*
December 31	Sekaten	*Repeat of January's festivities on Bali.*

Background Material

There are many fine books that discuss Indonesia, but few of them seem to have found their way into North American outlets. Check your local library for a bibliography. You can also pick up some books locally (Wirjosuparto and Kartini).

The Art of Indonesia by Frits A. Wagner, an *Art of the World* series book (Crown Publishers). Gives an excellent historical, sociological and religious background overview.

The History of Java by Sir Thomas Stamford Raffles (Oxford University Press, 1965, two volumes). More history to enjoy.

Rama Stories in Indonesia by Sutjipto Wirjosuparto (Bhratara Publishers, Jakarta).

Letters of a Javanese Princess by Raden Adjeng Kartini, translated by Agnes L. Symmers (W. W. Norton). Ibu Kartini is one of the country's most beloved folk heroines.

Ring of Fire by Lawrence Blair with Loren Blair (Bantam, 1988).

Islands of Fire, Islands of Spice by Richard Bangs and Christian Kallen (Sierra Club Books, 1988).

The New Indonesia Handbook by Bill Dalton (4th edition) (Moon Publications, 1993).

Insight Guides for Bali, Java, Indonesia (APA Productions, Prentice Hall) Check copyright page for most current update.

Ramayana and Mahabharata—two originally Indian epic poems on which lie all Indonesian arts. Gods, kings, demons and clowns in these tales are brought to life nightly by island's puppeteers.

Jakarta

JAKARTA IN A CAPSULE

*Capital of Republic of Indonesia...one of Southeast Asia's largest cities...
population of 13 million...located on northwest coast of Java...originally
a Hindu-ruled settlement called Sunda Kelapa...conquering Moslem
prince renamed city Jayakarta (City of Victory), June 22, 1527, a national
holiday celebrated every year...Dutch East India Company seized city in
1619 and renamed it Batavia...colonial rule lasted almost 325 years...dur-
ing Japanese-occupied period (1942-45), city was named Jakarta again...-
and it stuck...focal point of country's cultural, economic and political
forces...and a center for international businessmen and women.*

Jakarta is huge. Thirteen million people live in an area three times
the size of Singapore. This sprawling, polluted metropolis is home to
Indonesia's greatest achievements, as well as an undercarriage of extreme poverty that clings to the city's prosperity like resin. The
streets are crusty; the pungent air is rust-colored, thick with the un-
controlled emissions of automobiles, trucks and motorcycles
shrouding the skyscrapers. Many consider the traffic in Jakarta to be
even more congested than Bangkok, if that's possible.

Jakarta is the center of everything for Indonesia—commerce, communications, entertainment, manufacturing and the arts. Naturally,
it also boasts the highest per capita income rate in Indonesia. This
has spawned an incredible migration to the city from the Outer Islands, rural refuges with images of affluence. Nearly 50 percent of
Jakarta's inhabitants were born elsewhere. But this migration has
also bred disillusionment and incredible poverty.

Like many Southeast Asian cities that are both enjoying an economic boom and struggling to come to terms with the resultant social consequences, Jakarta is a city of amazing paradoxes. Beautiful
hotels, shopping malls, museums and restaurants have sprouted

from Jakarta's pavement in recent years—they bud in marked contrast with the city's filthy slums.

But there are a number of things to do in the capital. There are museums and temples; there's shopping and day-trips to the beaches at Pulau Seribu. And there is culture and the arts: the Taman Mini-Indonesia cultural park just outside Jakarta and the Taman Ismail Marzuki, which features cultural performances most nights of the week.

The heat here is intense. Planning activities around the midday hours would be wise. And the traffic...well...

WHAT TO SEE AND DO IN JAKARTA

Central Museum (Gedung Gajah) ★

Located at *12 Jalan Medan Merdeka Barat*. Also known as National Museum because it's the largest and finest in Indonesia. *Gedung Gajah* means Elephant Building; there's a bronze elephant statue in front, the gift of King Chulalongkorn of Thailand on an 1871 visit. The museum contains a wide collection of historical and cultural value, plus a library of social science. The **Treasure Room** is open on Sun. or by request only; open daily except Mon. from 9 a.m.-2:30 p.m., Fri. closing at 11 a.m., Sat. closing at 1:30 p.m.

Fine Arts Museum (Balai Seni Rupa)

Located on east side of **Fatahillah Square**. Formerly office of the Mayor of West Jakarta. Houses a fine arts painting collection of the Republic and includes contemporary works by Indonesians—plus a collection donated by Vice President Adam Malik. Hours same as Central Museum.

45 Generation Building (Gedung Juang 45)

Located at *31 Jalan Menteng Raya*. The place where revolutionary youth of Jakarta planned Proclamation of Independence in 1945 event occurred immediately following news of Japanese surrender to allies. Now a museum housing photographs from the revolutionary period.

Glodok (Chinatown)

Main square; boasts good food. Winding streets fun to wander.

Independence Pioneer Building

Located at *56 Jalan Proklamasi*. Original structure was a simple house where the late President Sukarno lived during the Japanese occupation. Sukarno and General Hatta proclaimed Independence of Republic of Indonesia here on Aug. 17, 1945. House was replaced by a high-rise. Proclamation Monument and Lighting Monument mark this historic spot.

Istiqlal Mosque

Located in Medan Merdeka area; said to be largest in Southeast Asia. A very modern and fantastic sight; huge white dome and minarets tower above surroundings. Visitors welcome (*please remove shoes*) except during Friday prayers.

Immanuel Church

Located in front of Gambir station; massive domed structure (resembles Jefferson's Monticello) was built in 1835. This was the church for Governor General of the Netherlands Indies; used as repository for ashes of Japanese troops during World War II. The present pulpit was formerly enclosure for Governor General and wife.

Jakarta Art Centre (Taman Ismail Marzuki)

Located at *73 Jalan Cikini Raya* (☎ *342605*). Both traditional and contemporary arts here; dances, music, plays, poetry. Regular performances for public; also cinema and planetarium here.

Jakarta Convention Hall

Located between city center and fashionable Kabayoran; a showcase of contemporary Indonesian art with the works of sculptors Sidharta and Soenarjo; artists Pirous, Prijanto and Sutanto and interior designer Adri Palar. Features a fine marble relief, wood and copper murals. The monumental sculptures were influenced by traditions of Tanimbar, Nias, Central Java and Bali. Also photographs of social and cultural life in Indonesia.

Jakarta Historical Museum (Fatahillah Museum)

Located on **Fatahillah Square** in Jakarta Kota area. The museum collection depicts the development of Jakarta since the 18th century, with maps, furniture, porcelain, paintings, etc. The building was the original Stadhuis (town hall) and dates from 1626; expanded in 1707. It played an important role in the Chinese massacre of 1742. Prince Diponegoro was once imprisoned here before banishment to Makasar. Hours are the same as Central Museum.

National Monument (Monas)

In Medan Merdeka Square, a towering gold-tipped obelisk; it's the most eminent landmark in capital. A memorial to Proclamation of Independence on Aug. 17, 1945. The eternal Flame of Independence is on top. The structure encompasses the Museum of National History, Hall of Independence. There's a viewing platform at the top of the obelisk and an equestrian statue of Prince Diponegoro. Open daily except last Mon. of each month from 9 a.m.-5 p.m.; admission charge.

Old Batavia (Taman Fatahillah)

Restored section of original Dutch-built city; features the Stadhuis and Jakarta Historical Museum and the **Balai Seni Rupa** Jakarta (the city's art gallery) housed in a Dutch period house. Also here is the Wayang Museum. Just northwest of Taman Fatahillah is the picturesque old drawbridge over **Kali Besar** (great canal); it's on the site of the old Kasteel (Batavia's venerable 17th-century fort). It was unfortunately demolished in the 19th century.

Pasar Ikan (Fish Market)

Located just northwest of **Kali Besar bridge** in old Batavia. The area is full of small lanes, warehouses and shops replete with articles made from the treasures of the sea. An actual fish market has auctions early every morning.

Presidential Palace (Istana Merdeka)   ★

Located on Jalan Merdeka Utara; it's the official residence of the head of state for Republic of Indonesia; formerly the home of a Dutchman, it became the official residence for Dutch governors in the mid-19th century.

Satria Mandala Museum (Armed Forces Museum)

Located at Jalan Jendral Gatot Subroto, this was formerly the residence of Dewi Sukarno, last and much despised wife of the late president. Museum depicts armed struggles from Proclamation of Independence until present. The 2 main buildings are General Sudirman Hall and General Urip Sumohardjo Hall; heavy armor exhibited on extensive grounds. Open Tues. to Sun. from 9 a.m.-5 p.m.

Senayan Sport Centre

Near Jalan Pintu IX, it's one of biggest games complexes in all Asia. Includes Sports Palace, swimming arena, basketball hall, hockey and softball fields. Built during one of late President Sukarno's sprees and opened in 1962 for the 4th Asian Games.

Sukarno-Hatta Monument

Located near Proclamation and Lightning Monuments, the monument honors the services of these two men toward the independence of the Indonesian people. Erected by order of President Suharto on Aug. 16, 1980.

Suropati Park

Located in front of National Development Planning Board at Jalan Imam Bonjo; contains monument to Raden Ajeng (Ibu) Kartini, Indonesia's most famous heroine. She espoused freedom in her writings, "*Letters of a Javanese Princess.*" She was born in 1879 of noble lineage; she died at age of 25 in childbirth.

Textile Museum

Located at *4 Jalan K. Satsuit Tubun.* Houses extensive collection of looms and other implements, as well as batik and weaving. Covers some 327 kinds of Indonesian batiks. There's historical data on the process of production, preservation, designing and other matters relating to the textile industry. Hours same as the Central Museum.

Wayang Museum (Puppet Museum)

Located at *27 Jalan Pintu Besar Utara*, it houses wayang collections from Indonesia, China, Malaysia and Kampuchea. The 2-story building was formerly a Protestant church built by the Dutch. Performances every Sun. in the museum, as well as all-night performances in the square once a month. Open Tues., Sat. and Sun., from 9 a.m. to 1 p.m., Fri. from 9 a.m. to noon.

Jakarta Environs/West Java

Bogor

This hill station is less than a 30-mile drive south of Jakarta. It's renowned for the **Botanical Gardens** (*Kebun Raya*), which were founded in 1817. There are 15,000 species of native flora and more than 5,000 kinds of orchids. Bogor features a Grecian-style monument to Olivia Raffles (wife of Sir Stamford) who died in 1814. Sir Stamford Raffles loved the place and was instrumental in designing the Botanical Gardens. The Presidential Palace is located within perimeter. It was built in 1745 by Baron Van Imhoff and restored in 1832. The palace was used frequently by late President Sukarno, who also built a weekend retreat called **Diah Bayurini**. The palace has an extensive painting and sculpture collection amassed by Sukarno. *Visitors welcome by prior arrangement.*

Bandung

This commercial and cultural city is 3 hours southeast of Jakarta by road. It was founded by the Dutch in late 19th century and still has a slight colonial atmosphere. It's also called Kota Kembang (*flowering city*) and sometimes Paris of Java and is the center of Sunda culture. The population is nearing 3 million including environs. Sukarno went to the Institute of Technology here.

The Gedung Merdeka (Concordia Sociteir) was built by Dutch architects in 1879 and was the site of Asia-Africa conference in 1955. It also features performances of *saung angklung*, music made from hollow bamboo tubes. Other cultural attractions here are the mask dance, wooden puppet show and ram fights.

Lubang Buaya (Crocodile Hole)

The **Hero Monument** (Pancasila Sakti Monument) is located near Pasar Rebo. The monument is dedicated to the heroes brutally murdered during the abortive Communist coup in fall of 1965. Official ceremonies are held here on Oct. 1 every year.

★ *Krakatoa*

This is one of the most famous volcanic islands in the world; located off the coast of Labuhan. The volcano erupted in 1883, killing more than 30,000 in the area and sending tidal waves across the Indian Ocean to Africa. Actually three islands now surround the new cone that rose in 1929. Scientists are fascinated by this area. Day trips are available for visitors from Labuhan, Carita, or Pasauran.

Sunda Kepala

There's an interesting museum in Sunda Kepala, which is in North Jakarta. The **Marine Museum (Bahari Museum)** is located on Jalan Pasar Ikan and opened in 1977. This collection contains old maps, naval equipment, models of historic vessels, as well as various woods used to construct ships. There are paintings of Tanjung Priok harbor. Hours are the same as the Central Museum.

Pulau Seribu (Thousand Islands)

These 60 small green islands with white sandy beaches are located in Bay of Jakarta. **Pulau Melintang** and **Pulau Putri** are becoming resort areas with scuba and skin diving centers, an amusement park for children, coral reefs and lovely beaches; reachable by boat or light plane.

Puncak

Located at the summit of Mt. Gede is Puncak, which lies at almost 4,000 feet. It's surrounded by **tea plantations** where the winding road from Bogor to Bandung climbs. Puncak Pass Inn, Cibodas Botanic Gardens and Cipanas Presidential Palace (built in 1750) all lie on slopes of Mt. Gede.

Pasar Minggu

Here you can find the **Ragunan Zoo** (Taman Margasatwa Ragunan). Situated about 10 miles south of Jakarta, this is one of the favorite outings for Jakarta inhabitants. Wonderful animals, like the Komodo dragon (lizards) and Bird of Paradise from West Irian are here. Also lovely orchid park. There's also **Taman Anggrek Ragunan**, where visitors can buy fresh orchid seedlings in bottles.

Slipi

The **Taman Anggrek Indonesia Permai Orchid Park**, located near Orchid Palace Hotel, has the largest collection of orchids in Southeast Asia. The garden is divided into several sections, each styled with different tribal and traditional houses. The gateway is made in the form of Candi Bentar, a typical Balinese gate. A real treat for orchid lovers.

Tanjung Priok/Sunda Kelapa Area

Taman Impian Jaya Ancol (Ancol Dreamland) is located on former marshland between port of Tanjung Priok and harbor of Sunda Kelapa; there are more than 340 acres of recreation area here. Also jai alai, bowling, hotels and nightclubs; drive-in theater, oceanarium, swimming pool complex. Also the **Pasar Seni** (Art Market), golf course and a racing circuit. There are massage parlors and a steambath, as well as a marina for yachts and motorboats. Also check out the Allied Troops' War Cemetery of World War II and 14th-century Chinese temple. Every Sunday *reog ponorogo* (peacock dancers from East Java) perform. Also *ondel-ondel*, gentle giant puppets.

Jakarta (South)

★**Taman Mini Indonesia Indah** (Beautiful Indonesia in Miniature) is located a few miles south of Jakarta proper, this is the pet project of Mme. Suharto, despite intense opposition over cost. This place depicts all aspects of Indonesian culture on 400 acres—typical Indonesian houses, orchid garden and a bird park. The Museum Indonesia houses many of the nation's cultural treasures. **Pancasila Flame Monument** symbolizes the struggle for independence. Also amusement facilities. Takes a full day to visit.

Tangkuban Parahu Mount

This is another famous **volcano** and one that's visible from Bandung at dawn. Ten eruptions have been recorded here. The crater **Kawah Ratu** has the shape of an upside-down boat. It still spews hot sulfur water.

★ Ujung Kulon

This is a nature reserve on the southwestern point of Java. It was originally established to protect Java Rhino, the white rhinoceros prized for its single horn. The trip here takes 10 hours from Jakarta, overland for 4 hours, then to the seacoast town of Labuhan. There are watchtowers for observing animals—Javanese wild cattle, rusa deer, wild boar, peacocks and over 250 species of jungle fowl. There are also canoe trips through the jungle and nature reserve. You could spend about a week here. Stay at a guest house in Pulau Peucang.

WHERE TO STAY IN JAKARTA

Borobudur Inter-Continental   ★★★★
Jalan Lapangan Banteng Selatan, P.O. Box 329. ☎ *380555. FAX: 359741*
• *1,172 rooms.* Located on 23 acres of landscaped gardens right in central Jakarta. Sanctuary of Indonesian marble and polished teak; attractively furnished. Fitness center and nightclub; Javanese-style lobby; new shopping arcade; business center. Convention facilities for

2,300 people. Jogging trail. Tennis, squash, minigolf, swimming pool and health club. Toba Rotisserie. Keio Japanese restaurant. Nelayan seafood restaurant. Bogor Brasserie (coffee shop). Pendopo lounge and bar. *Reservations: IHC.*

Grand Hyatt Jakarta ★★★★★
Jalan M.H. Thamrin. ☎ *3901234. FAX: 334321 • 450 rooms.* One of the city's newest and most luxurious. Convenient downtown location. Popular with traveling executives. Regency Club levels. Next to Plaza Indonesia shopping mall. Seven restaurants and lounges including Japanese and Chinese dining spots, a seafood restaurant and an Irish pub. Twenty-four-hour business center, meeting rooms, fitness center, lagoon-style pool with swim-up bar, tennis courts, squash courts, jogging track, mini-golf putting green, gardens. *Reservations: Hyatt.*

Horizon Hotel ★★★
Taman Impian Jaya Ancol, Jakarta Utara. ☎ *680008. FAX: 684004 • 350 rooms.* Major hotel at Ancol Dreamland. Sports and recreation complex on beach in northern Jakarta. International standards. Adjoins Copacabana Motel, restaurant and nightclub. Avoid during local holidays. Coffee shop. Japanese restaurant, seafood and regional dishes. Swimming pool and all sports available. Children's playground.
Reservations: Utell.

Hyatt Aryaduta ★★★★
Jalan Prapatan Raya 44-46, P.O. Box 3287. ☎ *376008. FAX: 349836 • 331 rooms.* Located in downtown area near the Presidential Palace and government offices. Regency Club and business center. French, Italian and Japanese-style restaurants. Coffee shop. Swimming pool. Closed-circuit video programs. *Reservations: Hyatt Int'l.*

Hotel Indonesia ★★
Jalan M.H. Thamrin 58, P.O. Box 54. ☎ *320008. FAX: 321508 • 575 rooms.* Downtown location. Member of Hotel Indonesia International Group. Continental, Chinese, Indonesian and Japanese restaurants. Coffee shop. Swimming pool and tennis courts. 5 bars. Secretarial services. *Reservations: INHOTELCOR.*

Jakarta Hilton International ★★★★★
Jalan Jend. Gatot Subroto (Senayan). ☎ *583051. FAX: 583091 • 1080 rooms.* Spectacular 32-acre garden setting. Minutes to downtown area; location adjacent to Jakarta Convention Hall. Has Indonesian Bazaar on grounds. Thirty typical ethnic houses for shops, handicraft and art galleries around man-made lake. Also Balinese Theatre, plus two residential towers. The Hilton recently added a 486-room wing and inaugurated the Jakarta Hilton Convention Center on the grounds of the hotel. Executive club. Oriental club with Juliana's of London Disco. Taman Sardi Grill. Peacock Cafe, a 24-hour coffee shop. Kudus Bar. Swimming pool, sports and health club. Pizzeria and Japanese restaurant. 31 executive lanai suites. *Reservations: Hilton.*

Mandarin Oriental Jakarta   ★★★★★

Jakarta Jalan M.H. Thamrin, P.O. Box 3392. ☎ *321307. FAX: 324669 •
455 rooms (19 suites).* An oasis of elegance in the heart of city; located
at Welcome Monument Circle. Impressive decor by Don Ashton.
Captain's Bar. Clipper Lounge. The Marquee coffee shop. The Club
Room. Spice Garden restaurant. Pelangi Terrace. Ballroom. Swimming pool, squash courts and health club. Executive services.

Reservations: LHW.

Kartika Plaza   ★★

Jalan M.H. Thamrin, P.O. Box 2081. ☎ *321008. FAX: 322547 • 331
rooms.* Downtown location next door to Hotel Indonesia. Comfortable and recently refurbished and upgraded. Continental and Chi-
nese/seafood restaurants. Bars. Swimming pool. *Reservations: Utell.*

Le Meridien Jakarta   ★★★★

Jalan Jendaral Sudirman Kav 18-10. ☎ *5711414. FAX: 5711633 • 265
rooms.* Decor of rooms and suites is pleasantly understated. French
restaurant is one of the city's best. Location close to business and
entertainment. French brasserie, seafood restaurant, lobby lounge,
poolside snack bar. Fitness center with squash courts, gym, sauna,
massage rooms, swimming pool. Meeting and banquet rooms.

Reservations: Meridien Hotels, Utell.

Sahid Jaya Hotel   ★★★

Jalan Jen. Sudirman 86. ☎ *570444. FAX: 583168 • 514 rooms plus
600-room extension.* Downtown location. Attractive native decor. All
rooms with refrigerator and minibar. Computer center. Mina's seafood restaurant, 24-hour coffee shop, Sahid Grill room, 2 bars, swimming pool, tennis court, business center, executive Club.

Reservations: Utell.

Sari Pan Pacific Hotel   ★★★

Jalan M.H. Thamrin, P.O. Box 3138. ☎ *323707. FAX: 323650 • 500
rooms.* Downtown location. Free airport transfer service. Member of
Japanese-operated Pan Pacific Hotel chain. Jayakarta grill. Fiesta coffee shop, Furusato Japanese restaurant, Melati bar, Pitstop disco,
swimming pool, business center, executive health center.

Reservations: Utell.

Shangri-La Hotel Jakarta   ★★★★★

Jalan Abdul Muis NO. 50. ☎ *5702658. FAX: 5702657 • 669 rooms.*
Opened in late 1993. Striking modern building integrated with terraced gardens. 7 Horizon Floor rooms and suites. Chinese, Japanese
and Indonesian restaurants, Western dining spot, lobby lounge, coffee
shop, poolside bar, entertainment center. Meeting and banquet
rooms. Business center with private meeting rooms. Health club with
outdoor pool, tennis courts, hot and cold Jacuzzi, gym, sauna, steambath and massage.   ***Reservations: Shangri-La Hotels.***

SAMPLING LOCAL FARE IN JAKARTA

Indonesian cuisine revolves around the rice kernel as well as an abundant supply of coconuts, peanuts, native fruits, vegetables and a treasure chest of tantalizing spices. No wonder Marco Polo called The Moluccas the Spice Islands in 1292 when he was the first European in a long line of traders lured by the taste of nutmeg, cloves, coriander, cardamon, cumin, ginger root, laurel and lemongrass—not to mention the tiny, hot chili peppers that sprout like weeds throughout Java and Sumatra.

The Indonesian word for a meal is *nasi*, the same word for rice so it is not surprising that rice is the center of every meal. *Nasi goreng* is fried rice and delicious for breakfast when topped with a fried egg. *Nasi putih* is steamed white rice and served with a series of side dishes and *sambal* (a fiery condiment made from mashed chilis and shrimp paste). Many of the side dishes have been simmered in coconut milk and then exquisitely spiced (the hottest sauces are made in Sumatra). One of the country's most delicious taste treats has Malayan origin—the *sate*, small pieces of skewered meat grilled over an open fire and then dipped into a spicy peanut sauce. Pure heaven!

It was the Dutch who dubbed ostentatious banquets in the palaces of the sultans *rijsttafel* (rice table) and the name has stuck. Indonesian restaurants throughout the world offer *rijsttafel*, a vast array of small dishes and condiments centered around a large bowl of rice. It's an excellent way to enjoy a variety of new food experiences and one should never pass up a proper *rijsttafel*, when offered. Some say that the *rijsttafel* today is only a shadow of its former self, but it's still a lovely way to enjoy an evening (especially when native music, dances and *wayang* are included).

Chicken, goat, fish, beef, lamb and egg dishes all accompany the rice, along with vegetables and fruits. Another important item is *krupuk*, shrimp paste potato chips. Pork is not served in Moslem society and therefore it is only available on Hindu Bali. Soups often have a coconut milk base and curried dishes are plentiful. A favorite salad among Indonesians is *gado gado* a mixture of bean curd and vegetables over which a peanut dressing is poured. (This one is definitely an acquired taste.) There is considerable Chinese influence on the local cuisine and noodle dishes are very popular. Wheat or rice flour noodles are either fried and topped with bits and pieces of things, or served in a tasty broth.

Because the archipelago is actually more water than land, fish is an important part of everyone's diet. Seafood restaurants abound in Jakarta and much of the fresh prawns, crab, eel, tuna and other more unfamiliar species of fish are cooked Chinese-style. Spring rolls made with tiny shrimp are a local specialty and are scrumptious. Nature has also provided an abundance of succulent fruits: several varieties of bananas, from miniature to oversized; pineapples and papayas and mangoes; rambutan and mangosteen; pomelos and the smelly durian (that can make you quite ill if it's mixed in your stomach with alcohol).

Alcoholic beverages are both scarce and expensive in Indonesia, but the local beers (Anker and Bintang) are pretty potent. There are many different fruit juices too, a delightful fragrant tea and strong coffee. It is best to avoid iced drinks outside the major hotels, so stick with bottled sodas and beer in the countryside. Wine by the bottle is available in the better restaurants, but European vintages are very, very expensive so why not give the Australians some business. (They are doing their best to ferment the grape.)

You can eat well indeed in Jakarta, as a metropolis of this size commands not only a great many good native restaurants but many quality European establishments. There are excellent Chinese, seafood and an ever-increasing number of Japanese restaurants available. As in all major Asian cities, the most consistent in quality, service, atmosphere and high prices are the food and beverage outlets in the top hotels. But don't leave town without spending an evening at the **Oasis**, located in a landmark Dutch colonial house formerly inhabited by an ambassador. Here, you can sip an aperitif in what was once the diplomat's chandeliered study and dine in the garden on either Indonesian or European cuisine. There is also romantic dancing under the stars. For years, the Oasis has been the smartest place in town—and well worth the price.

WHERE TO EAT IN JAKARTA

Indonesian Restaurants

Borobudur Intercontinental
☎ *370108*. Fri. evenings at poolside Kintamani garden bar. Dinner and cultural show from 7 to 10 p.m.

Hotel Indonesia
☎ *320008*. Oriental Restaurant features 150 dishes from 27 Indonesian provinces.

Jakarta Hilton
☎ *583051*. Best food and shows in town; great foodstalls in Indonesian Bazaar daily. Dance and musical performances at 7 p.m. (except Mon.) weather permitting. Free to hotel guests. Also rijsttafel buffet for lunch and dinner in Peacock Cafe every Fri.

Jakarta Mandarin
☎ *321307*. Every Fri. Kaki Lima from 7 to 11 p.m. Named after Jakarta's street vendors. Local fair with food carts; troubadors serenade guests.

Kartika Chandra
☎ *511008*. Excellent local restaurant.

Lembur Kuring
Jalan Pintu VIII, Senayan. Rusticity on outskirts of town. Freshly grilled fish. Eat with your hands. Cultural dances entertain at both lunch and dinner.

Oasis Restaurant
☎ *326397.* Popular setting. Wonderful for both Indonesian and European cuisine. Smart place.

Putri Duyung
Ancol Dreamland. Special Indonesian buffet; great for visitors.

Sabang Metropolitan
☎ *354031.* Small local hotel. Serves *rijsttafel* every Fri. evening.

Sahid Jaya
☎ *587031.* Mina's seafood restaurant, the best in town.

Senayan Satay House
Several locations. Best barbecue specialties.

Spice Garden
Jakarta Mandarin. ☎ *371208.* Szechuan cuisine.

Western Restaurants

Ambiente
In the Hyatt Aryaduta Hotel. ☎ *376008* • Attractive Italian restaurant serving superbly prepared Northern and Southern regional specialties.

Art and Curio Restaurant
Jalan Kebon Binatang 111/8A (Cikini) • Just that; good food among the antiquities. Charming atmosphere.

Brasserie Le Parisien
Hyatt Aryaduta Hotel. ☎ *376008* • French ambience and menu.

George and Dragon Pub/Restaurant
Behind the Hotel Indonesia. ☎ *345625•* Pleasant and basic.

Le Bistro
☎ *347475* • Located in converted home. Charming surroundings. Limited but reliable Continental menu.

Oasis Restaurant
☎ *326397•* A superb dining experience. Excellent European dishes too.

Pizzaria Indonesian Bazaar
Jakarta Hilton. ☎ *583350, ext. 613* • If you're craving for a slice, this is the place!

Rugantino Ristorante Italiano
☎ *714727* • Pasta and all that other stuff.

Swiss Inn
☎ *583280.* A nice spot for lunch or dinner in the Arthaloka building.

Taman Sari Grill
Jakarta Hilton Hotel. ☎ *583350, ext. 251* • As in all Southeast Asian Hiltons, the top European food in town.

Toba Rotisserie

Borobudur Intercontinental. ☎ *357611, ext. 2355* • Elegant dining in burnished copper setting. Daily deliveries of specialties from the U.S. and Europe.

The Club Room

Jakarta Mandarin Hotel. ☎ *371208* • Opulence galore; decor reminiscent of English club. Continental cuisine.

Seafood & Chinese Restaurants

Arithya Loka

Satria Mandala Museum. ☎ *582449.*

Coca Restaurant

☎ *775946.*

Dragon Gate

☎ *365293.*

Jade Garden

☎ *334104.*

King's Restaurant

☎ *357696.*

Mina Sahid Jaya Hotel

☎ *584151.*

Perahu Bugis

Horizon Hotel, Ancol Dreamland. ☎ *680008, ext. 111.*

Prince

☎ *345369.*

Ratu Bahari

☎ *774115.*

Yun Nyan

☎ *364063.*

Jakarta also has Korean, Indian, Thai, Japanese and lots of fast food chains. Grilled chicken, hamburgers and ice cream are very popular here!

NIGHTLIFE IN JAKARTA

There is plenty of fast-paced nightlife in Jakarta these days as well as sophisticated supper clubs at the international hotels. Discos also abound but be sure you know the admission fee before you embark, as tourists are easy prey. More magical and unforgettable is one of the many *"wayang"* theater performances where stories from the *Hindu Ramayana* and *Mahabharata* and *Bhagavad Gita* are played to the accompaniment of Gamelan music.

Wayang Museum

Wayang kulit (shadow puppets) performances Sunday mornings in Old Batavia and on second and last Saturday nights at Central Museum.

Aneka Ria Srumulat

Jalan Pintu VII, Taman Ria Remaja Senayan. Indonesian comedy daily from 7 to 9:30 p.m.

Bharata Jalan Kalilio

Wayang Orang (human drama). Nightly at 8 p.m. *Ketoprak* (an offshoot of Wayang Wong—also human drama) performed on Monday and Thursday with stories from popular folk legends and local history.

Taman Mini Indonesia

Indah cultural park outside Jakarta where regular drama and dance performances are scheduled.

The Tavern

Hyatt Aryaduta Hotel. ☎ *376008.* An informal, relaxing pub with live bands.

SHOPPING IN JAKARTA

Shopping for Indonesian souvenirs is like taking an immersion course in the country's many cultural treasures. The most popular of the crafts to tempt visitors' purchasing power is **batik**, for it appears in the dress of everyday life throughout Java, Sumatra and Bali. Few travelers leave without at least one **wayang puppet** to adorn a wall or niche. **Silver** items are also irresistible, especially the belts and bracelets made in Kota Gede, near Yogyakarta. More elaborate are the **kris**, or dagger with straight or wavey blade, whose scabbards boast local semiprecious stones (onyx, moonstone, jasper, agate, etc.). The art of **carving** is most prominent in Bali and some of the outer islands and native **baskets** are also attractive. Antique buffs can find plenty of old Chinese porcelains, coins and artifacts, although nothing more than 50 years old can be exported without permission.

Batik

The exact origin of the **batik** process, using drops of hot wax to create patterns on cloth, is rather vague and seems to have evolved from a pastime of court ladies to what has become a folk art. Today, the craft is also considered a "studio art," for framed batik paintings have become popular tourist items. The designs are from ancient interpretations of Hindu cosmology or modern abstractions of same and many are made with light boxes behind for more dramatic viewing.

Needless to say, making batik demands considerable time and patience. The white factory-made bolts of muslin must be treated and dyed. Then the pattern is drawn on both sides and the hot wax applied, either by hand *(batik tulis)* or with a copper stamp *(batik cap).* At least another month is needed for the dyeing and filling-in of the intricate designs.

The art of batik has become so refined that an educated eye can spot exactly which district in Java a particular piece was made. Most highly prized and best known are the designs from **Yogyakarta** and **Solo**, where the sultans preferred the colors of indigo, dark brown, blue and maroon (a court color in any language). Brighter colors, like green or red or yellow are more prevalent in northern Java and on Madura Island, while light browns and golds on blue-black backgrounds can be found in western Java.

Shopping for authentic, handmade batik with traditional designs and colors is a rewarding experience if you are willing to spend both time and money in the selection of fine work *(cheap imitations should be avoided)*. A local Javanese who designs beautiful batik on both cotton and silk, then creates high-style fashions for both men and women is *Iwan Tirta*.

A former lawyer turned couturier, Tirta has long been fascinated with the art of batik and has done much for both the craft and his country's fashion industry. He also has an excellent eye for antiques and serves as advisor to Mme. Suharto, First Lady of the Land, on many of her projects. Tirta's showroom and atelier is in his elegant old home at Jalan Panarukan 25 in central Jakarta (not far from the Mandarin Hotel) and definitely worth a detour.

Jakarta's Central and Textile **museums** are an excellent preview of the many other intricate fabrics found throughout the archipelago, especially *ikat*. This textile is made by either dyeing a pattern on the warp (long threads of the loom), or on the weft (thread woven across them), or on both, prior to the weaving. *Warp ikat* textiles are made by young girls with long, thin fingers and can be found on the islands of Sumba, Roti, Savu, Timor, Flores and Laimantan, while many of the shawls *(selendangs)* in South Sumatra are products of the *weft ikat* technique.

From other islands come intricately woven tubelike **sarongs** worn by women and ceremonial **shawls** for men. Some are richly decorated, with gold or silver threads and covered with small mirrors and other metallic adornments. They can be framed or used as wall hangings and are found in reputable shops in the main tourist centers. *(But watch out for factory-made copies with synthetic dyes and threads.)*

Wayang

The most popular form of entertainment in Indonesia is the **wayang**, or puppet play, that relates the many tales of the *Ramayana*. The moral of each episode performed is always the struggle of good against evil, with the former defeating the latter. *Wayang* performances can last all night and were originally a means of honoring one's deceased ancestors. The *dalang*, or puppeter, was considered the "medium" between the living and the dead and was treated as a holy person. Even today, the *dalang* is the producer, director and every player as well as conductor of the accompanying gamelan orchestra.

The **puppets** themselves make interesting souvenirs. The *wayang kulit*, popular in Central and East Java, are flat leather figures intricately carved and painted. They are made to perform against an erected white cloth that serves as a shadow screen, so the audience on the other side sees only silhouettes (*wayang* means shadow). There are also *wayang golek*, three-dimensional puppets made of wood and bamboo (with batik garments), characteristic of West Java. They make lovely doll gifts.

Silver

Indonesian silversmiths produce delicate lacelike silver filigree in butterfly and flower shapes in objects that range from jewelry to belts, coffee sets and candlesticks. Silverwork centers thrive where the Hindu influence was once (or remains) very strong, like Bali, South Sulawesi, Sumatra and the seaports of Java. The best known center is Kota Gede near Yogyakarta, but the fine works from Kendari on Sulawesi and Kota Gadang on Sumatra find their way into the tourist center shops.

Native Arts

Carvings and paintings from Bali are just about irresistible, especially if you take time to visit the villages where a single craft is the local cottage industry. **Ubud** is the center of Balinese painting and visits are encouraged to the studios of artists in residence. Ubud is also the home of the **Museum Puri Lukisan** (post 1920 paintings) and gallery. Mas and Peliatan are villages where carvers begin very early to make masks and winged garuda statues out of jackwood and ebony. Celuk is good for silver and goldsmiths; Bangli and Tampaksiring for carvings of bone and horn; Batubutan, Blaju and Gianjar for woven goods; and Puaya for puppets. Or you could just stop by the **Abian Kapas Art Center** in Denpasar to appreciate and purchase modern Balinese art. For serious buyers, Irishwoman Linda Garland (married to a Balinese) is a great help and her shop has the best of Bali. For an appointment, ☎ *28946* for a most enjoyable and rewarding time and good direction for other island galleries.

After Bali, **Yogyakarta** offers the best shopping opportunities, for this is still the cultural capital of the country and cottage industries thrive throughout the area. **The Batik and Handicraft Research Center** on Jalan Kusumanegara is a good place to begin one's research. Good shopping is also found on Jalan Malioboro, between the Sultan's Palace and the Pasar Beringharho market. Enticements include some antiques, batik, wayang kulit, brass and silver items.

Shopping in Jakarta can be fast and efficient if you stick to the fixed-price stores, but be prepared to pay more for the convenience. The **Sarinah Department Store** on Jalan Thamrin, **Ancol Dreamland's** so-called art market and the Hilton Hotel's **outdoor bazaar** offer a wide selection of crafts. Antique buffs should stroll along Jalan Agus Salim, Jalan Majahpahit and Jalan Surabaya for old coins, Ming kitchen china and porcelains.

Pasar Baru offers fabrics at a steal; **Pasar Burung** is famous for birds and birdcages; and **Taman Anggrek** is the most convenient center for orchid cuttings. Large general markets full of goods and local color are **Pasar Cikin** and **Pasar Minggu** *(watch your wallets and packages)*.

Java's ancient capital, **Solo**, offers excellent shopping opportunities for the more traditional items.

Pasar Trewindu is the city's flea market and known for interesting artifacts as well as brass oil lamps that sell for a song.

Pasar Klewer has an overwhelming amount of batik in the traditional cream, brown and indigo colors of central Java. There are also a number of batik "factories" in the area where visitors are welcome and purchases can be made. There is a **Toy Market** on the grounds of **Radyapustaka Museum** where doll houses, miniature gamelan sets and amusing paper items can be found. If luggage is no problem, fine furniture reproductions are made along **Jalan Slamet Riyadi** (Toko Parto Art) and **Jalan Kemasan** (Mirah Delima), with artisans said to be the best in the country.

The island of **Sumatra** has its own regional specialties that include embroidered **shawls** from Bukittinggi, **silver** items from Kota Gadang, **carvings** and hand-woven **Ulos cloth** made by the Bataks around Lake Toba and wonderful figures made from "old" coins that can be nicely framed.

Bali

BALI IN A CAPSULE

Formerly called Pulau Dewata...also known as the "Morning of the World"...people believe their island is just a loan from God...a 90-mile long beauty full of rice terraces and holy Mt. Agung...abode of the gods...a Hindu culture that supports 20,000 temples...60 religious holidays a year...some 2,000 different dance troupes...includes a Holy Monkey Forest where hundreds swing from trees to temples undisturbed...even the preparation of food here is a ceremony and an art form...no longer unspoiled...Bali still has an atmosphere in which visitors revel...life here is a continual festivity...and completely offbeat.

Many an ancient mariner proclaimed Bali, upon first sight of this emerald of Indonesia, as paradise on earth.

Bali is the westernmost island of the Lesser Sundas. It has the sometimes tainted distinction of being the most heavily touristed island in the Indonesian archipelago and, thus, features Indonesia's most developed infrastructure. It is an island characterized by volcanoes (Mt. Batur rises to 1,720 m and Mt. Agung to a spectacular 3,000 m), crystalline waters, beautiful temples, ancient cave stone carvings and—yes—a ton of tourists.

Bali is quite a bit different from the the rest of Indonesia. One big reason is that it's the only island in the chain where Islam didn't take a strong hold. The inhabitants of Bali are primarily Hindu, although Buddhist influences are evident.

To most tourists, Bali is known for its beaches. Some feature bone-crushing waves and attract a large Australian surfing contingent. Others offer placid azure waters that are kept that way by vibrant coral reefs teeming with kaleidoscopic undersea life. Kuta Beach was once known as a gathering spot for vagabond hippies on the route of "KKK" (Katmandu, Kabul and Katu). It's now a hodgepodge of sunseekers, drifters and surfers. It's become a little like an Asian Miami Beach, with its concentration of fast food chains, bars and discos. Sunar beach is a little less abbreviated.

Lake Bratan, Bali

On Bali, there are dramatic terraced rice fields and the vast moonlike setting of Mt. Batur. There is the unhurried charm of small villages, some of which haven't changed in 50 years, despite the boon in tourism. The temples themselves are worth a visit to Bali. Many are built high on top of hills, or precariously astride cliffs.

WHAT TO SEE AND DO ON BALI

Bat Cave (Goah Lawah)

Located between Kusambe and Padang Bai. Sinister sight; walls covered with bats. Cave said to extend all the way to base of Mt. Agung. Eerie but considered holy place.

Batubulan Stone Carvers

Statues of divinities and demons line edge of road through this village just northeast of Denpasar. Area also full of beautiful temples, especially **Pura Puseh.**

Batukaru Mountain and Temple

Coconut Shell Mountain and Shrine. Many shrines in the area (straight north from Denpasar); modestly decorated but dedicated to deities associated with **Batukaru.**

Batur Temple and Volcanic Lake

The people of **Batur** are building almost 300 shrines at foot of volcano; began ambitious rebuilding of **Pura Ulun Danu Temple** in 1927. The people of Trunyan village near Lake Batur consider themselves the original Balinese as descendents of the aboriginals who lived on

Bali before the Majapahit invasion. A very private and proud settlement. Not recommended to visit on your own. You will probably experience hostility and hustling.

Bedugul Mountain Village

Northwest from Denpasar through Mengui. Beautiful landscape surrounding the lake in the ancient crater of Mt. Bratan. Bedugul people honor **Dewi Danu**, the goddess of the waters, in the temple **Ulu Danau** above the lake. Colorful flower and vegetable market beneath village.

Bedulu Elephant Cave (Goah Gadjah)

Mysterious cave with carved entrance; a former Buddhist hermitage. The name taken from nearby Elephant River (*Lwa Gadja*). It's located near the village of Bedulu, where the mid-14th century king was known as He Who Changed Heads. The village lies in the shadow of holy volcano **Gunung Agung**.

Besakih Mother Temple

Most holy of all temples on Bali; thought to have been established in the 11th century before Hinduism even arrived. It was built to house holy spirit of **Gunung Agung**. Today, it's considered a royal ancestry sanctuary and is the principal state temple. It venerates Hindu trinity. Located in a large temple complex; watch for many festivals here.

Celuk Gold and Silver Works

Craftsmen have inherited the skills of their forebears in this tiny village not far northeast of Denpasar. Intricate designs and delicate artistry can be found here. A lovely stop en route elsewhere.

Denpasar Museum and Market

Name of Bali's capital means "north of market." The local museum was built by the Dutch government in 1932. It offers an excellent survey of Balinese culture. The architecture is of interest and depicts both the temple and palace of Bali. Visit also **Kokar Conservatory of Instrumental Arts and Dance** for student performances and don't miss the festival at **Pura Djagatnata Temple** every full moon. (It's next to the museum.)

Gillimanuk

Small port northwest of the island which connects to Java. Daily ferries available.

Gunung Kawi (Hindu Balinese Sanctuary)

Ancient burial towers hewn from solid rock; thought to have been constructed as royal memorials to King Udayana and family. Dates from around the 11th century.

Karangasem

One of the original kingdoms of the Gelgel dynasty, it cooperated with the Dutch at the turn of the century so the monarchy could be retained. Here is the palace of the last raja.

Puri Kanginan

Very European; another moated water palace located on the beach of Udjung.

Kintamani

Mountain village where a colorful bazaar is held every third morning. Local dances here are full of trancelike movement and quite unique to this village.

Klungkung

Seat of Gelgel dynasty which ruled Bali for over three centuries. Kerta Gosa Hall of Justice is known for klungkung style of painting and architecture and fantastic ceiling vignettes. Klungkung is also a good place for antique shops and stalls. Nearby is Gelgel, the early capital of the old kingdom.

Kubutambahan

This north coastal town is the site of **Pura Medrwe Karang**. Here is the Temple of Owner of the Land. It honors Mother Earth and the sun. Has a lot of folksy carvings.

Kusambe Fishing Village

Located on east shore opposite Nusa Penida island. Visitors can travel to the island from here.

Kuta Beach

Popular beach resort on southwest coast known for good surfing. It has become quite commercial. But the sunsets here are something special.

Kutri

Site of statue of Mahendradatta, or Queen Gunapriya, who died in A.D. 1006. The statue is now defaced. It was found in the rubble of the 1926 earthquake. Full of ancient rhythms and vibes.

Mas

Village famous for woodcarvers; the first Hindu priest in Bali settled here. Many claim descendancy from him. **Pura Taman Pule Temple** has frequent festivals. Many statues are carved here by young boys; good shopping.

Mengwi Temple

State temple of Pura Taman Ajun; former members of the royal family pay respect to their forebears here. The temple is in a moat. *Taman* means "garden with a pond." There are fine carvings on wooden doors.

Padang Bai

Small harbor on eastern coast; cargo and passenger vessels depart here for Lombok Island.

Pedjeng
Considered center of early Balinese dynasties; an ancient bronze drum dates from 300 B.C. It's called the Moon of Pedjeng because local Balinese legend says it fell from the sky one night. There are 40 ancient temples in the area. There's also a government archaeological office.

Sangeh Monkey Forest
Also called **Bukit Sari**, it is the home of hundreds of monkeys. It is a sacred place with a moss-covered temple in center. The monkeys are believed to have dropped to earth during Ramayana epic times and have stayed. This is one of the most popular spots on the island. Take along a bag of peanuts.

Sangsit
This town in northern Bali is known for **Pura Bedji**. The subak temple is dedicated to Dewi Sri, the goddess of agriculture. You'll find pink sandstone and carvings of mythical animals. Naga snakes guard entrance.

Singaraja
Capital of Buleleng district along Java Sea (in the north); important commercial center since early times. Bali was under Javanese rulers in 14th century here. The Dutch arrived in 19th century, so there are an interesting variety of influences in this cosmopolitan town.

Tabanan
Rice belt of the southern district also known as home of the famous gamelan orchestras and dancers. It's a little like Denpasar but much more unspoiled; lovely beaches here.

Tampaksiring
Holy spring of Tirta Empul—dates from legendary times. The waters are said to have curative powers. Balinese make annual pilgrimages here for purification. The primary festival occurs on and during the full moon of every 4th month. The temple was restored in the late 1960s. The late President Sukarno built himself a palace above here in 1954.

Tanah Lot Temple
Temple suspended on huge rock off southwestern shore; one of Bali's most famous shrines. It's at an odd placement in the sea. Balinese believe a huge snake dwells within. The temple casts a true Oriental quality when seen in the late afternoon.

Tenganan Village
Walled town and a very conservative village; it's said to date from pre-Hindu times. Interesting dance rituals here; women weave the famous cloth that protects wearers from evil vibes. This is a traditional and friendly Bali Aga village.

Ubud ★

A must-see for every visitor; this is a village of painters and galleries and studios. Don't miss the **Museum Puri Lukisan** (Palace of Fine Arts) founded in 1954. It houses an excellent collection of modern Balinese work—some of the most renowned are Ida Bagus Made Poleng, A. A. Gede Sobrat and I. Gusti Ketut Kobot.

Yeh Pula

Ancient ruins here and a small temple walled by a long frieze. The reliefs were excavated in 1925. This place is believed to date from the 14th century, but the exact meaning of carved figures is unknown.

BEACHES ON BALI

Children fleeing the surf, Bali. Bali's beaches, once the mecca of backpackers, today are attracting a more diverse tourist base.

Bali's beaches have been famous with Asian-hopping backpackers for several decades, even though the Balinese themselves (the older generation, to be sure) stay away because they feel an affinity with their mountains, from which good emanates. Aside from the fishermen, who must do their duty, Balinese feel that evil lingers beyond the smooth, palm-fringed sands.

Indeed, during the Hippie Age of the '70s, **Kuta Beach** was one of the three must "Ks" (the other two were Kabul and Kathmandu) for grouping and other activities. Kuta is still a favorite for most visitors but no longer the enclave of indigent Westerners from Australia and America; it is now a potpourri, consisting of young Indonesians and Balinese who want to mingle with visitors from all over the world. Kuta, though, still attracts some of the seedier elements of the West, as well as a collection of hedonists, beach bums and surfers. The French and the Aussies invade the area a number of times during the year.

All three of the well-known beaches—Kuta, Sanur and Nusa Dua—are in the south of the island and feature both excellent surfing and stunning sunsets. Each one, however, has a distinct personality and draws its own type of crowd. Each of the beaches boasts major resorts as well as small hotels, a plethora of restaurants, shops and local villagers just doing their own thing.

Kuta Beach

The legendary **Kuta** boasts both upscale properties as well as the many budget guest houses that have sprung up over the past three decades. Pertamina Cottages is located at the southern end of the beach away from most of the action. Closer in are Kartika Plaza's cottages and the Natour Kuta Beach Hotel, while the Bali Oberoi's villas are at the very end—at Kayu Aya on Legian Beach. Between are clothing and souvenir shops, vendors aplenty and restaurants serving everything from satay to burgers!

Sanur Beach

Sanur Beach is more stylish and quiet—known for the many artists and musicians who live in the area as well as for small inns, gracious restaurants and art shops. Sanur boasts the Bali Beach, the island's first major resort hotel, the Bali Hyatt and the Hotel Sanur Beach (the last major hotel allowed). Balinese bungalow resorts include Segara Village, the popular Tandjung Sari and Bali Sanur Bungalows.

Nusa Dua Beach

Nusa Dua Beach is a government experiment in resort planning—looked upon with some disdain by the locals, who feel it does not belong on Bali. Once an unpopular and inhospitable area on the east coast, the beach now is thriving with hotels, restaurants, tourist facilities and shops—all built in the past decade. The area's first major property was the Nusa Dua Beach Hotel, followed by Hotel Bali Nusa Dua, Hotel Bali Sol and a Club Med.

WHERE TO STAY ON BALI

Amandari Hotel ★★★★★

Kedewatan, Ubud. ☎ *95333. FAX: 95335 • 29 suites.* The first of three exclusive, luxurious Aman resorts to open in Bali (in 1989), the Amandari became an instant hit with celebrities and wellheeled travelers seeking an all-in-one hideaway. The hotel consists of 29 Terrace and Duplex suites, each with canopied beds and outdoor sunken marble baths. Convenient to artists' shops and galleries in Ubud. Restaurant serving Western and Asian dishes. Salt-water swimming pool, tennis court, library, antique gallery. The hotel arranges activities, such as whitewater river rafting, trekking and arts and antiques shopping expeditions. ***Reservations: Prima Reservations, Rafael Group.***

Amankila Hotel ★★★★★

Manggis. ☎ *21993. FAX: 21995 • 35 suites.* Opened in March 1992 overlooking a private beach in Eastern Bali, the hotel has 35 free-standing deluxe suites offering sweeping island views. Like its sister hotels, the furnishings and decor make use of traditional Balinese materials and design. Two restaurants and a bar. Beach Club, situated in a coconut grove, with a swimming pool and restaurant. Library, shopping gallery. ***Reservations: Prima Reservations, Rafael Group.***

Amanusa Hotel   ★★★★★

Nusa Dua. ☎ 72333. FAX: 72335 • *35 suites.* Opened in September 1992, the Amanusa is in a recently developed area of Nusa Dua and is situated on a high elevation, overlooking the Bali Golf and Country Club. Accommodations with views of Gunung Agang volcano. Bathrooms have sunken baths. Two restaurants and a bar. Swimming pool, library, gallery, golf course, tennis courts, cycling, watersports. Shopping trips available into nearby Kuta and Legian Beach.

Reservations: Prima Reservations, Rafael Group.

Bali Beach   ★★★★

Sanur, Denpasar. ☎ 88511. FAX: 87917 • *605 rooms.* One of the first luxury hotels; high-rise right on beach . Still one of the best. Baruna (seafood) Pavilion, Tirta bar, Bali Kopi shop and Beringin Coffee shop, Bali Hai supper club and lounge, Raja Room (Indonesian and Chinese), Swiss restaurant, Baris piano bar, extensive watersports, 3 swimming pools, tennis. golf, bowling. health club, heli-pad. $3.6 million renovation completed.   ***Reservations: Utell, SRS.***

Bali Hilton International   ★★★★★

P.O. Box 46, Nusa Dua. ☎ 71102. FAX: 71199 • *540 rooms.* Situated in landscaped gardens overlooking Nusa Dua Beach. Recently added an Executive Court with extra-large rooms and luxury appointments and services, Western and Asian restaurants, health and fitness center, business center, pool, tennis courts, squash courts.

Reservations: Hilton Int'l.

Bali Hyatt   ★★★★

Jalan Tanjung Sari, P.O. Box 392, Sanur. ☎ 88271. FAX: 87693 • *387 rooms.* Set on 36 acres at water's edge in structures no higher than a palm tree . A popular spot with Americans. Regency Club with special amenities. Indonesian buffet and dance performances nightly. Seafood restaurant, 24-hour coffee shop, disco, watersports, tennis, golf, health club.   ***Reservations: Hyatt Int'l.***

Bali Inter-Continental Resort   ★★★★★

Jalan Uluwatu, 45, Jimbaran Bay. ☎ 53783. FAX: 53784 • *450 rooms.* Opened in summer 1993. Variety of accommodations, including loft suites, Japanese suites, Executive Suites and two Presidential Suites with private swimming pools. Eight restaurants and lounges, including seafood and Japanese restaurants and an outdoor poolside dining spot serving pizza and barbecue. Business center, hairdresser/barber, health club, three swimming pools, beach, water-skiing, snorkeling, scuba diving, sailing, indoor and outdoor tennis courts, child-care center and outdoor cultural performances.   ***Reservations: IHC.***

Bali Oberoi   ★★★★★
Jalan Kayu Aya, Legian Beach, Box 351, Denpasar. ☎ *51061. FAX: 52791*
• *75 rooms.* Guests stay in private cottages. It's like a Balinese village;
a relaxing 34-acre resort. Villas have own patios, atriums and garden
bathrooms. A favorite with visiting celebrities. Dining room, coffee
shop, bar. Cultural shows in amphitheater. Swimming pool, tennis,
watersports, health club.   *Reservations: LHW, Utell.*

Club Mediterranee Bali   ★★★★
Lot N-6, Nusa Dua, P.O. Box 7, Denpasar. ☎ *71520. FAX: 71831* • *350
units.* Opened in 1986. Offers variety of recreational and social activities. Western and Asian dining, golf, watersports, children's activities.   *Reservations: Club Med.*

Four Seasons Resort Bali   ★★★★★
Jimbaran Bay. ☎ *71288. FAX: 71280* • *147 villas.* Spectacular new
hotel, opened in early 1993. Villas stretch along the hillside overlooking the bay; each has three thatched-roof living pavilions; air-conditioned sleeping pavilion has indoor and outdoor bathing areas, deep
soaking tubs, satellite TV, minibars and VCRs; outdoor pavilions
include dining area and lounging area with sun deck and private
plunge pool. Two-bedroom Royal Villas have swimming pool, sauna,
spa and live-in maid. Five restaurants and bar-cafes. Private beach,
swimming pool, watersports. Tennis Club and Spa with two flood-
lighted supergrass tennis courts, fitness and exercise studio, sauna and
plunge pool. Beauty spa. Meeting and banquet rooms.
                    Reservations: Four Seasons Hotels & Resorts.

Grand Hyatt Bali   ★★★★★
P.O. Box 53, Nusa Dua. ☎ *71234. FAX: 72038* • *750 rooms.* Arranged
in four "villages." Accommodations include deluxe suites and private
villas arranged amid lagoons. About six indoor and outdoor restaurants serving Indonesian, Japanese, Chinese, Italian and other Western cuisines. Pub with entertainment. Fitness center, squash courts,
tennis courts, swimming pool, jogging tracks, watersports, yachting,
deepsea fishing, nearby golf. Meeting rooms.
                              Reservations: Hyatt Int'l.

Kuta Beach Hotel   ★★★
Kuta P.O. Box 393, Denpasar. ☎ *51361* • *40 rooms.* Balinese-style bungalows adjacent to beach. Operated by Natour Ltd. Dining room, bar,
swimming pool and watersports. Barong and Ketchak dances upon
request.   *Reservations: Utell.*

Melia Bali Sol
P.O. Box 1048, Tuban, Nusa Dua. ☎ *71510. FAX: 71360* • *388
rooms.* Set in vast tropical gardens and lagoons. Attractive rooms with
balconies/patios. Good shopping arcade with antique gallery and jewelry boutique. Eight restaurants and lounges, including an open-air
theater offering Balinese dance performances. Health club with gym,

massage, three tennis courts, squash courts, lagoon-style swimming pool, watersports, beach, ping pong, volleyball, jogging track. Library, nearby 18-hole golf course, arrangements for sightseeing trips.   *Reservations: Utell.*

Nusa Dua Beach Hotel   ★★★★

Nusa Dua Beach, P.O. Box 1028, Denpasar. ☎ *71210. FAX: 71229 •* *450 rooms.* Located right on beach; four-story hotel spread over 20-plus acres. Operated by Aerowisata and a favorite conference venue. Restaurants. Airline and travel offices. Banks. Post office. Art shops. Meeting halls and performance stage. Swimming pools. Tennis courts. Watersports.   *Reservations: Utell.*

Pertamina Cottages   ★★★★

Kuta Beach P.O. Box 121, Denpasar. ☎ *51161. FAX: 52030 •* *249 rooms.* Just 5 minutes from airport. Owned by state-run oil conglomerate. Began as an executive retreat. Now a property with extensive grounds and tourist facilities. All suites. Dining room. Coffee shop. Bar. Disco. Cocktail lounge. Swimming pool. 3-hole golf course.

                                    Reservations: Utell.

Sanur Beach Hotel   ★★★

P.O. Box 279, Denpasar. ☎ *88011. FAX: 87566 •* *425 rooms in the main high-rise structure.* Located in a midst of palm trees . Convention facility hotel. 4 restaurants. 24-hour coffee shop. Bar. Tennis. Putting green. Windsurfing. Cultural shows. Watersports.

                                    Reservations: Utell.

Segara Village Hotel

Jalan Segara Ayu, Sanur, P.O. Box 91, Denpasar. ☎ *88407. FAX: 87242 •* *100 rooms.* Owned and operated by the Kompiang family who pioneered tourism to Bali at Sanur Beach in 1956. Atmosphere of a Balinese village with bungalows in the shape of rice storage barns. Connected by stone pathways. Lush gardens full of orchids and singing birds. Very personable; owners join guests for lunch.

                                    Reservations: Direct.

Sheraton Laguna Nusa Dua Hotel   ★★★★★

Kawasan BTDC Lot 2, Nusa Dua. ☎ *71327. FAX: 71326 •* *211 rooms.* Opened in 1991. Overlooking the beach. Facilities are connected by "swimmable" lagoons. Beautiful gardens. Three restaurants and two lounges with entertainment. Fitness center with sauna, steambath, plunge pool, Jacuzzi, tennis courts, golf nearby. Meeting rooms. Business center. Facilities for the handicapped. Trips to area attractions.

                                    Reservations: Sheraton.

Sheraton Legian Beach   ★★★★★

(Hotel is scheduled to open some time in 1994). Jalan Dyana Pura Ujung, Banjar Seminyak, Kuta. ☎ *52653. FAX: 588274 (Jakarta office) •* *395 rooms.* Hotel will be located on Legian Beach, close to the village of Kuta, a popular mid-level shopping and dining/entertainment area.

Four restaurants serving Western, Chinese, Indonesian cuisines and two lounges with entertainment. Swimming pool, plunge pool, sauna, steam room, massage, fitness center with gym, game room, two tennis courts. Shops, meeting rooms, business center.

Reservations: Sheraton.

Sheraton Nusa Indah Resort Hotel ★★★★

P.O. Box 36, Nusa Dua. ☎ *71566. FAX: 71908 • 367 rooms.* On the grounds of the Bali Convention Center, the hotel has good, standard rooms geared to convention groups. Sheraton recently (in 1993) took over the management of the hotel, which was developed as a member of the Aerowisata group and may have planned changes in the works. Four restaurants, three bars. Hotel has its own meeting and exhibition halls, in addition to those of the convention center. Free form swimming pool, tennis courts, watersports, adjacent 18-hole golf course.

Reservations: Sheraton.

Tanjung Sari Hotel ★★★★★

P.O. Box 25, Denpasar. ☎ *8844 • 24 two-story bungalows.* Charming seaside resort. A favorite of Bali afficionados; full of tropical gardens and private courtyards. Indoor/outdoor restaurant with best rijsttafel on the island. Swimming pool. Tennis and golf. Watersports. Horseback riding.

Reservations: Direct.

SAMPLING LOCAL FARE ON BALI

The foods of Bali are quite different from the rest of the Indonesian archipelago, for this is the only Hindu island in the large chain. Life on Bali is dominated by what the gods may think and every meal is considered a blessing from above. Because of the many festival days in every calendar year, food is constantly being prepared for presentation at the local temple. So a frequent and most attractive sight is a string of Balinese beauties carrying tiers of colorful rice on their heads as offerings to the gods.

Because the Balinese follow Hinduism, pork is not prohibited and no proper feast is prepared without a tiny suckling pig roasted slowly over a fire of wood. The succulent meat of the babi guling is flavored with a mixture of shallots, red peppers, garlic, coriander, lemongrass, Chinese celery and that ever present shrimp paste, while the skin crackles with crispness. Pork is also used widely here in the sate, skewered bits of meat grilled over coals and dipped into a spicy peanut sauce.

Another local specialty used for feasting as well as in soups and sate is the sea turtle, which is cajoled to dry land for fattening and eventual slaughter. An endangered species in other parts of the world, the sea turtle is considered quite a delicacy by the Balinese. However, since both suckling pig and the sea turtle are festival foods and affordable only on special occasions, the primary diet throughout the island consists of rice, chicken, duck, fish and the most wonderful array of fruits and vegetables that are definitely gifts from the gods.

The terraced rice fields of Bali are famous and so is the fluffy rice they produce. In fact, the Balinese insist that their two harvests annually offer no parallel in taste and fluffiness! So it is quite natural that one of the best rijsttafel (rice table) available in all of Indonesia can be found on a Saturday evening at Bali's **Tanjung Sari Hotel** on Sanur beach. Hotel food throughout the island is excellent and one can savor Indonesian, Chinese, Indian, Continental and American (hamburgers) foods. For delicious, fresh seafood specialties, the **Seahorse Restaurant** in the Sanur Beach Hotel is tops. But no one seems to combine the best of all worlds better than the **Bali Hyatt's Spice Islander** specialty restaurant which features a Balinese-style banquet along with dance performances.

NIGHTLIFE ON BALI

Bali has an interesting nightlife because of the many different types of people that are drawn to the charms of this island life. You can wander into native restaurants and spend the evening tasting local dishes and speaking with all kinds of fellow travelers. Or you can spend the evening hours in the various villages, enjoying the performances of dances, plays and *wayang kulit* (shadow puppetry). Evening comes swiftly on Bali—precisely at 6 p.m. year-round—and the nighttime hours are best for experiencing a cultural life that is unique to these people.

A native dancer on Bali

Dance Performances

Hotel shows are fine for offering a potpourri of what the different dances are, but attending performances in the village temple compounds is far more memorable and certainly worth the effort.

Baris

Traditional war dance. Word means a line or file (of soldiers). A good baris dancer must be well coordinated and supple. The dance was originally a religious rite, now just dramatic glorification of a Balinese warrior.

Djanger

Popular among villagers, the dance brings a dozen young men and young women together in song and dance. Action ranges from sublime to frenzied.

Djauk

Classic demon dance; renowned for solo performances. Dancer wears a frightening mask and long fingernails. Movements resemble a baris dancer's.

Kebyar

A most involved solo dance; the performer becomes infused with the music and must know every instrument intimately. *Kebyar duduk* (seated) is most popular in southern Balinese villages.

Ketjak

Most dramatic of all Balinese dances; 150 men simulate sounds of gamelan. It's also called the Monkey Dance because of the drama related to ramayana.

Legong

Classical dance of divine nymphs; one of most subtle and beautiful of all dances. Girls learn movements at age 5 and retire in their early teens!

Legong Kraton (of the palace)

This is the most beautiful and popular dance, featuring exquisite costumes and headdresses.

Oleg Tambulilingan

Modern dance choreographed for young men and women. It's cat and mouse play with a happy ending.

Ramayana Ballet

Traditional tales with modern humor; introduced to Bali by Kokar. Conservatory of Instrumental Arts and Dance. Very popular, especially because of the fanciful animals of the forest.

The Balinese are also fond of folk drama, in which tales of passion, intrigue, military prowess, romance and adventure are acted out to the accompaniment of gamelan orchestra. Some of the plays may be difficult for visitors to appreciate and comprehend, but the Balinese love them—especially the ever-present clowns who provide comic relief and never fail to send the audience into gales of laughter.

Ardja

Popular folk opera which begins around midnight and ends in the daylight hours, when the lovers are invariably reunited. This is one of the best, so stop by for an hour or so.

Barong and Rangda

Typical triumph of good over evil. Barong is a mythical forest creature danced by two young men. As his life is threatened, so is the life of the village. Rangda is eventually defeated.

Barong Landung

Giant Barong; considered sacred and can exorcise harmful influences when necessary. Interesting and sometimes raucous performances; giants striding around temple compound.

Tjalon Arang

Story of magic; often performed to appease magical powers of tjalon arang, who keeps the village safe.

Tjupak

Bali's notorious glutton: good over evil again. Quite an adventure play; full of comic relief.

Topeng

Mask play; also called chronicle play of Bali. The stories taken from old aristocratic families around the island. Good topeng actors use 30 or 40 masks and create many diverse characters.

The wayang kulit are also popular on Bali and the performances are full of raucous clowns as well as the usual good and evil chasing each other around the forest.

Yogyakarta

Yogyakarta

YOGYAKARTA IN A CAPSULE

Cultural capital of central Java...many centuries old...between 5th and 9th century A.D., center of Hindu-based civilization that constructed Prambanan Temple complex...just 25 miles away is largest Buddhist temple in the world...Borobudur, a "mountain" of carved stones and shrines...city is home of Indonesia's greatest university, Gajah Mada...and many other cultural institutions...Kraton or Sultan's Palace still plays important role in region...just 40 miles east is Solo...another ancient capital and thriving port...25 million live in Central Java area.

Visitors who go nowhere else in Java must not miss Yogyakarta, also affectionately known as "Yogya" (pronounced *Jogja*), for this is one of three special districts of Indonesia—the heart and soul of the country. The exact antithesis of noisy, bustling Jakarta (less than an hour away by air), Yogya boasts a calm and peaceful atmosphere where life is rather slow and laid back. Indeed, here the sign of a cultured and refined person means slowness in movement, speech and dance. (Westerners take note!)

The city is located at the foot of the active volcano Merapi and stretches to the Indian Ocean in the south. It is the main gateway to central Java and its fertile plain was the seat of the mighty Javanese empire of Mataram during the 16th and 17th centuries. It is still a Sultanate, now under the jurisdiction of Sultan Hamengku Buwono IX, a dynasty dating from 1755, when the Mataram empire was divided. Due to its location and history, the arts flourished in Yogyakarta and are nourished today through the patronage of the Sultan and his Kraton, or palace, which is the hub of the area's traditional life.

Yogya is a place to relax and let the variety of its traditional arts— gamelan music, classical and contemporary Javanese dances, Wayang

Kulit puppet theater, craftsmen of batik, silver and leather—cast a spell. Although its hotels (other than the Ambarrukmo Palace) and restaurants are not memorable, all is forgiven in the wonderful shops and the many spectacular places to visit both in the city and the environs.

The Sultan's palace is the center of life in Yogya. Here, visitors (with passes obtained from the local tourist office) may watch dance and music classes as well as the making of musical instruments and puppets for the wayang kulit. In fact, there are performances of the traditional arts daily throughout the city—either free or for a nominal charge. (Abbreviated versions of wayang kulit and Ramayana ballet are presented to guests at the Ambarrukmo Palace Hotel and gamelan music can be enjoyed at lunchtime in the lobby.) Batik and silver artistry are also popular with visitors and there are plenty of places to enjoy both the making and the buying!

A visit to Yogya takes at least three days because there is so much to see both in town and outside. The magnificent Shivaite temple of Prambanan is located in the village of the same name, about 10 miles east. Dating from the 9th century, this Hindu temple (in the center of the most popular Muslim country in the world) boasts parapets adorned with bas-relief depicting the legendary Ramayana story. Among its eight shrines are those dedicted to Shiva, Vishnu and Brahma. Prambanan is impressive by day but spectacular under a full moon from June to October, when performances of the Ramayana ballet are staged with the temple as backdrop.

Approximately 25 miles northwest from Yogya is the world's greatest Buddhist monument—Borobudur—truly an outdoor museum. Built between the 8th and 9th centuries A.D. , it is believed to predate Angkor Wat by 300 years and its exact purpose is not clear because it is definitely not a temple (there is no interior access). It is estimated that more than 80,000 people worked on the more than 2 million pieces of stone and some 1,500 relief sculptures carved into its walls. A visit to Borobudur—a spiritual experience and architectural achievement—is often the reason many travelers put central Java on their Far East itinerary.

WHAT TO SEE AND DO IN YOGYAKARTA

Affandi Museum

Located on airport road. Home of Indonesia's best-known painter. It's a private museum of his own paintings and those of his daughter, Kartika.

Batik Research Center

Located on eastern outskirts of city. Interesting permanent exhibition of batiks in both classic and modern designs. Both the hand-drawn and hand-stamped process of batik can be seen.

Kraton Palace of the Sultan of Yogyakarta ★

The formal name is Kraton Ngayogyakarta-Hadiningrat. It's a city within a city; surrounded by 4 walls about 1/2-mile long each. It's the pulse of cultural life here. Some of the structures used by Gajah Mada University, others for continuing native crafts. The compound dates from the 18th century and some of the buildings are European roccoco. Don't miss **Bengsal Kencono** or Golden Pavilion. Open to visitors most days. It's especially charming on Tues. and Fri. when hundreds from the *wayang kulit* collection of the Sultan are "aired." There's a shadow play performance offered on the second Sat. of every month. You can also see Ramayana ballet taught and performed here. This is a place not to miss.

Masjid Besar

Great Mosque next to the Kraton; very important to religious and political life of palace and city.

Sonobudoyo Museum

Also situated near Kraton; the museum houses a fine collection of central Javanese artifacts. See the gamelan and wayang kulit figures. The museum was designed by a Dutch architect (1935) in the traditional Javanese style.

Taman Sari

Water castle located slightly west of Kraton; once a fine castle designed by European descent architect but now eerie ruins. It was destroyed by an earthquake in 1865, but still worth a stop. Many studios here selling curios, batiks and batik paintings. Bird market at the north wall.

Yogyakarta Environs

★ *Borobudur*

Monastery on the Hill, located about 35 miles from Yogyakarta. Largest Buddhist monument in the world—dates from 9th century. Reopened (Feb. 1983) after an 8-year, $20-million restoration project. Built some 3 centuries before construction of Angkor Wat (Kampuchea) by Sailendra dynasty. But it's a mystery why this site was chosen. The temple has 504 statues of Buddha and more than 1,300 carved panels depicting scenes from his life; 432 alcoves and 1472 stupas; about 1-1/2 miles of carvings. Some of the missing artwork will never be replaced; restoration could not have taken place in such a short time without the help of technology. IBM provided computers to aid in the reassembling task. 10,000 workers cataloged fallen stones and then matched them correctly. Monument should be seen in moonlight as well as by day.

Borobudur is the largest Buddhist shrine in the world.

Dieng Plateau

A full day trip to an altitude of 7,500 feet offers breathtaking scenery and the oldest temple complex in Java; you can also see **Gunung Merapi**, one of Java's most volatile volcanoes, which erupts with regularity every 5-1/2 years. Known as "Mt. Fire" by Javanese.

Imogiri Tombs

Burial spot of Sultans since mid-17th century; located about 12 miles south of Yogyakarta. It's a beautiful spot to visit. It's a pilgrimage up some 345 shaded steps for an incredible view at the top. You must rent formal Javanese dress to enter the sacred compound. It's available for a few Rupiahs at the top. Why not?

Kasongan

Kasongan is a small village just southwest of Yogya. Known for artistic pottery and earthenware utensils and for its local artists who sell their wares at reasonable prices.

Kotagede

This village is famous for silver shops; located just about 4 miles southeast of Yogya. Supposedly founded in 16th century by founder of the second Mataram dynasty. His former Kraton is now occupied by a garden cemetery. Don't forget the silver shops.

Parang Tritis Beach

PTB is a seaside resort about 16 miles from Yogya. Important in Javanese mythology; Sultans make special offerings here in beachside ceremony called "Labuh."

Prambanan

This ancient Hindu Temple complex is located some 10 miles east of Yogya; it was built in 9th century and deserted 100 years later. It was restored between 1918 and 1953. Now it's most famous for the Ramayana ballet performances from May to October during nights with a full moon. A great experience; it should be visited both day and night.

Solo

The ancient city of Solo is located 40 miles east of Yogya, famous today for Kraton, a sleepy pace of life and excellent shopping for antiquities. Visit **Kraton Surakarta Hadiningrat** and **Mangkunegaran Palace**, as well as the **Royal Museum** and **Radyapustaka Museum**. There are good wayang wong performances at Sriwedari Park and annual festivals at 2 Kraton (palaces). There are two hotels in Solo.

WHERE TO STAY IN YOGYAKARTA

Ambarrukmo Palace   ★★★

P.O. Box 10, Yogyakarta. ☎ *88488. FAX: 63283 • 251 rooms.* Hotel has been through many lives (InterContinental, Sheraton, etc.); now it's owned and operated by Hotel Indonesia Corp. Still the most convenient to sightseeing and the most comfortable in the city. Pavilion restaurant in original building. Coffee shop. Borobudur restaurant with evening buffet and Ramayana dances. Cocktail lounge. Bar. Swimming pool. Tennis courts. Meeting facilities. Former palace.

Reservations: Utell.

Mutiara Hotel   ★★★

P.O. Box 87, Yogyakarta. ☎ *4531. FAX: 61201 • 90 rooms.* Dining room. 2 bars. Coffee shop.   *Reservations: Direct.*

Natour Garuda Hotel

72 Jalan Malioboro, Yogyakarta. ☎ *2316. FAX: 60374 • 120 rooms.* Originally built in 1911 with cottages around a courtyard; now two wings with a series of fine rooms and suites. A truly historic place; accessible to major attractions. Garuda Bar and Restaurant. Rooftop pool with good view of volcanic Mt. Merapi.   *Reservations: Utell.*

Puri Artha Cottage   ★★

Jalan Cendrawasih 9, Yogyakarta. ☎ *5934. FAX: 62765 • 60 rooms.* Located in Javanese garden setting outside the city. Only partial air conditioning in some accommodations. Dining room. Bar. Swimming pool.   *Reservations: Direct.*

Sri Wedari Hotel & Cottage ★★
Laksamana Adisucipto, Yogyakarta. ☎ *88288. FAX: 62162 • 70 rooms.* Indonesian, European, Chinese dining room. 2 bars. Cocktail lounge. Swimming pool. Native entertainment.   ***Reservations: Direct.***

Solo

Kusuma Sahid Prince Hotel ★★
P.O. Box 20, Solo. ☎ *46356. FAX: 44788 • 100 rooms.* Dining room. Bar. Coffee shop. Swimming pool.   ***Reservations: Utell.***

Mangkunegaran Palace Hotel ★★
Istana Mangkunegaran, Solo. ☎ *5683 • 50 Rooms.* Indonesian and Continental restaurant. Bar. Swimming pool.   ***Reservations: Direct.***

WHERE TO EAT IN YOGYAKARTA

Andrawina Loka Gudegbu Tjitro
Jalan Adisucipto (km 9) • Indonesian.

Ayam Goreng Candi Sari Kalasan
Candi Sari Kalasan • Indonesian, known for fried chicken specialty.

Garuda Bar & Restaurant
72 Jalan Malioboro ☎ *2113* • Indonesian, Chinese and Japanese.

Dewi Sri 1 Jalan
Solo C.T. XIV ☎ *3599* • Indonesian, Chinese, Japanese, European.

Gita Bujana Snack & Steak House
52A Jalan Diponegoro ☎ *3742* • Everything.

Puri Artha Restaurant
Puri Artha Hotel ☎ *5934* • Everything.

Sintawang
9 Jalan Magelang ☎ *2901* • Everything.

Srikandi
Arjuna Plaza Hotel ☎ *3063* • Indonesian, French.

Srimanganti
63 Jalan Solo. ☎ *2881* • Indonesian, European.

Wisma LPP Restaurant
8 Jalan Demangan Baru ☎ *88380* • Indonesian, European, Chinese.

WHERE TO SHOP IN YOGYAKARTA

Amri Gallery
67 Gampingan • Paintings Batik.

Ardiyanto
Many shops throughout Yogya • Batik.

Arjuna Art Shop
110 Jalan Sala • Statues.

Ganeca Art Shop
69 Jalan Ambarrukmo.

H.S. Silver Store
Jalan Mandongan, Kotagede • Silver items.

Indonesia Arts & Crafts
Jalan Kemasan No. K6V, Kotagede • Silver handicrafts.

Jul Shop Curio & Antiques
29, Jalan Pangeran Mangkubumi Wayang • Wood carvings, kris, masks.

Naga Art Shop
61 Jalan Malioboro • Paintings, statues, basketry.

Pak Djaelani
Kadipatenkulon KPI/300 • Distant member of royal family who has made leather puppets for decades; prices range from $10 to several hundred.

Pasar Klewar
Near Kraton Hadiningrat in Solo • Batik market.

Sidamukti Art Shop & Batik Painting
103 Jalan Taman Kampung III • Paintings, carvings, wayang.

Toko Terang Bulan
Jalan Malioboro/Jalan Jenderal Yani 76 • Batik at fixed prices.

Tom's Silver
Jalan Kotagede • Paintings, silver handicrafts.

Surabaya

SURABAYA IN A CAPSULE

Indonesia's second most important industrial area after Jakarta . . .3 million inhabitants...located on Kali Mas River...northern coast of East Java...Tanjung Perak Harbor important for exports to Europe, Asia and the Western Hemisphere...honored as the City of Heroes...Battle of Surabaya began less than three months after Proclamation of Independence had been read in Jakarta...not known for many cultural facets...but known for interesting excursions from the city...especially to Madura Island for the bull races...and Mt. Bromo.

With a population of more than 3 million, Surabaya is Indonesia's second most important industrial city; the number of its inhabitants has increased ten-fold since the Second World War. Although it's not particularly a mecca for tourists in itself, the city is a major trading center and is frequented by traveling business people.

The city was decimated in WW II after the Japanese surrendered and the Allies attempted to impose their sovereignty. The fierce resistance with which Surabayans countered Dutch and other allied forces was the impetus for the creation of Revolutionary Heroes' Day, a holiday that's celebrated across Indonesia.

Surabaya also serves as the gateway to both Mt. Bromo and Madura Island. Mt. Bromo is an active volcano that reaches to 2330 m. It's one of the most popular attractions on Java. Madura Island is on the other side of a 3 km strait from Surabaya and features the *kerapan sapi*—the bull races which occur in the late summer after the rice harvest—which attract most tourists to the island.

WHAT TO SEE AND DO IN SURABAYA

City Tour

The best way to enjoy Surabaya is via a quick tour, which takes a look at the Government House, Jogodolok Statue, Hero's Monument, the Arab sector, Chinatown, Tanjung Perak Harbor and the zoo.

Surabaya Environs

Madura Island

A 35-minute ferry ride across the harbor will bring you to Madura, famous for monthly bull races on the first Sun. of every month. The Grand Bull Race is in September following the harvest. You should take the time to observe this colorful and ridiculous pastime if you're in the area.

Mt. Bromo

Home of the God of Fire. You can visit the crater from **Ngadisari** through the Sea of Sands via horseback. It's also popular for watching sunrises from the crater. En route you can stop by the Tenggerese people, who maintain ancient Buddhist beliefs but have erected no temples.

Penataran Temple Complex

Built between A.D. 1200 and 1450, this complex is considered the creation place for the Hindu Javanese kings of Kediri. The temples reveal the culture of the Kediri kingdom. This was the era of famous King Airlangga. It's a full day trip from Surabaya .

Tretes Mountain Resort

Magnificent air and views just 40 miles south of Surabaya. This is an area famous for **Candra Wilwatika** open air theater and the classical dances performed from May through October during the full moon, with **Gunung Penanggungan** (almost perfect volcanic cone) in the background.

WHERE TO STAY IN SURABAYA

Hyatt Regency Surabaya ★★★★

124-128 Jalan Basuki Rakhmat. ☎ *511234. FAX: 521508 • 518 rooms.* In late 1993, the hotel opened a new Regency Tower wing with 250 rooms, Presidential Suites and Regency Suites, overlooking the pool and terrace. Seven restaurants, lounges and entertainment center. Fitness center with two swimming pools, three tennis courts, jogging track. Business center. Shopping arcade. Airline counter with city terminal check-in. *Reservations: Hyatt Int'l.*

Patra Surayabaya Hilton International ★★★★

Jalan Gunungsari. ☎ *582703. FAX: 574504* • *120 chalet-style rooms and four villas.* Opened in early 1993. Landscaped grounds; rooms with satellite TV and working desks; a 250-room tower to be added at a later date. Restaurant and poolside bar. Swimming pools for adults and children, 18-hole golf course nearby. Meeting rooms. Business center.   **Reservations: Hilton.**

Ramayana Hotel ★★

67-69 Jalan Basuki Rakhmat. ☎ *46321* • *100 rooms.* Dining room. Coffee shop. Chinese restaurant. Bar. Swimming pool. Tennis nearby.

WHERE TO EAT IN SURABAYA

Arumanis Terrace

Hyatt Regency Surabaya ☎ *470875* • Indonesian.

Cendana

Cendana Hotel ☎ *42251* • Indonesian, European, Chinese.

Ceshiang Garden

Hyatt Regency Surabaya ☎ *470875* • Chinese.

Chez Rose

12 Jalan Panglima Polim ☎ *45669* • Indonesian, European, Chinese.

Delby

145 Jalan Raya Darmo ☎ *66641* • Indonesian, European, Chinese.

Hugo's

Hyatt Regency Surabaya ☎ *470875* • European.

Mandarin

93 Jalan Genteng Kali ☎ *40222* • Indonesian Chinese.

Peninsula

Ramayana Hotel ☎ *45395* • Indonesian, European, Chinese.

Wijaya International

1-7 Jalan Bubutan ☎ *44088* • European, Chinese.

Zed Corner

1 Jalan Setail ☎ *68703* • Indonesian Chinese.

Sumatra

SUMATRA IN A CAPSULE

Indonesia's largest island...fifth largest island in the world...stretches some 182,859 square miles from the Andaman Sea in the north to Sunda Strait in the south...lies opposite southern flank of Malay Peninsula...forms southern boundary of long and strategic Strait of Malacca...island represents some 25% of Indonesia's land area...and 18% of its population...capital city is Medan...but Lake Toba is the most popular tourist attraction...island known for almost unlimited oil resources... most major American oil companies have joint ventures here.

With 30 million inhabitants, Sumatra is second among the Indonesian islands in population, yet its population density is about one-tenth of that on Java. After Bali and Java, the island ranks as the third most popular Indonesian tourist destination.

INSIDER TIP

Transmigration is the term used to describe what is perhaps the largest population resettlement program in the world. Since 1950, the Indonesian government has been moving inhabitants of overpopulated Java to the Outer Islands in the belief that this will alleviate the poverty and suffering inherent in urban overpopulation. In all, 6 million people have been displaced under the program, some 60 percent of them ending up on Sumatra. Human rights activists as well as environmentalists charge that the policy forces the relocation of indigenous people and is wreaking havoc on the environment, namely in swelling Indonesia's deforestation rate. In fact, it's gotten so serious on Sumatra that the island itself has a significant percentage of the population targeted for relocation.

The most spectacular topographical feature of Sumatra is the 1,000-mile long Bukit Barisan Range, a rugged chain of immense volcanoes that—in conjunction with incredible waterfalls and steamy jungles—looks right out of the Jurassic period. Many of the peaks are higher than 2,000 m, with Mt. Kerinci topping out at more than 3,800 m. Moving through the lush flora, you half expect an ancient raptor to snatch you out of the jungle for dinner.

Although that's something that couldn't happen to you today, it's darn close. Sumatra is famed for such wild beasts as tigers and leopards, bearded pigs, Sumatran rhinos, orangutans, tapirs and Indian elephants.

There are also a number of diverse cultures on Sumatra, including Stone Age and matriarchal tribes.

WHAT TO SEE AND DO ON SUMATRA

Brastagi

This is a popular mountain resort between Medan and Lake Toba and home of the Batak tribesmen. The native architecture features longhouses built high on stilts with very distinctive high-peaked roofs. Most Batak are now Christians, which explains so many churches in the countryside. Look for tribespeople en route to church every Sunday.

Bukit Tinggi

Bukit Tinggi nestled on the plateau on the lower slopes of **Bukit Barisan** mountain range. It's known as the center of **Minangkabau** people, who are skilled in woodcarving, weaving and metal-working—also for *silat* dance, which is considered a form of self-defense. The town lies at an altitude of 3,000 feet. You can see the great peaks of **Merapi** and **Singgalang**, both at 9,000 feet. Visit the beautiful caves of **Ngalau Kamang** with their enormous stalactites and stalagmites nearby.

Lake Toba

This is one of the great tourist attractions on Sumatra. It's a crater lake some 3,000 feet above sea level and surrounded by mountains. The lake is 50 miles long and about 110 miles south of Medan. It was once the sacred domain of local tribesmen. Outsiders once met with death if caught gazing at its dark and mysterious waters. It's now a tourist resort and hill station above the plains of Medan.

Medan

Medan is the bustling capital city of Sumatra. Today, it's full of American and Japanese traders dealing in oil, rubber, palm oil, tea, cocoa, sisal and Deli tobacco—all exported from the nearby port of Belawan. Visitors should see the **Palace of Sultan of Deli** (built in 1888) and the great mosque **Mesjid Raya**, built in 1906 and considered one of the country's finest. About 60 miles from Medan is the **Monkey Tour**. It's actually a sanctuary where hundreds of monkeys roam freely. It's considered a holy place and many people come here to worship.

Padang

Padang is a major seaport in West Sumatra. In fact, it was the main port along this coast during the 18th century, used then for shipments of gold and pepper. It's now an expanding area, known for the **Nirwana** beach resort and camping facilities. Padang is an important trading center on this island.

Parapat

This is a resort village overlooking Lake Toba. Lakeside accommodations can be found here at Parapat Hotel and Danau Toba Hotel. The main activities are swimming, waterskiing and antique hunting. The late President Sukarno was under house arrest here. Many tourists take a boat from Parapat to Samosir Island in Lake Toba. The village houses on Samosir are characterized by sway-backed roofs and facades elaborately carved and painted.

WHERE TO STAY ON SUMATRA

Medan

Danau Toba International Hotel   ★★
17, Jalan Imam Bonjol. ☎ 327000. FAX: 27021 • 259 rooms. Coffee shop. Japanese restaurant. Swimming pool. 4 Bars.
Reservations: Direct.

Dirga Surya   ★★
6, Jalan Imam Bonjol. ☎ 321555. FAX: 513387 • 60 rooms. Coffee garden. Bar. Restaurant with Indonesian, Chinese and European cuisine. Traditional dances.   *Reservations: Direct.*

Natour Dharma Deli Hotel   ★★
Jalan Balai Kota. ☎ 51362. FAX: 327153 • 183 rooms. Dining room. Bar. Swimming pool. Disco.   *Reservations: Utell.*

Parapat

Hotel Danau Toba   ★★
Jalan Pulau Samosir. ☎ 327000. FAX: 27020 • 50 rooms. Dining room. Japanese restaurant. Bar. Weekly entertainment.
Reservations: Direct.

Natour Hotel Parapat   ★★★
Jalan Marlhat. ☎ 410121 • 75 rooms. Dining Room. Bar. Folk entertainment. Tennis courts. Canoes and watersports. Lake resort.
Reservations: Utell.

Hotel Patra Jasa Parapat   ★★★
Jalan Siukar 1, Parapet. ☎ 41766 • 34 rooms. Dining Room. Bar. Entertainment. Swimming pool. Tennis. 9-hole golf course. Children's playground. Heli-pad. Boats. Stables. Waterskiing.
Reservations: Direct.

WHERE TO EAT ON SUMATRA

Medan

Bali Plaza
> *Jalan Kumango.* ☎ *321164* • Chinese.

Cape Demarati
> *Jalan Gatot Subroto.* ☎ *29141* • European.

De'Bour
> *Dharma Deli Hotel.* ☎ *322210* • Indonesian, European, Chinese, Seafood.

De'Plaza Garuda
> *Plaza Hotel.* ☎ *326255* • Indonesian, European, Chinese.

Fuji
> *Danau Toba Inn.* ☎ *22700* • Japanese.

Hawa Mandarin
> *Jalan Mangkubumi.* ☎ *27275* • Everything.

Kuala Deli
> *Dirga Surya Hotel.* ☎ *323433* • Everything.

Polonia
> *Jalan Jendral Sudirman.* ☎ *27380* • Everything.

Toshiko Yokohama
> *Jalan 7 Palang Merah.* ☎ *322319* • Japanese.

Parapat
> *Wisma Danau Toba Jalan P. Samosir* • Indonesian, European, Chinese.

Parapat

Lapaloma
> *Jalax Imam Bonjol/Jalan Gatot Subroto* • Indonesian, European, Chinese.

Metro
> *Jalan Jendrai Sudirman* • Everything.

Other Areas

Irian Jaya

This is the eastern-most territory of Indonesia and not yet a tourist center. It was first discovered by the Portuguese, but it was the Spanish who named it Nueva Guinea. The Dutch renamed it Nieuw Guinea but returned the island to Indonesia in 1963. Today, 200 to 300 primitive tribes live here. Some villages can be explored by the adventurous interested in sociology or photography. The most popular places are Biak, a tiny island off the north coast; Jayapura, near Lake Sentani; and Baliem Valley, discovered in 1938, where about 30 Dani tribes live. To enter Irian Jaya, special permission must be obtained from **Markas Besar Kepolisian (MABAK)**—department of police in Jakarta—or from a local tour operator.

Komodo Island

Komodo Island is located in the Flores Sea, east of Bali and its famous **Komodo dragon** (scientific name is *varanus komodoensis*), the largest lizard in the world, makes his home here. The island is sparsely populated. The inhabitants are outnumbered by about 300 counted dragons. The island is now considered a game preserve—a dragon sanctuary, if you will. The Komodo Dragon was discovered in 1912. It can weigh up to 300 pounds and grow up to 12 feet in length. Scientists say the dragon/lizard has remained unchanged for 5,000 years or more while other lizards in the world have undergone genetic changes. You must travel from Bali to Bima or Sumbawa to charter a boat to the island. Permission to visit must be obtained from MABAK in Jakarta, or from the CAGAR ALAM office in Bogor. Try a tour operator first.

Maluku

Previously called The Moluccas, the fabled Spice Islands lie in all shapes and sizes midway between Sulawesi and Irian Jaya, 900 to 1,000 bits and pieces of land of volcanic origin. The capital and main tourist attraction is **Ambon**, an island 14-by-30 miles filled with abundant clove and nutmeg trees. September through January are ideal for coral-viewing, snorkeling and skin diving here. The provincial capital, Ambon Town, is situated on rocky coastline. It has several tourist hotels and well-stocked shops, beautiful old homes and two jewel-like museums. 200 miles away are the villages of **Liang** and **Waai**, whose inhabitants welcome visitors to their homes. The fish in Waai's river are reputed to be so tame that visitors can stroke them!

Hila is a smaller village in the jungle where the scents of drying mace and nutmeg fill the air. The village also boasts an ancient fort called Nieuw Amsterdam and a wooden church dating from 1797. Peppercorns, nutmeg, clove and mace are plentiful, as well as ebony statues and handwoven fabrics from Tanimbar Islands.

Nias

Situated off the west coast of Sumatra, Nias is a remote and secluded island with a Stone-Age culture. It's just 30-by-80 miles—a 12-hour boat journey from Sumatra and light years away. The people are primarily Batak. Nias has one of the largest megalithic cultures in the world. No journey here is complete without a truck ride up to the fortress of **Bawomatalowa** to see the sun set at 1,300 feet above sea level. Ancient dances performed on site. It's an esoteric place but gradually becoming a tourist attraction. Islands such Nias are best enjoyed aboard a Society Expeditions' cruise ship.

Sulawesi

Formerly called the Celebes, Sulawesi lies just east of Borneo at the equator. This beautiful, lush, tropical island nourishes beautiful and rare wild orchids. The capital city of South Sulawesi is now called Ujung Pandang (formerly Makassar). More than half a million people live here along with old Fort Rotterdam—one of the great colonial sites. Ujung Pandang is also home of seafaring Buginese whose handmade two- and three-masted schooners, constructed entirely of teak, are still used in thriving inter-island trade. But the Toraja hanging graves are the most remarkable attractions on the island. Torajaland—land of the heavenly kings—is located about 300 miles north of Ujung Pandang. It's reached by jeep or minibus after a journey through the villages of Palawa, Marante, Nanggala and Siguntu. Torajas eagerly welcomes visitors. It features boat-shaped houses richly ornamented with geometric designs. Here there are funerals known as Festivals of Joy, where the deceased are displayed openly in hanging graves at Lemo, Longa and Ke Te. It's both interesting and colorful. South Sulawesi also has a resort and nature reserve at **Bantimurung**, where thousands of exotic butterflies can be seen against a background of high cliffs and waterfalls. North Sulawesi has colorful ports, spice plantations, lakeside resorts and hot springs. The capital, **Manado**, is a pleasant place to stay.

TOURS

Jakarta and West Java

Angklung Tour
> 3 hours, daily from Jakarta. Visit bamboo musical instrument work-shop in Padasuka village. Southeast of the city.

Bandung City Tour
> 3 hours, daily. Biological Museum, Zoological Gardens, Institute of Technology.

Bandung Volcano Tour
> All day. Tangkuban Prahu volcano and rim and Ciater hot springs. Lembang fruit market. Bogor Botanical Gardens and Puncak Pass.

Bandung Package
> 2 to 4 days. Visits Bogor and Puncak, Tangkuban Prahu and Ciater hot springs.

Bogor
> 5 to 6 hours, daily. Botantical Gardens and Presidential Palace. Eight-hour tour includes lunch at Puncak Pass.

Cirebon Tour
> 6 hours, daily. Sultan's Palace, Princess Cemetery, batik cloth center.

Garut and Tasikmalaya Tour
> 8 hours, daily. Craft centers and hot springs.

Jakarta City Tour ★
> 3 to 4 hours, daily. Presidential Palace, National Monument, Central Museum, Chinatown, Old Batavia restoration, Pasar Ikan (fish market), Senayon sports complex, batik factory.

Jakarta Night Tour
> 4 to 6 hours, daily. Ancol Dreamland Park, jai alai stadium. Dinner and cultural show.

Krakatoa/Ujung Kulon Package
> 4 to 6 days. Cruise to Krakatoa volcano in Sunda Strait. Land on the island it created. Continue on to Ujung Kulon wildlife reserve.

Mini Indonesia Tour
> 3 to 4 hours, daily. Tour of Indonesia in miniature; bird park, Museum Indonesia etc.

Yogyakarta and Central Java

Borobudur Temple Tour
> 4 hours, daily. Includes visits to Medut and Pawon temples. Longer tour also includes Prambanan.

Yogyakarta City Tour

3 hours, daily. Visits Sultan's Royal Kraton, Sonobudoyo Museum, batik workshop and silverworks at Kota Gede. Taman Sari Water Castle substitute on Moslem holidays.

Prambanan Temple Tour

3 tours, daily. Includes Plaosan and Kalasan temples. Evening tour to ballet performances during full moon nights from May to October.

Solo Tour

4 to 5 hours, daily. Also includes visit to Prambanan.

Surabaya and East Java

Bromo Sunrise Tour

10 to 12 hours. Departs at midnight by car. Traverses Sand Sea by horse for sunrise at volcano's rim.

Madura Island Tour

Full day. Ferry crossing to island. Drive, sightsee; bull races in season.

Mentawai Islands/Bukittinggi Package

7 days. Visits all islands off West Sumatra coast; by boat.

Sukamade-Baluran-Mt. Bromo Tour ★

7 days. Visits wildlife areas in Mt. Bromo, Surabaya, Jember, Sukamade, Baluran and Bayuwangi. Begins in Surabaya, ends in Denpasar, Bali.

Surabaya City Tour

3 hours, daily. Governor's palace, zoo, Hero's Monument and Jokodolok Statue.

Three Temples Tour

6 hours, daily. Calls at Singosari, Jago and Kidal temples.

Bali

Bali Packages

3 to 5 days. Includes dance performances, Kintamani and Sangeh/Mengwi tours. 5-day package adds Besakih.

Bedugul Lake Tour

6 hours, daily. Stops at Mengwi, Bedugul and Bratan Lake.

Besakih Tour

6 to 10 hours, daily. Combines Besakih with either Klungkung or Kintamani.

Dance Tours

Varying lengths. View barong and kris, kechak and legong dances.

Denpasar City Tour

Visits art and cultural center, Bali Museum and Le Mayeur Art Gallery, local market.

Kintamani Tour

8 hours, daily. Includes Celuk, Mas, Ubud, Bedulu, Penelokan, Tampak Siring, Kintamani and Bangli.

Sangeh, Mengwi, Tanah Lot Tour

4 to 8 hours, daily.

Singaraja Tour

Full day to top of Bali. Includes Mengwi, Bedugul and Singaraja.

Trunyan Village Tour

10 hours, daily. Same at Kintamani tour; adds drive along Batur Lake to Trunyan.

Ubud Tour

4 hours, daily. Calls at Ubud, Mas and Batuan.

Sumatra

Belawan Tour

5 hours, daily. Visit Medan's busy port. Seafood dining and nightlife along Strait of Malacca.

Brastagi Tour

Full day from Medan to Sembahe, Sibolangit Botanical Garden, Lawu Debuk-Debuk hot springs and Batak Karo houses.

Baharok Orangutan Reserve

10 hours to 2 days. Tour of Northern Sumatra reserve; special permit required.

Lake Toba Packages

2 to 6 days. Includes visits to Brastagi, Lingga, Prapat/Lake Toba, Pematang Purba and Tomok.

Medan City Tour

3 hours, daily. Grand Mosque, Palace of Sultan Deli, Heroes' Cemetery; shopping area.

Nias Island Package ★

Full day to full week. Includes visits to Teluk Dalam, Nias Village, a stay at the chief's house, stone jumping. Can be combined with Lake Toba tour.

Padang City Tour

3 hours, daily. Muara fishermen's village, open-air market, Chinese shrine.

Padang/Bukit Tinggi Package

2 to 4 days. Visits Sicincin Padang Panjang and Bukittinggi. Longer versions also cover Maninjau Lake, Anai Waterfall, Ngarai Sianok, Bungus Bay, Karang Tirta and Teluk Bayur Harbor.

South Sumatra Tour

3 days. Departs from Palembang; local tours and Musi River cruise.

Sulawesi

Toraja Land Package

3 days in South Sulawesi. Visits Lemo, Londa, Palawa, Siguntu and Rantepao. 4 days adds other villages.

Ujung Pandang City Tour

3 hours, daily. Visits Fort Rotterdam, Bundt's Orchid House and Coral Collection, Pinisi Wharf and local market.

Ujung Pandang Island Tour

4 hours. Visits Lae Lae Island, populated by fishermen and Samalona Island, a popular resort for watersports. Barrang Lompo Island offers excellent snorkeling and seashells.

Other Islands

East Kalimantan, Borneo Package

3 to 9 days. Visits Dayak tribal attractions; Mahakam River cruise.

Irian Jaya, New Guinea Package

7 to 8 days. Visits primitive areas of New Guinea when safe.

Komodo Island Tour

4 days from Bali. Visits famous "dragons" (giant lizards) on Komodo; also Sumbawa Island.

LAOS

Plain of Jars in Xieng Khouang province of Laos

LAOS IN A CAPSULE

Dramatic, scenic country of remote hill tribes and ancient kingdoms ...War torn country wedged between Vietnam, Cambodia, Myanmar, China and Thailand...Most primitive of all SE Asian countries....Incredible sights include the curious Plain of Jars, Pak Ou caves with thousands of gold/wood Buddha statues and Wat Phou for brilliant carvings...Li Phi and Khong Phapheng waterfalls are largest in SE Asia...a great destination for adventurers/history buffs.

143

With the exception of being able to get into Vientiane across the Mekong River from Nong Khai in Thailand for a limited stay in the capital, Laos has been mostly closed to tourism since 1975 and has only recently creaked the door open for travel elsewhere in the country. As a result of the 15-year ban, there have been little or no infrastructure improvements and you will be among the first Westerners to explore this heavily-damaged but interesting country. Much like Europe after 1945, many of its ancient monuments are damaged, many areas of the country are moonscapes; the consequences of our secret war against Laos are apparent.

Like Myanmar, the Laotian government directly controls where travelers can go and what they can see and do, although enforcement capabilities (and motivation, it seems) are lacking. You can get a short visa to gain entry and then try creating your own trip once in Vientiane. The fact of the matter is that the situation in Laos changes regularly regarding how you can enter the country and get around once inside. The "authorities" are hard pressed to keep track of you and, as it turns out, rarely do. If you're considering visiting this beautiful country, the best thing to do is question other travelers in places such as Bangkok, Saigon and Phnom Penh who have recently been to Laos themselves.

The best time to visit is November to March when it's cooler and drier. The higher elevations like Plain of Jars and Bolovens plateau can drop below freezing and the rest of the year it's hot, real hot.

Few governments envy Laos; a landlocked, rugged land populated by a diverse group of ethnic groups and bordered on all sides by pugnacious neighbors. With an annual per capita income of $180, most (75 percent) of the residents are agrarian subsistence farmers. Only 10 percent of the country lies anywhere near a road.

We don't want to ponder too long on the savagery of the undeclared war the U.S. wrought on Laos, but suffice it to say that Laos has the dubious distinction of being the most thoroughly bombed country in history. U.S. warplanes dropped more than two million tons of bombs on this primitive country for nearly nine years in the 60s and early 70s. That's more than the total tonnage dropped on Europe in WWII.

Little wonder why Laos has been living entirely on Russian aid until just a few years ago. Now with that source of income gone, Laos has looked to tourism to generate badly needed dollars. They do not wish to throw open their doors to unbridled commercialism and, like Myanmar, are taking it one step at a time. It may be too

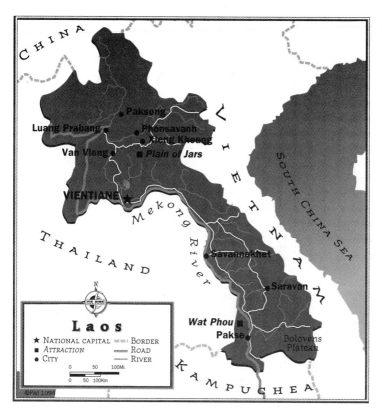

early for some and others may feel they are too late. In any case, a trip to Laos in 1994 will make you one of the vanguard who will see this country without makeup and in the cold light of its transition from communism to capitalism. Rather than take you through the tongue twisting list of rulers and dates, we will try to put some order to the various eras of Laos.

History of Laos

The mountains of Laos acted as a wall against the Mongols of Kublai Khan. The Tai tribes fled to Laos, gradually absorbing culture and influence from India rather than from China.

The Khmer empire was under the control of Lannathai in the 11th century and under the Sukhothai. It was not until 1349 with the fall of the Ayutthaya Dynasty that the kingdom of Laos was created.

Called **Lane Xang**, the land of a million elephants, it claimed as an empire an area similar to present-day Laos and was ruled from

Luang Prabang by Fa Ngoum, a prince from Angkor Wat in what is present-day Cambodia (Cambodia).

Therevada Buddhism was the official religion and the Golden Buddha, from which Luang Prabang gets its name, was a gift from Fa Ngoum's Khmer father-in-law.

In 1369, his son Samenethai took over and set up the current system of muangs which was in effect until 1975. When he died, Wat Manoram was built to house his ashes.

Chaiyachakkapat-Phaenphaeo ruled from 1441 until 1478, years that marked the beginning of Vietnam's incursions into Laos. His son, King Suvarna Banlang, drove the Vietnamese out of Luang Prabang. And King Visunarat, who ruled from 1500 to 1520, is remembered for building Wat Visoun in Luang Prabang. It was then Vientiane's turn to be Indochina's prominent center under King Phothisareth from 1520 to 1548. His union with a Chaing Mai princess created Setthathirat, one of Laos' best known and loved monarchs. He ruled from the new capital Vientiane and was responsible for building Wat Phra Kareo and bringing the Emerald Buddha (the same one that is now in Bangkok) inside. When he expired in 1574, the kingdom of Laos split into factions, with Vientiane (called Vieng Chan) ending up under Burmese rule and Luang Prabang in the north splitting away.

Seven years later the two kingdoms were unified under Nokeo Koumane, who ruled for five short years. His successor, Thammikarath, lasted from 1596 until 1622. The next ruler, King Souligna Vongsa, lasted until 1694 and it was about this time that Europeans caught their first glimpse of this strange and wonderful land. Jesuit missionaries and the Dutch trader Gerrit van Wuysthoff were some of the first. Laos was considered too remote and too poor; Europe's expansionist attention turned to the more lucrative lands of America and Indonesia. After the benign reign of Souligna Vongsa, Laos never regained its peaceful state again. The kingdom of Laos became a succession of small kingdoms, foreign-run vassal states and colonial empires.

In 1778, Vientiane (Vieng Chan) was sacked and both the Emerald Buddha and Phra Bang were taken to Bangkok. Run by the puppet King Anou, the Thais ruled Laos from afar. It wasn't until the French assumed control of Laos in 1887 that the country began to enjoy a 50-year period of *laisse faire* colonialism with the Chinese and Vietnamese given control of most of the country's trade.

The Japanese never technically invaded Laos but ousted the French administration in a coup in March of 1945. When the Japanese surrendered, the seeds of independence were planted in Lao minds, as they were in the minds of most of Asia. Faced with returning to their colonial landlords or fighting for independence, the Lao chose freedom. The governor of Vientiane, Prince Phaya Khammao, formed a national government and declared independence on September 1, 1945.

In typical fashion, the French fought to regain their colony and it wasn't until 1953 that the French granted Laos their freedom, being careful to make Laos a French protectorate.

The Pathet Lao, (the Lao Nation) who ruled the north, had different ideas and when the Viet Minh under Ho Chi Minh beat the French in Vietnam, the U.S. became concerned that Laos could fall to Communist influence from the north and begin destabilizing Southeast Asian countries one by one. The Domino Theory, as it was called, assumed that China or the Commies were bent on world domination. Laos plunged into a three-way civil war in the late fifties between left wing, right wing and neutrals. America chose to draw the line not in Vietnam, but in Laos in the early 60s.

America was determined to stop the flow of arms and supplies along the Ho Chi Minh Trail that ran through Laos into Vietnam. The concept was simple, but the execution was the stuff of pulp novels. The CIA, Army Special Forces (nicknamed the Green Berets), Thai mercenaries, Laotian soldiers and an amazing army of 30,000 Hmong tribesmen, all supported by a CIA-owned-and-run airline called Air America, began a war that would escalate into the Vietnam war.

At the time, the idea of remote wooden forts inhabited by A-teams, mercenary pilots in cowboy hats and jeans who flew soldiers and supplies in and opium out, sounded like the wild west; it seemed the stuff of fiction. It wasn't, but even the movie *Apocalypse Now*, written by John Milius, tried to capture the bizarre activities. Excess was the order of the day. The bombing of the area around the Ho Chi Minh Trail easily exceeded the ordnance dropped in WWII. Little is known or recorded about this covert war that virtually pushed Laos back into the stone age.

In August of 1975, peace came to Laos and the People's Republic of Laos was born. The monarchy was abolished and a period of darkness descended. We marvel at the dark ages of Europe and find it hard to fathom that it could happen in modern times. The communist government began to "reeducate" the population. Intellectuals were sent to concentration camps; village autonomy was ended. The king and his family were arrested; they died in squalor at a reeducation camp. In all, more than 10% of the population fled Laos between 1973 and 1975. 300,000 people, mostly educated property owners and shopkeepers, fled to the west or to refugee camps in Thailand.

Monks wait for dawn alms during That Luang festival in Vientiane

Today Laos is still run by an autocratic, Marxist regime but communism is definitely out of fashion. Same group, different song. You can decide if your tourist dollars are better spent in other countries. For now, we recommend Laos only to the most experienced independent travelers.

PLANNING AHEAD

TRAVEL RESTRICTIONS

There are limits to where you can and cannot go in Laos. You cannot go more than 15 km outside Vientiane (so they say). You do not have to travel in a group. Tourists must have a local guide approved or provided by Lao National Tourism. Guides can be hired on arrival for a daily fee ($12) expenses and tip. You may apply for permits to visit the following areas: Attapeu, Champassak, Luang Prabang, Saravane, Savannakhet and Xieng Khouang. Like Myanmar, the country is slowly opening up the area to tourism so do not be shy to inquire about any areas you would like to visit.

A couple of things to remember. Laos is not hung up on keeping people together in groups as long as you have your own guide. If you are discovered without the proper paperwork or without a guide, they do not fool around or look the other way. You will be detained, bounced out of the country and you will not have much luck in getting any prepaid portions of your trip refunded.

VISAS

To experience Laos you need sponsorship from somebody in Laos, a Lao citizen, company or travel company, who will issue an invitation combined with a telex issued by the Ministry of the Interior. These documents must be sent to the closest Lao embassy or consulate. There are offices in Canberra, Australia; Paris, France; Washington, DC, U.S.A., or Stockholm, Sweden. If you are in Asia, there are consulates or embassies in Bangkok, Hanoi, Phnom Penh and Yangon.

You will get a 15-day visa; it takes 2-7 working days, you will need half a dozen passport-sized photos and $77.50. Ask for a tourist visa, not a business or transit visa.

You can enter Laos from Bangkok, Thailand and there are many companies who will supply package tours.

This is the official line. If you plan to fly in, the best place to get a Lao visa is in Bangkok. It'll also be the cheapest place. But shop around. As it is with trying to get a visa for Cambodia, you'll run into as many procedures and prices as there are travel agents. And it seems that anyone who's got a phone in Bangkok does some moonlighting as a travel agent. Tourist visas typically cost less than U.S.$100 and you'll probably have to wait at least a few days to get one—but not the seven or 10 days many travel agents will say it takes. A transit visa takes less time and only about 20 bucks U.S. But, remember, a tourist visa will probably give you more freedom of movement in the country.

LANGUAGE

Lao is the language of the people. French is widely spoken by the older and more educated. And Russian is popular. Many people will try to speak English, so do your best. Government officials, shopkeepers and guides will have a basic understanding of English.

MONEY

Kip is the currency. There are about 700 kip to one U.S. dollar. There are no coins. You'll feel like a rich man because the largest bill is 500 kip. Carry U.S. dollars; travelers checks are hard to cash; there is no black market and U.S. currency and Thai baht are easy to spend in large cities. Out in the country spend your kip. Don't change too much unless you like to collect worthless third-world currency. It cannot be exchanged outside the country. Your credit cards are novelties and are only accepted at the largest hotels.

ELECTRICITY

220 volts/50 cycles in cities, 110 volts in the country. Bring a two-pin socket and a multi-voltage converter. Don't plan on having electricity 24 hours a day outside the main towns.

WEIGHTS & MEASURES

Metric. Drive on the right side of the road.

POSTAL

Mail service is not reliable. But try it for postcards. They might even arrive by the time you get back.

TELEPHONE, TELEX AND FAX

If you want to call home, use the major hotels or the international telephone office in Vientiane. The chances of being able to get a line from outside the country are slim to none. You must place the call through an international operator (dial 19); they will let you know when your call is ready. At this time, there is only one line to Western countries, so don't talk too long if you do get through!

Within the country there is better service, including faxes in major offices and hotels.

NEWSPAPER, TV, RADIO

VCRs and Thai TV stations are the most popular mediums. There is a national station. If you're dying for news, bring a shortwave radio. Government-controlled newspapers are of the old-school socialist type, good for souvenirs but not for news. *Khao San Pathet Lao News Bulletin* is published daily in English and French. You can also find Western publications in Vientiane, if you ask around.

TOUR PACKAGERS

In Bangkok, Thailand, you can contact the following: **Absolute Travel** (☎ *213-1277*); **Diethelm Travel**, *Kian Gwan Bldg. 2, 140/1 Wireless Rd., Bangkok 10300* (☎ *255-9150*); **East West Travel**, *46-1 Soi Nana Nua, Sukhumvit, Bangkok* (☎ *253-0681*); **Exotissimo Travel**, *21/17 Sukhumvit Soi 4, Bangkok 10110* (☎ *253-5240*); **MK Ways**, *18/4 Saint Louis Soi 3, Sathorntai Rd., Bangkok* (☎ *212-2532*); **Spangle Tours**, *205/1 Sathorn South Rd., Bangkok* (☎ *212-1583*); and **Thai-Vietnam** (☎ *237-7127*).

HEALTH

Technically, you will only need shots if you come from an infected area. But since you are coming into a third-world country with limited health or medical facilities, take all precautions. Make sure you are current on cholera, hepatitis, polio, tetanus and typhoid. Carry any medication and first aid. Take a prophylaxis for malaria, a small mosquito net, bug juice and wear long sleeve shirts and long pants. Domestic animals may have rabies.

Don't drink the water; bilharzia can be contracted from stagnant or slow moving water. Make sure whatever you stick in your mouth has been washed, watched, boiled and cooked properly.

There is a ratio of 1 doctor to every 1,362 people. Take a number if you get sick. There are two hospitals in Vientiane: Mahasot and Settathirath or you can visit the Australian or Swedish embassies. If you can wait, go to Bangkok.

ENTRY BY AIR

We recommend entry by air from Bangkok to Vientiane via Thai Airways ($184 return). You can also enter from Hanoi via Lao Aviation or Vietnam Airlines ($160 return, twice a week).

There are two flights a week from Phnom Penh ($240 return Wednesday and Thursday).

Internal flights rely on Lao Aviation's ramshackle collection of Russian and Chinese turboprops. You will long for the hot crowded buses after one circuitous up and down flight. Not recommended except for travelers with a lot of flight insurance and very few reasons to live.

INSIDER TIP

For white knuckle flyers we recommend sticking to Thai Airways to get to Laos and then ground transportation internally. Lao Aviation and Vietnam Airlines, in our opinion, are not maintained to Western safety standards and pose a serious safety hazard.

Wattay International airport is 3 km from Vientiane and there is a $5 departure tax.

BY LAND

There is entry from Nong Khai to Tha Dua, about 25 km from Vientiane. You can cross from Chomeck to Pakse as well, but it requires special permission if you leave this way. Once inside Laos, conditions go from primitive to nonexistent.

LOCAL TRANSPORTATION

There is not even a **bus** system for the locals—if you do find a bus, don't count on it getting there. There is bus service inside the prefectures. All roads are bad and there is erratic to nonexistent service between the states; some are subject to travel restrictions.

Taxis are rolling antiques and have no meters. Negotiate a day-rate in the main towns or a flat-rate for each trip. Count on spending a buck a mile or ten dollars for the day.

Trishaws are relatively plentiful. Agree on a price before you get in.

There is **car rental** in Laos. You can rent Toyota Land Cruisers, Volvos or nondescript passenger cars for anywhere from $25-$40 a day. With or without a driver.

Bicycles are popular for getting around town. And there are **boats** for river trips on the Mekong.

CUSTOMS

Customs allows 500 cigarettes, 2 bottles of wine and 1 bottle of hard liquor. You may bring in or take out as much currency as you wish. There is a limit on the amount of Thai baht (100,000 baht) that can be brought in. Do not attempt to export antiquities or any images of Buddha.

ACCOMMODATIONS

Hotels are basic, dull and uninspiring. If you are visiting the south, try to get into one of the colonial houses or chalets.

FOOD

Lao food is similar to Thai food—by way of China and without the variety. What you will eat in Laos either clucked, swam or was just yanked out of the ground. You may find yourself enjoying certain dishes more than others, as marijuana is a common addition to dishes. Some dishes include pounded raw meat marinated in lemon juice (*laap sin*). If it's made with fish, it's called *laap pa*. There's glutinous rice (*khaaw niaw*), fermented fish (*paddek of nam pa*) and soups such as bamboo shoot soup (*keng no may*), veggie broth and buffalo skin soup (*keng khi lek*). The soups are for the end or the middle of your meal. Don't go out of your way to find "typical" Lao home cooking because French cuisine is so popular. You also might want to patronize the Vietnamese or Chinese establishments in town. You may even think about opening a McDonald's franchise.

If you develop a thirst, there is a good but expensive selection of imported beer and alcohol. The local drink is rice wine that is a fine mixture of local river water and fermented rice (*lau-lao*). Try it but be prepared to suffer the consequences. You may want to bring home a bottle of Sticky Rice to impress your friends. At least they will have a doctor nearby.

SHOPPING

Laos is famous for textiles and weaving. Try to bring home some of the more ornate embroidered sarongs (*pha sin*) or shawls (*pha baeng*). Also look for silverware, tribal jewelry, wood carvings and antiques.

WEATHER

Precipitation increases with altitude. The average rainfall in Vientiane is 1,720 mm per year. The lowlands receive an average of 1,250 mm per year. And the highlands receive twice that. The rainy season is between May and October. In the highlands, it can drop below freezing in December and January. It is quite pleasant during the cool dry season, with temperatures between 10 and 20 degrees C from November to April. March to June is the hot dry season when temperatures climb to 35 degrees C plus.

TERRAIN

The majority of Laos's terrain (75%) is rugged mountains with the Mekong river being the only major commerical byway. It is heavily forested with high plateaus and has the lowest population density in Asia. Population is 4.1 million in 236,800 sq. km.

The high plateaux are grassy savannah, the northern area has pine forests and the lower elevations are hardwood forests. About 50% of Laos is primary forest. As with most Southeast Asian countries, timber is a lucrative source of quick cash and is being pulled out by Thai loggers at a fairly sickening rate (The government estimates that it exports 450,000 sq. meters a year). Another 100,000 sq. meters are cleared for swidden agriculture.

WILDLIFE

The wildlife of Laos is still very impressive with elephants, rhinoceroses and Asian elk still quite evident. There are many unique bird species; reptiles are in abundance—and predators such as leopards, tigers and bears liven up a jungle hike.

PEOPLE

The people of Laos are gentle and generally accommodating to foreigners, although many are fearful that contact with outsiders will somehow be construed as an act of treason by the secret police. There are many different tribes in Laos, generally comprised of one of three principal groups: the Thai-Lao of the lower valleys, the Indochinese of the highlands and the Tibeto-Burman peoples of the higher mountains. Theravada Buddhism is predominant in Laos.

INSIDER TIP

Use the wai when greeting: put your hands together as if in prayer and bow your head. Remove shoes in temples and private homes. Do not point. Ask permission before taking pictures. You should wear long sleeve shirts and long pants when visiting a religious site. Address people by their first name. Tipping is not widespread except for your guide.

SAFETY

One of the positive effects of totalitarian governments seems to be a lack of petty crime. Before you get too complacent though, you could end up being shot or injured if you are caught in a rebel attack while traveling in the Nam Ngum or Luang Prabang regions. As you are probably getting tired of hearing, the Golden Triangle area is not a good place to wander because of the tight and rather brutal control by opium smugglers.

INSIDER TIP

The Xieng Khouang province, The Ho Chi Minh Trail and the Bolovens Plateau will never be safe due to the thousands of unexploded cluster bombs delivered free of charge during the Vietnam War by the USAF. There are anti-personnel mines, unexploded cluster bombs and other unexploded ordnance in many areas of Laos.

FESTIVALS AND HOLIDAYS

January 1	New Year's Day	
January 6	Pathet Lao Day	*Parades.*
January 20	Army Day	*Public holiday.*
January	Boun Pha Vet	*Celebrates King Vessanthara's reincarnation.*
February	Magha Puja	*End of Buddha monastic term and prediction of his death.*
February	Chinese and Vietnamese Holiday	*Jan/Feb New Year. Businesses shut down for three days.*
March 8	Women's Day	*Public Holiday.*
March 22	People's Party Day	*Public Holiday.*
March	Boun Khoun Khao	*Harvest Festival.*
April	Lao New Year	*3-day holiday calling for rain and celebrating the Lao New Year.*
May 1	Labor Day	*Parades in Vientiane.*
May	Visakha Puja	*Celebrates the birth, enlightment and death of Buddha.*
May	Boun Bang Fai	*2-day Buddhist rain-making festival using bamboo rockets.*
June 1	Children's Day	*Public Holiday.*
June	Khao Phansa	*Start of Buddhist Fasting.*
August 13	Lao Issara	*Public Holiday.*
August 23	Liberation Day	*Public Holiday.*
August	Ho Khao Padap Dinh	*Celebration of the Dead.*
September	Bouk Phansa	*End of Buddhist fasting.*
October 12	Freedom from the French Day	*Public Holiday.*

FESTIVALS AND HOLIDAYS

November	That Luang	*Week long festival.*
December	Hmong New Year	
December 2	Independence Day	*Public Holiday.*

Tours

The country of Laos is wedged between Vietnam and Thailand. It has been crippled by three-quarters of its intellectual population fleeing before 1975 and the subsequent brutal restructuring of the country under the Communist regime. After a brief open-door policy in 1989, Laos decided to filter out the backpacker tourist and focus on big dollar, group tours.

In 1991 the government began to privatize tour packaging and began to encourage the influx of tourism dollars. A visit to Laos in 1994 means you are one of the vanguard of tourists to this little-seen treasure of Southeast Asia.

The North

Luang Prabang
    4 nights, $600

Xieng Khouang, Plain of Jars
    1 night, $230; 2 nights $300

The South

Saravane, Pakse, Wat Phou
    3 nights, $550

Khong Island, Pakse, Wat Phou, Saravane
    4 nights, $600

Khong Island, Pakse, Attopeu, Saravane
    4 nights, $600

These are approximate prices only and don't include personal expenses.

Vientiane

Si Muang temple in Vientiane

VIENTIANE IN A CAPSULE

Became capital of Laos in 1563...city was sacked by the Thais in 1827...many wats were lost...city remained empty until finally reconstructed by the French in the late 19th century...it became a colonial capital...most modern day attractions are of religious significance... architecture is a mixture of Eastern and Western influences...not as colonial looking as Phnom Penh or Saigon.

The capital city has a population of 400,000 made up of smaller villages (*ban*), built around their respective wats, that are then grouped into districts (*muang*) Most visitors will start their visit in the quiet river city of Vientiane. Not particularly distinctive or historic, it has a selection of religious monuments and a mix of old, colonial and drab buildings. Have fun getting around, since the streets are referred to by both their pre- and post-revolutionary names. This probably does not matter since there are no street signs to add to the confusion.

WHAT TO SEE AND DO IN VIENTIANE

That Luang

Built in 1566 by King Settathirat and plundered and restored at various times since then. The current restoration is from the 1930s. An important monument, it impressively commands the top of a hill 3 km northeast of the city.

Morning Market ★

Get here early and bring your camera and your kip. A good place to find souvenirs and local handicrafts. Rest assured that you will pay more than you should, even if your guide does the bartering for you.

Revolutionary Monument, Pathet Lao Museum and Victory Gate

A depressing contrast to the many beautiful religious monuments of Laos. Once you visit this monument on Thanon Phon Kheng, peek through the gates at the military surplus on the grounds and tour the Victory Gate, a huge tasteless monument to Anousacari. One wonders how communism can be so thoroughly, uninspiringly dull, especially in its portrayal of the artistic and religious skills of the Lao and other peoples. The Pathet Lao Museum is not open to the public. Admission to the Victory Gate is 30 kip.

Wat Sisaket and Wat Phra Kaeo Museums

Wat Sisaket is a traditional Lao monastery. Built in 1818, it is said to be the oldest existing wat complex in Vientiane. It is home to 2,052 Buddha statues dating from the 16th-19th centuries, as well as murals and typical architecture. Across the way, **Wat Phra Kaeo** was built in 1565 and restored in the 1950s. This is the original home of the Emerald Buddha now found in Bangkok. King Setthathirat brought the Buddha from Chaing Mai. It was stolen by the Thais in 1778 and then destroyed in 1827. Both buildings are museums worth visiting for their collections of Burmese, Khmer and Lao art from other wats in Vientiane. Admission is 200 kip. Open Tues-Sat., closed midday from 11:30-2:00p.m.

That Dam

This brick stupa features the legend of the 7-headed dragon designed to ward off invasions by the Thai neighbors.

Revolutionary Museum

Learn how the other side feels about colonial rule and the achievements of communism. It's worth seeing if only to open your mind to the thought processes of communist politicians. Like all good communist monuments, there is an admission charge. Here it's 200 kip. Open Tuesday-Sunday and closed midday from 11:30-2:00 p.m.

Wat Ong Teu, Wat Chan and Wat Simoung

The best place to experience the **That Luang Festival**, Wat Ong Teu is also home to a very large Buddha. Worth a peek for its carved wooden doors and interesting architecture. Wat Chan is the site of a bronze Buddha, although not much remains after the Thais wrecked the surrounding temple in 1827. Wat Simoung houses an undated Khmer boundary stone called a *lak muang*, or town pillar.

The Mekong River in Vientiane at sunset

Vientiane Environs

Tourists are not allowed more than 15 km outside the city without a special permit.

INSIDER TIP

If you decide to wander off towards the Hmong and Yao areas near Luang Prabang you may find the countryside is both scenic and dangerous. Hmong rebels will attack some convoys. For this reason foreigners are quickly deported if found.

KM-6 (Silver City)

6 kilometers south of Vientiane is an interesting area for those who have a military interest. This was the headquarters of the CIA staff and spotter pilots who ran the secret war in Laos up until 1975. After the Americans left, the communists made Silver City their headquarters and their operatives earned the nickname "Silvers." Ask your guide if he is a Silver—don't be surprised if he proudly confirms your suspicions.

Xieng Khonane
(Garden of the Buddhas)

Avoid this ticky, tacky Asian theme park built in the 1950s by a priest.

Saam Haa Yai (555 Park)

These gardens are about 14 km outside town. They're more inclined to serve the local need for recreation than to inspire wonder and amazement. Skip it.

Prabat Phonsanh

An impressively situated wat on a volcanic plug that contains a footprint of the Lord Buddha and a reclining Buddha. It's 80 km east of Vientiane towards Paksane.

Dane Soung

30 km north of Vientiane on the Luang Prabang road you will come across a semicave with sculpture of Buddha inside. There is supposed to be a footprint of the Lord Buddha at the entrance.

Ban Thalet and Nam Ngum Dam

90 km from Vientiane on Route 13. This is a large man-made lake that boasts a hydroelectric dam. The lake has a number of islands (actually submerged hilltops). Travelers are allowed to stay at the **Nam Ngum Hotel**. This is also a jumping-off point for adventurers heading north to Luang Prabang, who don't mind risking deportation and/or attack. And you ask what is so intriguing about northern Laos.

The Outer Limits

The lure of Northern Laos depends on whether your travels are for business or pleasure. If you are interested in traditional Hmong and Lao villages, then this is the place. You will need a guide (not an official one) and plenty of kip (it costs a lot to get around and to get out). The area between here and China is home to some of the least-visited tribes in the world. These tribes are tough, independent and very wealthy—wealthy because 60% of the world's heroin supply comes from this area. Myanmar and Afghanistan are the only two bigger producers of opium. Much of this wealth is used to pay for weapons and manpower to fight the current regime. How can you tell when you're in an opium smuggling area? Look for ponies. They are used for one purpose: transporting heroin over the mountainous terrain to Chaing Mai, Thailand.

If you are here on business, you know that the poppy fields are not for flower arranging. Raw material is transported overland to the Chaing Mai area of Thailand. There is also significant mining of sapphires. Timber poaching by the Thais is rampant.

Someday it would be fun to do the Ho Chi Minh Trail, but cluster bombs litter the trail like thistles.

INSIDER TIP

There are no "good guys" and "bad guys" out here and the line drawn between your deserving to be shot or allowed on your way isn't thin–it's anorexic. If the feuding between rival drug lords Khun Sa and Chao Nyi Lai isn't enough to spoil your Indochina "holiday," consider the other battles that are being waged in the hills, some reportedly by ethnic Hmong opposed to the Vientiane government. In fact, right-wing American and Australian Hmong have reportedly been staging covert military operations in Laos as of late. Hmong, loyal to resistance leader Gen. Vang Pao, who have resettled in Western countries have been sent back to Thailand and financed to carry out military strikes inside Laos, Vientiane government officials charge. Watch out.

Van Vieng

A very scenic area 150 km north towards Luang Prabang not open to foreigners. Ask and maybe it will be open by the time you decide to go.

Luang Prabang

Not much left of this historic but oft-razed city. Worth a trip for its over 60 temples, 30 of which are still in good enough shape to visit.

Many of the wats are locked so make sure you contract with a local guide.

Buddhas in Pak Ou Caves, Luang Prabang

WHAT TO SEE AND DO IN LUANG PRABANG

Royal Palace (National Museum)   ★★

Built in 1904, the palace has been the repository of some of the most important and revered Buddha figures in Laos. Make sure you see the 15th-17th century statues and the Khmer bronze drums. The Golden Buddha inside is a copy; the original is 90 percent solid gold, 83 cm high and weighs over 90 kg. It was created in Ceylon in the first century, brought to Cambodia and then to Vientiane in 1563 by King Setthathirat. It was taken to Thailand in 1779 and then returned in 1839. It was "rediscovered" in 1975 in the palace chapel. Much of the decor is modern (1960-1970) as befitting for the last king, Sissavong Vattana. There are a variety of state gifts from other countries on display (there's even a moon rock from the Apollo missions). You will need to arrange for special entry with the LNT office if it is not part of your tour.

Wat May

This wat took more than 70 years to complete. It features beautiful architecture and facade.

Mount Phousi   ★

An enormous, exotic rock. Climb it for the view early in the morning for sunrise or at dusk for sunset. Enjoy the very Asian, very spiritual feeling that this rock has inspired for centuries. **Wat Chom Si** sits on the summit. The anti-aircraft guns dampen the mystical feeling somewhat. Along the main road, there are a number of important religious sites. **Wat Phra Bath Nua** features a 3-meter-long footprint of the

Lord Buddha. **Wat Sene** was built in 1718 and is a Thai-style temple. **Wat Xieng Thong**, built in 1559, is a well-cared-for royal wat with a reclining Buddha which was shown at the 1931 Paris Exhibition on a 12-meter-high, gilded funeral chariot used to transport the burial urn of King Sisavang Vong. **Wat Pak Khan** has a pretty location but not much else. **Wat Visoun** was built in 1513 and rebuilt in 1898. It's an ancient-looking wat with a good collection of religious art and the largest Buddha in town. Its neighbor, **Wat Aham**, was built in 1823 and has 2 Bodhi trees. **Wat That** is known for its ornamental doors and pillars. **Wat Phra Bath** features a large Buddha footprint in a scenic setting. **Wat That Luang**, built in 1818, is the burial place of King Sisavong Vong, the last king. **Wat Manorom** is the site of a 2 ton Buddha from 1372; it's one of the oldest Laotian Buddha images.

Wat Phra Phone Phoa

Just out of town and modeled after the Shwedagon in Yangon, Myanmar. Check out the rather absurd depiction of the fates that await a variety of sinners.

Luang Prabang Environs

Ban Chan

This place downriver is a good place to buy large water jars and other pottery. Ban Hat Hien (near the airport) is known for its knives made from scrap.

Ban Phanom

Old village 3 km out of town known for weaving. 300 years of weaving and selling to visitors makes this a tough place to cut a deal on the beautiful fabrics that were originally made for the royal family.

Henri Mouhouts Tomb

If you'd like to pay your respects to fellow explorers, here's your chance. The discoverer of Angkor Wat was buried here in 1860—he died of malaria—but his grave was just discovered in 1990.

Pak Ou Caves

25 km upriver from Luang Prabang. We recommend the boat trip and the sacred caves, **Tham Thing** and **Tham Phum**, for their thousands of gold and wood statues of Buddha. In April, hundreds of townspeople journey upriver to celebrate Pimay. The caves used to be the home of monks.

Royal Cemetery

Not all people can be cremated, so the remains of the royal family who died as infants or from contagious diseases are buried here. Do you believe in ghosts? You will after you see the look on the face of your guide when you ask to visit here.

Wat Chom Phet

Wat Chom Phet is a popular scenic viewpoint.

Wat Long Khoun

Wat Long Khoun dates from the 18th century. There is a carved door which dates from 1937.

Wat Tham

This wat is a dark, dank cave with steps and carved-out stone. Bring a flashlight to see the dilapidated Buddhas inside.

Xang Hai

If you develop a terrible thirst or a death wish, head upriver about 20 km to the home of lau-loa. The distilled wine is potent and definitely an acquired taste. If you visit the source, they take great pleasure in watching you grimace as you sample their wares.

WHERE TO STAY IN LUANG PRABANG

Luang Prabang Hotel (Mittaphab)

In town, ☎ *7233* (no international calls from Luang Prabang city). Air conditioning, pool and passable restaurant.

Phousi, Kitarath Settharhirat

Air conditioning; restaurant; bar.

Xieng Khouang

Travel outside Vientiane requires a special permit and a tour (with guide). The site of severe bombardment during the Vietnam War, it is also known for the curious Plain of Jars.

WHAT TO SEE AND DO IN XIENG KHOUANG

Phonsavanh

The major town has a daily market and a Revolutionary Museum with some unimpressive, but authentic momentos of the war. From Phonsavanh there are only two side trips allowed—the first 10 km southeast to the Plain of Jars.

Plain of Jars   ★

Maybe one of the better known areas in Laos to Westerners. The Plain of Jars is exactly that. It is a 1,000-sq. meter plateau which is covered with more than 300, 1-to-3.5-meter-high jars that have yet to be accurately explained. Some say that they are 2,000-year-old burial urns with the size of the jar being relative to the deceased's station in life. No one is sure how they came to be here and exactly what their purpose was. In February 1970, the U.S. began bombing this area. B-52s on their way back to Thailand from Hanoi used the area to jettison their bombs—putting the total tonnage dropped here well above the official estimate of half-a-million tons of explosives.

This area was also the site of fierce fighting between the Hanoi-backed Pathet Lao and U.S.-backed Hmong mercenary forces.

Xieng Khouang

Another town that was destroyed during the war, this is the site of many temples that are now totally destroyed or defaced by shrapnel. **Wat Phia Wat**, **That Chomsi** and **Wat Si Phoum** are the only sights worth seeing here. Tha Joh and Ban Na Sala are typical Hmong villages. The latter is the more traditional of the two.

INSIDER TIP

You will see plenty of war surplus in this area, including unexploded bombs. Keep to the paths and touch nothing. Dozens are killed every month in Laos from unexploded bombs.

Muang Kham

Muang Kham is the location of Tamp Phiu Cave the scene of a 1968 air attack that killed eleven families. Used as an air raid shelter, it is now a war memorial. The remains of the dead still poke through the dirt next to the cave mouth. For those with a more hedonist bent, there is a hot springs near the Nam Mat River.

WHERE TO STAY IN XIENG KHOUANG

Hotel Plaine de Jarres
Just outside Phonsavanh on road to Muang Khoune.

Phou Phieng Xieng Khouang
1 km east of Phonsavanh. This is a relatively new hotel with a good view.

Saravan

This province was decimated during the war—in particular, the town of Saravan. Perhaps the biggest attraction here are the heaps of war material that were cleared away when the airport was reconstructed. The area is also home to vast numbers of bombed-out temples, as U.S. war planes followed no rules of avoiding striking pagodas during their metallic carpeting of Laos. The market in the town of Saravan is stocked with the riches of the jungle surrounding the Ho Chi Minh Trail, including wildlife that would (and does) give U.S. Fish and Game Department officers conniptions.

WHAT TO SEE AND DO IN AND AROUND SARAVAN

Savannakhet
This is a bustling and highly entrepreneurial town with a population of maybe 25,000, that serves as a gateway to the south for travelers.

Although it isn't of much interest to travelers in itself, there are some nice surrounding areas. Kengkok is an especially nice village to visit. **That Inheng** is in Savannakhet and is worth a stop.

Ho Chi Minh Trail

This is a surprisingly undisturbed part of the country, which may have to do more with the amount of unexploded bombs found here than its inaccessibility. The trail itself was heavily bombed during the Vietnam War and the undeclared war on Laos. There is dense jungle vegetation found here, as well as a lot of exotic animals, if you can spot any.

Bolovens Plateau

This is an agricultural area (coffee and tea center) interesting for its diverse ethnic mix and the impressive lost city of **Wat Phou**. Many villages were destroyed during the Vietnam conflict, but there are very colorful and unusual ethnic centers.

Tha Teng

Village known for its export of wild honey collected from the surrounding hills.

Ban Khian and Tad Soung

Unusual Alak villages with grass-thatched huts. The Alak family head builds the coffins for his family out of hollowed logs and then stores them under the rice huts.

Ban Paleng

Tay-Oy Village which is the site of a 3-day sacrificial festival in February or March. A water buffalo is donated by each family and then sacrificed.

Paksong

This is a small town known for its proximity to the **Tad Phan** waterfall, which is 130m high. We recommend staying at the **Tad Lo Resort** built at the top of the falls. This is a very scenic location and the resort is a relaxing chalet-type facility.

Pakse

A town of 25,000 known for its fading colonial buildings and nearby Khmer ruins of **Wat Phou**.

Boun Oum Palace

This is the 6-story home of Prince Boun Oum of Champassak. This is an unfinished monument to waste, bad taste and excess.

Wat Luang

This is the oldest wat in Pakse, built in 1830 and restored in 1990. It's near the site of the largest monastic school in southern Laos.

Ban Saphay

Village known for its silk weaving and a wat featuring the statue of Ganesh, Indra and Parvati.

Champassak

This is the closest town to Wat Phou, 8 km from town.

★★ *Wat Phou*

If you come to Laos for one reason this is it. 200 years older than Angkor Wat and discovered in 1866 by French explorer Francis Garnier, the lost city of Wat Phou features brilliant carvings, impressive scales and a fantastic setting with the majestic mountain **Linga Parvata** in the background. There is ongoing restoration and archeological work and a small charge for entry and photography.

Hindu sculpture at Wat Phou. Most of the temples at Linga Parvata date from the 5th and 6th centuries.

Oup Moung

This is a romantic ruin about a half-hour walk from the river. Built around the same period as Wat Phou, there is little left of the 6th-century temple. The full extent of this site has yet to be explored.

Mekong Islands

There are around 4,000 islands in the wide Mekong in southern Laos on the Cambodia border. They're covered with lush tropical foliage. Worth visiting for the impressive **Li Phi** and **Khong Phapheng Falls**, the largest waterfalls in Southeast Asia and the working elephants at **Pha Pho**. There's even an amethyst mine where you can try your luck.

Don Khong is the largest island in the river and there's even a town here, called **Muang Khoune**. You can visit **Li Phi Falls** by taking a boat from **Ban Nakasong**. On Ban Khone Thai (**Don Khone**), there's a short railway line that was built by the French during the colonial era. It was the only railway built by the French in Laos.

Just to the east of Don Khone are the **Khong Phapheng Falls**, which offer great views.

An amethyst mine is located a few kilometers off the main road linking Ban Thang Beng and Attapeu. The stones are primarily bought by the Thais (who else?).

WHERE TO STAY ON THE MEKONG ISLANDS

Government Resthouse
Khong Island.

WEST
MALAYSIA

EAST MALAYSIA

MALAYSIA

Majestic Mt. Kinabalu (13,450 ft./4100m) is Southeast Asia's highest peak.

MALAYSIA IN A CAPSULE

A confederation of 13 separate states and almost 130,000 square miles of the Malay Peninsula...between southern Thailand and Singapore...includes Sabah and Sarawak on the northern coast of Borneo...known for rubber, tin, palm oil and timber...Spectacular Parks: Taman Negara, Mt. Kinabalu, Gunung Mulu and more to come...Rugged island of Borneo, oldest tropical forests on planet...many unique species: animal, plant, bird and insect...Islamic, widespread English, gentle friendly people, unspoiled by tourism...a beautiful and fascinating place to visit...adventure tourism hotspot.

Tell your neighbors you have come back from Malaysia and they will probably give you a puzzled shrug. Thailand, Indonesia and even tiny Singapore score better on awareness. But this is good. Malaysia just may be the best undiscovered adventure destination in Southeast Asia. Jungle trekking, white water rafting, caving, scuba diving, indigenous cultures, exotic scenery and the best food in Asia all await the curious traveler. And, oh, is it cheap! But, wait a minute why are we telling you? The longer Malaysia remains a secret, the longer it can be enjoyed by those in the know; so only invite your close friends.

The National Mosque in Kuching, Sarawak

Bad points? Well it can get a little dull if you don't like jungles, beaches and conservative lifestyles. Malaysia does not have the energy of Thailand or the dark mystery of Vietnam. In a nutshell, Malaysia is nice. Middle of the road or even quaint. There is little of the creaking colonialism found in Myanmar. The architecture is utilitarian and the people are quiet and reserved. But let's get back to the high points. Anyone who comes to Malaysia has to experience its ancient jungle. My favorite part of Malaysia is Borneo. The states of Sabah and Sarawak will fill your head with sights and experiences like the world's largest cave chamber, with its millions of bats exploding out of its cool depths at sunset. Or misty jungle plateaus inhabited by noble, exotic-looking peoples. Spend a night with an ex-headhunter to get past the tourist hype and put on your jungle boots at least once to understand the word primeval. Spend an afternoon in an old Chinese timber town to experience the warmth and good will of its immigrants. Wander through the backroads of the hill resorts

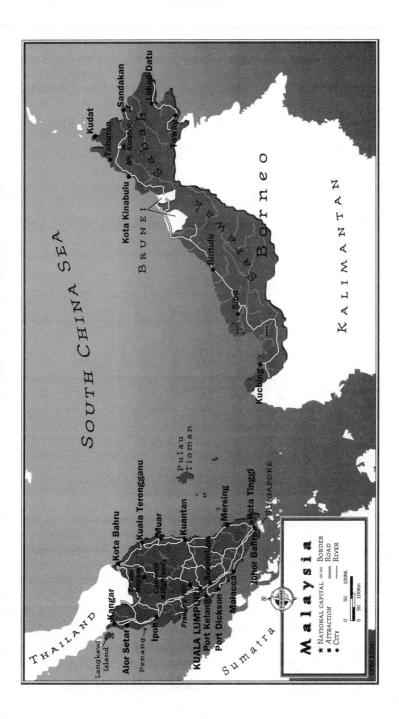

and take tea with the Tamil workers. Malaysia can still provide a feeling of discovery.

Try everything on the menu at a Kuala Lumpur restaurant. And, oh, is it cheap! But we've already told you too much. Just go, pick your place, take your Malay dictionary and you won't be disappointed.

Malaysia is the perfect destination for people who want to understand the vibrancy and growth of Asia and want to experience its awe-inspiring ecosystems.

History of Malaysia

It is impossible to describe the typical Malaysian, for he or she is everyman: a Straits-born Chinese Buddhist whose family is most likely involved in commerce and may even control one of the great export fortunes in rubber or tin or timber; a Moslem descended directly from one of the original Malay settlers; a Hindu whose ancestors were brought to the peninsula from India by the British for much-needed labor; or one of the almost one million tribal members living on the northern coast of Borneo, whose ancestors are said to have inhabited this area as early as 37,000 years ago.

Although Eastern man flocked to the Malay Peninsula very early after the birth of Christ (to confirm rumors of precious minerals in the ground) and the great Marco Polo boasted about his sail through the Straits of Malacca at the end of the 13th century, things really didn't begin to pop until the beginning of the 15th century. A favored date is 1403, when a Sumatran prince named Parameswara seems to have founded the city of Malacca—the city that became the primary trading post between India and China for over 300 years. The place was obviously destined for success because two years later, in 1405, the colorful Admiral Cheng Ho came to call and gave the port the blessing of the Ming Court.

China was so impressed by this new settlement that in the 1460s, the emperor sent his daughter Princess Hang Li Poh to marry the reigning sultan, Mansor Shah. She did not come alone, so the sultan created a special residential area for her entourage of 500 ladies-in-waiting. Today, Bukit China covers 160 acres and is the largest Chinese cemetery outside the mainland; many of the tombs date from the Ming Period.

Portuguese, Dutch and British Control

By 1500, the Portuguese fleet was looking for some Eastern real estate; they took control of Malacca just over a decade later. Although they only held the port for a little more than a century, the Portuguese left their legacy in the Eurasian community that still exists and speaks a medieval dialect only its proud members can understand. The Portuguese were replaced by the Dutch in 1641 as the dominant force in Malacca and the architecture took on a pink hue with bricks brought all the way from Holland.

The Dutch traded their booty to the British in 1786, the same year that Captain Francis Light claimed the island of Penang for the British Crown. The Straits settlements were falling into place and Britain would control the destiny of the Malay Peninsula for the next 155 years. Kuala Lumpur, the "muddy estuary," was founded at the confluence of the Klang and Gombak rivers in 1864 on the notion that tin could be mined nearby. The town was an unimpressive outback until the turn of the century when the British began to fill its swampland with colonial-style structures and made it the capital of the Protected Malay States.

Born administrators, the British also became planters on a grand scale. Some Brazilian rubber trees sent from Kew Gardens as an experiment became an unexpected bonanza; Malaysia is now the world's largest single supplier of the raw material. Tin mining is another lucrative export and two-thirds of the land covered with jungle supplies much of the world's timber. Life was pleasant for all concerned and progressing nicely until the Second World War, when two decades of jungle warfare ensued.

World War II and the Emergency

The Japanese sank a few British battleships patrolling the South China Sea and arrived at the northeast corner of the Malay peninsula on December 8, 1941—within minutes of their colleagues' attack on Pearl Harbor. From Kota Bahru, the army made its way south via anything with wheels (including bicycles) and took the seemingly impregnable island of Singapore within two months. While the British kept their big guns pointed in the other direction, the Imperial Army simply crossed over the causeway and marched most of the white population off to Changi POW camp. Meanwhile, the British on the peninsula fought beside Chinese and Malay in their own battle against the invaders.

The official war was over in 1945, but peace did not last long. A communist revolt began in 1948 that lasted 12 bitter years. The British called it "The Emergency" and used their considerable resources and intrigue to flush communist guerillas from the Malayan jungles. Due to the absence of support from the other populace, the

British Military Administration launched the Resettlement Programmes for villages near the jungles. The Emergency did hasten the independence of Malaya, however, for it took all purpose away from the CTs (communist terrorists) who claimed they were just attempting to rid the country of colonial imperialists.

Malaysia's Independence

As the fighting continued through the 1950s, the British could no longer hem and haw. Finally, on August 31, 1957, independence came to the Malay peninsula and its 11 states were symbolized in a new flag with an 11-point star. On September 2, the new king and ruler of the Federation of Malaya kissed the blade of his gold kris (dagger) and took office. His official title was the Yang di Pertuan Agong and he would govern for a period of five years, after which one of the other ten sultans would be elected king. It is a most sensible and democratic solution, fair to the individuality and autonomy of each state and its sultan or ruling family.

Malaya became known as Malaysia in September 1963, when the former British colonies of Sabah, Sarawak and Singapore joined the federation. But 14 states did not prove to be an auspicious number and Lee Kuan Yew split Singapore away in December 1965, making it a fully independent republic. The prime minister and his Malay counterparts just never saw eye to eye and historians now feel that an independent Singapore was his scheme all along.

With such a diversity of cultures and people living tolerably together, travel in Malaysia is a constant surprise. Visitors may come across an Islamic festivity, Chinese celebrants lighting joss sticks in a colorful Buddhist temple, or Indians chewing betel nut by the side of the road at the same time. Pork will be on the menu in a Chinese restaurant, but you will probably find that only beef or chicken sate are available. And your flavorful Indian curries are more likely to be vegetarian than not. From the Borneo chieftain to the sultan's daughter, the people of Malaysia cling tightly to their traditions and customs.

While the original inhabitants of the Malay Peninsula were aborigines (Senois, Negritos and Temiars) as well as Malays, the 15th century Chinese arrivals resulted in a new group called the Peranakans. This is a mixture of Chinese/Malay in food, traditions and language. When the Portuguese arrived in the 16th century, however, their offspring from marriage to the locals were and still are considered Eurasians. Today, there is relaxed intermarriage among the ethnic groups (something the British never encouraged)—especially between professionals like administrators, politicians and teachers.

The range of experiences for travelers in Malaysia may make many think they are actually touring several countries at once. You can join the Pesta Menuai festival in Sabah to welcome the rice spirit Bambaazon. Shop to your heart's desire at Kota Belud's famous *tamu*, or weekly open-air bazaar. Continue on to Sarawak for a trip upriver and a stay in one of the Dayak longhouses. Watch turtles lay their eggs along the East Coast beaches in peninsular Malaysia. Shoot the rapids in Taman Negara, the national park that spans three states. Lose a bundle at the Genting Highlands casino, or join the chic on the golden sands of Penang's Batu Ferringhi, or Foreigner's Rock.

You can revel in the colonial atmosphere of Kuala Lumpur and eat like a prince or princess, or relive the fiery past of Malacca where the oldest Anglican church in Southeast Asia still stands. You can visit the new industrial town of Petaling Jaya, an experiment in living and a national showpiece, or watch the tapping of rubber trees, a method unchanged for years. Tin mines, timber trucks bound for ships in the port of Singapore, batik and kite-flying contests are also part of the Malaysian scene.

There are countless idyllic islands off Malaysia's vast coastline.

It is a colorful and fascinating tapestry that beckons the traveler to visit again and again. In fact, Malaysia expects to welcome more and more visitors annually and is preparing a great many new tourist facilities. In addition to more hotel rooms, Kuala Lumpur boasts one of Asia's largest convention centers, the Putra World Trade Center. The 12-acre site features a 35-story tower, exhibition hall and hotel in an architectural design that combines the traditional cultural features of the country's many varied regions.The Malaysia Tourism Promotion Board, which kicked off the decade with a year-long Visit Malaysia Year in 1990, is staging an even bigger (in terms of number of events) Visit Malaysia Year in 1994. The public and private sector are cooperating on the festivities, which will take place in Kuala Lumpur and elsewhere throughout the country.

PLANNING AHEAD

THE MALAYSIA TOURISM PROMOTION BOARD

(MTPB), also known as Tourism Malaysia, is working hard to welcome more and more visitors every year. Major tourism projects have been included in the Fourth Malaysia Plan, the country's blueprint for development. Highway extensions, railroad improvements, more first-class hotel rooms in Penang and Kuala Lumpur and a $7 million cultural zone in the capital are all scheduled for the future.

Headquarters for the MTPB is *24th-27th floors, Menara Dato Onn, Putra World Trade Centre, Jalan Tun Ismail 50480, Kuala Lumpur (☎ 03 2935188)*. Visit the regional offices—in Penang, Terengganu, Johor Bahru, Kota Kinabalu and Kuching—for excellent maps and brochures.

Unfortunately, the only U.S. branch is the Malaysian Tourism Promotion Board, *818 W. 7th St., Los Angeles, CA 90017 (☎ 213-689-9702; FAX: 213-689-1530)*. The MTPB office in Canada is at *830 Burrard St., Vancouver, B.C. V6Z2K4, Canada (☎ 604-689-8899; FAX: 604-680-8804)*.

VISAS

Visas are not required of travelers holding valid U.S. passports, for a stay of up to 14 days, which can be extended to three months. Proof of solvency, respectable dress and airline tickets are necessary for receiving an extension.

INOCULATIONS

Inoculations are not required for entry, unless you are coming from an endemic area. We advise getting updates on all shots to be effective. Check with your doctor. Malaria is a very real threat in the logging camps and remote areas of Borneo. Check with the Center for Disease Control in Atlanta or your local doctor for the latest in preventative medicine.

INSIDER TIP

Please note that most mosquitoes are resistant to quinine based medication. Larium is not successful in preventing malaria. Since Fansidar is banned in the U.S. but is commonly prescribed by Asian and African doctors, know the pros and cons of malaria before you venture into remote regions.

ENTRY BY AIR

Entry by air will probably be into Kuala Lumpur's glamorous airport at Subang, about a half-hour ride from the capital. The New Kuala Lumpur International Airport is under construction in nearby Sepang, Selangor and is scheduled to become operational in stages, starting in 1997. Travel time between the new airport and K.L. will take about 45 minutes. In addition to airport buses and taxis, a new express train will take travelers from the airport to the city in about 35 minutes. Departure tax is M$5 for domestic flights and M$20 for all international flights, including Singapore. There is also daily service to about 35 other domestic destinations, including Penang, Malacca, Kuantan, Kota Kinabalu and Kuching. Kuala Lumpur is a mere 35 minutes by air from Singapore and about 80 minutes from Bangkok. Malaysian Airline System (MAS), which has extensive regional service and from North America, ranks as one of the best airlines for efficiency and service in Asia. **Departure tax** is M$3 for domestic flights, M$5 for flights to Singapore and M$15 for international flights.

ARRIVAL BY SEA

Arrival by sea is via the historic island of Penang or Port Klang (for Kuala Lumpur). Penang is the more popular of the two and several cruise lines call here annually on their global voyages, such as: Seabourn Cruise Line, Crystal Cruises and Windstar Cruises.

ARRIVAL BY LAND

Arrival by land offers many opportunities. There is **train** service between Bangkok and Singapore right through the Malay Peninsula, if you can bear to sit for two days straight. I took the train once from Bangkok to Penang (Butterworth) and it was a very, very long ride. Also, in September 1993, the new Eastern & Oriental Express train inaugurated service. Conceived by the same people who revived the Venice Simplon-Orient Express, the new rail service features luxurious vintage trains reminiscent of the heyday of Far Eastern rail travel (but with the welcome addition of air conditioning) and carries passengers from Singapore to Kuala Lumpur and Bangkok. Fares for the complete three-day/two-night trip start at $1,100, including all meals on board, but shorter sectors, such as Singapore-Kuala Lumpur, are also available, starting at $390. Call the U.S. booking office (☎ *800-524-2420*). Better yet are shared **taxis** that run frequently between Johor Bahru and Penang on a pay-per-destination basis. Malaysia's road system is pretty good and you never know who your companions will be.

You can also rent a **car** in Singapore and drive to Kuala Lumpur or along the east coast, if you don't mind fighting with timber trucks that use the same route. In fact, be prepared to pay extra insurance if you tell the car rental people of your plans to drive into Malaysia.

The roads along both coasts are generally excellent and a new east-west highway has been cut into the main Range Mountains in the north and reduces travel from Penang to Kota Bahru from 621 miles to 225 miles. It also offers lovely views of formerly inaccessible areas. Driving in Malaysia is on the left.

INSIDER TIP

Once you get on those fast, new roads in your shiny Proton rental car, don't be surprised when you get pulled over for speeding by a pleasant motorcycle cop. (Radar has come to Malaysia.) He will be so pleasant that he will probably offer to take the fine back to the station for you, since the police station will be a long way in the other direction to where you are travelling. We both know how far your "fine" will get so be sure to only have half of the amount he requests on you in cash. If by some stroke of bad luck you hit an honest cop, do not try this ploy.

DUTY FREE

The usual items are duty free, but beware: pornography, narcotics, daggers and walkie-talkies are prohibited. Trafficking in illegal drugs in Malaysia carries the death penalty.

THE CURRENCY

The currency of Malaysia is the dollar or **ringgit** and there are approximately M$2.40 to U.S.$1, although the exchange rate fluctuates slightly. The Malaysian dollar used to have the same approximate worth as the Singapore and Brunei dollar but no longer and it is no longer interchangeable with the Singapore dollar. Bona fide tourists may import not more than M$10,000 and export not more than M$5,000. The importation of traveler's checks, letters of credit, or cash in foreign currency is unlimited. Credit cards are accepted widely throughout the country, although some shops add a surcharge.

LOCAL TIME

Local time in Malaysia is Greenwich Mean Time plus 8 hours, in the same zone as neighboring Singapore. The entire Malay Peninsula and the separate states of Sabah and Sarawak on Borneo were finally synchronized on New Year's Day 1982 as a symbol of unity.

LOCAL CURRENT

The current is 220 volts 50 cycles, but don't expect appliances to work too well outside the leading hotels. You will probably even have a problem with razors in this country. Some luxury hotels will have 110 volt outlets for shavers but don't count on it.

LOCAL WATER

Local water is potable throughout Malaysia, which boasts an extremely high standard of living and excellent health facilities. There is an abundance of bottled water and soft drinks available for the timid. When you get out of town the usual "watch it, wash it or boil it" rules apply.

THE OFFICIAL LANGUAGE

The official language is Bahasa Malaysian, but Tamil is spoken by the Indian population and either Cantonese or Hokkien by the Chinese. English is still spoken widely by the educated class. Even in small towns, someone will be old enough to remember enough English to be helpful. If you truly want to get lost, just stand with an open map at any corner and you will be amazed at how many wrong, but sincerely helpful directions you'll receive in order to get to your destination.

There are three English language newspapers published daily, The *New Straits Times*, *The Star* and *The Malay Mail*; they'll have to make do since it is difficult to find much outside reading material. Tune into the English broad-

cast on Radio Ibukota from 6 to 7 p.m. daily for weather, money exchange rates, music and local events in Kuala Lumpur. Most imported television programs are in English with Malay subtitles.

BUSINESS HOURS

Hours of business differ widely throughout the Malay Peninsula. Government offices usually operate from 8:15 a.m. to 12:45 p.m. and from 2 to 4:15 p.m. (Mon.-Fri.) with a little extra time off on Friday noon for communal Jumaah prayers at the many mosques. Offices and shops open at 9 a.m. and close anywhere from 5 to 9 p.m. Saturdays are usually half days for office work and Sunday is a holiday. However, the five states in the eastern part of the peninsula still maintain the traditional Moslem half-holiday on Thursday, full holiday on Friday (the holy day) and business as usual on Saturday and Sunday. The best rule is to always confirm appointments and check hours of business.

TIPPING

Tipping is not considered compulsory in Malaysia and a 5% service charge is added to most hotel and restaurant bills. However, you should still always reward service rendered with a smile. Malaysians are sincere, honest people and the gratuitous dispersal of money can sometimes be taken the wrong way. Park your wallet and break out a smile.

TELEPHONE, TELEX AND FAX

These services are quite good in Kuala Lumpur, not as good elsewhere in Malaysia (with one major exception; many remote places like Borneo have an excellent cellular network!). Most hotels in Kuala Lumpur offer excellent services for overseas calls and telexes and fax service is widely available at hotels and public offices. Or you can use the Central Telegraph Office located in Bukit Mahkamah, open 24 hours daily. There is also a Telegraph Office at the Kuala Lumpur International Airport, open from 7:30 a.m. to 11:30 p.m. daily.

Direct calls can be made from telephones with International Subscriber Dialing (ISD) facility to Australia, Japan, United Kingdom, Germany, Hong Kong, Bangkok, Switzerland, U.S., Italy and Tahiti, but expect to pay heavily for this service. Self-dialing facilities are available to all cities within Malaysia as well as to neighboring Singapore and trunk calls (long distance) are charged at reduced rates between 6 p.m. and 7 a.m. Keep in mind, Jahatan Telekom Malaysia has just in the last year changed all telephone numbers in Selangor and the Federal Territory of Kuala Lumpur from six to seven digits long. If you need assistance or information regarding a new number, contact the Assistance Centre by dialing 1060 and give them the old number. Local calls within each city limit are M$.10.

WHAT TO WEAR

Wear what the Malaysians wear—cool, light, comfortable and very conservative clothing. The local batik is lovely. In this country women may be requested to don a covering when visiting a mosque or other holy place. People "dress" in the evening in Kuala Lumpur, where a jacket and tie are expected for gentlemen, a long skirt or pantsuit for women. However, batik sport shirts and casual clothes are worn elsewhere.

It can really rain on the Malay Peninsula, so some sort of protection is suggested at all times. An umbrella is ideal for those short torrential storms that come from nowhere and leave after several drenching moments. Ponchos or plastic wraps can be sweaty and get mildewed. The country is hot and humid most of the time, but the luxury hotels and restaurants are over air-conditioned, so carry a shawl or sweater when dining out. Sandals are worn by everyone and are not a bad idea considering the rain and the fact that shoes are not allowed in Moslem monuments. Inexpensive straw hats are also helpful to those not accustomed to the hot tropical sun. Don't rely on too much choice in large size clothing when you get to Malaysia. But there are excellent stores with great prices for just about any casual wear you might need.

INSIDER TIP

Save space. Pick up a cheap umbrella, a straw fedora and any cotton clothing you might need in the main cities. But don't expect much selection if you are tall or large. Give 'em away before you leave.

Dress in the highlands or hill resorts is quite different, as the temperatures drop very low at these heights and wool slacks are often necessary, especially in the evening. At some of the more colonial-style hostelries (e.g. Foster's Lakehouse in the Cameron Highlands), life is a bit formal and stuffy in the evening, so be prepared. Never venture toward the hill resorts without a few extra layers, as you will be very uncomfortable and definitely get a chill.

LOCAL TRANSPORTATION

Transit throughout the country is excellent and consists of constantly improved **railway** service, **highways** along both coasts connecting east with west, local **buses** and share **taxis**. A major new five-lane highway connecting the north and south of Peninsula Malaysia also recently became operational.

In the capital and smaller cities, there are local buses and taxis, even a few **trishaws** (three-wheeled vehicles). You should bargain in advance for the trishaws, which are terrific for sightseeing in Penang or Malacca. Catch them quickly, before they disappear forever!

A new multimillion-dollar bridge (the third largest in the world) now connects Penang to the mainland. Thirteen and a half kilometers in length, it has a lifespan of 400 years and was built to withstand earthquakes measuring up to 7.5 on the Richter scale.

In Penang, a **ferry** operates around the clock between Georgetown (on the island) and Butterworth on the mainland. There are two terminals on each side, one for passengers and vehicles, the other for vehicles only. Departures are every 7 to 10 minutes during the day, every 10 to 30 minutes from 10 p.m. until 5:30 a.m. and rates are very reasonable (M$.40). Penang also has a cog **railway** that goes up to Penang Hill, with departures about every 30 minutes and rates about M$3 per adult (round trip).

Domestic **air** services are provided by Malaysian Airline System (MAS), Malaysia Air Charter Company and Wira Kris Udara Malaysia. The latter two companies are headquartered at Kuala Lumpur International Airport in Subang.

FESTIVALS AND HOLIDAYS

It almost seems that Malaysians celebrate every festival known to man, since their calendar includes holidays belonging to Christians, Hindus, Buddhists and Moslems—as well as many local and national events. It is quite a calendar and visitors are certainly encouraged to participate in any celebration under way! Public holidays are marked with an asterisk*. In addition to the annual holidays and festivals, a number of special events are being planned for Visit Malaysia Year 1994.

*January 1	New Year's Day	*Not a holiday in the states of Johor, Kedah, Kelantan, Perlis and Terengganu.*
January	Gengguland Day	*The Orang Asli aborigines in South Perak lay a feast for the spirits and deities as well as for themselves.*
January	Thaipongal	*The first day of the Tamil month of Thai. Harvest Festival and pongal, or new grain, is cooked.*
*January	Birthday of Prophet Muhammad	*Born April 20, A.D. 571. Processions and chanting of holy verses held throughout the country. Also a large rally in Kuala Lumpur's Merdeka Stadium.*
January/ February	Chinese New Year	
February	Thaipusam	*A day of penance for Hindus, who offer milk, honey and fruit carried on kavadi (a steel arch with long thin skewers attached) to shrines of Lord Subramaniam. Celebrations in Kuala Lumpur take place at Batu Caves with a colorful procession (celebrated only in Penang, Perak (Selangor and Negeri Sembilan).*
*February 1	Federal Territory Day	*Public holiday celebrated only in Kuala Lumpur and Labuan. Decorations and cultural shows throughout the capital.*
February	Birthday of Tien Kung	*Chinese God of Heaven.*
February	Chap Goh Meh	*15th day of the Chinese New Year.*
February	Birthday of Chor Soo Kong	*Deity of the Snake Temple in Penang.*
February	Tua Pek Kong	*Festival of burning paper money, houses and cars for deceased relatives. Main celebration at San Ten Temple, Kuching, Sarawak.*
February	Ban Hood Huat Hoay	*Gathering of Ten Thousand Buddhas. Devotees pray for world peace at Kek Lok Si Temple in Penang.*
March	Hari Raya Puasa	*End of month of fasting for Moslems. Great festivities with prayers, delicacies and offerings to the poor (date changes yearly, as it falls on the first day of Syawal, the 10th month of the Moslem calendar).*

FESTIVALS AND HOLIDAYS

March	Maha Siva Rathiri	*Pujas (ceremonies) performed in Hindu temples through the night. Devotees sing hymns in honor of Lord Siva.*
March	Pangguni Uttiram	*Day of prayers for Hindus that commemorates the marriage of Rama and Sita, hero and heroine of the Ramayana epic.*
March	Kuan Yin	*Day of worship for Chinese Goddess of Mercy, guardian of children.*
March 25	Police Day	*Recognition of service to the country by the police force.*
April	Good Friday	*Celebrated only in Sabah and Sarawak.*
April	Easter Sunday	
April	Cheng Beng	*All Soul's Day. Chinese pay homage to ancestors.*
April	Udhadhi	*New Year for Telegu-speaking Hindus.*
April	Sri Rama Navami	*Marks descent of Lord Rama, seventh Avatar of Vishu Rama and hero of the Ramayana epic. Pujas performed by Hindus.*
April	Songkran	*New Year of the Thais. Water Festival.*
April/May	Chitra Pauranami	*Hindus offer pujas, carry kavadis and pay homage to Lord Subramaniam in temples throughout the country.*
May	Sipitaxg Tamu Besar	*Blowpipe competitions and ladies' football matches held in Sipitang, a coastal town in Sabah.*
May	Kota Belud Tamu Besar	*A tamu (open market) in Kota Belud, Sabah, with cock fighting, native dances, buffaloes for sale and handicrafts.*
May	Migratory Giant Turtles	*Giant leathery turtles from South China Sea make annual visits from May to early September to east coast beaches.*
*May 1	Labor Day	
*May 7	Hari Hol	*Public holiday in Pahang only that marks the anniversary of death of Sultan Abu Bakar.*
May	National Youth Week.	
*May	Kadazan Harvest Festival	*Traditional thanksgiving by Kadazan farmers only in Sabah.*
May	Hari Pesta Menuai	*Festival for Kadazan farmers to appease rice spirit for good harvest.*
May	Ascension Day	
May	Teacher's Day	

FESTIVALS AND HOLIDAYS

May	Vesakhi	*Sikhs celebrate New Year.*
*May	Wesak Day	*Commemorates birth, enlightenment and passing away.*
May	Isra' and Mi'raj	*Isra' is the journey by night of Prophet Muhammad from Al Haram Mosque in Baitul Muqaddis. Mi'raj is the ascent of Prophet Muhammad from Al Aqsa to Heaven to meet Allah. It was on this occasion Prophet Muhammad received orders from Allah to introduce the practice of praying five times daily to Mecca.*
June 1-2	Gawai Dayak	*Festival celebrates successful padi (rice) harvest. Dayaks offer traditional tunk, or rice wine and a bard recites poetry.*
*June 2	Birthday of Dymn Seri Paduka Baingda Yang Dipertuan Agong	*Thanksgiving prayers offered in mosques, churches and temples throughout Malaysia.*
June 4	Martyrdom of Guru Arjan Dev	*Religious ceremonies in all Sikh temples.*
June	Dragon Boat Festival (Tuan Wu Chieh)	*Marks death of a Chinese minister, scholar and poet, who drowned himself rather than live corruptly like his colleagues.*
June	Nisfu Syaaban	*Moslems perform their religious duties at this time.*
June	St. Peter's Feast	*Celebrated by fishermen at Portuguese settlement in Malacca.*
June	Bird Singing Competition	*Contests held throughout country, but primarily in Kelantan.*
July 1	International Cooperative Day	
July	Awal Ramadhan	*Beginning of month of fasting for Moslems. (Public holiday in Johor.)*
July	St. Anne's Feast Day	*Celebrated by Christians at Bukit Mertajam and Malacca.*
July	Nuzul al Quran	*Holy verses of the Koran were revealed to Prophet Muhammad in Mecca; Moslems celebrate this day by religious gatherings. (Public holiday in Kelantan, Malacca, Perak, Perlis, Selangor and Terengganu only.)*
July	Heroes Day	*In remembrance of all Malaysians who fought and died for their country.*

FESTIVALS AND HOLIDAYS

August	Farmer's Day	
August	Festival of Seven Sisters	*A Chinese festival for single girls to pray for a happy marital future.*
August	Hungry Ghosts Festival	*A festival to celebrate the Chinese custom of offering food, joss sticks and paper money to ghosts who apparently come down to earth for a month and mingle with real people.*
August	Sri Krishna Jayanti	*Marks the descent of Sri Krishan as the eighth Avatar of Vishnu and hero of the Mahabharata epic of the Hindus.*
August 31	National Day	*Parade, cultural performance and musicals abound; the highlight of the celebration is in Kuala Lumpur.*
September	Moon Cake Festival	*A time of great significance for Buddhists.*
September	Fire Walking Ceremony	*Devotees walk across a pit of glowing embers to fulfill their vows—most apparent at Hindu temple in Gajah Berang, Malacca.*
September	Hari Raya Haji	*Moslem celebration for those who have become haji (those who visited the holy city of Mecca).*
September	Vinayaka Chaturti	*A special day for Hindus, when they worship Ganapathy, the elephant-headed god who blesses devotees.*
September	Armed Forces Day	
October	Deepavali	*The Hindu festival of lights marks the victory of light over darkness, good over evil and wisdom over ignorance.*
October	Awal Muharram	*First month in the Hijrah (Islamic) calendar. Marks the journey of Prophet Muhammad from Mecca to Medina.*
October	Universal Children's Day	
October	Festival of Loy Krathong	*Buddhist festival of lights. Candles are floated on artificial lotus flowers in memory of Lord Buddha's footprint.*
November 1	All Saints' Day	
November	All Souls' Day	
November 30	Birthday of Guru Nanak	*Founder of Sikhism. Day of prayers, hymns and religious lectures.*

FESTIVALS AND HOLIDAYS		
December	Tung Chih Festival	*Chinese pay homage to ancestors. Marble-sized rice balls (tung yuan) are served to symbolize family reunion.*
December 25	Christmas Day	
December	Pesta Pulau Pinang	*Month-long carnival in Penang.*
December	Prophet Mondi's Birthday	

Background Material

The Jungle Is Neutral by Spencer Chapman (Corgi Books). One of the best on the jungle warfare of World War II.

Great Short Works of Joseph Conrad (Perennial Classic). Many of the stories are taken from Conrad's experiences in this part of the world as a seaman. Read especially *The Lagoon*. His first novel, *Almayer's Folly* (written in 1889) is based on the village of Berau in Borneo.

World Within: A Borneo Story by Tom Harrison (Cresset Press). Very good on Sarawak.

Malayan Safari by Charles Shuttleworth. Tells of the national parks and east coast islands.

The Cultural Heritage of Malaya by W. J. Ryan. Summarizes this multiracial society.

The Singapore Story by Noel Barber (Fontana paperback). Includes some interesting vignettes on Malaysia and "The Emergency."

W. Somerset Maugham's *Borneo Stories* and *Land Below the Winds* and Joseph Conrad's *The Shadow Line* and *Lord Jim* provide insights into Malaysian life.

East Coast

There are nearly 1,000 miles of crystal-clear waters to frolic in along Malaysia's east coast.

EAST COAST IN A CAPSULE

Peninsular Malaysia's largest tourist region consists of four large states—Johor, Kelantan, Pahang and Terengganu—plus the islands Tioman and Rawa...stretches from the Thai border to the causeway separating Singapore...almost 1000 miles of shoreline and beautiful, unspoiled beaches...the craft center of the country—batik, silver, kites, weaving, wood carving and traditional theater...turtles, singing birds and top-spinning contests...a 1737-square-mile national park that boasts the peninsula's highest mountain, river trekking and unexplored jungles...it's another world altogether...with such expanse of natural beauty and such differing cultures...Malaysians insist you have not truly experienced their country until you have seen the East Coast.

The east coast of Malaysia is about ambience, "vibes" if you will. There is not much to recommend this area in the way of history, scenery or culture. You will however find a truly simple way of life. Any village will welcome you. Children will laugh and wrestle as they pose for pictures and the men and women will welcome you into their simple homes to share a few moments of friendship. If you arrive between November and January, be prepared to be stranded by flooded roads and torrential downpours. You will not see many tourists unless you visit Tioman Island or any of the mini-resorts. Highlights are the beaches, islands (**Tioman** is worth an entire vacation), fishing villages and the incomparable **Taman Negara National Park**.

Johor

Desaru

The Village of Casuarinas is where Johor's newest beach resort is; about a 90-minute drive from Johor Bahru. Desaru is situated along 20 km of unspoiled golden beaches at Penawar in the southeast corner of the peninsula. This place has been called the "last unspoiled corner in Southeast Asia." It was developed by Kejora (Johor government agency) and offers private chalets with Minangkabau roofs, as well as verandas overlooking the South China Sea. There's a Malay restaurant, watersports and golf. First-class high-rise hotels are planned. Skip it if you came here for exotic; go to Tioman instead.

Johor Bahru

This is the Johor state capital and city just across the causeway from neighboring Singapore. It's perhaps best known for **Istana Besar**, palace of the sultan, which can be visited mornings (except Fridays and holidays) by prior arrangement. The palace is also famous for its gardens, with a replica of a Japanese teahouse and the adjoining **Johor Zoo**. The sultan actually lives at Bukit Serene, overlooking the river. See also **Abu Bakar Mosque** and pineapple plantations outside the city. **Johor Lama** (Old Johor) is located about 18 miles upriver and was the original seat of the sultanate until the Portuguese destroyed the town and fort in 1587. **Air Hitam**, northwest of the capital, is the center for Aw pottery works; and **Lombong Waterfalls** are popular with tourists.

Kota Tinggi

Located 56 km east of Johor Bahru (see "Hill Resorts"), this area is noted for its 36-meter waterfalls at the foot of the 624-meter Gunung Muntahak. Visit it for a refreshing dip in one of the pools at the base of the waterfalls. Admission is 1 ringgit. Also visit here for **Kampong Makam**, royal mausoleum for sultans of Johor.

Mersing

Situated on the mouth of Mersing River, Mersing is known as a quiet fishing port and most of the visitors here are simply waiting for a ride out to the islands. But this quaint town is worth a look. Just a few miles north of town there's a decent beach.

★★ *Pulau Tioman*

Catch the Merlin Inn launch for this idyllic island 2-1/2 hours off the coast or 30 minutes by air. This is another beautiful resort area where no automobiles are allowed. If you want to get away from it all, we suggest Tioman Island. This island was one of the settings for the film *South Pacific* (along with Hawaii) and it can be said without exaggeration that this is "Bali Hai" of James Michener's *Tales of the South Pacific*. Compared to Bali, Bora Bora or Hawaii, Tioman is right up there. Mountainous peaks with crystal clear waterfalls, virgin forests, snow white beaches and solitude (if you want it). Make sure you avoid the crush. (Off season is Nov. to Feb. when, surprise!, it's monsoon season.) Head for the east side of the island.

There are a number of activities besides the standard diving, sunning and funning. Turtles lay their eggs at night; there are bats, lizards, birds and mouse deer, the smallest and most nervous member of the deer family. Jungle hikes will take you to deserted beaches and spectacular views. And you can do it on the cheap or in style. A Fielding Recommendation.

INSIDER TIP

If you came to Tioman for the diving and the scenery check out Ben's Diving Center in Kampung Salang. Get a basic but rustic hut at one of the nearby "hotels." If you are into "the real thing," charter a boat from Mersing to the island of Tinggi. Just the basics in accommodations but a real mind-blower for its dramatic sheer cliffs, Eden-like jungle and crystal clear ocean. No facilities, no tourists, no worries...you may never leave.

Pulau Rawa

Pulau Rawa is a smaller island and closer to the peninsula. It's known for white coral sand, tall palm trees and many caves.

Pulau Sibu

This is another little-visited but utterly romantic tropical isle. Simple A-frame digs can be had at the Sea Gypsy Resort.

Pulau Tinggi

Don't tell anyone about this place. See "Insider Tip." Shhh!

Muar

A peaceful fishing town en route to Malacca, Muar is known for great restaurants and foodstalls that offer local delicacies for barely a song. It's a traditional Malay village, full of ghazal music and **Kudang Kepang** dances that are said to induce trances.

Telok Mahkota

At Jason's Bay, located just before the eastern coastline town of Mersing. There are about 10 km of sandy beach sheltered from the South China Sea. It's popular with locals as a weekend retreat.

WHERE TO STAY IN JOHOR

Desaru

Desaru Golf Hotel
☎ *07-821-101* • *100 rooms.* 3 restaurants, 18 hole Robert Trent Jones golf course. *Expensive*

Desaru View Hotel
☎ *07-838-221* • *134 rooms.*
Swimming pool, four restaurants, beach. *Expensive*

Desaru Holiday Resort
☎ *07-821-240* • Chalets for families. *Moderate*

Johor Bahru

Desaru Golf Hotel ★★★
P.O. Box 50, Kotatinggi, Tanjung Penawar. ☎ *821107. FAX: 821480* • *100 rooms.* Resort on the beach in Johor's newest playground. Malaysian and Western cuisine. Bar. Tennis. Riding. Swimming pool. Golf.
Reservations: Utell.

Holiday Inn Crowne Plaza Johor Bahru ★★★
Jalan Dato Sulai-man Century Gardens. ☎ *323800. FAX: 318884* • *200 rooms.* Meisan Szechuan restaurant. Red Baron cocktail lounge. Entertainment. The Boulevard coffee shop. Satay and seafood terrace. Swimming pool. Movies. The Millennium disco. Hey, if you came all the way here to stay in a Holiday Inn we aren't going to stop you.
Reservations: Holiday Inn.

Merlin Inn Johor Bahru ★★★
10 Jalan Bukit Meldrum. ☎ *237400. FAX: 248919* • *104 rooms.* Futuristic architecture overlooking the Straits. Malay and Continental cuisine. Coffee terrace on seafront. Bar. Conference facilities overlooking the Straits. *Reservations: Utell.*

Tropical Inn Hotel

15 Jalan Gereja. *07-247-888* • Another choice in air-conditioned comfortable hotels. Pool; restaurant.

Mersing

Mersing Merlin Inn   ★★★

1-1/2 Mile, Jalan Endau. *791312. FAX: 793177* • *34 rooms.* Restaurant/disco with Western and Chinese cuisine. Coffee terrace. Launch for Tioman Island here.   *Reservations: Utell.*

Tioman Island

Berjaya Imperial Beach Resort   ★★★

Pulau Tioman Island. ☎ *445-441. FAX: 445-718* • *375 rooms.* The former Tioman Island Resort has been completely rebuilt and expanded and is now one of the area's most expansive resort hotels on the island of Pulau Tioman. Western and Asian restaurants. Conference rooms. 18-hole golf course, snorkeling, scuba diving, circle island trips, horseback (and pony) riding, tennis courts, swimming pool. You can't go wrong here as long as your credit card holds out. Book ahead.   *Reservations: Utell.*

Note: There are many places that are downright cheap around Kampung Tekek and Kampung Air Batang. You'll be slumming it compared to the Berjaya Imperial Beach Resort, but you can always spend the money you saved on the hotel tab for activities at the resort during the day.

Kelantan

Kota Bahru

Kota Bahru is the capital of Kelantan and primarily Malay (Kelantan is also known as the cultural state), featuring Makyong and Menora dance dramas, Wayang Kulit (shadow puppetry), traditional Malay music, silverware, kain songket and batik and even berok monkeys, who work the coconut palms in tandem with their masters. Kota Bahru is also great for kite-flying, top-spinning and bird-singing competitions. Kota Bahru has *one of the best market squares in Southeast Asia*. There's also old-world charm in **Istana Balai Besar**, the Sultan's palace built in 1844 and still used for royal weddings. The palace also houses a barge called "Flower of the Gods, the Splendor of Kelantan." A must-see for lovers of culture, color and memorable experiences.

Kuala Krai

Kuala Krai is about 64 km from Kota Bahru. It's famous for its fine zoo of local wildlife, including the *kijang* (deer). Game hunting for wild deer, elephant and *seladang* (wild buffalo) can be arranged through the State Game Warden here. Make sure that you can return to the states with your trophy. It's a popular place for well-heeled Malaysians to use their very expensive imported guns. Definitely a "skip it" for "PC" travelers. And it's a very expensive, very dull trip for NRA'ers.

Pantai Dasar Sabak

Here's a popular beach lined with casuarina trees located about 13 km from Kota Bahru. Turtles come ashore here to lay eggs. It's also known because *the Japanese opened World War II in the Pacific here in December 1941 about 95 minutes before the Pearl Harbor attack began*. Between here and the capital is another beach known romantically, but incorrectly, as **"Beach of Passionate Love"** (Yeah, sure).

Other lovely beaches are **Pantai Dalam Rhu** near the fishing village of Semerak and **Pantai Irama** (Beach of Melody) near Bachok town. The turtle-laying spectacle here attracts a lot of locals and tourists who are somewhat insensitive to what actually is occurring here. We suggest one of the islands for this impressive display of stamina and survival. Don't even bother to begin your search until midnight; then be prepared to spend hours watching the beasts lumber out of the dark surf to lay their precious cargo. The sight of egg collectors calmly collecting the fruits of the poor turtles' labors might shock some, but relax; they are going to the Fisheries Department to be hatched and released.

Pulau Perhentian

This is an island in the South China Sea about 2 hours by boat from Kuala Besut. There's a government rest house here for those who wish to spend a few quiet days.

Waterfalls

Waterfalls are in abundance throughout the state of Kelantan. In the district of Pasir Puteh alone are **Jeram Pasu**, **Jeram Tapeh**, **Cherang Tuli** and **Jeram Lenang**. Of the lot, Jeram Pasu is the most popular, especially at holiday time. Reach it via an 8 km path through the jungle.

WHERE TO STAY IN KELANTAN

Khota Bahru

Hotel Perdana ★★★
Jalan Mahmud, P.O. Box 222. ☎ *785000. FAX: 747621 • 136 rooms.*
Golden Jade seafood restaurant. Wayang lounge. Rebana coffee shop. Children's playground. Private beach. Squash and tennis. Bowling alley. Health center. Disco.
Reservations: Specialty Tours ☎ *(800-421-3913).*
VIP Reservations: ☎ *(800-822-8101).*

Pahang

Pahang is a photographer's paradise. There's no shortage of subjects.

Beserah

This is a fishing village about 10 km north of Kuantan known for its friendly and serene people. The village people enjoy visitors and have plenty of souvenirs to offer them, including giant tops for the local spinning contests, carved fishing boats and shellcraft items. Photographers love it here.

Cherating

This is the site of Asia's first **Club Med Holiday Village**. Malaysians are proud of this joint venture between TDC and Club Med of Paris. It's the biggest tourist complex on the East Coast. Styled in traditional Malay architecture, the 2- and 3-story buildings offer accommodations, 2 restaurants and indoor recreational facilities, as well as a disco. Of course, you'll find watersports and everything else here, as befitting a Club Med. Guests can take night tours to Kuantan's famous evening market and longer excursions to other East Coast towns. Local villagers will demonstrate the art of pandan weaving, congkak, or offer performances of Wayang Kulit or Rodat, a traditional dance involving elaborate hand movements. Because of Cherating's popularity, there are many simple but pleasant bungalows and chalets. We should warn you that there is very little to do and that the ocean can become muddy in monsoon season.

WHERE TO STAY IN PAHANG

Cherating

Club Mediterranée Holiday Village   ★ ★ ★

Cherating, near Kuantan, Pahang. ☎ *591-131. FAX: 591170 • 300 rooms.* 250-acre resort. Asian/French restaurant. Bar. Disco. Theater. Library/bridge room. Tennis. Watersports. Basketball, volleyball, calisthenics, yoga, etc. 2 swimming pools. Children's pool and other activities.   ***Reservations: Club Med.***

Note: There are many inexpensive chalets and bungalows within 200 meters of the beach.

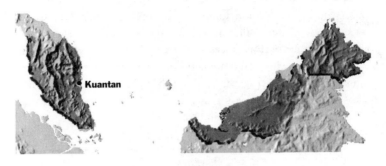

Kuantan

Kuantan is the capital of Pahang, the 3rd largest state in Malaysia. The city is an important East Coast port and noted for its fine beaches. **Telok Chempedak** is just a few kilometers from the town center. There's also **Chendor Beach** in the north. **Turtle-watching** is a unique pastime here. Many villages around Kuantan offer cultural traditions, such as kite flying, top spinning, Wayang Kulit, wood carving, batik printing, brocade and pandan weaving. The Brocade Weaving Center features kain songket, in which intricate designs of gold and silver are added to the silk. Bersilat, the Malay art of defense, is another tourist attraction. Demonstrations of all the crafts can be arranged.

Lake Chini

The Loch Ness of Malaysia. Go 60 km west of Kuantan, then left to Lubok Paku and from there by boat. Mythical monsters are reputed to lurk in the mysterious waters. There are indications that a Khmer city existed near the site. It's an interesting sidetrip from the beaches, but only for the adventurous. We suggest you take both jungle and camping equipment along.

Marathandhavar Temple

This Hindu temple can be found along the jungle-lined Jerantut/ Maran road between Kuantan and Taman Negara. Devotees flock here in March to celebrate the colorful **Panguni Uthiram Festival**.

Pekan

The Royal Town is situated near the mouth of peninsular Malaysia's longest river, the Sungei Pahang and is about 45 km south of Kuantan. It is the site of **Istana Abu Bakar**, the royal palace of the Sultan of Pahang. The palace is an impressive modern structure that overwhelms the rather quaint little town. A 4-day cultural and sporting festival is held here every year to celebrate the sultan's birthday.

★★ *Pulau Tioman*

Largest of a group of 64 volcanic islands near Malaysia's coastline in the South China Sea, Pulau Tioman belongs to the state of Pahang but is reachable from Mersing. It's covered with beautiful beaches and jungle. The Gunung Kajan peak stretches to 1037 meters. Coral beds around the island offer superb scuba diving. All other watersports available.

★★★ *Taman Negara*

Taman Negara is a 4,343 square km national park featuring jungles, rivers, mountains and streams, all pristine. This park is remote and amazing. There are no roads. Activities include jungle walks, game viewing, river trips, bird watching and checking out the bizarre insects. The park is located in the world's oldest tropical rain forest, which is 130 million years old and located in the north central area of the state. It covers part of Kelantan and Terengganu as well. The park is a photographer's dream. There are exotic animals to watch. Journey to Jerantut from Kuantan by train or bus, then to Kuala Tembeling by taxi or bus. Then it's a 3-hour boat ride upriver to park headquarters at Kuala Tahan. There are comfortable lodges, chalets and government rest houses that provide accommodation. This is the real thing so don't expect Yellowstone park facilities. Definitely for the outdoor set.

INSIDER TIP

Don't expect to see much in the way of large mammals. The jungles of Malaysia have a low biomass and very timid animals. Go out as far as you can from habitation, stake out the salt licks, go out in heavy rain and, make no noise and wait. All these tips still won't guarantee sightings but are good tips if you want to see anything during your trip.

Many people are quite surprised to see the lack of wildlife, facilities and access that many Western parks offer. The key to Taman Negara's beauty has been the undisturbed solitude and balance of rain, heat, fertility and lack of natural disaster. Even the current flow of visitors drives animals miles into the jungle and disturbs the gentle balance. Enjoy the park for what it is, knowing that other than the poles or the ocean, you are experiencing one of the few primeval wonders left on this earth. A Fielding Recommendation.

WHERE TO STAY IN KUANTAN AND AREA

Hyatt Kuantan

Telok Chempedak. ☎ *525211. FAX: 501755 • 185 rooms.* 8 acres on sandy beach near mouth of Kuantan River. Kampong coffee shop. Hugo's continental restaurant. Chinese restaurant. Sampan bar. Renang bar at pool's edge. Disco. Tennis and squash. Health studio. Watersports. Golf course nearby. Swimming pool and kiddie pool. Convention facilities. The hotel is building a new Regency Tower wing that will add 168 one- and two-bedroom suites by 1995.

Reservations: Hyatt Int'l.

Merlin Inn Resort

Telok Chempedak. ☎ *511388. FAX: 503001 • 106 rooms.* Next door to Hyatt. All rooms face South China Sea. Chempedak Restaurant. Open-air patio. Magic Circle bar. Disco. Watersports. Swimming pool. Fishing and golf. Squash courts and health center. Bunga Raya ballroom.

Reservations: Utell.

TIPS ON ENJOYING TAMAN NEGARA

Plan enough time; 1 week is a minimum.

Book ahead, preferably with a group (it will reduce costs).

Prepare to get wet (either from rain, sweat or humidity).

Prepare for leeches and mosquitoes (bring bug juice).

Visit between Mar. and Sept. (the park is closed mid-Nov to mid-Jan and Hari Raya).

Bring the basic camping equipment (some can be bought on site).

Bring fast film, binocs, plastic bags and patience.

GAME VIEWING

Janut Tahan (near center)	*Artificial salt lick, crowded, barren, skip it.*
Jenut Tabing (1 hour from Kuala Tahan)	*Deer and tapir. 8 beds, toilet and mandi. River nearby.*
Jenut Belau (1-1/2 hour walk from center)	*Civit, deer and tapir, no water.*
Jenut Kumbang (5 hours from Kuala Tahan or by boat)	*Elephant, tiger, gibbons, tapir, six bunk beds, toilets.*
Jenut Cegar Anging (1-1/2 hour walk from Kuala Tahan)	*4 bunk beds, toilet and mandi, river nearby.*

HIKES

Bukit Teresek	*1 hr. hike to Bukit Teresek (344m). Good views from summit.*
Teresek Spring	*1/2 day hike. Good rainforest intro.*
Gunung Gendang	*1 day hike to 590 meter summit.*
Kuala Tahan-Bukit Teserik-Tabing Hide-Lata Bekoh-Kuala Tahan	*Good hike with boat section (beginner rapids). Leave 9 a.m., finish 4 p.m. Guide fee.*
Kuala Tahan-Bukit Indah-Kuala Terengganu-Kuala Tahan	*Hike white water section to cool you down. Leave 9 a.m., finish, 4 p.m. Guide fee.*
Gunung Tahan	*9 day hike to 2187 meter summit. Tough.*

BOAT TRIPS

Kuala Terengganu-Kuala Kenyan-Kuit Batu	*Limestone cliffs, fruit trees, 1-1/2 hrs.*
Kuala Tahan-Lata Berkoh	*Good rapids, swimming hole, 1 hr.*
Kuala Tahan-Kuala Terengganu	*Seven hairy rapids, gorges, our pick if you can only do one, 45 minutes.*

FISHING

Lake Bertoh	*Fishing Lodge.*
Kenyam River	*Camping trip upriver.*
Kuala Perkai	*Fishing Lodge.*
Sepia River	*Remote camping trip.*
Tahan River	*Above Kuala Terengganu.*

Note: *Most of the above activities may require rental of equipment, guide, a boat and some preplanning. Boats are expensive. Check with the tourist office Kuala Lumpur for up-to-the-minute prices and availability.*

INSIDER TIP

For those who would rather donate blood to the Red Cross instead of Taman Negara's leeches, exploration by boat is recommended. You can always combine hiking, or a visit to a blind or even a little fishing. You'll also find it cooler and easier to spot bird life along the river banks. It is obviously more expensive, but might be a more productive use of a shorter stay.

Terengganu

Kemaman

A small fishing village on the Terengganu/Pahang border marks the beginning of a charming and scenic area along the coastline traveling northward through the villages of **Teluk Mengkuang** and **Kemasik** and on to **Dungun**, another seaside town. For the next 64 km north, the shoreline offers a series of peaceful sights—small villages, casuarina trees and beautifully carved *perahus* (boats). It's well worth a detour to drive along the South China Sea.

Kuala Terengganu

Here is the state capital. The city is known for its **Central Market** on the river. The sultan's historic palace is across the road from his modern residence. It features fine wood carvings and intricate patterns with inscriptions from the Koran. Life is easy here. Expect to travel slowly around town in a trishaw. Take in the local color and spend some time in the villages around the capital. The homes are full of cottage industries and all the crafts are for sale.

Pulau Kapas

An island famous for its coral and seashells, located just 6 km offshore from village of Marang, which is about 10 km south of Kuala Terengganu. It's great for swimming and snorkeling; but there aren't any accommodations yet.

Pulau Perhentian

This is considered one of most beautiful islands in the area. It's located about 20 km offshore from the village of Kuala Besut in the most northern point of Terengganu state. Fishermen will ferry tourists over and back for a fee. Take along your refreshments; a modest government rest house is available.

Rantau Abang

A turtle-watching village. Giant leatherneck turtles reputed to be 1000 years old come ashore in this small village to lay their eggs. They can be seen from May to Sept.; the best months are July and Aug. The star attractions are giant turtles that weigh over 2000 pounds. The government prohibits the collection and sale of the eggs to protect the species. Turtle watching is a big hit with East Coast visitors, but you must obey the rules.

WHERE TO STAY IN TERENGGANU

Kuala Terengganu

Primula Beach Hotel

Jalan Persinggahan, P.O. Box 43. ☎ *622100. FAX: 633360 • 260 rooms.* Beach location, a mile from town. Rhusila coffeehouse. Local corner supper spot. 2 cocktail lounges. Swimming pools. Pony riding. Watersports. Children's playground. Supper club, coffeehouse, Bayu bar and Cascade grill, library. ***Reservations: Utell.***

Tanjong Jara Beach Hotel

8 miles off Dungun. ☎ *841801 • 100 rooms.* Operated by TDC. Traditional Malay architecture. Village-style setting reminiscent of sultan's palace of Terengganu. All rooms have view of South China Sea. Danau Chinese/Indian/ Western restaurant. Nakhoda lounge. Disco. Swimming pool and bar. Tennis and squash. Watersports. Fishing. Saunas and gym. Boating. ***Reservations: Direct.***

Hill Resorts

Cameron Highlands

HILL RESORTS IN A CAPSULE

Malaysia has six hill resorts...visitors can recharge their energies in cool and invigorating climates found only in the higher altitudes...lovely vistas of mountain peaks and tea plantations, peaceful jungle areas...active sports like golf, tennis, swimming and climbing...as well as the promise of a log fire every evening...most of the areas were discovered and founded by the British, who never could stand the heat and humidity of Asia...expect to find colonial overtones in your accommodations and food...Foster's Lakehouse and the Tudor-style Smokehouse (which was on the verge of being sold at this writing and may soon have a new name) are examples of the change-of-pace available in the Cameron Highlands...golfers will enjoy the many fine and beautiful courses but should avoid the peak months of April, August and December.

Few things refresh like a visit to the classic hill resorts of Malaysia. There cannot be a more sublime climate with its crisp evenings and delicious days. Most golfers dream of playing forever on the brilliant green courses; nature lovers will babble endlessly about the orchids, flowers and greenery; die-hard colonials will take their tea and scones in tudor hotels while watching lawn bowling and tennis. Adventurers will head into the hills to enjoy the rugged cool highlands, tea plantations, farmlands and untravelled back roads. Once you escape the rank tropical heat below and bathe yourself in the cool soft air and genteel surroundings you will wonder why the hill resorts aren't reason enough to visit Malaysia.

A few tips: Cameron Highlands is the best hill resort. The resorts are very busy during school holidays (April, August, December). There is a good selection of cheap to medium hotels. And don't just assume hill resorts are for golfers and tea fanatics. There are some excellent jungle treks and remote regions accessible from the highlands.

WHAT TO SEE AND DO AT THE HILL RESORTS

Cameron Highlands ★★★
The Cameron Highlands are 1,524 meters above sea level with a population of 20,000. They are linked by a winding mountain road to town of Tapah, on the highway between Kuala Lumpur and Ipoh. Cameron Highlands was discovered by government surveyor William Cameron in 1885. There are many tea plantations, vegetable farms and flower nurseries here. There are also jungle walks and magnificent waterfalls, as well as tennis, golf and swimming. Accommodations include the 65-room **Merlin Hotel** with disco and television and the 30-room **Golf Course Inn**; the quaint and conservative 20-room **Smokehouse** should be a definite stop to sample the locally grown tea and colonial ambiance. Smaller hotels and government-sponsored bungalows rent for a song, especially in Tanah Ratah. There's also the **Strawberry Park** hotel and apartment complex. This is my favorite hill resort whether camping or hoteling it. This is where all the old Land Rovers are used by farmers to lug produce to town.

INSIDER TIP

If you can, take a free visit to the Boh Tea Estate. The tea makes great souvenirs, light, inexpensive and to be savored over your travel stories. Open between 9 a.m. and 4:30 p.m.

Fraser's Hill ★
Fraser's Hill is 1,524 meters above sea level. It was named after Louis James Fraser who built himself a shack up here and traded tin. It was

surveyed in 1919 and developed into one of Malaysia's most popular resorts. Located north of Kuala Lumpur. The junction to the mountain road is Kuala Kubu Bahru; the last 5 miles from the gap to Fraser's Hill are along a narrow winding road that alternates to one-way traffic at posted hours. It has a lovely 9-hole public golf course, tennis, sports complex, swimming beneath **Jeriau Waterfalls**. There are jungle walks with panoramic views of the states of Selangor and Pahang as well as Straits of Malacca. There's a minizoo and park on some 10 acres. There are real English gardens everywhere. The social centers of Fraser's Hill are **The Tavern** and **Hillview**. The local development corporation runs bungalows and chalets with full catering facilities for up to 20 people. There's also the 109-room Merlin Hotel.

Genting Highlands

Genting Highlands is 1,714 meters above sea level and easily accessible from Kuala Lumpur by helicopter (10 minutes), or about one hour by road. It's the country's latest and most Las Vegas-style resort. It opened in 1971 with 5 huge modern hotels, gambling casino, artificial lake, indoor stadium, 18-hole golf course, convention facilities, 1200-seat theater restaurant, cable-car system and **Chin Swee Cave Temple** (opened Sept. 1979). There are 1116 hotel rooms. This is not a true hill resort but a glossy recreation area which can boast the only legitimate gambling casino in the country.

Kota Tinggi

Kota Tinggi is 634 meters above sea level. It's located in the state of Johor and just an hour's drive from Johor Bahru, Malaysia's southernmost town (just across the causeway from Singapore). It's popular for cooling off in the many waterfalls and natural pools in the area. Visitors can also practice a little mountain climbing or carry on down to Teluk Mahkota where a sandy bay stretches 6 miles and is sheltered from waves of South China Sea. Accommodations at Kota Tinggi feature seven self-contained chalets; there's a 2-story restaurant and large car park. Buses run regularly from Johor Bahru.

Maxwell Hill   ★

Maxwell Hill is 1,035 meters above sea level. It's also called Bukit Larut and known as Malaysia's oldest hill resort; just 9 km from Taiping Town in Perak State. There's access by Land Rover only up winding, hairpin turns. The only accessible summit is the Cottage. At the top you can see the coastline from Pangkor Island to Penang on a clear day. There are accommodations in fully-contained rest houses and bungalows at various levels of the mountain range.

Penang Hill

Penang Hill is 692 meters above sea level and situated in the middle of Penang Island; it's accessible by funicular railway. There is a 12-room hotel at the top of the railway station and several small government-run bungalows. Spend a few hours up here—having lunch or a drink on the lawn overlooking the city and Kedah Peak.

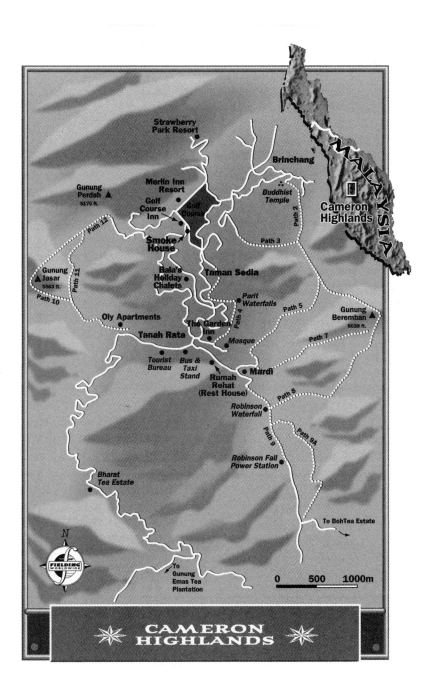

Strawberry
Park Resort

Brinchang

Gunung
Perdah
5170 ft.

Merlin Inn
Resort

Buddhist
Temple

Path 2

Cameron
Highlands

Golf
Course
Inn

Golf
Course

MALAYSIA

Path 12

Smoke
House

Path 3

Gunung
Jasar
5563 ft.

Path 11

Bala's
Holiday
Chalets

Taman Sedia

Parit
Waterfalls

Path 5

Gunung
Beremban
6038 ft.

Path 10

Oly Apartments

Path 4

The Garden
Inn

Tanah Rata

Mosque

Path 7

Tourist
Bureau

Bus &
Taxi
Stand

Mardi

Rumah
Rehat
(Rest House)

Path 8

Robinson
Waterfall

Path 9

Path 9A

Robinson Fall
Power Station

Bharat
Tea Estate

To BohTea Estate

N

FIELDING
WORLDWIDE

To
Gunung
Emas Tea
Plantation

0   500   1000m

CAMERON
HIGHLANDS

WHERE TO STAY AT THE HILL RESORTS

Cameron Highlands

Golf Course Inn ★★
Tanah Rata, Cameron Highlands. ☎ *901411. FAX: 941462 • 35 rooms.*
Chinese and European restaurants. Coffeehouse. Games room. Bar.
Tennis. Golf course. Are we in Southern California? Expensive.
Reservations: Specialty Tours ☎ *(800-421-3913).*

The Lakehouse Hotel ★★★
Ringlet, Cameron Highlands. ☎ *996152. FAX: 996213 • 12 rooms.*
European food; forest walks. Dining room. 2 bars. Sports activities.
Good for tea or pub snacks. *Reservations: Direct.*

Merlin Inn Resort Cameron Highlands ★★★
P.O. Box 4, Tanah Rata. ☎ *941205. FAX: 901178 • 100 rooms.* Hill
resort 6,000 feet up. Malay and western cuisine replaces "Rajah restaurant." Asli bar. Sidewalk cafe. Marquerite lounge. Tennis and badminton. Golf course. Gym. Video movies. Conference room. Good
views. Posh but nothing special. Expensive. *Reservations: Utell.*

Strawberry Park Motel ★
Brinchang. ☎ *05-941-166 • 172 rooms.* Biggest resort in Cameron
Highlands. Strangely out of the way. Expensive.*Reservations: Direct.*

Ye Old Smokehouse ★★★
☎ *05-941-214 • 20 rooms.* A British country inn in the middle of
South East Asia? Oh heck, why not. A crackling fire, creaky floors,
ticking grandfather clock, it's all here. Frayed at the edges, musty and
terribly British. They get their stars for atmosphere not luxury. Moderate to Expensive. *Reservations: Direct.*

Fraser's Hill

Fraser's Hill Holiday Bungalows ★★
Fraser's Hill. ☎ *382044. FAX: 382273 • 69 rooms.* Dining room. Bar.
Tennis and squash. Golf course. Swimming pool. Pony rides and children's playground. Jungle walks. Mini-zoo. Health center. Mini-train
and Ferris wheel. *Reservations: Direct.*

Merlin Inn Resort Fraser's Hill ★★★
Fraser's Hill. ☎ *82300. FAX: 382284 • 90 rooms.* Restaurant. Coffeehouse. Bar. Games room. 9-hole golf course. Riding. Swimming pool
and health center. Children's playground. Skating rink. Tennis and
squash. Mini-zoo and mini-train. *Reservations: Utell.*

Genting Highlands

Genting Highlands Resort ★★★
Genting Highlands Resort, 9th Floor, Wisma Genting, Jalan Sultan Ismail,
50250, Kuala Lumpur. ☎ *211118 • 675 rooms.* Theater restaurant.
Western, Malaysian and Chinese restaurants. Casino. 24-hour coffee-
houses. *Reservations: Utell.*

Kuala Lumpur

Kuala Lumpur

KUALA LUMPUR IN A CAPSULE

Malay name means "muddy estuary"...situated at the confluence of Klang and Gombak rivers...city founded around 1858 or so at the beginning of the tin boom...made capital of Federated Malay States in 1895... one of Asia's most beautiful, green and tidy places...offers a spacious and good life for over one million inhabitants...a multiracial society of Malays, Chinese, Indians, Arabs, Eurasians and Europeans...was important transportation and administration center during British rule in Malaya...an impressive array of structures in the Islamic, Gothic, Tudor and Colonial styles...home of country's elegant and modern National Mosque... a lovely capital known affectionately as K.L. by both locals and frequent visitors.

Kuala Lumpur, or "K.L." as everyone calls it, could just be the Dallas of Southeast Asia. The city is exploding with futuristic skyscrapers, businessmen chattering on cellular phones and thousands of shops bursting with every possible type of goods at unbelievable bargains. Tucked between the high-rise office buildings are a few quaint reminders of K.L.'s past—Chinatown, the temples, rows of sedate colonial mansions and a few notable monuments to Malaysia's British heritage. I thoroughly enjoy K.L. with its nonsensical street system, endless shopping centers, its polyglot people and the busy, happy hum of a city that is well on its way to becoming a world business center. Spend a few days here shopping and enjoying the nightlife before you head into the jungle or toward the beaches.

WHAT TO SEE AND DO IN KUALA LUMPUR

Central Market ★

Huge collection of shops and food stalls adjacent to Putra World Trade Center downtown; just across the street from Chinatown; wonderful for browsing, souvenirs, snacks and watching the city's colorful and varied residents. **Chan See Shu Yuan Temple** built in 1906; features typical Chinese temple; open courtyards and symmetrically organized pavilions; serves as both religious and political venue.

Chinatown ★

Home to many of the city's almost half million Chinese residents; concentrated in one of the city's busiest areas; bounded roughly by Jalan Petaling, Jalan Sultan and Jalan Bandar; everything on sale from dawn to dusk. (Gee do you think those are real Rolex's for 25 bucks? Buy a sackful as gifts, your in-laws will never know.) Great open-air bazaar, **Pasar Malam** located mid-section on Jalan Petaling at dusk; see **Chinese Assembly Hall** at junction of Jalan Foch; birdcages on Jalan Sultan; visit also **See Yeoh Temple**; oldest and most venerated of the city's Chinese shrines. **International Buddhist Pagoda** stands between bodhi tree and shrine; built in 1894 by Sinhala Buddhists; pagoda represents contemporary architectural design of pagodas; images and replicas of pagodas enshrined in octagonal hall at base of pagoda; example of great religious freedom and tolerance of beliefs throughout Malaysia.

Istana Negara

Official residence of their majesties, the elected rulers; set on over 20 acres of beautifully landscaped grounds; originally built in 1928 by a local millionaire; occupied by the sultan elected king for a 5-year term; VIPs received in audience in the west wing; state banquets and official functions held in the east wing; their majesties occupy private quarters on the first floor above ground.

KUALA LUMPUR

Key

1) Lake Gardens
2) National Monument
3) Parliament House
4) National Museum
5) Kuala Lumpur Railway Station
6) Malayan Railway Administration Headquarters
7) Masjid Negara (National Mosque)
8) Sultan Abdul Samad Building
9) Masjid Jame
10) National Museum of Art
11) Chinatown
12) Sri Mahamariamman Temple
13) International Buddhist Pagoda
14) Chan See Shu Yuen Temple
15) Merdeka Stadium
16) Istana Negara
17) Ming Court Hotel
18) Federal Hotel
19) Regent of KL
20) KL Hilton
21) Equatorial Hotel
22) Holiday Inn
23) Hotel Istana
24) Shangri-La Hotel

Jalan Ampang

Ampang Road; lovely old mansions and official embassy residences line this street; many a bit dilapidated; but some now beautifully restored and ready for business; like the famous **Bok House**, one of the best French restaurants in town (**Le Coq d'Or**).

Kampung Bahru

Open-air night bazaar; just 10 minutes from the city center; one of the great experiences of K.L.; especially interesting on Sat. evenings; food and other items to tempt even the tightest pocketbook!

Karyaneka Handicraft Village

Just behind the Hilton International and near the sprawling race club; crafts from various regions of Malaysia displayed in traditional dwellings in a landscaped park; a crafts museum and the opportunity to buy samples of local handicrafts from the entire country; folkloric shows on Saturdays.

Kuala Lumpur Railway Station

Moorish-style structure built by British in 1911; basic design beneath Islamic-influenced exterior, supposed to resemble large glass-and-iron train sheds constructed throughout England at the close of the 19th century.

Lake Gardens

Part of K.L.'s "green belt;" gardens laid out in 1888 by Englishman named A.R. Venning; located in their midst is **Tasik Perdana** or Premier Lake—artificial water on which boating is available; entire 160-acre parkland open daily to the public.

Malayan Railway Administration Headquarters

Located opposite K.L. Railway Station; imposing structure with elements of Islamic design; houses offices of the country's railway authorities.

Masjid Jame

Old mosque built at confluence of Klang and Gombak rivers; close to where first settlers landed; mosque nestles within coconut grove; 2 minarets rise to the height of the palms; prayer hall has 3 domes and opens onto walled courtyard called Sahn.

Masjid Negara (National Mosque)

Pride of Malaysia and one of the largest in Southeast Asia; center of Islamic activities in the country; contemporary structure finished in 1965; on approximately 12 landscaped acres behind the railway station; consists of grand prayer hall, mausoleum, library, offices, open courtyard and 245-foot minaret; dome is umbrella-shaped with 18-pointed star to represent the 13 states of Malaysia and 5 pillars of Islam; courtyard partly covered by 48 concrete parasols to provide both shade and architectural interest; fountains for ablutions located on floor below; marble columns placed to signify the many rubber plantations that are so important to country's economy; mosque open to public from 8 a.m. to 6 p.m. Sat. through Thur. and after 2 p.m. on Fri.; ladies have separate entrance; visitor's gallery from which to witness some proceedings.

Merdeka Stadium

Outdoor stadium with capacity for 50,000; the venue where one of Malaysia's most historic events occurred; Declaration of Independence (Merdeka) signed here in 1957; sports events and competitions now held here regularly; main axis lies north-south so players need not face the evening sun.

National Monument

It's located in Lake Gardens; constructed in 1966 to commemorate Malaysia's national heroes, many of whom died in the cause of freedom and peace; seven bronze figures represent triumph of forces of democracy over evil; entire monument designed by Felix W. de Weldon, creator of famous Iwo Jima Memorial in Arlington National Cemetery across the Potomac River from Washington, D.C.

National Museum

Muzium Negara; completed in 1963 on site of old Selangor Museum which was destroyed during World War II; built in old Malay-style architecture with 2 large Italian-mosaic murals by local artist Cheong Lai Tong on front; depicts life and customs of Malaysians; design of main doors by Kelantanese artist Wan Su Wan Othman; carvings by team of local craftsmen under direction of Samsuddin bin Haji Tahir of Terengganu; exhibits depict history, culture, arts and crafts, currency, flora and fauna and major economic activities of country; open daily from 9 a.m. to 7 p.m.; closed Fri. from noon to 2:30 p.m.; admission free.

National Museum of Art

Located in the old Majestic Hotel; permanent collection of works by local Malaysian artists; plus exhibitions of international nature throughout the year; open daily from 10 a.m. to 6 p.m.; closed Fri. from noon to 2:30 p.m.; admission free.

Parliament House

Located on elevated grounds in Lake Gardens; a contemporary 18-story structure dominates complex; includes low building containing House of Representatives, Senate, various offices, library, banquet hall and committee rooms; visitors may enter Parliament House when in session, with prior arrangement; formal national dress of Malaysia or Western lounge suit required; women must have hemline below the knee.

Royal Selangor Golf Club

Located at junction of Jalan Bukit Bintang and Jalan Pekeliling; about 15 minutes from city center; oldest golf club in Malaysia and scene of annual Malaysian Golf Tournament; elegant club with many fine facilities; visitors should inquire about exchange privileges.

Selangor Club

One of the capital's most historic landmarks; located opposite Sultan Abdul Samad Building; founded in 1884 to provide recreation for British civil servants; today stands as a reminder of country's colonial past; membership drawn from top strata of K.L. society.

Selangor Turf Club

Racecourse located in Jalan Ampang; provides lovely green spot in eastern area; site acquired in 1895 when racing allowed for first time in State of Selangor; club founded in 1896 and still thriving; modern grandstand opened in 1966; the best view of the area is from the top of the K.L. Hilton.

Sri Mahamariamman Temple

Hindu Temple built in 1873; one of country's largest and most ornate; elaborate design incorporates gold, precious stones, Spanish and Italian ceramic tiles; located at corner of Jalan Bandar and Jalan Davidson.

Sultan Abdul Samad Building

Formerly known as State Secretariat; one of K.L.'s most distinctive and most photographed landmarks; opposite Selangor Club; built in 1894-97 by the British in Moorish-style architecture; clock tower, domes and curving arches; design considered a little ahead of its time by then British appointed governor of Straits Settlements (what the place was called before turn of century); don't miss the **Dewan Bandaraya** (City Hall), along the same lines; an altogether impressive representation of a time gone by.

Wisma Loke

Located in city center at Medan Tuanku; one of oldest buildings in the capital; fine old mansion with porcelain balustrades from China, Malaccan tiles and traditional Moongate; became first private residence in K.L. to be lit by electricity in 19th century; first owned by Cheow Ah Yeok, close ally of Yap Ah Loy (a founder of Kuala Lumpur); later bought by famed millionaire Loke Yew; century-old house now renovated into antique shop.

Titiwangsa Gardens

Former mining land; landscaped area of about 130 acres; lake called **Tasik Titiwangsa** for boating; tennis courts and children's playground; open daily until 6:30 p.m.

Kuala Lumpur Environs

Batik Factory Selayang

Located north of K.L.; demonstrations daily from 8:30 a.m. to 5 p.m.; material for sale here; no demonstrations from 1 to 2 p.m.; special requests honored.

Batu Caves

Sacred place of worship for Hindus; great mass of limestone cliffs just north of K.L. The largest cavern houses Hindu shrine of Lord Subramaniam; climb 272 steps to entrance. Hindus make pilgrimage annually during festival of Thaipusam; open daily except Wed. and Fri. from noon to 2 p.m.

Mimaland

A 300-acre tourist recreation complex some 30 minutes from K. L.; guitar-shaped lake; largest natural water swimming pool in Southeast Asia; prehistoric center; golf course; children's play-grounds; 24-room motel overlooking lake; 10 bagans (Malay-style houses); floating restaurant and Western-style restaurant.

National Zoo and Aquarium

Located in Ulu Klang, just 13 km from K.L.; zoo has some 200 species of animals, birds and reptiles; aquarium has 25 species of ma-rine exhibits and 81 species of freshwater fish; elephant, boat and train rides for children; open daily from 9 a.m. to 6 p.m.; admission charge.

Rubber Plantations

Malaysia is world's largest producer of natural rubber; visits ar-ranged by tour operators to view trees being tapped.

Selangor Pewter Factory

Located at Jalan Pahang on the outskirts of K.L.; largest pewter factory in the world; watch demonstrations of the material being made from Malaysian tin, antimony and copper; open from 8:30 a.m. to 4:30 p.m. daily; duty-free shopping.

Templer Park

Near Batu Caves, along same north/south highway just 22 km from K.L.; beautiful retreat of some 3,000 acres of cool and green parkland; streams and waterfalls; paths through forest; home to but-terflies, flying lizards and birds; very friendly monkeys; named after Sir Gerald Templer, High Commissioner in former Federation of Malaysia.

Tin Mines

Malaysia produces some 40% of the world's tin making it the single largest supplier; several large mines can be viewed along Malaysian highways, especially in Batu Caves and Templer Park area; visits arranged by tour or travel agencies.

Morib

A weekend and holiday beach resort some 64 km from K.L.; a favorite for picnics and family gatherings. There's a 20-room government rest house, a 9-hole golf course, aviary and open-air foodstalls.

Port Kelang

The country's most important seaport, located about 40 km from K.L., where the original founders of the capital started up river; It's known for excellent seafood restaurants; the Sultan of Selangor's Palace is in Kelang town.

Port Dickson

This is a favorite resort area about 1-1/2 hours west of K.L. by car. The beaches are about 18 km long; there are watersports and fishing facilities. The Yacht Club has reciprocal arrangements. Government rest houses and first-class hotels are available; located about 34 km from Seremban.

Seremban

Here is the capital of Negri Sembilan. Seremban is the Malay word for a federation of 9 states. It's located about 66 km southeast of K.L. It's the commercial and administrative center of the Minangkabau state of Negri Sembilan. It's known for its distinctive architecture, an open-air museum at Lake Gardens and for the royal town of Sri Menanti, a few kilometers to the west. This state is also traditionally matriarchal; women inherit rights over property and land to the exclusion of men.

WHERE TO STAY IN KUALA LUMPUR

Equatorial Hotel
Jalan Sultan Ismail. ☎ *2617777. FAX: 2619020 • 300 rooms.* Golden Phoenix Chinese, Swiss Chalet and Japanese Kampachi restaurants. 24-hour coffeehouse. Disco. Swimming pool/health club.
Reservations: Utell.

Federal Hotel
35 Jalan Bukit Bintang. ☎ *2489166. FAX: 2438381 • 450 rooms.* 20-story, 300-room addition called **Imbi Hotel** behind existing hotel; on Jalan Imbi; with 3 bars and restaurants; swimming pool and convention center. Mandarin Palace Chinese restaurant. Kon Tiki room

Western restaurant. 5 bars. Federal Club and Sky Room nightclub. 24-hour coffeehouse. Swimming pool and health center.

Reservations: Utell.

Holiday Inn On The Park ★★★

POB 10483, Jalan Pinang. ☎ *2481066. FAX: 2435930 • 200 rooms.* Rooms with TV, in-house video-movies, minibar, coffee/tea-making facilities. Three restaurants serving Western and Asian dishes. 24-hour coffee shop. Health club with sauna, exercise machines, pool, tennis, children's playground. Meeting rooms. *Reservations: Holiday Inn.*

Hyatt Saujana Hotel and Country Club ★★★★

Subang International Airport Highway. ☎ *746 1188. FAX: 7462789 • 250 rooms.* Opened in 1987 in the midst of two 18-hole championship golf courses; 30 minutes from downtown K.L. and 3 minutes from the airport; a variety of restaurants as well as meeting facilities.

Reservations: Hyatt International.

Hotel Istana ★★★★★

73, Jalan Raja Chulan, POB 12919. ☎ *2419988. FAX: 2440111 • 516 rooms.* Opened in 1992. Striking building blending Malay and Western design; good location in the city's business, financial and shopping district. Club and Istana floors with private elevator and butler service. 10 restaurants and lounges, including Ristorante Bologna, Japanese and Chinese restaurants and the Ahambra Musictheque, a multipurpose nightclub-entertainment centre. Business center. Shopping arcade. Fitness center with sauna, steam bath, spa, gym, massage. Outdoor swimming pool, two tennis courts, three squash courts, arrangements for golf. *Reservations: LHW.*

Kuala Lumpur Hilton ★★★★★

Jalan Sultan Ismail (P.O. Box 577). ☎ *2422222. FAX: 2438069 • 589 rooms;.* First luxury hotel in town and still holds its own as one of the best; located in the heart of the business district; has loyal following; excellent views right over the Royal Selangor turf club. Melaka grill for businessmen's lunch and nouvelle cuisine. Inn of Happiness Chinese restaurant. Planters' Inn 24-hour coffeehouse. Nirvana ballroom. The Tin Mine disco. Swimming pool and health club. Tennis and squash courts with full-time coach. Champagne check-in.

Reservations: Hilton Hotels.

Melia Kuala Lumpur Hotel ★★★★★

16, Jalan Imbi. ☎ *2428333. FAX: 2439479 • 300 rooms.* One of the city's newest; well-furnished rooms with many amenities; good French restaurant; Chinese restaurant, coffee shop, poolside snack bar, French restaurant, lounge, disco. Health center with gym, sauna, massage. Outdoor pool. Meeting and banquet rooms. Business center.

Reservations: Utell.

Ming Court   ★★★

Jalan Ampang. ☎ *2618888. FAX: 2612393* • *447 rooms.* 13-story structure featuring swimming pool, disco, restaurants and conference seating for 1,000 persons; owned by Malayan United Industries.
Reservations: Specialty Tours ☎ *(800-421-3913).*

Pan Pacific, Kuala Lumpur   ★★★★★

Jalan Chow Kitbaru, P.O. Box 11468, Kuala Lumpur. ☎ *4225555. FAX: 4417236* • *571 rooms (15 suites).* Situated in commercial sector of the capital; part of the Putra World Trade Centre; Japanese chain. Atrium lobby lounge. Atrium bar. La Pattisserie. The Continental restaurant. Selera coffee house. Keyaki Japanese cuisine. Hai-Tien-Lo Chinese restaurant. Pacific ballroom. Health club. Tennis and Squash courts. Pacific Executive floors (28th and 29th). No-smoking floors (20th and 21st). The Splash swimming pool.   *Reservations: Pan Pacific.*

Petaling Jaya Hilton   ★★★★

2 Jalan Barat Petaling, Jaya. ☎ *7553533. FAX: 7553909* • *388 rooms.* Formerly known as Jaya Puri Hotel; hotel located between K.L. and airport; taken over and refurbished by Hilton; counter at Subang airport to aid guests of both properties. Grill room. Coffeehouse. Nightclub. Chinese restaurant. 2 bars. Disco. Swimming pool and health facilities. Ballroom and theater-style seating for 1300.
Reservations: Hilton Hotels.

The Regent of Kuala Lumpur   ★★★★★

160 Jalan Bukit Bintang. ☎ *2418000. FAX: 2430535* • *469 rooms.* Not to be confused with the old Regent of Kuala Lumpur, the new Regent is situated in the heart of the city's Golden Triangle shopping, business and entertainment district; all rooms offer panoramic city views; butler service on every floor; signature Regent bathrooms with marble fittings, king-sized bathtub and separate glass-enclosed shower; Six restaurants, including a grill room, brasserie, Japanese restaurant, Chinese eatery and poolside terrace. Pastry shop. Business center. Function rooms. Outdoor swimming pool. Health center with supervised gym, sauna, steambath, spa pool. *Reservations: Regent Hotels.*

Shangri-La Hotel Kuala Lumpur   ★★★★★

11 Jalan Sultan Ismail, K. L. 04-01. ☎ *2322388. FAX: 2301514* • *722 rooms.* Deluxe high-rise hotel and the showcase of the city; welcome to the world of polished marble; boasts largest guest rooms in K.L., all with city views; combines business with resort hotel; large and well-equipped function rooms for conventions. Swimming pool. Squash and tennis courts. Nadaman Japanese cuisine. Shang Palace Cantonese restaurant. Restaurant Lafite. The Coffee Garden. Club Oz. The Pub.   *Reservations: Shangri-La Int'l.*

WHERE TO STAY IN PORT DICKSON

Mul Beach Hotel   ★ ★ ★
Port Dickson, Negri Sembilan. ☎ *795244* • *165 rooms.* 7-1/2 miles from town. Pelangi grill room. Kontiki coffee shop. Coral Reef lounge/disco. Tiupan lounge. Swimming pool. Private beach. Tennis and golf on request. Indra Negri banquet hall. **Reservations: Utell.**

Si-Rusa Beach Resort   ★ ★
7th mile Coast Rd., P.O. Box 31, Port Dickson, Negri Sembilan. ☎ *405233. FAX: 405332* • *160 rooms.* Dining room. Cocktail lounge. Watersports. Boating and fishing. Golf on request.

Reservations: Direct.

SAMPLING LOCAL FARE IN KUALA LUMPUR

What would you get if you crossed English, Indian, Chinese, Thai, Arabic and Malay cooking? Well the simple answer is Malaysian food. I can't describe the hundreds of taste sensations that await you in Malaysia. There are only a handful of Malaysian restaurants in North America but I would urge you to seek one out. It may be enough to convince you to visit K.L.

Malaysia's capital offers visitors continual dining experiences that range from fun-filled foodstalls full of enticing aromas of local spices and colorful sights, to sophisticated settings and nouvelle cuisine to match any European restaurant.

The first step to enjoying Kuala Lumpur's eating pleasures is to immerse yourself in the local cooking, where great pains are taken not only in the preparation, but especially in the presentation of all edibles. This is the home of *satay*, that succulent dish of skewered meat kebabs marinated in coconut milk and spices and barbecued over glowing embers. *Satay* is usually consumed at any number of open-air foodstalls; dip it in the peanut and chili sauce that tries not to knock your eyes out.

The staple of ★ ★ **Malay food** is, of course, rice and it is often eaten with one's fingers with a variety of curries, sambals (a hotter, dry curry), vegetable dishes and fried foods. Many local spices and santan (coconut cream) give the food an unusual and rich flavor. Specialties range greatly between the 13 states and the southern manner of cooking is quite different from the north. *Nasi dagang* is unique to Kelantan State, while *assam pedas* is a Johor-style fish curry with a tamarind-based sauce. Favorites at open-air foodstalls *(gerai)* are *mee jawa* (boiled noodles) or *mee goreng* (fried noodles) or a variety of *nasi* (rice dishes) with all sorts of accompanying meat, vegetables and condiments. Chilis are a necessary ingredient in Malay cooking and they are used as much as in neighboring Thai cuisine.

You can feast mightily on **Chinese food** in the nation's capital and every region is well represented. Cantonese, Pekingese, Szechuanese, Hokkien, Teochew, Hakka and Hainanese. All differ from one another and the range of taste treats stretches from dim sum (little dumplings) and Canton for breakfast or lunch to Peking duck and steamed pork buns for dinner. The Hokkiens are famous for their noodle dishes (such as fried *mee*) and

Teochew food features porridge and salted side dishes. Hakka offerings include *yong tau fu*, stuffed bean curd and vegetables with a sauce for dipping, while Szechuanese dishes are fiery and use chilis and garlic. Hainanese chicken rice is a bland but popular favorite as a midday repast.

More interesting yet is **Nonya cuisine**, an original and spicy blend of Chinese and Malay cooking. *Nonya* is the local term for a Straitsborn Chinese woman (*Baba* is the male equivalent). Although Nonyas are notorious for jealously guarding their family recipes from generation to generation, there are some modest restaurants in K.L. now serving authentic Nonya dishes. Most of the recipes begin with a generous helping of *rempah* (mixture of ground spices), which are considered a matter of *agak* (estimation) by the cook at hand. Some of the more recognized dishes are curry *kapitan*, an unusual chicken curry; *otak otak*, a sort of fish pâté flavored with spice and coconut cream and wrapped in leaves and grilled; *inche kabin*, a spicy deep-fried chicken; and *poh piah*, a savory stuffed pancake.

★**Indian food** available in Kuala Lumpur represents both northern and southern traditions. Northern cuisine is rather more fitting to the Western palate; it tends to be less hot and pungent. Tandoori chicken and *nan*, a flat bread baked in a round clay oven, are world-renowned dishes. There are plenty of Moghul-inspired curries available as well as the other breads (*chappatis* and *puris*) to go with them. Southern Indian cooking is more available in K.L. and many local coffee shops offer rice with hot curries served on banana leaves (consumed without utensils). For breakfast, try *dosal*, a pancake served with coconut chutney, or one of the many vegetarian dishes always on the menu. Afficionados of Indian Muslim food should not miss the many restaurants along Jalan Tuanku Abdul Rahman in the capital.

There are many elegant **European-style** restaurants, a few with real U.S.-bred steaks, a growing number of Thai and Japanese eateries and the inevitable fast-food chains that are slowly overtaking the good taste of the world. Hamburger, french fries and a milk shake anyone? You wouldn't really waste a dinner at the *Hard Rock Cafe* or *McDonalds, Kentucky Fried Chicken*, or *A&W* would you?

WHERE TO EAT IN KUALA LUMPUR

Malay Restaurants

Budaya Restaurant and Snack Bar
Lorong Medan Tuanku Satu, Jalan Tuanku Abdul Rahman. ☎ *2921381.*

The Hut
Shah's Village, Lorong Sultan, Petaling Jaya. ☎ *2569322.*

Indahku
3rd Floor, Kuwasa Building, Jalan Raja Laut. ☎ *2931372.*

Rasa Utara
Bukit Bintang Plaza, Jalan Bukit Bintang. ☎ *2438324.*

Satay Aneka
kit Bintang Plaza, Jalan Bukit Bintang. ☎ 2483113.

Satay 'n' Steak House
Ground Floor, Wisma Central. ☎ 2420570.

Yasmin Restaurant
Ampang Park Shopping Complex. Jalan Ampang. ☎ 2415605. One of the best in town.

Warong Rasa Sayang
Jalan Raja Muda Musa. ☎ 2923009.

Chinese Restaurants

Dragon Court Hotel Merlin
Jalan Sultan Ismail. ☎ 2480033.

Fatt Yow Yuen
Jalan Balai Polis. ☎ 2480491. Vegetarian.

Golden Phoenix
Hotel Equatorial, Jalan Sultan Ismail. ☎ 2422022.

Inn of Happiness
Kuala Lumpur Hilton, Jalan Sultan Ismail. ☎ 2422122.

Imperial Room
Malaysia Hotel, Jalan Bukit Bintang. ☎ 2427862.

Kuala Lumpur Restaurant
Hotel Malaya, Jalan Cecil. ☎ 2427721.

Kum Leng
119 Jalan Pudu. ☎ 2483637.

Mandarin Palace
Federal Hotel, Jalan Bukit Bintang. ☎ 2427701.

Marco Polo Restaurant
1st Floor, Wisma Lim Foo Yong Jalan Raja Chulan. ☎ 2425595.

Metro Restaurant
3rd Floor, Wisma MPI Jalan Raja Chulan. ☎ 2424505.

Ming Court
Town House Hotel, Jalan Tong Shin. ☎ 2424273.

Rasa Sayang Seafood
Jalan Imbi. ☎ 2439890. Outdoor dining in relaxed ambience.

The Pines
297 Jalan Brickfields. ☎ 2741194.

The Plaza Court Chinese Restaurant
Plaza Hotel, Jalan Raja Laut. ☎ 2920535.

Indian Restaurants

Akbar
>   *Medan Tuanku, Jalan Tuanku Bdul Rahman.* ☎ *2920366.*

The Bangles
>   *Jalan Tuanku Abdul Rahman.* ☎ *2983780.*

Bilal
>   *33 Jalan Ampang.* ☎ *2320804.*

Ceylon Restaurant
>   *Malay Street.* ☎ *2924708.*

Devi Restaurant
>   *Jalan Brickfields.* ☎ *2485505.*

Kassim
>   *53 Jalan Tuanku Abdul Rahman.* ☎ *2928240.*

Shiraz
>   *Medan Tuanku Abdul Rahman 7.* ☎ *2910035.*

Simla Restaurant
>   *95 Jalan Ampang.* ☎ *2328539.*

Vazeer Restaurant
>   *147A Jalan Imbi.* ☎ *2840744.*

Western Restaurants

Castell Pub & Grill
>   *81 Jalan Bukit Bintang.* ☎ *2428328.* One of the big favorites among the expatriates and visiting foreigners.

Chalet Restaurant
>   *Hotel Equatorial, Jalan Sultan Ismail.* ☎ *2422022.* Swiss cuisine.

Cock & Bull Steak House
>   *Jalan Bukit Biatang.* ☎ *2422855.*

Hacienda Grill
>   *Hotel Fortuna, Jalan Berangan.* ☎ *2419111.*

Kontiki Room
>   *Merlin Hotel, Jalan Sultan Ismail.* ☎ *2489166.*

La Terrasse
>   *243 Jalan Ampang.* ☎ *4573803.* Fine classic French cuisine served in a former colonial villa, about a 10-minute ride from the city center.

Le Coq d'Or
>   *121 Jalan Ampang.* ☎ *2429732.* A good choice for quaint atmosphere and delicious, Continental cooking.

L'Espresso
>   *G22 Wisma Stephens, Jalan Raja Chulan.* ☎ *2413669.*

Melaka Grill

Kuala Lumpur Hilton, Jalan Sultan Ismail. ☎ *2422122.* May be the best restaurant in K.L., complete with gorgeous surroundings.

The Ship

10-1 Jalan Sultan Ismail. ☎ *2418805.*

NIGHTLIFE IN KUALA LUMPUR

There's a surprisingly healthy nightlife scene in K.L. Typically, the more upscale hotels offer the best in international-type discos.

Campbell Nightclub and Music Hall

Jalan Campbell. ☎ *2929655.*

Epitome

Petaling Jaya Hilton, Petaling Jaya. ☎ *2553533.*

Federal Club

Federal Hotel, Jalan Bukit Bintang. ☎ *2489166.*

High Voltage

Massdisco LB29, Lower Basement 2, Sungei Wang Plaza. ☎ *2421220.*

Kira's Nite Club

Bangunan Angkasaraya. ☎ *2420556.*

Pertama Cabaret

Pertama Complex, Jalan. Tuanku Abdul Rahman. ☎ *2982533.*

Pink Coconut

Hotel Malaya, Jalan Cecil. ☎ *2232772.*

Pyramid Club

3rd Floor, Wilayah Shopping Complex, Jalan Munshi Abdullah. ☎ *2923092.*

Sapphire

Plaza Yow Chuan, Jalan Tun Abdul Razak. ☎ *2430043.*

Shangri-La Night Club

Bangunan Hentian Puduraya. ☎ *2321174.*

Sky Swan Nightclub

22 Jalan Tong Shin. ☎ *2420233.*

Starship Disco

Wisma Central, Jalan Ampang. ☎ *2427581.*

The Cave

Jalan Ampang. ☎ *2481589.*

Tin Mine

Kuala Lumpur Hilton, Jalan Sultan Ismail. ☎ *2422222.*

Toppan Club

Wisma Stephens, Jalan Raja Chulan. ☎ *2489304.*

Traqs

Wisma Central, Jalan Ampang. ☎ *2426529.*

Malacca

The mouth of the Malacca River was significantly wider during the Portuguese and Dutch periods of the 16th and 17th centuries.

MALACCA IN A CAPSULE

City of Living History...125 miles northwest of Singapore...2- to 3-hour's drive from Kuala Lumpur...founded in 1403 by a fugitive prince and named after Malacca tree...seat of a Malay kingdom...Islam entered the peninsula from here...Portuguese arrived in 1511 and were supreme for about 130 years...Dutch took sovereignty in 1641 and lasted for 150 years...British destroyed A Famosa, largest fortress in the East in 1807...won Malacca in Treaty of Holland in 1824 and made it part of their Straits Settlements crown colony in 1867...100,000 people now inhabit this remarkable, much fought over trading post...most of them Straits-born Chinese (Nonya and Baba) plus large Portuguese Eurasian settlement who speak Cristao, a medieval dialect from the 16th century.

Malacca (or Melaka) is one of the great historical cities of Southeast Asia. Not in a monumental way but more for being the focal point for six centuries of soldiers, conquerers and traders. This was one of the first homes of the Chinese traders in 1405, then a colonial prize that went to the the Portugese in 1509, the Dutch in 1641, the British in 1795, back to the Dutch in 1807, back again to the Empire in 1824 and then to the Japanese during WWII; it finally became a part of Malaysia in the 1960s. Although most of what was built was destroyed, there is still the dark ancient patina of history around every corner that makes it the most historic city in Malaysia.

Malacca is also a city made for exploring on foot. Wander down the crooked streets packed with tumbledown houses, temples and shops. Stop and admire the way people have carved out their lives in a pattern of history. Take pictures of the fanciful architecture, share a joke with a Chinese merchant and just enjoy the people and feeling of Malacca.

WHAT TO SEE AND DO IN MALACCA

Baba Nyonya Heritage
Lovely old home at 50 Jalan Tun Tan Cheng Lock; museum of artifacts and lifestyle to preserve diminishing community of *Babas* and *Nonyas*; Chinese men and women born in the Straits; full of 19th-century Nonya wares and furniture of blackwood or namwood inlaid with mother of pearl, or embroidery designed backs; also carved floral and pictorial motifs; ask for Mr. Chan—great-grandson of original owner—to guide you; tours at 10 a.m., 11:30 a.m., 2 p.m. and 3:30 p.m.; small admission fee; ☎ *06-2222065.*

Bukit China
China Hill; site of first Chinese community in Malacca; hill is a gift from Sultan Mansur Shah (c. 1460) to his Chinese princess and her 500 ladies-in-waiting; some of oldest Chinese relics in Malaysia are here. With *Bukit Gedong* and *Bukit Tempurong,* it forms the largest Chinese cemetery outside the mainland; more than 106 acres; *Perigi Raja*, or Sultan's Well, at foot of Bukit China is said to possess an extraordinary purity; person who drinks from it will return to Malacca; you may also throw a coin.

Cheng Hoon Teng Temple
Oldest Chinese temple in Malaysia; plaque commemorates A.D. 1406 visit of Admiral Cheng Ho, envoy of Ming Emperor; one of the most traveled and celebrated figures in Chinese history of the time; gables and eaves richly decorated with figures from Chinese mythology; porcelain and glass carvings inside welcome visitors.

Church of St. Peter

Built in 1710; known for its unusual facade that mixes Oriental and Occidental architecture; testimony to numerous cultures in Malacca during its heyday; stained-glass windows of note and ancient tombstones within.

Church of St. Paul's

Atop Residency Hill, overlooking famous Straits of Malacca; built in 16th century; apparently used by St. Francis Xavier during his visit to Malacca; considered another relic of early Portuguese era; although the Dutch gave it its present name; only the walls remain, along with memorials and tombs of Dutch notables; lovely spot to just rest and contemplate after the hefty climb!

Malacca's 18th century Dutch-built First Christ Church

First Christ Church

Built in 1752; one of the town's many unusual salmon-colored buildings dating from the Dutch era; built of bricks from Middleburg, Zeeland and covered with red laterite; features louvered windows topped with fan-shaped decorations; heavy wooden doors and tiled roof; interior most interesting; antique silver vessels bear Dutch coat of arms; today the church is Anglican.

Jalan Gelenggang   ★★

Formerly called Jonker Street; narrow, one-way street full of trishaws and bicycles; known world-over for antique shops and dilapidated shops featuring Peranakan architecture (symbolic of earliest Chinese settlers in Malaya); lots of junk stores here, too; good if you know your stuff; you must obtain an export permit from the Director General of the National Museum in Kuala Lumpur.

Malacca River

A mere shadow of its former self; it must have been quite strong and wide during the 17th century to have brought so many traders to the port; walk across the bridge at Jalan Gelanggang and use your imagination to recapture the romance and adventure that took place here centuries ago.

Porta de Santiago

Gateway to **A Famosa**; greatest Portuguese fortress built in the East in the 16th century; fell to the Dutch in 1641 and almost totally devastated by British in 1807; only this gateway stands; the Dutch East India Company's coat of arms still intact.

Stadthuys

Oldest building of Dutch origin in the East; salmon-colored City Hall built between 1641 and 1660; thick masonry walls and heavy hardwood doors; windows with wrought-iron hinges have stood the test of time; dominates main square just as it has for almost 3-1/4 centuries; one of Malacca's most photographed landmarks; everyone must witness the clock tower at noon; also houses the **Malacca Museum**; a gentle view of the past and some artifacts from the ancient Malays and Chinese as well as the intruders—Portuguese, Dutch and British. Open daily; admission charge.

Strait of Malacca

Narrow channel of water between Malay Peninsula and Sumatra; on the route from Indian Ocean to South China Sea; monsoon winds meet at the mouth of the Malacca River; most favorable spot for ships from East and Middle East to meet and exchange goods; Joseph Conrad sailed through these straits at age 25 just before his ship blew up off Bangka Island, Sumatra; led him to write "the East of the ancient navigators, so old, so mysterious, resplendent and somber; living and unchanged, full of danger and promise."

Tranquerah Mosque

Built about 150 years ago; Sumatran design; provides a link to British colonial era in Malacca; within mosque lies tomb of Sultan of Johor, who signed cession of Singapore to Sir Thomas Stamford Raffles in 1819.

WHERE TO STAY IN MALACCA

City Bayview Hotel Melaka ★★★★

Jalan Bendahara. ☎ *239888. FAX: 236699* • *182 rooms.* Deluxe rooms and balconies on Executive Floor have views of the Straits of Malacca; elegant public areas. Five restaurants serving Chinese-Szechuan and international cuisines. Poolside bar. Health club with gym, massage, sauna, steambath. Swimming pool. Business center. Meeting rooms.
Reservations: Utell.

Malacca Village Park Plaza Resort
Ayer Keroh. ☎ *323600. FAX: 325955 • 147 rooms.* Opened in 1983. Malacca dining room. Japanese restaurant. 2 bars. Swimming pool. Tennis, squash and health club. The Club. Businessman's center.

Reservations: Utell.

Melaka Renaissance Hotel ★★★★
Japan Bendahara, P.O. Box 105. ☎ *248888. FAX: 249269 • 295 rooms.* 24-story high-rise in heart of Malacca; only luxury hotel in town until Shangri-La opens; special Renaissance Floor (23rd) with club room, lounge, continental breakfast, etc. Taming Sari grill. Famosa lounge. Long Feng Cantonese restaurant. Summerfield's coffee shop. Stardust disco. Health center. Squash courts. Business center. Malacca Garden swimming pool, bar and restaurant. Bunga Raya ballroom.

Reservations: Ramada Int'l.

Shah's Beach Resort Hotel
6th mile Tanjong Keling. ☎ *511120. FAX: 511088 • 50 chalets.* Very restful. Open-air dining room. Bar. Swimming pool. Lovely private beach. Boating and watersports. Out-of-town location.

Reservations: VIP Reservations ☎ (800-822-8101).

Penang

PENANG IN A CAPSULE

Pulau Pinang, or Island of the Betel Nut; one of Malaysia's 13 states...situated just 3 to 13 km off mainland from Butterworth...once an uninhabited hideout for pirates plundering ships leaving Malacca...natural harbor attracted British captain, Francis Light...negotiated lease of island from Sultan Abdullah of Kedah in 1786...Light built Fort Cornwallis and named capital Georgetown after King George III...Penang became first British settlement in Straits of Malacca...and first member of crown colony...British left their colonial architecture but Chinese, Indians, Arabs and indigenous Malays have contributed their own flavor and culture to the island...today it is one vast melting pot of Asia with 500,000 inhabitants...one of most popular resorts in the Far East...beautiful beaches...interesting sights...friendly, no-hurry people...calls itself Pearl of the Orient.

British history abounds on this cosmopolitan island. There's Fort Cornwallis and other areas where the colonial architecture gives you the impression you're in quite a different part of the world than the Orient.

Because of the island's booming popularity with tourists and the construction of the Penang Bridge, both the beaches and the ocean have become dirtier in recent years; the coral at Batu Ferringhi, the most popular beach on the island, has all but vanished. But there have been some efforts to clean the area up. The hotels along the strip at Batu Ferringhi, for instance, are highly protective of their own beachfront areas. The northwest part of Penang possesses perhaps the best and least crowded beaches on the island. The southern part of Penang also has some decent beaches.

Georgetown, the provincial capital on the northeast coast of the island, is a bustling, creative community comprised primarily of Chinese. It is a college town and home to many of Malaysia's most influential artists, writers and intellectuals.

There are myriad shops and great places to eat in Georgetown and it can be toured easily on foot or by trishaw. Or you can rent a bike.

It seems half the visitors to this popular resort destination are here on vacation and the other half, expats living in Thailand, here to get their visas renewed. If you've got to leave Thailand for a few days, Penang's a pretty good place to wait it out.

WHAT TO SEE AND DO IN PENANG

Batu Ferringhi Beach

Foreigner's Rock is the draw for most visitors; a most beautiful silver beach along the island's northern coastline; many luxury hotels; sumptuous food at open-air restaurants; watersports; artists and galleries; sunseekers from all over the world; Europeans during the winter months; Australians during the summer; Americans from the oil fields of Indonesia year-round; great for a few days at a time; a regular call for many luxury cruise ships.

Batu Maung

Shrine dedicated to Admiral Cheng Ho; famous envoy of Ming Emperor whom overseas Chinese later deified and gave the religious name of Sam Po; although history says he was just a bejeweled eunuch of the Ming Court who spent far too much time traveling; located at southern tip of Penang; about 3 km from Bayan Lepas Airport; near small fishing village of Batu Maung; early inhabitants believed Admiral Ho left his footprint here; another footprint can be found on Langkawi Island to the north; both are supposed to bring good luck to those who light joss sticks.

Botanical Gardens

Considered among the finest in Malaysia; located about 8 km from center of Georgetown in lovely 75-acre valley surrounded by jungled hills; green rolling lawns, secluded lily ponds, ornamental pools; tropical flowering plants of every variety; children love to feed the friendly monkeys that roam around.

Clock Tower

A relic of the colonial period; located next to Fort Cornwallis, the tower was presented to Penang by Cheah Chin Gok; to commemorate the diamond jubilee of Queen Victoria; also known as empress of all Eastern colonies.

Fort Cornwallis

Originally built of wood by Captain Light; rebuilt between 1808 and 1810 by convict labor; pretty much as it stands today; although local children play on the ramparts; includes cannon called Meriam Timbul; presented to the Dutch by sultan of Johor in 1606; later captured by Portuguese; spent some time in Java; then captured by pirates and thrown into Straits of Malacca; brought up from the bottom in 1880 and taken to Selangor; eventually found its way to Penang; Malaysians call it the "traveling cannon."

Guillemard Reservoir

Located on Mount Erskine; a lovely spot and often viewed first by passengers flying into Bayan Lepas Airport; reservoir surrounded by casuarina trees; artfully planted.

Kapitan Kling Temple
Pitt Street; built around 1800 by Indian Moslem merchant, Cauder Mohudeen, also known as Kling Kapitan (headman); occupies site of first mosque in Penang; dome-shaped minaret reflects Islamic architecture of Moorish influence.

Kek Lok Si Temple
Finest and largest in Southeast Asia; entire complex known as "Monastery of the Western Paradise of the Pure Land Sect of Buddhism;" built from 1890 to 1910; actually a series of altars built along the hillslopes of Ayer Itam; midway between the village and the dam of the same name; complex dominated by **Ban Hood Pagoda**; also known as "10,000 Precious Buddhas Pagoda;" 7-stories high and filled with images of Lord Buddha from various parts of the world; building itself is influenced by Thai, Burmese and Chinese architecture; a complicated and interesting place; great tourist attraction; crowded with devoted Chinese on weekends and holidays.

Khoo Kongsi
Khoo clan house located near Cannon Square in Georgetown; *kongsis* or clan houses originated in China centuries ago; they were associations for people with the same surname. *Leong San Tong* (the Dragon Mountain Hall) of this structure is considered most elaborate and elegant of its kind in Malaysia; rich carvings and decorations and architecture reflect influence of ancient China; 200 members of Khoo clan began construction on the house around 1835 and it went through a series of designs; the first considered far too ostentatious for mere mortals; took 8 years to complete; Khoos came from China to Penang around the turn of the 19th century.

Kuan Yin Ting
Goddess of Mercy Temple on Pitt Street; Penang's oldest Chinese temple; one of its most humble; attracts working-class devotees; built in 1800 by the first Chinese settlers; dedicated to the most popular of Chinese gods who is revered by Buddhists, Taoists and Confucianists at the same time; also houses the God of Prosperity; very popular at holiday time when joss sticks are lit to tempt good luck through coming year; lots of festivities around Kuan Yin's birthday on March 17.

Malay Mosque
On Acheen Street; known for finely balanced minaret; reminiscent of Egyptian architecture; quite a departure from Moorish influences brought by Indians to Penang.

Nattukkotai Temple
On Waterfall Road; largest Hindu temple in Penang; dedicated to Bala Subramaniam; in front of the shrine is a peacock given to Subramaniam by mother Parvathi; important rites and ceremonies here during Thaipusam festival.

Peng Buddhist Association

Modern-looking structure on Anson Road built in 1929; considered Buddhism's most serene shrine in Penang; 7-tiered pagoda at entrance; shrine hall is filled with devotees reciting prayers to 6 huge Carrara-marble statues of Lord Buddha and his disciples; under glass chandeliers from Czechoslovakia; teak tables inlaid with mother-of-pearl from China hold offerings.

Penang-Butterworth Ferry

A 24-hour ferry service operates between Weld Quay in Georgetown and Butterworth; the 4 km ride is free from the mainland to Pulau Pinang (island of Betelnut Palms) and costs just a few pennies on the return to the mainland; ferry also transports bicycles, motorcycles, cars and commercial vehicles.

Penang Hill

Rises some 830 meters in the middle of the island; considered one of Malaysia's 6 hill resorts; but I think it's more suitable as a day trip; take the 30-minute funicular railway journey from 6:30 a.m. to 9:30 p.m. for a cool and refreshing change; temperature drops to at least 65 degrees during the day; lovely place to view the city of Georgetown and have a pleasant meal or drink; service on the funicular extended until midnight on Wed. and Sat. nights.

Penang Museum and Art Gallery

Located in interesting colonial structure on Farquar Street; fine collection of historical documents including the will of Captain Francis Light; Chinese carvings and furniture; Chinese room, bridal chamber, island room, Tunku Abdul Rahman room; art gallery on first floor has batiks, oils, lithographs and Chinese ink drawings plus exhibitions by Malay artists throughout year; open 9 a.m. to 5 p.m. daily (except Sun.); free admission.

Snake Temple

Also known as Temple of the Azure Cloud; located about 5 km north of Bayan Lepas Airport; dedicated to deity Chor Soo Kong; contains poisonous snakes who are not supposed to bite; Buddhist devotees pet and coddle them; are even photographed with them; snakes allegedly made drowsy during the day due to incense fumes; become themselves at night; temple very busy and colorful during Chinese New Year festivities.

Siva Mariamman Temple

On Dato Keramat Road; dedicated to the third God of Hindu Trinity; worshiped as a preserver, destroyer and creator all at once; priests chant their prayers at sunset to beat of drums and pipes.

Sri Mariamman Temple

On Queen Street; dedicated to the Hindu goddess of Mariamman; she is bedecked with gold and silver, not to mention precious stones of diamonds and emeralds; quite a sight.

St. George's Church

Located on Farquhar Street; built in 1818; considered the oldest Anglican church in Southeast Asia; architect was Captain R. Smith; British colonial officer whose etchings of early life in Penang can be seen at the museum; built by convict labor; memorial canopy to Captain Francis Light on front porch; see also double-spired Cathedral of the Assumption and Christian Cemetery along the same street.

Telok Bahang Forest Recreation Park

About 22 km from Georgetown; about 250 acres of park surrounded by jungle; designed for people's recreation as well as to preserve trees; also a center for botany and zoology; has arboretum and forest museum; freshwater pools, footpaths, Malaysian-style rest huts and children's playground; open from 8 a.m. to 6 p.m. daily; free admission.

Wat Chayamangkalaram

Thai Buddhist Temple; houses third largest reclining Buddha in the world (108 feet); behind statue are niches where ashes of devotees are stored; photography not allowed inside temple; interesting Thai architecture.

Penang Environs

Alor Setar

Alor Setar is the capital of the state of Kedah. It's also known as Malaysia's rice bowl. Visit **Balai Besar**, the Great Hall where the sultan of Kedah still holds ceremonial functions. Also see the *padang*, the green square in the middle of town. The **Zahir Mosque** is considered one of the most beautiful in the country. There is interesting old and new architecture here.

★ *Gunong Jerai*

Here rises Kedah Peak, the highest mountain in the northwest at 1202 meters. It welcomes climbers and adventurers; also amateur or professional archaeologists. More than 40 archaeological sites have been discovered on its slopes. Studies include the migrations of Hindus from India to this peninsula.

★★ *Pulau Langkawi*

This is a chain of 99 islands lying off the northwest coast of peninsular Malaysia. They offer some of the most beautiful scenery in the entire country. They're quiet and secluded. The area is called the Land of Legends. Visit **Tasek Dayang Bunting** (Lake of Pregnant Maiden), a freshwater lake on Dayang Bunting, second largest island in the chain. Also see the **Tomb of Mahsuri, Gua Cherita** (cave of stories), the **Seven Pools** and **Gua Langsir** (cave of marble-shaped pebbles). The largest island is Langkawi; its people have both Thai and Malay origins. The islands are a 40-minute air ride from Penang. They offer great beaches, fishing and watersports. Check out the Langkawi Country Club, which is operated by TDC and offers 100 rooms on 100 acres. There's tennis, golf and riding; a first-class international resort.

Pulau Pangkor

Pangkor Island is a peaceful and lovely parcel of land off the southern coast of Perak State. This is another former pirate hangout which was ceded to Britain by the Sultan of Perak in 1876. It's now just a cluster of charming villages that rely on fishing. There are few international tourists and it doesn't have a "swinging" reputation. It is reachable from the peninsula through Lumut. The ferry makes the 35-minute voyage several times daily. There are a few interesting accommodations on the island, including the Seaview Hotel at Pasir Bogak, the Princess Hotel on Oyster Bay and the Pangkor Laut Resort. There's also a somewhat dilapidated government rest house used chiefly on weekend outings by local university students.

WHERE TO STAY IN PENANG

Bayview Beach Hotel   ★★
Batu Ferringhi. ☎ *812123. FAX: 812140 • 74 rooms.* Dining room. Bar. Freshwater swimming pool with sunken bar. Private beach. Tennis and badminton.   *Reservations: Utell.*

Casuarina Beach Hotel   ★★★
Batu Ferringhi. ☎ *811711. FAX: 812155 • 175 rooms.* Dining room. Coffeehouse. Swimming pool. Tennis and badminton. Children's playground. Private beach and watersports.   *Reservations: Utell.*

Eastern & Oriental Hotel   ★★

10 Farquhar Street. ☎ *635222. FAX: 634833 • 100 rooms.* A great view of the bay; central Georgetown location; very Old World atmosphere. Two restaurants. Cocktail lounge. 2 bars. Swimming pool.
Reservations: Specialty Tours (☎ *800-421-3913).*

Hotel Equatorial   ★★★
1 Jalan Bukit Jambul, 11900. ☎ *838111. FAX: 848000 • 415 rooms.* One of the new hotels built for Penang's busy convention trade; not on the beach but adjoining an 18-hole golf course; Japanese, French and Chinese restaurants plus a 24-hour coffee shop; tennis and squash courts with a health club.   *Reservations: Utell.*

Ferringhi Beach Hotel   ★★★
Batu Ferringhi Rd., 11100 Batu Ferringhi. ☎ *805999. FAX: 805100 • 350 rooms.* One of the newer hotels on Penang's most popular

beaches; sits on a hill overlooking the water; there is a pool, health spa and disco, as well as Continental and local cuisine.

Reservations: Utell.

Holiday Inn Penang   ★★
Batu Ferringhi Beach, Penang. *811601. FAX: 811389 • 165 rooms.* Baron's Table German gourmet restaurant. Rock Garden cocktail lounge. Matahari seafood terrace. Mutiara coffee house/sidewalk cafe. Bayan bar. Pool Deck. Penthouse Garden suites. Watersports.

Reservations: Holiday Inn.

Palm Beach Resort Hotel   ★★
Batu Ferringhi Beach, Penang. *811621. FAX: 811051• 145 rooms.* Located on beach between Rasa Sayang and Golden Sands; under same management; considered their budget hotel. Watersports. Beach terrace. Swimming pools, tennis, etc., next door. Special food festivals in evening. Meeting facilities.   *Reservations: Shangri-La Int'l.*

Penang Mutiara Beach Hotel   ★★★★
1 Jalan Teluk Bahang. *812828. FAX: 812829 • 442 rooms.* Beach-front hotel. Modern, well-equipped rooms with balconies. Chinese, Japanese, Italian and seafood restaurants. 24-hour Garden Terrace, two lounges and a disco. Fitness center with steamroom and sauna, Jacuzzi, massage. Two swimming pools, four squash courts, volleyball, netball, four tennis courts, jogging tracks, watersports. Golf nearby. Conference and banquet rooms.   *Reservations: Utell, JAL.*

Shangri-La Golden Sands Hotel   ★★★★
Batu Ferringhi Beach, P.O. Box 222, Penang. *811911. FAX: 811880 • 389 rooms.* Situated on the island's best stretch of beach; all rooms with balconies; lovely landscaped gardens; many social activities and special events in the evening; barbecues, steamboat dinners, Chinese buffet and Malam Pulau Pinang—local cuisine plus music and dance. Bunga Raya restaurant for Chinese/Malay/Indian food. The Grill continental menu. Coffee House terrace. Kuda Laut bar by free-form swimming pool. Sunset lounge. Watersports.

Reservations: Shangri-La Int'l.

Shangri-La Hotel Penang   ★★★★
Victoria St., Georgetown, Penang. **☎** *622622. FAX: 626526 • 426 rooms (16 suites).* 18-story hotel located in heart of Penang's shopping district; spacious lobby faces Magazine Road. Chinese restaurant. Coffee house. Lobby lounge. Swimming pool and poolside bar. Health center. Business center. Ballroom and meeting rooms.

Reservations: Shangri-La Int'l.

Shangri-La Rasa Sayang Hotel   ★★★★
Batu Ferringhi Beach, P.O. Box 735, Penang. *811811. FAX: 811984 • 305 rooms (13 suites).* Ferringhi Grill. Furusato Japanese restaurant.

Coffee Garden. Tepi Laut bar. Cinta, a Juliana's of London disco. Meeting rooms. Executive center. Swimming pool and all water-sports.   *Reservations: Shangri-La Int'l.*

SAMPLING LOCAL FARE IN PENANG

Penang's multi-racial population offers the adventurous eater a vast array of tastes and native specialties. Because it is an island, you can dream of the succulence that comes from the sea; there are many casual seafood restaurants along the beaches at **Tanjong Tokong** that feature crab, prawns and several varieties of freshly caught grilled fish.

In the evening, mobile foodstalls crowd **Padang Brown**, **Gelugor Road**, **Gurney Drive**, or along the **Esplanade** in Georgetown. Their tempting aromas indicate that the national pleasure—*satay*—is in the vicinity. These tender bits of chicken or beef are skewered and barbecued, then dipped into a spicy peanut and chili sauce. You should also try *kari kapitan*—tender pieces of chicken cooked with coconut milk, sugar, oil and lemon juice and served with the ever-present staple, rice. Anyone interested in beef noodles in a delicious broth and topped with bits and pieces of things should venture over to Victoria Street and demand *goo bak kway teow.*

Nonya-type food (belonging to the Straits-born Chinese) is a frequent specialty throughout the island of Penang; no dish is more popular than *laksa assam*, a creation of rice noodles in a sourish fish-based soup. Tamarind, onions, chilis, shrimp paste and mint leaves are added to the broth—which is then poured over a bowl of special white *laksa* noodles. Shredded cucumber and slices of an edible, fragrant, pink flower known as *bunga kantan* are sprinkled on top while the concoction is very hot.

Laksa lemak—originally a Thai dish—is slightly milder in taste than *laksa assam*, because coconut milk is used instead of tamarind. However, the ingredients are basically the same.

Nasi kandar is what the Malaysians call a meal-on-a-plate; it's quite special to Penang. Available at open-air stalls or local coffee shops, it is a plate of steaming white rice on which as many beef, chicken, fish, shellfish and vegetable curries as you choose have been added—a nutritious, filling and inexpensive meal.

Visitors may also be interested in the local pizza, called *murtabak*. It is the Indian-style flatbread filled with mutton and onions and usually served with *dhal*, a mild curry cooked with *brinjals* (white beans). Another fun dish (and great ice-breaker) is steamboat, the Malaysian equivalent of a fondue. A pot of boiling water is placed in the center of the table and guests cook their own assortment of meat, seafood and vegetables as they wish. Later, the broth from the cooking pot is served as a soup to aid the digestion.

Western food is readily available at the major hotels, like the **E & O**, **Merlin**, **Holiday Inn**, **Golden Sands** and **Rasa Sayang** out at Batu Ferringhi; but Penang is a town where you should strike out and enjoy the local foodstalls and small hideaways that line the streets. In the evening, there is plenty of action at hotels in Georgetown or down at the beach, where plenty of visitors from the Western world come to have a good time. At the **Eden Restaurant** you can catch cultural shows daily.

Sabah

Panar Laban resthouse at more than 3,300m atop Mt. Kinabalu

SABAH IN A CAPSULE

Land Below the Wind...so-called by early Sulu pirates because the area is south of the typhoon belt...formerly British North Borneo...known for Mt. Kinabalu (13,450 feet)...highest peak in Southeast Asia...beautiful national parks...Gomantong Caves for edible birds' nests...Sepilok Orangutan Sanctuary...coral beaches and offshore islands...Bajau sea gypsies, Illanun pirates, Kadazan farmers, Murat blowpipe hunters, Rungu villages with stilt houses, Muruts who live in longhouses, etc....plus mix of Malay, Chinese and Hindus...colorful and interesting spot to visit...reachable by air from peninsular Malaysia and other Southeast Asian cities...one of the future eco and adventure tourism hotspots.

Welcome to the wild east. One can imagine America in the 1890s having much of the appeal of Sabah in the 1990s. Tattooed ex-head-hunters stroll down hastily constructed towns next to young Chinese businessmen on their cellular phones. Air-conditioned shopping malls are minutes away from virgin rainforest. Towering mountains, dark swamps, massive caves are all within a half-day's drive of the main city, Kota Kinabalu. Not as exotic as Sarawak, more rugged than the mainland, Sabah is home to an industrious and forward thinking people. Everyone seems to have business here; hotels and transportation are expensive, designed more for business travelers than tourists. The road system is evolving from logging roads to paved highways and tourism is a relatively new but rapidly growing industry.

There are many fortunes to be made here in the next decade and it seems exporting raw timber will probably be one of the most popular. So you better be fast if you want to discover the mythical, verdant island of Borneo. They are cutting the great canopy forests down as fast as they can. The only hope is that the impact of tourism will provide an alternative source of income to slow the rapid loss of one of the world's great ecosystems.

We don't recommend driving around Sabah unless you have a sturdy 4WD vehicle, a good guide and like to eat dust and dodge 50-ton logging trucks. Malaysian Air Service usually has a special fare for travel between airports in Sabah and Sarawak. Once you arrive, taxis can be hired for an entire day. They will take care of your luggage, recommend bad restaurants and laugh at your jokes. Local tour operators are also a good deal since they usually are just like you (and your companions) and prefer to avoid nasty surprises (like getting lost on new logging roads).

WHAT TO SEE AND DO IN SABAH

Batu Punggul   ★

You will always remember the impressive sight of Batu Punggul as it looms out of the mist. The 200m-high white rock is a massive ridge of karst that is punctured by **spectacular caves** and fissures. There are also a variety of jungle walks. You can climb the rock (leave early!) or explore the impressive caves. If you're squeamish about wading in about 1-2 feet of bat droppings, cockroaches, spiders or bats, you may want to pass. The caves are large, open to the light and very interesting. Recently opened to visitors is a KPD (Korperasi Pembangunan Desa or local development agency) rest house. There is also a very nice replica of a Murut longhouse. Arrange a tour at KPD, Inanam at the corner of Jalan Tuaran and Jalan Kelombong; ☎ *(088) 428910,* ext. *240.* If you can get to Sapulot there may be a chance to arrange a boat up the river. It's actually cheaper to book a tour. They typically like to book the tour for groups so they can drag the nearby villagers up to put on a cultural show for you. After you have done your obligatory *taipai* chugging contest and made a fool out of yourself on the *lansaran* (an ingenious native trampoline), they will leave you in relative peace as the villagers polish off the rest of the rice wine. Boats from Sapulot to Batu Punggul are M250 per boat (maximum 6). Don't bring too much luggage. You will need a guide for jungle trekking, M20 to see the caves and M30 to climb the rock.

Beaufort

100m from KK, Beaufort is a curious backwater town known more for being the terminus of the ancient railway built in 1905. The tiny railroad only carries about 10-12 passengers and hobbles between Beaufort and Tenom. What makes the 2-hour trip worthwhile is the view of the Padas river and its gorge. (The front seats have the best views.) After you have seen how angry the river is, you may want to think twice about arranging a **white water rafting** tour out of KK. If you wondered why the old wooden buildings near the river are so high off the ground it is because of the flooding during the heavy monsoons. There is a market on Saturdays.

There are a handful of simple Chinese-run hotels in Beaufort—the Beaufort and the Padas across from the fishmarket. We recommend the Beaufort for obvious reasons.

Danum Valley

How can a logging company also be a social agency *and* the owner of a large forested park? Easy, when that company is the Sabah Foundation. Despite my incessant criticism of logging practices in Borneo, I have to praise Clive Marsh and the Sabah Foundation. Clive worked to create this area to find new and better ways of forest management. To do this, he has invited scientists from around the world to help him. By doing so, he has also made it very difficult for anyone to cut down his 438-sq.-km outdoor laboratory. You can stay in the simple visitors' quarters, which may be full of visiting schoolchildren or crane-necked birdwatchers. Meals are served and you will bump into the scientists (who work across the way and live up the road) at coffeebreaks or teatime. They study everything from ants to orangutan nests and are a storehouse of knowledge, as well as pleasant company. There are 220 species of birds here alone. They have yet to identify all the tree species.

INSIDER TIP

Don't be too impressed by the number of species rattled off in nature guides. Asian forests may have a high diversity of species but a low biomass. This means you will be amazed at the species you see but unlike East Africa don't expect to see a whole lot of animals, birds or insects in one place at one time. The animals are not only shy but need large habitats to survive in these meager conditions.

Danum's uniqueness lies in its lack of habitation and natural disasters. (Clive admits that there may have been a major burn centuries ago and a few nomadic hunters.) Here you will find all the major land mammals—birds, insects and more plant species than the entire continent of Europe and America combined. If you came to Borneo to see elephant, kijang, argus pheasant—or just to jungle walk—this is the place.

INSIDER TIP

Elephants and other animals are best seen along the road leading into the park boundaries. Elephants like to move in heavy rain and in aging logging cuts...Start out at dusk and be patient.

There are no set itineraries or programs for visitors, but your guide or the staff can set up an itinerary for you. Ask if there has been any activity recently. The 30 km of trails include the survey plots laid out across the river. There are also elevated blinds that offer excellent viewing and an unusual tree platform that will work up a sweat. I recommend spending the night in a blind or on the tree platform. You won't see much but it is a great experience. There is a **Rainforest Lodge** in the planning stages built along the lines of Treetops in Africa or Tiger tops in India. I visited the site and can only describe it as idyllic. The walk that winds up into the jungle and back down along the river is among the most beautiful I have experienced in my 5 years in remote Malaysia. Inquire at the Sabah Foundation for the status.

You can buy maps, a guide map and rent binoculars in the sparse store. Spend about a week here if you can; you will truly learn to love the lowland dipterocarp forest.

Gomantong Caves

Part of the Sandakan/cruise ship tourist rut that also includes Sepilok, Turtle Islands and the Crocodile Farms. Still worth a visit; 32 km south across the bay the main cave is Black Cave and the smaller White Cave. See it at sunset for the memorable sight of 2 million bats going out for dinner. Famous for its collection of edible birds' nests. They don't eat the nest, just the saliva used to glue them to the wall. The best ones are higher up. They are collected with bamboo poles 2-3 times a year.

Labuan Island

Labuan Lalang (also known as Teluk Terima) was the stuff of myths. A deep-water harbor and coal reserves made this an excellent spot for Rajah James Brooke to fight pirates. The former penal colony and then colonial administration center for the British North Borneo was manned by drunken civil servants who were the source for many of the despondent, besotted characters created by Conrad and Maugham.

Today Palau Labuan is tax-free Federal Territory that has generated much notoriety as a center of smuggling and piracy. A bustling center of commerce and barter for raw goods and finished luxuries between the Philippines and Malaysia. Filipinos trade raw goods and leave bulging with expensive manufactured goods. For all you cautious travelers, we should warn you that you must check your weapons when you enter the port just as the heavily armed sailors must. The marine police will return them to you when you leave. Labuan is also a military base, a major oil drilling center and a **WWII battle site**.

Labuan Lalang is and excellent spot for a **wreck dive**. Borneo Divers, KK, offers an intriguing 6 day dive trip (18 hours by boat.) Also contact Coral Island Cruises, KK.

Lahad Datu

You will probably pass through this grubby backwater town on your way to Danum Valley. Lahad Datu is famous for pirates, illegal immigrants from Timor and the Philippines and oil palm plantations. If you get hungry or get tired hanging out to absorb the seediness, try the fish and chips at the Evergreen Snack Bar and Pub.

Maliau Basin ★

You will probably hear stories of the Maliau Basin or the Lost World of Borneo. It is a truly remote and unexplored place. An uninhabited plateau shaped like a tiara with Gunung Lotung being the highest peak at 5,468m. It is protected by sheer cliffs and surrounded in mist. Once in the lost world, you are surrounded by *podsol* (heath) forest that ranges from lowland dipterocarp to mossy forest. The tea-colored water drains out of the Basin through a network of table-like rivers that ends in a series of dramatic waterfalls. Being a member of one of the first expeditions into this region I was disturbed to find just how quickly Sabah is moving to turn the area into a coal mine. There is an area put aside for research and conservation. In the future, it may become a popular adventure destination. If you want to explore the Maliau, contact Jon Rees at **White Water Adventures** in KK. All supplies will have to be hiked or helicoptered in. The cost will depend on whether you want to be dropped in by chopper or hike in from the steadily encroaching logging roads.

Keningau

If you want to see the rate at which Sabah is bleeding timber, spend a few hours sipping ice cold beer and counting the timber trucks. Keningau is an outpost before you head into the maze of logging roads that vein Sabah. I always seem to end up in Keningau to get fuel or supplies, but I would not recommend it to anyone who wants anything but cold beer.

Kinabalu National Park ★★

Site of Mount Kinabalu and home of the spirits of departed Kadazans, who still hold the mountain sacred. It's a popular peak for dimbers.

Huts line the slopes and the summit should be ascended in early morning. The park itself boasts some 800 varieties of orchids and 500 species of birds as well as giant earth worms, mouse deer, tree shrews and red leaf monkeys. The tour through the park takes about 2 hours by Land Rover; it's a drive through jungle tracks and mountain streams. It's worth it for the scenery and panorama of the countryside. Mt. Kinabalu is not an overly-daunting mountain, so it is strange that it was not climbed until 1851. Today, you will find yourself huffing behind a group of schoolchildren or geriatric bird watchers. There is a simple but scenic rest house just below the tree line that allows visitors to take their time in the ascent.

The ascent is a muddy path pressed between gnarled roots so be careful your trip doesn't end with a trip.

INSIDER TIP

Pick up the guidebook to the park at the park office. As you ascend, try to let the groups pass you and take a few detours off the path to rest and take in the constantly changing plant species and birds. Remember that as you change altitude, the species of plants will change.

Mt. Kinabalu is not a mountain climb; it is a hike. It can get awfully tiring if you aren't in shape or have just finished a 20-hour plane ride. You might want to save the climb towards the middle or end of your trip to Sabah. Carry water, an extra layer of clothing for the crisp weather at the summit and protection against the sun and rain.

Location	Elev./Dist./Time	What to look for
Timpohon Gate	1,830m/0km/0min	Nepenthes fusca, thick oak forests.
Pondok Kandis	1,981m/0.9km/20min	Tree ferns, Kinabalu balsam.
Pondok Ubah	2,095m/1.7km/15min	Nepenthes tentaculata off the trail.
Pondok Lowii	2,286m/2.3km/30min	Nepenthes lowii, moss forest, orchids .
Pondok Mempening	2,518m/3.1km/45min	Bamboo forest, birds, look for nests.
Carson's Camp	2,621m/3.9km/30min	Rhododendron lowii, Nepenthes villosa (unique to Kinabalu), mist.
Pondok Villosa	2,942m/4.9km/45min	Scrubby vegetation, thin air.
Pondok Paka	3,052m/5.3km/30min	Paka cave, vegetation thins.
Panar Laban	3,300m/5.8km/1hr.	Overnight rest house, edge of "tree line."
Summit	4,101m/8.5km/3hrs	Go slow due to thin air, leave by 10:30 a.m. due to heavy mist.

The most important experience is seeing how the environment changes as you slowly gain altitude. Spend as much time as you can on the way up since you will not have the same sense of wonder on your way down. The lack of trees at the summit is caused by lack of soil scraped off 3,000 years ago by glaciers, not cold. In fact you will be frozen, then broiled as the sun comes up. You are supposed to hire a guide for your ascent of the mountain, so by all means, bring all the camera gear and nature guide books you need, up to 11kg. The guide will help find any particular plants or birds you seek.

Note: *The best way to do Mt. Kinabalu* is to stay below the first evening to get a good night's sleep. Set off early in the morning to make it to Laban Rata Guesthouse in 8-10 hours (take the bus to the power station). Get up at 2:00 a.m. to leave at 4:00 a.m. See the sunrise on the summit and spend the next night in the first hotel of choice or Poring Hot Springs. You will sleep very well. Book well in advance and try to avoid weekends and holidays. From KK, call Sabah Parks reservations at ☎ *088-211-585* or visit the Sabah Parks office in person at Jalan Tun Fuad Stephens in KK, 8 a.m.-12:45 p.m. and 2 p.m.-4:15 p.m., Monday-Friday and Saturday a.m. only.

INSIDER TIP

Watch for pitcher plants (nepenthes), rhododendrons and orchids. Despite what the other guidebooks tell you, pitcher plants are not carnivorous and the water found in the base of the plant is quite refreshing. Use your teeth to strain out the bugs.

Kinabatangan River

The longest (560 km) river in Sabah meanders through a very important basin. Here you can find the Jimmy Durante-nosed, beer-bellied, proboscis monkey with great regularity. Orangutan nests and rhino tracks are common; traces of Asian elephants are very easy to spot. Whether you actually see the latter animals or not is a matter of luck and stealth. This is one of the last areas for accessible wildlife spotting. Best bet is actually a tributary of the Sungai Menanggol, where you can see the curious-looking proboscis monkey (*nasalis larvatus*) in the trees above. Thankfully, the female of the species is more attractive, with a pert upturned nose. Since the area is mostly mangrove swamp, the monkeys spend each evening and morning socializing, eating and mating in the trees.

Book a tour in KK or contact the caretaker in the village of Sukau to stay at the rustic lodge 6 km down from Sukau. You will need a guide and a boat.

Kota Belud

This is a small Bajau town about 77 km from Kota Kinabalu known for its Sunday morning market; biggest and most colorful *tamu* in the state. Local products for sale by the Bajaus and Kadazans—fruits and vegetables as well as handicrafts.

Kota Kinabalu

This is Sabah's capital with a population of about 130,000; it's known as KK and was flattened by the Allies in WWII. It's now an unappealing mix of dull modern structures and dull older structures. Visit the gold-domed **State Mosque** with its contemporary Islamic architecture; and the **Sabah Museum** for exhibits of tribal artifacts. Walk the crowded Chinese section, which stands in unique contrast to the Western-style high rises. Journey out to **Kampung Ayer** or Water Village to see houses and sidewalks on stilts. You will end and start any journey in dull but friendly KK, definitely a boom town. It is the best place to arrange your adventures from. Mt. Kinabalu trips should be booked here first. Sabah Parks office is at ☎ *088-211-585 (Block K of Sinsuran Kompleks on Jalan Tun Fuad Stephens)*; the TDC office can be reached by calling ☎ *088-211-732*; it is in the Wing Onn Life Building on *Jalan Segunting.*

Kudat

Kudat is the home of the Rungus people and located about 4 hours drive from Kota Kinabalu. Inhabitants live in longhouses. The women wear black ankle-length *sarungs* (sarongs). They weave baskets and hats, make beaded adornments and metal jewelry.

Penampang Village

13 km from Kota Kinabalu, Penampang is popular with tourists, who can get quick view of the Kadazan tribe at work, their traditional structures, activities and handicrafts.

Poring Hot Springs

Most people don't realize there is another side to Mt. Kinabalu National Park. 43 km from the park headquarters is an attractive group of chalets and rest houses with **nature trails**, **hot springs**, **orchid gardens** and a semi-zoo. There is also a very unique **canopy walk** sponsored by the Smithsonian that will take you up into the canopy of a Southeast Asian rainforest. You won't see much but you can tell people you have been there. The canopy walk is a stiff hike up a hill and then along a series of swaying aluminum platforms supported by cables. Try to experience the canopy early in the morning and at dusk. Ask the ranger if there are any rafflesia in bloom and to see what animals are in captivity at the zoo.

Choose from the **Mamutik Rest House** (8 people), **Manukan Chalet** (4 people), **Poring New Cabin** (4 people) or **Poring Old Cabin** (6 people). Camping is also permitted. Good for a refreshing couple of days or to recuperate from your ascent of Gunung Kinabalu.

Ranau

Ranau is an agricultural area known more for its **war memorial** in Kundasang than for its scenery. After the Japanese had forced Australian and British prisoners of war to build the airport at Sandakan, they force-marched 2,400 of them (mostly Australian) to Ranau. Only 6 prisoners survived the 11-month, 240 km march. This act killed more Australians than any other single event in WWII. There is a particularly disturbing monument with a plaque that describes the beating, torture and death of one Australian. Read it, lest we forget.

Sandakan

Sandakan is the former capital of North Borneo. It lies on the east coast about 180 degrees from Kota Kinabalu. Sandakan is a modern city at the edge of the sea, known for the **Sandakan Orchid House** with its exhibits and collections of rare orchids. See the **Forestry Exhibition** for displays of local handicrafts and tribal hunting weapons.

Pulau Gaya near Semporna

Semporna   ★

You will probably end up here on your way to Sipadan but non-divers will enjoy the Dragon Inn, a rustic resort built out over the water with a restaurant that asks that you choose your dinner from the holding tanks. Charter a boat and visit the Sea Bajau, their stilt villages and the volcanic islands in the surrounding bay. They once had pearl farms here. Semporna is the least known but probably the most diverse Marine Park in Asia. There are 73,000 acres with 70 genera of coral and over 200 species of fish. Make sure you sample at least 3 or 4 of the species at the restaurant before you go diving.

Sipadan   ★ ★ ★

Sipadan is an offshore island that features 200m wall dives, caves, overhangs, placid snorkeling, large ocean fish, pristine coral reefs, sea turtles and a sense of untouched perfection. Once a secret, it's now on the verge of being overdeveloped. And it is very easy to overdevelop a tiny island that has the attractions that Sipadan offers. Sipadan is another unique and threatened area that makes early travel to Sabah important. Here, on this tiny limestone island, you will find nothing of interest. But walk 10 short meters from the dive shack and plunge into the ocean and your mind will be blown. You will be soaring 200 km above the ocean floor on one of the most impressive wall dives in the world. Dive sites throughout the world tout themselves as being great, but Sipadan is magnificent. A must-see for divers and lovers of marine life.

INSIDER TIP

Try to visit between mid-February and mid-December, when visibility is a staggering 50-60 meters. If your interest is the turtles laying eggs, then August and September are the best times. There is no one best spot but ask what's happening when you arrive. Try to get in shape before you go—you'll be doing a lot of diving!

Bring all the supplies you need for photos or special interests, because even the drinking water has to be brought in. Don't be too unnerved by the visiting Malaysian warships. Indonesia would like their island back, but both sides have agreed to a peaceful solution.

Contact **Borneo Divers** in KK, *Rooms 401-404, 4th floor, Wisma Sabah, Kota Kinabalu;* ☎ *222226; FAX 221550.* Or **Palua Sipadan Resort**, *2nd Floor, 188 Jalan Bakau, Tawau;* ☎ *772689; FAX 763575.* I recommend trying Borneo Divers first, even though you will end up in the same place. Equipment can be rented, but make sure they have what you need first.

Sepilok Sanctuary

24 km outside Sandakan is the most popular of Borneo's three Orangutan rehabilitation centers (40,000 visitors a year). The others are Tanjung Puting in Southern Kalimantan—run by Canadian scientist Dr. Birute Galdikus—and Semonggoh in Sarawak, 32 km from Kuching. Sepilok is a 4,530 hectare forest reserve used to protect orphaned or recaptured orangutans and to help them grow to maturity—to eventually be released in the wild. There are an estimated 5,000 animals left in the wild, so each one is important.

Take a taxi to the preserve, go to Platform A just before 10:00 a.m. (there is another less well attended feeding at 2:30 p.m.). The youngest apes will come from out of nowhere to feed on bananas and milk. You can then take a rigorous hike out to Platform B for the 11:00 a.m. feeding. Don't be surprised if no one shows up, since this is where the older apes are released. I advise you to spend a couple of hours at platform A. If you are taking pictures, a couple of words of advice: first, use a tripod and fast film. And do not leave your possessions unattended, because as you're concentrating on one ape, another will calmly swing down and steal your camera bag, hat, sunglasses or even your entire video outfit. It's all in good fun, but you may not get it back in one piece. Keepers try to discourage human contact, but once you hold the soft hand of a young orangutan and look him directly in the eyes, you will know there is someone in there. Scary.

There also is a pair of Sumatran rhinos that are being cloistered so they'll breed. Visitors are no longer allowed without special permission. Worth a trip. Admission fee. Open 9:00 a.m. to 4:00 p.m. Monday through Sunday.

Tambunan

This is the usual base of operations for trips to **Crocker National Park**. Tambunan was also the stomping grounds of Mat Salleh, the charismatic rebel leader and military fort builder of the late 1800s. Mat Salleh initiated a series of "terrorist acts" against the British North Borneo Company who were stealing tribal land. He outwitted the various military forays against him and built a great fort of stone and wood in Tambunan that withstood 10 days of shelling, until he was killed by a stray bullet in January of 1900. Today, he is considered a national hero by Sabahans.

Tanjong Aru

Capital's seaside resort features beautiful beaches. **Prince Philip Park and Recreation Center** is located just 5 km south of Kota Kinabalu International Airport. It's a lovely spot to enjoy the sunset.

Tawau

The famous hot spring is in the southeastern part of Sabah. Tawau is a jumping-off point for Tarakan in Kalimantan, Indonesia. Take a plane or a ferry; get your visa first.

Tenom

Home of the Muruts, Tenom is reachable by Sabah's only railway. It's very quaint. From Tanjong Aru, the 154 km journey takes you through the towns of Papar, Sipitang and Beaufort. You'll cross the Crocker Range and skirt the banks of the Padas River. Transits Padas Gorge, Tuaran.

Tenom is a popular tourist area about a 30-minute drive from Kota Kinabalu. There are some interesting visits to the agricultural station of Tamu on market day. **Mengkabong Bajau** village is built over water. **Tamparuli** is for handicrafts, local specialties. Stroll across Sabah's longest suspension bridge. And make sure you visit the **Agricultural Research Center** (also called the Cocoa Research Station) about 10 km from Tenom. Although most people can't imagine why they would want to visit a cocoa research center, you will be pleasantly surprised. My friend and renowned botanist, Tony Lamb (now retired) has created one of the most unique botanical attractions in Asia. His collection of over 450 Bornean **orchids** and thousands of **wild fruits and plants** is second to none and he has managed to create a collection of every possible type of wild and domesticated tropical plant that could be useful to man. The goal is to discover new agricultural products and resiliant strains for export. As you may or may not know, Malaysia's major agrarian exports—rubber, cocoa and palm oil—came from other countries and were adapted for their conditions.

INSIDER TIP

If anyone was looking for a reason to save the rainforests this is it. The center contains many unusual plants that have yet to be fully tested on humans: medicinal plants, artificial sweeteners and potentially even a cure for AIDS. It's all here.

The orchid center is the only place where you will see some of the world's most exotic epiphytes in one place. Also, the acres of hundreds of different fruits, nuts, fibres and medicinal plants are an education in themselves.

Mt. Trusmadi

Gunung Trusmadi is the poor brother to Kinabalu. Most people see Mt. Trusmadi from Gunung Kinabalu but never go there. It is the second highest mountain in Malaysia (2,642m) and offers a truly challenging set of 2 climbs and a large and very rare pitcher plant to seek out. (*nepenthes trusmadiensis*). There is a northern route that takes 4 days up and 3 days down. The 2-day southern route is more difficult but takes less time. Stop in at the district office in Tambunan to hire guides and porters.

Tunku Abdul Rahman National Park ★

This park is comprised of islands just offshore of Kota Kinabalu and is a sanctuary for beautiful coral and many varieties of fish. The beaches are uncrowded and offer superb snorkeling. Also popular for weekend picnics. Boat trips can be arranged with local fishermen. The islands are Pulau Gaya, Pulau Sapi and Pulau Manukan.

Turtle Islands National Park

If you are in Sabah between July and October don't miss seeing the dozens of green and hawksbill turtles coming out of the water to lay their eggs. There is activity year-round if you can't make peak season. The females will come up after 8:00 p.m., while the male waits offshore. Be patient; it takes about 90-120 minutes for the laborious process. The number of spectators is limited to 20 and permits are required from the Sabah Parks Office in Sandakan. There are only three chalets, so taking a tour is best.

WHERE TO STAY IN SABAH

Batu Punggul

Batu Punggul Resort

The word resort is ambitious here. Very simple accommodations complete with stray cats and very large spiders. Don't be surprised if you are mobbed by one of the local tour groups, or kept up all night by the party animals 100 meters away in the longhouse. There are cooking facilities as well as meals provided by the simple canteen. Inexpensive.

Murut Longhouse

If you really want to get rustic this is it. You enter along a notched log and sleep on woven platforms. All this and bedding for about M6. If you signed on for the "typical Murut welcome" don't bother trying to get any sleep. Be careful where you walk. I spent most of my time trying not to crash through the flimsy split bamboo floor.

Campsites

You can camp out for next to nothing. You can even rent a tent.

Danum Valley

Sabah Foundation

Technically not a tourist attraction, but you can apply at the Sabah Foundation in KK ☎ *354496* (the big shiny skyscraper that looks like a tree stump) or the Forestry Division in Lahad Datu ☎ *81092*. The rooms are inexpensive and the meals simple. It is a beautiful lodge situated with a sweeping view of the jungle. The company of the resident scientists can also make it a very educational experience.

Kota Kinabalu

Hotel Capital   ★★

P.O. Box 23, Jalan Haji Saman. ☎ *231199* • *102 rooms.* Dining room serving Western/Chinese cuisine. Cocktail lounge. Nightclub. Watersports and boating. 20 feet from ocean.   ***Reservations: Direct.***

Hyatt Kinabalu International   ★★★

☎ *221234. FAX: 225972* • *345 rooms.* Chinese and Malaysian restaurants. Hugo's grillroom. 24-hour cafe. 2 bars. Cocktail lounge. Entertainment. Swimming pool. Health center. Regency Club. Businessman's center. Well worn, slighty musty business hotel.

Reservations: Hyatt Int'l.

Shangri-La's Tanjung Aru Resort   ★★★★

Locked Bag 174. ☎ *225800. FAX: 217155* • *500 rooms.* Recently revamped and expanded. Rooms and suites with balconies and panoramic ocean views. Restaurants serving Continental, Italian, Chinese, seafood and other Asian specialties. Lounge, poolside bar, disco-pub. Fitness center, two swimming pools, beach, outdoor Jacuzzi, four tennis courts, 9-hole pitch-and-putt golf course. Jungle treks, island tours, watersports, 9- and 18-hole golf courses nearby. Business center. Meeting and banquet rooms. A great oasis and the only place to stay if you want to have a little fun and recreation while in KK.

Reservations: Shangri-La Int'l.

Mt. Kinabalu

Laban Rata Guesthouse

Below the summit of Mt. Kinabalu • 54 beds. The commute is a bitch but there isn't much competition up here. The simple bunks and cheerful restaurant (that opens at 2:30 a.m.) will seem like the Ritz by the time you drag your weary carcass up the mountain. And you can't beat the view. You can rent sleeping bags here as well as use their cooking kit. Probably doesn't matter what kind of rating it gets. Inexpensive.

Kinabalu Lodge

On main road just outside of park. Rooms sleep up to 8 people. Expensive.

Hotel Perkasa Kundasang

Towards Ranau. ☎ *088-79511 • 74 rooms.* Moderate.

Note: *There are three huts at the 3,300 meter level. Ask your guide just how big the rats are on Mt. Kinabalu. He will not exaggerate, they are the largest in the world. If you wonder what they eat to get that big, ask your guide how big the earthworms are. They reach 7 feet in length. Yummy. Not recommended, except for masochists. Inexpensive.*

Sipadan

A-frames

You don't have much choice and you won't care. Both of the dive companies offer simple clean A-frames to lay your weary body in. You will be in the water from dawn to dusk.

Tenom

Tenom Hotel or the Sri Jayar.

Try these two. Or for kicks, try the palatial 7-story **Perkasa** above town.

Orchid Research Station

I recommend this scenic rest house (Rehat Lagud Sebren) with its sweeping views of the valley and pleasant breezes (they never did explain the chopped-up monitor lizard in the freezer!). At M15 a night, it's a treat. You will need a car since it is a 5 km drive from the research center.

TOURS

There are a number of tour companies in Kota Kinabalu. They will essentially send you to the same people with the same subcontractors. Compare price and specifics. You can cut a better deal if you are flexible.

City and Countryside Tour

4 hours, daily. Combines Kota Kinabalu with Menkabong fishing village and view of Mt. Kinabalu.

Kampong Scenic Tour

4 hours, daily.

Kinabalu National Park

Full day to several days. Can include ascent of Mt. Kinabalu and visits to Ranau as well as to the Australian war memorial.

Kota Belud Tamu

6-8 hours, weekly. Visits the most colorful and exciting market in Malaysia.

Kota Kinabalu City and Suburb Tour

2-3 hours, daily. Visits State Mosque, Tanjong Aru, coastal highway, Signal Hill, Sembulan water village and Sabah Museum.

Kota Kinabalu Penampang Tour

4 hours, daily. Capital sightseeing and Kadazan village.

Labuan Island

All day, daily. Visits war memorial and site of Japanese surrender. Only duty-free port in Malaysia.

Penampang Papar Tour

5 hours, daily. River cruise to Kadazan village and Pantai Manis beach.

Rungus Long House

12 hours, daily.

Rungus Long House

2 days, with accommodations.

Sabah Interior Tour

2 days, by road and rail to Tambunan, Keningau and Tenom.

Sandakan and Orangutan Sanctuary

Full day, daily.

Tunku Abdul Rahman National Park Tour

All day excursion to one of the off-shore islands.

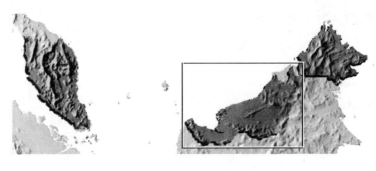

Sarawak

An Iban chief on the Skrang River exhibits his ancestors' handiwork.

SARAWAK IN A CAPSULE

Land of the Hornbills...formerly known as the Land of the Headhunters...Malaysia's largest state...peninsula lies southwest of Sabah...on northwest coast of Borneo...originally under sultanate of Brunei...placed under administration of British adventurer James Brooke when he quelled a rebellion...became part of the Malaysian federation in 1963...present population estimated over 1 million...rich in natural resources but many are unexplored...many jungles, mountains, rain forests, swamplands and rivers...Kuching, on the banks of Sarawak River, is the state capital...accessible from Southeast Asia by air.

Sarawak is the exotic Borneo that most people imagine. Headhunters, longhouses, unexplored jungles and semimythical creatures. Sarawak, like Sabah, has a colorful history thanks to adventurer James

Brooke, who managed to finagle a kingdom from the Sultan of Brunei for keeping the infestation of pirates down. Today, Sarawak is an excellent destination for those who seek the exotic and the wild. Not as rugged as Sabah, not as industrious as mainland Malaysia, Sarawak is a country unto itself. The high points are both cultural and natural: the Iban people, the town of Kuching, the Sarawak Museum and Gunung Mulu National Park and the miles of riverine adventure that await.

Visiting Longhouses

Longhouses are the indigenous housing of choice. Built on stilts for security and comfort, they are now becoming modernized—and they look curiously like government housing instead of the massive fortresses they once were. Some used to run as much as half a kilometer long and sit 7 meters off the ground. At night they would pull in the entry logs to keep out raiding parties. Today, most are between 10 and 20 doors long and are about 2-3 meters high. Color TVs, linoleum and electric kettles are not unusual. There is still a common area and then private apartments off the common veranda or *ruai*. Ancient longhouses made of *bilian* or ironwood are often rebuilt.

If you want to visit one of the 1,500 or so longhouses in Sarawak, there are a few things you should know. First, it can be excessively tedious to have to drink home-made hooch and dance like a chicken until dawn, especially when accompanied by the dissonant banging of gongs. Second, choose your longhouses carefully so that you get the real thing, not a carbon copy. The best longhouses for short stays are at Iban settlements downriver; for longer stays, you'll probably want to get to know the upriver longhouses of the Kayan and Kenyah. They are the aristocrats of the Dayaks and do not have the boisterous nature of the Iban.

TIPS ON VISITING A LONGHOUSE

Make sure you have an invitation or are part of a tour. You can usually ask around and find a way to be invited if you are not part of a tour. Longhouses prefer to have tours visit since it is a big event for them. But single travelers will receive traditional hospitality if the headman is receptive.

The best time to visit is in June when the gawai or harvest festival is in full swing. Most longhouses will be partying up a storm whether they have visitors or not.

Bring gifts not only for the headman (tuai rumah), but also the other residents (there will be many). Cigarettes, alcohol, souvenirs of your country will do for the headman. Toys, photos or pens are good for the others.

Make a ceremony of giving the gifts as well as meeting the members of the longhouse. I bring a Polaroid and make a big deal of presenting each photo. You can also make a speech in lieu of a gift. The Iban will also make speeches.

If you are with a large group and are asked to dispatch (kill) your dinner before entering (usually a pig) make a clean cut through the throat with the proffered spear.

Take your shoes off just as you enter. Observe most rules of conduct for Asian cultures. Ibans are animist or Christian.

You will be expected to take a sip from each of the proffered bottles. If you do not drink or have had too much, touch the the rim of the glass with your fingers and then your lips with a thank you nod. Do not use your left hand.

You may be invited to take a wash in the river. Men and women always bathe wearing some type of light clothing such as a sarong or shorts.

If you see a white flag (a sign of mourning) or feel that your reception is rather chilly, offer a gift and beat a hasty retreat.

You may get hit up for souvenir sales such as weavings or parangs. People may also ask for payment for photographs when in costume.

The Ibans are hams and love to mimic guests. Don't take it personally; you can join in and mimic them. Be warned, if you are really popular they may make you repeat your performance until you keel over from exhaustion.

If you drink too much or act like a fool, don't worry—the Iban are party animals and have probably behaved much worse than you.

WHAT TO SEE AND DO IN SARAWAK

Bako National Park

This was Sarawak's first national park. It is 2728 hectares of mangrove, heath forest and dipterocarp forest about 2 hours by speedboat upriver from Kuching. There are fascinating plants and animals, including the pitcher plant, dwarf palm, proboscis monkey, flying lemur, civet cat and over 150 species of birds. It has a good choice of hiking paths and government rest houses. **Tanjung Sapi** is the most dramatic of the many sculptured coves and headlands. There's good swimming in secluded bays located about 1.5 hours from Park headquarters. Teluk Pandan Kecil is probably the best bet.

Bandar Sri Aman

Site of Batang Lupar, a river with a mean tidal bore that almost drowned Somerset Maugham in 1929. The episode inspired *Yellow Streak* in his book *Borneo Tales*. Also to see is Fort Alice, which was constructed in 1864 as a base for Brooke's pirate-quashing forays against the Ibans.

Belaga

This is for folks who really like to get backcountry. This place was originally set up by Chinese traders to deal in truly raw materials like beeswax, bezoar stones (monkey gallbladder stones), gutta-percha and rhinocerous horn. You will need a permit to get here (from the State Government Complex in Kapit). I hope you don't mind taking a hell-bent-for-leather ride in a 12-cylinder Ekspres speed boat, watching bad kung fu movies and shooting the 2.5 km long Pelagus Rapids, all inside an hour into your trip to Belaga. Longhouse tours are popular; ask around to make sure you get the name of the type you like and then see if you can weasle an invite.

Bintulu

This is a good place to leave from. Bintulu is the site of a monstrous refinery complex. Niah caves are nearby, as are about 2 dozen long-houses (authentic but not unvisited) on the Kemena River. There are modern and inexpensive hotels in town (compared to Kuching).

Gunung Mulu National Park

Only an estimated 400 visitors a month visit Gunung Mulu, but it is a treasure of global proportions. It contains not only one of the world's largest cave systems (there may be one bigger recently discovered in China) but is home to the Penan (or Punan), a nomadic people who are very quickly running out of forest to live in. The discoveries in Mulu are coming fast and furious. It was only in 1984 that the Sarawak Chamber, the largest cave chamber in the world, was discovered. There are 27 caves, with over 200 km of passages. The vast size of the cave area will require years to explore.

As for the Punan, they have been incongruently settled in government-built longhouses in Batu Bungan upriver from Park Headquarters. One suspects it's been for the benefit of tourists rather than for the Punan. I visited them in 1989 and found their conditions questionable and their reaction to their new homes diffident.

As for species of flora and fauna, the numbers are staggering: 20,000 animal, 3500 plant, 282 bird, 280 butterfly, 75 amphibian, 67 mammalian, 50 reptile and 9 fish. Each new expedition records new species.

Gunung Mulu is the adventure of a lifetime, for I can think of nowhere else to find such vast primeval beauty—accessible and mysterious—waiting to be truly explored. A Fielding recommendation.

To see the park you will need a guide. I recommend letting a Miri-based outfitter take care of everything. Plan at least a week to really see it all. Here is a chart of just some of the things that await you.

Exploring Gunung Mulu National Park

Although the park was gazetted in 1974, there is much still to be discovered. Only a third of estimated cave system has been explored. The sheer size (52,866 ha) and remoteness of the park invites discovery. Hard-core cavers and climbers can organize trips at HQ or through tour companies. Here are the highlights:

Clearwater Cave	*40-mile long underground river. At 62 km, the longest underground passageway in SE Asia.*
Deer Cave	*World's largest entrance, highest passage (22m), 1.2 km long. Look for nightly exit of over one million bats. Visit Garden of Eden.*
Lang's Cave	*Lit cave, impressive stalagmites and stalactites.*
Cave of the Winds	*Visit King's room, constant breeze and interesting formations. Linked to Clearwater.*
Sarawak Chamber	*World's largest cave chamber (600m long, 450m wide, 100m high). Open with advance notice. 4- hour walk from river. Big! Can hold 16 football fields. Bring powerful light sources.*
Melinau Gorge	*2-3 hr arduous climb to see the dramatic 1580m limestone cliffs visible intermittently through the thick canopy. Crystal clear, ice cold river and swimming hole (brrrr) await the hardy.*
The Pinnacles	*45m razor sharp needles at 1200m, 2-hour boat ride, then 5 km trek to Camp 5. Short morning ascent is 3 km (4-6 hours up, 4-5 down) of hell. Tough but worth it. Bring gloves or you will get cut by razor-sharp limestone.*
Gunung Api	*3-day trek to 1710 summit. The experienced climb. First climbed in 1978. Hot, dangerous and a newsworthy accomplishment if you can climb it. (Same goes for the unclimbed Gunung Benarat across the river.)*
Gunung Mulu	*4-day climb over ridge trail to 2326m summit. Shelters eliminate need for tents. Fixed ropes near summit. Medium tough.*
River Trips	*You can content yourself with the rip upriver or to the cave mouths.*
Jungle Treks	*There is plenty to keep you occupied if you just hike between camps or to the caves.*

We strongly recommend spending time setting up your trip with a Miri-based guide company to get the most from your stay.

Kelabit (Bareo) Highlands   ★★

This is truly the remote heart of Borneo (along with its Indonesian border twin, the Apo Kayan in Kalimantan). Shrouded in mist and hidden even from modern satellite mapping, the Kelabit Highlands (sometimes called the Bareo Highlands) is the Holy Grail of hard-core trekkers. The gentle Kelabit inhabit a 1000m-high plateau of fertile fields and mountainous scenery. The area is surrounded by a circle of mountains that has left this area remote and relatively unaffected by outsiders. I say relatively because the highlands have been heavily proselytized by Christian missionaries and were the center of very successful Allied guerilla activities against the Japanese during WWII. Led by Tom Harrisson, it is a modern day Lawrence of Arabia story that few have heard. The area today provides truly rugged mountaineering, hiking and trekking. The dramatic twin-peaked **Bukit Batu Lawi** (6,703ft./2,043m) seems to draw the most climbers. Also there is Sarawak's highest peak, **Gunung Marudi** (7,950ft./2,423m). Both require climbing equipment and skill. To explore the Kelabit Highlands, you must be self sufficient, since there are no facilities other than one rest house in Bareo. And make sure you identify yourself to the Penghulu, or chief; he will let you stay with him at Bareo Bahru. You can fly into the small landing strip from Miri or Marudi. You are best advised to set up your trip with one of the major outfitters in Miri. The best conditions for entry and travel are between March and October.

INSIDER TIP

Before you get all excited about what the backpacker guides tell you about hiking Borneo, be forewarned. Jungle trekking can be tedious, frustrating and debilitating due to the dank forests, oppressive heat, long distances, constant wetness, slippery slopes, river crossings, hungry leeches and low caloric food. Expect to be bored, lose weight, get lonely and dream of alpine snowfields and ice cold beer. But c'est l'adventure.

Limbang

If you like to do things the hard way like me, you will visit Brunei or Gunung Mulu Park through the back door. It is a thin strip of land that must drive the Sultan of Brunei crazy because it has cut his country in half ever since his forebears gave a bunch of it to Brooke in 1890. In any case, this route provides a very different and unusual way into the park and you won't see anything twice. You can get here from Lawas, then take a boat or you can fly into Limbang from Kuching or you can come directly from Brunei.

Kapit ★

Kapit is the last outpost before heading "ulu," or upriver, on the Rejang. The first of the two places to visit is the museum, which features an Iban longhouse and wood carvings. Fort Sylvia was used by Brooke to keep the Iban away from the Kayan and Kenyah upriver and vice versa. Kapit is a very colorful city because of its importance as a trading center and wilderness outpost. Popularized by Redmond O'Hanlon in his hilarious book *Into the Heart of Borneo.* Worth a visit.

Kuching   ★ ★

Kuching is the Riverine capital of Sarawak—it's name comes from the word "cat" in Malay; the population is about 70,000. The river bisects the city and most people prefer to travel back and forth by boat. The city was under White Rajah rule until 1941, when the Japanese invaded. It became part of the British crown colony of Sarawak in 1946 and a state of Malaysia in 1963. The **Sarawak Museum**, built in 1891 by Rajah Charles Brooke, houses wonderful tribal artifacts. **Istana** (palace) is now the residence of Sarawak's governor. **Fort Margherita** (named after Brooke's wife) is now a police museum but is still considered among the best colonial architecture left in Southeast Asia. **Masjid Besar** (Main Mosque) is famous for impressive contemporary architecture. Completed in 1968, the mosque incorporates the design of some of the first buildings constructed on the site, dating from 1852. There are many impressive Chinese temples, including **Tua Pek Kong** (1876); **Hian Tien Shian** (1877), dedicated to god of heaven; the **Temple of Kuan Yin** (Chinese god of mercy), which dates from 1908; and **Tien Hou** (goddess of seamen), built in 1927. Upriver are traditional villages accessible by small craft.

A typical bridge made from hardwood logs

Miri

Miri is a big expatriate center for Shell Oil employees. It is also the origin of trips to Gunung Mulu National Park and the Bareo and Kelabit Highlands. Alo Doda and Tropical Adventure have a lock on the Mulu trips because of their lodgings within the park. If you are planning to go to Mulu or beyond, I would strongly suggest one of these companies. They will be glad to customize your trip. It will not be cheap, but at least it will happen in the time alloted for the money alloted.

Niah National Park

In 1959, Tom Harrisson, curator of the Sarawak museum, changed the way people viewed Asia's role in the evolution of man when he found evidence of human habitation as early as 37,000 years ago. Today, Niah is Sarawak's most popular tourist site. Take the longboat from Park headquarters to visit the caves. There is a 4 km plank walk to the mouth of the Great Cave. Continue through the cave to visit the Painted Cave, where you'll see the 32m-long cave paintings. Make sure you experience the spectacle of the bats leaving the cave at sunset. You will need a permit to visit the Painted Cave, which is available from the Museum in Sarawak or Niah Park headquarters. If you want to watch the tri-annual collection of birds' nests, plan on visiting in August to December or January to March. The nests hang from the roofs of the caves and collectors bring them down by long bamboo poles equipped with scrapers. Birds' nest soup is a delicacy in China and sells for up to U.S.$400 a kilo in Hong Kong. It's not so popular in Borneo, probably because the Chinese don't watch the nests tumble into the cockroach-infested guano!

A guide is recommended. There are rest houses at the park or cheap hotels in Batu Niah, 4 km away.

Santubong Resort

Santubong is a seaside resort about 32 km from Kuching and was an important trading center during the Tang and Sung dynasties from 7th to 13th centuries A.D. Ancient rock carvings are found at **Sungai Jaong**, just upriver from the village. But, today, it's just a popular place for swimming and fishing. Government chalets may be booked through the District Office in Kuching.

Sarawak Cultural Village

About the only way you will be able to see just how the Dayaks of Borneo lived is in this well-executed recreation of various ethnic villages. Although this cultural Disneyland, complete with native dancing and gift shops will make veteran travelers run screaming, it is the only way most visitors will see how authentic longhouses are made, use real blow pipes, taste rice wine and see what goes into making the handicrafts. You can even take a class in one of many cultural handicrafts. It does, though, smack of the ticky-tacky pseudo-cultural villages of Hawaii, East Africa and Mexico. I recommend it if only for the massive authentically-built longhouses. *Open 9:00 a.m.-5:30 p.m., Monday to Sunday. Admission charge.*

Sarawak Museum

Worth a trip in itself just to understand the art and culture of the peoples of Borneo. Originally housed in the 1891 building, it was expanded in 1983, as a new wing was added. This museum, in conjunction with the Cultural center, is one of the best introductions to a country's indigenous peoples I've seen. *Open 9:00 a.m.-4:00 p.m., Monday to Sunday. Admission charge.*

Sibu

This is the second largest city in Sarawak. A Chinese timber trading town, Sibu is the springboard for Kapit and the river trips up the Rejang River, a colorful and photogenic area.

Similajau National Park

The park is a long (32 km), thin (1.5 km) strip of beach and coastal estuarine. Visit to see the beaches (Pasir Mas), coral reefs (Batu Mandi), birds (185 species), turtles, dolphins, small mammals and the feared saltwater crocodiles. Sarawak was once the home of the world's largest crocs, but domesticated cattle (which crush the crocs' nests) and hunting (they eat people) has thinned their ranks. The area's not very well known, but the park is a great place to spend a couple of days hiking, swimming and birding. Get a permit in Bintula at the Bintilu Development Authority and stay at the chalet at Park headquarters.

Skrang River

This area is home to the Iban, who settled in this area in the 16th century. Because of their proximity to the ocean and their alliance with sea-going Malays, the people were called Sea Dayaks. The Iban are warlike and the only group to make head hunting a sport rather than a tool of war. Head hunting had a very positive and spiritual significance to each longhouse. The heads are still kept in many longhouses though their protective magic has long worn off.

Conquered by James Brooke in 1849 on behalf of the Sultan of Brunei, the adventurer was given this area as a reward. Thus began Sarawak and the steady erosion of the Sultan of Brunei's land.

If you want to take a river trip complete with a longhouse stay, try to get past the longhouses near Lamanak and Pias (unless you want the standard tourist fare). You have to wonder if the Iban develop liver problems, with visitors showing up for a party and booze binge every day of the week! The concept of riverine hospitality has developed into a floor show of souvenir sales in some longhouses. Frequent visitors to Borneo will do anything to avoid another night in a longhouse. Once is enough for most. The area is 135 km from Kuching.

WHERE TO STAY ON SARAWAK

Kuching

Aurora Hotel   ★★★

Jalan Tanjong Batu, Bintulu. ☎ *240281. FAX: 425400 • 108 rooms.* Continental cuisine. Coffeehouse. Swimming pool. Watersports. Tennis and squash. Garden restaurant.   ***Reservations: Direct.***

Kuching Hilton Hotel ★★★★
Jalan Tunku Abdul Rahman, PO Box 2396. ☎ *248200. FAX: 428984 •*
322 rooms. Close to beach. Executive floors. Western and Asian restaurants. Business center. Health club. Swimming pool. Meeting
rooms. ***Reservations: Hilton Hotels, Utell.***

Holiday Inn Kuching ★★★
Jalan Tunku Abdul Rahman, Kuching. ☎ *423111. FAX: 426169 • 165*
rooms. Serapi restaurant and terrace. Banquet rooms. Rajang bar. Coffeehouse. Chinese restaurant. Disco. Swimming pool. Tennis. Health
club. Minigolf. ***Reservations: Holiday Inn.***

Hotel Long House ★
Abell Rd., Kuching. ☎ *55333 • 50 rooms.* Dining room. Coffee shop.
Snack bar. ***Reservations: Direct.***

TOURS

Bako National Park
8 hours, daily.

Kuching City
3 hours, daily. Visits Sarawak Museum, State Mosque, Malaysian market, Istana, Fort Margherita and Hong San Temple.

Kuching Longhouse Tour
5 days. Visits Kuching city, plus sea and land Dayaks by bus and
motorized longboat.

Land Dayak Longhouse
3 to 4 hours, daily. Visit to Iban longhouse and native lunch.

Niah Caves
Full day to 2 nights. Includes longboat trip and visits to caves. Longer
versions visit Miri city, oil palm and cocoa plantations.

Sea Dayak Longhouse
Full day, daily. Visits Iban longhouse and includes a native lunch.

Skrang River Safari
2 days. Land and longboat transportation to longhouse accommodation, including a pepper plantation visit.

Skrang River Ulu Longhouse
2 days. All of the above but more native food and accommodations.

SHOPPING IN MALAYSIA

The souvenirs in Malaysia will vary from state to state, as many of the
traditional handicrafts are regional. The wonderful batiks from the East
Coast are familiar to collectors all over the world and Selangor pewter is
highly prized for its fine workmanship. However, visitors should be prepared for such temptations as Aw pottery from Johor; Sarawak vases; Labu
pottery from Perak state; wood carvings typical of Kelantan, Terengganu,
Malacca, Kedah and Negri Sembilan; silverware from Kelantan; Songket

weaving from the East Coast region; rattan from Kuantan to Kuala Terengganu; Padan weaving from the state of Terengganu; kites from Kelantan
and birds' nests (yes, for soup) from the caves of Sabah and Sarawak.

Batik is everyone's favorite purchase, as the lovely materials can be used
for many things and for all occasions. Clothing is the most popular usage
and Malaysians themselves dress both formally and casually in their batik.
You can also find such items as tissue box covers, hats and bags, cushion
covers, bedspreads, curtains and table mats or napkin sets. The batik industry is concentrated in the East Coast and visitors may have the opportunity
to visit factories to observe the production first-hand and make their purchases on the spot.

Songket is another indigenous fabric and the pride of Malaysia. It is a
fabric much entwined with the country's history and culture; it has long
been worn by royalty and used by the courts for ceremonial occasions. It
has also been successfully adapted for Western evening wear. Songket is
woven with the finest silk available and the gold-threaded patterns are reproduced from ancient designs (which are often a secret passed from generation to generation). The art of weaving songket dates from as early as
the 15th century and it is said that no two pieces of the cloth have ever
been alike. Even the design of the loom has not changed with time and
many weavers now employ valuable antiques in their making of the cloth.
Naturally, a piece of songket (1.8m in length) is expensive in comparison
to other Malaysian traditional crafts, but anyone able to purchase one will
never fail to enjoy its exquisite beauty.

Batik painting has become, in recent years, another of Malaysia's contri-
butions to the world of art. The batik artist needs the same skill, craftsmanship and patience necessary in the making of batik. The only difference
between the maker and the artist is that the artist's patterns may be bolder
because the cloth is sized and framed and not worn on the body or used as
household accessories. Batik paintings make excellent souvenirs because
they can be framed later and take up little room in a suitcase.

The Malay is known for his fine **wood-carving** abilities, as evident from
the shutters and railings found on the stilt houses in Penang, Negri Sembilan, Malacca and the environs of Kuala Lumpur. Carving is a very old
craft on the Malay Peninsula and the timber resources have provided a variety of woods. Visitors are always impressed by the decorative carvings
found throughout the country, especially in the Istana Balai Besar, built in
1840 for the sultan of Kelantan, or the Istana Lama Sri Menanti, built at
the turn of the century for the sultan of Negri Sembilan. Both wooden palaces are still used for ceremonial occasions. Visitors interested in traditional carvings are encouraged to haunt the antique shops, or contact the
National Museum in Kuala Lumpur for a list of modern wood carvers.
There are also some interesting wood sculptures available, namely from the
Mah-Meri and the Jah-Hut groups. The former offers more sophisticated
works, while the latter live a rural life in Pahang (where the jungle and

mountains are the inspiration for their art). The Mah-Meri wood sculptures are best known in the Kuala Lumpur area.

Pewter is synonymous with Malaysia and one of the world's oldest crafts. Pewter drinking vessels were thought to enhance the flavor of wine in first-century Rome. The craft was introduced to Malaysia in 1885 by Yoon Koon, who emigrated from the Chinese pewter province of Swatow. He founded Selangor Pewter and is called the "Father of Malaysian Pewter." The factory, just outside Kuala Lumpur, produces every item you might desire in this alloy of tin, copper and antimony, that is cooled and then highly polished. A pewter article takes about three weeks to be produced and personal engraving can be ordered. Visitors are welcome at the Selangor pewter factory and, of course, there is a retail shop attached—for everyone's convenience.

Silver items made in Malaysia come from the East Coast state of Kelantan, where silversmiths work the old-fashioned way to craft bowls, trays, salad spoons and tea sets. Filigree work is still a long, tedious process, although machines are now used to make the silver sheets into wire. It is a cottage industry that has not changed much and many of the designs even show a Hindu influence that dates back approximately 600 years.

Locally made **pottery** is also a strong candidate for souvenirs.

Aw pottery is made at Air Hitam (about 80 miles north of Johor Bahru) by Aw Eng Kwang and his family, who've been in the craft for five generations. Aw's pottery follows the Chinese method of making ceramics and his products range from vases and lampstands in earth tones of amber and burnt sienna to more delicate tea sets and figurines. His kiln is considered the largest outside China.

A more primitive type of pottery is made by the Labu people, whose Malay villages are found on the banks of the Perak River in Perak state. The charm of their pottery lies in the ancient craft by which it is made, uninfluenced by modern techniques. The tools employed to work the clay consist of bamboo strips for cutting, a smooth stone for polishing and small wooden rods for stamping designs. The Labus can be found at Lenggong in Upper Perak, Sayong (near Kuala Kangsar) and Pulau Tiga in Lower Perak.

The colorful **vases** of Sarawak come from the capital, Kuching, where Chinese from Kwantung province brought their skill. The vases are quite unusual, however, because the hand-applied designs feature local folklore. You can appreciate figures of Iban hunters, Murut men in traditional dress, or the stylized dragons from the Bidayuh, Kayan and Kenyah tribes.

Pandan weaving is another cottage industry in the East Coast state of Terengganu. The short pandan, or screw-pine leaves are used to make narrow sleeping mats, fans, baskets, tobacco pouches, slippers, purses and colorful table mats. The longer mengkuang leaves are used for floor mats. Visitors who wish to see this interesting weaving process can visit several village houses, open daily, from Kuantan to Kuala Terengganu. Primarily a woman's vocation, the process includes a great sense of camaraderie as the women chat and laugh together while they work. Though the craft looks simple, even a small purse may take an entire day to complete. Considered an East Coast tradition, the weaving is also popular among the women of Malacca, Selangor and Negri Sembilan.

Rattan, or *rotan* in Malay, is abundant in this country because it is a jungle vine that thrives in dense, tropical rainforests. The furniture made from this vine is inexpensive, attractive and extremely durable. Basketware is also popular. Although a bit difficult to transport in a suitcase, rattan can be viewed at handicraft centers throughout Malaysia.

Kites are very important to local culture and many ceremonial occasions are preceded by the flying of kites. Children are taught kite legends from an early age and they fly *layang-layang* during the windy season. Adults have their own kite, called the *wau*, which requires skill, discipline and stamina to maneuver. The *wau* is considered so important to one's well being that even the Malaysian national air carrier MAS uses the *wau* as its logo. Needless to say, kite fanciers the world over will always appreciate a fine specimen from Malaysia.

Finally, the "caviar of the East" is said to be the **birds' nests** found in the Niah caves and Baram in Sarawak and the Gomantong caves and Madai in Sabah. The Chinese insist that the birds' nests not only are tasty and nourishing, but also have aphrodisiacal powers. Uh, huh. So does bat stew. If you don't have the time or interest to collect your own, good quality nests are available from medicine shops (expensive) or packed in plastic bags at supermarkets. You don't eat the nest, rather the saliva that's used to keep them together. Before you tell all your friends with a wok what to expect, check with the U.S. Department of Agriculture. Birds' nests may be classified as plants and not allowed to be imported individually.

Malaysian handicrafts are readily available at the government-sponsored handicraft centers in major cities as well as the duty-free shops in Kuala Lumpur and Penang. However, the best and most enjoyable way to purchase your souvenirs is at the local markets. The famous Sunday night market in Kuala Lumpur (actually held on Saturday night) is located in Kampung Baharu, the exclusively Malay section of the capital. It is a wonderful place to eat and shop on a Saturday night and the handicraft stalls are overwhelming.

The **Pasar Malam**, or night market, in Penang is another emporium not to miss, so inquire about its current location as soon as you arrive. Penang also has some exciting shopping streets, like Jalan Pinang for imported items, Jalan Campbell for Chinese goods and Rope Walk for antique or junk shops. Chinese opium beds were the rage when I lived in the Far East, but they cost a fortune to be shipped—and then to be repaired after they arrive in pieces! It is far more sensible to stay with the local fabrics and crafts which can be carried home and enjoyed immediately.

TOURS

Countryside Tour

3 hours, daily from Kuala Lumpur; visits Batu Caves, rubber plantation, batik demonstration center, Lake Gardens, National Monument,
Parliament House and State Secretariat Building; can be combined
with K.L. city tour for full day.

Kuala Lumpur City Tour

3 hours, daily; visits National Museum, National Mosque, Parliament
House, Railway Station and other colonial-era buildings.

Kuala Lumpur Night Tour

3 hours, nightly; visits Chinatown plus offers a Malaysian dinner and
cultural show.

Kuala Lumpur/Fraser's Hill

3 nights; includes morning tour of K.L. and roundtrip transportation
to hill resort.

Kuala Lumpur/Genting Highlands

2 nights; includes return helicopter fare.

Kuala Lumpur/Cameron Highlands/Penang

5 nights.

Kuala Lumpur/Port Dickson

8-10 hours, daily.

Kuala Lumpur/Malacca

8-10 hours, daily.

Kuala Lumpur/Malacca/Singapore

5 nights.

Kuala Lumpur / Penang / Kota Bharu / Tanjong Jara / Kuantan / Singapore

10 nights.

MYANMAR

Thousands of pagodas dot the landscape of Bagan.

MYANMAR IN A CAPSULE

An undeveloped country continually beset by war and natural disasters ...paradoxically, a safe and exotic location but with restricted mobility...the world's greatest collection of religious pagodas...people known for gentleness, graciousness and devotion to their Buddhist doctrines... repressive government with poor record of human rights...can be safely experienced through government tours of up to 14 days in approved areas...or adventurers can go solo into smuggling regions or areas contested by guerillas...opening its doors just a crack at a time to the outside world...a Fielding recommendation for 1995/96.

It will take a long time for newly named countries like Bosnia-Herzegovina, Burkina Faso, Sri Lanka and now Myanmar to regain their previous romantic associations. In 1988, the Burmese government officially changed the name of the country to Myanmar and the name of its principal city, Rangoon, to Yangon. Other cities that underwent name changes include Prome, now known as Pyay and Pegu, now called Bago. Like many third-world countries that wish to discard the baggage of ancient or colonial names, Myanmar is still striving to seek an identity that is on par with most Westerners' recollection of the fabled land of Burma.

Myanmar is among the most enchanting and exotic of all Asian countries to visit. Overlooked by most travelers because of a 20-year ban on tourists and ongoing internal strife, Myanmar is slowly coming out of the darkness. At Fielding, rarely do we ever suggest taking an organized tour. But with Myanmar, this is one of the few instances where we do, because this is the only way most people will get a chance to see this rough-edged but charming country.

INSIDER TIP

Visitors are allowed to stay a maximum of 14 days and are required to stay only at official hotels and visit approved sites. And there's no wandering out of approved areas. There are ways around this restriction, but we do not recommend them at this time.

Any tour of Myanmar is comparable to stepping back several decades from the 20th century, assimilating some 2500 years in cultural history. The internal problems are not new and will not be solved for many years, if ever. In the meantime, the government's martial grip of the majority of the country results in a virtually crime-free environment with some unusual warnings. Forget about ecotourism since the mountainous north is off limits; the great forests are in the control of rebel groups. You will have to be content with seeing the major highlights of Myanmar with a few tantalizing glimpses into what could be. New sites are continually being opened up to visitors. One former forbidden marvel is the famous balancing pagoda of Kyaiktiyo, a gold leaf-covered rock capped with a pagoda, that seems to teeter on the edge of a great cliff.

There are also many areas that will not and may never be open to outsiders due to guerilla warfare or the smuggling of opium, timber or gems. Journalists have snuck in to cover the armed struggle of the Karen National Union, but there is always a price to pay for this type of travel. Other adventurers have managed to talk their way through

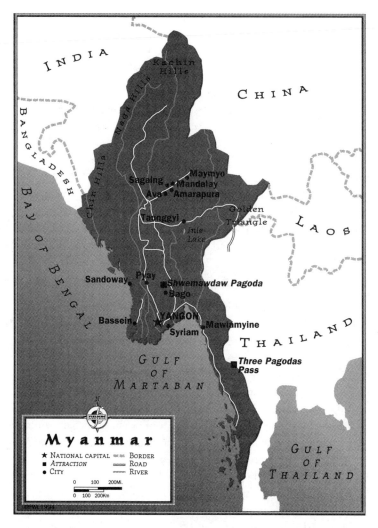

the Golden Triangle, but please remember that, under the regime of Dictator Ne Win, all bets are off once you leave the government defined tourist circuit.

Some savvy travelers are concerned that the tightly controlled flow of tourist dollars directly benefits this repressive regime, while others hope that the continual existence and pressure of visitors will force a positive change. Our opinion is that the increased presence and effect of Western visitors will be beneficial in pressuring Myanmar to create a positive image and a more liberal government. For now, visit Myanmar for the awe-inspiring sight of Shwedagon Pagoda, the world-class vision of Bagan with its thousands of pagodas stretching off into the distance and the lasting memory of gentle, laughing people who will stay in your heart long after your slides have faded.

History of Myanmar

Burma means "first inhabitants of the world." Records show that the Mons people laid the cornerstone for the Shwedagon Pagoda in 588 B.C. on a site that was already considered sacred. Rebuilt over the ensuing centuries, it has become the most important living monument in the Buddhist world. It not only dominates Yangon, the capital city, but the entire country. This is the **Land of Pagodas**, with many of them featuring brilliant golden domes and *hti* (umbrellas) encrusted with precious stones on their flights to heaven. Some say the Burmese practice the purest form of the religion—Theravada Buddhism. It permeates the everyday life of 80 percent of the people.

A Union Divided

That the Socialist Republic of the Union of Myanmar is "socialist" can be readily affirmed; however, it has been anything but a "union" since its inception. Situated on the crossroads between the Indian subcontinent and the Indo-Chinese peninsula, the country has been trampled upon, fought among and over for far more than 25 centuries. Even today, it consists of many separate ethnic minorities—including the Chins, Kachins, Shans, Karens, Kayahs, Mons and Arakense. These are only some of the more than 60 racial groups in Myanmar who speak more than 200 languages. The territory of Myanmar is the third largest in mainland Asia, after India and China and boasts the mighty Irrawaddy River, which flows some 1350 miles from the foothills of the Himalayas down to the Andaman sea. The Irrawaddy, together with its tributaries the Chindwin and Mu rivers, is the heartland and powerplay of the country. It provides access from China to the rest of the world. The first kingdom was founded along its banks and its overflow provides for both an abundant rice and bread bowl.

Burmese history becomes intriguing only in A.D. 1057, when King Anawrahta conquered the neighboring Mons capital of Thaton and returned with enough "loot" to establish the first Burmese Empire in Bagan. Among the 30,000 prisoners—including monks, craftsmen and builders—the king brought to the banks of the Irrawaddy River in Upper Burma a culture, a new language and Theravada Buddhism. As a fresh convert, the king began constructing what was to become "the most remarkable religious city in the world." In only

200 years, no less than 13,000 sacred monuments were erected on this fluvial plain as successive monarchs tried to "win merit" in the eyes of Buddha and their own predecessors.

A hundred years ago, Shway Yoe wrote, "Jerusalem, Rome, Benares—none of them can boast the multitude of temples and the lavishness of design and ornament that make marvelous this deserted capital on the Irrawaddy. For eight miles along the river bank and extending to a depth of two miles inland, the whole space is thickly studded with pagodas of all sizes and shapes, the ground is so thickly covered with crumbling remnants of vanished shrines that according to the popular saying, you cannot move foot or hand without touching a sacred thing."

The Destruction of Bagan

The glory lasted until A.D. 1284, when the emperor of China sent a vast army to avenge the murder of an ambassador and Bagan's King Narathihapate "pulled down a thousand arched temples, a thousand smaller ones and four thousand square temples to strengthen the fortifications." Unfortunately, however, he lost his courage and fled to the south. Today, less than 2000 of these magnificent structures are standing—due to both man-made and natural devastations (including a disastrous earthquake in 1975)—but it remains a place of pilgrimage for travelers from all over the world.

The Golden City of Mandalay

The founding of **Mandalay**, at a bend in the Irrawaddy in Upper Burma in 1857, represents another colorful chapter in the country's history. According to legend, Gautama Buddha and his disciple Ananda visited Mandalay Hill and proclaimed that on the 2,400th anniversary of his teaching, a great metropolis of Buddhist learning would be established there. King Mindon found this irresistible and moved his palace from nearby Amarapura to a spot below the sacred mount of Mandalay Hill.

Between 1859 and 1885, when King Thibaw surrendered the "Golden City" to the British and went into exile, several dozen ambitious monuments to Buddhist teachings were erected. Mandalay became not only the capital of Upper Burma but the cultural center of the entire country. Most of its structures were built of teak, exquisitely carved and decorated by local craftsmen, but, unfortunately, very few are standing today. All that remains of the renowned royal palace are the walls (1-1/2 miles long) and the moat. The magnificent teak pavilions turned to ashes during the Second World War. Mandalay today is a shadow of its former self, although it is still

a center for Buddhist teachings and many of the country's indigenous crafts.

Colonial Rule

On January 1, 1886, the independent kingdom of Burma ceased
and became a province of British India. From that day until full independence on January 4, 1948, Burma was under British colonial
rule, although the country was granted some sort of self-govern-
ment in 1923 and became a separate colony (no longer annexed to
India) in 1935. In 1941, the Japanese invaded Burma and persuaded
the Burmese Liberation Army, led by Aung San, to help them drive
the British back to India.

What ensued were perhaps the bloodiest and bitterest campaigns of
the entire war—most of them in the treacherous jungles of Upper
Burma. Somehow, all the "biggies" arrived at this crossroads of Asia
and most lived to tell about their own brand of jungle warfare. There
was "Vinegar Joe" Stilwell and the 114 Chinese soldiers he got safely
to Delhi, General Wingate and his famous "**Chindits**," General
Claire "Old Weatherface" Chennault and his "**Flying Tigers**," General Frank Merrill and his "**Marauders**," not to forget those who
built the Ledo Road. This 500-mile stretch, through territory man
never dared attempt before, was to connect with the famous **Burma
Road**; it was never completed. Nonetheless, it is said to have cost exactly "one man per mile."

At the turning point in the raging conflict, Aung San transferred
his troops and his allegiance to the Allies and the Japanese surrendered on August 28, 1945. Intense feelings about the "Burma Campaign" have not been mollified very much with time. In fact, Queen
Elizabeth's uncle, Lord Mountbatten (whose other title was 1st Earl
of Burma), specified that no Japanese representative be allowed at
his funeral a few years ago. After 30 years, he was still incapable of
forgiving the fate of British troops in Burma.

Independence

According to a local astrologer, the most auspicious moment for
Burma to become independent (once and for all) was at exactly 4:20
a.m. on January 4, 1948. And so it happened with Burma, the first
former colony to sever ties with the Commonwealth. Unfortunately,
the nation's premier leader, Aung San and six of his future ministers,
were assassinated just months before independence and were placed
in a marble mausoleum near the sacred Shwedagon Pagoda in
Rangoon (now Yangon). Since 1962, General Ne Win has been the
Number One figure in Burmese politics and is now the chairman,

while U San Yu has assumed the presidency. Although isolated and introverted since independence, Myanmar has not been without its world statesmen—like U Thant, secretary-general of the United Nations in the 1960s.

The abrupt resignation of U Ne Win during the summer of 1988 followed a period of political, social and economic unrest that arose as government corruption became more apparent. The general had bankrupted the country during the past two and a half decades while amassing a reputed U.S. $1 billion-plus fortune in Europe for himself and his six wives; his ministers are also said to be multimillionaires. During the general's tenure, Myanmar disintegrated from one of the world's great rice producers to just one that provides bare subsistence for its own people. Its famous teak wood and gemstones are not part of the GNP (although the general is said to have had first pick) but smuggled out of the country by a select group for markets in Thailand.

In 1990, after civil unrest, elections were held for a new head of state. The winner was the newly formed National League for Democracy's candidate, Aung San Suu Kyi. The results of the election were disregarded and Ms. Suu Kyi, winner of the 1991 Nobel Peace Prize, was placed under house arrest where she remains.

The Golden Triangle and the War Lords

The infamous "Golden Triangle" falls largely in Myanmar's Shan Sate, although it covers parts of Thailand, Laos and some of China's Unman province. This is where the raw material for opium and heroin is grown and it is definitely not a safe place to visit. The area is currently controlled by war lords who control the lucrative drug trade and the passage of adventurers.

Following the unrest of the summer of '88, the Myanmar government closed its doors to visitors—especially journalists. However, a desperate need for hard currency has prompted a slight opening with tours of up to 14 days paid for in U.S. dollars. Visitors are watched carefully and advised not to make contact with the local populace. A change of government with democratic elections is promised— which is particularly significant to the youth of Myanmar—but whether it will take place is another matter.

A Word About Pagodas

The word pagoda is derived from the Sanskrit to mean "relic shrine" and is "properly allied only to a monument raised over some of the remains of the Lord Buddha." These include pieces of flesh, hair, teeth, bone, or sacred items used by the Teacher. Somehow, the

Burmese seem to claim more personal relics of the Lord Buddha than could have possibly existed. The number of pagodas raised in Myanmar far exceeds those built by pious Buddhists in Sri Lanka (Ceylon), Tibet, or China. It is said that a Burman does not notice the multitude of religious edifices in his country until he leaves it and sees how sparing other people have been.

Yangon woman gives blood without the benefit of sterile equipment.

There is a reason: no work of merit is so richly rewarded as the building of a pagoda, according to the form of Buddhism practiced by the Burmese. Actually, the word *pagoda* does not exist in the Burmese language. Such a structure is called a *zedi*, meaning offering place or place of prayer; but the expression *paya* is most frequently employed in reference to the more famous places of worship in this country. The greatest and most venerated of all the *payas* in Myanmar is the **Shwedagon** in Yangon, followed by the **Shwemawdaw** (lotus-shrine) in Bago, the **Shwesandaw** (depository of the sacred hair) at Pyay and the **Mahamyatmuni** (temple of the most exalted saint) at Mandalay. All were founded by individuals who received strands of the great Master's hair.

Another reason for the proliferation of religious shrines throughout this country is that one only gains "merit" from building anew, not from repairing those that are crumbling. In fact, the pious Burman felt it was enough to gratify the feeling of the moment, therefore, most religious monuments were built of crumbling, sun-dried bricks that had no business lasting as long as they did!

Language, Culture and Architecture

As the people, language and culture of Myanmar differ from north to south and east to west, so does the architecture of the *payas*. In **Lower Burma**, the forms are simple, patterned after the rice-heap or lotus-bud. They are solid, pyramidal cones of undistinguished design (except when covered with solid gold leaf) and topped with those lyrical *hti*, or umbrella spires formed of concentric rings from which bells or precious stones sway in the breeze.

The architecture of the Bagan temples is completely different in styles from all other parts of Myanmar. In fact, they differ one from another—some even resemble Christian shrines, laid out as they are in the form of a Greek cross. The earliest ones, built by King Anawrahta, who established the city, were modeled exactly after monuments built in Thaton—the kingdom he had previously conquered. (No wonder, since Anawrahta brought all the craftsmen and builders with him as booty.) Later monuments show a continued sophistication of the designs begun by Anawrahta, as well as Chinese and Indian influences.

The **Upper Burma** area of Ava, Amarapura and Mandalay have quite different monuments altogether. Native teak—and local craftsmen—were abundant and the temples were shrines of merit to all who labored upon them. Unfortunately, only the stone portions remain and even these take some imagination to recall their rightful glory. Of all, the Kuthodaw or Royal Merit House, built by King Thibaw's uncle, is one of the most compact and tastefully adorned of all the pagodas. The texts of Buddhist Scripture it contains are considered the best extant. This truly is the Land of Pagodas.

PLANNING AHEAD

MYANMAR TOURS & TRAVEL (MTT),

previously called *Tourist Burma, is the country's only official tourism agency and tour operator.* Headquarters is *77-79 Sule Pagoda Rd.* in Yangon (☎ *78376*). Although there are no MTT offices abroad, there is an office in the U.S. called the **Myanmar National Tourist Office**, *2524 University Dr., Durham, NC 27707* (☎ *919-493-7500*). However, it appears to actually be a tour operator rather than an information source and in any event, *travelers should be forewarned that the office doesn't answer its phone for weeks on end.*

Visitors will do much better to contact **Diethelm Travel**, the best-known and most knowledgeable of Myanmar tour operators, at *Kian Gwan Bldg., 1/F, Wireless Rd., Bangkok* (☎ *255-9150*), or one of the tour operators in the U.S. experienced in handling travel to Myanmar and use Diethelm as their local operator.

Among these is **EastQuest**, *1 Beekman St., New York, NY 10038* (☎ *212-406-2224*), whom the Myanmar Consulate in New York recommends not just as a tour operator but as an unofficial travel information source. EastQuest's president, Patricia Cunneen, is partly Burmese and spent much of her childhood there. The company offers independent and group tours of Myanmar.

You can also contact the **Myanmar Embassy**, *2300 S St., NW, Washington, DC 20008* (☎ *202-332-9044*) and the Consulate General-Mission to the *United Nations, 10 E. 77 St., New York, NY 10021* (☎ *212-535-1310*).

Due to the volatile political situation in Myanmar, the U.S. State Department occasionally issues travel advisories. For up-to-date information, call the department's Citizens' Emergency Center (☎ *202-547-5227*). Overseas, contact the U.S. Embassy in Yangon (☎ *82055, ext. 223*), or in Bangkok (☎ *252-5040*).

VISAS

Visas are *required of all travelers to Myanmar,* aged seven years and above, for a stay of up to 14 days only. It takes about four weeks for a visa to be processed and costs $16. Tour operators process visas for travelers on their organized tours. Tourist visas are not extendable but are easily obtained with plenty of notice—at least two weeks. If you are in Bangkok and planning to travel via a Diethelm tour, a visa will be forthcoming in two days' time for about $38. Once inside Myanmar, a business visitor may possibly apply for an extended visa with the invitation and recommendation of a state enterprise.

INOCULATIONS

Shots for smallpox are not required for entry. If you arrive within six days from an infected area, certification of immunization against cholera and yellow fever is required.

ENTRY BY AIR

Entry by air into Myanmar is via Yangon's Mingaladon Airport, the country's only international gateway. There are daily flights that take less than an hour between Bangkok and Yangon. The U.S. State Department currently advises tourists not to fly Myanmar's national airline, Myanmar Air, due to its poor safety record, although the airline has recently purchased new aircraft for use on its routes to Singapore. Thai International offers far superior service than Myanmar Airways between the two capitals but only three times a week. There are also direct flights available from Singapore, Calcutta, Kathmandu, Dacca, Moscow and Beijing on a variety of third-world airlines.

Mingaladon Airport is situated about 19 kilometers northwest of Yangon and there may or may not be a BAC bus to transport passengers into the major hotels. If you are traveling on a package tour, transfers are definitely provided. Expect to pay about $6 if using local taxis (and don't forget to bargain a little).

DEPARTURE BY AIR

Leaving Myanmar is definitely more organized than arrival, especially if your visa is running out. BAC buses will transport passengers from city hotels to the airport for flights in good time for baggage inspection (black market goods and many artifacts may not be exported), foreign currency conversions and what duty-free shopping is available.

Departure tax (about $6) is included in tour package prices.

ARRIVAL BY SEA

Getting there by boat is the only other option available, since the land borders along Myanmar have long been closed and are considered extremely unsafe. Yangon is the country's major port and it lies at the mouth of the Irrawaddy River. Visitors are welcome to travel upriver on private cargo ships or conveyances owned by the government-run Inland Water Transport Corporation to either Mandalay or Nyaung-U (for Bagan). The journey is hot, picturesque and overly time-consuming for those with only a seven-day visa in hand.

Cruise ships in the Far East area often schedule calls at Yangon but thus far, no company has been successful in arranging regular visits.

ARRIVAL BY LAND

With the opening of an overland route between Thailand and Myanmar, visitors may now travel from Mae Sai, Thailand to Kengtung, Myanmar, an eight-hour trip by road each way. Travelers using this route are limited to a three-day/two-night trip (EastQuest and others offer tours). The opening of a China overland route, from Kunming in Yunnan province, is currently under consideration.

DUTY FREE

Duty free is an expression the Burmese have not yet learned. Bona fide visitors may import 200 cigarettes, 50 cigars, or a half-pound of tobacco; one quart of liquor; and one pint of perfume or toilet water, for personal use only. *Customs inspection is lengthy and tedious upon arrival* and all valuables (jewelry, cameras, tape recorders, typewriters, radios, etc.) must be listed in detail and the list must be attached to your passport. *Be sure to carry enough film and batteries for the entire trip.* All foreign currency and credit cards should be included and everything must be exported or you will be requested to show cause. *Although it is very tempting to buy semiprecious gems on the flourishing black market, they cannot be exported without a receipt from the government-owned store. Be careful also of many artifacts, which may not be allowed out of the country* (despite assurances from the seller). *Emptor caveat*, as they say.

CURRENCY

The currency of Myanmar is the **kyat** (pronounced chat) which is divided into 100 *pyas*. The official rate of exchange is approximately 7 kyat = U.S. $1.00. Notes are used in denominations of ks. 1, 5 and 10; make sure markings are in both Burmese and Arabic numerals. Coins are available in denominations of 1 kyat and 1, 5, 10, 25 and 50 pyas. Coins are difficult to decipher because they are marked only in Burmese numerals.

Unlimited amounts of foreign currency, whether in cash or traveler's checks, may be brought into the country. But *remember that what is declared upon entry must be accounted for upon departure.* There are plenty of taxi drivers and tourist guides eager to offer a "better than official rate" for your dollars, so proceed at your own risk. Keep the currency conversion form with you at all times and present it to the customs officials upon exit. *Loss of this document can be very troublesome.* Unless your entire tour has been prepaid in U.S. dollars outside the country, your hotel may demand payment in foreign currency or by credit card. Keep the receipt as an extra precaution.

It is illegal to carry Burmese currency in or out of the country (despite the terrific exchange rates available in Hong Kong, Singapore and Bangkok) and the government does not deal lightly with found offenders. Unspent kyats can be reconverted to U.S. dollars at the time of your departure.

INSIDER TIP

Although we do not want to encourage illegalities of any kind, may we brashly remind you that in artificial economies such as Myanmar, barter is the tourist's best friend. May we suggest purchasing your full allotment of Johnny Walker Scotch and cigarettes (2 liters of booze and 200 cigarettes) in-flight and then exchanging or selling these items once in country.

LOCAL TIME

Local time in Myanmar is Greenwich Mean Time plus 6-1/2 hours. Yangon is half an hour behind Bangkok, 1-1/2

hours behind Hong Kong and 2-1/2 hours behind Tokyo. If it is noon today in Myanmar, it is 12:30 a.m. today in New York and 9:30 p.m. the night before in California.

LOCAL CURRENT

Current is 200-250 volts 50 cycles. *It is best not to count on using fancy electrical gadgets in this country* as you may blow out the entire hotel.

LOCAL WATER

Tap water should not be consumed unless it has been boiled or properly treated. Local fruits and vegetables should be avoided unless peeled with your very own (clean) hands and/or cooked. You should also contact your physician for antimalarial medicine and take it regularly before and after your stay in Myanmar. Experienced travelers also carry their own mosquito coils for use at night. They are available at any Southeast Asian street stall.

OFFICIAL LANGUAGE

The first language is Burmese, spoken by 80% of the population, with a script derived from Sanskrit. Chinese, Tamil, Hindi and minority state dialects are also spoken throughout the country. However, the most important Western language employed is still English and many official signs are left from the colonial period.

There are two English language daily newspapers in Yangon, *The Working People's Daily* and *The Guardian*, which provide some news of the world outside (if you don't expect an impartial opinion). The Myanmar Broadcasting System offers daily programs in English at 8:30 a.m., 1:30 p.m. and 9:30 p.m. There is no television. Books and periodicals in English can be found in the large libraries and universities as well as at both the American and British embassies.

INSIDER TIP

If you pride yourself on picking up the local lingo wherever you go, forget it. Not only do the Burmese have there own unique language but there is constant confusion of old names and new names. If you did knuckle down and pick up the banana leaf derived script (there are few straight lines to allow writing on palm or banana leaves without tearing) from Southern India you would be hard pressed to keep up with the machine gun patter of the Burmese. If you need help, search out the oldest geezer you can find. Hopefully they still recall the queen's English from their colonial days.

BUSINESS HOURS

Businesses are open in Myanmar generally from 9:30 a.m., although banks do not open to the public until 10 a.m. The Myanmar Socialist Program Party and the military begin at 8 a.m. Everyone closes early, so try to do the important business in the morning. Offices are open half-days on Saturdays. No one except private shopkeepers seems to work on Sunday. Most restaurants in Myanmar finish service early (8 or 9 p.m.) so don't plan on a late dinner. The Burmese eat early and apparently retire early. There is no "nightlife" in this country. The fact that the people are under martial law and are used to curfews doesn't encourage all-nighters.

TIPPING

Tipping is *not expected* in Myanmar although service people who are exposed to the major hotels may have heard about the practice. A 10% service charge in the government-run hotels will be added to your bill and nothing else is expected. Helpful guides and taxi drivers frankly prefer new ballpoint pens, lighters and other hard to find Western trinkets.

INSIDER TIP

Since tourism has yet to screw up this country, I strongly advise not to tip service people but to exchange gifts as tokens of friendship and gratitude.

TELEPHONE, TELEX AND FAX

Service in Myanmar does exist, but *expect delays and frustration.* Overseas calls can be made from Yangon but must be booked in advance and placed in order. For some reason, calls to North America are not accepted on Sundays! The Central Telegraph Office in Yangon is located at the corner of Pansodan St. and Maha Bandoola Rd. They're open from 7 a.m. to 8 p.m. and Telex services are available.

The **General Post Office** is located on Strand Road and Bo Aung Gyaw Street in Yangon and operates during normal business hours. Mail for North America and Europe leaves the country twice weekly, on Monday and Friday nights. Another post office at Mingaladon Airport will receive all but registered letters 24 hours daily. The GPO also sells very attractive stamps.

WHAT TO WEAR

Cool, comfortable and conservative clothing. The Burmese dress simply in sarongs and sandals; *footwear is prohibited in religious monuments.* Since many of the touristic sites are temples and other places of worship, visitors are expected to dress with respect. Short skirts and short shorts should not be worn sightseeing. The Burmese are gentle and moral people and are offended by provocative or incongruent dress. No Howard Stern or Madonna wanna-bes please. Long sleeves and long skirts or slacks are also excellent defense against the sun and mosquito bites. *(Watch out for deadly snake bites,* too—which occur more in Myanmar than any other country worldwide.)

Be sure to pack plenty of toilet tissue and other necessities of travel (wash-and-drys, etc.) for a country that has progressed from having little to almost nothing in consumer goods.

LOCAL TRANSPORTATION

Transit in Myanmar consists of vintage vehicles for bumpy roads, the train and the domestic arm of BAC. Somehow, the Burmese have a way with 30-year-old cars and trucks that should have gone to their peaceful rest long ago but still manage to make yet another trip. So have faith, you too will be transported in relative comfort from here to there! In Bagan, it is possible to find a guide with a Jeep or Land Rover. If all else fails, there is still the romance of the horse and buggy (**tonga**) in this country as well as plenty of bicycles with sidecars. These **trishaws** are inexpensive and a wonderful way to enjoy the local scenery.

Taxis have red license plates and can usually be found outside major hotels, but make sure to agree on the fare before setting off.

City **buses** are overly crowded and not recommended for Westerners, who tend to take up too much room and cause a terrible commotion if they don't understand something. MTT operates buses from Yangon up-country, but the journeys I've taken have been tortuous and take too much precious time. For example, a Tourist Burma bus leaves Mandalay at 4 a.m. and arrives in Bagan ten hours later (maybe); another bus leaves Mandalay at 5 a.m. and arrives in Taunggyi about 12 hours later (lucky passengers). True diehards should inquire at MTT for a complete schedule—and always reconfirm the information. Departing and arriving on time is not a virtue of this country's local transportation system.

There are two **trains** daily from Yangon to Mandalay, departing the capital at 7 a.m. and approximately 7 p.m. Both are "express" (only four intermediate stops) and travel time is about 11 hours. There is an Upper Class for about $14, but carry your own food and drink. Some trains have sleeping accommodations and you'll save a whole day if you travel through the night.

Unfortunately, the best way to travel between Myanmar's tourist centers is via BAC, the state-run airline that offers daily flights from Yangon to Mandalay, Bagan, Taunggyi and Sandoway aboard Fokker Friendship equipment. Air tickets must be purchased in foreign currency and are slightly cheaper if booked abroad—but reconfirm again and again, because the state often sees no reason to inform its visitors of a change in schedule.

Passengers may also be hit with a jet surcharge, but it's only a few dollars and not worth arguing about. As flights are often delayed throughout Myanmar, it is wise to carry good reading material along with some snacks, water and other essentials.

CUSTOMS

Customs in Myanmar are similar to those in Thailand and the same do's and don'ts apply. Visitors are expected to respect the national flag, the socialist state, the deep religious feeling that permeates the country and the people themselves. Burmese are extremely polite to one another and employ several different pronouns denoting rank before their names. "*U*" is a title of respect for a man and used before one's proper name (as in U Thant). *Bo* is a title used for members of the military,

Kodaw when addressing monks and *Ko* for men and *Ma* for women of the same rank.

The usual rules apply: Restrain yourself from touching people (Americans love to tousle those cute Asian children) especially on the head and try not to point or sit akimbo with your feet pointing at people. Don't get mad, try not to shout when people don't understand you and remember that things will get screwed up so try to make the best of it.

As yet, *there are no family or surnames among the Burmese,* but this may change when modernization sets in and the people need a stronger identification. So far, names are bestowed upon newborns by soothsayers, who apparently consult the heavens and their own consciences. That completed, parents begin by addressing their young with *Maung* which means "inferior" or *Ko Maung* (if the given name is just one syllable). Like the Thais, the Burmese enjoy spouting a mouthful of words whenever they must speak.

FESTIVALS AND HOLIDAYS

Festivals in Myanmar revolve around the many renowned pagodas. There are plenty of pagodas, as well as plenty of national and regional holidays, so plan to encounter at least one colorful celebration during your seven-day stay in this country. Religious events are guided by the lunar calendar and change from year to year, while political commemorations are dictated by the Roman calendar and therefore take place on the same date annually. Public holidays are marked with an asterisk(*).

*January 4	Independence Day	*Marks Myanmar's independence from the British in 1948. Nationwide sporting events and other festivities.*
*February 12	Union Day	*Marks the country's union in 1947 through efforts of Bogyoke Aung San. Week-long political rally and festival.*
February/ March	Enshrinement of hair relics of Lord Buddha in Shwedagon Pagoda more than 2500 years ago	*Occurs on the day of the full moon of the lunar month Tabaung. Special htamane rice dish offered to monks and Buddhist images.*
*March 2	Peasants' Day	*Similar to our Labor Day.*
*March 27	Armed Forces Day	*Commemorates Burmese resistance against the Japanese. Military parades and evening fireworks display.*
*April	Burmese New Year	*Thingyan (water festival) lasts three to four days with great merriment. Throwing of water denotes good luck.*
*April/May	Kason Lunar Month	*Triple celebration of Buddha's birth, enlightenment and attainment of Nirvana upon his death. Major ritual at Shwedagon Pagoda.*
*May 1	May Day	*Workers' holiday in the socialist world.*
*June/July	Waso Festival	*Marks the beginning of Buddhist Lent. Three-month period of abstinence.*
*July 19	Martyrs Day	*Commemorates 1947 assassination of Bogyoke Aung San and cabinet. Memorial wreaths laid at Martyrs Mausoleum.*

FESTIVALS AND HOLIDAYS

*October	Thadingyut (Festival of Lights)	*Occurs on full moon in the lunar month of Thadingyut and marks the end of Buddhist Lent. Much dancing, feasting and merriment.*
*November	Tazaungdaing Festival	*A festival of lights. All-night weaving contest at Shwedagon Pagoda.*
*December 25	Christmas Day	*The birthday of Jesus Christ.*

Background Material

Burma by Wilhelm Klein and photography by Gunter Pfannmuller, Apa Productions (HK) Ltd., first edition 1981. A wonderful memento of your trip. Well written and beautifully photographed.

Burma Through Alien Eyes by Helen G. Trager, Asia Publishing House, 1966. Missionary views of the Burmese in the 19th century. Available in Yangon.

Burmese Days by George Orwell, available in paperback. Novel about British rule and written in the 1930s. Good atmosphere of colonialism.

Burmese Proverbs by Hla Pe, a UNESCO publication. A charming source of Burmese wisdom. Available in Yangon.

Historical Sites in Burma by Aung Thaw, Director of Archaeology. Published by the government and available in Yangon. Bad reproduction but the best offered.

Harp of Burma by Michio Takeyama (translated by Howard Hibbett), a UNESCO collection of contemporary works published by Tuttle in paperback. If you read nothing else, don't miss this beautiful story of Japanese POWs in Burma. The novel is among recommended world literature classics for high school students.

Rangoon: A Guide for Tourists and Mandalay and Environs, published by U.S. Embassy in Yangon and written by the American Women's Association. Excellent and practical.

Road Past Mandalay by John Masters, Penguin Books, paperback. Memorable account of young British officer during World War II.

Stilwell and the American Experience in China 1911-1945 by Barbara W. Tuchmann, available in paperback. A great document of the Burma campaign by one of our best historians.

The Burman by Shway Yoe (also known as Sir James G. Scott, His Life and Notions). Author spent over 30 years as a British civil servant in Burma and captures the essence of the country, even a full century after it was first written.

The Great Railway Bazaar: By Train Through Asia by Paul Theroux. Available in paperback. Thoroughly entertaining train experiences by a popular writer.

We Burmese by Helen G. Trager, Ph.D. and former visiting professor at the University of Yangon. Published in New York by Praeger. This book explains a great deal about Burmese life and culture.

Yangon

YANGON IN A CAPSULE

*Capital of the Socialist Republic of Myanmar...over 3 million people live tranquilly along the edge of Irrawaddy River delta...city surrounded by water on three sides...an ambience of yesteryear, of 19th-century colonialism left by the British...the writings of Rudyard Kipling and Somerset Maugham still ring true...landscape dominated by one of Buddhism's most important monuments, the 2500-year-old **Shwedagon Pagoda** whose golden dome glistens from dawn to dusK.*

Decaying, fading, with an unmistakable aura of past glories, Yangon will usually be the traveler's first exposure to Myanmar. Unlike typical Asian centers with grey boxlike cities complete with frenetic hordes of scooters and buses, Yangon is a soft gentle city with much to recommend for those who like cities with ambiance. Stroll around the streets, take in the dilapidated buildings and quaint charm of this once romantic colonial outpost. Sit in the bar at the Strand Hotel nursing a gin and tonic while you read your well thumbed paperbacks by Kipling and Maugham. Make sure you spend enough time as you need to take in the many moods of Shwedagon Pagoda. Chat with the people about life and beauty. You will soon come to understand the magical spell Myanmar has had over Westerners who have had the privilege to visit or live here.

WHAT TO SEE AND DO IN YANGON

Botataung Pagoda

A rare hollow pagoda, Botataung is 40 meters high and a 20-minute walk directly east of the Strand Hotel. The original monument, more than 2,000 years old, was destroyed by Allied bombs in 1943, but rebuilt after the war. It contains relics of Buddha as well as several hundred bronze statues.

Chauk Htat Gyi Pagoda

Another contemporary Buddhist monument; several hundred monks live and study here. Known for the enormous reclining Buddha image which is larger than the Buddha in Bago. It's worth a visit.

Kaba Aye Pagoda

1952 monument, 34 meters high, built by U Nu (independent Myanmar's first prime minister) just north of Inya Lake, 11 km from the city. It was dedicated to the cause of world peace and contains relics of two Buddhist disciples. U Nu also built **Maha Pasan Guha** (artifical cave 139 by 113 meters) on the grounds. Skip it unless you want to see the Buddhist sculptures inside.

Kandawgwi Lakes

Tranquil spot in middle of city which features **Bogyoke Aung San Park** and statue of the country's most revered martyr. Show up between 4 and 6:30 p.m. to get great shots of the Shwedagon Pagoda.

Koe Htat Gyi Pagoda

Located on Campbell Road, the pagoda features a huge sitting Buddha image some 5 stories high. See it, because most guides won't tell you it's bigger than the one in Bago.

Martyrs Mausoleum

Just north of Shwedagon Pagoda, the mausoleum contains **Tombs of Aung San**, father of Myanmar's independence and seven other statesmen assassinated with him in 1947. This is the country's most important nationalistic monument. Visit it for the view of the city.

National History Museum

Located on southern shore of Royal Lakes, the museum features some of the best examples of the country's flora and fauna. The area also encompasses horticultural and zoological gardens and Yangon Zoo, where visitors can ride camels and elephants every afternoon.

National Museum

Located a few minutes' walk behind Strand Hotel, the National Museum has interesting displays of artifacts, the most renowned item being the Lion's Throne from the royal palace at Mandalay. Other beautifully carved teak pieces from King Thibaw's reign are also on display here. Make sure you don't miss the upper floors which contain instruments and prehistoric artifacts. Hours are 10 a.m.-3 p.m. Monday to Thursday. Saturday 1 p.m.-3 p.m. Closed Sunday, national holidays and Fridays. A must see for lovers of art and exoctica.

Shwedagon Pagoda

There are special places in the world where architecture, setting, scale and ambiance all come together. The Great Pyramids, The Eiffel Tower and the Shwedagon Pagoda are a few of these unique experiences. You will feel the mystery and power of Asia here. Just under 100 meters high (The Great Pyramid in Egypt is 107 meters high by

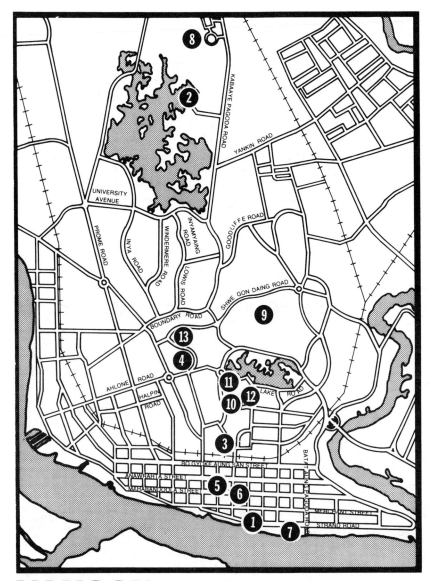

YANGON

Key

1) Strand Hotel
2) Inya Lake Hotel
3) Thamada President Hotel
4) Shwedagon Pagoda
5) San Khantha Hotel
6) Sule Pagoda
7) Botataung Pagoda

8) Kaba Aye Pagoda
9) Chouk Htat Gyi Pagoda
10) National Museum
11) National History Museum
12) Kandawgyi Hotel
13) Martyrs Mausoleum

comparision) on 5.6 hectares, the temple dominates the surrounding countryside. One of Buddhism's most important and impressive monuments. It should be visited at least three times—at dawn, midday and dusk. 78 smaller pagodas are clustered around the base. The pagoda is the center of life for all Burmese and said to possess more gold than the Bank of England, as well as containing precious stones from local mines. The top vane contains 1,100 diamonds and 1,383 other precious stones. The very tip holds a 76-carat diamond (don't tell Liz Taylor!) below 13,153 plates. 30 cm sq. cover the area directly below the *hti* and the entire structure is covered with gold leaf. It takes a climb of over 100 steps to the sacred compound and many important temples and pavilions along the way. Look for the massive bronze bell that the British tried to steal in 1824, but was saved by the Burmese through native ingenuity. Every visit to Yangon should begin and end at this site. And ask the flight attendant which side of the plane will offer the best view when flying out of the country. Admission $5. Camera permit $5.

INSIDER TIP

See it at dawn and dusk, walk around clockwise, take off your shoes (watch out; it gets hot!). Only men are allowed to climb the plinth terrace; check out the east shrine hall if you are in a hurry.

State School of Music and Dance

Located on Shwedagon Pagoda Rd. Visitors may observe classes in traditional Burmese dances and music here during weekdays. Also a special performance on weekends. Inquire at MTT.

Sule Pagoda

Located in the heart of the city, it's the tallest structure in the midtown area. Originally called Kyat Athok, the pagoda is supposed to contain a hair from the Lord Buddha. It's the second most important religious monument in the capital and busy with devotees and merchants.

Yangon Arts and Science University

Located on southern shore of Inya Lake, the university boasts some 10,000 students and an impressive library. Get to know the real people of Myanmar—but try not to discuss politics, there are many informers.

WHERE TO STAY IN YANGON

Dagon (Orient)

256-260 Sule Pagoda Rd. ☎ *71140 • 12 rooms.* In center of town; great in a pinch. Inexpensive.

Inya Lake Hotel   Not recommended

Kaba Aye Pagoda Rd., P.O. Box 1045. ☎ *50644 • 222 rooms.* Built by the Russians ('nuff said). Out of town and difficult to get back and forth. Lovely setting but no atmosphere. Western/Oriental dining room. Coffee shop. Two bars. Swimming pool (if it works). Putting green and tennis court. Hong Kong-based New World Hotels International acquired the management of the Inya Lake and Strand hotels and launched complete renovations, which were expected to be finished by late 1993/early 1994. Somehow I don't think it will matter with this property. Rooms start at about $50 to over $300 (ouch!) for a suite.   ***Reservations: New World (U.S.*** ☎ ***800-538-8882).***

Kandawgyi Hotel

On Kandawgwi Lake on the way to Shwedagon Pagoda ☎ *82255.* Formerly a yacht club and the Natural History Museum. A luxurious but curious hotel with its towering T-Rex dominating the garden. Gentle views, good service (they train hotel staff for other MTT hotels here) and good food. Lakeside bungalows are available. Our second choice in Yangon.

Thamada (President) Hotel

No. 5, Signal Pagoda Rd. ☎ *71499 • 58 rooms.* Situated in the center of town. In-between accommodations. Burmese/Chinese/European dining room. Bar. Coffee shop. $40–$60   *Reservations: MTT*

Sankhantha Hotel

At the railway station ☎ *82975 •* Definitely for those who like their travel seedy and romantic. If , by the time you get to Yangon, all the famous hotels are Asian Ho Jo's, try this place. You better like trains, tropical decay and be willing to pay the $40-$45. Check out the bar.

Strand Hotel   ★★

92 Strand Rd. ☎ *81533 • 100 rooms.* Very Old World. The only place to stay; the spirit of Somerset Maugham still hangs heavy. One of the great old colonial edifices of Southeast Asia, worth the whole journey itself. Helpful staff. Old World dining room serving Burmese/Chinese/European food. Great bar—where locals come to visit. Entertainment of sorts. Our first pick for a taste of old Burma. After the renovation, all bets are off. We'll keep you posted. As mentioned above, New World Hotels International acquired the management of the Strand Hotel and launched complete renovations, which are expected to be finished this year.

         Reservations: New World (U.S. ☎ ***800-538-8882).***

INSIDER TIP

Once the renovations are completed on the Strand, Inya and Thamada hotels they will change from seedy colonial curios to upscale tourist resorts. Rates are expected to double from their currently reasonable range of $30–$60 to the $100–$200 range. Check before you go.

SAMPLING LOCAL FARE IN YANGON

Burmese food leans heavily on a vast number of different curry dishes, ranging from sweet to mild to quite hot, that accompany the daily portion of rice. The Burmese eat everything: fish, fowl, available meats and plenty of fruits and vegetables. Some dishes can be spicier than others, but visitors do not have to worry about the danger of chili overkill that is so prevalent in neighboring Thailand. In fact, the curry dishes are more reminiscent of Indian recipes than of anything else and plenty of bland sticky rice helps soothe your stomach. Some of the most popular local dishes that visitors seem to enjoy are *hinga*, a sweet and sour soup of vegetables; *sibyan*, a fish or meat stew with mild sweet flavoring; and *mohinga*, rice noodles with bits of fish, egg, onions and banana leaf. Condiments, or little side dishes, like *nagapi* or *ngapigyaw* or *balachaung*, should be tried with some trepidation for they all have a chili and fish base and do not always appeal to the Western palate.

Tea is, of course, the national drink and should be quite safe since the water has been boiled. Bottled sodas and People's Brewery Mandalay Beer as well as locally made rum, gin and whiskey are available where tourists gather. Frequent visitors stick to the local beer or bring in their own name-brand spirits.

Western food is available in the dining rooms of the Inya Lake and Strand hotels but most of it is "BB" (Bad British) and tastes as if it were prepared in the last century. (I have always said that the British should have taken their recipes back when they returned independence to these countries.) However, Chinese cuisine and real Indian curries and breads are excellent here.

WHERE TO EAT IN YANGON

Bamboo House
3 Thapye Nyo St., near President Hotel compound in West Yangon ☎ *20018.* Noted for Burmese dishes in a pleasant setting.

Burma Kitchen
141 Shwegondaing Rd. ☎ *50493.* Respected for local dishes and frequented by Westerners.

Dagon Hotel (Orient)
256-260 Sule Pagoda Rd. ☎ *11140.* One of the best for authentic Indian cuisine.

Great Wall
196 Pansodan St. Chinese.

Hla Myanma Rice House

(also nicknamed **Shwe Ba** after local actor who lived nearby.) *27th St. next to Shwedagon Pagoda.* Burmese Food. The "local" place we all look to for home cooking, great food and great prices. No tourists and hard to find. Take a cab and ask for "Shwe Ba" and make eating motions. Say no more.

Inya Lake Hotel

Kaba Aye Pagoda Rd. ☎ *50574.* Burmese, Chinese and Western food in socialist setting. Worthy of a detour for the view, in my opinion.

Kandawgyi Hotel

(in hotel) An exception to big hotel food since the trainees seem to excel at preparing Western and local dishes.

Karaweik Restaurant

Located on eastern shoreline of Royal Lake. ☎ *52352.* A fun but touristy experience for Burmese, Oriental and Western dishes and the cultural show. If you just want to peek inside the replica of a Burmese floating palace, be prepared to pony up 1 kyat. If you like your culture in a neat package, just check out the 10:00 p.m. show with Burmese dancing, singing and rattan ball playing—all accompanied by the somewhat discordant local music. If you can skip the dinner, do so.

Myananda Restaurant

Across from Strand Hotel. Open only in the evening and operated by Strand; great for simple Indian dishes in the open air.

Myanmar Patisserie

Sule Pagoda Rd. and Bogyyoke Aung San St. A tea shop where you can sip tea and try the many different snacks. A colonial English and now Burmese tradition.

Nan Yu

81 Pansodan Street. Chinese (Cantonese).

Nilar Wins's Cold Drink Shop

377 Mahabandoola St. Not a restaurant but a great place to escape the heat and throw back a yogurt/fruit *lassi* or any number of mouth-watering combinations.

Palace

84 37th Street. Great Chinese food, ample portions; ask for costs before you order.

Strand Hotel

92 Strand Rd. ☎ *11533.* Dining room never turned the century. Good Chinese food here though; Western cuisine just passable. Old World atmosphere. A memorable experience for ambience, not the quality of the cooking.

Thamada Hotel

5 Sule Pagoda Rd. ☎ *71499.* Excellent Chinese dishes; located in town center.

Various Street Stalls

41st Street. If you want to try a little of everything, make sure you have a cast iron stomach and are pretty much at the end of your trip. This is the place to catch all those little bugs that cause intestinal upset so make sure it is boiled, fried or cooked well and served hot.

NIGHTLIFE IN YANGON

In a country where you would be arrested for being on the street after 11 p.m. up until 1992, you can imagine that chatting, watching TV or sleeping is about it for excitement. There is the **cultural show** at Karaweik restaurant, a few bad movies (unless you like C grade Kung Fu and Rambo-like imported movies) and hotel bars. If you want to see the real thing, we recommend asking around for *zat pwes,* or **people's theater** festivals, held during temple festivals and fairs (some will be out of town). The theater-like festivals start about an hour before midnight and continue till pre-dawn. *Zat pwes* are typically held during a full moon on temple grounds during the dry season.

INSIDER TIP

Book your trip to Myanmar during a full moon in the dry season (between October-May) if you wish to see a real zat pwe.

Yangon Environs

Until recently, the Burmese government kept Western travelers from visiting certain specific touristic areas to prevent potential harm that might come from warring minority factions within Myanmar. This is still in effect today in the famous Golden Triangle/opium dealing states. However, government policy has become considerably relaxed and visitors who wish to tour places of definite historical and cultural significance may do so by applying to MTT in Yangon and persisting with a gentle firmness.

Pathein

Pathein is the largest town in the Irrawaddy delta (after Yangon), 190 km west of Yangon and a 30-minute flight due west or an 18-hour river journey from the Capital. Formerly known as Bassein, it's inhabited today by Karen and Akan tribes and some Christian converts. The town is famous for three pagodas: **Shwemokhpaw**, **Tagaung** and **Thayaunggyaung**. It's a sleepy port town known for colorful umbrella cottage industries as well as exports of rice and jute. If you're in town for a day or more, try the Pathein Hotel, for about $25-35 a night.

Mawlamyine

Mawlamyine is a picturesue town at the mouth of Salween River—a 40-minute flight southeast from Yangon, 6-8 hours by train (you must take the ferry from Martaban across river when you arrive), which leaves Yangon at 6:30 a.m. and arrives at 12:30 p.m.; returns at 2 p.m. and arrives at Yangon at 8 p.m. Once the country's major teak port, visitors can travel into the forests to see the elephants at work. The town is noted for **Kyaikthanlan Pagoda** which Kipling immortalized in *Mandalay*. There are splendid views of the city and port from the hilltop. See also **Uzena Pagoda** and the **caves of Hapayong** and **Kawgaun** with their Buddhist images. They're an hour south of the city near the town of **Thanbyuzayat**, where there's an Allied war cemetery that commemorates POWs who died constructing the infamous Thailand-Burma railway system for the Japanese.

★ *Bago*

A must see for pagodas. Bago is an easy 50-mile road or train journey north of Yangon. Daily tours are available from MTT. It's the ancient capital of the Mon people, who enjoyed a 270-year Golden Era here from the mid-11th to late 13th centuries. Bago was also the country's greatest seaport in 16th and 17th centuries, however, the river changed course and silted up.

A magnificent landmark is **Shwemawdaw** (Great Golden God) Pagoda, 114 meters high (14 meters higher than Shwedagon). It contains two Buddha hairs. Destroyed by an earthquake in 1930, it was rebuilt in the early 50s. Also impressive is **Shwethalyaung**. The 55 meter long reclining golden Buddha is considered the country's most beautiful and largest reclining Buddha image. Look for the **Mahazedi** (Great Stupa) **Pagoda** that dates from 1560 but has been extensively reconstructed. En route from Bago to Yangon is **Kaikpun Pagoda**. It was built in the 15th century and is a lovely spot to picnic. Detour also to the British War Cemetery where 27,000 Allied soldiers are buried.

Syriam

Syriam is 45 minutes by ferry across the Bago River. It's a small industrial town southeast of Yangon and worthy of a daytrip only if you've seen everything else. The town is the center of Indian life in the country and was a great trading center in the 18th century. Now it's just an oil refinery and home of the People's Brewery (the local beer). But two interesting pagodas are in the vicinity, **Kyaik Khauk** and **Kyauktan**.

Sandoway

This beach resort is on the southeastern side of Bay of Bengal and a few hundred miles northeast of Yangon. There are daily flights to Sandoway via BAC. The area features some pristine stretches of sand as well as some interesting pagodas; a few decent hotels can be found here. No one travels to Myanmar for the beach life, but if you have the time, an entirely different experience awaits you here.

Mandalay

MANDALAY IN A CAPSULE

Golden City founded by King Mindon in 1857 who moved his capital from nearby Amarapura...tradition says that Buddha prophesized that a great center of Buddhism would spring up at the foot of Mandalay Hill in the 2400th year of his religion (A.D. 1857)...most monuments date from mid-19th century...Mindon built a magnificent fortified city...was succeeded by King Thibaw in 1878...but British annexed upper Burma in 1885...city soon lost its cultural glory...devastated by the Second World War...heavy fighting when Japanese took area...fire in May 1981 destroyed many existing monuments and left 35,000 homeless...today Mandalay is a sleepy city of approximately 600,000...full of cottage industries where the arts still flourish.

You already know about the Kipling poem and the old image of Mandalay—but what is there *now*? Mandalay is definitely on our "must see" list for Southeast Asia. When you see how fragile many of the wooden monasteries and temples are you may be glad you went sooner than later. Shwenandaw Monastery is worth the trip alone. Be advised that, like most Asian cities that were flattened in WWII, there is a lot of utilitarian 1950s architecture and a fetid climate that can flatten the hardiest. Pick out your "must sees," travel by taxi and then move out into the countryside. But make it a point to see the treasures of Mandalay before they fall down or burn down!

WHAT TO SEE AND DO IN MANDALAY

Atumashi Kyaung

Known as the Incomparable Monastery before destroyed in 1892. Only the foundation and stairway remain. Atumashi Kyaung was once famous for its beauty and intricate carvings. If you want to skip it and just see what is not there, there are old photos in the Shwenandaw Monastery nearby.

Eindawya Pagoda

Built in 1847 in the midst of the city, this is a lovely shrine. The Buddha image was carried back from India. Worth a visit but hard to find.

Kythodaw Pagoda

"Royal Merit House" is located at base of Mandalay Hill and known as the world's largest book. It's also known for **Maha Lawka Marazein Pagoda**. Features more than 700 surrounding pitaka pagodas built to house marble tables on which entire Buddhist canon Tripitaka is written. It took 2,400 monks and six months just to recite it. Then it took stone cutters six years to inscribe the sacred Pali text on 729 stone slabs. It dates from 1857, when King Mindon founded Mandalay and 1872, when the 5th Buddhist Synod (ecclesiastical council) was called here.

Kyauktawgyi Pagoda

Located near southern base of Mandalay Hill, this pagoda dates from 1853-78. It's known for the seated Buddha carved from a single block of marble.

Mahamuni Pagoda

Located a few miles south of Mandalay on the road to Amarapura. The pagoda is also called **Arakan** or Payagyi (Great Pagoda). It was originally built in 1784, but destroyed by fire and rebuilt a century later. Mahamuni is famous for **Mayamuni Buddha**, a 12-foot bronze seated figure now covered thickly with gold leaf. The figure has been to and fro during local wars. Legend says that Lord Buddha meditated under the bodhi tree in the back garden for an entire week. The stalls are full of interesting artifacts that line the route to the temple. It's best to visit in February during its own festival and time of pilgrimage. Admission $4.

Mandalay Hill

This is the focal point of the city. You can begin your sightseeing with a pilgrimage up the 1,700-plus steps to the top (barefoot, please), past merchants, soothsayers and local school children. The stone walk is covered and cool and there are plenty of places to rest. Small temples and statues line the way. **Shweyattaw Buddha** points to the site of the royal palace; the statue dates from before 1857. See also **Sanda Moke Khit**, a statue of a woman said to be reborn as King Mindon of Mandalay. The view from the top is well worth the climb. Here a plaque tells the story of the heavy losses suffered here by British and Indian troops during World War II.

INSIDER TIP

If you want the best view or photo make sure you beat both the tropical heat and haze and get to the top as early in the morning as you can.

Mandalay Palace

The palace dominates the city even though only a few walls and the moat remain. It was built in the 1860s by King Mindon. The palace is renowned in 19th-century writings for exquisite teak carvings and buildings. It was conquered by the British in 1885 and devastated in 1945 during heavy fighting between British/Burmese troops and the Japanese. Today the palace is known as Mandalay Fort and serves as headquarters for the Burmese Army. King Mindon's Mausoleum and the watchtower are still extant, but not worth a detour.

National Museum and Library

Located near **Shwe Kyi Myint Pagoda** and West Moat Rd., the museum houses artifacts and historical documents salvaged from the turbulence that has prevailed in this Golden City.

Sandamuni Pagoda

The pagoda is located near **Kuthodaw Pagoda**, built over the spot where King Mindon's younger brother, Crown Prince Kanaung was assassinated in 1886. The site is also where Mindon lived during construction of the royal palace; it contains a Buddha image cast in 1802 and over 1,700 marble slabs inscribed with Buddhist canons.

Setkayathiha Pagoda

Located along Shweta Canal, the pagoda dates from 1814 and contains a 5-meter-high bronze Buddha image cast in nearby Ava, as well as a rather creative back-lit halo. Worth a visit and a photo; a bizarre clash of old and new. Who says disco died? The bodhi tree was planted by independent Myanmar's first prime minister, U Nu. If you can't get up to Kyaiktiyo, check out the large reproduction of this fascinating monument to balance and faith.

Shweinbin Kyaung

This monastery contained 13th-century teak carvings; some of them still exist.

Shwe Kyi Myint Pagoda

Built by King Minshinzaw of Bagan in the 12th century, this is one of few extant religious monuments to predate the founding of Mandalay. The Buddha image was dedicated by the king. The pagoda is also known for other images in gold, silver and crystal salvaged from the royal palace during British occupation in 1885.

Shwenandaw Kyaung

Located just east of Atumashi monastery, Shwenandaw Kyaung was built by King Thibaw in 1880. The materials came from the apartment owned by King Mindon. It's renowned for fine carvings and scenes from the 10 great Jataka and is one of friendliest monasteries in Mandalay.

State School of Fine Art, Music & Dance
Located near the royal palace along East Moat Rd. Visitors may attend rehearsals as well as performances.

Mandalay Environs

Amarapura

This is the Immortal City founded by King Bodawpaya in 1781 that served as capital of Upper Burma until 1882. Amarapura is located just a few miles south of Mandalay and reachable by taxi or public bus. The original city was a perfect square with a moat surrounding walls of brick; little is left of the citadel today. Most of the bricks were dismantled and moved to Mandalay by King Mindon. Still standing are 4 pagodas: **Kyauktawgyi Pagoda**, built by King Bagan in 1847; **Patodawgyi Pagoda**, built by King Bagyidaw in 1820 and the twins on the bank of the Irrawaddy River, **Shwekyetyet** and **Shwekyetkya pagodas**—both built in 12th century. U Bein Bridge over Taungthaman Lake is considered the oldest bridge in the country. Amarapura is known today for its fine weavers.

Ava

Ava is called the City of Gems (*Ratnapura*). It's located where the Irrawaddy and Myitnge rivers meet in Upper Burma, just east of Amarapura by bus from Mandalay. It was founded in A.D. 1364 and was the seat of a kingdom until 1841 when it was abandoned in favor of Amarapura. It's in ruins today but **Maha Aungmye Bozan Monastery** is worthy of a detour. The building is a beautiful white structure with an eerie air. Also check out **Htilainshin Pagoda**, built by King Kyanzittha during the Bagan era. In the south of the city are **Leitutgyi** and **Lawkatharaphu pagodas** and **Ava Fort**. Modern Ava Bridge in the northern section was built by British in 1934. The Brits blew it up in the retreat of 1942. It was reconstructed in 1954 and is still the only bridge that crosses Irrawaddy River.

Inle Lake

Inle Lake is reachable by daily flights from Mandalay or Yangon and is often included in 1-week tours of Myanmar. It's a beautiful area located in Shan state; the main attractions are famous Shan legrowers on the lake, who maneuver long boats with one leg wrapped around the oar. The local weaving industry is famous, but handwoven Shan shoulder bags are often cheaper elsewhere. It's highly controlled by the government here.

Maymyo

This hill station is some 2-1/2 hours by road northeast of Manda-lay and was popular with British colonials for the breathtaking views at 3,500 feet and pleasant temperatures. It boasts an Old World hotel called Candacraig and a 175-acre botanical garden. There's also golf and waterfalls for swimming and picnics. There's a strictly 19th-century atmosphere here. Maymyo is known as **Pyinulwin** by the Burmese. Relax and enjoy the surroundings in horse-drawn carriages. Get up early to enjoy the crisp air and take in the morning market and the Shan people who trade here. The more athletic may want to hike the 9 km down to Anisaka to see the five waterfalls.

This was also the site of the Burma Road that supplied Chiang Kai Shek. Loss of the road to the Japanese then forced U.S. troops to fly the Hump, which claimed over 600 aircraft and the lives of over 1,000 servicemen.

Most people take the 8-passenger taxi jeeps that leave from the town. The trip takes 2-1/2 hours up and about 45 minutes less back. Be prepared for breakdowns, water stops and a sore rear end. Grab a seat up front. Train buffs may wish to take the laborious 5-hour train trip from Mandalay that huffs and puffs up the mountain in a series of tortured switchbacks. Catching the train at 5 p.m. won't be too tough since there will be little nightlife to distract you.

Mingun

A great day trip for the boat ride and the experience. Mingun boasts a 200 year old, 90 ton **Mingun Bell**, the largest ringing bell in the world and a massive 50-meter-high brick foundation for unfinished **Mingun Pagoda**. Mingun is one hour by boat from Mandalay. King Bodawpaya took temporary residence on this island in the Irrawaddy River while building Mingun Pagoda on the west bank between 1790 and 1797. It would have stood 150 meters high, but, unfortunately, it was never finished and is now considered the largest pile of bricks in the world (the base is 72 meters on each side). The 5-meter-wide Mingun bell was cast for the pagoda. The present pagoda is one-third the size of the intended monster pagoda. Visitors can strike the bell; you can even stand inside while you do it. Mingun is a popular place for day outings for Mandalayans.

INSIDER TIP

If you want to avoid the overpriced tourist office package, just buy a ticket on the riverboats that leave the 26th St. Pier (every hour in the mornings). It takes an hour each way for the 11 km trip and the last boat returns to Mandalay at 4 pm.

Sagaing

This was the capital of Shan kingdom from A.D. 1315 until it moved to Ava in 1364. It's located on the right bank of the Irrawaddy River south of Mandalay, just across Ava Bridge. The landscape is beautiful and dotted with religious monuments. There are at least 600 monasteries and 5,000 monks live here. The air is alive with the ringing of bells and chanting of prayers. Notable pagodas include 15th-century **Htupayon**. **Hsinmyashin** was built by King Monhyin of Ava in A.D. 1429 and destroyed by an earthquake in 1955, but still contains some valuable images and votive tablets. The **Kaunghmudaw** (Rajamanicula) was built by King Thalun in 1636 and enshrines a tooth relic of Lord Buddha. The **Aungmyelawka** was erected in 1782-1819 and the **Ngadatkyi** was built in 1657. Also see the **Ponnyashin Zedi**, which contains 2 relics of Buddha and **Onhmin Thonze** (30 Caves) Pagoda. **Tilawkaguru cave temple** was built about 1672 with rare artifacts of the Ava period. You can ask to overnight in a Buddhist monastery.

Taunggyi

Taunggyi is a hill station north of Inle Lake and reachable by daily flights from Mandalay or Yangon to Heho; then by bus. The stop is only for those with plenty of time. The local museum is worthy of a visit.

WHERE TO STAY IN MANDALAY

Don't expect much from the government approved hotels, but we would recommend spending at least one night in Maymyo just to experience the English country-house hotel.

Mandalay

Htun La Hotel

27th Rd. ☎ *21283* • *10 rooms.* Some with air conditioning and private bath, some without. Restaurant serves Burmese, Chinese and Western food. Beer garden and swimming pool (when functioning). 5 minutes from Mandalay Hotel.   ***Reservations: MTT.***

Inwa (Ava) Inn

66th St. near Mandalay Palace. Newer hotel.

Mandalay Hotel

26 B Rd. ☎ *21004, 22499* • *68 rooms.* Best hotel in town, just across from the royal palace. Reserved for tourist groups. Comfortable motel-like accommodations. Restaurant serves Burmese, Chinese and Western food; bar and beer garden. Cheaper rooms are fan cooled, more expensive come with air conditioning.   *Reservations: MTT.*

Mya Mandala Hotel

Near Mandalay Hotel • *50 rooms.* Mildly interesting hotel that caters to budget tour groups. Pool, popular bar.

Manmyo Hotel

78th St. Near the railway station. Popular and moderate in price.

Maymyo

Candacraig Hotel

(Maymyo Hotel or Pyin Oo Lwin Government House) *Center of town up the hill* A classic English county manor built from solid teak. Built in 1906 for the single male employees of the Bombay Burma Trading Company (a company set up to extract teak from the surrounding forests). We recommend making a special detour just to experience this hotel and its attentive staff. You can order roast beef, enjoy locally grown strawberries, have a port in front of the roaring fire and enjoy this time-warp hotel that brings back dreams of the empire and adventure.   *Reservations: Direct.*

WHERE TO EAT IN MANDALAY

The best plan in Mandalay is to stay with the menus available at the Htun La or Mandalay hotels for Burmese, Chinese and Western dishes. Both hotels also offer a plentiful supply of Mandalay beer from the People's Brewery. Nyaung Bin Yin on 29th Rd. is a local Burmese restaurant that caters to Western palates and there are some good Chinese establishments in town—someone at either hotel will guide you to a favorite. If you want to wander out, there are no distinctive restaurants, but you can try Shan food, which is similar to Thai food, in the many small eateries.

Needless to say, there is no nightlife in Mandalay.

Bagan

Bagan's structures have withstood the ravages of war, time and nature.

BAGAN IN A CAPSULE

Formerly called Pagan...Deserted capital on the Irrawaddy...seat of kingdom of Myanmar from A.D. 1057 to 1284 and center of Burmese Buddhism....10,000 religious monuments built during its Golden Age...now only a few thousand left on a plain 8 miles along the river bank by 2 miles inland...structures have suffered ravages of war, time and natural disasters (including devastating earthquake in 1975)...Area thought to have been settled as early as 2nd century A.D....and known by classical name Arimaddanapura...today just a dusty plain with many breathtaking vistas...reachable by daily flights from Yangon and Mandalay to small airport near Nyaung-U...then a half-hour ride to the banks of the Irrawaddy.

The normal question travelers ask before they plan their trip is "What is there to see?" Bagan is a place where there is so much to "see" that you may want to dedicate a major part of your trip just to take it all in. What there is to "see" are not individual attractions so much as the massive sight of thousands of different pagodas dotting the landscape (there are over 5,000 sites). If you were to visit one place that conveys the power of Burmese religious fervour and exotic artistic tastes, it would be Bagan.

INSIDER TIP

Bagan was formerly referred to as Pagan and in many guidebooks, is listed under Pagan. If you get confused by all the name changes, all we can say is welcome to Myanmar (Burma), the world's record holder for new names.

Many visitors also come away with a powerful feeling of place. A mysterious and tangible feeling of being at the center of a very important spiritual center. Even the nonspiritual admit that there is something here that inspired the Burmese to construct these thousands of religious monuments. Like all great wonders of the world, I urge you to see it for yourself and form your own opinion.

INSIDER TIP

All temples and pagodas are considered sacred—the area of Bagan more so because of the many people who come here for religious reasons: You might want to make sure you show up in Bagan with clean laundry. Dress conservatively and cleanly; no shorts, no long T-shirts, women should not be overly exposed. You won't necessarily be shot or arrested, but you'll suffer the wrath of indignant locals.

If you spend some time in Bagan, you will learn that there are two basic types of religious buildings: pagodas—also known as *ceityas*, *chedis* and *dagobas* (yes, that is where George Lucas got the name of the planet in Star Wars and no, Yoda does not live here)—*stupas* and *zedis*. These are the gentle bell-shaped structures that usually entomb a piece of the Buddha. They are Indian in origin and are the most common. The other type is the temple, which tends to be hollow and is similar to the Christian church, where people enter to reflect and meditate. The structure of the temple can be curiously reminiscent of our Gothic cathedrals, with spires that reach up to the heavens. The only major difference is that Buddhists build temples as places to revere the concept and principal of a man, rather than a god (Buddha).

INSIDER TIP

The best way to see Bagan is to rent a jeep and a guide. That way you can concentrate on the spots and the timing that interest you (important for photographers). A guide can take you to some of the lesser-frequented shrines that are locked. He will have the grounds keeper open them up for you.

WHAT TO SEE AND DO IN BAGAN

To get the most out of your trip, concentrate on the temples closest to the village. Start as early as you can to visit the pagodas or stupas, leaving the temples or museums for midday when the heat and haze build. Late in the afternoon, or near sunset, try to capture some of the more spectacular sites like Thatbyinnyu, or the view from Mt. Popa.

Abeyadana Temple

Located in Myinkaba village (just 2 km south of Bagan's city walls), this temple was named after the wife of Bagan's King Kyanzittha (1084-1112). The site is where she waited for the king when he fled the wrath of his brother King Sawlu (1077-1084). It resembles Nagayon nearby with its red brick and perforated windows. There's a bell-shaped stupa and interesting frescoes.

Ananda Temple   ★

The best known of Bagan's monuments, this is a whitewashed structure that dominates the landscape. It was built by King Kyanzittha to resemble the snowcapped Himalayas. The golden pinnacle of tapering pagoda glistens in the sun; the temple is planned like a perfect Greek cross. The four large corridors and many narrow passages are lit naturally. The upper terraces are decorated with 389 scenes illustrating Jatakas. The temple also houses the largest collection of glazed plaques found on any shrine. A colossal Buddha is enshrined within the structure. Plus, there are many, many smaller images. Earthquake damage to the temple was repaired by Myanmar's archaeology department. Ask to see upper terraces for views, especially near sunset. A must see: the two Buddha footprints.

Bupaya Pagoda

Located on the banks of Irrawaddy River, Bupaya's claim as the oldest pagoda built in Baganhas has not been substantiated. The original structure was commissioned by King Pyusawti during the 2nd century A.D. The bulbous shaped dome definitely predates King Anawrahta and the Golden Age of Bagan.

Dhammayangi Temple

This is Bagan's largest shrine, built by King Narathu (1167-1170) to atone for past sins. This is also one of best preserved temples; it resembles Ananda Temple in plan. It features brilliant masonry but the structure was never completed. Narathu was assassinated by an Indian prince. The temple is located southeast of city walls.

Gawdawpalin Temple

Located near the Irrawaddy. Built in Burmese style by King Narapatisithu (1173-1210), it is one of the area's most impressive monuments, with two stories of splendor. Unfortunately, it was badly damaged during a 1975 earthquake. Good views from the top, though.

Htilominlo Temple

This temple is located between Bagan and Nyaung-U and was constructed by King Nantaungmya (1210-1234), whose other name was Htilominlo. It is considered the last Burmese-style temple built in Bagan. Htilominio is in the same class as Sulamani Temple. Check out the stucco carvings.

Kubyaukkyi Temple

Located in Myinkaba village, near Bagan, this temple was built by Rajakumar following the death of his father, King Kyanzittha in A.D. 1112. It has many features of the early Bagan temples—dark corridors lit by perforated stone windows. This is an excellent example of its period. There are fine Jataka prints and Buddha images inside, as well as Mayazedi stone inscribed in four languages: Burman, Mon, Pali and Pyu. It's kept locked to avoid thefts of frescoes. Check with attendants for keys.

Kyaukku Umin

This cave temple near Nyang-U was built against the side of a deep ravine; its long tunnels have been excavated. A huge seated Buddha faces the entrance. Kyaukku Umin was attributed to King Kyanzittha. The upper stories date to King Narapatisithu's reign (1174-1211).

Lokananda Pagoda

One of three pagodas built by King Anawrahta, it was erected in A.D. 1029. There's a graceful white stupa with a tall, cylindrical golden bell. Also, the pagoda has three octagonal terraces; the lower two can be ascended by stairs on all four sides.

Mahabodhi Temple

Constructed during the reign of Nantaungmya (1211-1234), the temple is an exact replica of an Indian temple where Buddha achieved enlightenment. It features the only architectural style of its kind in Myanmar.

Manuha Temple

Manuha was built in A.D. 1059 by King Manuha of Thaton, whom Anawrahta deposed and captured. The king was brought to Bagan, along with numerous Mon architects, artists and craftsmen to begin the Golden Age of construction. Manuha worried he would become a temple slave, so he built this monument to gain heavenly merits. Unfortunately, the second story collapsed during the 1975 earthquake, but was restored. The temple is known for four large enshrined Buddhas; one of them is reclining. The temple is very cramped; skip it if you are pressed for time.

Mimalaungkyaung Temple

This temple is located near the south gate of the old city; it was built in A.D. 1174 by King Narapatisithu. It's a small and square structure, with a tall spiral pagoda. Narapatisithu avenged his brother (then king) and murdered him for wife-stealing. Narapatisithu then ascended to the throne (1173-1210).

Mingalazedi Pagoda

Located just south of Bagan, this is the last of the great stupas built during the Golden Age. Its construction is said to precipitate the fall of Bagan. It was built by King Narathihapate in A.D. 1284, but his own arrogance dethroned him. He was forced to tear down many fine temples in the area to rebuild fortifications, as the army of Kublai Khan was on its way. Nonetheless, this monument represents the pinnacle of Burmese architecture. It's noted for unglazed Jataka plaques around its terraces. Put on your must-see list.

Myinkaba Pagoda

Myinkaba is located on the banks of Myinkaba River in a village of the same name. It marks the spot where Anawrahta killed his half-brother Sokkate in A.D. 1044 and took the monarchy. Anawrahta erected the temple to expiate his crime. There are low round terraces and an elongated bell. The pagoda is almost cylindrical in shape, in the very early style.

Nagayon Temple

Stands on the site where Kyanzittha hid from brother Sawlu, his predecessor on the Bagan throne. Here he was given protection by a naga. The structure has an elegant form; there are corner stupas on all terraces and a graceful pinnacle. Also found are lovely paintings in the corridors and a double life-size Buddha image under the hood of an enormous naga (serpent). The temple is locked, so ask for the key to see the Buddhas and murals inside.

Nanpaya Temple

This temple is said to have been captive King Manuha's residence in Myinkaba. It was later converted to a temple. It's built in the very early style—brick faced with stone, perforated stone windows and a crenelated roof line. This is a great place for being under house arrest.

Nathlaungkyaung Temple

Constructed in A.D. 931 by Taungthugyi, the temple was dedicated to Hindu god Vishnu. It was Bagan's great Hindu temple during its Golden Age, but now only the main hall and superstructure are still standing. The exterior of the building and the porch are also lost. The

famous central **Vishnu statue**, seated on the Garuda, was carried off to
the Berlin Museum at the turn of this century. A standing image of
Siva in the Bagan Museum may have once been here.

Ngakywenadaung Pagoda

Attributed to King Taungthugyi and constructed in the 10th century,
this pagoda definitely belongs to the pre-Anawrahta period. It is similar in style to Bupaya Pagoda with its bulbous-shaped structure on a
cylindrical base. Now it seems like an unaesthetic pile of bricks.

Bagan Museum

Located near Thiripyitsaya Hotel, the museum contains displays of
what the Burmese have managed to salvage of the artistic wealth of the
area—statues, paintings, architectural embellishments, etc., as well as
votive panels collected in the region. They are written in Burmese,
Mon, Pyu, Pali, Tamil, Thai and Chinese—quite a meeting of Asian
minds.

Pebingyaung Pagoda

Constructed in the 12th century and noted for its Sinhalese type of
stupa with a square chamber between the bell and finial, the pagoda
confirms the close ties that existed between Ceylon and Burma during
this period. King Anawrahta sent ships and supplies to squelch a
Hindu Cholas invasion of Ceylon. He also sent monks to strengthen
the future of Theravada Buddhism in Ceylon.

Pitakat Taik

This was King Anawrahta's library, built to house elephant loads of
scriptures brought to Bagan from Thaton following his conquest. The
structure is 51 square feet and 60 feet high. The entrance is on the
east side, with 3 perforated stone windows on the other sides. The
interior conforms to the plan of early Bagan temples. This is one of
the few secular structures preserved in Bagan. Unfortunately, it was
altered in 1783 by King Bodawpaya. It also had finials added to the
corners of five roofs.

Sarabha Gateway

This is the eastern gateway into Bagan from Nyaung-U and the only
section of King Pyinbya's 9th-century city walls still standing. Bagan's
guardian spirits, Nga Tin De and sister Shwemyethana, have prayer
niches here—these are the most important spirits in Myanmar after
King of Nats and Thagyamin.

Shwegugyi Temple

Located on the road to Nyaung-U, this temple was built by King
Alaungsithu in A.D. 1131. The king died in the temple at the grand
old age of 81. The temple faces north toward the former royal palace
site and stands on a brick platform. The hall and inner courtyard are
lit by large windows and doors, which denotes the Burmese style
architecture that evolved here.

Shwesandow Pagoda

This pagoda was erected by King Anawrahta in A.D. 1057 following his victorious return from Thaton. The stupa enshrines hairs of Lord Buddha sent to Anawrahta by the king of Bago. It's also called the Ganesh Temple because elephant-headed Hindu god images stood at the corners of all 5 terraces.

Bagan's golden age began with the conquest of Thaton.

Shwezigon Pagoda

One of the most venerated in all Myanmar, the pagoda was begun by King Anawrahta (1044-1077) and finished by Kyanzittha (1084-1112). It is the most important shrine in Bagan. Buddha's collar bone, frontlet bone and tooth are here. Pilgrims from throughout Myanmar arrive every autumn for the Shwezigon Pagoda Festival; it's one of the most popular in the country. This is considered the prototype of later Burmese stupas, featuring an elegant structure with a golden dome and hti, despite the many renovations done on it by subsequent rulers. This is a favored place to visit.

Sulamani Temple

Located midway between Bagan and Minnanthu village, this is one of Bagan's fine two-storied monuments. It was built by King Narapatisithu (1173-1210) 10 years after ascending the throne. The upper story sits on a pillar and there are seated Buddha images on all four sides of the lower floor. There are also some 18th-century paintings.

Thandawgya Image

This is a huge seated Buddha built by King Narathihapate in A.D. 1284; it stands almost 20 feet high. Its hands signify the moment of enlightenment. The Buddha has a slightly jaundiced appearance, but is nonetheless important to the Golden Age monuments. It's located near Thatbyinnyu Temple.

Thatbyinnyu Temple

This is the temple of omniscience and the tallest structure in Bagan. The temple was built by Alaungsithu (1112-1167) and consists of two enormous cubes. The upper story is reached from the inside staircase. There is a Buddha image here, as well as a wonderful view of the Bagan plain. Thatbyinnyu resembles Ananda Temple, but it's not designed in the Greek cross-style. It's also small.

Tally Pagoda

The pagoda is built from the same bricks as the temple. Ruins of bell pillars in a former monastery are nearby.

WHERE TO STAY IN BAGAN

As in other popular areas in Myanmar, there is a desperate need for mid-range lodging—both comfortable and culturally sensitive. Needless to say, you won't find it in Bagan. Hopefully, as the demand rises, there will be a better selection of places to stay. For now, you can choose between luxury (Thiripyitsaya Hotel), simple (Ayeyar Hotel) or cheap (Bagan Hotel). The more adventurous or impecunious can choose from a cluster of cheap guesthouses.

Bagan Hotel

Near the main road near Ayerar Hotel. 2 story guesthouse with fan-cooled rooms. Chalet-style bungalows available with air conditioning are more expensive. Ask for a river view room. Inexpensive.

Ayeyar Hotel (Irra Inn)

Near Bupaya Pagoda, about a mile from Thiripyitsaya Hotel. ☎ *24 • 27 rooms.* Singles, doubles and a suite with private bath; no air conditioning. Ask for river-side junior suites with fridge and a view. Restaurant with Burmese, Chinese and Western menu. Bar. Inexpensive.

Reservations: MTT.

Thiripyitsaya Hotel   ★★★

Overlooking Irrawaddy River in the midst of the ruins. ☎ *A28 • 36 rooms.* Modern resort hotel style; large clean rooms with air conditioning and private bath. Only place to stay in Bagan. Very good restaurant with Burmese, Chinese and Western menu. Bar. Gift shop. Nice grounds. 6 bungalows with verandas available. Accepts Amex-card. Moderate to expensive.   *Reservations: MTT.*

WHERE TO EAT IN BAGAN

The best bet in Bagan is the dining room of the Thiripyitsaya Hotel. Otherwise there are a number of inns scattered among the ruins: the **Irra** near Bupaya Pagoda, the **Cooperative** near Gawdawpalin Temple, the **Moe Moe** near Mimalaung-kyaung, the **Burma Rest House** near the BAC office and the **Aung Mahaya Lodge** near Shwegugyi Temple.

Visitors to Bagan are grateful for the lack of nightlife, for fatigue sets in soon after dinner from all that walking among the ruins. For times when there is a full moon, keep your eyes peeled for the tell-tale bamboo stage scaffolding that tips you off to *zat pwe* ceremonies. There are fewer people in this area, though, due to the 1990 uprooting of the old Bagan village.

SHOPPING IN MYANMAR

Myanmar's shopping specialties include lacquerware, painted parasols, traditional shoulder bags, precious gems, tapestries, wood and ivory carvings and puppets.

Myanmar may be an isolated, so-called third-world country, but inveterate shoppers will find a treasure trove here of local handicrafts and natural resources Some of the world's finest **semiprecious** and **precious stones** are mined in Myanmar's soil, including Blood Ruby and Imperial Jade (which even the Chinese admit is superior in quality to anything found in their country). Other splendid gems available for adornment include sapphires, aquamarine, topaz, emeralds, amethysts and lapis lazuli. Indeed, the abundance of such gifts from nature explains why the annual February Gems and Pearl Emporium at the Inya Lake Hotel in Yangon is an exciting event and draws dealers from all over the world to bid upon what the government controlled industry places in auction.

If you are not an expert gemologist, but still plan to make some major purchase in unset stones, the government advises that visitors not stray from the Tourist Department Store (formerly the Diplomatic Shop) on Sule Pagoda Rd. (and its various branches throughout the country). Here, in something that resembles the Friendship Stores in the People's Republic of China, are cases and cases of gems in the full range of brilliance, quality and weight. The prices are set by the government and payment must be in hard currency (U.S. dollars or traveler's checks). Street peddlers and relatives of your driver and/or guide will have stones at better prices, gems so well-made that even top jewelers often cannot tell that they are synthetic. Artificial stones are everywhere in Myanmar and there is no such thing as a bargain-basement authentic ruby!

The Black Market

Since we are on the subject of tricky dealings we should explain what the black market is and isn't. The government of Myanmar wants your Western currency and they don't want to pay retail. If you are paid in kyats at the real value of about 100K to the dollar, the government wouldn't make any money—so they feel more comfortable forcing you to spend at about 6K to a U.S. dollar. This means you could spend a lot or a little for the exact same service or product. It is **illegal** in Myanmar to:

- import kyats

- export kyats

- **change money** at any place other than official banking establishments

Now anybody who has traveled more than 1000 miles is thinking about how to take advantage of this artificial system. First of all, it is not illegal to barter or exchange products. Second of all, you can keep a second wallet as long as you don't plan on leaving the country with any kyats and, finally, they'll get your bucks on the airfare, hotel and meal portions of your trip. Since we cannot advise anyone to break the law, all we can say is that large U.S. bills bring the best rates and the best place to do it (which we know you won't) is in Yangon.

Myanmar's shopping attractions include lacquerware, parasols, gems, wood and ivory carvings and tapestries.

The Tourist Department Store

The Tourist Department Store should be everyone's first stop, for two reasons. First, it gives a general idea of the beautiful handicrafts available throughout the country. Second, it allows you—as a foreigner—to buy goods like cigarettes and then walk outside and sell them for an immediate profit. After you are finished taking advantage of this loophole, you can spend your time admiring the exquisite lacquerware from the Bagan area, gold leaf and teak carvings from Mandalay, silverwork from Sagaing, copper and brass items from Mandalay, beautiful handwoven material lengths and embroideries and the popular Shan shoulder bags. Although prices are higher in this state-run store, the one-stop shopping is convenient. With all the sightseeing that you may wish to pack into a seven-day stay (not to mention the transportation delays), you'll find there is often not enough time to do extensive shopping while touring. Fortunately, there is a small branch of the Tourist Department Store at the airport for last-minute items, but the secret of departing Myanmar with invaluable souvenirs is to buy what you simply can't live without when you first see it.

Market people will love the sights and sounds of the vast local outdoor emporia in both Yangon and Mandalay. In addition to imported consumer items (most of them smuggled over the border from Thailand), there are stalls and stalls of foodstuffs and local craftsmen selling their artistry. Yangon's largest and most prosperous marketplace is the **Bogyoke Aung**

San, which the British always called the Scott Market. It is located across from Yangon's red-brick Moorish-style railway station, at the corners of Sule Pagoda Rd. and Bogyoke Aung San St.—and it has everything! A great place for photographers as well as for a little bargaining.

Other spots of interest for frenetic activity and lots of local color are the **Open Air Market** off Shwedagon Pagoda Rd. and the **Thein Gyi Zei** (also known as the Indian Market), with its ample supply of fruits and vegetables. If your nostrils can take the pungent odors, it's worth a walk through. Yangon also has a large Chinatown section and the **Chinese Market** can be found on Lan Ma Daw Rd., not far from the Chinese Temple.

SHOPPING IN MANDALAY

Around Mandalay's Diamond Jubilee Clocktower (erected in honor of Queen Victoria's 60th year as monarch) is the **Zegyo Market**, which brings together the varied ethnic groups of Central and Upper Myanmar. At night, the Zegyo Market has the flavor of Istanbul's great bazaar and about as much variety in goods for sale. And since Mandalay was created as the artistic and religious center of Myanmar, you can find beautiful handicrafts as well as curious antiques. Shan shoulder bags can be bought here cheaper than where they are made and the renowned teak carvings of Mandalay are less expensive here than in the Tourist Department Store. In any event, the Zegyo Market is about the only diversion in Mandalay during the evening hours, so you should not miss it.

SHOPPING IN BAGAN

Bagan has no great market, but the area is full of lacquerware cottage industries where you can pick up gold leaf wedding baskets and such. Local guides will be delighted to act as agent/interpreter—for a nice tip, of course. In any event, save some money for shopping in Myanmar—and enjoy the experience.

PHILIPPINES

Mactan Island is famous for its guitars and ukuleles.

PHILIPPINES IN A CAPSULE

7,000-odd archipelago on the edge of the South China Sea...land mass slightly smaller than Japan but coastline twice that of United States ...largest islands–Luzon and Mindanao–represent 65% of the total land area; discovered by Spanish traders in 1521; Malays arrived as early as 700 B.C. from Indonesia...islands came under U.S. administration in 1898 following Spanish-American war...fully independent on July 4, 1946....Since February 1986 and the election of Mrs. Corazon Aquino, the Philippines is undergoing a "rebirth"...almost 50 million Filipinos...national languages are English and Pilipino (Tagalog).

With an archipelago some 7,000 islands strong and a shoreline twice that of the United States, it is not surprising that the Philippines plays host to over 100 different ethnic groups who speak at least 80 separate languages and dialects. This country is a contradiction in itself, an anomaly in the midst of Southeast Asia. Its people range from the fairest of fair, who only follow European trends, to the fiercest and darkest of hilltribes, who rarely see the light of day. And, of course,there are the tribes who'd like you to believe that they're the fiercest and darkest of hilltribes. By day, they parade around naked with threatening looking speers and sneers for the "adventure" tourists who "just happened" to stumble into their "undiscovered" villages with their guides and, by night, kick back in their Levis to swill a couple of San Miguels and take in a Dodger game on the dish.

If there's any evidence that exists about bogus tribes in the Philippines, it probably has something to do with the sweet, gentle Tasaday, who many anthropologists have been arguing for years live in a totally unaltered Stone Age milieu. The Tasaday were "discovered" in the early 1970s by loggers deep within the Mindanao rainforest. This prehistoric tribe made fire with a drill and lived in caves. They took their food from trees and streams and used stone tools. Since their discovery, the debate surrounding the Tasaday's authenticity has raged in the scientific community. How many scientists have come back with that once-in-a-lifetime shot of a banana-leaf clad Tasaday princess breast feeding her child, blown it up to 900 percent and mounted it in the library? Are the Tasaday really the cave-dwelling people whom Filipino aid organization director Manuel Elizalde described as "not knowing there is a country. They didn't know there was a sea. The simplest things like rice; they did not know what it was, nor do they even have a name for it?" Or are they the scientific hoax of the century? Recently an anthropologist showed up at a Tasaday village in the rainforest unannounced. He found the tribespeople fully dressed in sarongs, Western T-shirts and jeans and photographed a family. Two journalists, who were expected, dropped by only a week later and discovered and shot the same villagers clad only in orchid leaf loincloths and skirts, the women barebreasted. So much for the noble savages.

Despite the fact that hotel, travel and food prices are some of the lowest in Asia, the Philippines remains largely untouristed. Many Americans perhaps fear the anti-U.S. sentiment that has grown over recent years in urban areas. But the fact is that Filipinos are some of the warmest people in Asia. And the Philippines is an outdoorsman's

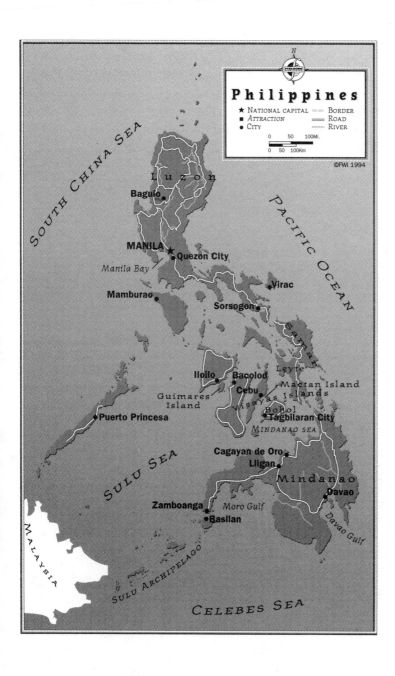

paradise. There are beautiful jungles and pristine white sand beaches that border gently lapping crystalline seas. The diving here (among 30,000 sq. km of kaleidoscopic coral reefs!) is considered unmatched in the world. There are volcanoes and the spectacular rice terraces of northern Luzon. There are mountains that shouldn't be climbed by anyone but experts and others that offer easy hiking.

Unlike other destinations in the Far East, there isn't a lot worth seeing here in the way of magnificent temple ruins or religious architecture. The Philippines should be enjoyed more for its natural beauty.

INSIDER TIP

Although the Philippines offers an abundance of lush jungles and unspoiled natural surroundings, this country, like so many others in the tropics, is witnessing a horrifying rate of deforestation. During the last 40 years, it's estimated that the Philippines has lost nearly three quarters of its rainforests due to relentless population growth, unabated slash-and-burn agriculture in marginal upland areas and the commercial rape of its jungles for hardwoods. The government has initiated conservation programs, but some researchers predict that the country's forests will be denuded entirely by 2010.

The Philippines also has the distinction of being the site of the defeat of two men that history books never fail to mention: Ferdinand Magellan, who was stabbed to death on Mactan Island in 1521; and General Douglas MacArthur (U.S.A.), who was airlifted off Corregidor Island in 1942 and made good his famous promise; "I shall return."

History of the Philippines

When Magellan and his pals stopped by on their circumnavigation of the world, they found an already viable commercial area, since traders from India, Arabia and China had exchanged their wares and infiltrated the local culture since the 10th century. Along with spices, silks and porcelains, they had also brought Islam. To this day, the majority of Mindanao Island is Moslem. Magellan himself is said to have planted the first Christian seed, so offending a local chieftain named Lapulapu that the Spanish explorer never made it to the next port. (A piece of cross he planted still exists and is one of Cebu City's most historic monuments.)

Spanish expeditions to the islands continued and by 1565 the archipelago had been named "Felipinas" in honor of Spanish King Felipe the Second. A treaty was maneuvered and Miguel Lopez de Legazpi installed himself as the first governor-general and Manila was established as the capital of Spain's new colony. Legazpi defeated the Moslems throughout Luzon Island and Christianity became the official religion. Baroque churches were built for centuries after and Spanish culture influenced the architecture, cuisine and education of the people. Trade strengthened with other Spanish-dominated countries, namely Mexico, which exported silver from its plentiful mines.

Toward the end of the 19th century, Filipino leaders began to demand a stronger role in their own country. People like physician, poet and patriot Jose Rizal fanned the flame and his writings eventually made him a martyr. He was executed by the Spanish in 1896 at a site immortalized by Rizal Monument in the Luneta. With the monument, he was born again as "father of his country." By the end of the century, the Philippine Republic was declared and its first president inaugurated.

But independence was short lived. As a result of the Spanish-American War, Puerto Rico, Guam and the Philippines were ceded to the United States for $20 million. After decades of more wrangling, the Philippines became a Commonwealth in 1935, with Manuel Quezon its first president. It became a fully independent nation on July 4, 1945. The dream was only delayed a year (1946), for the Japanese invaded the islands just two days after Pearl Harbor in 1941 and stayed for four disastrous years.

The war was not kind to the Philippine Islands. The fall of Corregidor and Bataan and the retaking of Manila are still vivid to those who were there. The infamous "Death March" to Capas cost thousands of lives and the route is still remembered. This was also the only country in Southeast Asia where the Japanese occupation impeded independence rather than enhanced it. But the glorious day finally arrived and the Republic of the Philippines was declared on July 4, 1946, with Manuel Roxas the first president. Defense Secretary Ramon Magsaysay, who successfully quelled Communist-inspired internal problems in the early 50s, became the country's third and (to date) most popular president and served his people well until his tragic death in 1957 in an airplane crash. He was succeeded by Carlos P. Garcia, Diosdado Macapagal and a lawyer/war hero named Ferdinand Marcos.

For over 20 years, President Marcos was chief of state, with an authority that became more and more absolute and corrupt. The president and his first lady ruled the country as well as most of the industry, banks and media. In September 1972, Marcos declared martial law, which suppressed the opposition and totally crippled any semblance of a free society. Many fine Filipinos fled the country, taking refuge in the United States, including Mr. and Mrs. Benigno Aquino.

The assassination of Benigno Aquino, one of Marcos' strongest opponents, upon his return from exile in 1983 began the finale for Marcos. In early 1986, Aquino's widow Cory ran against Marcos in an election that was rife with fraud and cheating. Marcos proclaimed himself the winner and had himself reinaugurated, but hours later was forced to flee the country with his family and an entourage of some 60 fellow corruptors.

Mrs. Aquino was immediately recognized to assume the presidency the world believed was rightfully hers. It was an impressive and peaceful transition led by "rebels," General Ramos, Defense Minister Enrile and thousands of concerned citizens. It was a wonderful show to the world that democracy is a much wanted and viable instrument in this country and Filipinos can be proud of their unity and behavior in a tense situation that led to the end of the Marcos regime. Mrs. Aquino has tremendous popular support and has been transformed astonishingly from a simple housewife to a self-assured and sympathetic leader determined to put her beautiful country back on its feet and into the world stream, politically, socially and economically.

The Philippines is a fascinating combination of people, cultures and experiences. With a Mexican-like devotion to the Virgin Mary, it is a country full of colorful religious holidays and communal festivities. On Good Friday each year, young men volunteer themselves for the honor of being "crucified" just as it was done centuries ago and "flagellants" take to the streets to beat themselves bloody. Even the public transport vehicles—those unavoidable "jeepneys"—are full of Christian images, symbols and offerings of devotees.

Despite an uneven distribution of the riches and a lack of opportunity for betterment in many areas, Filipinos are a happy and spirited people with sincere hospitality. Language is rarely a problem here since Tagalog and English are often spoken simultaneously, even outside metropolitan regions. There is plenty to see and do throughout the islands and music everywhere! No one who has ever heard a Philippine band can resist the temptation to have the ensemble "play it again." This inherent talent is amazing and Philippine bands play in every major Southeast Asian nightspot. In the arts, Filipino works and crafts display the original Malay culture as well as European/ American influences and many young painters and sculptors are receiving serious attention from abroad.

Manila is not the Philippines, but it certainly reflects all that the 7,000 islands have to offer. It is a typical, overcrowded and quite exasperating Southeast Asian capital, but it also has great beauty, charm and sophistication. The restoration of the elegant Manila Hotel was one of Mme. Marcos' finer moments. Manila is yet another "hotel town" and, if you can stand the over-used air conditioning everywhere, hotel-hopping is the best way to watch how the elite of Manila live. But you should also take the time to walk around Intramuros, the original walled city built by the Spanish, or delve into bustling Chinatown in the district of Binondo. I also suggest a courtesy call at the Rizal Monument in the Luneta, the large and most popular public park fronted by the sea. Save a moment to enjoy the sunset over Manila Bay. It is one of the great sights in the Far East and never fails to provoke thoughts of history, adventure, romance and intrigue.

PLANNING AHEAD

THE PHILIPPINE TOURIST INFORMATION CENTER

PTICs are located at Ninoy Aquino International Airport (☎ 828-4791/ 828-1511), Nayong Pilipino Complex, Airport Road (☎ 828-2219) and on the ground floor, Philippine Ministry of Tourism building near Rizal Park in Metro Manila (☎ 501-703). Field offices are situated in Pampanga, Baguio, Legazpi, La Union, Bacolod, Cebu, Iloilo, Tacloban, Cagayan de Oro City Davao, Marawi and Zamboanga.

In North America, the Philippine Tourist Office is located in *Philippine Center, 556 Fifth Ave., New York, NY 10036* (☎ *212-575-7915*); *Suite 1212, 3460 Wilshire Blvd., Los Angeles, CA 90010* (☎ *213-487-4525*); *Suite 1111, 30 North Michigan Ave., Chicago, IL 60602* (☎ *312-782-1707*).

VISAS

Visas are not required of travelers holding valid U.S. passports, provided they possess tickets for onward or return journey. Visitors wishing to extend their stay may apply to the Commission of Immigration and Deportation.

INOCULATIONS

Shots for smallpox and cholera are not required for entry, but cholera shots are suggested when the Philippines appears on a weekly summary of areas infected (according to the World Health Organization). Yellow fever vaccinations are required of all travelers arriving from infected areas.

ENTRY BY AIR

Arrival into the Philippine Islands from abroad is primarily through **Ninoy Aquino International Airport**, a modern facility with 14 jetways. Located in nearby Pasay City, the airport is less than 30 minutes away by car to any major hotel and services an average of 170 international flights weekly. Manila is just over an hour by air from Hong Kong, 3 hours from Singapore, 5 from Tokyo, 17 hours from San Francisco and 22 hours from New York.

Several Southeast Asian regional carriers have direct flights into Zamboanga, Mindanao and proposed international airports are due for Cebu City and Zamboanga. Domestic flights connect Manila daily with about 50 other towns, cities and rural areas. Where scheduled flights do not serve, there are aircraft for charter. Local service is bare-bones basic, with nothing but a plastic cup of water available. Allow plenty of time before departure for security inspection.

BY SEA

Around this archipelago there are inter-island vessels with first-class accommodations that sail between several different ports daily. There have been some luxury-liner calls in the past and interest is picking up again.

DEPARTURE BY AIR

Leaving from Ninoy Aquino International or Domestic Airport can be a drudge because of the tight security and zealous inspections. The airport taxes are P200 for international flights and P25 for domestic flights.

DUTY FREE

Duty free items' allowances for incoming visitors (bona fide tourists) are 200 cigarettes or 50 cigars or 250 grams of pipe tobacco (or an assortment of the above), two bottles of alcohol and as many personal effects as necessary and appropriate for use. These personal items include jewelry, toilet water, camera equipment, portable radios and typewriters, tape recorders and sports equipment as well as tools of the trade.

Bona fide tourists are not required to complete a customs declaration and their luggage is generally exempt from inspection. However, travelers with a scruffy appearance may very well be stopped and searched.

Visitors may not import into the Philippines any seditious or subversive materials, pornographic materials, ammunition or weapons of war, gambling equipment or contrivances and articles of precious metals that are not imprinted with the international code of quality.

CURRENCY

Philippines currency is the **peso** (P), which is divided into 100 centavos. Approximately P24.00 equals U.S.$1, although the exact exchange rates fluctuate daily. Coins are in 1, 5, 10, 25, 50 centavo and 1 peso denominations. Five-peso coins are also available. Bills are in 2, 5, 10, 20, 50 and 100 peso denominations.

Hard foreign currency and traveler's checks are easily converted throughout the Philippines at banks, hotels and authorized money changers. Always demand a Central Bank receipt, however, as it is necessary to show it in duty-free shops. Credit cards are also widely accepted in shops, restaurants and hotels. Some international hotel chains now offer their own credit-card systems as well.

LOCAL TIME

Local time in the Philippines is Greenwich Mean Time plus 8 hours, i.e., exactly 13 hours ahead of Eastern Standard Time, 14 hours in advance of Eastern Daylight Time. Add another hour for each mainland U.S. time zone (add 5 for Hawaii). Manila is in the same time zone as Beijing, Taipei, Macau, Kuala Lumpur, Singapore and Hong Kong, but 1 hour ahead of Seoul and Tokyo. It is 1 hour ahead of Bangkok, Jakarta; and 1-1/2 hours ahead of Yangon.

LOCAL CURRENT

The local current is 220 volts/50 cycles, but don't expect power all the time when out in the provinces. Electric razors can be used in major hotel multifitting bathroom plugs, but most hair dryers will need converters.

LOCAL WATER

The local water is generally potable, except for remote rural areas. Those with squeamish stomachs should stick with bottled water at all times, not use any ice and avoid all fresh, raw vegetables. Fruits that you peel yourself are always considered safe. Drink only bottled beverages that are opened in your presence.

OFFICIAL LANGUAGES

The official languages in the Philippines are English, Tagalog and Spanish. The national language is actually called Pilipino, of which Tagalog is one of its 87 dialects, but Tagalog is the tongue most tourists encounter. English is widely spoken and understood throughout the country and few visitors have any communication problems.

The Philippines are a media person's dreamland, with four major English morning newspapers and two evening papers in Metro Manila (quite heavily censored in the past), plus a host of provincial and local dailies and weeklies in both English and Filipino.

Filipinos love their radios and television; there are five major channels in the Metro Manila area as well as over 250 radio stations throughout the country. *What's On in Manila* and other visitor-aimed magazines discuss what local entertainers are "hot" at the moment and how to enjoy their music or songs.

BUSINESS HOURS

Hours of business in the Philippines are from 8 a.m. to 5 p.m. Monday through Friday, with most offices closed from noon to 1 p.m. or so. Banks open from 9 a.m. to 4 p.m. Monday through Friday. Shops in major tourist centers open at 9 or 10 a.m. until at least 7 p.m. daily. The smaller, family-owned shops outside Metro Manila are open whenever and for as long as the spirit prevails.

Metro Manila (the city proper plus environs) is quite a Far East business center, both on the reclaimed land along Roxas Boulevard and in Makati. The **Asian Development Bank** is headquartered here and there are over 80 other banks with offices in Manila. There are also three stock exchanges (Manila, Makati, Metropolitan) that trade in the Philippine market from 9:30 a.m.-1:30 p.m. Monday through Friday. There are several local professional clubs and organizations in Metro Manila, including Kiwanis and three branches of Rotary. The **Manila Overseas Press Club** is located at Orense in Makati (☎ 855-981). The **United States Embassy** is situated in a beautiful building near the Manila Hotel, on Roxas Boulevard (☎ 598-011). **The Canadian Consulate** is located on the fourth floor of the Philippine Air Lines Building, Ayala Avenue in Makati (☎ 876-536).

TIPPING

Tipping in the Philippines is not a problem. A service charge of 10% (15% in the top-class establishments) will be included in hotel and restaurant bills. Additional tipping is optional. Taxi drivers are not tipped, unless special service has been rendered. Porters, barbers and W.C. attendants get a peso or two and the rate per suitcase at the airport is clearly marked P10. If you do not have any pesos, a dollar bill per couple's luggage will bring smiles.

TELEPHONE, TELEX AND FAX

These services in the Philippines are good, although communication with the outside world is slightly slower than you'll find in other parts of the Far East. Overseas calls take from 30 minutes to an hour to put through, as there is no direct dialing in most hotels. Overseas calls can be costly and frustrating from this country because hotels add a 20% or more surcharge and you must pay even though no connection was made.

Telex services are available at all major hotels on a 24-hour basis, usually in the Businessmen's Center (now an important part of many travelers' existence). Bilingual secretarial services, current publications, complimentary coffee and a conference area are also available here.

Local calls are about P5 for three minutes from your hotel room, about P10 from a red public phone. However, connections are not always clear and phone lines have a habit of breaking down. Patience is the key word here!

Fax service is available at all the better hotels and most businesses.

WHAT TO WEAR

What to wear in the Philippines is what you would wear in any hot, humid tropical climate. Although synthetics pack well, cottons wear better in humid climes. Sweaters are necessary in the mountain areas. Discreet cover-up clothing for both men and women (this is a predominantly Catholic country) is appropriate by day. At night, life is quite formal in the fine restaurants and nightclubs of Manila, much much less so in the other cities. Local women wear the *terno*, or butterfly sleeve, long gown for formal occasions, while the men all don the *barong* tagalog, or Tagalog shirt. The barong is a transparent, embroidered overshirt (T-shirts are in order underneath) that makes a fine gift for informal occasions at home. The shirt dates from the 19th century and was a symbol of Filipino patriotism.

December to May is the drier and cooler season in the Philippines and, indeed, the locals may be shivering! Remember that mountain resorts, like the popular Baguio, are at least 20 degrees cooler than the plains and visitors can be quite chilly here if not dressed properly. Expect wet and warm weather from June to November, with high humidity and a never-ending procession of tropical storms.

LOCAL TRANSPORATION

Transit in the Philippines consists of a national **railway** that serves the island of Luzon, from Legaspi in the south to San Fernando, La Union in the north. **Buses** also connect major tourist areas and both chauffeured and self-drive **automobiles** are for hire. Traffic does move along the right-hand side, but similarities in driving styles stop there. Watch out if you intend to drive yourself! Actually, the colorful and cheap **jeepneys**, colorfully decorated former U.S. military vehicles that carry about 12 passengers each, are the fastest and most entertaining way to get through the clogged byways. Just hop on, tell the driver your destination and he or she will inform you of the fare. Metro Manila also has a series of **Love Buses**, fast and clean and with a fixed rate between stops throughout the city. All major cities also have a large fleet of licensed **taxis**, some more decrepit than others, that are amazingly inexpensive provided both you and the driver know where to go!

FESTIVALS AND HOLIDAYS

Holidays and festivals are sustenance to the Filipinos, who will use any excuse to celebrate patron saints days, mythical figures, or historic events. Festivals throughout the Philippines, whether local or national, are colorful and fun. Try not to miss one if you happen to be in the neighborhood. The "fiesta" spirit is quite catching, but don't expect to get much business accomplished during this time. Public holidays for 1994 are marked with an asterisk (*).

*January 1	New Year's Day	*Begins with early morning Mass. The evening before is a family gathering with fireworks, merry making and a midnight repast.*
January 6	Feast of Three Kings	*Pageants in Santa Cruz, Gasan and Marinduque.*
January 9	Feast of the Black Nazarene	*Traditional procession in Quiapo, Metro Manila.*
January 10	Fiesta de Santo Niño	*Feast of the Holy Child celebration all week in Cebu City.*
January	Pipigan	*Preparation of native delicacy in Noval-iches, Rizal. Toasted malagkit rice is pounded into pinipig to tune of guitars.*
January	Appey	*Three-day thanksgiving rites for a bountiful harvest. Celebrated in Bontoc, Mt. Province.*
January	Mannerway	*Exotic dance festival to awaken the Bontoc rain gods. Bontoc, Mt. Province.*
January	Ati-Atihan	*Rowdy Mardi-Gras-style fiesta involving Kalibo townsfolk dressed as either aboriginal Atis or seafaring Borneans for three days of dancing and carousing in the streets. Watch for the festivities in Kalibo, Aklan.*
January	Constitution Day	*National celebration during third weekend to commemorate amended Philippine Constitution.*
February	Hari Raya Hadji	*Celebrated throughout the Moslem provinces to commemorate devotees annual pilgrimage to Mecca.*
February	Chinese New Year	*Dragon dances, opera and plays on streets of Chinatown.*
February 2	Feast of Our Lady of Candelaria	*Fiesta for patron saint of Jaro, Iloilo.*
February 11	Tinagba	*Harvest festival and parade in Iriga City.*
February 11	Feast of Our Lady of Lourdes	*Processions and masses held at the Shrine of the Virgin in Quezon City and the Grotto in Novaliches, Rizal.*
February 14	Valentine's Day	*Celebrated nationally.*

FESTIVALS AND HOLIDAYS

February 22-25	People Power Anniversary.	*National holiday celebrating unity.*
February 24-25	Bale Zamboanga Festival	*Cultural shows, fairs, regattas and religious services for both Christians and Moslems in Zamboanga City.*
March	Saranggolahan	*Regional kite-flying contests as prelude to summer season.*
March	Baguio Festival	*Week of culture and celebration in Philippines' summer capital, Baguio City.*
March	Iloilo Regatta	*Sea becomes dotted with racing paraws (native sailboats) in Iloilo City's bay.*
March 10-16	Araw Ng Dabaw	*Religious processions, military parades, cultural fairs and carnivals to mark founding of Davao City.*
March 25	Sinulog	*Exotic tribal dance of religion and folklore preserved by Mundos tribe at Ilog, Negros Occidental.*
Lenten Week	Palm Sunday	*National holiday that ushers in the Holy Week.*
Lenten Week	Moriones Festival	*Marinduque townspeople hold spectacular Holy Week street pageant recalling the passion and the legend of Roman centurion named Longinus. Climax is the beheading of Longinus.*
Lenten Week	Holy Week	*Celebrated nationwide. The most solemn of all Philippine religious festivals. Good Friday is a public holiday.*
*April 9	Bataan Day	*Tribute to the bravery of the defenders of Bataan Island during World War II. Filipinos and foreigners visit Ang Dambana ng Kagitingan, the Mt. Samat Shrine.*
April 24	Magellan's Landing in Cebu City	*Local festival commemorates Ferdinand Magellan's historic landing in 1521 to "discover" the Philippine Archipelago for the Western World. Celebration takes place in Cebu City.*
April	Handugan	*Landing of ten Bornean datus on Panay Island. Celebrated during fourth week of April in San Jose, Antique.*
April	Feast of Virgen de Turumba	*Devotees jump, fall, leap, or dance while following image of Our Lady of Sorrows in procession. Pakil, Laguna.*
*May 1	Labor Day	*National holiday to honor Filipino work force.*
May 1-30	Santacruzan	*Cherished nationwide Filipino tradition of month-long Maytime festival. Procession-pageant recalls the quest of Queen Helena and Prince Constantine for the Holy Cross.*

FESTIVALS AND HOLIDAYS

May 1-30	Flores de Mayo	*Evening processions and floral offerings nation-wide to honor the Blessed Virgin.*
May 1-30	Feast of Our Lady of Peace and Voyage	*Month-long pilgrimages to the shrine of travelers' miraculous patroness, Nuestra Sra. de la Paz y Buen Viaje in Antipolo, Rizal.*
May 6	Fall of Corregidor	*Ceremonies in Corregidor commemorate the Battle of Corregidor in 1942.*
May 7-8	International Sea Fair	*Annual international aquatic sportsfest in Balangit, Bataan.*
May 14-15	Carabao Festival	*Farmers in carabaos pay respects to their patron saint, San Isidro Labrador, prior to games, contests and merriment. Major festivities in Pulilan, Bula-can; Nueva Ecija; Angono, Rizal.*
May 15	Harvest Festival "Pahiyas"	*This is another colorful celebration that honors San Isidro, in Lucban and Sariaya Quezon.*
May 17-19	Fertility Rites	*Triple religious rite to honor San Pascual Baylon, Santa Clara and Virgen de Salambao. Childless cou-ples who participate in the fertility dance, it is said, will become parents. Obando, Bulacan, hosts the festivities.*
June	Pista Ng Krus	*Bountiful harvest procession. Obando, Bulacan.*
June 12	Philippine Independence Day	*Nationwide celebrations. Most impressive is the military parade at Rizal Park.*
June 24	Halaran Festival	*Re-enactment of the purchase of Panay Island by Bornean datus. Riotous tribal-type parades in Roxas City, Capiz.*
June 24	Feast of St. John the Baptist	*Celebration of the baptism of Christ, in San Juan, Rizal.*
June 24	Lechon Parade	*A procession that includes a crispy roast pig parade honors St. John the Baptist, in Balayan, Batangas.*
June 27	Our Lady of Perpetual Help	*Major religious procession at Baclaran church in Rizal.*
June 28-30	Saint Peter and Paul	*Celebrations highlighted by a procession of images along the Apalit River in Apalit, Pampanga.*
June 29	Feast of San Pedro	*Elegant fair in honor of Davao City's patron saint.*
July 1-30	Harvest Festival	*Tengao Fagfagto is a combination of Pagan and Christian rituals for a good harvest. The celebra-tions to see are in Mountain Province.*

FESTIVALS AND HOLIDAYS

*July 4	Filipino-American Friendship Day	*Public holiday throughout the islands.*
July	Bocaue River Festival	*Colorful barge procession the first Sunday in July, in Bocaue, Bulacan.*
July 29	St. Martha River Festival	*This barge procession is held in Pateros, Rizal.*
August 1-7	Dance of the Aetas	*Exotic tribal dances and songs at Bayombong, Nueva Ecija.*
August 26	Cry of Balintawak	*National celebration commemorates the commencement of Filipino revolution against Spain.*
August 28	Cagayan de Oro City Festival	*Colorful, rowdy pageants, parades, etc. in Cagayan de Oro City.*
September	Sunduan	*Traditional ritual when young men with parasols fetch young girls from their homes in La Huerta, Paranaque.*
September	Penafrancia Festival	*Image of the Blessed Virgin is returned to its home shrine via the Naga River in a spectacular boat procession. Held during the third week in Naga City, Camarines Sur.*
*September 21	National Day	*Public holiday commemorates the proclamation of Philippines' New Society by President Ferdinand Marcos in 1972.*
October	Davao Tribal Festival	*Highlanders perform tribal dances, songs and traditional rituals. Held during the first week of October in Davao City.*
October	La Naval de Manila	*Night procession in honor of the Lady of the Holy Rosary to commemorate Filipino-Spanish victory over Dutch marauders in 1646. Held during the second Sunday in October at Santo Domingo Church, Quezon City.*
October 3	Our Lady of Solitude	*Feast of the Blessed Virgin whose image was said to have been found in the sea. Festivities take place in Porta Vega, Cavite.*
October 12	Feast of Our Lady of the Pillar	*Commemorates an apparition at Fort Pilar. Celebrated in Zamboanga City.*
October 20	Landing of the Liberation Allied Forces	*Commemorates the World War II landing on Red Beach, Palo, Leyte.*
October 21-24	Great Sibidan Race	*Native canoes race in Legaspi City.*

FESTIVALS AND HOLIDAYS

October	Pista Ng Apo	*Religious procession in honor of Jesus Christ and the Virgin Mary is held on the last Friday of October with sumptuous meals in Angeles City, Pampanga.*
October	Feast of Christ the King	*National all-male processions held throughout the country on last Sunday in October.*
*November 1	All Saints Day	*National holiday to pay homage to memories of the departed. Filipinos have their own versions of happenings on Halloween, the evening before.*
November 2	All Souls Day	*Catholics throughout the country pray for souls of the dead.*
November	Hari Raya Poasa	*Moslem festival marks the end of Ramadan, the 30-day fasting period.*
November 23	Feast of San Clemente	*Viva San Clemente parade in Angono, Rizal.*
November 15-30	Yakan Harvest Festival	*Celebrated in Basilan, Zamboanga.*
November 18-20	Kaamulan	*Tribal dances and rituals in Malaybalay, Bukidnon.*
*November 30	National Heroes' Day	*Celebrants pay homage to the country's heroes.*
December 8	Feast of Our Lady of the Immaculate Conception	*Evening processions, cultural presentations, pageants, etc. in Roxas City, Capiz; Vigan, Ilocos Sur; Pasig, Metro Manila.*
December 8	Malabon Fluvial Parade	*Procession in Malabon, Rizal.*
December 8-9	Taal Fluvial Festival	*Rustic river procession is set against the country's twin volcanoes in Taal, Batangas.*
December 12	Pagsanjan Town Fiesta	*Bamboo arches are set up in this town, famous for its gorge and rapids.*
December 16-25	Simbang Gabi	*Longest Christmas in the world is ushered in by a nine-day novena in pre-dawn masses throughout the country.*
December 24	Panunuluyan	*Regional Christmas Eve pageants.*
December 24	Lantern Festival	*Christmas Eve parade of "paroles" in San Fernando, Pampanga.*
*December 25	Christmas Day	*Most joyous occasion in every Christian Filipino home.*
December 26	Bota de Flores	*Floral offerings to the Neustra Sra. de Guia at the Ermita Church, Metro Manila.*

FESTIVALS AND HOLIDAYS

December 28	Holy Innocents' Day	*Filipino version of April Fool's Day throughout the country.*
*December 30	Rizal Day	*National celebration to honor Dr. Jose Rizal, greatest of Filipino heroes.*

Background Material

Philippines (apa productions). Excellent photos and text.

Readings in Philippine History by Father Horatio de la Costa.

Traditional Handicraft of the Philippines by Roberto de los Reyes.

The Culinary Culture of the Philippines by Gilda C. Fernando.

A Question of Identity by Carmen Guerrero.

Things Filipino

The art of making nets is passed through the generations.

This fun-loving country is most hospitable to visitors. Filipinos enter right into the spirit of whatever is happening, wherever they are and expect you to do the same. Return the smile and you will be returning a favor. The following are a few things that may not be particularly useful in your travels around this archipelago, but they are certainly of interest.

Lambanog

A potent alcoholic drink, especially popular in the provinces; natives of Samar are said to have offered it to Magellan.

Bagoong
Popular condiment often called the poor man's caviar; fermented mixture of fresh anchovies and salt; used to flavor vegetable dishes.

Bayanihan
Embodiment of closeness that Filipinos feel for one another; Pilipino term for "old team spirit."

Canao
Religious rite performed by mountain provinces' natives; sacrificial pig is roasted; much native wine drunk; dancing lasts for several days.

Harana
Shy swains sing love songs on moonlit nights; still popular in the provinces; although songs have changed somewhat.

Ulog
Communal courting place for young people of the northern mountains; test their compatibility here; mountain marriages very stable.

Yo-yo
The world's favorite toy is said to have its origins in the Philippines; once used as missile weapon; skillful Filipinos can do amazing tricks.

Manilla

Manila

Schoolchildren on a field trip in Manila

MANILA IN A CAPSULE

9 million plus people in the metropolitan area...originally a small Moslem settlement...old city founded in 1571 by Spanish conquistadors...encompasses Intramuros as well as Ermita, Pasay City, Baclaran, Makati commercial district and Quezon City...Cultural Center of the Philippines, built on land reclaimed from Manila Bay, was the pride of Mme. Marcos...90-acre Nayong Philipino (Philippine Village) located near international airport offers touristic view of entire country...Roxas Boulevard follows Manila Bay and has become the hotel and entertainment center of city...one of most colorful, vibrant and sophisticated areas in entire Far East; complete contraposition to rest of archipelago.

Like so many of the Asian capitals discussed in this book, Manila is an anomoly, a city of garish contrasts. The steel and black glass pillars of Asian progress rise into the polluted heavens in monolithic splendor while the ooze of urban squalor seeps into the Pasig River. Many of Manila's nearly 9 million residents have no running water or electricity. The level and quantity of poverty here is not to be believed. Burning trash pits are the ovens to cook the meager meals of questionable and usually unmentionable origins. In no other city in Southeast Asia does one get the feeling so strongly that the economic extremes that exist here are codependent—that each is the prerequisite for the other's existence.

But Manila is a thriving, bustling and insatiable metropolis, racing toward the 21st century on new foundations built from the ashes of World War II. Though the city was founded in the 16th century, Manila is a new gotham. The historical attractions are few and it's not particularly exotic (perhaps because of more than 300 years of Spanish dominance). You won't find the ancient pagodas and wats found elsewhere in Asia, but there are parks and antique shops, Spanish forts and ornate cathedrals. Don't miss the Metropolitan Museum, Manila Zoo and the spectacular Malacañang Palace.

And, of course, there's Manila's nightlife, probably the most bizarre and hedonistic daily festival in Asia. Manila's bars, nightclubs and strip joints in the tourist district make Bangkok's Patpong look like a couple of geisha girls serving tea and crumpets at Raffles. A hodge-podge of cross dressers, wide-eyed tourists, hookers and children parade along Mabini and Del Pilar in a fustian regatta of splash and gaudiness. It's a scene not to be missed.

WHAT TO SEE AND DO IN METRO MANILA

Chinatown

Older than the city itself; center of a flourishing trade in the 12th century; considered primary ghetto for over one million Filipino-Chinese. You can enter by foot or *calesa* (horse-drawn rig) at the corner of Rizal and Recto streets. Sidestep the touts; the local restaurants and herbal shops excellent; there's also handmade jewelry. Plaza Santa Cruz on Calle Florentino Torres fronts the church built by Jesuits in 1608 for Chinese converts. Take a taxi to **Chinese Cemetery**, a garish blend of Catholic and Buddhist mausoleums with two dragon-temples in the center.

Cultural Center

Pride of the former first lady and governor of Metro Manila, Imelda Marcos, it was built on 1,700 acres of land reclaimed from Manila Bay at a cost of untold millions and millions. It was primarily designed by Leandro "Lucky" Locsin, the country's favorite local architect; the complex contains design and exhibition halls, performing arts centers, libraries, museums and studios; an impressive convention complex includes Philippine Plaza Hotel. The 90-day wonder **Folk Arts Theatre**

MANILA

Key

1) Cultural Center
2) Design Center
3) Folk Arts Theater
4) Fort Santiago
5) Malacanang Palace
6) Manila Hotel
7) Rizal Park
8) Century Park Sheraton
9) Holiday Inn
10) Hyatt Regency Manila
11) Manila Pavilion
12) Philippine Plaza
13) Silahis International
14) Roxas Boulevard
15) Ermita

was hastily constructed for the 1974 Miss Universe Pageant; reclamation continues as the complex threatens to become a new and self-contained city. Don't miss the **Tourism Pavilion**, **Manila Film Centre** and the **Design Centre of the Philippines**.

Ermita

Section of Metro Manila known as the "tourist strip;" foreigners frequent bars, restaurants and shops and fraternize with local bohemians of an artistic nature; it's popular now with bus loads of Japanese.

Escolta

Old shopping center; originally the commercial center of Manila; reachable by MacArthur Bridge across Pasig River. Part of the avenue leading to **Binondo** is still cobblestoned. The proud old buildings are still standing, though they are less fashionable now. The area also leads to the Plaza Santa Cruz.

Fort Santiago   ★

Located along old Aduana St. It took 149 years for the Spanish to complete this bastion on the site of Raja Sulayman's (Manila's defeated ruler) original bamboo stockade; it is the former military headquarters of occupying forces and is now a popular tourist site; it contains the **Rajah Sulayman** open-air theater and a museum honoring national patriot Dr. Jose Rizal. There are nice walks among preserved ruins.

Intramuros

Walled city of Manila; it offers a glimpse of the colonial past. Portions of the walls, gates and ramparts are restored; it was originally built by the Spanish in the early 16th century. It was attacked by Chinese warlord Lim Ah-hong in 1574, gutted by fire in 1583 and rebuilt in 1590; a moat was added in 1603 when all entrances to the city were closed at night. The moat was filled during the American administration to combat disease; the old city remained intact until bombing raids and fires at end of World War II; a sense of history still stands.

Makati

A former airstrip, it's now a plush commercial section of the city with modern high rises and hotels, shopping malls and parks. It's edged by the **Santa Ana Race Track** and fabulous **Forbes Park**, where the elite all live behind high walls topped with broken glass. The **Ayala Aviary** is located at Greenbelt. **Ayala Museum** depicts Philippine culture and history through dioramas. Visit also **Libingan Ng Mga Bayani** (Graveyard of the Heroes) **American Memorial Cemetery** where 1700 allied soldiers are buried; it's the largest U.S. military cemetery in another land.

Las Piñas Church

Built in 1794 by Spanish friar Diego Ceva; it's best known for its famous Bamboo Organ. It was constructed in the early 19th century of 950 bamboo pipes; the church was damaged in 1850 and the organ lay undiscovered until 1972. The organ was shipped to Germany for restoration and has been in service regularly since 1975; the church is located just past the Paranaque section on the way out of the city.

Malacañang Palace ★★★

Official residence of Philippine heads of state; the name means "A noble lives in that place." It is a large complex of elegant state apartments and guest houses, luxurious gardens, fine collections of Chinese trade porcelains, Filipino paintings and Asian and European treasures. It is an important tourist attraction, located in the San Miguel section between J. P. Laurel Street and the Pasig River; the gardens are occasionally accessible. Mme. Marcos' shoe collection can be viewed as the palace is now open to the public.

A colonial facade in Manila

Manila Cathedral

Across from Fort Santiago; the original church on this site was built in 1571 of nipa (Philippine palm). Natural disasters and fire caused four additional cathedrals to be constructed here. The latest devastation took place during the bloody Battle of Manila at the end of World War II; the present structure dates from modern times; Italian sculptors are responsible for the frontal statues and the bronze doors; **Plaza Roma** facing cathedral is the sister to Piazzale Manila in Rome.

Manila Hotel

A national landmark overlooking the bay at end of Roxas Blvd., it was commissioned by American governor-general William Howard Taft in 1908 and designed by New York architect William Parsons in California mission-style. It opened for business in 1912 and immediately became a watering hole for the city's elite set; a 5th-floor penthouse was added in the late 1930's when the "American Caesar," General Douglas MacArthur, insisted upon accommodations equal in luxury to

Malacañang Palace. It was headquarters for the Japanese during World War II, who shot up the interior before retreating. It's a fine monument to Philippine history and culture and not to be missed. The MacArthur Suite has been renovated and is filled with memorabilia of the general, including numerous photographs and some of his medals.

Nayong Pilipino

Located in Pasay City adjacent to International Airport, this is a 90-acre tourist attraction showcasing Filipino traditions and cultures among the multi-island ethnic groups; there are village miniatures from different regions and typical architectural styles, products and cottage industries from throughout the archipelago—plus replicas of famous tourist attractions. Handicrafts are available in small "authentic" shops and the main administrative building. It's open daily with a small admission charge; it was another pet project of Mme. Marcos.

Quezon City

Part of Metro Manila but the antithesis of the Makati and Roxas Blvd. areas. It is the center of the University of the Philippines as well as government service buildings. It's a rather sprawling and ugly area—overpopulated and overcongested with automobiles.

Quiapo

District in the heart of Manila famous for the church with the **Shrine of the Black Nazarene**, a life-size image in black wood carved by Mexican Indians in the 17th century and brought to Manila by a Spanish galleon. The feast of the Black Nazarene is celebrated by a mammoth January afternoon procession; barefooted devotees carry the image through local streets. The church fronts historic **Plaza Miranda**. This is a colorful area full of itinerant vendors, good for photographs and curio seekers.

Rizal Park

Named in honor of Filipino martyr and national hero Dr. Jose P. Rizal; the monument stands on the exact spot where he was executed in 1896. It's an oasis at the end of Roxas Blvd. There are Chinese and Japanese gardens and a topographical map of the Philippines, lighted pools and a multicolored Agrifina Circle Fountain ideal for skating. A band offers open-air concerts late afternoons. Visit also the planetarium with its 16-meter dome; it accommodates 300 viewers.

Roxas Boulevard

One of the finest boulevards in the Far East, it extends along Manila Bay from the airport to the old city. It's lined with deluxe hotels, shops and restaurants. The area is dominated by the new Cultural Center complex and office towers, the Manila Yacht Club, the U.S. Embassy, the Army and Navy Club and the **Museum of Philippine Arts**; all are located on the bayside of the boulevard. It's quite an experience and quite a sight.

San Augustin Church

Originally built of nipa in 1571, the present structure dates from 1599-1606 and is considered the oldest stone church in the country. It was miraculously spared during the 1945 World War II bombings of Intramuros. The church is located near the intersection of General Luna and Calle Real streets and guarded by Chinese stone lions. The interior was decorated by Italian painters and displays chandeliers from France. There's also a hand-carved Philippine wood choir-loft. The cloister and gardens are beautiful and the monastery-museum houses an extensive collection of religious art, valuable manuscripts and artifacts of note.

University of Santo Tomas

Founded in 1611, it is the oldest university in the Far East; it beats Harvard by 25 years. It's known affectionately as U.S.T. by Filipinos and is a source of great pride to the country. The university press is housed in a small building on campus; it was founded in 1592. The university also has a first-rate museum with a rare manuscript collection of some 12,000 volumes. The campus is located at Mendoza and Espana avenues, a short taxi ride from Malacañang Palace.

WHAT TO SEE AND DO ON THE LUZON ISLANDS

Baguio

Only heaven could be more refreshing; this resort town and cultural center is nestled some 5,000 feet high in the Cordillera Mountains. The year-round temperatures average 65° F. It was developed by colonial rulers as a summer retreat from the heat of the lowlands. Several universities here bring in many interesting youths who stay on. Bountiful flowers and vegetables are available in the public market daily. There are beautiful vistas, comfortable accommodations and plenty of recreation available. There is **Rizal Park** with the **Tower of Peace** as well as the Filipino-Chinese Friendship garden. Also see **Burnham Park** and **Mines View Park**. There are silversmiths making items at St. Louis University. See the Easter school with its Igorot hand looms. **Mansion House** was the official summer residence of the former first family. Also see Camp John Hay U.S. Air Force recreation center, the 900-plus **Philippine Military Academy** and **Mirador Hill**, with its unobstructed view (beneath power lines) of Lingayen Gulf, the Ilocos coastline and the South China Sea. It is about 5 hours' hard drive from Manila and less than an hour by scheduled flights. Watch the runway.

Banaue Rice Terraces   ★★

This is a monument to the skill and patience of Ifugaos tribal artisans some 2000 years ago. It's considered the "eighth wonder of the world" by locals; the terraces rise like a giant stairway to the sky for almost 2 miles. Placed end to end, they would be 10 times longer than the Great Wall of China. They are irrigated from the top by man-made waterfalls cascading down through walls to the valley below; it's a photographer's paradise. Ifugaos still inhabit the countryside. The area is several hours' drive from Baguio; helicopter tours are available. Some of the best rice terraces are found outside Banaue, such as Batad, Banga-an, Duclingan and Mayoyao. April to July are the best months. Visit also the small villages along the way.

Batangas

Historic province southwest of Manila and accessible by land, air and sea. Known as the birthplace of Philippine heroes and statesmen, i.e., Apolinario Mabini and Jose Laurel. It was originally called Bonbon or Balayan; the rich soil was formed from eruptions of **Taal Volcano**. There are many tourist attractions such as **Matabungkay Beach** situated on China Sea. Taal Volcano is reputed to be the smallest volcano in the world. Also see **Lobo Submarine Garden**, **Submarine Caves** beneath the slopes of Mounts Pulangsaya and Kamantigue in San Juan town; **Taal Church**, reputed to be largest in Far East, was constructed in 1858. Its facade, which resembles St. Peter's Basilica in Rome, can be seen for miles. Mabini Shrine and Mausoleum contains relics of Filipino patriotism in Bo Talaga. There's also **Isla Verde**, resort island with white sand beaches.

Corregidor

This is The Rock at the entrance of Manila Bay. Here Filipino and American forces made their last stand during the Japanese invasion. The mile-long barracks and anti-aircraft guns on this rocky fortress immortalize this famous battle of 1942. The name means "to correct" in Spanish and was named so because all ships entering Manila Bay stopped here for documentation checks. The island is now reachable from the city by a 50-minute hydrofoil ride. There are plans and funds by both U.S. and Filipino congressmen to restore the island and create overnight facilities for visitors.

Ilocos

North of Luzon; its best reachable by air. The region has a romantic past with many baroque churches. **Paoay Lake** is said to contain remains of a town that sank due to a curse; **Paoay Church** was built in 1699 and is famous for its mixture of Gothic, baroque and Oriental architecture. **Vigan** is a virtual museum town, known as Intramuros of the north. It's the portrait of a Spanish colonial town. **St. Paul Metropolitan Church** was built three centuries ago; it features a lavishly adorned gold altar.

Legaspi   ★

Southern Luzon; it's best reached by air. The spectacular attraction here is semiactive, 8,000-foot Mayon Volcano; its conal shape is said to be one of the most perfect in world. It erupts about every decade. Visit also the ruins of Cagsawa. Only the church steeple and a few walls remain from the once busy town after it was buried by lava and mud flows.

Los Banos

Nestled at the foot of mystical Mt. Makiling, this town is famous for its thermal springs and the health-restoring properties of the waters. The University of Philippines Agricultural College is located here. It features a magnificent setting and is an excellent environment for learning.

Pagsanjan

Rather quaint Laguna town with Spanish look; it's most famous for its waterfalls. Shooting the rapids in a *banca* (dug-out canoe) through the churning currents is not for the meek. Although expert boatmen steer, the craft shoots between boulders at top speed.

Tagaytay

Resort some 2,250 feet above sea level; it's perched on a ridge overlooking Lake Taal and is the lowest volcano in the world. Lake Taal boasts the only volcano with a crater rising out of the lake of its original crater. The new crater has its own lake and an island; it's interesting to see. It's situated about a 1-1/2-hour drive south of Manila.

La Union

Located about a 1-1/2-hour drive southeast of Baguio. The towns of San Fernando (founded in 1850 in honor of King Ferdinand of Spain), Agoo (founded in 1578 by Friar John Baptist of Pisaro) and Bauang (dates from 1815 and the word means "garlic" in Ilocano) are the primary tourist destinations. Bauang is actually the "beach resort capital" of the country. There are many small resort hotels available here; it's a good base for watersports and exploring.

TOURS

Manila and Suburbs

3 hours, daily; begins at the Cultural Center and goes along Roxas Blvd. to Rizal Park, Intramuros, Church of San Augustin, Manila Cathedral, Fort Santiago, Pasig River; to the University of Santo Tomas, Makati, Forbes Park, Manila American Cemetery Memorial.

Manila Bay Sunset Cruise

2 hours, daily; comfortable cruiser departs Manila Yacht Club to sail along the edge of one of the world's finest natural harbors; city lights sparkle from afar; drinks available at the cash bar; romantic guitar music highlights the mood.

Nayong Pilipino (Philippine Village)

3 hours, daily; situated near Manila International Airport; 90-acre site represents 6 major regions of the Philippines—Moslem, Visayas, Mountain Provinces, Ilocos, Southern Tagalog, Bicol; transportation around grounds by motorcoach, jeepney, or on foot; Museum of Philippine Traditional Cultures has life-size models and rare artifacts from different ethnic groups; visit cave-dwelling Tasadays or seafaring Bad-jaos; tour also includes Manila American Cemetery and Memorial in Fort Bonifacio.

American Memorial Cemetery in Manila

Manila by Night

3 hours, daily; begins at jai alai fronton where Spanish and Filipino pelotaris vie; dinner and show at elegant supper club; popular night-club for dancing.

Museum Tour

3 hours, daily; begins at Cultural Center of the Philippines; view Fili-pino paintings in main gallery; collection of porcelains, antique jew-elry, Moslem artifacts and ethnic musical instruments; National Museum at Rizal Park to view permanent collection; Intramuros and San Augustin Church to visit museums there; ends at Ayala Museums in Makati; dioramas of historic events; Filipino costumes; models of ships and boats used by early inhabitants.

Corregidor Tour

4-6 hours, daily; hovercraft across Manila Bay to The Rock; last Filipi-no-American fortress to fall during Japanese invasion; allied troops on Corregidor held enemy at bay for 5 months; will always be honored for their perseverence and bravery; considered one of the most bitter episodes of World War II; many veterans who survived the Bataan Death March make a pilgrimage here; The Rock was recaptured by American parachute troops in early 1945; the suffering here cannot be described; among the historic sites visited are Malinta Tunnel; Gen-eral Douglas MacArthur's headquarters, field hospital and supply depot during siege; Pacific War Memorial and eternal Flame of Free-dom; silent plain at Bottomside where gallant Filipino-American gar-rison, some 10,000 men strong, finally surrendered.

Tagaytay

4 hours, daily; features drive to Tagaytay ridge to view Taal volcano; visit to Church of Las Pinas to see world's only bamboo organ; tour of a local jeepney factory.

Pagsanjan

8 hours, daily; colorful country scenery, volcanoes, Laguna de Bay (country's largest lake), native villages; highlight is "shooting the rapids" in banca through waterfalls from 300-foot cliffs; take your bathing suit and a plastic bag for your camera; tour may also include a drive through Lake Caliraya and brief stop at International Rice and Research Institute in Los Banos where "miracle rice" was developed.

WHERE TO STAY IN MANILA

Metro Manila

Century Park Sheraton

Corner of Vito Cruz and M. Adriatico avenues. ☎ *50-60-41* • *510 rooms.* All accommodations with private balcony; 20-story high rise 2 blocks from Roxas Bld. and Convention Center; 6-story high atrium lobby; rare tropical birds in huge cages; adjacent to Harrison Plaza, one of largest shopping complexes in the Philippines. Top of the Century cocktail lounge with buffet lunches and dinners on 19th floor. Badjao Filipino restaurant serves American breakfast buffet from 7-9 a.m. AOI Japanese restaurant. Peacock Chinese restaurant. Cafe in the Park for coffee and pastries on lobby floor. Iberia grill. Kachina Lounge for nightclub entertainment. Cellar disco. Half-acre swimming pool and health center. Convention facilities and businessmen's area. Medical, travel, airline offices in-house. *Reservations: Sheraton Int'l.*

Holiday Inn

3001 Roxas Blvd. ☎ *59-79-61* • *370 rooms.* Another high rise; directly across from Cultural Center; nice views of Manila Bay from all rooms; typical Holiday Inn style and atmosphere. Baron's Table continental restaurant. Baron's Bar. Cafe Vienna coffee shop. El Camarote bar with live entertainment. Delicatessen corner. Tsismisan lounge in lobby. Paseo del Sol poolside snack bar. Outdoor swimming pool. Embassy ballroom. Business center. *Reservations: Holidex.*

Hyatt Regency Manila

2702 Roxas Blvd. ☎ *80-26-11* • *265 rooms (31 suites).* Flagship of the Hyatt chain in the Philippines; designed by Filipino architect Leandro Locsin; plush appointments by Dale Keller Associates; 9 guest room floors; all accommodations with private balconies and fine views over Manila Bay and Cultural Center; 8th floor Regency Club. La Hacienda 24-hour coffee shop. Mandarin Room Chinese and Tempura-Misono Japanese restaurants. Calesa bar. Hugo's gourmet restaurant. The Gallery for local art exhibitions. Crystal ballroom. Outdoor swimming pool with cascade waterfall and bar. Medical/dental clinic. Businessmen's centre. *Reservations: Hyatt Int'l.*

Manila Pavilion   ★★★

United Nations Ave., Ermita. ☎ *57-37-11 • 416 rooms (23 suites).* A 22-story tower; one of the city's tallest buildings; terrific views from top; nonsmoking rooms on the 15th floor; Executive 19th floor; 2 rooms for handicapped guests; hotel loaded with activity and entertainment; considered one of the "older" and more established hostelries in town. Hilton has relinquished its operating contract with this hotel; has been sold to Australian investment group. Ecumenical chapel on 5th floor for daily masses, weddings, etc. Top of the Hilton luncheon buffets with fashion shows, later Supper Club with Karilagan Dance Group. Rotisserie grillroom. Cafe Coquilla (coffee shop). Toh Yuen Chinese provincial cuisine. Swimming pool with terrace on 5th floor and health club. Sultana lobby piano bar. The Music Room cocktail lounge with local musical entertainment. Coral ballroom.

Manila Hotel   ★★★★★

Rizal Park. ☎ *47-00-11 • 570 rooms.* Owned by Philippine government; one of the former first lady's pet projects; a national landmark; originally built in 1908; fully renovated in 1976 by the team of architect Leandro Locsin and interior designer Dale Keller; one of the most historic and renowned hotels in the Far East; lousy mañana-type service when I was there; guest book reads like an international Who's Who since 1912; barring war and local disasters, the hotel has been in service for 75 years; MacArthur Suite in original building still a draw; sells for over $1,000 per day; Penthouse Suite in new 18-story tower overlooking Manila Bay is over $1,500 per day. Lovely old-world lobby with adjacent lounge/bar. Tap Room bar with local entertainment. Apres disco. Sea Breeze grill (outdoor barbecues). Champagne room with 1890s atmosphere and Manila Symphony violinists. Maynila Filipino cuisine and entertainment restaurant. Cowrie grill for steaks and seafood. Rome Ristorante Italiano. Cafe Ilang-Ilang coffee shop. Bay Club sports center, with swimming pool, tennis courts, sauna. Executive Services Center.

Reservations: Distinguished Hotels.

Manila Inter-Continental   ★★★★★

Ayala Ave., Makati Commercial Center. ☎ *89-40-11 • 420 rooms.* Pioneer luxury hotel in Makati; splendid long-time reputation; a favorite with business executives; large acreage amid the commercial center; overlooks fabulous Forbes Park; also known as millionaire's row; accommodations not so splashy and plush as some newer hostelries in town; but always under impeccable management. La Terrasse for light snacks off lobby. Gambrinus businessmen's club—women welcome after 5 p.m.! Le Boulevadier cocktail lounge. Romantic Prince Albert Rotisserie. Bahia seafood restaurant on rooftop, with elegant buffets. Colorful and fun Jeepney coffee shop. Large swimming pool in the shape of a female figure with tennis club and Bermuda-grass grounds. Jogging map in every room takes executives through paved section of

Forbes Park. Sol y Sombra poolside snack bar. Where Else disco. Meeting facilities. Adjacent to Makati Commercial Center.

Reservations: IHC.

Mandarin Oriental Manila ★★★★

Corner Makati Ave. and Paseo de Roxas. *816-3601 • 470 rooms (20 suites).* Member of prestigious Mandarin chain; offers fleet of white Mercedes Benz 200s; circular lobby; overly air-conditioned high rise designed by Filipino architect Leandro Locsin; interiors by British consultant Don Ashton have just received $11.5 million refurbishment throughout; 18th floor has Mandarin Suite with own private outdoor swimming pool; plus 5 other special suites (Persian, Georgian, Hong Kong, Philippine, Oriental); artwork and ambience a blend of European and native works; convenient to Makati commercial buildings; very tedious and over-trafficked ride to downtown Manila. Carousel bar off 2-story lobby. Clipper lounge overlooking lobby. Tivoli restaurant. New Cantonese-style restaurant. L'Hirondelle French restaurant. Marquee coffee shop. Large swimming pool with bar and Barrio Fiesta buffets on Sunday evenings. Nash room for private functions. Business center with IBM/PC.*Reservations: LHW.*

Manila Peninsula ★★★★

Ayala and Makati avenues. *85-77-11 • 537 rooms (21 suites).* Member of the famed Peninsula Group; opposite Makati Commercial Complex; terrific 4-story lobby with 24-hour life; most gracious personnel in town; 2 high-rise towers of 11 floors each; helipad with direct access to Presidential Suite; fleet of Ford and Mercedes Benz limousines for guest transportation; public relations/social directress (Mila Magsaysay Valenzuela) is the daughter of a beloved former Philippine president; a lovely person who adds grace and dignity to the hotel; however, still some distance from downtown Manila. Old Manila grillroom. La Chesa Swiss specialty restaurant. La Bodega coffee shop. Tipanan cocktail lounge with nightly entertainment. The 4-story Lobby—a modern edition of the famed lobby in The Pen (Hong Kong). Rigodon ballroom. Business centre. The Cake Shop. Swimming pool and snack bar. Hatch & Reed fitness center. The Valet Shop. 3,000-square-foot Presidential Suite with accommodations for guard plus valet and easy access to helipad. *Reservations: SRS.*

Philippine Plaza ★★★★

Cultural Center complex, Roxas Blvd. *832-0701 • 676 rooms (62 suites).* Owned by the Cultural Center; chairman and founder was former first lady Imelda Marcos who maintained the Royal Suite for private parties and friends; designed inside and out by Leandro Locsin; located within Cultural Center complex; dramatic lobby area; large adjacent convention facilities; spectacular outdoor pool and gardens on edge of Manila Bay; built entirely on reclaimed land; hotel managed by Westin International; vies with Manila Hotel for title of nation's guesthouse; definitely worth a visit just to admire interior if nothing else. Most spectacular outdoor pool in Asia, with Treasure Island bar in middle. Pistahan cultural show and buffet dinners at pool-side. Plazaspa resort/health club with 4 tennis courts. Abelardo's Continental restaurant with serenades. Pier 7 Steak and Seafood. The Galley bar/pub. Cafe Fiesta coffee shop. Siete Pecados cocktail/entertainment lounge. Lost Horizon disco. Lobby Court cocktail lounge. Executive Center. Fleet of Mercedes-Benz and complimentary shuttle service to Makati commercial area.

Reservations: Westin Hotels.

Silahis International Hotel

1990 Roxas Blvd. ☎ *57-38-11* • *600 rooms.* Flagship of Sulo Group hotels; Philippine owned and managed; famous as home of the Playboy Club of Manila; Silahis means "rays of the sun"; excellent location between Cultural Center complex and Rizal Park; unimpressive structure and decor. Playboy Club of Manila on 3rd floor, with game/library/conference rooms, VIP grill, Playmate and Bunny bars and health club. Sunburst coffee shop. Bienvenida piano bar. Capriccio Italian cuisine restaurant. New Stargazer lounge on 19th floor, with glass elevator. Los Mares ballroom. *Reservations: Utell.*

Manila Environs

Banaue Hotel and Youth Hostel

Banaue, Ifugao ☎ *386-4088, FAX: 386-4048* • *20 rooms in hotel/30 beds in dormitory.* Perched on mountainside; overlooking Poitan Rice Terraces; all hotel rooms have balconies with panoramic views; about 240 steps to a typical Ifugao village; famous Banaue viewpoint about a 20-minute drive from the hotel; new Trade Center full of local souvenirs about a 29-minute hike; best accommodations in area; owned and operated by Tourism Ministry. Fabulous vistas from both hotel and hostel. Outdoor swimming pool. Filipino/Continental restaurant and bar.

Reservations: Philippine Tourism Authority.

Baguio Park Hotel

Harrison Rd./P. Claudio St., Baguio City. ☎ *56-26* • *65 rooms.* Rajtour; located in front of Baguio's famous Burnham Park; easily accessible to middle of town; not up to Hyatt standards but better than most of the others. Cafe by the Park. Beer patio. Liu Fu Chinese restaurant.

Reservations: Rajah Tours/Philippines, Inc.

Cresta Ola Beach Resort Hotel

Bauang, La Union. ☎ *09-2983* • *20 rooms.* Also owned and operated by Tourism Authority; situated on Lingayen Gulf; swimming pool; air-conditioned rooms; Filipino/Continental restaurant; good watersports. *Reservations: Philippine Tourism Authority.*

Hyatt Terraces Baguio

South Drive, Baguio City. ☎ *56-70/57-80* • *303 rooms (49 suites).* The only deluxe establishment in town; interesting design; unusual interior; similar to Hyatt Regency in U.S.; all rooms with balconies and views; but I'd check out amenities (showers, plugs) before unpacking; property adjacent to Camp John Hay's extensive sports facilities (golf, tennis); 4 duplex penthouse suites available. Copper Grill gourmet restaurant. Hanazono Japanese restaurant. Kaili coffee shop. Hunter's Pub for mood music. Gold Mine disco. Indoor heated pool. Conference/ banquet rooms. ***Reservations: Hyatt Int'l.***

International Spiritual Center and Resorts (ISCR)

Lucnab, Baguio City. ☎ *69-06 • 55-plus rooms.* Offers seminars in spiritualism and psychic knowledge; 16-acre property; main lodge plus cottages; hotel-like rooms. Japanese gardens and teahouse. Interfaith chapel. Fish pond. Swimming pool. Shuttle service to city center. Restaurant. 100-room beach resort in San Fernando, La Union also in progress. ***Reservations: ISCR.***

Pagsanjan Falls Lodge and Summer Resort

Pagsanjan. ☎ *645-1251 • 28 rooms in cottages and houseboats.* Nothing fancy; but if you want to shoot the rapids more than once this is the place to stay. ***Reservations: Direct.***

Pagsanjan Rapids Hotel

Pagsanjan. ☎ *645-1258 • 38 rooms.* Take your pick; but only if you enjoy rusticity. ***Reservations: Direct.***

Mt. Data Lodge

Mt. Data (100 km) Mountain Province ☎ *812-1984, FAX: 812-1164 • 8 rooms.* Located halfway between Baguio and Banaue; 8-room lodge owned and operated by Tourism Ministry; nestled in mountains some 7200 feet above sea level; very quiet; recommended highly for honeymooners or mountain climbers.
Reservations: Philippine Tourism Authority.

Puerto Azul Beach and Country Club

Ternate, Cavite. ☎ *6395-574-731, FAX: 6395-597-074 • 350 rooms.* Located at Puerto Azul beach; about a 75-minute drive from Philippine Village Hotel in Manila; operated by same Sulo Group; buses run 3 times daily between 2 properties; accommodations in cluster of cottages; rooms all have balconies and deluxe amenities. Wide variety of watersports. Horseback riding. Outdoor swimming pool, jacuzzi and health spa. Game rooms. 27-hole golf course. Sports village with 12 tennis courts, squash courts, pelota/ badminton courts, bowling, etc. Meeting and convention areas. 6 separate dining/entertainment areas. ***Reservations: Utell.***

Ruff Inn

1 Maryhills, Loakan Airport, Baguio City. ☎ *22-18 • 30 rooms.* Rustic lodge located near airstrip; in a former Benguet village; family-run inn; friendly atmosphere; simple ambience in accommodations; some attic apartments with fireplaces for family groups. Home-style dining room. Conference facilities. Hotel-organized tours.

Reservations: Direct.

Taal Vista Lodge

Tagaytay City c/o Resort Hotels Corp., Alco Bldg., 391 Buendia Ave. Manila. ☎ *818-0811 or 88-23-82* • 25 deluxe rooms with private patio. Situated some 2500 feet above sea level; overlooks Taal volcano and lake; great views everywhere; hotel tourist bus daily to and from Manila; about one hour by road; good place to relax after shooting the rapids at Pagsanjan Falls; first ladies of the world met here during the 1960s. Restaurant, bar, disco. Conference facilities. Camping grounds adjacent. Some sports.   *Reservations: Resort Hotels Corp.*

Mindanao Islands

MINDANAO IN A CAPSULE

Second only to Luzon in size...southernmost of the Philippine archipelago's 11 largest islands...varied in shape and topography...dramatic and beautiful...abundant in natural resources...minerals, iron, nickel, wood, copper, silver, gold and perhaps oil...agriculturally important with pineapple, corn, coffee, cacao, etc....home of the Moro (Moslem) who have now become a minority in their own land...hence, considerable unrest here between the traditional population and the newly arrived Christians from neighboring Visayas...also home of one of the world's most interesting tribes, the Tasaday...island less than 2 hours from Manila by jet.

Searching for some excitement? If you've come to Mindanao, you've come to the right place. Searching for some peace and relaxation? If you've come to Mindanao, you've come to the right place.

This is the exotic south of the Philippines, with beautiful mountains and dense tropical jungles. It's a more kick-back type of place than Luzon. Although the area has been relatively highly developed, it remains one of the most pristine destinations in the Philippines.

But it is not all peace here. Militant communist groups, such as the New People's Army and radical Muslim self-rule groups do control areas of Mindanao and are not particularly approving of Westerners—read that Americans. Regardless, Mindanao is overall a very safe destination for North Americans.

The islands off Mindanao close to Surigao are simply beautiful. There are verdant mountains and gorgeous untouristed lakes, such as Lake Sebu in the southwest.

INSIDER TIP

The communist New People's Army (NPA) does engage government troops in sporadic tit-for-tat firefights, primarily with artillery fire in remote areas. The big concern in Mindanao are groups such as the Moro National Liberation Front and other smaller radical Muslim groups that are participating in ongoing efforts to bring independence to the nation's Muslims. Before venturing out on your own (especially for areas such as the Sulu archipelago and Lake Lanao), check with local authorities as well as with the U.S. Embassy in Manila for current political conditions in the south.

WHAT TO SEE AND DO

Anguinaldo Pearl Farm

Situated on Samal Island, an hour from Davao City across the gulf. There's a pleasant resort with a beach and paddleboats as well as a nonfunctioning pearl farm. This is an excellent area for swimming and scuba diving.

Barter Market

Tax-free items from neighboring countries; don't expect more than sandalwood soap, some tape recorders and the local noodles, *sotanghon*. There are Chinese porcelains, Moslem brass and the handwoven tribal cloths are good buys. But remember; play the game and bargain!

Buddhist Temple

Located on Leon Garcia St. in city center, Davao has the largest Chinese population in Mindanao. It is also known as Little Japan and plenty of kilawin or sashimi is available in local restaurants.

Cagayan De Oro

City of Golden Friendship; it lies on a plain in the midst of the north coast and is surrounded by lush and rolling hills. It's along the Philippine-Japanese Friendship Highway and is the gateway to the Del Monte Pineapple Plantation; excellent harbor; many government offices and banks.

Cagayan River

The river flows through the middle of the sprawling city. Visit Gaston Park on the west bank, also San Augustin Cathedral and Lourdes College. Xavier University has interesting museums. Huluga Caves is an exciting excursion from the city center; Machambus Caves is also popular with visitors, especially for the view overlooking the river.

Camiguin Island

Reachable by ferry or small aircraft, the island is dominated by Hibok-Hibok, one of seven volcanoes on the island. Information available from the Volcanology Station. Mambajao, the capital, is a sleepy, Spanish-style town. Bonbon was the original capital but it was covered by a lava flow in the late 19th century. A 64-kilometer road circumnavigates the island.

Camp Philips

Headquarters of Philippine Packing Corporation, it is said to be the largest pineapple plantation in the world. General Douglas MacArthur flew from this airstrip to Australia after the fall of Corregidor. This is a beautiful estate, but visitors may prefer nearby Bugo, where guided tours take visitors through the canning factory.

Davao

This is a boom town and the second largest city in terms of land area the world over. It features mostly unspoiled countryside and is the center for Durians, lanzones, mangosteens, oranges and pomelos. There is fruit from fruit stalls, candied or preserved. Experience a relaxing and resortlike atmosphere here, 1-1/2 hours from Manila by jet.

Fort Pilar

300-plus-year-old fortress, now moss-covered; it has survived attacks by Moslems, the Dutch, the British and the Portuguese through the centuries. The Lady of Del Pilar, the patron saint of Zamboanga, is enshrined here; pilgrims flock here with candles on the weekends. The fort is located near Lantaka Hotel.

Iligan

Drab, industrial city where steel, fertilizer, cement, pulp and paper mills abound; it's best known for Maria Cristina Falls about 9 km south. It is supposed to be the most beautiful and largest waterfall in the country at 58 meters high. Permission to visit must be obtained from the Philippine Constabulary in Iligan for travelers on their own. There is a good observation platform at the hydroelectric station.

Menzi Citrus Plantation

This is the agricultural plantation of the South; there are vineyards, mango orchards and a modern citrus processing plant.

Mount Apo

Highest mountain in the Philippines; it dominates the landscape of Davao. It's home to the monkey-eating eagle, the world's largest and only example of the species. Mt. Apo is a dormant volcano some 3000 meters high; it's considered a sacred abode of the local gods. It is a fine peak for climbing, especially during April and May. Most enthusiasts plan a 4-day safari up and back; guides are available in Kidapawan, about a 2-hour ride from Davao. The starting point of the climb is Ilomavis; the first portion is through gentle landscapes. Agko Blue Lake is located at 1,200 meters, Marbel River at 1,800 meters and Lake Venado at 2,400 meters. From here it's a rocky climb to the summit; it's worth it for the extensive panoramas from the peak.

Pasonanca Park

Just 7 km north of Zamboanga; there are recreational facilities plus a treehouse for overnight guests. Lovely flowers bloom year-round; swimming pools are fed by mountain springs. View spectacular brass objects in Salakot House opposite. The deluxe Zamboanga Plaza Hotel is also nearby. The park offers memorable sunsets over the bay.

Plaza Pershing

Named in honor of the American general who was also the first American governor of the area. It's located in the center of town, behind the wharf and near city hall, not far from the old-world Lantaka Hotel by the sea. Tourism offices are located here. There are terrific views of the local hustle and bustle from the terrace.

Rio Hondo Village

Home of the seafaring Samal tribe; it's fast losing its charm as urban development spreads. A few houses are still on stilts like the old days; brightly colored sails are still hoisted over the local *vintas*, or small boats. Small children in their birthday suits still play in the waters where the bridge joins the village proper.

Santa Cruz Island

30 minutes by motorboat from Zamboanga City, it's noted for its pink and white beaches as well as its colorful coral reefs. This is the perfect place for swimming, waterskiing and coral diving. The ride over and back is wet; no facilities on the island of great comfort.

Talomo Beach

Site of landings made by the Japanese army in 1942 and the Americans and their allies in 1945. It's one of many lovely beaches outside Davao City if you like black sand; it is excellent for fishing, snorkeling and scuba diving.

Taluksangay Village

19 km from the city but well worth the visit. There are houses on stilts and a dramatic mosque with towering silver-domed minarets. Cultured pearls of good texture are produced here. There's also another Samal village.

Zamboanga

Considered the traveler's prize catch in Mindanao, this is the melting pot of Christian and Moslem cultures. The city is full of tradition and charm; the Castilian heritage is apparent in the local dialect. This is a colorful, still slightly exotic city with many flowers and fruits; there are native handicrafts on every corner. The houses are built on stilts. It is the cargo center between the southern islands and Borneo/Malaysia.

WHERE TO STAY ON MINDANAO

Cagayan De Oro

Alta Tierra Hotel

Carmen St., Cagayan de Oro City. ☎ 36-61; 36-62 • 32 rooms. Western/Asian restaurant. Bar. Pelota court. Conference room. Swimming pool. *Reservations: Direct.*

Caprice Hotel by the Sea

Lapasan St., Cagayan de Oro City. ☎ 48-80 • 23 rooms. Restaurant. Bar. Swimming pool. Conference room. Car service between hotel/port and airport. Room service. *Reservations: Direct.*

Mindanao Hotel

Corner Chavez and Corrales streets, Cagayan de Oro City. ☎ 30-10; 35-51 • 53 rooms. Newish hotel. Same as Alta Tierra but bigger and slightly more plush. Disco. Executive health center. Sports.

Reservations: Resort Hotels Corp.

Davao

Apo View Hotel

J. Camus St., Davao City. ☎ 7-48-61 • 86 rooms. Swimming pool. Coffee shop. Function rooms. Transport service. Tour office. Car rental. Seafood/barbecue mall. *Reservations: Direct.*

Davao Insular Inter-Continental Inn

Lanang (P.O. Box 144), Davao City D9501. ☎ (35) 7-60-61 • 153 rooms. A member of the Inter-Continental group; resort with a beach setting. Beautiful facilities. Swimming pool. Bilaan coffee shop. La Parilla grill. Vinta bar. Maranaw dining room. Badjao pool bar. Transport service. Pelota, basketball and tennis courts. Minigolf course. Car rental. Worldwide reservation network. *Reservations: IHC.*

Imperial Hotel

Claro M. Recto Ave., Davao City. ☎ 7-84-81 • 52 rooms. Coffee shop. Ballroom and convention room. Supper club. Gift shop. Pelota court. Car service. Swimming pool. *Reservations: Direct.*

Zamboanga

Lantaka by the Sea

Mayor Valderosa St., Zamboanga City. ☎ 39-31 • 132 rooms. Historic hotel; located near harbor; lovely views from the verandah. Restaurant and coffee shop. Talisay bar. Swimming pool. Scuba diving gear. Room service. Conveniently located in town. *Reservations: Direct.*

Zamboanga Plaza Hotel

Pasonanca Park. ☎ 20-51 • 210 rooms. Deluxe hotel right in the park. Restaurant and dining room. Bars. Coffee shop. Swimming pool. Convention facilities. Tennis and pelota courts. Orchidarium. Shops and all services available here. Resort hotel located away from town.

Reservations: Direct.

The Visayas

Sunrise on Mactan Island

THE VISAYAS IN A CAPSULE

6 major and several lesser islands right in the middle of the Philippine archipelago...home of 20 percent of the country's total population...Magellan landed here in 1521...lost his life to a local chieftain from Mactan...Cebu is capital of Central Visayas and the oldest city in the Philippines...original settlement of Zubu an important trading center long before arrival of the Spanish...still known as Queen City of the South...other islands of interest are Samar...Leyte, where General Douglas MacArthur landed in 1945 and said, "I have returned"...Bohol, with its chocolate hills...Negros Oriental and Occidental...and Iloilo, famous for its 17th- to-19th-century architecture...most areas in the Visayas are just an hour's flight from Manila.

If you've got some time and we mean a lot of time, hit the Visayas. If you're just over in the Philippines for a week or two, forget them.

Forget 'em totally. Because once you see them, you just may not leave them. These islands are perhaps the most beautiful in the country and offer the best resorts. If you want to get away—really away—this is the place. The pace of life here is so slow, the locals bet on snails.

As with most of the Philippines, the attractions of the Visayas are natural. But here you won't find the industrial trappings of the north. The people are friendlier—if that's possible—and offer a more fundamental side of Philippine culture. On the other hand, the islands represent the nadir of Philippine life as well. Poverty abounds in these lush surroundings—and they are also the site of the greatest concentration of incidents between NPA guerrillas and government soldiers. But fear little, these clashes are almost uniformly confined to the most remote of areas.

With the exception of Cebu City, the islands offer little in the way of "nightlife" and "entertainment." But once you've reached them, your definition of these words will have changed anyway.

WHAT TO SEE AND DO IN THE VISAYAS

Anhawan Beach Resort
Some 12 km from the city, the resort offers cottages, a good seafood restaurant, lagoon, convention pavilions, a sea-shell collection and handicraft store. It's excellent for swimming, sunbathing and fishing for the day.

Arevalo
Flower village some 6 km from Iloilo City. All sorts of arrangements are produced here. The Dutch and the British attacked the town in the late 16th century. The Spanish finally built Fort San Pedro in 1617 and kept the others out.

Bacolod
Sugar capital of the Philippines; it's 1 hour by jet from Manila and offers Old World charm and natural beauty.

Basilica Minore Del Santo Nino
Built in 1565 by Legazpi (who colonized the islands for Spain and established Cebu as the capital), it was constructed to house the country's oldest religious relic: the image of Senor Santo Niño de Cebu. It is much venerated by Cebuanos and establishes this city as the center for Christianity in the Far East. It's located on Juan Luna Street in the old section of town.

Bohol Chocolate Hills   ★
This is a major attraction. They are located about 60 km from Tagbilaran City, the capital of Bohol Island. The chocolate hills are actually hundreds of oval limestone mounds; they change color from green to

brown during summer season. There are recreational facilities located on two of the highest hills; but the whole chain is best seen from the air.

Bohol Island

Small but industrious, this island features the largest coconut area in the Philippines. Local weavers are involved in thriving cottage industries and sell handicrafts in the Manila markets.

Cebu Island ★

The most important island in the Visayas, Cebu City is the oldest city in the Philippines; it is industrial capital of the south and second only to Manila in commerce and history. Ferdinand Magellan was considered first Western tourist here in 1521; he lost his life in a battle with a local chieftain. There are many Spanish monuments and relics here, as well as some of the best rattan furniture factories in the world. It is also home to the manufacture of finely tuned guitars and ukuleles. It's an hour by jet from Manila.

Chapel of St. Joseph the Worker

A colorful altar mural made from soda bottles in a psychedelic design, it depicts Christ with dark-skinned saints in native dress. It's on the grounds of the Victorias Milling Company, which is claimed to be the largest mill and sugar refinery in the world.

Cockfight Galleries

Not for the fainthearted, this is a Sunday passion with the people of Iloilo. The galleries include Molo Gamecock Jungle, Gallera de jaro, Gallera de la Paz, Jaro Square Garden and Gallera de Arevalo.

Colon Street

Oldest thoroughfare in the Philippines; it was laid down by the Spaniards who landed in Cebu in 1565 under Legazpi.

Fort San Pedro

Also begun by Legazpi in 1565, but not completed until 1738. It is a triangular-shaped fort built on a spit of land near the then seashore; it is one of the oldest Spanish structures in the Philippines. It's now undergoing reconstruction; it houses the local tourist office. The property has been in continual use since the 16th century.

Iloilo ★

The most colorful city in the Visayas; it's a 2-hour boat ride from Bacolod, one hour by jet from Manila. Some Gothic architecture is still standing, as well as a collection of churches founded by the Spanish. The city still retains much of its colonial character.

Kanlaon Volcano ★★

Twin craters rising some 2,500 meters above sea level; one is extinct and the other active. It's popular with mountaineers, especially during Holy Week. Serious climbers never miss the chance to peer down both craters.

Mactan Island

Home of the Magellan monument, erected in 1886 in memory of Magellan's slaying by the local chieftain Lapu-Lapu. A mural beside the monument depicts the historic event. Lapu-Lapu has his own monument nearby; he is considered a national hero. Cebu International Airport is also located on Mactan Island. Maribago is here too, which is famous for its guitars and ukuleles. Visitors can watch the instruments being made by hand and listen to an impromptu musicale. Sales are not discouraged.

Magellan's Cross ★★

This is the most famous landmark in Cebu City and located in a kiosk on upper Magallanes Street. The cross was apparently left by Magellan in 1521. He is considered the first foreign tourist to the Philippines—as well as a marauder.

Mambucal Summer Resort

Located on the slopes of Mt. Kanlaon about 45 minutes from Bacolod City. A drive through lush landscapes rises 400 meters. There is a cool and refreshing climate year-round. There are at least a dozen waterfalls as well as hiking trails, curative hot springs, hotel and cottage colonies, swimming pools and other recreational facilities.

Samodal Flowers

This is a major cottage-industry attraction in Bacolod; colorful flowers are made from dyed wood shavings and are displayed and sold in many houses throughout the city.

Suarez Orchid Collection

The collection contains more than 100 different varieties of rare orchids: cattleyas, green giants, leilanis, etc.. There are several greenhouses; seedlings and cuttings are for sale.

Taoist Temple ★

A monstrous new structure atop Beverly Hills; this is Cebu City's fanciest residential area and considered an architectural landmark. It attracts many visitors (most of whom have little choice). Taoist ceremonies are held on Wed. and Sun.; nonbelievers can still light joss sticks and have their fortunes read. Farther north by car is the Chapel of the Last Supper in Mandaue City. Life-size statues of Christ and the apostles were carved during the Spanish occupation.

University of San Carlos ★★

Founded in 1596, it is one of the most important cultural centers in the Philippines. It houses a museum of mosaic prints made from butterfly wings, as well as antique collections of jars, jewelry, porcelains and weaponry.

Fort San Pedro

Built at the mouth of the Iloilo River by the Spanish in the 17th century as defense against the British, French and Moslems.

Guimaras Island

A 15-minute ride by motorboat from Iloilo, this has been a favorite place for picnics since Rizal's time. There are lovely beaches, falls, springs and the Roca Encanta (the enchanted rock).

Iloilo Museo

Showcase of pre-Hispanic art and culture in the Visayas; a museum houses collections of fossil shells, pre-Spanish burial coffins, relics from a 19th-century shipwreck, Victorian china, flake tools of early man and elephant fossils. It's located on Bonifacio Drive.

Jaro

The religious center of the Western Visayas, the district is just 3 km from the city. It has a romantic and colonial air. Antillan houses line its streets. There are private collections of colonial art and relics; also a Gothic-fronted cathedral. This is a center for weaving; hand embroidery of native *pina* and *jusi* and traditional fabrics for the *barong* tagalog.

Miagao Church

Fortress church located about 40 km southeast of Iloilo City; it is yellow sandstone in the baroque style. The facade bears a relief carving of St. Christopher amid native papayas, coconuts and shrubs. The structure was built in colonial era for protection from pirates.

Molo Church

A Gothic-Renaissance monument in Molo district about 3 km from city. It was completed in the early 19th century. The district is also known for fine *tiongco* antique collections and local Chinese noodle dishes.

San Joaquin Church

One of the most beautiful churches in the area; it's 53 km from Iloilo City. It dates from 1869 and is built of gleaming white coral. A facade depicts the historic battle of Tetuan in Morocco in high-relief style. The sculpture even depicts the pained expression of wounded soldiers.

WHERE TO STAY IN THE VISAYAS

Cebu

Argao Beach Club ★★★★

Casay, Dalaguete, Cebu Island. ☎ *6332-314-365* • *77 rooms.* Lovely beach resort; 2 km of coastline in town of Dalaguete; 3 coves and coconut groves; 2 hours by boat from Tambuli Beach Resort; much longer from Cebu City over dusty, bumpy roads; be prepared to stay awhile; great wind surfing and scuba diving; also glass-bottom boat for viewing marine life and coral formations; great for honeymoons; very quiet. Tan Awan native seafood and international cuisine restaurant with Casay Bar. Swimming pool. Tennis courts. Gift and pro shop. Duwaan game room. ***Reservations: Direct.***

Cebu Plaza

Barrio Nivel, Lahug, Cebu City. ☎ *611-29* • *450 rooms.* A low-rise building; with new 300-room tower; overlooking city and Mactan Island. Under new ownership and management. Cafe del Monte coffee shop. Lantau native seafood restaurant. 2 swimming pools. Garden setting. Tennis court. All services in new tower.

Magellan International Hotel

Gorordo Ave., Cebu City. ☎ *7-46-11* • *200 rooms.* Most attractive place; tropical building; plenty of grounds; lush planting. Swimming pool. 18-hole golf course. Plenty of services. Zugbu coffee shop with old plantation atmosphere. Sigay cocktail lounge named after a colorful Philippine sea shell. El Balconaje Lounge for sunrise and sunset refreshments. Puerto Galera restaurant. Camarin Filipino restaurant, highly recommended and closer to town.

Reservations: Global Service Inc.

Montebello Resort Hotel

Banilad, Cebu City. ☎ *7-76-81/3* • *142 rooms.* Spanish-style hacienda on 12 acres of beautiful grounds; an oasis in the midst of a bustling city; comfortable rooms. Swimming pools. Conference facilities. Restaurants and bars. Pelota Court. Services and disco.

Reservations: Direct.

Tambuli Beach Resort

Buyong Beach, Mactan Island, Cebu City. ☎ *7-00-52* • *52 rooms.* An overcrowded resort out near the airport; watch out for the day transients; especially those who wash their hair in the shower by the pool; dirty when I was there; tacky; I'd avoid it. *Reservations: Direct.*

Iloilo City

Hotel Del Rio

M. H. del Pilar, Molo Iloilo City. ☎ *7-55-85* • *57 rooms.* The least of all evils; convention facilities; bar and dining room; swimming pool; coffee shop; room service and that exquisite modern invention—piped-in music! *Reservations: Direct.*

TOURS

Manila/Cebu/Manila

3 days and 2 nights; by air to Cebu City; sightseeing in second largest metropolis in the Philippines; Magellan's Cross; Basilica San Minore del Sto. Niño; Fort San Pedro; University of San Carlos; old Colon Street; Taoist Temple; cruise along coast of Cebu and Mactan; time for skin diving and swimming; return to Manila on 3rd day.

Manila/Bacolod/Ilolio/Guimaras/Manila

3 days and 2 nights; by air to Bacolod City; capital of Negros Occidental and home of "sugar barons;" tours of Victorias Milling Company; St. Joseph the Worker Chapel; Iloilo City; museum and markets; Anhawan Beach resort for Filipino seafood specialties; Guimaras

Island hideaway; motorized outrigger to other small islands surrounding Guimaras; MacArthur built present wharf at Buenavista; return to Manila by air from Iloilo City.

Manila/Davao/Cagayan de Oro/Manila

4 days and 3 nights; by air to Davao; city tour of waterfront, suburbs and Alde-vinco Commercial Center for handcrafts, brassware and shell products; full-day visit to Samal Island; depart by air for Cagayan de Oro to visit Del Monte pineapple plantation in Bukidnon; one of largest in the world; overnight and morning tour before return flight to Manila.

Manila/Zamboanga/Manila

3 days and 2 nights; by air to Zamboanga; city of flowers; melting pot of Christian and Moslem cultures in the Philippines; 17th-century moss-covered Fort Pilar; old Zamboanga City Hall once General Pershing's headquarters; Rio Hondo Moslem village with houses on stilts over the water; Cawa Cawa Blvd.; Pasonanca Park; Zamboanga market for brassware, antiques, batik and native woven cloths; motorized vinta ride to Santa Cruz Island; return by air to Manila.

Manila/Cebu/Davao/Zamboanga/Manila

6 days and 5 nights; most comprehensive tour of the southern Philippine archipelago; by air to Cebu City for touring and overnight; by air to Davao for touring of city and Cagayan de Oro and overnights; by air to Zamboanga for city tour; a day at Santa Cruz Island and 2 overnights; return to Manila by air.

Visayas Aquasports Tour

4 days and 3 nights; by air from Manila to Cebu; transfer for flight to Dumaguete City; cruise to Sumilon Island for diving at Silliman University Marine Reservation; day at Apo Island to see coral formations, mackerels, jacks and prowling barracudas; cruise to Siquijor Island where coral ledge extends full length; also snappers, Napoleon wrasses and giant pumphead parrots along the reef; overnights in Dumaguete City; return by air to Manila.

SAMPLING LOCAL FARE IN THE PHILIPPINES

Food—glorious food—is abundant throughout the Philippines, where rice is the staple and there are almost as many varieties of fruit as there are islands in the archipelago. However, true Filipino food is the culmination of several overlapping cultures and influences—Spanish, American, Malay and Chinese—which tends to allow for a pretty fair blending of East and West every time the table is set. And it goes without saying that the Filipinos love to eat—whether a gift of nature straight from the vine, at one of the many turo fast-food centers in major towns, at home with family, or in a formal restaurant where the barong tagalog substitutes for Western jacket and tie. Casual about their dining habits (you use your fingers for most dishes) and superbly hospitable, the Filipinos pay special attention to enjoying every morsel in sight and having a wonderful time doing so!

Even world explorer Ferdinand Magellan was pleased with the many new types of fruits he encountered in these islands and later visitors wrote favorable reports on the abundance of thirst-quenching edibles bestowed by nature. One of the oldest fruits cultivated by man is the **mango**, reputed to be known for over 4000 years. From its origin in India, the mango found its way to the Philippines in the early 1600s; today there are some 41 varieties available. The two most important types are the **carabao** (named after the Asian buffalo) and the **pico**, both of which make excellent appetizers, desserts, candies and jellies. The mango has also found favor recently in nouvelle cuisine and is delicious served with seafood in a light curry sauce.

The **watermelon** is no stranger to the Philippine palate; it is known locally as the **pakwan**. Its first cousin the **canteloupe**, brought to the islands by the Spanish, is also abundant. The **avocado** was introduced around the turn of this century and grows in many shapes. It is eaten as is, with salt and salad dressing, or mashed with sugar and milk. The offensive-smelling **durian** is an acquired taste and travelers are requested not to bring the fruit aboard Philippine Airline flights, because fellow passengers do complain about the odor. A favorite of the tropics for many visitors is the **guava**, especially when used in jelly and spread on breakfast toast.

The **papaya** is one of the mainstays of the Filipino fruit diet and a delicious way to begin each day. **Bananas**, whose origins lie in India and southern China, are memorable in these islands and their sweetness extends to some 277 varieties. Most unusual are the clusters of "finger" bananas which grow wild along the roadside. **Jackfruit, pineapple, mangosteen** from Malaysia, **santol, tamarind** and **rambutan** are among other local fruits. The **pomelo**, resembling a grapefruit, is sold from street stands throughout the Philippines but has very little taste and less juice. The most popular drinks are sugar-cane juice, sometimes called **halo halo** when mixed with other fruits or ice cream and **buko**, or the juice made from young coconuts (the fleshy white meat is used for salads). Aficionados of the pina colada will often taste fresh coconut and pineapple juices mixed with their tot of rum.

Some typical Filipino dishes feature **adobo**, chicken and/or pork stewed in soy sauce, vinegar, garlic, peppercorn and other spices, or **arroz valenciana**, a local version of paella without the squid and various other trimmings. A specialty like **balut** is only for the very brave, as it consists of a duck's egg with a half-formed chicken inside; it's considered an aphrodisiac. **Pata** is a pig's thigh deep fried to a crisp and dipped in vinegar seasoned with garlic and chili.

Dinuguan is pork innards stewed in fresh pig's blood and served with chili, **pan de sal** (small buns) or **puto** (rice cakes). **Inihaw** is anything grilled (chicken, pork, fish, shrimp) and dipped in a dish of vinegar with crushed garlic and hot chili.

Lechon, suckling pig roasted whole over an open fire and brushed with spices, is the highlight of any barrio festival. By tradition, its crisp slices of meat are then dipped into a liver sauce.

Kare kare is oxtail or knuckles stewed in a thick peanut sauce, in to which rice and other vegetables are thrown. It is served in an earthen pot and accompanied by **bagoon**, a paste made from tiny shrimp and similar in taste to anchovies. **Alimango** is a large crab whose grilled meat is dipped in the popular vinegar sauce. **Achara** is a native relish of unripe papaya, carrots, peppers and onions carved into a flowered design and served with grilled specialties. **Banana-cue**, a popular snack, consists of bananas on a stick dipped in brown sugar and deep fried. **Champurrado** is glutinous rice prepared with thick chocolate and served with beef tapa (dried beef), tenderloin tips, or for breakfast.

Filipino soups are simply made by simmering food in plain water and adding a dash of salt. Some of the more popular soups are **tinolang manok**, chicken with green papaya, garlic, onion and pepper leaves; **sinigang na baboy**, a pork stew with a slightly sour taste; and **batsoy**, a thick and tasty soup of pork meat as well as the liver, heart and kidneys.

Seafood from the waters surrounding these 7,000-plus islands is abundant, inexpensive and truly delicious! Oysters are quite often served fresh from the sea as appetizers. Large crabs are steamed or grilled, torn apart with one's hands and dipped into that popular vinegar sauce. **Lapu lapu**, known as the king of the Philippine fish species, is named after the famous native chieftain encountered by Ferdinand Magellan. It is actually a large-mouthed grouper that can be prepared in any number of ways. Local shrimps and prawns are often found in **sinigang na hipon**, the Philippine version of bouillabaisse, or as a snack with noodles and condiments.

Chinese Food

The Philippines also boasts excellent Chinese cuisine and the restaurants range from family-style to very fancy, indeed. You can opt for a several course banquet or stop in for some local noodles with bits of this and that on top.

Western Food

There is no dirth of impressive Continental or European/American restaurants in the Metro Manila area. In fact, there are many more than you can possibly sample in a few days' visit. The better restaurants are located in the deluxe hotels that line Roxas Boulevard and Makati Avenue and each one has its own personality and ambience.

The Filipinos love to eat out, frequently with the entire family and prices are always reasonable (except in some of the top hotel specialty restaurants). San Miguel beer and sodas are plentiful and cheap, but imported wines and spirits are not. Those with tender stomachs should drink only bottled water, avoid raw vegetables and eat only fruit that you peel yourself. Patronizing roadside snack stands in any country is asking for trouble—so, why tempt fate? The wise traveler chooses his food carefully and enjoys every meal no matter how simple or fancy. However, good Filipino restaurants can be found on every main boulevard both in Metro Manila and throughout the country. Below are some of the best known.

WHERE TO EAT IN MANILA
Filipino Restaurants

Aristocart
> Roxas Bvd., Metro Manila ☎ 502621 • Cozy and informal; specialties are chicken barbecued or baked in honey; try also alimango (crabs wrapped in banana leaves).

Badjao
> Century Park Sheraton, Roxas Blvd., Metro Manila ☎ 506041, ext. 736 • Specialties are kare kare; inihaw or anything grilled; beefsteak Pilipino; folk dances.

Barrio Fiesta
> Buendia Ave., Makati ☎ 874728 • Try crispy pata and sinigang here.

Bulakena
> 2102 Roxas Blvd., Metro Manila • This is a salu-salo, or eating together Filipino-style restaurant; specialties are kilawin (oysters marinated in vinegar, onion and garlic); paksiw fish; rellenong bangus (stuffed milk fish); crispy pata.

Cafe Ilang Ilang
> Manila Hotel, Metro Manila ☎ 470011 • A coffee-shop atmosphere; try lapu lapu broiled in banana leaves.

Evelyn's
> Corner Roxas Blvd. and Concepcion St., Metro Manila ☎ 505130 • Local lobsters and prawns; regional dishes; very reasonable.

Fisherman's Hut
> Makati Ave. and Durban St., Makati ☎ 8189458 • Specialties include kare kare, bulalo, all kinds of sinigang; also many types of adobo, inihaw meats and kinilaw (seafood).

Grove
> 7850-C Makati Ave., Makati ☎ 898383 • Specialties are kuhol (local escargot cooked in coconut milk); laing (vegetables cooked in same).

Kamayan
> Pasay Rd. and Santillan, Makati ☎ 883604 • Eating is by hand here; crabs, lobsters and shrimp right from the sea.

Maynila
> The Manila Hotel, Rizal Park, Metro Manila ☎ 470011 • Expensive but includes show of traditional dances and songs; halabos na banagan (steamed lobster) and chicken pakan na manok (cooked in a young coconut shell) are specialties.

Via Mare
> La Tasca Bldg., Legaspi Village, Makati ☎ 852306 • Lobster; grilled lapu lapu, Pampano and maliputo (freshwater fish from Lake Taal).

Zamboanga Restaurant
8739 Makati Ave., Makati ☎ *894932* • Grilled lobster, prawn, crab and fish; entertainment nightly with Filipino folk dances.

Chinese Restaurants

Aberdeen Court
7842 Makati Ave., Makati ☎ *899372* • Peking duck; seafood.

Cathay House
PV Kalaw Bldg., Metro Manila ☎ *497821* • 6-course banquets; shark-fin soup; abalone with mushroom sauce.

Green Patio
1014 Pasay Rd., Makati ☎ *878215* • Considered one of the best in town; small; lemon chicken; Taiwanese noodles; shrimp; Green Patio; maki noodles.

Mandarin Room
Hyatt Regency Hotel, Metro Manila ☎ *802611* • Expensive; lavish service; presents special festivals of food.

Marco Polo Restaurant
750 Shaw Blvd. Metro Manila ☎ *709077, also 7872 Makati Ave., Makati* ☎ *8189446* • Peking chicken.

Peacock
Century Park Sheraton, Metro Manila ☎ *506041, ext. 1838* • Cantonese-style; boasting Hong Kong chefs.

Tai Hang Lau
816 Pasay Rd., Makati ☎ *886793* • Specialties include birds' nest soup with coconut milk; abalone in oyster sauce; roast pigeon; minced beef soup.

Western Restaurants

Abelardos
Philippine Plaza Hotel, Cultural Center Complex, Metro Manila ☎ *8320701* • Elegance plus; serenaders accompany menu of imported items; worth a visit.

Au Bon Vivant
1133 L Guerrero St., Ermita; and Makati Commercial Center, Makati ☎ *875950/875802* • An old favorite among the locals; 5 private dining rooms; specialties include tournedos perigourinde; chateaubriand with sauce bernaise; steak au poivre.

Baron's Table
Holiday Inn, Roxas Blvd., Metro Manila ☎ *597961* • Continental cuisine; dark, Germanic atmosphere.

Champagne Room

Manila Hotel, Rizal Park, Metro Manila ☎ *470011* • A lovely dining experience; romantic ambience; beautiful setting; French cuisine with music; best service in hotel.

Chesa

Manila Peninsula Hotel, Makati ☎ *857711* • Swiss specialties in chalet-like setting; a regular in Peninsula hotels.

Cowrie Grill

Manila Hotel, Rizal Park, Metro Manila ☎ *470011* • Steaks and seafood in pleasant surroundings.

Guernica's

1326 MH del Pilar, Ermita ☎ *500936* • Old Spanish tavern atmosphere; try paella here; also lengua and steaks.

Hugo's

Hyatt Regency Manila, 2702 Roxas Blvd., Metro Manila ☎ *802611* • The chain's gourmet restaurant throughout the Far East; Continental specialties; good wine list.

L'Hirondelle

Manila Mandarin, Makati ☎ *857811* • French restaurant; interiors by Don Ashton; very expensive.

Iberia Grill

Century Park Sheraton, Roxas Blvd., Metro Manila ☎ *506041, ext. 534* • Roast beef on the cart; grill items; wine list; businessman's 3-course luncheon offered weekdays.

Old Manila

Manila Peninsula, Makati ☎ *857711* • Beautifully decorated grillroom; off lobby level; lovely atmosphere.

Pier 7

Philippine Plaza Hotel, Cultural Center Complex, Metro Manila ☎ *8320701* • Seafood and steaks in pleasant atmosphere.

The Steak Town

1840 Makati Ave., Makati ☎ *866267* • Old West atmosphere; steak and lobster specialties.

The Filipinos are also fond of buffets, often all you can eat is combined with song and dance or a fashion show. The major hotels are very busy during the lunch hour and some offer buffets in various restaurants three times daily. For example, the Manila Hotel offers buffet breakfast in the Lobby Lounge, buffet lunch in both Maynila and Champagne Room and buffet snacks in Cafe Ilang Ilang. The Hotel Inter-Continental has an international buffet daily in the Bahia, while the Century Park Sheraton utilizes both the Iberia Grill and Cafe in the Park. The Philippine Plaza offers a breakfast buffet in Cafe Fiesta, luncheon buffet in Pier 7 and a native dinner buffet in Pergola with folk dances. Look also for Barrio Fiesta evenings at poolside in most hotels.

NIGHTLIFE IN MANILA

The Filipinos are music mad and their bands are the best in the Far East. So, it is no coincidence that the sounds of the cities are to the latest beat. Popular singers and musicians are abundant here and the "stars" make albums, have their photos splashed in the media, are called the "Frank Sinatra of the Philippines" or the "Diana Ross" and drive around town in the back of limousines. Who's Who and Who's In throughout the entertainment field is very important and seems to be the No. 1 diversion of most young people. While most visitors can probably take or leave the evening hours, the local scene is worth some attendance because it is so much of the current culture.

DISCOS AND WATERING HOLES

Apres
> *Manila Hotel* • Live music and disco records until 1 a.m.

Another World
> *Greenbelt Park, Makati* • Disco dancing until 2 a.m.

Birds of a Feather
> *802 Tomas Morato St.,Quezon City* • Jazz pub.

Cellar Disco
> *Century Park Sheraton* • Minimum charge.

Circuit
> *Hyatt Regency Manila* • Disco with minimum charge.

Coco Banana
> *610 Remedios St., Malate, Metro Manila* • Gay bar. Entrance fee.

Grape Escape
> *1038 A. Mabini St., Ermita* • House band. No cover.

Hobbit House
> *1801 A. Mabini St., Ermita* • Various folk singers.

Lost Horizon
> *Philippine Plaza Hotel* • Showband alternates with disco records. Open until 3 a.m.

Playboy Club of Manila
> *Silahis International Hotel* • Members and guests free of charge. Considered very plush. Good drinks.

Stargazer
> *Silahis International* • Lavish atmosphere. Drinks and dancing. Cover charge of about $10 a person.

Tipanan
> *Manila Peninsula Hotel, Makati* • Live music until midnight.

Where Else
Hotel Intercontinental, Makati • Cover charge.

HOTEL MUSIC AND ENTERTAINMENT

Century Park Sheraton
Atrium Lobby from 4:30 to 8:30 p.m. Kachina Lounge from 7 to 11:30 p.m. Top of the Century until 1 a.m.

Holiday Inn
Braukeller from 9:30 p.m. Cafe Vienna from 7:30 p.m. Baron's Table from 8 p.m.

Hotel Inter-Continental
Bahia lounge and restaurant until 11 p.m. Le Boulevardier until 1 a.m. Prince Albert Rotisserie until 11 p.m. La Terasse at noontime and Gambrinus until 10 p.m.

Hyatt Regency Manila
Calesa Bar until 1:45 a.m.

Manila Hotel
Champagne Room with 11-man string ensemble until 11:30 p.m. Tap Room bar until 1 a.m. Lobby lounge with piano cocktail music. Fiesta Pavilion special shows. Maynila Room dinner shows.

Manila Mandarin
Carousel bar from 8:30 p.m. L'Hirondelle until 11 p.m.

Manila Peninsula
Tipanan nightly performances from 6 to 9 p.m.

Philippine Plaza Hotel
Abelardo at lunch and dinner. Lobby Court pianist in the afternoon. Pier 7 Filipino entertainment. Siete Pecados until 1:30 a.m.

Silahis International Hotel
Bienvenida bar and music until 12:30 a.m.

SHOPPING IN THE PHILIPPINES

The Philippine archipelago is often called a "giant bazaar" of local handicrafts, which tells a tale of the many influences that these people have come under. Serious shoppers can fill their suitcases with a wide range of mementoes and gifts found in both the bountiful native markets (where bargaining is definitely part of the game) and the modern commercial centers full of sophisticated specialty stores. Boutiques along the public areas of major hotels are just teasers for what lies beyond, once you begin to explore the great outside. And enthusiasm for more shopping builds as discoveries include santos, the comfortable barong tagalog, handwoven baskets and cloth from the mountain provinces, finely crafted guitars, local cigars and rum, San Miguel beer as it's never tasted before, custom-made shoes and handbags, Kapiz jewelry and novelties, brass and bronzeware, fine embroideries and high-quality bamboo/rattan/wicker furniture that can enhance the most splendid of decors.

Some of the most popular shops for tourists these days feature "**antiques**" and seem to concentrate on three specific types: porcelains, santos and furniture. An abundance of Chinese-style porcelains have allegedly been found recently in excavations of early grave sites throughout the country and are claimed to be of the T'ang and Sun periods. Among the most prevalent of these so-called early Chinese porcelains, obtained during trade and buried with the dead, are the early brown and white, the red and white, the early blue and white and the celadon. But buyers must be aware that reproductions are not uncommon, even among the most reputable and expensive dealers.

Only slightly less suspect are the shelves and shelves of carved **santos**, or statues of favorite saints. The early Spanish friars always encouraged their Filipino flock to consider these statues necessary to home devotion and the more affluent boasted up to a dozen fine pieces that were imported from Mexico or Spain. The average folk were content with more primitive carvings of their patron saints, but both types of religious artifacts seem to have found their way into the antique shops. Again, be cautious and purchase only what pleases you (despite the claims of dealers). There are many worthy reproductions around, carved yesterday from old wood. A favorite trick is to chip off the aquiline nose of the Santos, because Filipino revolutionists in former days would associate the statue's profile with that of Spanish tyrants and desecrate the faces.

Hardly suitable for your suitcase but nonetheless a worthy purchase for antique aficionados is early Filipino **furniture**, ornately carved and heavily influenced by Spanish tradition. Most interesting are the gallineras, or long wooden benches that have an undercage for prized cocks. Also unusual are the amarios, or low canopied cupboards for the storage of sleeping paraphernalia. However, the Filipinos show their superb craftsmanship in the top-of-the-line furniture made from bamboo, rattan, or wicker that is produced daily in local factories. Hand-bent bamboo frames that take many intricate steps to accomplish are shipped to our West Coast where they are refinished and upholstered for U.S. tastes and then sold through exclusive interior designers. Check the mouth-watering advertisements of McGuire and Company in your favorite magazine for just such products.

Perhaps the most widely recognized Philippine handicraft is the **barong tagalog**, the national dress shirt that is both comfortable and cool. The garment was originally made of woven pina cloth or pineapple fiber and derives its name from the Tagalog Province where fine needlework is a tradition. Unfortunately, most of the ready-to-wear racks of barong tagalogs today are made from synthetic materials and the embroidery is obviously by machine. However, the popularity of this garment among Western men never wanes as it is a cool alternative to a coat and tie at any formal gathering in this warm climate. (The shirts are transparent, so it is customary to wear a T-shirt underneath for modesty's sake.) Neither has this traditional costume bypassed ladies' wear; both dresses and pantsuits are available.

Name designers have added high fashion to the garment for men and women and a popular version now is the Mandarin collar, which President Marcos wore on many occasions. Both **Tesoro's** and **Rustans** are popular stores for the barong tagalogs and both have many branches throughout Metro Manila. If you don't mind paying a high premium, the natural fibers of ramie (China grass), jusi (banana silk) and pina, with hand embroidery, are beautiful for evening clothes and table linens.

Other natural fibers—rattan, bamboo, nipa and various palms are used to make decorative **baskets** in various sizes and for many different purposes. Smoked, old-age-type baskets from northern Luzon are considered worthy of collecting and eventually can become heirlooms. **Mats** made from the same products are plentiful in the markets and their uses range from beach mats to wall hangings. Brightly colored mats with floral designs come from the Visayas, while more exotic geometrics can be found in Mindanao. The Moslems in Mindanao also make lovely **brassware**, such as jugs and urns and trays etched with intricate geometric designs. Among the favorite pieces available as souvenirs are sarimanok, or Moslem teapots and kulintang, a Moslem xylophone.

The **hardwood** of the Philippines also makes fine, carved objects, especially when crafted by Igorot tribesmen. Statues, salad bowl sets, curios, kitchen equipment and a variety of containers are plentiful. Paete wood carvings from the town of Paete in Laguna are popular tourist items for their elaborate floral and foliage designs. Furniture, wall panels and dividers are also available. But **kapiz** is the most frequently associated product in the world of Philippine handicrafts. Kapiz shells, plain or pearlized, are made into a variety of novelties such as coasters and table mats, lamp shades, chimes, etc. Mother-of-pearl shells are used for buttons, brooches, ashtrays and jewelry, while other shells that are called "cat's eyes" are set with silver or gold-plated filigree and sold as more expensive adornments. The ornamental hairpieces made by tribal craftsmen are especially interesting and can be found in both native markets as well as Metro Manila boutiques. Look also for coral or tortoise-shell jewelry.

The mountain tribes of northern Luzon also make fine **handwoven cloth**, for use as place mats and napkins, blankets or beach bags and even as draperies and upholstery materials. You can find exquisite hand embroideries or evening bags, blouses and other garments, table sets, etc. A visit to local centers, such as in Baguio, will yield not only a feast for one's eyes but also some good bargains. Handmade silver flatware from Baguio is also a good buy as it is sold by weight (visit the silvershop at St. Louis University).

The distinctly flavored Philippine **cigars** are said to be among the best in the world and their prices are certainly reasonable. Among the best known brands are Tabacalera and Alhambra and the attractively boxed items make fine gifts (as long as they are smoked far, far away). San Miguel **beer** is no stranger to most American visitors either, although I hear that its taste is quite different in the Philippines than it is abroad. **Rum**, another local beverage, comes in four different types: light, pale, dark and special five-year-old. Most of the rum available is manufactured by three firms—*Manila*

Rhum, Anejo Rhum and La Tondena distilleries. They all claim to have won international rum competitions.

Local **tailoring** in the Philippines is excellent should you wish to have something whipped together for a special occasion. Custom-made **shoes** are also a bargain and the beaded sandals for evening wear are a steal (if you don't expect them to last forever). Another female temptation is the kimona, the loose-fitting embroidered or beaded blouse worn over a long skirt for formal occasions.

For tourists who wish to supplement their purchases with imported goods, there are many tourist duty-free shops available where tax-free privileges are rendered upon presentation of passport and confirmed flight departure. You can walk out with two bottles of liquor, two cartons of cigarettes, two ounces of perfume, four ounces of toilet water, three pieces of soap and one of any other kind of merchandise (designer scarves, handbags, briefcases, pens, etc.) for personal use. Additional items may be purchased but only collected at the Manila International Airport predeparture area. In addition to the airport, duty-free shops can be found at the Makati Commercial Center, the Philippine Plaza Hotel and Convention Center, the Manila Hotel, Manila Hilton Hotel, Hyatt Regency shopping arcade, in Cebu City and at Zamboanga International Airport. The shops are truly a godsend, but don't get caught buying for anyone else but yourself!

The exportation of National Cultural Treasures (rare and unique cultural properties) is prohibited unless authorized in writing by the director of the National Museum and only for the purpose of exchange programs or for scientific scrutiny and shall be returned promptly following the exhibition or study. Travelers are warned that when buying antiques, only the stamp of the National Museum attests that a particular piece has been authenticated. (The word is: Buyer beware.)

SINGAPORE

Centrepoint Shopping Center on Orchard Road

SINGAPORE IN A CAPSULE

Island republic of approximately 240 square miles...completely surrounded by sea...closest metropolis to the equator (87 miles north)...annual rainfall almost 100 inches...average daily temperature 80° F...present city founded in 1819 by Sir Thomas Stamford Raffles as a free port...present population about 2.7 million, half under the age of 20...population mix is 76% Chinese (majority hokkien origin), 15% Malay (original inhabitants), 7% Indian, 2% others...official national language is Malay...median salary (S$2,000) is second only to Japan in the Far East.

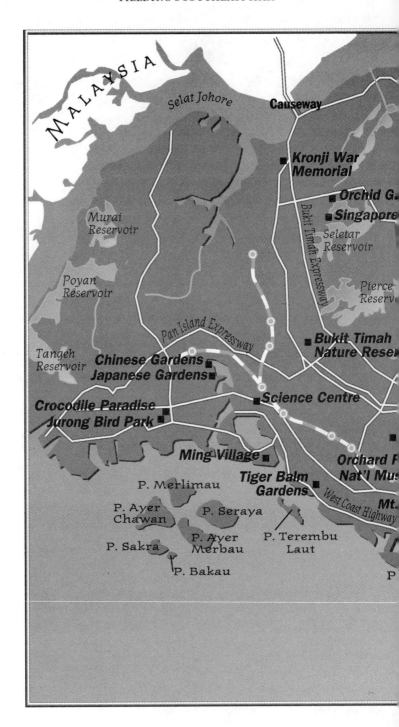

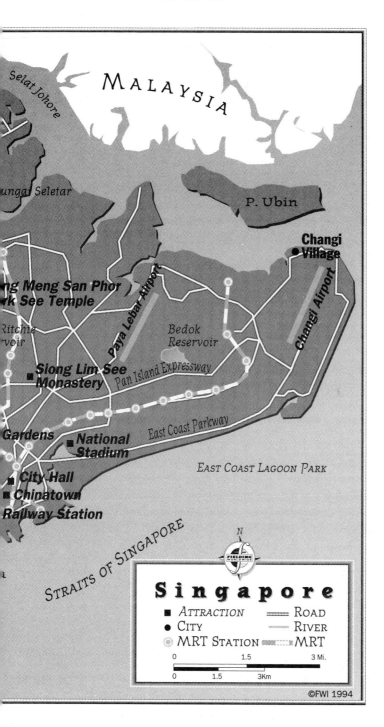

Singapore

■ ATTRACTION ═══ ROAD
● CITY ─────── RIVER
◉ MRT STATION ▭▭▭▭ MRT

0   1.5   3 Mi.
0   1.5   3Km

©FWI 1994

If you like clean and we mean *really* clean, Singapore is pure heaven to visit. Nowhere in the world are the gardens so lovingly cared for and enjoyed. Nowhere are the streets so clean, the laws so well obeyed, the food so abundant and enticing. With four cultures intermingling peacefully, nowhere can you catch such a perfect glimpse of Instant Asia. And, unless you're Felix Unger, it's almost enough to make you sick. You can get arrested for selling chewing gum (contrary to popular belief, it's legal to chew gum in Singapore—it's just illegal to buy it or sell it), tossing a cigarette butt on the ground and not flushing a public toilet. It's one of the few places left on earth where a customs officer will ask to see a man's ongoing ticket out of the principality if he wears his hair longer than a Marine corporal. Or, if the visitor happens to be Malay, they'll just cut it off in a side room at the customs post on the other side of the bridge at Jahore Bahru.

These inconveniences aside, Singapore is the most advanced region in Asia and is a strikingly beautiful, sun-drenched city, most of which was built only within the last 25 years. Actually, Singapore exists as it does today because of the efforts of two people: Stamford Raffles nearly two centuries ago, and Lee Kuan Yew in the last 30 years. In many ways, Singapore is more Western than the West. It is a center for high-tech products and the financial hub of Southeast Asia. With Hong Kong moving to Chinese rule in 1997, Singapore is poised to become one of the next great financial centers of the world.

If you like shopping, you've come to the right place. The entire city can seem like one giant shopping mall. Even Changi Airport, the airport cited as the world's best by most travelers, belies its purpose; row after row of duty-free, high-end retailers line its corridors like Rodeo Drive with a roof over it. Most shopping malls look more like airports. The fact that they also fly airplanes in and out of this place seems simply like a ho-hum, value-added service.

Singapore is a land that is both elegant and ethnic. Although Chinese make up three-quarters of the population, the principality is heavily influenced by the presence of its Malay, Tamil and European minorities. Even though Singapore has been independent since 1967, a strong colonial British presence endures here—in both mind and matter.

But don't be mistaken, Singapore is also very, very Asian. Hinduism, Islam and Buddhism co-exist peacefully, be prepared for some of the best Asian culinary experiences of your life.

History of Singapore

It will always be somewhat of a mystery to me why the name Singapura—Sanskrit for "lion city"—was bestowed upon this island settlement situated just below the Strait of Malacca. The existence of lions has never been verified, although tigers and an abundance of rather nasty crocodiles in the surrounding swamplands have been well recorded. Nonetheless, the name has withstood both time and several upheavals, mainly because founding father Sir Thomas Stamford Raffles readily accepted it as he stepped ashore on January 29, 1819.

That Sir Raffles is synonymous with the success of Singapore is no mean happening. This self-made English fellow (scholar/historian/politician/businessman), who snuck around the Dutch to claim this place for his country, always considered Singapore his own child. Although he spent no more than the total of one full year here (on three separate occasions), he laid the cornerstone for present-day Singapore. Until the Japanese occupation, his laws banned slavery, cockfighting, brothels and other nuisances. As a final official act before his departure in 1823, he established Raffles College, which has educated a number of noteworthy Singaporeans (among them, Prime Minister Lee Kuan Yew).

Raffles insisted that this island settlement, caught as it was amid the sea-lanes between the East and Middle East, become a free trading port under the aegis of England. His grand scheme bore quick results, for not three years after the Union Jack was first raised here there were dozens of ships anchored in the harbor; the total trade figures were quite astounding. Population figures boomed along with business and, by 1867 (a year after Raffles' death), Singapore became a British Crown Colony. Two years later, the Suez Canal opened and ships came through in half the time.

Life was very pleasant and very colonial, especially for "white Singapore" whose members had big houses with full domestic staffs; there were parties and teas. There was Sunday tiffin at what was to become Raffles Hotel; there was the Singapore Cricket Club at one end of the padang (playing field) and the Eurasian Sporting Club at the other. Life was also rather inexpensive (being duty free, as it was) and residents drank a lot of tax-free gin and whiskey—either as pahit (a short drink) or the famous stengah (half liquor/half water). There was entertainment galore, plenty of companionship for the English bachelors and daily business was mainly conducted on credit. Although people had plenty of money, they didn't like to carry it about because of the heat and humidity!

The Japanese and World War II

The fun and frolic lasted until Monday, December 8, 1941, when the Japanese attacked (among other places) the east coast of Malaya. Two months and one week later, the government of Singapore surrendered to the Japanese invaders. It was hardly one of England's finest hours and paved the way for the end of colonial rule in Singapore. Now, in hindsight, historians agree that Japanese battle victories in the early part of World War II destroyed (more than anything else) white supremacy in Asia. However, the local populace first had to deal with the captors who changed the name of Singapore to Shonan (it didn't stick) and generally ruled with malice. Their one contribution to mankind's progress was the introduction of trishaws (three-wheeled pedicabs) versus the traditional rickshaws (pulled by single runners), because the latter were considered inhumane.

The British reassumed control of Singapore when the war ended (many of the officials coming straight from the ranks of the famous Changi prison), and the statue of Raffles was reinstated beside the river, but as one writer put it, "People looked at him a little differently." The yellow brick road to independence was being laid, held back briefly by the 1950s Emergency (Communist rebels) that struck the Malay peninsula. Finally in June 1959, a 36-year old Cambridge-educated Baba (the local name for a Straits-born Chinese male) won the first election and became the first prime minister of the independent state of Singapore. His name was Lee Kuan Yew and he long ago earned his place in history books right next to that of the founding father.

The New Singapore Emerges

For 30 years Prime Minister Lee has dedicated himself to making miracles happen and disproving that well-known "white epitaph"— *Here Lies a Man Who Tried to Hurry the East*. Through a combination of strategy, cunning, imagination and very, very hard work (some say Calvinism), Lee Kuan Yew transformed this island republic into the most modern Asian nation possible. He was ruthless at every step (all white clubs that did not open their doors to others would be closed forever), but he was also frequently touted as the only incorruptible politician in all of Asia (perhaps the world). In November 1990 after Lee stepped down, Goh Chok Tong became prime minister of Singapore and Lee assumed the post of senior minister.

After reclaiming land at an alarming speed (making maps obsolete) for more high-rise housing projects, more golf courses and parks, more factories and entertainment facilities, Singapore has responded to negative reactions by visitors and slowed development, even recreating sections of Old Singapore that had been demolished in the name of progress. And when early morning traffic in the city center threatens paradise with its fumes and congestion, barriers are erected to keep cars out, despite the inconvenience. Yet Singaporeans continue to celebrate an annual tree-planting Sunday that keeps theirs a "garden city." An amazing number of festivals and public holidays celebrate the traditions and religions of the four cultures that live together so peacefully on this island.

Lee Kuan Yew proved that the good old Protestant work ethic will produce success every time (he is often said to have manners "more English than the English"). The Singapore he shaped is booming in trade, local industries, banking and finance; and the number of annual visitors (for business or pleasure) has surpassed the total local population. He also created one of the most literate of Asian societies, although the media is strictly controlled and "bad" outside influences are not tolerated.

PLANNING AHEAD

SINGAPORE TOURIST PROMOTION BOARD (STPB)

It is located at *Raffles City Tower, #36-04, 250 North Bridge Rd., Singapore 0617.* ☎ *339-6622,* and the hours are 8:30 a.m.-5 p.m. weekdays and 8:30 a.m.-1 p.m. Saturday (closed Sundays and public holidays). Receptionists assist visitors with information and complimentary maps and publications. They will also arrange for the (paid) services of an official tourist guide if you like. Brochures are also available at the STPB Information Center in the arrival hall of Changi Airport from 6 a.m.-10 p.m. daily, and two additional offices in town: *01-19 Raffles City Centre, 250 N. Bridge Rd.,* open 8:30 a.m.-6 p.m. daily, and *02/03 Scotts Shopping Center, 6 Scotts Rd.*

The STPB has four regional offices in North America: *590 Fifth Ave., New York, NY 10036* (☎ *212-302-4861*); *8484 Wilshire Blvd., Suite 510, Beverly Hills, CA 90211* (☎ *213-852-1901*); *333 N. Michigan Ave., Suite 818, Chicago, IL 60601* (☎ *312-220-0099*); *175 Bloor St., East, Suite 1112, North Tower, Toronto, Ont. M4W3R8, Canada* (☎ *416-323-9139*).

VISAS

Visas are not required of travelers holding valid U.S. or Canadian passports, for stays of up to 14 days, for purposes other than employment or residence. Valid passports are required of all visitors.

INOCULATIONS

Required for smallpox or yellow fever only if travelers have arrived from an area infected within the preceding 14 days.

ENTRY BY AIR

Entry is at Singapore's impressive International Airport at Changi. Often singled out by frequent travelers as their favorite airport, Changi has been voted the world's best airport on several occasions by readers of *Business Travel International.* Among the many amenities offered in its two terminals are day rooms with private bathrooms, a fitness center, supermarket and medical clinic. Changi is located about 10 miles from the city center. Taxis cost about US$12 to downtown hotels (there is a surcharge for taxi rides originating at the airport).

Departure tax is S$15 for all international flights, including flights to Malaysia and Brunei.

ARRIVAL BY SEA

Arrival in the world's busiest harbor can be aboard any number of **passenger vessels**, ranging from the Queen Elizabeth 2 to Royal Viking Line, Royal and Pearl Cruises, Seabourn, Windstar, Princess and Renaissance Cruises. Singapore is a favorite port on around-the-world cruises as well as the many ships departing from Australia on year-round sailings. Entry formalities and port taxes are the responsibility of the individual shipline, and the Singapore Tourist Promotion Board is on hand with a mobile information service to greet all passengers stepping ashore from Keppel Harbor.

ARRIVAL BY RAILWAY

Rail is yet another alternative transportation to and from Singapore. The Express Rakyat takes exactly 24 hours to Bangkok, with stops at Kuala Lumpur and Butterworth (for Penang Island). There are air-conditioned coaches and berths as well as a dining car. Tickets can be purchased three days in advance from the railway station on Keppel Rd. (☎ *222-5165*). In September 1993, the Eastern & Oriental Express inaugurated rail service linking Singapore with Kuala Lumpur and Bangkok. The luxury vintage train service is operated by the same company as Europe's Venice Simplon-Orient-Express. Fares for the complete three-day/two-night trip start at US$1100 per person, including all meals. Shorter sectors can also be booked, starting at $395. ☎ *(800) 524-2420* for information.

BUSES

Buses to and from Malaysia run daily. Departures are every 10 minutes via the Causeway to Johor Bahru from Rochor Rd. Terminus and every 15 minutes from Queen St. or Bukit Timah Rd. Malacca buses leave from the Beach Rd. Terminus six times daily; while Kuala Lumpur, Penang, Butterworth, Mersing and Kuantan buses all depart from the New Bridge Rd. Fringe Car Park Terminus.

DUTY FREE

Duty free is the case for most items in Singapore. There are no currency restrictions on the amount allowed imported or exported in either local or foreign notes. Incoming travelers are allowed (except when coming from Malaysia) duty free one bottle of spirits; one bottle wine; one bottle beer, ale or stout. All can be purchased at the Duty free Emporium at the airport arrival hall. Dangerous weapons are prohibited, and household pets from other than the U.K., Ireland, Australia, or New Zealand are subject to quarantine at owner's expense for at least 30 days.

Teenagers of all ages should take note that the "hippie look" is not tolerated in Singapore and possessing or trafficking any kind of drug or narcotic is a severe offense and punishable by jail, fine, or death. Drug abuse in this republic is not to be taken lightly.

CURRENCY

The unit of currency is the **Singapore dollar**, written as S$. The present exchange rate is about S$1.50 equals U.S.$1.00. Notes are used in the denominations of S$1, S$5, S$10, S$20, S$50, S$100, S$500, S$1,000 and S$10,000. There are 100 cents to each dollar and coins can be found in 1 cent, 5 cents, 10 cents, 20 cents and 50 cents.

Like Hong Kong, Singapore is an important Far East financial capital and there are more than 80 banks and some 75 insurance companies doing big business here. Banking hours are 10 a.m.-3 p.m. Mon. through Fri. and 9:30 a.m.-11:30 a.m. on Sat. Branches of the Development Bank of Singapore remain open until 3 p.m. on Sat. However, licensed moneychangers often give the best rates and don't deduct a surcharge when converting foreign currency for tourist purchases. Look for them at shopping complexes and commercial areas. Exchange rates at hotel desks are always too low.

LOCAL TIME

The time in Singapore is Greenwich Mean Time plus 8 hours. When it is noon Sun. in Singapore, the local time on the west coast is 8 p.m. Sat. and on the east coast 12 a.m. Sun. morning. Singapore time is the same as Hong Kong, Taipei, Manila and the entire Malay peninsula. It is one hour in advance of Jakarta and Bangkok.

LOCAL CURRENT

Local current is 220-240 volts AC, 50 cycles. Most hotels have a transformer to reduce the voltage to

110-120 volts, 60 cycles, if necessary for electric shavers, hair dryers, etc.

LOCAL WATER

The water is pure and potable. Tap water is safe to drink anywhere and it is wise to drink at least six glasses daily while adapting to this tropical and somewhat debilitating climate. There is no water shortage in Singapore, but you still must take care not to waste any water.

OFFICIAL LANGUAGES

Languages in Singapore are English, Mandarin, Malay and Tamil. English is the language of business, administration and tourism. Most Singaporeans are tri-lingual (at least). Schools are required to educate children in their mother tongue as well as English.

One English-language newspaper is published daily, the *Straits Times* (morning). For outside news, look for the *International Herald Tribune* and the *Asian Wall Street Journal* in addition to the weekly news magazines. English radio service airs from 6 a.m. to midnight daily, FM stereo from 6 a.m.-11 p.m. Color television programs are broadcast in all four languages on Channel 5 (3 p.m. to midnight) and Channel 8 (6 p.m.-11 p.m.). Two stations from Malaysia can also be received.

Singapore is also a publishing capital and there are any number of excellent books available, so don't pass by the local stores without looking in.

BUSINESS HOURS

Business hours in Singapore range from 8 a.m.-5 or 6 p.m. Singaporeans are industrious and serious in their work. Shops stay open from 10 a.m. until at least 9 p.m. seven days a week and the Chinese emporiums until 10

p.m. Stores are open in the large centers on Sunday.

TIPPING

Tipping is not supposed to be a way of life in Singapore. It is prohibited at the airport, in hotels and restaurants that add a 10% service charge and in restrooms. Taxi drivers do not expect much, but it is nice to offer small change. Bellboys should be tipped for services rendered. Away from the tourist centers, a smile suffices.

TELEPHONE, TELEX & FAX

These services in Singapore are excellent. Local phone calls (except in public booths) are free of charge. The telephone system is extensive throughout the city and it is even possible to speak with a vessel in Keppel Harbor (dial 105 for operator) or a ship at sea (dial 907). The city also has IDD (International Direct Dialing).

Telex and cable services are available 24 hours a day at your hotel, or from the General Post Office, Fullerton Building (☎ 983111). You can mail cards and letters at the front desk of your hotel or with the concierge. In addition, the post office at Changi Airport and at Killiney Rd. are both open from 8 a.m.-8 p.m. Monday-Saturday. Postcards to other parts of the Far East are S$.20, to the U.S. S$.30; airmail letters to the U.S. are S$.75 (for the first 10 grams).

WHAT TO WEAR

The lighter the better is the key to what makes comfort in this hot and humid climate. Casual cotton clothing (skirts, short-sleeve blouses for women and slacks and shirts for men) is best for daytime wear, with something more formal for the evening. Singapore is actually a very casual city (open shirts or safari suits for men), unless you plan to attend business meetings daily and to dine in a premier hotel restaurant every evening. Coat and tie are required in many restaurants and clubs; forget them if you're wandering out for some satay or to your favorite curry place. But blue jeans and T-shirts are frowned upon, even at some of the better discos where they are considered unacceptable. And if your visit is scheduled during the rainy season (Oct. through Jan.), expect to be drenched from time to time in heavy downpours. An umbrella, light slicker and rainhat are necessities during these winter months. And at any time of the year, pack enough wraps for evening to protect yourself against too-cold air conditioning after a day in tropical heat.

LOCAL TRANSPORTATION

Local transit is clean and efficient in Singapore. There are more than 10,000 air-conditioned, metered taxis, with a maximum allowance of four passengers each. Fares begin at S$2.20 for the first 1.5 km, plus S$.10 for each subsequent 250 meters traveled and for up to every 45 seconds of waiting time. Add a surcharge of S$.50 for each third or fourth passenger and each piece of luggage is an additional S$1. In addition, there is a 50% surcharge for service between the hours of midnight and 6 a.m.

If your hotel or morning destination is located within the central business district, you may experience some difficulty arriving and departing between the hours of 7:30 a.m. and 10:15 a.m. Mon. to Sat. (except public holidays). A "restricted zone" in the city center has been designated to alleviate traffic congestion in the morning hours. Unless you are in a vehicle carrying at least four persons, you can not enter this zone without a permit or Area License. It's all rather complicated and totally annoying if you have to be somewhere

within this zone in the early morning. The best advice I can give is to have the taxi driver drop you as close as possible to your destination, then WALK!! If you have any taxi complaints, do not hesitate to direct them to Registry of Vehicles, Sin Ming Dr., Sing. 2057 or the STPB at its headquarters. A dial-a-taxi service is available 24-hours daily. ☎ *452-5555* and ☎ *250-0700*. London cabs, which seat five, may also be reserved by ☎ *481-1211*. City buses run from 6 a.m.-11:30 p.m. Fares are computed by distance, in stages that average about four-fifths of a kilometer in length. The fares range from S$.40 to S$.80 and exact change is required. Bus guides and routes are available for about S$.50 at local hotel shops and bookstores. The Singapore Explorer ticket allows holders unlimited use of the local bus service for one or three days (S$5, S$12). Trishaws are still "in" and an interesting way to explore the back alleys of the older sections of the city. Find out the going rate from someone in your hotel or at the STPB and then settle the amount before you enter the "cab." And be a little sensitive about the differences in size between East and Western bodies. Should a 60-pound trishawist, who lives on a few bowls of rice, cart around a 200-lb steak-and-potatoes American? Many cyclists will say NO—for any price.

Singapore introduced air-conditioned passenger train service in 1991. The Mass Rapid Transit (MRT) system serves 42 stations and operates from 6 a.m. to midnight at three- to eight-minute intervals. Singapore's new trolley service is also a convenient and inexpensive way to get around town. For a flat fare of S$6 for adults and S$3 for children, trolley passengers can hop on and off at 22 stops.

In the early morning or the cool of the evening, Singapore is a walking city and you will find the streets much more revealing after dark than at anytime during the day. The sidewalks of Chinatown become one great open-air cafe, with odors of regional specialties mingling together to tempt bypassers. Local street operas, mini-festivals and block bazaars only occur when the sun has gone to rest and the workday stops. Have a taxi driver aim you in the right direction, then get out to walk, eat, watch and ENJOY!

Whether by night or day, jaywalking is a severe offense in Singapore, punishable by a S$50 fine. Cross streets at traffic lights only (especially as you may not be accustomed to left-hand drive) and if there is an overhead bridge or underpass for pedestrians, use it.

SOME USEFUL INFORMATION

Littering is also a grave offense against the city, and even a cigarette butt dropped is risking a S$500 fine. In fact, smoking in general is discouraged by the government and absolutely forbidden in some taxis, all public buses, elevators, theaters and government offices.

Seeing Singapore by water is a delight. Bumboats offer a half-hour ride along Singapore's waterway and operate 9 a.m.-7 p.m. daily, every hour, from the pier at Raffles Landing. Fares are S$6 for adults and S$3 for children under 12.

Singapore is reputed to be one of the safest cities in the Far East and travelers find little difficulty in getting about on their own. There are a great many rules and regulations in this city and it's best to obey them while you are a paying guest. Apart from charity draws, certain lotteries and betting through the Singapore Turf Club, gambling is illegal.

Always deal with a licensed money-changer and NEVER get into a discussion or promotion of drugs with ANYONE.

FESTIVALS AND HOLIDAYS

Holidays and festivals permeate life in Singapore; the holidays of four different religions are celebrated with equal fervor. The Chinese celebrate feasts in honor of hungry ghosts, monkey gods, Confucius, mooncakes and dragon boats, as well as the birthday of Buddha. The Moslems observe Ramadan without fail and Hari Raya Puasa at the finale is a time of much feasting. The Hindu population has Thimithi, its fire-walking festival, and the Taoists honor the birthday of the Third Prince with a street procession. Christians deck the hall with bows of beautiful poinsettias at Christmastime and with abundant wild orchids at Easter. Visitors are always warmly invited to all the festivities. The following are holidays scheduled for Singapore each year. Only those marked with an asterisk (*) are public holidays.

*January 1	New Year's Day	
January	Maulidin Nabi or Hymns for the Prophet Mohammed	*Devotees gather in mosques to chant Murhaban hymns of praise and recite the Berjanzi, the book on the life of Mohammed. Visit Sultan Mosqueoon, North Bridge Rd. for the biggest celebrations. (Women are not permitted in certain parts of the building.)*
January	Ponggol or Harvest Festival	*A four-day festival from Southern India in which Tamils honor the Sun God with prayers of thanksgiving and offerings of rice, sugar cane, spices and vegetable curry. The prasadam (sacred food) is then distributed...visit the Perumal Temple on Serangoon Rd.*
*January/ February	Chinese New Year	*The most important festival in the Chinese lunar calendar. Two days of Kung Hei Fat Choy—feasting and visiting, goodwill and merrymaking all around. Most businesses open the third day, but the holiday continues until the 15th day.*
*February	Chingay Procession	*Decorated floats held on the first weekend of the Chinese New Year along a predetermined route. Lion dances, drums, martial artists, stiltwalkers, swordsmen, beautiful young ladies, etc.*
February	Birthday of Monkey God	*A colorful festival in honor of T'se Tien Tai Seng Yeh, celebrated lavishly twice annually in several Chinese temples around the city. Wayang (Chinese street opera) and puppet shows are performed in temple courtyards and processions are held at temples on Eng Hoon St. and Cumming St.*
April	Birthday of the Saint of the Poor	*The image of Kong Teck Choon Ong is carried in a palanquin by worshipers and spirit mediums from White Cloud Temple on Ganges Ave. on a tour of the neighborhood.*

FESTIVALS AND HOLIDAYS

April	Ching Ming Festival or Remembrance of Ancestors Day	*A tradition since the Han Dynasty, Chinese families clean and freshen ancestors' graves and then have a picnic on the site. A splendid outing.*
*April	Hari Raya Puasa	*The end of Ramadan arrives with the sighting of a new moon and the beginning of the tenth month in the Moslem calendar. The holiday means much feasting, visiting and weaving new fabrics. Date varies from year to year.*
April	Songkran Festival	*The Thai Buddhist festival celebrated with throwing holy water at believers signifies the start of the year's solar cycle, when the sun returns to first position in the zodiac. Visit Ananda Metyrama Thai Buddhist Temple at Silat Rd. or Sapthapuchaniyaram Temple on Holland Rd., but be prepared for a drenching!*
*Lenten Week	Good Friday	*Solemn services held at all Christian churches, plus a candlelight procession in the grounds of St. Joseph (Catholic) Church in Victoria St.*
End of Lent	Easter Sunday	*Hotels and restaurants have special menus with gifts for the children.*
May	Birthday of the Third Prince of the Lotus	*A temple in his honor is located at Clarke St./North Boat Quay near Chinatown. Here on the day of celebration are pantomimes, Chinese wayangs, mediums in a trance and charms written in blood. Go if you must.*
*May	Vesak Day	*In honor of the Lord Buddha's birth, death and enlightenment. Free meals are offered to the poor, birds are released from their cages, and devotees go vegetarian or fast altogether. The Temple of 1000 Lights (Sakya Muni Gaya Temple) on Race Course Rd. and Pher Kark See Temple on Bright Hill Dr. are centers for this celebration.*
June	Dragon Boat Festival	*One of the most colorful and fun of the entire calendar, this festival commemorates the ancient Chinese poet Ch'u Yuan, who drowned himself in protest against injustice and corruption. International dragon boat races highlight the festival as well as the consumption of chang (glutinous rice dumplings) that legend says fishermen threw into the water to sustain the drowning hero.*

FESTIVALS AND HOLIDAYS

June	Hari Raya Haji	*A Moslem festival of pilgrimage with praises to Allah, alms for the poor, and the forgetting of old quarrels. Celebrations at all mosques in Singapore, especially Sultan Mosque on North Bridge Rd. Date varies from year to year.*
June 1	Commencement of Ramadan	*The first day of the ninth month of the Moslem calendar, when devotees observe daylight fasting until the next new moon. Stalls behind Sultan Mosque sell colorful cakes for evening, when the fast is broken, and Arab St. livens up after sundown.*
July	Market Festival	*A month-long festival held in conjunction with Feast of the Hungry Ghosts and celebrated lavishly by stallholders. Street operas are popular to entertain the spirits, especially throughout Chinatown. Visit also the Cuppage Rd. Hawkers' Center off Orchard Rd.*
August	Festival of Seven Sisters	*Dedicated to young lovers and celebrated since the 8th century B.C., this festival signifies the meeting of a cowherd and a spinning maid every year on the 7th day of the 7th moon (in the lunar calendar).*
*August 9	National Day	*Displays by Singapore's cultural mix and a huge parade that ends in the National Stadium at Kallang to celebrate the formation of an independent Republic in 1965.*
August	Feast of the Hungry Ghosts	*A Chinese tradition since the 6th century during the month of the 7th moon. Celebrations are held on a grand scale at temples, market places and even neighborhood street corners. The Chinese stay home on the last night, lest their spirit get carried away by a ghost returning to the underworld.*
September	Mooncake Festival	*Another Chinese legend about a lovely young lady in the heavens, but the more practical prefer the story about the patriots who communicated through messages hidden in cakes while attempting to overthrow the Mongols. To commemorate liberation from foreign domination, Chinese traditionally eat mooncakes and light lanterns on the 15th night of the 8th moon. The cakes are filled with bean paste, lotus seeds, orange peel, egg yolks, etc. There are also lantern processions, lion dances, concerts and competitions with children in ancient costumes.*

FESTIVALS AND HOLIDAYS

September	Kusu Pilgrimage	*Every day for a month or so, Taoist devotees flock to the turtle-shaped island of Kusu to pray for prosperity, fertility and good luck at the Chinese temple of Tau Pek Kong, or a Malay Kramat (shrine). It is better to avoid this islet during pilgrimage time.*
September/ October	Emperor Gods and Double Ninth	*From the first to the 9th day of the 9th moon, nine Chinese Emperor Gods are venerated with street operas and float processions. Their spirits cure ailments, bring luck, wealth and longevity and are said to possess their images in sedan chairs, etc. On the 9th day, whole families take to the hills for a picnic or visit Kusu Island on pilgrimage.*
October	Thimithi Festival or Fire Walking	*Held to honor the purity of Hindu Goddess Durobatha, supplicants pray to the goddess and then walk across burning coals to pay a debt for wishes granted. If you can stand it, visit Sri Mariamman Temple on South Bridge Rd.*
October	Navarathi Festival	*A 10-day homage to the consorts of the three gods of the Hindu trinity. The first week is spent in worship; the last days are for feasting and merrymaking. Goddess Durga, also known as Parvathi, consort of Lord Siva the Destroyer, commands the attention of the devotees during the first three days of the festival; the next three are for Lakshmi, Goddess of Wealth and consort of Lord Vishnu the Protector; and the final three belong to Saraswathi, Goddess of Education/Literature/Music/Eloquence and consort of Lord Brahma the Creator. On all nine evenings of the festival, classical Indian musical shows from 7 p.m.-10 p.m. are staged at the Chettiar Temple on Tank Rd. On the 10th day, traditional Hindu families teach their young how to write om, the universal word and Hari (Vishnu). The festival closes with a grand procession from Chettiar Temple through the nearby streets.*
*October	Hari Raya Haji	*The 10th day of the 12th month of the Moslem calendar has special significance for all who have completed their pilgrimage to Mecca. (They wear white caps and the men are addressed as Haji, women as Hajjah.) This day is observed at most mosques with prayers from 8 a.m.; goats are sacrificed to Allah in remembrance of the prophet Ibrahim's sacrifice of his son.*

FESTIVALS AND HOLIDAYS

*October or November	Deepavali	*The Festival of Lights is a traditional Hindu celebration centuries old. Legends disagree exactly why this festival is celebrated–either the triumph of Lord Krishna over the demon king Nasakasura or the one day of the year when Lakshmi returns to earth. Hindu temples are colorful sights on this day, especially Perumal Temple on Serangoon Rd.*
*December 25	Christmas Day	*If you happen to be in town, you will find everything here but the snow.*

Background Material

The Singapore Story by Noel Barber is the very best and most readable history of Singapore (from Raffles to Lee Kuan Yew). It is available in Fontana paperback at hotel bookshops throughout Singapore, for about U.S.$4. The British Barber, a former foreign correspondent, is author of some 27 books. Others of interest and also in paperback are *Sinister Twilight* (the fall of Singapore and Japanese occupation) and *The War of the Running Dogs* (the Emergency years after the war).

King Rat by James Clavell is a fictionalized account of life in Changi prison during the Japanese occupation. The book rings very true (because Clavell was, indeed, interned there) and is one of his best.

Raffles Hotel by Ilsa Maria Sharp is the first book by this local resident. It's a history of Singapore's most famous hostelry. It should be a fascinating account of the years from 1887 to present and who did what, when. Especially, if you stay at Raffles.

Lord Jim, The Nigger of the Narcissus, Almayer's Folley and *The Shadow Line* by Joseph Conrad are all products of his visits to Singapore several times as a seaman. It is still possible to see something of Conrad's Singapore along the river—Cavenaugh Bridge (oldest bridge still in use), the godowns where goods are still unloaded and stored, the Old Ice House (now occupied by the TaiThong Rubber Works).

Singapore (APA Productions) is also highly recommended.

WHAT TO SEE AND DO IN SINGAPORE

Alkaff Mansion

Telok Blangah Green. The restored Arab trading family's mansion overlooking Singapore Harbour is open daily for lunch, tea and dinner. Continental cuisine and rijstafel served.

Arab Street

Between Singapore River and Rochor Canal. The Muslim Malay quarter is dominated by the Sultan Mosque. Herbs and spices from Moluccus islands permeate the air here. There are good buys also in Middle Eastern materials, rugs, baskets and jewelry.

Botanic Gardens ★★

Cluny and Napier Rds. If you can only visit one of the city's lovely green spots, pick this. It's close to hotel-land. Malaysia's thriving rubber industry began here when Henry Nicholas Ridley experimented with hevea seeds and gave them to planters across the causeway. The gardens are now a well-planned oasis with lily ponds, happy swans, orchid pavilions and an herbarium. This is one of the most popular spots in town. There are 80 lush acres and paths for joggers. It's known for Tai Chi followers, lovers (newlyweds come here for photographs after the big event) and whole families on picnic. Open from 5 a.m.-11 p.m. weekdays, to midnight on weekends and holidays. Admission is free.

Bukit Timah Nature Reserve

Upper Bukit Timah Rd. More for residents who must escape the city steam than for visitors. Nonetheless, this is a well-kept, 185-acre retreat with footpaths, a jungle atmosphere, shelter huts and great views. Walkers can take the road to the summit (no vehicles allowed). Plan a half-day for communing with nature. Admission is free.

Cenotaph

Connaught Dr. This towering landmark dedicated to the dead of two world wars was unveiled by the late Duke of Windsor (then Prince of Wales) in 1922.

Chinatown

Bounded by New Bridge Rd. and South Bridge Rd. Some of the scenes here have been unchanged for more than 100 years. You cannot visit Singapore without spending some time here. It's a constant hubbub of activity from dawn until after midnight; more than 100,000 people occupy one square mile and wouldn't dream of moving. Businesses and trades thousands of years old are carried on daily. Walk through slowly to do it justice. Surprises and new sensations are at every turn.

Chinese and Japanese Gardens

Off Yuan Ching Rd. Jurong's 32-1/2 acres make it the largest of its kind outside Japan. The gardens are in the traditional Kaiyu-chikuyo-marinsen style; carefully manicured with ponds, bridges, a waterfall and quietude. Open daily 9 a.m. to 7 p.m. Monday-Saturday; 8:30 a.m.-7 p.m. Sundays and holidays. Admission is S$4 for adults; S$2 for children.

East Coast Park

East Coast Parkway. Eight hundred sixty-five acres of seaside recreational facilities off the highway between Changi Airport and the city proper. There's swimming, jogging, tennis, golf, barbecues, squash, etc.—plus a Crocodilarium (admission S$2 for adults; S$1 for children) with more than 1000 crocodiles and a man-made lagoon for 6,000 bathers. It's great if you like crowds. There's also windsurfing lessons and boards for rent.

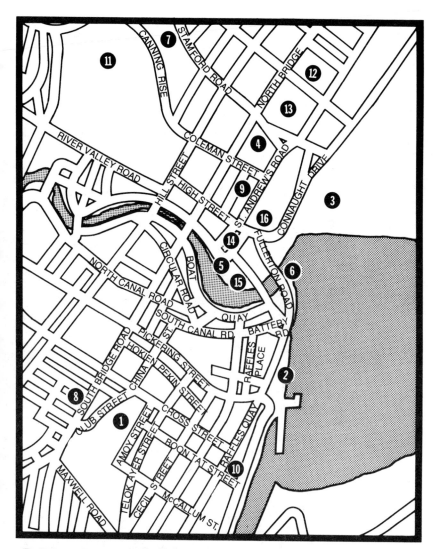

SINGAPORE

Key

1) Chinatown
2) Clifford Pier
3) Elizabeth Walk
4) St. Andrew's Cathedral
5) Sir Stamford Raffles Landing Site
6) Merlion
7) National Museum and Art Gallery
8) Sri Mariamman Temple

9) Supreme Court and City Hall
10) Telok Ayer Market
11) Fort Canning Park
12) Raffles Hotel
13) Westin Plaza & Westin Stamford
14) Victoria Theatre and Memorial Hall
15) Empress Place
16) Singapore Cricket Club

Elizabeth Walk

At the other end of Merlion Park. Sit on the rustic benches and imagine what colonial Singapore was like. Look across the road at the **Padang,** the famous green of the **Cricket Club,** where so many good times have taken place (as well as some nasty ones). Best known for the evening, when the **Satay Club** begins, with skewers of meat barbecued and consumed in the open air.

Empress Place

A new museum created from one of the old British colonial office buildings within walking distance of Raffles City and the Cathedral. It captures much of Singapore's history in the building itself, with exhibits devoted to the country's various historical traditions. The opening exhibit featured the personal effects of the last emperor of China.

Fort Canning Park

Clemenceau Ave. Founded in 1859 as a fortress to protect the port of Singapore. It features a historic cemetery, a floral clock and the national theater.

Hajjah Fatimah Mosque

Beach Rd. Built in 1845-46 in honor of a Malay woman from Malacca. She stands in a grove of glam trees which provided medicinal oil to the Malays and bark for their boats. The daughter and son-in-law of Hajjah Fatimah are buried in the back yard. This is an inspiring and charming small mosque. Open daily.

House of Tan Yeok Nee

Junction of Clemenceau Ave. and Somerset Rd. (opposite Singapore Shopping Centre). Built in 1885 of carvings and granite pillars imported from China for a prominent Teochew Chinese gambler and pepper merchant, it's now Salvation Army headquarters and preserved by National Monuments Board.

Jurong Bird Park

Jalan Ahmad Ibrahim, Jurong. Fifty acres in the heart of Jurong, the park features 3,500 birds from all over the world, some 400 species. There's a 5-acre walk-in aviary where more than 3,000 birds (65 varieties) fly free. The park is open from 9 a.m.-6 p.m. weekdays; to 7 p.m. weekends and holidays. Admission is S$5.00 for adults; S$2.50 for children. There are tram and camera surcharges.

Jurong Crocodile Park

Jalan Ahmad Ibrahim. Here there are 2,500 crocodiles on view. There's a breeding enclosure in a landscaped setting. Open daily. Admission is S$4.50 adults; S$2.50 children.

Kuan Yin Temple

Waterloo St. The temple is dedicated to the Goddess of Mercy, who devoted her life to helping mankind. It's a humble temple with few adornments—one a lustrous image of the goddess, adorned in silk vestment. The temple is jammed at New Year's time as supplicants flock to seek favors for the coming year.

Little India

Serangoon Rd. This is a stretch along Kandang Kerbau populated by Singapore ethnic Indians. Visit from 8 a.m.-9 p.m. any day. Jasmine garlands and barrels of spice sweeten the air. Gold bangles are heard even before they're seen on the sari-clad women. Sikhs fill the streets; vegetarian restaurants abound. There are good bargains if you know where to look.

A landmark in Singapore's Little India. Indians account for just under 10 percent of Singapore's population.

Marina Square

Designed by American architect John Portman on reclaimed land, the new square is accessible from Nicoll Highway, Bras Basah Road and East Coast Parkway; it's an enormous complex of 3 large hotels, landscaped gardens, 4 department stores, some 240 retail outlets, entertainment and sport facilities and parking for 2,300 cars. The hotels here are the top-rated Oriental and Marina Mandarin, as well as the Pan Pacific—a division of Tokyo International Hotels that will appeal to the Asian trade. Of the three, The Oriental boasts the distinctive Portman atrium concept.

Merlion

This is the symbol of Singapore, a 26-foot statue with a lion's head (*Singapura* means lion city) and the body of a fish (*Tumasek* is Javanese for sea) that guards the harbor. It's situated at the mouth of Singapore River and spews a constant flow of water. A rainbow often forms on the horizon because of this tropical climate. You can't miss this fellow.

He's one of the city's most popular camera subjects. The statue also commands the vista of Merlion Park, a small green area fronting the sea.

Singapore's Merlion guards the entrance to Singapore Harbor.

Mt. Faber

Off Kampong Bahru Rd. Mt Faber is a 385-foot hill with an excellent view of the city and harbor. It's reachable by cable car from Jardine Steps or from Sentosa Island station. There's an art gallery/restaurant on top. The last cable car departs from the top of the hill at 6:30 p.m.

National Museum and Art Gallery   ★★★

Stamford Rd. This was an idea Sir Stamford Raffles talked about in 1823 and actually began in 1849. It moved to its present building in 1887. The collection includes archaeological artifacts, Chinese bronzes and porcelains, Nonya fabrics (Chinese/Malay design), costumes and furniture, maps and paintings of old Singapore, contemporary artworks, plus the Haw Par 385-piece priceless jade collection—the largest of its kind in the world. Open 9 a.m.-5:30 p.m., Tuesday-Sunday. Admission is S$4.50 adults; S$2.50 children.

Orchid Gardens

Mandai Lake Rd. Ten acres of orchids to feast the eyes; all varieties and all colors. This is an entire hillside covered with wild orchids, including Singapore's national flower, the Vanda Miss Joaquin. There are two hundred hybrids here. Open 9 a.m.-5 p.m. daily. Admission is S$1.50 for adults; S$.50 for children.

Pasar Malam (Night Market)

The night market is a newly created weekly tourist attraction which takes place daily from 6 to 10 p.m. and 4 to 10 p.m. on weekends. It specializes in handicrafts.

Raffles City ★★★

This modern complex, conceived and designed by Chinese-American architect I.M. Pei, incorporates all the features of a city-within-a-city. It occupies 8 acres in the heart of downtown Singapore. It features 4 separate towers, including a 42-story tower connected by a 7-story enclosed space. This is truly a 21st-century version of the town square. The 71-story Westin Stamford and twin-core 28-story towers of Westin Plaza offer more than 2,000 rooms, 18 restaurants and lounges—and the ultimate in meeting and exhibit facilities, a 3,500-seat Convention Center. Raffles City provides the ultimate in technology, convenience and comfort. It's the largest convention and meeting center in the Far East.

Raffles Hotel ★★★

Beach Rd. Asia's most famous grande dame hotel underwent a complete restoration several years ago. It reopened in September 1991 with 104 suites and the renowned Long Bar, birthplace of the Singapore Sling. It's much more than just a hotel; it's a world-renowned institution. Raffles "stands for all the fables of the exotic East" wrote Somerset Maugham. It was originally a tiffin house but turned into a luxury hostelry by the Sarkie brothers in 1886. It became a Far Eastern stopover for many acclaimed authors: Maugham, Coward, Conrad and Kipling. It's also home of the Singapore Sling—have one at the Long Bar, although they're not what they used to be.

Singapore Cricket Club ★

Stamford Rd. and Connaught Dr. This is one of the oldest institutions in the city, located on the site of the home of Singapore's first resident. It faces the famous Padang or playing field, where "white" Singapore once frolicked. Now 4 cultures coexist on good terms.

Singapore Science Centre

Off Jurong Town Hall Rd. Opened 1977, there are 4 galleries and over 300 exhibits; great for children. The center also features the Omni Max Theatre and Planetarium. Open Tues. through Sun. from 10 a.m.-6 p.m. Admission is S$2 for adults; S$.50 for children.

Siong Lim See Monastery

Jalan Toa Payoh. Also known as Twin Grove of the Lotus Mountain Buddhist Temple, the monastery is set in a bamboo grove off the Pan Island Expressway; it's guarded by the **Four Kings of Heaven** in full military regalia. There are statues of **Gautama Buddha** and **Goddess of Mercy, Kuan Yin**. Murals depict adventures of the Patriarch, the Monkey God and "Piggy" on a mission for the Jade Emperor.

Sir Thomas Stamford Raffles Statue & Landing Site

Empress Place. This bronze lifesize statue of the founder of Singapore was sculpted by Thomas Woolner. Raffles' eyes peer toward Singapore

River, the spot where he landed on Jan. 29, 1819. Another statue of the city's founder can be found on the east bank of the river which also marks his historic arrival in 1819.

St. Andrew's Cathedral

Coleman St., between the Padang and Raffles City. This is another fragile relic of the past. The foundation stone was laid in 1853; the church was built by Indian convicts. One of the stained glass windows is dedicated to Sir Stamford Raffles himself. This is a designated national monument. Open from 7 a.m.-6 p.m. daily.

Sri Mariamman Temple

South Bridge Rd. Singapore's most photographed temple is located on the fringe of Chinatown on land donated by a Tamil Hindu from Penang who arrived in Singapore with Sir Stamford Raffles. The temple was decorated by Indian artisans. Prayers offered for the price of a banana or coconut. Open daily from 6 a.m.-noon and from 4:30-8:30 p.m.

Sultan Mosque

North Bridge Rd. This is the city's biggest Moslem structure. Muezzin broadcast daily at 5:30 a.m. from the tallest minaret. It's filled with worshipers every evening and Fri. at noon. It was built more than a century ago with money donated by Sir Stamford Raffles. Open from 8 a.m.-5:30 p.m. daily. *Remove your shoes and wash your feet before entering.*

Supreme Court and City Hall

St. Andrew's Rd. These are neoclassical structures built between 1929 and 1939. The Japanese surrender in 1945 and declaration of the Republic in 1965 took place in city hall. Worth a look as you drive past.

Tang Dynasty City

Jurong. This is the re-creation of a 7th-century Tang Dynasty village, featuring replicas of the Great Wall and the Forbidden City, as well as depictions of craftspeople and village life of the period. Open 10 a.m.-7 p.m. weekdays; 9 a.m.-7 p.m. weekends and holidays.

Telok Ayer Market

Raffles Quay. First built in 1825 and rebuilt in 1894; the octagonal **Lau Pa Sat** (old market) stands proudly beside high rises. The prefabricated cast-iron building is believed to have been made in Europe and shipped here. Now it's a giant outdoor market filled with foodstalls. Great for lunch, but get there early.

Telok Ayer Street

There are three national monuments here all within walking distance: **Thian Hock Keng Temple**, which is dedicated to Ma Chu Poh, the Queen of Heaven and the patron saint of sailors; the **Al-Abrar Mosque** at No. 192, which was built in 1850-55 from a humble shack and is now a holy place for Singapore's Moslems; and **Nagore Durgha Shrine** at No. 140, which is a mosque erected by southern Indian Moslems in 1829-30. There's a mixture of Eastern and Western architecture.

Temple of 1000 Lights

Race Course Rd. This is a 50-foot statue of Lord Buddha framed by hundreds of lights. The temple was built by a Thai monk named Vutthisasara. Relics include a replica of Buddha's footprint and a piece of bark from the bohdi tree. Open from 9 a.m. until after 4:30 p.m. Prayers daily.

Thian Hock Keng

Temple of Heavenly Happiness at Telok Ayer St. This is the oldest Chinese temple in Singapore, built in 1840 by Chinese immigrants in honor of **Ma Chu Poh** (Queen of Heaven). It's believed her blessings got them to safety in Singapore; her birthday is celebrated here with great gusto. The temple is embellished throughout with intricate pillars and stone carvings imported from China.

Thong Chai Medical Institution Building

3 Wayang St. This is an ornate building in the heart of Chinatown; it began as hospital around 1830. Now it's a showplace for Chinese architecture and curios. It's a fascinating, well-preserved monument that is worth a stop.

Tiger Balm Garden

Pasir Panjang Rd. The garden was recently restored via an S$80 million facelift and the addition of the latest technology. This theme park depicts Chinese mythology and folklore. It was built by the Aw family whose fortune was made in Tiger Balm medicines. This place was full of what I thought were badly sculpted tableaux with morals to preach. It's a depiction of how the Chinese view life, at present and during salvation. My advice is to avoid this place if you can. Free admission. Open daily from 8 a.m.-6 p.m.

Underwater World

Sentosa Island. Asia's largest tropical oceanarium is open 9 a.m.-9 p.m. daily.

Victoria Theatre and Memorial Hall

This is one of the few colonial structures still standing. It was built in 1906; the clock has stopped only on 3 occasions; the last time was during the fall of Singapore in 1942. The theater and hall are used for symphony concerts and professional dramas.

War Memorial

Beach Rd. Memorial Park Land. The memorial commemorates the thousands of civilians who died during the Japanese occupation of Singapore during World War II. Four tapering white columns representing four cultures of Singapore were erected on the site where the Japanese were said to have murdered so many. There's a memorial ceremony held here every Feb. 15.

Yu Hwa Yuan Chinese Garden

Off Yuan Ching Rd., Jurong. This is something new; it's based on Peking's famous Summer Palace gardens, with some of the architectural traditions of the Sung Dynasty. There are 32-1/2 acres of bridges, pagodas, stone lions, lotus ponds and bamboo groves. It's a favorite with families in neighboring **Jurong Town**, which houses workers from 600 factories. It's also a popular site with newlyweds for wedding photos. Check out the the White Rainbow Bridge or the Cloud-Piercing Pagoda. Open daily from 8 a.m.-6 p.m. with S$2 admission for adults, S$1.00 for children.

Zoological Gardens

Mandai Lake Rd. This is ranked one of the world's top ten zoos. More than 1300 animals of some 140 different species roam around an open zoo. There are 70 acres of landscaped park and one of the world's largest collections of orangutans. The animal showtime with elephants and sea lions is entertaining. One highlight is breakfast (or high tea) with an orangutan. In June 1994, a S$60 million Night Safari, inhabited by nocturnal creatures in their natural habitats, will make its official debut at the zoo. Hours are 8:30 a.m.-6 p.m. daily. Admission is S$7 adults; S$3 children.

Sentosa and the Southern Islands

Buran Darat

Situated right next to Sentosa; Buran Darat covers some 37-1/2 acres. There's a great swimming lagoon. The island is being developed into a marina and a bridge to Sentosa is also under consideration.

Kusu

This is also called Tortoise Island and is probably the most popular of the 42 islands in the so-called southern chain. It's only 3-1/2 miles from Singapore. The land was recently reclaimed and enlarged to 21 acres with a 3,000-plus foot beach.

Tua Pek Kong

A Chinese Taoist temple juts into the lagoon here. There's also a Malay kramat; both are visited by devotees. Additionally, there's a tortoise sanctuary, swimming lagoons and changing huts. Ferries depart from the World Trade Centre pier from 9 a.m.-6:20 p.m. daily. The return fare is about S$3 adults, S$1.50 children.

Lazarus

It's called Pulau Sekijang Pelepah in Malay. The isle is some 81 acres of lush ground between Kusu and St. John's. There's no regular ferry service here; you must hire your own boat.

Pulau Hantu

Also called Ghost Island, it's about 4 miles from the mainland and popular with swimmers for its 1-1/2 miles of sandy beach on 32 acres of land. There are 3 beautiful lagoons. It's busy on weekends.

Pulau Renggit

This little island is 3 miles from the mainland. It lies near St. John's and Lazarus islands. It's been reclaimed to 30 acres now.

Sentosa

Sentosa is also called the "Island of Tranquility." It is Singapore's resort island, accessible by cable car from Mt. Faber and Cable Car Towers or by ferry from the World Trade Centre Ferry Terminal. Each is less than a 15-minute ride. It offers many attractions: nature and history, recreation and fantasy, a nature walk, coralarium, butterfly park, Underwater World. Pioneers of Singapore Museum depict Singapore's history up to the re-enactment of the Japanese surrender. A number of hotels exist on the island, including the new Shangri-La Rasa Sentosa Resort and the Beaufort Singapore. A monorail circles the island. Ferry to Sentosa operates 7:30 a.m.-11 p.m., Monday- Thursday; 7:30 a.m.-midnight, Friday-Sunday. The cable car runs 10 a.m.-9 p.m. Monday-Saturday; 9 a.m.-9 p.m. Sunday and holidays.

St. John's

This island (Pulau Sakijang Bendera) was a former leprosarium 4 miles from mainland. There are 93 acres of gentle hills and shade trees, a mile-long beach made for the picnic crowd and holiday camps and bungalows for government workers. There are many facilities here. The ferry is the same as for Sentosa.

Sisters Islands

Subar Laut/Subar Darat are the Sisters Islands, reclaimed to a total of 13-1/2 acres. They're 5-1/2 miles from Singapore and feature sandy beaches; overnight camping is allowed.

Terembu Retan Laut

This is a 30-minute ride from Jardine Steps. The 37 acres are sheltered beautifully. The Singapore Yacht Club leases the western part of the island for mooring facilities.

TOURS

Arts and Crafts of Singapore

3 hours. Instant Asia cultural show, Singapore Handicraft Centre, crocodile farm, batik factory, pewter factory, gem-cutting factory.

Changi and East Coast Tour

3-6 hours, by arrangement only. Batik factory, Changi Prison (chapel and roof garden), Selarang barracks, Changi murals, Changi Village, East Coast Park, Singapore Handicraft Centre.

City Tour

3-1/2 hours, daily. Elizabeth Walk, Merlion Park, Supreme Court and City Hall views, Singapore River, Chinatown, Sri Mariamman Hindu Temple, Mt. Faber, Instant Asia cultural show, Tiger Balm Gardens, Queenstown Housing estate, Orchid Pavilion at Botanic Gardens, National Museum and sometimes Singapore Handicraft Centre.

East Coast Tour

3-1/2 hours, daily. Merdeka Bridge, National Stadium, East Coast Park, villages and fishing ponds, rubber and coconut plantations, crocodile farm, Siong Lim Temple and garden, Temple of 1,000 Lights.

Flora and Fauna

3-5 hours, by arrangement only. Mandai Orchid Garden and Zoological Gardens.

Genting Highlands Tour

2 days. By coach to Kuala Lumpur via Ayer Itam, Yong Peng, Segamat Seremban and Kajang. On to Genting Highlands and casino. Pass through Malacca on return.

Harbour Tour

2-1/2 hours at 10 a.m. and 1:30 p.m. weekdays; harbor, islands and 20-minute stopover at Kusu Island.

Johor Bahru Tour

3-1/2 hours, daily. Sultan's old palace, Bukit Serene (new palace), Sultan Abu Bakar Mosque, sarong weaving factory, rubber plantation.

Junk Cruise

2-1/2 hours at 10:30 a.m., 3 p.m. and 4 p.m. daily.

Jurong Tour

3-1/2 hours, daily. Jurong Bird Park, Jurong Town and Chinese Garden.

Malacca Tour

8-12 hours, by arrangement only. Johor Bahru, drive past rubber and pineapple estates, past fields and villages, Malacca, Dutch churches, Portuguese fortress, Malaysia's oldest Moslem mosque and first Chinese temple.

Our People, Our Heritage
> 3 hours. Thian Hock Keng Temple, Chinatown, Little India on Serangoon Rd., Sri Srinivasa Perumal Temple, Sultan Mosque on North Bridge Rd., Arab St.

Pulau Tioman Tour
> 3 days. By coach to Mersing, by launch to Tioman, tour of village, swimming, water skiing, scuba diving and fishing.

Sentosa, Southern Island and Cable Car Tour
> 3 hours from 9:30 a.m. and 3:30 p.m. weekdays. Tour of harbor, stop at Sentosa to visit attractions, cable car return to Singapore.

Sunset Cruise
> 1-1/2 hours, daily at 7:15 p.m. A cruise around harbor plus Kusu and St. John's islands.

Temple Tour
> 3-1/2 hours, by arrangement only. Siong Lim Buddhist Temple, Sultan Mosque, Sri Mariamman Hindu Temple, Buddhist Temple of 1,000 Lights.

Trishaw Tour
> 1-3 hours, by arrangement only. Start from Raffles Hotel to seafront, through Chinatown.

Ulu Tiram Tour
> 6-7 hours, Wed. and Sat. Johor Bahru, Sultan Abu Bakar Mosque, Ulu Tiram Estate (oil palm, toddy, rubber taping, rubber factory).

West Malaysia Tour
> 7 days, by arrangement only. Malacca, Kuala Lumpur, Penang, Cameron Highlands, Genting Highlands.

WHERE TO STAY IN SINGAPORE

ANA Hotel Singapore ★★★★

16 Nassim Hill, Singapore 1025. ☎ *732-1222. FAX: 235-1222 • 456 rooms (19 suites).* Quiet location a few minutes from Orchard Rd. Cabana rooms with terraces by 2nd-floor pool. Superb views compared to other accommodations; pleasant atmosphere with paneled lobby and bar. Owned by All Nippon Airways; one of the better Sheratons in Asia. Facilities: Hubertus Grill, Fountain Lounge and Cafe in the Park coffee shop on ground level. Ridley's Has the Rubber (one of the hottest discos in town) on mezzanine. Unkai, attractive Japanese restaurant, on 1st floor. Secretarial services. Steam bath, sauna and swimming pool. ***Reservations: ANA Hotels, Utell.***

Boulevard Hotel ★★★★

200 Orchard Blvd. ☎ *737-2911. FAX: 737-8449 • 520 rooms (20 suites).* Convenient to shopping and business districts. Rooms with many amenities. Facilities: Cantonese and Japanese restaurants. Fitness club, two swimming pools. Disco, Alcove lounge with music, 24-hour coffee house. Executive Center. Meeting rooms. Shops and drug store.   *Reservations: Utell, Golden Tulip.*

Crown Prince Hotel   ★★★★

270 Orchard Rd., Singapore 0923. *732111. FAX: 732-7018 • 303 rooms.* Managed by Prince Hotels of Japan. Expect to find little touches like bedroom slippers; attractive structure with spacious atrium lobby. Facilities: Fen Cheng Lou Teochew Chinese cuisine. Cafe de Prince. Sushi Kaiseki Nogawa. The Lounge. Swimming pool. Business center. Presidential and Corner Executives suites with steam and whirlpool baths. Meeting rooms.

Reservations: Utell, Prince Hotels.

The Dynasty   ★★★★

320 Orchard Rd., Singapore 0923. *734-9900. FAX: 733-5217 • 400 rooms (72 suites).* Dramatic structure on the Singapore skyline. 33-story pagoda-style hotel linked to C.K. Tang's new department store; roof tiles from China. Dramatic 3-story lobby. Interiors by Don Ashton; energy-saving exteriors and the latest in guest-room locks. Unusual concept here. Facilities: Bill Bailey's bar, Golden Dew coffee-house and sidewalk cafe on ground floor. La Vendome restaurant on 2nd floor. Tang Court Chinese restaurant on 3rd floor. The Executive Club in lower basement. Fifth-floor Chinese garden, pavilions and swimming pool. Pedestrian walkways to Orchard and Scotts roads. Executive services. IDD.   *Reservations: Utell.*

Goodwood Park Hotel   ★★★★

22 Scotts Rd., Singapore 0922. *737-7411. FAX: 732-8558 • 235 rooms (43 suites).* Original tower built in 1900 as Teutonia Club. Fifteen acres of grounds; fantastic Brunei suite with private lift, dining room with roof garden and octagon-shaped lounge area. 64 Parklane suites with balcony in separate wing. 2 swimming pools. 7000-plant nursery. Old-world charm and Commonwealth clientele. Watch out for visiting "royalty." Facilities: L'Espresso indoor-outdoor terrace cafe, coffee lounge, Highland bar and Gordon grill on lobby level. Former West End Club closed. Shima Japanese restaurant. Carlton bar. Gourmet market on lower ground level for suite kitchenettes. York Hotel next door (same ownership) offers another swimming pool, squash courts, Mario's Italian restaurant and Bamboo Court for Chinese cuisine. Goodwood Park group also owner/manager of Ladyhill and Malaysia hotels, manager of Ming Court Hotel.

Reservations: SRS, Preferred Hotels, Utell.

Hilton International Singapore   ★★★★

581 Orchard Rd., Singapore 0923. 737-2233. FAX: 732-2917 • 435 rooms (43 suites).* A longtime favorite with businessmen; dependable and efficient. Opened 1970 and constantly refurbished; exclusive 21st floor of suites designed by French couturier Hubert de Givenchy, with private balcony, whirlpool bath, crystal decanters of liquors, butler/

maid service, complimentary laundry/valet, etc. Try the "Suite Life." Facilities: Rooftop garden with swimming pool (23rd floor) and health club (22nd floor). Tradewinds foodstalls featuring local ethnic snacks and feature films on Sun. (23rd floor). Inn of Happiness Cantonese and Szechuan restaurant (23rd floor). Harbour Grill (2nd floor). Orchard Cafe coffee shop (ground floor). The Music Room (2nd floor) for afternoon teas, drinks and music. Lobby bar (ground floor). Executive business centre with worldwide courier service, word processing service, electronic pagers and overnight film developing service.   *Reservations: Hilton Hotels.*

Holiday Inn Park View

11 Cavenagh Rd., Singapore 0922. ☎ *733-8333. FAX: 734-4593 • 320 rooms.* Strategically located for shopping just off Orchard Rd., this is a lovely, unpretentious hotel with a friendly feel to it. Facilities: New Orleans restaurant and bar, Fragrant Blossom restaurant for Chinese food, The Tandoor for Indian, a coffee shop and Clemenceau's for cocktails; executive lounge and executive floor.

Reservations: Holiday Inn.

Hyatt Regency Singapore

10-12 Scotts Rd., Singapore 0922. ☎ *733-1188. FAX: 732-1696 • 1174 rooms (421 suites).* An excellent hotel; reputed to have very good feng shui. Well managed and quite capable of holding its own against the competition; walking distance to Orchard Rd. activities. Fine shopping in Serendipity Row off the lobby. A leading business and convention hotel. Can't beat the pampering of the Regency Club. Don't miss Malam Singapura cultural show and splendid barbecue three times a week. Facilities: Gallery 10-12 for European/Asian artist showings and sale on mezzanine. Regency Club for guests on 19th, 20th and 21st floors with own concierge, butler station, complimentary continental breakfast and cocktail hour, personalized stationery, etc. Nutmegs art deco specialty restaurant on mezzanine. Hugo's gourmet restaurant with French provincial decor and dishes on mezzanine level. Scott's bar off lobby. Chinoiserie membership club/disco on mezzanine. Pete's Place pizza and Italian menu restaurant on lower level. Swimming pool with daily buffets/barbecues and health center on 4th floor. Businessman's Centre with full services and IDD telephones. Elegant, new 350-room extension, Regency Terrace, with tennis and squash courts, fitness center and landscaped pool with 4-story waterfall!   *Reservations: Hyatt Hotels.*

The Mandarin Singapore

333 Orchard Rd., Singapore 0923. ☎ *737-4411. FAX: 732-7361 • 1200 rooms (59 suites).* Lavish public areas; impossible to find one's way about without effort. Enormous lobby in Venetian/Tang Dynasty style; guest-oriented energy-saving systems in rooms, all with excellent views. Well-appointed bathrooms; 6 restaurants; 5 cocktail lounges; 2-tiered sundeck; good conference hotel. Kuan Dai (means hospitality in Mandarin) service arranged by Leading Hotels of the World; includes airport greeting, complimentary cocktail, fruit basket, express check-out. Facilities: Full banking facilities on the property. 24-hour call medical clinic. 3-story shopping arcade. Recreation and health center with minigolf course, tennis and squash courts, sauna, hydropool and gym on 38th floor. Outdoor swimming pool with sundeck and snack bar on 5th floor. Belvedere gourmet restaurant on 5th floor. Chatterbox coffeehouse on ground floor South Wing. New Tsuru-No-Ya Japanese restaurant on 3rd floor. Pine Court Peking restaurant on 36th floor. Top of The M revolving restaurant on 40th floor. The Stables grill room on 5th floor. (Mandarin also manages Neptune theater-restaurant on Collyer Quay.) Act I bar adjacent to lobby. Clipper bar and Mezzanine lounge on mezzanine floor. Observation lounge on 39th floor. 3 airline offices in hotel. Kasbah nightclub on 36th floor. The Library club/disco for members only. Mandarin Executive Service (secretarial, etc.) on mezzanine.

Reservation: LHW.

Marina Mandarin Singapore ★★★★★

6 Raffles Blvd. #01-100, Singapore 0103. ☎ *338-3388. FAX: 339-4977 • 640 rooms (29 suites).* Located in heart of town at Marina Square; largest atrium in Asia; scenic views of Marina Bay and city. A brand-new and exciting hotel; part of Mandarin Singapore Int'l Hotels. John Portman exteriors. Don Ashton interiors—fabulous! Facilities: Swimming pool. Squash and tennis courts. Health center. 250 shops. Les Oiseaux French restaurant with dinner music. Ristorante Bologna Italian specialties. The Cricketer Pub. House of Blossoms, Teochew Chinese cuisine. Brasserie Tatler (coffee shop). Reading Room disco. Video recorder rentals. Banquet and meeting rooms. Poolside restaurant/bar.

Reservations: LHW.

Melia at Scotts Hotel ★★★★

45 Scotts Rd. ☎ *732-5885. FAX: 732-1332 • 249 rooms (4 suites).* Across the street from the Newton Circus Hawker Centre's food emporia. Royal Service floor with butler service. Facilities: Spanish and Continental dining. Bar, piano lounge, music and dance lounge. Shops, drug store, tailor shop. Health club. Swimming pool. Business center. Function rooms. *Reservations: Melia Hotels, Utell.*

Le Meridien Singapore ★★★★

100 Orchard Rd., Singapore 0923. ☎ *733-8855. FAX: 732-7886 • 414 rooms (16 suites).* Six-story hotel managed by Air France subsidiary, in the heart of the business district. Facilities: French, Continental and Indonesian restaurants. Le Rendezvous lounge. Le Club President level. Fitness center. Shopping arcade. Business center. Conference rooms. *Reservations: Meridien Hotels.*

Le Meridien Changi-Singapore ★★★★

1 Netheravon Rd., Upper Changi Rd., Singapore 1750. ☎ *542-7700. FAX: 542-5295 • 276 rooms.* Situated in a garden setting near Changi

International Airport, just a few minutes from the beach. Guests have plenty of watersports opportunities as well as access to golf and tennis nearby. Offshore island tours and junk cruises. Facilities: La Veranda restaurant. Changi Cafe. Lotus bar. Lobby bar. Swimming pool. Meeting rooms. Business center. ***Reservations: Meridien Hotels.***

New Otani Hotel ★★★★

117A River Valley Rd. ☎ *338-3333. FAX: 339-2854 • 408 rooms (22 suites).* Located adjacent to a busy, multi-use development; recently renovated; rooms overlooking the water are the best. Facilities: Japanese, Chinese and American restaurants, beer garden and lounge. Swimming pool. Business center. Shopping arcade. Meeting rooms.
Reservations: Utell.

Novotel Orchid Singapore ★★★★

214 Dunearn Rd. ☎ *250-3322. FAX: 250-9292 • 442 rooms (30 suites).* Set in a five-acre garden compound; shuttle bus service to Orchard Road shopping district; rooms for the handicapped; Orchid Club. Facilities: Chinese restaurants, 24-hour coffee house, Music Pub with live entertainment, Limelight lounge, karaoke bar. Business center. Health club, swimming pool, cycling, jogging, golf putting green. Shopping arcade. ***Reservations: Utell.***

Omni Marco Polo Singapore ★★★★

247 Tanglin Rd., Singapore 1024. ☎ *474-7141. FAX: 471-0521 • 603 rooms (30 suites).* Lovely 4-acre setting with landscaped gardens; well managed with small hotel friendliness; excellent accommodations in the better rooms. Minutes from Botanic Gardens. Step away from Handicraft Centre and Rasa Singapura; impressive service except in early a.m. checkout. Complete 9th floor for nonsmokers; pool-side terrace rooms for fresh air fiends. Facilities: Full business center (off lobby) and IDD service in guest rooms. Clark Hatch physical fitness centre (men only). Beautiful swimming pool and gardens on 2nd floor. Marco Polo lounge for meetings and cocktails. Marco Polo steak house, San Marco gourmet restaurant, Brasserie la Rotonde, La Pinata coffee shop and El Patio all on ground level. Marco Polo cake shop in shopping arcade and The Club disco in basement.
Reservations: Omni Hotels, SRS, Utell.

The Oriental ★★★★★

6 Raffles Blvd., Singapore 0103. ☎ *338-0066. FAX: 339-9537 • 580 rooms (62 suites).* Operated by the Hong Kong-based Mandarin Oriental Hotel Group. Beautiful hotel in Marina Square complex designed by John Portman. Distinctive 21-story triangular-shaped structure; luxurious accommodations overlooking harbor and city. 7th hotel in Mandarin Oriental's portfolio; all top-rated. Interiors by Don Ashton. Facilities: Fourchettes continental restaurant. The Gallery for coffee, tea and cocktails. Captain's bar. Cafe Palm brasserie. Cherry Garden Chinese restaurant. L'Aperitif bar. Taeping and Ariel suites for private parties. Atrium lounge. Swimming pools with Marina bar and barbecue. Health center. Air-conditioned squash courts. Executive center. 240 shops. Oriental Ballroom. *Reservations: LHW.*

Pan Pacific Hotel Singapore ★★★★★

7 Raffles Blvd., Singapore 0103. ☎ *336-8111. FAX: 339-1861* • *837 rooms (37 suites).* Located in Marina Square, it reflects the latest in hotel design and construction. Convenient to the business district, Raffles City, sightseeing attractions and adjacent to subway stop for shopping areas. Glass bubble elevators, atrium and the largest shopping complex in Southeast Asia. Facilities: 10 restaurants and bars serving every kind of food imaginable; fully equipped health spa and gym, 24-hour business center, breathtaking views from every room.

Reservations: Utell.

Raffles Hotel ★★★★★

1 Beach Rd. ☎ *337-1886. FAX: 339-7650* • *104 suites.* Asia's most famous grande dame hotel underwent a complete restoration several years ago; reopened in September 1991 with 104 suites and the renowned Long Bar, birthplace of the Singapore Sling; more than just a hotel—a world-renowned institution. "Stands for all the fables of the exotic East," wrote Somerset Maugham. Originally a tiffin house but turned into a luxury hostelry by the Sarkie brothers in 1886; became a Far Eastern stopover for many acclaimed authors: Maugham, Coward, Conrad and Kipling. Home of the Singapore Sling; have one at the Long Bar, although they're not what they used to be. *Reservations:Direct*

The Regent of Singapore ★★★★★

No. 1 Cuscaden Rd., Singapore 1024. ☎ *733-8888. FAX: 732-8838* • *443 rooms (44 suites).* Three-acre site across the road from Marco Polo Hotel. Interesting design by Atlanta-based architect John Portman; guest rooms and public areas spaced around sky-lit 12-story interior atrium; east and west accommodations have large balcony areas. Opened in 1988, Regent is in the process of putting its highly distinctive touch on the hotel and has already created the most elegant property in Singapore. Facilities: Maxim's de Paris (since 1893) is exact replica on 2nd floor. Summer Palace Cantonese restaurant on 2nd floor. Tea Garden coffee shop on 1st floor. Two atrium lobby bars. Swimming pool and health center on ground level. Lobby filled with 40,000 yellow chrysanthemums. Business Centre.

Reservations: Regent Hotels.

Royal Holiday Inn Crowne Plaza Hotel

25 Scotts Rd., Singapore 0922. ☎ *737-7966. FAX: 737-6646* • *511 rooms (18 suites).* Recently renovated and upgraded; a cut above your average Holiday Inn—especially for travelers who like sea-green interiors. Convenient location; near Shaw Centre across from Hyatt Hotel and Far East Plaza. Facilities: Department store and nightclub next door. Winter Garden lobby bar and Cafe Vienna 24-hour coffeehouse with live music in evenings. Baron's Tavern/Baron's Table (German provincial) restaurant. Treetops bar. Meisan Szechuan restaurant. Rooftop swimming pool, minigolf course. Health center. Business Center. ***Reservations: Holiday Inn.***

Shangri-La Singapore ★★★★★
22 Orange Grove Rd., Singapore 1025. ☎ *737-3644. FAX: 733-7220 • 809 rooms.* Located on 12-1/2 acres in a lovely residential area; 24-story main tower plus Garden and Valley wings; spacious and soothing accommodations; nice views; excellent service and restaurants; beautiful grounds; waterfall connects 2 buildings. Absolutely one of the top hotels in Singapore. Facilities: Recreation facilities with swimming, squash, tennis, golf and health club. La Tiara rooftop supper club with international cabaret. Spacious lobby bar (where much business is conducted over drinks). Golden Peacock continental restaurant and Peacock bar with country-and-western music (a favorite with the oil crowd) off lobby. Shang Palace Cantonese restaurant on upper level. Waterfall cafe on ground level of Garden Wing. 24-hour coffee garden on lower level. Full business center.
Reservations: Shangri-La Int'l.

Sheraton Towers Singapore ★★★★
39 Scotts Rd., Singapore 0922. ☎ *737-6888. FAX: 737-1072 • 406 rooms.* Follows Sheraton's Towers concept, designed to appeal to upscale travelers. 21-story tower featuring many elegant touches for guests; butler service on every floor; 24-hour pressing service. Complimentary coffee and tea in rooms; complimentary continental breakfast and hors d'oeuvres. Terry bathrobes; special personal care amenities. Facilities: Domus continental cuisine. Li Bai Chinese restaurant. Terazza coffee shop. Health club. Swimming pool. Business center. Disco. ***Reservations: Sheraton.***

The Westin Plaza ★★★★★
2 Stamford Rd., Singapore 0617. ☎ *338-8585. FAX: 338-2862 • 796 rooms (47 suites).* Located in Raffles City complex. Two 29-story towers connected to sister-hotel Westin Stamford by air-conditioned multitiered complex of shops, meetings rooms, restaurants, lounges and atria. Facilities: 5 restaurants. 2 cocktail lounges. Disco. 4 air-conditioned squash courts. 6 tennis courts. 2 swimming pools with snack bar. Health food shop and bar. Executive Busines center. In-house fitness expert. ***Reservations: Westin.***

The Westin Stamford
2 Stamford Rd., Singapore 0617. ☎ *338-8585. FAX: 337-1554 • 1257 rooms (80 suites).* Billed as the world's tallest hotel; guests can enjoy spectacular views of neighboring Malaysia and Indonesia (so they say) from their private balconies; quite a sight if you don't mind the height. Facilities: Palm Grill. Canton Garden. Szechuan Court. Somerset's bar. Inagiku Japanese restaurant. The Terrace lounge. Prego.

L'Express. The Raffles Deli. Scribbles. The Compass Rose. Health club shared with Westin Plaza. Executive business center. Convention center.   *Reservations: Westin.*

SAMPLING LOCAL FARE IN SINGAPORE

Satay is one of Singapore's specialties.

To say that Singaporeans love to eat is an understatement—they live for their food. And they do so in four major cultures, with another dozen or so cuisines ready on the back burners. Dining in this city is a continual taste treat, and not so much a planned event but a spontaneous happening. As a visitor, you will probably become so tantalized by the mixture of cooking odors from shops and sidewalk foodstalls that sudden hunger will demand a nibble here and another there. Voila! You have just consumed a spectacular meal of *satay, kai fan* and *mee goreng* and a bottle of local beer for just a few dollars— totally unplanned and more enjoyable than you ever imagined. Here, more than any other city in the Far East, you can be adventurous and daring, for the food is fresh, delicious and completely safe.

The majority of dishes found in Singapore are Chinese to satisfy that 75 % of the population—but Indian, Malay and Indonesian cuisines also prevail. There is also *Nonya* food, a combination of the most delicate of Chinese and Malay. Western cuisine here is comparable to anywhere in the world and if you must have your American steaks and hamburgers or pasta or Swiss fondue—none is difficult to find. Most of the restaurants and especially the food stall complexes, require only the most casual of attire and manners. Do not be put off by the lack of utensils offered—Chinese dishes are eaten with chopsticks (known as *fai tse* or nimble brothers to Singaporeans), but both Malay and Indian food are often consumed with either a spoon or your fingers. Only in hotel restaurants and the better independent places will you find the table fully laid with the gamut of silver flatware and dressed with starched cloth and napkins. Of course, at these places you are expected to dress accordingly (and leave fingers in your lap). Otherwise, open shirts and cool slacks are the norm for gentlemen—something equally informal for women.

Chinese Food

Cantonese cuisine, with its emphasis upon freshness and retention of the taste of the original ingredients is still the most prevalent of all Chinese cooking in Singapore. And you can count upon an endless array of dim sum (which is called tim sum here) for breakfast or lunch. But most Singaporeans are descended from Fukien province families and Hokkien cooking features fresh seafood dishes, stews and the best soya sauce in all of China. Hokkien mee (wheat-flour noodles in a soup with bits of shrimp and other seafoods) is a favorite of food carts, along with poh piah (spring rolls of the thinnest rice- flour pancake filled with shrimps and egg, bean sprouts and dried squid, vegetables and chili).

It's interesting that in such a tropical climate, something known as Steamboat is on most menus. This is a chafing-dish meal that comes from the Teochew district of Kwantung province and resembles the Mongolian Hot Pot popular in Hong Kong during the winter months. Steamboat features plates of thinly sliced fish, meat and just-picked vegetables, cooked individually in a broth (that is then consumed at the end of the meal). It is meant to bring a group of diners together, much as Westerners treat cheese or beef fondues.

Other Teochew dishes to savor are roast suckling pig, roast goose and orr chian (tiny oysters cooked into an omelet). From the island of Hainan comes chicken rice, flavored with ginger and chilis. Neither can you miss the chilis and fire in Hunan and Szechuan (Sichuan) dishes, which are guaranteed to keep you warm inside and out (order extra bottles of beer)! If you are a Peking duck afficionado, there is plenty to behold, as well as Shanghainese beggar's chicken and bird's nest soup. Taiwanese food is also represented here, with a porridge surrounded by foods such as oysters, mussels and pork stewed in a rich, black sauce.

Indian Food

You may think that a curry is a curry is a curry, but some of them are blends of over 20 different spices. And not all are HOT. India boasts over 15 centuries-old cuisines, evenly divided (if you can) between north and south. The northern dishes are milder, with flavors added to meats and vegetables that are considered more subtle and somewhat less stomach--clutching. One of the most well known of all northern Indian delicacies is tandoori chicken, in which the skinned fowl is halved and marinated in yogurt and spices and then grilled in an amphoralike clay oven. This dish is accompanied with grilled onions, mango chutney and naan (unleavened bread baked on the side of the tandoor oven). The result is absolute heaven! Chicken tikka, kebobs of mutton and chicken and subtle but aromatic curries can also be found on the menu.

Southern Indian food is as hot as you like, to be diluted with saffron rice, chappati bread or puri (a deep-fried pancake) and plenty of beer or tea. Some favorites among the hot dishes are chicken beryani, mutton Mysore and prawn curry. You can also attempt several variations of vegetarian curries with boiled white rice, a glass of yogurt, or pepper water. A tray of condiments may include several types of chutney, fresh onions, cucumbers, yogurt and cottage cheese.

Malay Food

There are curries blended with rich coconut milk and there are the exquisite satay sticks. The curries are of beef, fish, prawns and vegetables and eaten with white rice, sambals (chili, onion and tamarind) and ikan bilis (tiny anchovy-like fish). The satay is something very special in the Far Eastern diet. These are tiny pieces of beef, mutton, or chicken marinated in crushed spices, skewered and grilled over charcoal. Although the magic is in the grilling, they say, these tasty morsels of meat are not complete until dipped into a sauce of ground peanuts, coconut milk and other spices. You then alternate eating a stick of meat (with bits of raw onion and cucumber) with cubes of glutinous rice steamed in banana-leaf wrappings. Satay tastes best at the open-air food stalls for which Singapore is justly famous.

Other Asian Foods

Indonesian cuisine is similar to Malay, with rice (nasi) as the main staple, accompanied by a variety of spicy dishes, coconut milk and peanuts. Popular dishes available in Singapore are beef rendang, chicken curry, udang sambal (prawns) and the famous gado gado (salad with spicy peanut dressing). A good way to enjoy what this cuisine offers the palate is the rijstaeffel, or rice table, a Sunday buffet the Dutch seem to have invented.

Nonya food is a fragrant blend of Chinese and Malay and owes its descent to the fact that so many Malay and Chinese have intermarried. There is generous use of ginger, scented laos root, lemongrass and dried shrimp paste (blachan) in many Nonya dishes. Singaporeans prefer to frequent food stalls for their Nonya specialties, especially laksa (noodles in spicy coconut and herb broth).

Piquant **Thai** dishes and seafood are also well represented in Singapore as well as **Korean** bulgogi (thin slices of beef marinated in soya, sesame and garlic and grilled) and the entire gamut of **delicate Japanese** cuisine.

Western Food

If you must, there is a Kentucky Fried Chicken and a McDonald's on Orchard Rd. For more genteel dining, there are several fine grill rooms (English, Scottish, Continental) in the top hotels as well as French, Italian, Swiss, Russian, German, Spanish and Mexican specialty restaurants. Prices tend to be higher, the atmosphere more gracious and dress codes more formal at these Western establishments. Reservations are recommended and major credit cards are accepted.

Seafood

In a city completely surrounded by the sea, it is natural that the fruits de mer will be succulent. All the more formal restaurants below serve delicious seafood, but the local populace prefers to consume such delicacies as crab, jumbo prawns, cockles and mussels in a casual manner—with their fingers. Much of the seafood offered is cooked quickly in a succulent chili sauce (not hot) or as for prawns, in a sweetish, black sauce. Try the food-stalls at Albert St. if you are in town, or drive out to the **Seaview** or **Palm Beach** restaurants at East Coast Park. Here, you sit on tiny stools at make-shift tables in what looks like the back of a garage. But the chili crab, steamed prawns (jumbo and you peel your own), fried squid, mussels in soya bean sauce and huge bottles of beer transform the place into a palace. Hot towels and finger bowls arrive to clean your hands. Great fun and dress accordingly. For perhaps the best seafood of all, try Ponggol Village at the northern tip of Singapore (40 minutes by car). What's lacking in elegance is more than made up for in an abundance of dishes featuring every kind of fish, mullusk and shellfish imaginable. A favorite with the locals.

Fruits

It is impossible to discuss the abundance of food in Singapore without mentioning the many unusual tropical fruits available. In addition to the familiar coconuts, pineapples, bananas, watermelons and limes, you can also indulge in long, skinny papaya—the juiciest papayas ever! Why not also try the hybrid mangosteen or the smelly durian, which Singaporeans are fond of calling the "king of all fruits" (do not take one into your hotel room because of the odor). Then, there is the jambu ayer, to be cut and dipped into a mixture of soya sauce, sugar and chilis, or the jambu batu (also known as guava). Ranbutan is a weird-looking fruit, but starfruit looks like a star when cut cross- wise; it's a good thirst quencher. Other thirst quenchers seen in marketplaces in huge plastic containers are kam chia chui (sugar cane water) and ya chui (coconut water).

If you feel like a little pick-me-up in the warm weather, buy some pieces of fruit from one of the street vendors with iced carts. It's perfectly safe and so refreshing.

Many of these eating places are simply "walk in off the street," and there is little need for reservations except in the top hotels which might have a full house. Try both the plain and the fancy establishments. However, there is a local superstition that the less rich the decor, the more appetizing the meal (because that's where the owner puts his money). However, suit yourself and loosen that belt!

WHERE TO EAT IN SINGAPORE

Chinese Restaurants

Huan Long Court
Apollo Hotel, Havelock Rd. • Hunan-style with minced pigeon in bamboo cup, spicy honey ham, deep-fried scallops.

Chiu Wah Lin
Mosque St., Chinatown • Teochew roast suckling pig and roast goose.

Imperial Herbal Restaurant
Metropole Hotel, Seah St. • A Hakka restaurant featuring fried bean curd stuffed with pork and vegetables (*yong tau foo*), fish in rice wine (*ng teow chou sui tong*) and fried intestines of pig with vegetables; definitely for the most adventurous.

Canton Garden
Westin Plaza Hotel • A gracious setting for China's most popular regional cuisine; located in the Westin complex that includes a dozen restaurants, shops and two hotels.

Golden Phoenix
Hotel Equatorial, Bukit Timah Rd.• Glamorous surroundings for spicy Szechuan dishes with chilis and smoked duck.

Great Shanghai
Armenian St.• Crab meat and sweet corn soup, braised fish heads, fried eels.

Hillman Restaurant
Cantonment Rd., Manhill, Pasir Panjang Rd. • Nothing elaborate, but terrific for "clay pot" dishes like chicken, prawns and fish heads.

Hung Kang
North Canal Rd. • Popular for Teochew Steamboat.

Inn of Happiness
Hilton International Singapore. ☎ *7372233* • Cantonese/Szechuan; chili prawns, abalone with broccoli, three mushrooms.

Min Jiang
Goodwood Park Hotel • The interesting blend of excellent Chinese cuisine in a quiet, colonial hotel setting.

Moon Pavilion
Orchard Parade Hotel • Excellent and very popular dim sum lunches; take the mooncakes home and compare, as one friend did.

Omei
Hotel Grand Central, Orchard/Cavenagh Rds. • Szechuan smoked duck, chicken with dry chilis, braised beef on fire pot.

Peking Restaurant
International Building, Orchard Rd. Also **Eastern Palace**. *Supreme House, Penang Rd.* • Specialties are Peking duck with all the trimmings (skin, succulent meat, soup from the carcass), shark's fin, prawn ball soup and beggar's chicken.

Pine Court
Mandarin Hotel • Reputed Peking duck, baked tench, shark's fin and marinated lamb on the 36th floor. Weekend dim sum buffet lunches, with northern Chinese specialties.

RuYi
Hyatt Regency • Probably the most elegant Chinese restaurant in Singapore, with food to match.

Shang Palace
Shangri-La Hotel. ☎ *737-3644* • Considered one of the best and very posh. Dim sum for lunch and Cantonese specialties for dinner; try crystal prawn ball and abalone with kailand.

Swee Kee
Middle Rd. • Hainanese chicken rice a specialty.

Tai Tong
Mosque St., Chinatown • Popular among locals for dim sum breakfasts; reputed to have the best mooncakes in Singapore.

Indian Restaurants

Banana Leaf Apollo
Racecourse Rd. • If you must, they will give you a spoon but mostly it's with the fingers; chili prawns and other hot dishes.

Jubilee Cafe and Islamic Restaurant
North Bridge Rd. • Two eating places side by side. Don't go by the decor; chicken madras curry and mutton bombay; it's hot here, so come prepared to suffer.

Moti Mahal
Food Alley on Murray St. • Specializes in Kashmiri and Punjabi dishes. Forget the decor, concentrate on the food.

Rang Mahal
Oberoi Imperial Hotel, Jalan Rumbia • Northern Indian and bound to be excellent; featured dining spot in an Indian hotel chain.

Malay Restaurants

Aziza
Emerald Hill Rd. • Serves Malay dishes in Western surroundings. The restaurant most recommended for visitors.

Satay Club
Elizabeth Walk • Not so much a "club" as a nightly happening, with dozens of stalls grilling satay before your eyes and offering other Malay dishes.

Tradewinds Foodstalls
Poolside at Singapore Hilton, Orchard Rd. • A delightful way to relax in comfort and taste all the local offerings.

Asian Restaurants

Korean Restaurant
Specialists' Centre, Orchard Rd. • For your kimchee, origuljot (oysters) and bulgogi.

Luna Coffee House
Apollo Hotel, Havelock Rd. • Noted for Nonya dishes, especially satay babi (pork), tangy broths and laksa.

Rendezvous
Bras Basah Rd. • Nothing fancy, but everyone loves the place across the street from the Cathay Building. If you don't know what the dishes are, just point to the display case and be pleasantly surprised. The best Indonesian food in town, they say.

Shima Restaurant
Goodwood Park Hotel, Scotts Rd. • Specializes in prime beef for teppanyaki, sukiyaki, yakiniku and shabu shabu.

Thai Seafood Restaurant
Cockpit Hotel, Oxley Rise • Well known for seafood dishes as well as popular Indonesian rijstaeffel on both Sat. and Sun. lunchtimes.

The New Tsurunoya
Mandarin Hotel, Orchard Rd. • Elegant Japanese restaurant with sushi flown in daily from Tokyo and Osaka.

Unkai Restaurant
ANA Hotel Singapore, Nassim Hill • One of the most attractive Japanese restaurants in Singapore. Special sushi and tempura sections; private rooms for parties.

Inagiku
Westin Plaza. • Traditional Japanese cuisine in a contemporary setting; one of a chain of restaurants founded in 1905; separate dining areas for tempura, sushi and teppanyaki.

Western Restaurants

Baron's Table
Holiday Inn, Scotts Rd. ☎ *737-7966* • German groaning board, if you can take it in this climate.

Compass Rose
Westin Stamford • A blend of east and west on top of the tallest hotel in the world. Elegant dining with French dishes presented Japanese style, using seasonings and condiments inspired by Eastern cultures.

Elizabethan Grill   ★★
Raffles Hotel, Beach Rd. ☎ *337-8041* • Very old-world atmosphere, with food and service to match.

Gordon Grill

Goodwood Park Hotel, Scotts Rd. ☎ *737-7411* • Noted for Scottish fare and good steaks; stop first in the Highland bar.

Harbour Grill

Singapore Hilton, Orchard Rd. ☎ *737-2233* • Award-winning nouvelle cuisine and Continental menu; 5-course Chef's Surprise gourmet menu nightly.

Hubertus Grill

ANA Hotel Singapore, Nassim Hill. ☎ *737-9677* • Another Continental-style grill room with decent food, but a sour-faced maitre d'hotel (when I was there).

Hugo's

Hyatt Regency, Scotts Rd. ☎ *737-5511* • French provincial decor with special Captain's Table for 10 diners; et menu and a la carte; exclusive wine cellar.

La Rotonde Brasserie

Marco Polo Hotel, Tanglin Rd. ☎ *647141.* • The most charming French-style bistro outside of Paris; a definite favorite. Choose chef's specialties chalked on The Mirror.

La Vendome

The Dynasty Hotel, Orchard Rd. ☎ *235-4188* • French cuisine in the spectacular new pagoda-style hotel.

Le Chalet

Ladyhill Hotel, Ladyhill Rd. ☎ *737-2111* • Swiss fondues, raclette, etc. in chic atmosphere; quiet and comfortable.

Palm Grill

Westin Plaza Hotel • A luxurious bit of Olde England in the Far East, complete with Chippendale furniture, an international cuisine and extensive wine list.

Marco Polo Restaurant

Marco Polo Hotel, Tanglin Rd. ☎ *647141* • Gracious setting with scenes from old Singapore; recently redesigned as a steak/ grill room.

Maxim's De Paris

Regent of Singapore, Tomlinson Rd. ☎ *913211* • A replica of the original on Rue Royale since 1893, with a staff trained by Parisian personnel; sounds intriguing and expensive.

Nutmeg's

Hyatt Regency, Scotts Rd. ☎ *737-5511* • The former Islander now in art deco and most attractive; seafood in tanks; homemade ice cream and cheesecake; fashion shows at Tues. lunch.

Pete's Place

Hyatt Regnecy, Scotts Rd. ☎ *737-5511* • Don't know who Pete is, but this is one of the most swinging places in town; live music in evening; pizzas, pastas, carafe wines, great desserts.

San Marco

Marco Polo Hotel, Tanglin Rd. ☎ *647141* • A recent addition to the Italian restaurant scene and pride of general manager Dario Regazzoni; bound to be a success.

Tangle Inn

Tanglin Rd. • Local favorite with colonial atmosphere and traditional English fare.

The Stables

Mandarin Singapore, Orchard Rd. ☎ *737-4411*• English inn theme with gaslight and brass. Rustic charm and steak/kidney pies, oxtail stew, daily roasts, sherries and wines.

Top of the M

Mandarin Singapore, Orchard Rd. ☎ *737-4411* • Revolving restaurant on 40th floor; salad bar and East/West menu. Go for the superb view both day and night.

NIGHTLIFE IN SINGAPORE

CHINATOWN: Spend several hours here at nighttime and see a different side: fortune tellers, letter writers, Sago Lane (the funeral parlor road), block parties, local entertainers and ever-present foodstalls. It's all here. Enjoy before this historic section becomes a massive high rise. Get a guide from STPB if you feel timid and remember not to photograph the superstitious old folk.

CINEMAS/THEATER/TV: There are over 50 air-conditioned cinemas in the city, many of them with Western films. There is a national theater with first-run dramas and a symphony orchestra with its own hall. The television shows shown here are terrible (as they are everywhere), but some hotels (like Pavilion Inter-Continental) are now offering in-house movies.

CULTURAL SHOWS: Check with hotel concierge.

Discos

Kasbah

Arabian nights style at the *Mandarin Hotel.*

El Morroco

At the *Oberoi Imperial.*

Black Velvet

At the *Century Park Sheraton.*

The Library

At the *Mandarin* (for members and hotel guests only).

The Club
> At the *Marco Polo* (members and hotels guests only; no T-shirts or blue jeans).

Chinoiserie
> This is tres chic at the *Hyatt Regency.*

The Music Room
> At the Hilton.

Fabrices
> In the *Dynasty Hotel.*

Xanadu
> In the *Shangri-La Hotel.*

Fire
> At *150 Orchard Rd.*

Zouk
> At *17/19/21 Jiak Kim St.*

Top 10
> At *Orchard Towers.*

Tornado
> In the *Specialist Centre.*

Night Tours

There are a few organized evening tours, with one drink here and another there, but you're much better off on your own. Or you can try a trishaw tour. Singapore is a safe and clean city, so enjoy the cooler hours.

Supper Clubs

There is the posh **Belvedere** with live music at the Mandarin. **La Tiara** is on the rooftop of the Shangri-La Hotel, with an international cabaret. Then there is the **Neptune Theatre Restaurant**, with Cantonese cuisine and lavish revues; the **Grand Restaurant and Niteclub** (Chinese) in Shaw Towers; the **Tropicana Theatre Restaurant** in the Tropicana Building on Orchard Rd., with Chinese dinner and international shows.

Wayang

Wayang is Chinese street opera with grand performances on festive dates and holidays, especially during Feast of Hungry Ghosts in Aug./Sept. Singapore is the best place in the Far East to enjoy this ancient entertainment. Special platforms erected in heart of Chinatown; watch for them. They're also held in housing estates and parks.

SHOPPING IN SINGAPORE

Singapore can certainly be considered a "shopper's paradise" but I would hardly call it the "bargain basement of Asia" as local promotions claim (because there is no such creature). However, shopping here is on a par with Hong Kong, as all tourist-interest goods sold are duty free and often at prices below retail cost in the country of origin. These include the inevitable photographic and stereo equipment, watches and jewelry in 18K gold, electric shavers, silk and leather goods (excluding ready-made clothing), pearls and precious stones, ivory and antiquities, luxury smoking paraphernalia, calculators, perfumes and imported apparel from Europe. People used to think that prices in Singapore were slightly higher than in Hong Kong (mainly because the stacks were more orderly), but that doesn't mesh anymore and studies have shown that most items are competitive.

As in Hong Kong, just about everything you would ever want but don't need is available in Singapore either today or early tomorrow. And the young Singaporeans are buying everything they can! The shops are loaded with electronic gadgetry, computer-age games, elegant fashions from all over the world, gold Swiss watches plus counters and counters of the less expensive Japanese brands, locally made leather goods and pewter, imported goods from mainland China, accessories and furnishings from all over Asia. If you want something copied or tailored, there is a shop around the corner (or your hotel concierge will call a friend).

However, the Singapore Tourist Promotion Board suggests that you seriously compare prices before buying, avoid touts, insist upon official records of purchase and world warranty (if available) and shop at approved STPB stores. Shopping hours are approximately 10 a.m. to 6 p.m. including Sun., with the most crowds predicted from noon to 2 p.m. (lunch-hour browsers). Credit cards are widely accepted, but the shops may add a surcharge (which is highly illegal but common). It is also suggested that you clarify customs regulations for the U.S. and Canada if you plan on purchasing extraordinary items, i.e. ivory and other wildlife products.

With the exception of the many new department stores and the elegant, European-style boutiques, definitely bargain. Test the water a bit first if you happen to be patronizing a large appliance store. However, if it's the **Thieve's Market** or **Change Alley**—well, merchants there would think you were crazy if you didn't make a counter offer! And always remember, you get what you pay for and you will be happy with your purchases.

One of the more rewarding aspects of shopping in Singapore is in discovering the abundance of so many handicrafts and arts from neighboring countries. For a capsule of what is available here, walk over to the Singapore Handicraft Centre on Tanglin Rd., directly fronting Rasa Singapura. This well-planned complex of shops does not intimidate the casual browser and offers arts and crafts from all over Asia—from China to Sri Lanka. There is everything on display and sale from costume jewelry to batik shirts and dresses to rugs from India and furniture made from Thailand teak. If you have your heart set on a sari, look here first before canvassing the scented shops of Serangoon Rd. Chinese carpets, batiks, brass and pewter are all well displayed at the Handicraft Centre.

Antiques

Antiques are sought after the world over and it is not impossible to find some lovely items in Singapore—if you know what you are buying. Chinese porcelains, Malaccan chests, opium beds, Victoriana, Indonesian carvings, Burmese buddhas, etc. are all here, but it is wise to frequent the better shops if you plan to spend good money (as opposed to a few dollars). Orchard Rd. has always been known for fine antique shops and many have moved into the new shopping plazas. If you prefer out-of-the-way places, try the **Changi Junk Store** on *Changi Rd.* or **Katong Antique House** on *East Coast Rd.* Items over 100 years old can be imported to the U.S. duty free, but unless they are packable (or you hand carry them on the plane), the expense of shipping and insurance can be quite a burden. Other areas include:

Arab Street

Arab Street is frequented by the Moslem community, with its own variety of spices and intriguing smells. Baskets, brassware, Malay and Indonesian batiks, Haji hats, dried fruits and woven flowers are just some of the items spilling from the shops that line this street.

Change Alley

This area has changed little since the good old days when sailors jostled through the narrow tunnel of bizzare fantasies just off the waterfront. That it still exists is somewhat of a miracle, jostled as it is between multimillion dollar high-rise office buildings. For a bit of local color and perhaps a bargain or two, Change Alley is certainly worth a visit, but take your skepticism along and plan serious shopping elsewhere.

High Street

High Street is a mere quarter-mile stretch in the middle of town with high quality shops of luxury items: pearls, breathtaking jewelry, gold watches, crystal and brassware as well as imported dress materials. Prices match value but custom-made jewelry is available here.

Little India

Little India is the nickname of that wonderful area along Serangoon Rd., filled with spices and fragrant garlands and exquisite women in saris with gold bangles up and down both arms. This is also where you can buy your own hand-dyed cottons and silks, colorful pillows and bedcovers and pounds of curry powder. No special time to shop here, but don't expect to do much business on one of the Hindu holidays.

North Bridge Road

This is just a stone's throw from High St., but seething with electrical bargains and some of the less expensive brands of watches. Shop around here because the game is to "sell"—even at a bigger discount than desired.

Orchard Road

This area has a long history of interesting shopping in Singapore although its face has changed in recent years. Gone are all the quaint single-story buildings, replaced by high-rise hotels and shopping plazas. Still known as "up market," you can enjoy a delightful spree wandering among the elegant boutiques in hotel arcades as well as the variety of shops in such huge complexes as **Far East Shopping Centre**, the **Chinese Emporium** in the International Building, **Lucky Plaza** (one of the most popular), **C. K. Tang's** remodeled department store. At the northern end of the thoroughfare, which becomes Tanglin Rd., there are still a few of the old-time antique shops and specialty stores (including 24-hour tailoring).

People's Park

This was once an area of the old Singapore. It is now a showplace of the new Singapore, with clean streets, high rises and organized street bazaar businesses all packaged in a modern high-rise shopping complex.

Raffles Place

Raffles Place was once the domain of the famous Robinson's Department Store, which supplied the "colonials" with everything from soup to swans. But that was all before the war, occupation and independence and Robinson's has moved northward to become a less important establishment. The Place is now a garden mall surrounded by high-rise office towers on most sides. If you're lucky, you may still be able to visit a few of the old-time shops on the western edge.

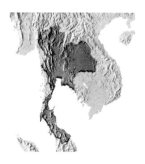

THAILAND

Doi Step Temple, Chiang Mai

THAILAND IN A CAPSULE

518,000 square miles of land with more next-door neighbors than any other Far East country; bordering on Myanmar, Laos, Cambodia and Malaysia in the extreme south as well as Gulf of Thailand and Andaman Sea...known as Siam until 1949...population approximately 57 million. 80% still agrarian...constitutional monarch...a long and turbulent political history...the only country in the Far East that never succumbed to colonization by the Europeans...a proud and independent people whose gentleness is an endearing quality...the annual growth rate of the Thai economy is among the highest in Asia.

If any country could be considered the archetypical Southeast Asia country, it would be Thailand. It's on the front bumper of Asia's missile-like dash toward dominance in the world economy. With a per annum double-digit growth rate and a Bangkok skyline that seems to change as fast as a seismograph in an earthquake, Thais are embracing the fruits of their industriousness enthusiastically. But this prosperity is not without its growing pains. Bangkok's transportation system is an oozing, foul-smelling, anarchic nightmare. Frequently, the headlines announce another industrial or commercial tragedy in the nation—a hotel collapsing, or a garment factory burning down. The army brutally quelled a bloody student uprising in May 1992. Thailand *is* growing in leaps and bounds—the infrastructure is perhaps the most rapidly accelerating in Asia—but it has to be careful that it doesn't build itself upon a house of cards.

More than five million people visit Thailand (*Muang Thai*) each year. It is one of the most topographically and culturally rich countries to experience on the continent. The kingdom's national park system is vast; there are more than 50. Restored ancient ruins and magnificent temples are found all across this lush, tropical landscape. In the south, on both the shores of the Gulf of Thailand and the Andaman sea, are beautiful white sand beaches and crystalline water. And the elephants that could once be found hauling teak out of the forests in the north can now be seen doing tricks for tourists; one can be occasionally spotted being led down a congested Bangkok street by a lone tattered shepherd, passing a Pizza Hut and oblivious to the cavalry of exhaust-spewing two-stroke motorcycles screaming by.

Thailand is also known for the honesty and generosity of its people. Whereas Westerners tend to compete for what they can accrue from life, Thais seem to try to out muscle one another with their extraordinary capacity for giving.

Thailand, for what it's worth, is home to the world's largest sex industry. Groups of Europeans, Americans, Middle Easterners and other Asians arrive in Thailand in droves on 10-day sex junkets, crowding the nighttime neon-splashed *sois* of Patpong and Soi Cowboy in Bangkok (and the discos of Chiang Mai and south Pattaya) in a bizarre frenzy that's straight out of a Fellini movie. Men decades older than their Thai partners splash in this surreal fountain of youth for a few short days, then dejectedly come to grips with themselves on their jumbo jet rides back home. Some never go home. Hundreds of thousands of Thai girls are employed in the sex trade, most coming from small villages in the provinces. Much of the money they make they send home to their families.

HIV infection is a growing problem in the kingdom. Although it has affected the number of sex tourists, the trade remains a thriving one.

Finally, the shopping in Thailand is unmatched anywhere in Asia. Bargains galore on silk, electronics, gold and crafts can be found among the thousands of stalls that pack city sidewalks. However, the police have pretty much put to an end (or at least relocated) the bustling and lucrative pirated goods trade. It's now a little harder to find that 500-baht Rolex.

History of Thailand

The colorful Kingdom of Thailand is the only country in Southeast Asia that never served time as a European colony, although various parts of it have been occupied by not-so-friendly neighbors through the ages. Until 1939 it was called Siam, a Sanskrit word meaning "gold" or "green," but history is unclear which color actually applied. There are a few gold mines in the southern part, but traditionalists say the beautiful green color that covers the mountains and fields and lies along the rivers must have inspired the name. Alas, when the "absolute" monarchy was abolished in the 1930s and a "constitutional" monarchy established, Siam became known to the world as Thailand—land of the free—splendid but less romantic.

The origin of the Thai people is somewhat vague, but scholars believe migrations probably occurred from the Chinese province of Szechuan (Sichuan in Pinyin) around the 1st century A.D. However, discoveries since the Second World War in the caves of Kanchanaburi (near the Burmese border) and the tiny village of Ban Chiang (in the northeast) have led archaeologists to proclaim that a sophisticated culture existed here that predates even the Chinese. Furthermore, it can be documented that a mysterious kingdom of Indian origin was established around the 3rd century B.C. in the Nakhon Pathom area, where the country's largest and most important Buddhist monument now stands. Add to this migrations of the Mons from the West and the Khmers from the East and that is the makeup of the present Thai people.

The Kingdom of Sukhothai

Thai history really begins with the founding of the independent kingdom of Sukhothai in A.D. 1238, for it gave the people a distinction and marked a period of great cultural development. The "cradle of Thai civilization" lasted just a century, during which time the tiny kingdom absorbed elements of neighboring cultures. From China came fine potters who established the famous kilns at Sawankhalok, and over the trade route contact was made with India. (The influence of Indian art can be appreciated at the ruins of Sukhothai today.) From Cambodia, the Sukhothai kingdom absorbed elements of administration as well as architecture.

King Ramkamhaeng the Great (1277-1317) is the most famous leader of this era and best known for creating the Thai alphabet and introducing a uniform system of currency. He also initiated political and cultural relations with China and opened the door to diplomatic relations with the world outside.

When King Ramathibodi assumed the throne in 1350, he moved his kingdom to Ayuthaya where it flourished for over four centuries in one of the world's most fertile rice bowls. A succession of 33 kings ruled over the capital situated where three great tributaries join to form the mighty Chao Phraya River, at a point just 110 kilometers from the sea. During the first 200 years of the Ayuthaya period, the kingdom prospered and annexed neighboring territories. The Portuguese came to call in 1511 and diplomatic relations were established. However, the Burmese arrived in 1569 and occupied the country until King Naresuan the Great "liberated" Siam in 1584.

During the 17th century, the country opened its door to the West. In 1612 the British were granted permission for a small settlement on the banks of the Chao Phraya River in Ayuthaya. During the next decade, envoys were received from both Denmark and Japan. King Narai the Great was coronated in 1656 and arranged an exchange of ambassadors with the French court of King Louis XIV in 1685. Siam had its place in the world and was known for its fine cloth, spices, metals and semiprecious stones.

But the Burmese, who had waged war with Siam almost continually since the 15th century, arrived again and completely sacked Ayuthaya in 1767. Phya Tak is credited with driving the aggressors away and became known as Taksin the Great. He established a new capital at Thonburi, across the river from present day Bangkok. Unfortunately, he was "seized by religious delusion" some 15 years later (he actually went mad). So one of his generals, Chao Phya Chakri, on return from a victorious campaign against Cambodia, proclaimed himself king in 1782. He called himself Rama I, founder of the Chakri Dynasty and moved his capital to the eastern bank of the Chao Phraya River as a precautionary measure. It was named Krung Thep, or Bangkok.

Reign of the Ramas

Rama I reigned for some 27 years and successfully kept the Burmese at home. He also set about recreating the glory that was Ayuthaya in this new "city of angels." He brought the legendary Emerald Buddha (first discovered near Chiang Mai in the 15th century) back from Laos during another victorious military campaign. The small emerald image (in reality, made of jasper) was housed in an elegant new temple, Wat Phra Keo, and given the supreme place of honor it still enjoys in the palace compound (indeed, the kingdom).

Rama IV or King Mongkut (1851-1868) is considered one of the country's enlightened monarchs, for he established modern Thailand. He was known as a scholar, having spent some 27 years as a Buddhist monk before assuming the throne. He was fluent in English, studied Latin and was knowledgeable in astronomy and astrology as well as Western sciences. He was also the innovator who brought an English governess to his court, resulting in one of the most delightful (but hardly accurate) stories of all time—Anna and the King of Siam. During Mongkut's reign, foreign trade flourished and some 200 foreign vessels were calling at the port of Bangkok annually.

The eldest of the alleged 39 sons of King Mongkut ascended the throne in 1869 and became known as Chulalongkorn the Great (Rama V). He ruled for over four decades and was so admired that the people built him a statue—while he was still alive! He abolished slavery, instituted social reforms, public education and reorganized the courts of law. He brought such stability to the country that it was the only Asian nation able to resist the sweeping European colonization of the late 19th century. (However, that did not prevent him from sending a few offspring to Europe for their education and fresh ideas.) Chulalongkorn is still so beloved that both students and government workers lay wreaths before his statue in front of the National Assembly on October 23, the day he passed away in 1910.

Thailand's present monarch, King Bhumibol Adulyadej (Rama IX) assumed the throne in 1946 upon the mysterious death of his brother in the Grand Palace. He is a thoroughly modern and gentle man, who was born in Cambridge, Massachusetts, in 1927 (where his father Prince Mahidol was attending Harvard University Medical School). Although his present duties are more spiritual and social than anything else, Bhumibol is highly respected by his people. They are proud of his many accomplishments as a sailor, poet, historian and Buddhist scholar. He plays no less than eight different musical instruments and has appeared with professional jazz musicians throughout the world! He and his beautiful consort, Queen Sirikit, are familiar sights all over Thailand and give their time most generously to all occasions.

The Subtle But Firm Military Presence

Thailand is also the only Asian country that was not devastated by World War II. The government capitulated immediately to the Japanese invasion to avoid "unnecessary bloodshed of its people." However, the Thais did not totally ignore the Allies and were very helpful to the POWs building the "Death Railway" over the River Kwai. They have tried to remain neutral to the warring factions that line their many borders, but that is not an easy task. There have also been internal political difficulties over the past few decades, including bad student riots in 1973 and 1992 and a coup d'état in 1976. The military runs the country, but they do it with subtlety. You are only aware of their presence because the number of olive-drab uniforms almost matches the number of saffron-robed monks seen everywhere!

Thailand is a wonderful place to visit and must be included on every Far East itinerary. Its people are gentle and warm, smiling and helpful. They are devoted to their land, their Buddhism and their royal family. Their manners are impeccable and you can learn much from their respect for life and the living.

PLANNING AHEAD

TOURISM AUTHORITY OF THAILAND

(TAT) works admirably to foster and serve the kingdom's more than two million international annual visitors, who spend well over $1 billion directly related to tourism. TAT has offices around the world and publishes an array of literature describing the delights of Thailand as well as information on special festivals and lavish photographs of the beauty spots. All TAT employees are knowledgeable, courteous and efficient and they are fluent in English.

TAT's head office is at *372 Bamrung Muang Rd., Bangkok* (☎ *02-226-0060*). There are also 14 branch offices around the country. The principal ones are: *381/2 Chaihat Rd., South Pattaya 20260* (☎ *428750*); *105/1 Chiang Mai Lamphun Rd., Amphoe Muang, Chiang Mai 50000* (☎ *213666*); and *73-75 Phuket Rd., Amphoe Muang, Phuket 83000* (☎ *212213*).

The TAT has three offices in the U.S.: *3440 Wilshire Blvd., Suite 1100, Los Angeles, CA 90010* (☎ *213-382-2353*); *5 World Trade Center, Suite 3443, New York, NY 10048* (☎ *212-432-0433*); and *303 E. Wacker Dr., Suite 400, Chicago, IL 60601* (☎ *312-819-3990*).

VISAS

Two-week transit visas do not have to be obtained in advance, but are issued on arrival in Thailand for stays of up to 15 days for U.S. and Canadian citizens in possession of valid passports and confirmed onward tickets.

INOCULATIONS

Shots are required only of travelers who have been in a smallpox infected area within 14 days of arrival, or in a yellow fever infected area within six days of arrival in the kingdom.

ENTRY BY AIR

Most people enter Thailand via Bangkok's modern Don Muang Airport, about 15 miles from the city center. Bangkok serves as a Southeast Asian junction for over 700 international flights weekly from Europe, the Middle East, South Pacific and Western Hemisphere. An average of 3,500 travelers pass through the airport daily and make use of the local Tourist Authority of Thailand information bureau as well as the reservation service operated by the Thai Hotels Association. Porterage and limousine service are controlled by the airport and travelers are advised to use only authorized baggage handlers and taxis into town, at least until you become a master at the custom of bargaining over the fare. The airport also has restaurants, an inoculation center, banks and shops.

In addition to regular air-conditioned airport bus and limousine service into town, there are shared-seat **minibuses** operating between the airport and hotels for about $12 per person. **Taxis** fares vary, depending on your destination, but are quite reasonable. To destinations within Bangkok from Don Muang, the rates are set, which are about the only routes where they are. If you're staying at the Shangri-La or the Royal Orchid Sheraton, you can take advantage of a new eight-passenger **helicopter** service, operated by Si-Chang Flying Service (☎ *662-254-3481, FAX: 662-254-3765*), provided you're willing to spring for the approximately $120-$140 per person fare. Flights have to be booked at least seven days in advance. The same company also operates helicopter service to Pattaya, Rayong, Hua Hin and Si Chang Island.

A second international airport is under construction in the Bangkok area, at Nong-Ngu Hao in Chachoeng-sao province, about 18 miles east of the capital. When it becomes completely operational in 1999, Don Muang will become a regional airport.

In addition to Bangkok, there are international airports at Chiang Mai, Phuket, Hat Hay and Chiang Rai.

Thai Airways International (THAI) has contributed to making Bangkok an important hub for air traffic and instituted the Amber One air route to Hong Kong a few years ago which saves at least an hour's flying time. The Thai Airways Company (TAC), the kingdom's domestic carrier, was among the first to schedule passenger flights to China and to reopen service to Laos, Vietnam and Cambodia. Bangkok is still the only doorway to Yangon from the east, to Vientiane from the south and to Cambodia from the west.

Departure tax is approximately 200 baht, or about U.S.$8.

ENTRY BY SEA

Entry by sea is likely to be via the Eastern Gulf of Thailand into Pattaya, a popular beach resort some two to three hours by road from Bangkok and Phuket, the resort island off the southern tip of the country. Indeed, the great world cruise liners have "discovered" this port of entry versus Sattahip a few miles south, home of the Royal Thai Navy and where most of the country's shipping is handled. Passenger ferries connect Bangkok with Samui and Songkhla (the port for Hat Yai) and hydrofoil service with Pattaya, Hua Hin, Chumphon, Samui and Songkhla. Cruise passengers are expected to "tender into shore" (be transported in small craft) for sightseeing excursions in

Bangkok or relaxing on the beaches of this Acapulco-like playground.

Cunard Line, Cunard/NAC, Royal Cruise and Royal Viking Line often schedule port calls in Pattaya, and the average length of stay in the Eastern Gulf is just under 48 hours.

ENTRY BY LAND

In September 1993, the Eastern & Oriental Express (☎ *800-524-2520*), which was developed by the same people who revived the Venice Simplon-Orient Express, launched service linking Singapore, Kuala Lumpur and Bangkok. The luxury trains, similar in concept to the European version, offer train buffs an opportunity to recapture the heyday of luxury Far Eastern rail travel. Fares for the complete three-day/two-night trip are from $1,100 per person, including all meals. Shorter sectors can also be booked, starting at $390.

DUTY FREE

Duty-free allowances for bona fide tourists include 200 cigarettes or 250 grams of smoking tobacco, one quart of wine or liquor and personal effects. Narcotics, obscene photos or literature, firearms and ammunition, certain types of fruits, vegetables and plants are all prohibited. The importation of currency is limited to 2000 baht per person or U.S.$2000 per person (unless a higher amount has been declared upon arrival). 500 baht, however, is the limit, per person, on departure.

NOTE

Imported goods are heavily taxed in Thailand, so visitors should bring what they will need in cigarettes, spirits, film, cosmetics, etc. (Wine seems to have an especially heavy duty here.)

CURRENCY

The currency of Thailand is the **baht**. Each baht is worth about 4¢ and there are roughly 25 baht to the U.S. dollar. (The exchange rate is pretty much fixed, but it does hover between 22.5 baht and 26 baht to the buck.) The baht is divided into 100 satangs, just for confusion's sake. Notes are used in denominations of 10 baht (brown), 20 baht (green), 100 baht (red) and 500 baht (purple). Coins come in 25 satang, 50 satang, 1 baht and 5 baht pieces. Traveler's checks are accepted everywhere but best cashed at authorized money changers, like banks and most hotels or tourist shops. Hotels notoriously offer terrible rates, even though the baht does not tend to fluctuate very much. Since the Vietnam War, American money is quite well recognized and some shops will take it directly.

LOCAL TIME

Local time in Thailand is Greenwich Mean Time plus 7 hours. For our purposes, Thailand is exactly 12 hours ahead of Eastern Standard Time (and just about halfway around the world from New York City), 11 hours in advance of Eastern Daylight Time. Add another hour for each mainland U.S. time zone (5 hours for Hawaii). Thailand is in the same time zone as Jakarta, Kuala Lumpur and Phnom Penh; one hour behind Hong Kong, Manila and Taipei; 2 hours behind Tokyo and Seoul; 1 hour behind Singapore and 1/2 hour ahead of Yangon.

LOCAL CURRENT

The local current is 220 volts/50 cycles, with adaptors available in most city and resort hotels.

LOCAL WATER

The water is considered quite safe to drink in the major deluxe hotels, but the cautious should always stick with bottled mineral water and sodas. The Thais are a clean and hygienic people; in fact, their sanitary habits are certainly admirable in a country so hot and humid. Expect ice in major hotels to be potable, but not from street stalls or small shops. Green Spot soda and Thai beer are available ice cold everywhere and are excellent antidotes for the fiery dishes served. Thai beer tends to be rather potent, however and should be avoided during the heat of the day.

OFFICIAL LANGUAGE

The official language in the kingdom is Thai, which has origins in Chinese, Khmer, Sanskrit and Pali. In the southern region, Malay words are interspersed with the Thai. The written language dates from the late 13th century and is an art unto itself. In a week's visit, it is impossible to conquer more than the polite greeting *Sawadee* (followed by *khrap*, spoken by a man and *kha*, spoken by a woman). However, visitors can be assured that English is widely used in major hotels, tourist attractions, shops, restaurants and bars. There are also many Roman-lettered signs around the center of Bangkok, Chiang Mai, Pattaya and Phuket Island. Thai is a very polite language, which explains much of the behavior of the Thais themselves.

There are two English-language dailies in Bangkok, the morning *Bangkok Post* and *The Nation*. Do not expect much in the way of enlightening coverage of major international events, but they cover Thailand well and are useful for getting a general idea of what's happening in the rest of the world—if you even care. There are also some tourist newspapers that offer helpful information on sightseeing, food and entertainment in English, German and French. Otherwise, the *International Herald Tri-*

bune and the *Asian Wall Street Journal* can be found at the concierge desks in major hotels—and generally as a complimentary bonus with your breakfast tray. Newsstands also carry the latest issues of *USA Today, Time, Newsweek* and *Asiaweek.*

The BBC "World News Tonight" is broadcast on Thai radio via an FM station and more programs with English subtitles or sound are becoming available in the better Bangkok hotels. As is true elsewhere in Asia, top hotels in Bangkok also carry CNN broadcasts. And martial arts fans can view any number of the latest films in theaters throughout Thailand.

BUSINESS HOURS

Business hours in Thailand range from 8 a.m.-9 p.m. Government offices are open from 8:30 a.m.-4:30 p.m., with an hour lunch break at noon (avoid this hour). Private offices have working hours from 8 a.m.-5 p.m. with an hour at noon free. Banks are open from 8:30 a.m.-3:30 p.m. except branches in major hotels and tourist attractions. Major shops are open from 10 a.m.-7 p.m. while family-run places set their own hours—long ones! Only the Tourism Authority of Thailand (TAT) is open for service on weekends and holidays, but call ahead to be sure.

Local trade associations and multinational company offices are located easily through the English language telephone directory in your hotel room. The American Chamber of Commerce is located at *140 Wireless Rd., Bangkok* (☎ *2511605*) and the Foreign Correspondents Club is now in the shopping plaza across from the Oriental Hotel. The U.S. Embassy can be found at *95 Wireless Rd. in Bangkok* (☎ *2525040-9*) and working hours are 7:30 a.m. to noon, 1-4:30 p.m. The Canadian Embassy is at *138 Silom Rd., 11th floor, Boonmitr Bldg.* (☎ *2374125/2374452*), with office hours from 8 a.m.-12:30 p.m. and 1:30-4:30 p.m.

TIPPING

Tipping is strictly optional in Thailand because most people here aim to please anyway. The visitor who wishes to show his appreciation for good service should follow the European or American standards for tipping, but note that offering 1 baht (about U.S.4¢) is considered an insult—so get the coins organized. Most hotels and better restaurants add a straight 10% to 15% service charge to the bill, so additional tipping is optional. You do not need to tip in taxis or trains unless the service was exceptional. Porters at the airports and railway stations have a set fee and you are required to pay a central cashier before retrieving luggage. Guides will, of course, take anything; their remuneration is up to your conscience. A 10-baht note (40¢) is plenty to tip in both beauty and barber shops.

TELEPHONE, TELEX & FAX

These services in major hotel chains are fine and many also have Businessman's Centers, where secretarial help and translation can be arranged. Try not to tax your patience and knowledge of the Thai language by trying to telephone outside the hotel, especially without use of a telephone directory in English. **Cables** can be sent through the Post and Telegraph Department on New Rd., Bangkok, or via your hotel concierge. Don Muang Airport, the Erawan Hotel and other major hostelries have small post office branches for the purchase of stamps and mailing small items.

WHAT TO WEAR

Dressing for this hot and humid tropical climate can be a problem because synthetic materials are not comfortable in this weather. March to May is very, very hot and humid; June through October is the official rainy season; and the months from November through February are more pleasant and cooler (but still very hot to the unsuspecting). Cottons and seersucker suits are preferable to polyester pants, even though the cotton material tends to wrinkle in the heat. However, life is very casual in Thailand; very few restaurants even require jackets and ties (check in advance). Women should dress modestly at all times because the Thais are offended by too much "skin" in public and tradition calls for being properly covered (no short shorts) when visiting temples. The evenings are lovely, especially during the winter season and gentlemen usually wear a short-sleeved shirt while the ladies don colorful long cotton skirts. At all times, you should carry a light sweater or wrap as defense against the air conditioning.

LOCAL TRANSPORTATION

Transportation in Thailand ranges from good to bad and can be a bit tricky unless you know the ropes. **Taxi** drivers have the annoying habit of keeping the meter running continually, so each new passenger must bargain over the fare before the journey even begins. Bangkok especially has a crazy traffic system and you can expect constant noise, fumes and heat at every curve in the road. The city must have thousands of three-wheeled *tuk-tuks* that also serve as taxis, albeit much cheaper than the others. Many hotels advise their guests to use the hotel taxi system, which is air-conditioned, trustworthy and expensive, but it's not a bad idea for a short visit. Just be certain the vehicle is air-conditioned or you will quickly perish from the dreadful fumes. Although the air is cleaner in Bangkok than it was just a few years ago, the capital needs considerable help in cleaning up the heavy, putrid air.

There is excellent transportation from Bangkok to other parts of the country, via bus, train, or domestic plane service.

Buses run regularly from the city to Pattaya (2-1/2 hours) as well as to the north, east and south. There are three different bus terminals, so be sure you are at the Southern Bus Terminal (Khonsong Sai Tai) to embark on a bus traveling southward! Fares are very reasonable (about 80 baht for a 9-hour journey) and most of the vehicles are "air-conditioned." Carry your own refreshments.

Railway service within Thailand is also excellent, although the trains are not super modern as in Japan. Nonetheless, they are well-run and most often on time. There are three classes of service on lines that run to the north, northeast, east and south as well as a Malayan Express that can be embarked upon between Butterworth (Penang) and Singapore. (However, it's a 24-hour journey from Bangkok to Butterworth and another 19 hours to Singapore so pack a few cushions!) **Trains** in Thailand and neighboring Malaysia are an excellent way to see the lush, tropical landscape and the fares are relatively reasonable, especially in second class. Example: the 3,076 kilometer ride to Singapore from Bangkok is about U.S.$130 one way. The 13-hour overnight trip to Chiang Mai from Bangkok (751 km) is about $45 one way in first class and $32 in second class. Thai Airways, the mostly government owned and operated domestic carrier, is one of the best carriers in the Far East. There are frequent daily flights between the capital city and the popular tourist areas: Phuket, Chiang Rai, Songkhla and Chiang Mai. In contrast to the local service in other Far Eastern countries, Thai Airways offers smiling attendants and such creature comforts as the late edition newspaper, fresh coffee and a full hot breakfast on the less-than-one-hour early morning flight to Chiang Mai. Sandwiches and drinks were offered on the late afternoon return, a few days later. For travelers planning to do a lot of air travel in Thailand, there is a special Discover Thailand's Natural Heritage fare. In 1993, the fare was $239 for four coupons (i.e. four domestic flights), plus $50 for each additional coupon up to a maximum of eight. The offer is expected to remain in effect for 1994 and fares should be about the same (or slightly higher). Call ☎ *800-426-5204* for information.

Rivers and **klongs** (canals) are a vital part of life in Thailand. For over four centuries, the kingdom's former capital of Ayuthaya was situated on an artificial island in the Chao Phraya River and crisscrossed by some 55 kilometers of waterways. A similar intricate network of klongs was devised when the capital was transferred to Bangkok in 1782. Unfortunately, many of these picturesque old klongs have been sacrificed to "progress" and high rises, but the Chao Phraya (River of the Kings) still plays a majestic role in big city life and is an important thoroughfare for the transportation of cargo and food. There are plenty of interesting river trips still available to visitors, mainly from the pier beside the Oriental Hotel. Here, you can find regular **ferries** that go up-river past Wat Arun (Temple of the Dawn), Wat Po and the Grand Palace.

Or, you can bargain a bit with one of the boatmen and make your own sightseeing tour for just a few dollars. The Oriental Hotel operates the posh Oriental Queen riverboat on daily trips to Ayuthaya and on dinner cruises every evening.

Touring the *klongs* by *hang yao* or **long-tailed motorized boats** is one of the highlights of anyone's stay, for here one can view a most lively panorama of typical Thai life. The ramshackle huts beside the water have antennae and large color televisions, but the inhabitants still bathe in the water below. Most colorful are the daily floating markets at which the locals trade wares and offer themselves to amateur photographers. Alas, Bangkok's famous floating market has moved across the river to Thonburi and there is another popular one in Ratchaburi Province. The price of a seat in one of these *hang yao* is only a few baht apiece, or you can charter your own for about 50 baht an hour. Be warned, however, that these craft are not the most seaworthy you have ever encountered so photographic equipment and small children should be safely guarded at all times. (And dress in boat clothes as you are apt to be splashed by muddy water from other drivers in a hurry.) Water tours outside of Bangkok are also popular but may be slightly dangerous at these times. The State Department advises that travelers do not venture unaccompanied along the waterways of the "Golden Triangle" area, center of the world's opium trade, because local bandits have been known to harrass and rob tourists. The northeast, along the famous Mekong River valley, borders Cambodia and the natives may not be friendly on the other bank. During the 1960s, it was something of an adventure to take the train to Nong Khai (624 km from Bangkok), cross the Mekong River by boat to the Laotian side and hop a dilapidated bus into the dusty capital of Vientiane. Alas, these days are over and the adventure now just a happy memory of youth.

If you can't stay away from the sea, there are boats to two islands offshore from Pattaya, called Koh Sak and Koh Larn (also known as "Pattaya 2"). In Southern Thailand, the island of Phuket can be reached from a causeway from Khok Kloi and is a highlight of any visit to *phak tai* as the southern region is known. On the Eastern coast of the Thai isthmus is Ko Samui, the country's largest island and accessible only by ferries from Ban Don in Surat Thani Province but note that the "express" takes about three hours. Songkhla is another seaside resort on the southeastern coast and famous for an inland lake dotted with islands. It is linked to the Gulf of Siam by only a tiny channel at one end.

CUSTOMS

Customs in Thailand are special enough to deserve their own category and the government advises a few "dos" and "don'ts" so that unsuspecting Westerners do not offend their charming and hospitable hosts. The Thai people have a deep reverence for their royal family and the National Anthem is played at all public events, with all in attendance standing silently. They are also very serious about their Buddhism and anyone acting in a manner insulting to religious custom will be severely punished. Shoes are never worn inside a chapel where the principal image of Buddha is kept. Buddhist priests are forbidden to touch (or be touched) by a woman, or to accept anything from the hand of one. Buddhist images are regarded as sacred objects and are not to be handled.

In **social behavior**, Thais do not normally shake hands but greet one another with palms pressed together in a prayerlike gesture. This is known as a *wai* and Thais are very honored when Westerners return the polite gesture. It is considered rude to point your foot at a person, so try to avoid doing so when seated. Thais are also insulted to be touched on the head (so don't ever pat the heads of young ones). In fact, public displays of affection are frowned upon and even holding hands is rarely seen. The people are among the most friendly and polite in the world and visitors are expected to keep a cool head (especially when angry) and conceal emotions at all times. Finally, don't be surprised if you are always addressed by your first name, as this is the manner in which Thais refer to one another.

FESTIVALS AND HOLIDAYS

Festivals and holidays in Thailand are colorful, slightly exotic and loads of fun. Most of them relate to monarchial and religious traditions and floral processions with monks in their saffron robes are the main spectacle. In addition to the main fetes, there are such charming customs as buying the chance to free caged birds and making a wish (which is supposed to be granted). Of course, the birds are quickly recaged and the next innocent falls into the trap, but it's an enjoyable few moments for very little money!

The following are public holidays and festivals throughout Thailand in 1984, when there is great rejoicing and very little business accomplished. Public holidays are marked with an asterisk (*).

*January 1	New Year's Day	
*January	Red Cross Fair	*Held throughout the month in Bangkok under the patronage of Her Majesty Queen Sirikit.*
February to April	Kite flying season	*Contests held at Royal Ground in Grand Palace in Bangkok, weekday afternoons. Fine Arts Department stages dances and concerts every Friday and weekend afternoons in National Museum Compound throughout season.*
February	Flower Carnival in Chiang Mai	*Colorful flower floats and parades, expositions of tropical flowers and orchids, country fair and bazaar, workshops for floral arrangements. Usually held in second week of month.*
February 1	Phra Buddhabaht Fair	*Buddhist devotees make annual pilgrimage to the Shrine of Holy Footprint near Saraburi (236 km north of Bangkok). Temple fair, country music, plays and bazaar.*
February (early)	Chinese New Year	*Thailand's several million Chinese close their shops, feast with their families and visit their temples to offer prayers for prosperity in the coming year.*
March	Magha Bucha	*Commemorates preaching of Lord Buddha to 1250 disciples who gathered without summons. Candlelit processions around main temple buildings and full moon throughout kingdom.*
March	Kite flying season continues	*Official kite flights on weekday afternoons at Sanam Luang in Bangkok.*
*April 6	Chakri Day	*Honors King Rama I, first monarch of present Chakri Dynasty who established Bangkok as capital in 1782. Extensive bicentennial celebrations took place in city during 1982.*

FESTIVALS AND HOLIDAYS

*April 13-15	Songkran (water) Festival	*Traditional Thai New Year's Day marking entrance of Sun into Aries. Folk festival features sprinkling water upon Buddha images, monks and family elders. Fish and birds set free. Colorful processions in Chiang Mai and Paklat.*
*May	Royal Ploughing Ceremony	*Rice seeds are blessed by Buddhist monks and distributed to farmers for good luck. Graceful Bhraminical processions in white and gold, with soldiers in red, at Royal Grandstand in front of Grand Palace. His Majesty the King presides.*
*May 5	Coronation Day	*Their majesties, King Bhumibol and Queen Sirikit, proceed to Royal Chapel for ceremony commemorating their coronation in 1946. Government officials in full dress pay respects.*
May	Rocket Festival	*Falls between the harvest and rainy season. Drumming, dancing, singing and shooting rockets into the sky as a plea for rain. Best celebrated in Yasothorn, northeast of Bangkok. Generally last weekend in May.*
*June	Vishaka Bucha	*Commemorates birth, enlightenment and death of Lord Buddha. Floral arrangements and candlelit processions around main temple buildings with full moon throughout kingdom.*
*July	Asanha Bucha	*Commemorates first sermon delivered by Lord Buddha to first five disciples. Candlelit processions around main temple buildings in full moon throughout kingdom.*
*August	Khao Phansa (Buddhist Lent)	*Marks the return to the monastery of all monks to resume study and meditation during rainy season. Youths of 20 years of age are ordained during this period. Best celebrated in Ubon with colorful Lenten candle processions in the town streets.*
*August 12	Queen's Birthday	*Queen Sirikit attends religious ceremonies and presents offerings to monks at Chitralada Palace as well as other places in Royal Household program.*
October	Boat races at Nan	*Celebrates end of Buddhist Lent. Colorful processions along streets and boat races on local rivers. Best celebrations occur in Nan Province, Northern Thailand.*
October	Thot Kathin Ceremony	*Lasts a full month to mark end of rainy season and Buddhist Lent. Time of annual offering of new yellow robes and necessary utensils to monks. Colorful processions along streets and rivers of people who sing and dance their way to monasteries with gifts.*

FESTIVALS AND HOLIDAYS

October	Phra Chedi Klang Nam Fair	*Colorful processions, boat races, amusing games as part of celebration in worshiping of pagoda at Paknam, south of Bangkok.*
*October 23	Chulalongkorn Day	*Commemorates death of beloved King Chulalongkorn, son of King Mongkut and grandfather of present king, who died in 1910. Floral tributes and incense placed at foot of equestrian statue at end of Ratchadamnoen Avenue in Bangkok.*
November	Golden Mount Fair and Phra Pathom Chedi Fair	*Buddhist devotees make pilgrimage to relics at temple of Golden Mount in Bangkok and the Phra Pathom Chedi in Nakhon Pathom.*
November	Loi Krathong Festival (Festival of Light)	*Rivers, streams, canals and ponds throughout kingdom full of tiny flickering flames from thousands of banana leaf and lotus petal cups containing candles and incense. A thanksgiving to Mae Khongkha, goddess of all rivers and waterways, during full moonlight. Best celebrations are in Sukhothai (first capital of Thailand) where Lady Nopphamat invented first flower lantern some 700 years ago. Also grandly celebrated in Bangkok and Chiang Mai.*
November	Elephant Roundup at Surin	*Elephant demonstrations, races, roundup show, soccer match, tug-of-war between 100 men and an elephant. Town streets closed for elephant rides, country fair and bazaar. Held every third weekend of November.*
December 3	Trooping of the Colors	*Parade of Royal Guards in honor of His Majesty King Bhumibol's birthday.*
*December 5	King Bhumibol's Birthday and National Day	*Celebrations throughout kingdom with colorful pageantry. Public buildings and houses decorated with spectacular night illuminations.*
*December 10	Constitution Day	
*December 31	New Year's Eve Celebration.	

Background Material

Anna and the King of Siam by Margaret Landon (adapted from the original *An English Governess in the Court of Siam* by Anna Leonowens) tells the story of a prim Victorian who taught at the court of King Mongkut (Rama IV) during the late 19th century.

Bridge Over the River Kwai by Pierre Boulle. The story of the "Death Railway" built by POWs over what the Thais called the Meklang River, but known to the world as the River Kwai.

The Legendary American by William Warren (Houghton Mifflin). A fascinating account of Jim Thompson, the man who is credited with reintroducing Thailand's silk industry to the world and the facts of his strange disappearance in 1968.

The House on the Klong by William Warren (Weatherhill, Tokyo). A sketch with photos of Jim Thompson's beautiful teak museum/house in Bangkok.

From the Hands of the Hills by Margaret Campbell. Published locally and researched/written by a Canadian teacher, this beautifully photographed volume describes the customs and crafts of the hill tribes.

Thailand (apa productions). Beautiful photos and text.

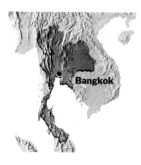

Bangkok

Bangkok's Grand Palace is the backdrop for this pickup soccer match.

BANGKOK IN A CAPSULE

Established in 1782 on eastern bank of Chao Phraya River by Rama I, founder of present Chakri Dynasty...originally called Rattanakosin. Name changed to Krung Thep by Rama III...always known as Bangkok to foreigners...means City of Angels...6 million inhabitants live here in chaos...with occasional patches of serenity...capital is part boomtown, part traditional...a hub of traffic between East and West. Not a place you love at first sight...but its dawn to dusk vitality and ever-changing face give the city a strong character...the unexpected in sight and sound is very much a part of the Bangkok scene.

Bangkok has to be one of the grimiest cities on the planet and one of the most magnetic. Travelers leave this sprawling urban blob either with a deep appreciation and fascination for the capital, or an absolute disdain for it.

The streets are perpetually shrouded in a gray-brown toxic cloud of carbon monoxide left by the millions of cars, buses, motorcycles and *tuk-tuks* (open tri-wheeled taxis)—all traversing the avenues at a crustacean's pace. The mugs of traffic policemen and pedestrians alike are wrapped with surgical masks to keep the dense toxicity out of their lungs. The unmuffled wailing of the tinny, two-stroke motorbikes can reach noise levels that make a heavy metal concert seem like someone humming Brahm's Lullaby during nap hour at a pre-school.

And Bangkok is hot, perhaps the hottest city in the world; there is no respite at any time of the year from the high humidity and temperatures that typically hover around the mid-90s F.

But the City of Angels offers an abundance of sights and attractions, of outstanding cuisine and unbelievable shopping bargains. There is the magnificent Grand Palace and dozens of beautiful wats sprinkled across the city. There are festival-like markets, the spectacle of Thai boxing and beautiful traditional dances. There are the floating houses, the floating markets and unforgettable long-tail speedboat rides up the Chao Phraya River.

Bangkok is a city that takes time to fully appreciate. You won't "get it" in a day or two here. It's a state of mind. And, as with any other state of mind, you have to surrender to its annoyances to appreciate its joys. As the Thais have. Rarely will you find such a content people in such a raw place.

WHAT TO SEE AND DO IN BANGKOK

Chao Phraya River

This is the lifeline of Bangkok, which was founded by King Rama I 200 years ago. The original city was located between a dramatic, sweeping curve of the river and an elegant klong built to meet it. From here can be viewed the **Grand Palace Complex**, **Wat Phra Keo** (Temple of the Emerald Buddha) and **Chatuchak Park**, where colorful weekend markets are held every Sat.

Grand Palace Complex

Built by King Rama I in 1782 for the Chakri Dynasty; it's an interesting potpourri of Eastern and Western architectural styles from Thai to Italian Renaissance; used only for state occasions and royal ceremonies. Visitors may tour formal reception rooms of Chakri Maha Prasad (royal residence of Grand Palace) daily. The dress code stipulates coat and tie for men, no slacks or shorts for women. The tour is very worthwhile and led by knowledgeable guides. Since the untimely

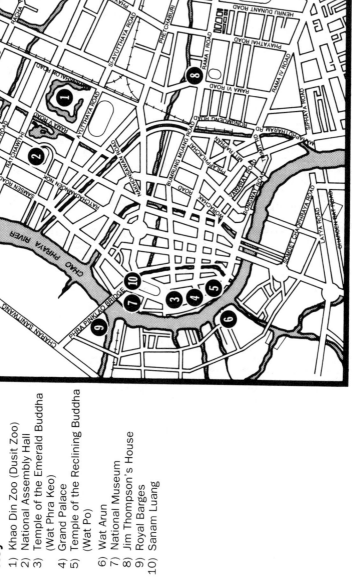

BANGKOK

Key

1) Khao Din Zoo (Dusit Zoo)
2) National Assembly Hall
3) Temple of the Emerald Buddha (Wat Phra Keo)
4) Grand Palace
5) Temple of the Reclining Buddha (Wat Po)
6) Wat Arun
7) National Museum
8) Jim Thompson's House
9) Royal Barges
10) Sanam Luang

death of the present king's brother in 1946, the royal family lives down the road not far from the Marble Temple. Hours: 8:30 a.m. to noon, 1 to 4 p.m. Admission is 30 baht.

Jim Thompson's House   ★

Located at Soi Kasemsan 2, opposite National Stadium. A former architect and military intelligence officer, the late American Jim Thompson adopted Thailand as his permanent residence; he's credited with contributing substantially to the growth of the Thai silk industry after World War II. It took a combined 6 traditional teak structures to make his house; it's filled with a collection of valuable artifacts—even chandeliers from 18th- and 19th-century Bangkok palaces. He opened the house to the public to aid Thai charities. Thompson himself disappeared in 1968 during a visit to the Cameron Highlands, Malaysia. No clue to his whereabouts has surfaced in the ensuing years. The house now belongs to the James H. W. Thompson Foundation which preserves the legacy of his creativity and deep love for all things Thai. Hours: 9:30 a.m. to 3:30 p.m.; weekdays only. Admission is 50 baht for guided tour.

Khao Din Zoo

Located on Rajawiti Rd. The name means Mountain of Earth; manmade hill in middle for picnics and family outings; also known as Dusit Zoo. Animals from all parts of the world as well as domestic ones can be viewed. Hours: 8 a.m. to 6 p.m. daily. Admission is 10 baht for adults, 5 baht for children; also a small charge for cameras.

Lak Muang

City Pillar; located at southeast corner of Sanam Luang in Inner City. Considered the foundation stone of the capital; visited daily by believers. Lavishly costumed dancers perform here in honor of the spirits; they're paid by those whose wishes have been fulfilled. Distances throughout the city are measured from this shrine.

National Assembly Hall

Sri Ayuthaya Rd. This is the original throne hall; constructed of white Italian marble; lavish gold leaf interior. Statue of King Chulalongkorn, grandfather of the present king, dominates the square in front. Statue festooned with flowers every Oct. 23, the day of his death in 1910. Hours: Mon. through Fri., except Thurs., by prior appointment.

National Museum   ★★

Located next to Thammasat University on Naprathat Rd. One of the largest museums in the Far East, with 26 different low structures and exhibition halls. It traces the history of Thai culture from 5600 B.C. to present Chakri dynasty. There are many Buddha images from Ayuthaya and Sukhothai periods; many objects from the royal household, including a whole pavilion of funerary coaches and palanquins. The buildings are not air-conditioned, so try to visit early in the day;

extensive walking is necessary to see the majority of exhibits. Hours are 9 a.m. to noon, 1 p.m. to 4 p.m., Tues. through Thurs.—and the same on Sat. and Sun.; closed Mon. and Fri. Admission is 20 baht, free on Sat. and Sun.; English guidebooks are available and docent tours daily—check times through your hotel.

Royal Barges

Klong Bangkok Noi, Thonburi side. Parked farther upriver from Wat Arun, these richly carved barges are used in ceremonial processions, especially when the king offers gifts and new robes to the monks of Wat Arun. The most impressive of the boats is the Sri Supannahong, or the Royal Barge, where the king sits in a golden pavilion and is transported by over 50 oarsmen.

Royal Pantheon

Located in Grand Palace complex. Contains life-size statues of Chakri Dynasty kings; only open to public on Chakri Day (April 6). But don't miss the mythological figures that adorn it; see detailed model of Angkor Wat nearby. Built by Rama IV when the temple was in Thai territory.

Sanam Luang

Pramane Ground. A 32-acre oval expanse in the heart of Inner City, it has been the historic site of royal cremations and the annual Ploughing Ceremony since the birth of Bangkok. The kite flying contests held here from Feb. to April are an annual tradition.

Siam Society

Located at Soi Asoke and Sukhumvit Rd. Founded under royal patronage at the turn of the century to promote the study of anthropology as well as the history and zoology of Thailand; interesting publications available here as well as a good reference library. Kamthieng House from Chiang Mai also worth a visit; guided tours available. Hours: 9 a.m. to 5 p.m.; weekdays only.

Snake Farm and Pasteur Institute

Corner of Rama IV and Henri Dunant roads. King cobras kept here, along with varmints. Venom is extracted from the snakes for use in serum; only the hardy should stop off here. Hours: daily except holidays; venom extracted at 11 a.m. Admission is 40 baht.

Suan Pakkad Palace

Sri Ayuthaya Rd. This is the residense of the present king's aunt, Princess Chumbhot. The princess is one of Thailand's leading gardeners and art collectors; the palace is a series of small structures brought to this site, some dating from mid-19th century; it's furnished authentically and filled with fine antiquities; landscaped gardens with flora brought back from all over the world by the princess—plus a lacquer pavilion discovered near Ayuthaya by the late prince was reassembled here. Hours: 9 a.m. to 4 p.m. Mon. through Sat. Admission 50 baht and well worth it.

Thieves Market

Located in Thevet district of Bangkok. Not for thieves, but for plants. Thousands of orchids sold here along with every other tropical species possible; a great place to visit for both gardeners and photographers. Don't miss the picturesque bridge across Klong Krung Chasum.

Vimanmek

The world's largest teakwood mansion and one of the country's major new tourist attractions, this was the residence of King Chulalongkorn during the early 1900s. It had been unoccupied since 1910 (but for a few months during 1925) and reopened in 1982 by Queen Sirikit as a period museum; its collection includes glassware, porcelain and "collectibles" (all considered treasures) that display the tastes of the court at the turn of the century. Open Wednesday through Sunday, 9:30 a.m. to 4 p.m.

Yaowaraj

Chinatown. A bustling section of the city—full of amusing markets. The Chinese were the original traders here. They now number 1/3 of the population. The traditional (birds nest soup) to the ridiculous can be found here.

TEMPLES

The **wat**, or temple, of Thailand is what makes the skyline so unique. Although similar in style to the structures found throughout the lands of their neighbors (Laos and Cambodia to the east, Myanmar to the west), the wat of Thailand is more sophisticated and refined in architectural manner and decorative elements. Thai fancy appears in the colorful, multitiered roofs and carved gables juxtaposed upon striking Indian, Khmer (Cambodian) and Chinese influences. The wats found in Bangkok are especially refined and sophisticated because none of them is more than two centuries old. When Rama I founded the city in 1782, he began a palace and temple building program that anyone today would envy!

No less impressive than the outside view of these many temples scattered throughout the capital is the inside view of the **bot**, or main chapel that holds the Buddha image, for many are filled with an awesome display of precious stones and metals. Look also for the brightly painted murals, often scenes from the Ramakien or Thai version of the Indian-origin Ramayana epic. Devotees arrive at these chapels all day long, bearing gifts of fruit and flowers as well as paper-thin pieces of beaten gold that are pressed to the images in gratitude for favors bestowed.

The Thais are a reverential people with a highly sensitive etiquette toward their religious monuments. In addition to heeding the advice offered in "Customs," visitors should note that no cameras of any type are allowed inside a bot and only still or 8 mm cameras in the compound.

Wat Arun1

Temple of the Dawn, Arun Amarin Rd., Thonburi. Located on the Thonburi side of the Chao Phraya River. Easily reached by tour boat or water taxi; also known as Wat Chang because of the original temple on this site, parts of which date from before 1782. You'll see the tall prang (Angkorean spire), which is often used in travel posters. The view is splendid from the central tower across the river to the Grand Palace, Wat Phra Keo and Wat Po; bot built by King Chulalongkorn. Some ashes of King Rama II are at Wat Arun, so the present king travels across the river aboard the royal barge to bestow gifts at the end of the rainy season.

Wat Benchamabophit

Marble Temple, Sri Ayuthaya Rd. The name actually means Temple of the Fifth King; built by King Chulalongkorn and finished just after his death in 1910. It was called the Marble Temple because the main buildings are constructed of Carrara marble. Two huge marble lions guard the entrance to the bot. It houses a famous collection of Buddhist images; don't miss the bodhi tree in the rear courtyard. It's 70 years old and supposedly descended from a tree in India where the Lord Buddha was born.

Wat Pathum

Lotus Temple, located near Siam Intercontinental Hotel. This is part of the former palace area the hotel grounds now occupy. The temple is noted for blossoms in the lotus pond behind it. Also favored by taxi drivers who come to have their vehicles blessed.

Wat Phra Keo ★★★

Temple of the Emerald Buddha, located in Grand Palace complex. This is the most famous temple in Thailand; built by King Rama I in 1782 to house the image of the Emerald Buddha. It's a small image whose origin is lost in legend. It was found at Chiang Rai in northern Thailand in 1434. At the beginning of each season (summer, rainy and winter), the king dresses the Emerald Buddha in appropriate costume, a ritual instigated by King Rama I. The figure of a single piece of jasper from southern China sits on a golden throne flanked by other decorated Buddha images; it's surrounded by offerings from kings, royal princes and commoners—truly the most important Buddha image in Thailand.

Wat Po ★

Temple of the Reclining Buddha, located on either side of Jetupon Rd. just south of Grand Palace. Enormous complex covering almost 20 acres; also known as "Thailand's first university" because of its educational value. The first four Chakri Dynasty kings favored Wat Po and added greatly to its art treasures. The Temple of the Reclining Buddha is just one of many structures here. Look at the old murals depicting daily Thai life.

Wat Rajabopitr

Located near Klong Lawd and near Ministry of Interior. Seldom visited by tourists; it's an interesting example of King Chulalongkorn's interest in the West. It was built by the king in 1863 and combines Western and Thai architectural styles. European influence is also seen in the bas reliefs.

Wat Sraket

Washing the Hair Temple, Boriphat Rd. The name derives from legend that Rama I stopped here for a washing while en route to Thonburi to be crowned; a Bangkok landmark because of Golden Mount on top; gilded chedi containing relics of the Buddha (presented to Rama V by Lord Curzon, then Viceroy of India). Golden Mount started under Rama III and completed by Chulalongkorn. There's a circular stairway of 300-plus steps to the top which offers a panoramic view of the capital. The temple is most impressive during the annual Nov. fair when worshipers make a candlelight processional all the way to top of Golden Mount.

Wat Suthat

And the Giant Swing, Dinso Rd. Suthat means "God Indra's heavenly monastery." The temple faces Giant Swing or Sao Ching Cha. Two tall red poles are joined at the top with carved beam. The swinging ceremony no longer takes place; used to honor Brahman god who came down to earth in Jan. Suthat has the tallest chapel in Bangkok; the 14th-century bronze Buddha image was brought from Sukhothai by Rama I.

Wat Traimit1

Temple of the Golden Buddha, Yaowarat Rd. The temple was built about 1238; 10-foot golden Buddha weighs more than 5 tons. It was discovered by accident by construction workers who found it covered with stucco which cracked during a severe storm, revealing pure gold Sukhothai-style image. It's believed to have been covered in the 18th century to prevent theft by invading Burmese.

Bangkok Environs

Ancient City

The country's largest outdoor museum is located in Samut Prakan Province, some 33 km from Bangkok. There are 200 acres of spectacle; 65 of Thailand's most impressive temples and historical monuments are reconstructed here, many of them full size. There are also restaurants, elephant rides, streams and waterfalls. There's a simulated rural village for wandering. Hours: open daily from 8 a.m.-7 p.m. Admission is 150 baht per person; further information is available from The Ancient City Co., Ratchadamnoen Ave., Bangkok.

★★ Ayuthaya

Capital of Thailand for a period of 417 years; site of magnificent ruins, archaeological excavations and restorations; located 88 km from Bangkok and reachable by bus, car, train, or boat. Operated by the Oriental Hotel's "Oriental Queen." Founded by King U Thong in A.D. 1350. During the Ayuthaya period, some 33 kings reigned over the territory. The ancient capital was invaded by the Burmese in 1767 and destroyed beyond repair. Principal monuments are **Chandra Kasem Palace**, the 13th-century **Phra Maha That Temple**, **Ratchaburana Temple**, **Na Pramen Temple** (also 13th century), **Memorial of Queen Si Suriyothai, Temple of Golden Mount Pagoda, Elephant Kraal**, 14th-century **Chao Phraya Thai Temple** just outside the area and 14th-century **Phanan Choeng Temple** on the river bank south of the town. Hours: open daily from dawn to dusk; 2-hour bus ride and 90-minute train trip from Bangkok.

Bang Pa-in

Former country residence of Ayuthaya monarchs; also used by Chakri kings Mongkut and Chulalongkorn. The Royal Summer Palace complex consists of 5 buildings, 2 of them in the classical Greek style. There's also a Gothic church and a replica of the Beijing Palace, along with fine examples of Thai architecture. Hours: the Royal Palace open daily except Mon., 8:30 a.m.-3 p.m.; permission to visit is necessary but easily obtained.

Crocodile Farm

Located in Paknam, some 30 km from Bangkok. There are 10,000 crocodiles on view here. The best time to visit is 6 p.m. when animals are fed. There's also a demonstration on how to catch a crocodile barehanded. Hours: 8 a.m.-6 p.m. Admission is 80 baht.

The floating market of Damnoensaduak in Bangkok

Floating Markets

Venice of the East; two of the most popular floating markets for tourists are the Wat Saiin Thonburi (just across the Chao Phraya from Bangkok) and the Damnoen Saduak in Ratchaburi Province some 104 km from the capital. Early morning hours are the best. Men and women hidden by huge straw hats guide their sampans (narrow boats) full of rice sacks, mounds of colorful fruits and vegetables, local liquor, whole sides of beef and pork, flowers and other goods. The waterways are crowded and the air vibrates with hawkers' calls. It's a photographer's dream, but don't drink the water.

Hua Hin

Summer residence of royal family—and a popular resort on the West Coast of the Gulf of Thailand since King Rama VII built a summer palace in 1920. Located about 200 km south of Bangkok, the area has beautiful white sandy beaches, a good golf course and tennis courts and nice surrounding countryside. Small hotels are available, and there are small shops in town for browsing. Accessible by car, bus, or train.

Kanchanaburi

Here is the Bridge over the River Kwai . It's one of Thailand's most attractive provinces, featuring spectacular waterfalls, wild jungles and rugged terrain—but it's more renowned for the atrocities that occurred here to Allied POWs during World War II. British, Dutch, American, Indian and Australian soldiers lost their lives during construction of famous Death Railway, which included a bridge over Kwai River built to link the valleys of Kwai Noi with Kwai Yai. The railway was to carry war supplies into Myanmar. Visit the sobering cemetery and the JEATH Museum. The Sound and Light program at the River Kwai is the most spectacular we've seen.

Khao Yai

National Park and Hill Resort; total area consists of 542,000 acres. Approximately 50,000 acres are rolling hills and gentle slopes. The average elevation is 2,500 feet above sea level, but the highest peak is Khao Khieo at 5,000 feet . The park is for the preservation of wildlife. There's hiking, fishing, 6 waterfalls, open grass and golf. A motor lodge and small bungalows are available for accommodations.

Lop Buri

Noted for historical significance during Dvaravati period (6th to 11th century), Phra Narai Rachanivet Palace houses ancient artifacts. Prang Sam Yot (Sacred Three Spired Pagoda) is believed to be the work of Khmer craftsmen. Wat Phra Si Ratana Maha That was built by Khmers during the 12th century. The Hindu shrine dates from the 10th and 11th centuries. Phra Kan Shrine is from the 17th century, during the reign of King Narai. Nakhon Kosa monastery may have been a Khmer Hindu shrine. Lop Buri is located about 150 km north of Bangkok and reachable by car, bus and train. Simple hotel accommodations are available.

★ Nakhon Pathom

This is the oldest city in Thailand. Buddhism was first introduced to the Thais here, but the city dates from 150 B.C. Phra Pathom Chedi is one of the largest in the world. The 3-day fair in Nov. is the highlight of the year. Four viharas (halls) at 4 points of the compass contain Buddha images. The Chedi is an enormous inverted golden bowl of almost 380 feet. It can be seen from all over. A museum is in the courtyard of this great temple complex and it contains priceless relics. East of Phra Pathom Chedi is Nakhon Pathom Palace built by King Mongkut (1861-1868). Another palace slightly south is Sanam Chan, which was built by King Vajiravudh (1910-1925) and now is used as government offices and clubs. In front of the Mongkhon Asna building is the bronze statue of King Vajiravudh's favorite dog Yaleh.

Pathum Thani

This sanctuary for open-billed storks is located about 45 km north of Bangkok. It's reachable by car or boat. The most famous monument is Wat Phai Lom.

Petchaburi

These limestone hills pocketed with Buddhist shrines are located about 150 km south of Bangkok. The Palace of King Mongkut and Khao Luang Cave are the 2 main attractions. Kaeng Krachan Dam, some 60 km from Petchaburi, is a scenic man-made lake. Cha Am is a popular beach resort among the Thais. Accommodations are available. The area is reachable by car, bus, or train.

Rose Garden

Suan Sam Phran, located about 32 km southwest of Bangkok (on the way to Nakhon Pathom), is a private recreation area of 50 acres, featuring landscaped flower gardens, 18-hole golf course, Thai houses, hotels and thatched cottages for accommodations; 5 restaurants, 2 swimming pools and large convention rooms. The highlight is the performance of local arts and crafts every afternoon. Good if you have the time, otherwise there are much more enriching places to visit. Hours: daily from 8 a.m.-6 p.m. Admission is 10 baht, plus 140 baht for Thai classical shows.

Sattahip

This is the biggest commercial port in the country; it was built as part of the American war effort in Vietnam. It's now home of the Royal Thai Navy. About 20 km south of Pattaya, Sattahip was also known for large cruise vessels, but they now come into the Gulf of Siam at Pattaya.

TOURS

Floating Market
5 hours, daily. Cruise by motor launch along Chao Phraya River into klongs; the market itself is on Thonburi side of river; stops at Wat Arun (Temple of the Dawn) upon return.

City Tour
3 hours, daily, at 9 a.m. and 2 p.m. Visits to Marble Temple, Reclining Buddha and Golden Buddha—or Wat Trimitr with its 5-1/2-ton Buddha image of pure gold.

Grand Palace ★
3 hours, daily, at 9 a.m.-2 p.m. Visits entire royal complex—Temple of Emerald Buddha, Coronation Hall and replica of Angkor Wat of Cambodia .

Ancient City
4 hours, daily, at 8:30 a.m.-1:30 p.m. A drive to an outdoor museum some 30 km from Bangkok. Parkland features reconstructions of more than 60 of the kingdom's famous temples and monuments.

Rose Garden
4-1/2 hours, daily, at 1:30 p.m. An hour's drive from Bangkok to this new resort area. Man-made klongs and gardens; hotels and restaurants. Thai Village Show allows a taste of the local culture.

Damnoen Saduak Floating Market ★
10-1/2 hours, daily, at 7:30 a.m. A 110 km drive to the most colorful market in the country, followed by a rice barge ride to the Rose Garden. You'll attend a Thai Village cultural show.

Rice Barge Cruise
3-1/2 hours, daily, from 3 p.m. A quiet cruise along the klongs of Bangkok; a visit to a riverside house, some residential areas, rice farms.

Canal Trip by Speed Boat
3 hours, daily, from 3 p.m. Exciting journey along klongs of Bangkok by long-tailed speed boat. Dress casually and watch your camera lenses; they can get splashed easily.

Jim Thompson's Thai House ★

2-1/2 hours, Mon. and Fri. only, from 9 a.m.-2 p.m. Visit the museum-like house of legendary Jim Thompson, the American credited with developing the Thai silk industry after WWII. An exquisite compound of Thai architecture and oriental antiquities.

Crocodile Farm

4 hours, daily, from 8:30 a.m.-2 p.m. A drive outside the capital to one of the world's largest crocodile farms. Watch how beasts are bred, fed and raised. Also features a wrestling match between beast and man. The visit may also be combined with a tour of the Paknam fish market.

National Museum ★★

3 hours, daily, from 9 a.m.-1:30 p.m. This is a chance to see the kingdom's many art and historical treasures; this is one of the most enjoyable museums in the Far East. The tours are guided by charming and competent docents; highly recommended.

Thai Dinner and Dance

3 hours, daily, from 7:30 p.m. This is a dinner of Thai delicacies (even for the non-Thai palate), plus a performance of classical dances, folk dances and demonstrations of Thai martial arts.

River Cruise with Dinner

3 hours, daily, from 5:30 p.m. and 7:30 p.m. Evening cruise on the Chao Phraya River aboard either the Tasanee Nava rice barge or the Oriental Queen.

Ayuthaya

8 hours, daily, from 9 a.m. Tour of former ancient capital, some 90 km north of Bangkok. Tour visits ruins with an informed guide; lunch and a visit to Bang Pa-in, the previous royal summer residence.

Ayuthaya via Oriental Queen

9-1/2 hours, daily, from 7:30 a.m. Cruise one way between the Oriental Hotel and the ancient capital, the other way by bus with a stop at Bang Pa-in. A buffet lunch is served aboard the vessel.

Kanchanaburi and the River Kwai ★

1 to 4 days. A 130 km drive north from Bangkok to Thailand's most attractive province. A visit to the famous bridge over the Kwai River. Observe the remains of the Death Railway in cemeteries and museums. There are lovely waterways and falls, adventures by jeep, long-tailed boat, train and elephant back to visit waterfalls, caves, local villages and large plantations. Accommodations at River Kwai Village Hotel.

Thai Boxing ★

4-1/2 hours, daily, from 5 p.m. Boxing with fists, feet, elbows and knees; a local tradition, but not for the timid.

Kickboxing is Thailand's national sport.

Pattaya and Coral Islands

1 to 2 days. Pattaya is but a 2-1/2-hour drive from Bangkok; a beautiful beach resort; its off-shore islands are also filled with coral wonders. You can take a trip out to them on converted fishing boat.

Phuket

3-day packages minimum; by air from Bangkok to Phuket. This is a tropical island of sweeping bays and uncrowded beaches. Also see the caves of Phangnga and the fishing village of Koh Panyee and the small town of Phuket.

Phimai

2-day tour. This is the Angkor Wat of Thailand. Designed by the same architects, this area was an important center of the Khmer Empire and is linked by a road 240 km long to the original Angkor. The visit includes an overnight stay, combined with a visit to Khao Yai National Park, or in Khorat, where you'll get a view of Phimai's ruins and museum; on return you'll see the famous Wat Phra Buddhabadh.

Chiang Mai   ★★

2 to 3 days; by air from Bangkok. A visit to handicraft villages and the Doi Suthep and Meo hilltribes; also includes visits to temples and local industries, such as umbrella-making, lacquer and carving.

Chiang Rai   ★

2 to 3 days as extension to Chiang Mai tour. Thailand's northernmost province borders on Myanmar and Laos. There are fascinating hilltribes such as the Akhas, Yaos, Lahus; still unspoiled but not always safe for tourists. Also a drive north to Fang and Thathon via Chiang

Dao and a boat journey of 5 hours, stopping at hilltribe villages along the Kok River. Also a drive to Mae Chan to visit Akha and Yao before returning to Chiang Mai.

Old Kingdoms

3 days. Visits to Bang Pa-in, Ayuthaya, Phitsanulok, Sukhothai and Si Satchanalai to explore ruins and old temples. A 6-day extension is available to Nakhon Sawan, Kamphaeng Phet, Lampang, Chiang Mai and Lamphun.

Trekking in the West

3 or 7 days. This shorter tour features a night on floating rafts on the River Kwai. You'll take a tour by boat and jeep to Three Pagodas Pass near the Burmese border. Also a visit to Mon hilltribe villages and the surrounding jungle. The longer version includes more hilltribe visits, more bamboo forests, jungles and tin mines. This is a new tour.

Trekking in the North

8 days; by air to Chiang Mai for an overnight; by bus and boat to Ban Mai via Fang—overnight in Shan village. A 2-hour trek on the 3rd day to Three Hills; overnight at Lisu village. There's trekking every subsequent day through spectacular forests, jungles and green valleys; an off-the-beaten-track sort of tour.

Around Thailand

7 days; several variations possible. Most include visits to Khorat and Phimai; Khmer temples and an overnight at Kaho Yai National Park; Lopburi's famous temples; Phra Buddhabadh to see the shrine with the holy footprint of Lord Buddha; overnight at Phitsanulok. Also the ancient towns of Sukhothai and Si Satchanalai; overnight at Bhumibol Dam guesthouse. Chiang Mai and Lamphun, Chiang Dao and Fang, Chiang Rai and Mae Chan. Return by air to Bangkok.

South Thailand

7 and 14 days. The tour with a "difference" according to past travelers. Ethnic, cultural, gastronomic, scenic and relaxing; those are the bywords. See the unspoiled beaches of Nakhon Si Thammarat, the spectacular Wat Mahathat and the provincial scenes of Krabi, Thar Bokkha Thoranee National Park, Phangnga and Phuket. The tour begins in Bangkok, by train south and by air back to the capital.

WHERE TO STAY IN BANGKOK

Ambassador Hotel & Convention Center

171 Sukhumvit Rd. ☎ *251-0404. FAX: 253-4153 • 942 rooms (many suites).* Enormous hotel/convention complex, but rather away from city center . Guest rooms in tower most attractive; nice grounds. Several restaurants include Hong Teh Cantonese, Chiu Chau Chinese, Tokugawa Japanese, Cafe Ambassador open 24 hours, Amigos grill featuring Spanish and Continental specialties, Dickens pub, Le Bistro, Garden cafe (coffee shop) and Ambassador seafood restaurant. Also lobby lounge, garden bar and The Club for non-stop live music. Largest swimming pool in the capital and sun terrace. Post office and secretarial services. **Reservations: Utell.**

Dusit Thani Hotel   ★★★★

Rama IV Rd. ☎ *236-0450-9. FAX: 236-6400 • 525 rooms (18 suites).* The name means "town in heaven;" a huge hotel with lobby that is reminiscent of your favorite railway station; great hotel for conventions; the presentation makes a big impact on delegates. Centrally located, well-established property. Restaurants: Castillion Garden, 22nd-floor Tiara Buffet, lounge and nightclub, Sukhothai traditional Thai feast and dancing, Shogun Japanese restuarant, Pavilion cafe (coffee shop). Also Bubbles discotheque and Cookie Corner (for take-away snacks). Swimming pool. Tennis courts. Health club. Shopping arcade. Executive center in new 14-story Executive tower.

Reservations: Utell.

Grand Hyatt Erawan   ★★★★★

494 Rajdamri Rd. ☎ *254-1234. FAX: 253-5856 • 400 rooms.* Located in the city's fashionable Raddamri Rd. shopping, business and diplomatic district; surrounded by beautiful tropical gardens. Regency Club levels. Thai, Chinese and Italian restaurants. Several bar-lounges and cafes, including the Garden lounge and bakery with espresso bar. Club Erawan fitness spa, outdoor swimming pool with swim-up bar, tennis court, squash courts, jogging track, Aromatherapy and other massage treatments. Business center. Meeting and banquet rooms. **Reservations: Hyatt Int'l.**

Hilton International Bangkok   ★★★★★

2 Wireless Rd., off Ploenchit Rd. ☎ *253-0123. FAX: 253-6509 • 389 rooms (43 suites).* Located in the 8.5-acre Nai Lert Park; in midst of Bangkok's diplomatic and business districts; all guest rooms have private balconies overlooking lush gardens; curved atrium building with Thai motifs throughout; low-rise structure with 3 atrium lobbies and thousands of bougainvilleas for effect. Garden restaurant and terrace (Thai/Western specialties). Ma Maison French restaurant. Genji Japanese restaurant. Lobby lounge. Juliana's of London Club. Swimming pool. Health club. Tennis and squash courts. Thai Village handicrafts and folkloric entertainment. Executive service center.

Reservations: Hilton Hotels.

Holiday Inn Crowne Plaza   ★★★

981 Silom Rd., Bangkok. ☎ *238-4300. FAX: 253-3190 • 662 rooms.* The former Holiday Inn Bangkok recently became a member of the company's business traveler-oriented Crowne Plaza division after an expansion and renovation and the addition of such facilities as a business center. Orchid Terrace coffee house. Chef's Table restaurant. Tropicana disco. La Rotisserie. Embassy lounge. Swimming pool. Executive business center. **Reservations: Holiday Inn.**

Imperial Hotel ★★★★

Wireless Rd., 370. ☎ *254-0023. FAX: 253-3190 • 400 rooms.* Set in 6 acres of garden in Embassy section of town; designed for business travelers; large convention facilities. Tennis and squash courts. Jimmy's Kitchen coffee shop. Tudor grill. Jarmjuree seafood restaurant. Garden Room for luncheon buffet. Peep Inn nightclub. 2 swimming pools. *Reservations: Utell.*

Indra Regent Hotel ★★★★

Rajprarob Rd., 439. ☎ *252-1111. FAX: 253-3849 • 500 rooms (24 suites).* Dark interior lobby; commercial atmosphere but some nice amenities; centrally located; near Prahunam market. Indra grill room. Ming Palace. Garden bar. Pratunam cafe (coffee shop). Sala Thai, replica of 13th-century aristocratic home for traditional Thai dinners and dances. Indra Sky Room on 18th floor. The Den Night Club. Swimming pool on 4th level and massage parlor. Indra Cinema, only cinerama-equipped theater in Thailand. Convention facilities for up to 1500. *Reservations: Utell.*

The Landmark of Bangkok ★★★★★

138 Sukhumvit Rd. ☎ *254-0404. FAX: 253-4259 • 360 rooms and 55 suites.* Video text system in all rooms provides a range of information, messages, remote checkout; rooms have fax, word processing and telex capability; 24-hour business center; mobile phones available for guests who use limousine service; four-floor shopping arcade; Seafood, Thai, Chinese and Western restaurants, as well as the Rib Room, a pub and bar-lounge. Business center, executive lounge and bar. Meeting rooms. Health club, swimming pool, squash court, sundeck, outdoor Jacuzzis, sauna, steambath, massage. Shops, including the Chinese Emporium. *Reservations: Summit Int'l. Hotels, Utell.*

Mandarin Hotel ★★★★

662 Rama IV Rd., Bangkok 10110. ☎ *238-0233. FAX: 237-1620 • 343 rooms.* Reputable chain of Asian hotels; luxury category. Restaurants, nightclub, coffee shop, swimming pool, conference facilities and shopping arcade. *Reservations: Utell*

The Menam ★★★

2074 New Rd., Yannawa. ☎ *289-1148. FAX: 292-1048 • 727 rooms.* Menam offers first-class amenities with superior service; you be the judge!; claims sundecks as big as a beach; amidst acres of the landscaped gardens. Jogging tracks, squash, tennis, health club. Floating seafood restaurants. Thai, Chinese and French cuisine. Riverside terrace. Cocktail lounge. Disco. Large shopping arcade.
Reservations: Utell.

Mansion Kempinski ★★★★

75/23 Sukhumvit Soi 11. ☎ *255-7200. FAX: 253-2329 • 120 rooms, 7 Penthouse suites.* Well-furnished, spacious rooms; each has three IDD phones with two lines; VCR and CD players; P.C. and fax outlets in rooms. Western and Asian restaurants, lobby bar, lounge, evening musical entertainment. Outdoor pool, whirlpool, garden. Meeting rooms. Business center.

Reservations: Kempinski Hotels (the hotel division of Lufthansa).

Le Meridien President

135/26 Gaysorn Rd. ☎ 253-0444. FAX: 253-7565 • 377 rooms. Convenient to business district; popular karaoke bar. Caters to many French and Japanese guests, especially business travelers. Six restaurants and bar-lounges. Business center. Swimming pool, health club. Shopping arcade. Conference rooms.

Reservations: Meridien Hotels (Air France's hotel subsidiary).

Montien

54 Suriwongse Rd. ☎ 234-8060. FAX: 236-5218 • 496 rooms (20 suites). Privately owned and operated by local Thais; lovely lobby and gracious atmosphere throughout; a nice departure from the big "hotel chain" mentality; well located; sumptuous furnishings throughout; one of the most pleasant hostelries in Bangkok. Le Gourmet grill with award-winning French chef. Ruenton coffee shop. Jade Garden Cantonese restaurant. Montientong cocktail bar with unusual Thai interiors. Casablanca nightclub on lower lobby. Secretarial service center. Swimming pool in rooftop garden setting. Post office. Convention facilities for up to 1500.					*Reservations: Utell.*

### Novotel Bangkok					★★★

Siam Sq. Soi 6, Bangkok 10500. ☎ 255-6888. FAX: 236-1937 • Novotel is one of the largest European hotel chains, with properties all over Africa and Asia. Restaurant, barber shop, coffee shop, shopping arcade, convention facilities and swiming pool.

Reservations: Pullman-Sofitel, Utell.

The Oriental

Oriental Ave. ☎ 226-0400. FAX: 636-1937 • 402 rooms (21 suites). Situated on the banks of the Chao Phraya River; romantic views of this muddy water from all guest rooms; began as a colonial structure in 1876; modern tower block added in 1958; River Wing in 1976; managed by Mandarin Int'l since 1974; considered the best hotel in Asia by readers of the financial publication Institutional Investor; a favorite of Somerset Maugham and Noel Coward (I saw the latter there in 1968). Prestigious rooftop Normandie grill. Verandah coffeehouse and Riverside terrace. Bamboo bar. Lord Jim's seafood restaurant. Author's lounge. Riverside cafe for barbecues. 2 swimming pools. River cruises aboard hotel's *Oriental Queen* and *Orchid Queen*. Squash/tennis courts. Health centre. Business service center. Diana's disco. Ballroom. Sala Rim Naam for Thai buffets and cultural shows—across river from hotel. In late 1993, the hotel opened the Oriental spa, just across the Chao Phrya River from the hotel, with 14

Thai-style rooms and suites where guests are accommodated while luxuriating in a range of health and beauty treatments.

Reservations: LHW.

The Regent of Bangkok ★★★★★

155 Rajadamri Rd., Bangkok. ☎ *2516127. FAX: 253-9195 • 424 rooms.* The former Peninsula property; beautiful structure with masterpiece lobby designed by one of Thailand's most famous artists; tropical paradise inside and out; rooms overlook Royal Bangkok Sports Club, poolside terrace, or city. Combinations of suites and interconnecting rooms. Lobby lounge. Spice Market Thai cuisine. La Brasserie. Le Cristal continental restaurant. Garden Terrace. Rommanee lounge, piano bar. Business center. Largest hotel pool in Bangkok and Rimsra Terrace. Fitness Center with squash courts, jaccuzzi, massage, health bar and gymnasium. *Reservations: Regent Int'l.*

Royal Garden Riverside ★★★★

257/1-3 Charoen Nakorn Rd., Bookalo, Thonburi. ☎ *476-0022. FAX: 476-1120 • 427 rooms and suites.* Striking Thai-style complex with red tile roofs; three low-rise wings, surround a swimming pool and gardens; large shopping center with designer boutiques. Restaurants include Thailand's first Trader Vic's and first Benihana, as well as Chinese and barbecue dining spots and several bar-lounges. Fitness/aerobics center, outdoor pool with Jacuzzi, tennis courts. Shopping arcade. Business center. Meeting and banquet rooms.
Reservations: Royal Garden Resorts Group ☎ *(800-637-7200), Utell.*

The Royal Orchid Sheraton Hotel & Towers ★★★★

Captain Bush Lane, off Siphya Rd., ☎ *234-5599. FAX: 236-8320 • 776 rooms (78 suites).* Built on former site of Hong Kong and Shanghai bank; just 450 meters upriver from The Oriental; all rooms with uninterrupted view of Chao Phraya River from 28-story Y-shaped structure; 10 minutes by boat to Grand Palace; hotel provides river transportation to Don Muang International airport. The Gazebo Terrace Mediterranean and seafood restaurant. The Bird Cage coffee shop with river view. Bank Vault grill room. Japanese restaurant with river view. River Wharf bar off lobby. Giorgio's grill alfresco on riverside terrace. Silk's nightclub on 2nd floor. Open air swimming pool. Secretarial services. Tennis court. *Reservations: Sheraton Hotels.*

Shangri-La Hotel ★★★★★

89 Soi Wat Suan Plu, New Rd., Bangkok 10500. ☎ *236-7777. FAX: 236-8570 • 650 rooms (47 suites).* All deluxe accommodations with uninterrupted views of Chao Phraya River; palatial lobby looking onto river; $100 million structure; intent upon attracting convention and incentive groups to Thailand; large ballroom with meeting and board rooms; 30 stories; adjacent to South Sathorn bridge. Executive 21st floor with 24-hour purser. Business center. Coffee Garden and barbecue terrace. Poolside snack bar. Sala Thai banquet room. Palm Court.

French specialty restaurant. Shang Palace Chinese restaurant. Swimming pool. Tennis and squash courts. Health Club.

Reservations: Shangri-La Int'l.

Siam Inter-Continental   ★★★★★

Srapatum Palace Property, Rama I Rd. ☎ *253-0355. FAX: 253-2275 •* *411 rooms.* Built within 26 acres of tropical gardens and a pond that backs up to the Srapatum Palace; this hotel presents an oasis of calm in the middle of Bangkok; recently extensively refurbished; good service and peaceful atmosphere; lovely gardens in which to stroll; even a minizoo; 12-room royal suite; stupendous! Sivalai coffee shop. Talay Thong seafood restaurant. Avenue One European/Oriental gourmet restaurant. Naga bar. Thai Night buffet poolside. Business center. Bank and post office. 2 tennis courts, 2 jogging trails. Croquet.

Reservations: IHC.

Sukhothai Hotel   ★★★★★

13/3 S. Sathorn Rd. ☎ *287-0222. FAX: 287-4480 •* *222 rooms, including 76 suites.* Beautiful Thai-style design motifs; proximity to embassies; attracts the international trendies. Elegantly decorated rooms with silk wall-coverings and Thai-inspired decor. A member of the Beaufort Hotels group. Celadon (Thai) restaurant, an alfresco Italian dining spot, a Continental dining room and several bar-lounges. Fitness center with sauna, whirlpool, steambath, gym and massage treatments. Large swimming pool, two squash courts, nearby golf. Business center. Shops. Butler service for every room.

Reservations: ☎ *(800) 421-1490.*

Tawana Ramada   ★★★

80 Surawongse Rd. ☎ *236-0631. FAX: 236-3738 •* *265 rooms (7 suites).* Much needed refurbishing has brought it back to snuff; guest rooms completely redone; suites sport Thai silk interiors; marble lobby. Bon Vivant grill room overlooks pool and garden. Port of Call lounge. Cavern bar nightclub/disco. Swimming pool. Massage and steam baths.

Reservations: Ramada.

SAMPLING LOCAL FARE IN BANGKOK

Thai food can best be described as Hot, Hotter and Hottest since every recipe begins with "take a handful of chiles;" they may be tiny but they pack a mighty wallop in the mouth of unsuspecting visitors. Spicy and fiery are the two adjectives most used in Thai cookery from sweet-and-sour soups to curries and fish dishes. In addition to the basic ingredient of chiles, other frequent seasonings are coriander, garlic, basil, cardamom and local vegetables. Regular, sticky rice is, of course, the mainstay of every Thai meal and the centerpiece of every family table. It is accompanied by side dishes of curries, meat, fish, vegetables and soup, the whole eaten with a large spoon. Chopsticks are employed in authentic Chinese restaurants and may turn up elsewhere if noodles are on the menu.

However, there are many excellent Thai restaurants that cater to the foreign palate and temper the degree of garlic and chiles. The Thai Night buffets, such as found around the pool at the Siam Inter-Continental Hotel, have been carefully planned with Western stomachs in mind. A sample menu features *kuay tiaw* (rice noodle soup), *yam koonchiang* (sweet Chinese sausage salad), *kaeng kai noh mai* (chicken curry with bamboo shoots), *hoh mok pla* (fish pudding in banana leaves), *phad priew wan pla* (sweet and sour fish), *poh piah* (spring rolls), *phad Thai* (Thai-style fried noodles) as well as beef, pork and chicken satays, spare ribs and other barbecue items.

As in all Southeast Asian countries, Thailand can boast a long list of delicious fruits, some of which are quite new to most visitors. Familiar favorites abound, like succulent pineapples (*saparot*) and finger bananas (*klue khai*) that are frequently used in desserts. The mango (*ma-muang*) is probably the most popular and typical of Thai fruits and incomparably sweet and delicious. Familiar to Westerners but still foreign to Thais is the guava (*farang*), which is both used in jelly or consumed right from the tree with a little sugar and salt. The longan (*lamyai*) is abundant in northern provinces and, in fact, brings an annual income of about U.S.$4 million to Chiang Mai. It is considered quite a delicacy in Bangkok. Other sights in local markets are the langsat (*langsard*), pale brown berries with sweet flesh and the mangosteen (*mang-khud*) whose purple rind covers delicious white segments and the rambutan (*ngo*) with a hairy exterior and translucent interior. The sapodilla (*lamood*) is eaten much like the mango and has an equally luscious pulp. The apple family is no stranger in Thailand, for there are plenty of crabapples (*pood-sa*) the size of a small plum, custard apples (*noi-na*) that must be eaten with a squeeze and a spoon for it is difficult to separate the seeds from the flesh and roseapples (*chompoo*) that are shaped like a miniature pear and have a pink waxy surface. This fruit has a subtle sweetness and is usually preferred with a dash of salt.

Thai desserts are sweet and sticky, often combining rice with syrups and fruits and served in the leaves of local plants. You can taste sticky rice baked in bamboo (*kow laam*), bananas in sweet coconut milk (*gluay buad chee*), or that old favorite egg custard (*maw gang*). Drinks available include bottled sodas, tea and coffee in all guises, lemonade with or without salt, bottled fresh, or soybean milk, juices and beer. Wines and hard liquor are very, very, very expensive in Thailand, so pay close attention to the bar bill. Frankly, the local beer is potent enough and should be consumed very slowly.

WHERE TO EAT IN BANGKOK

Thai and Asian Restaurants

Akbar
1/4 Soi 3 Sukhumvit. Indian/Moslem dishes.

Bakee Pochana
1784-8 Corner Soi Pae Sa. Hunanese Chinese.

Celadon
   13/3 South Sathorn Rd. in the Sukhothai Hotel. Superb Thai cuisine.

Chanphen Restaurant
   1031/1 Rama IV Rd. Thai specialties.

Charmchuree Restaurant
   287 Bangkok Bazaar. Cantonese.

Chit Pochana   ★
   1082 Phaholyothin Rd. and Sukhumvit Soi 20. Most comprehensive Thai menu in town.

Chiu Chau Chinese Restaurant
   Ambassador Hotel. Chiu Chau dishes.

Daikoku Restaurant
   960/1 Rama IV Rd. Japanese food.

Dragon Gate
   894/1-3 Rama IV Rd. Taechew Chinese.

Fu Lu Su Restaurant
   23-27 Raiprasong Rd. Hakka Chinese style.

Himali Cha Cha
   1229/11 New Road. Indian/Moslem tandoor, kebabs and vegetarian dishes.

Intown
   66-70 Soi Tontan, Rama IV Rd. Chinese fish restaurant.

Jade Garden
   Montien Hotel. Cantonese cuisine in elegant setting.

Ming Palace
   Indra Regent Hotel. Cantonese dishes prepared by Hong Kong chefs; lavish decor. Chinese music and entertainment.

Moghul Room
   1/16 Soi 11, Sukhumvit Rd. Indian/Moslem menu.

Moti Mahal
   18-20 Old Chartered Bank Lane. Indian/Moslem menu.

Nang Phya
   38/16-17 Soi Pratuchai, Suriwong Rd. Also Indian/Moslem dishes; tandoori and kebabs.

Omar Khayyam
   2/7-8 Soi 3 Sukhumvit Rd. Arabic, Indian, Iranian and Pakistani dishes; extensive menu.

Peking Restaurant
   187/1 Rajdamri Rd. Shanghai-style food, believe it or not.

Rochana
> *President Hotel.* Thai food.

Salanorasingh
> *20 Sukhumvit Soi 6.* Thai-style cuisine.

Shalimar
> *Opposite Ambassador Hotel.* Indian/Moslem menu.

Shangrila
> *154/4-5 Silom Rd.* Shanghai-style Chinese cuisine.

Sheesh Mahal
> *1/22 Nana Nua Sukhumvit Soi 3.* Indian/Moslem menu.

Shogun
> *Dusit Thani Hotel.* Japanese, of course.

Shu Shi Kin
> *9/23-24 Thaniya Rd.* Japanese noodles and such.

Siriwan
> *Siam Square Soi 2.* Thai soups, curries and spicy dishes.

Sorn Daeng
> *Near Democracy Monument.* Good menu and plenty of less fiery Thai dishes; tempered to visitors.

Talay Thong
> *Siam Inter-Continental Hotel.* Excellent seafood restaurant; fixed Thai style.

Teppanyaki Steak House
> *Ambassador Hotel.* Meats and seafood grilled before your eyes.

The Spice Market
> *Regent Hotel.* Superlative Thai food, prepared with a sensitivity to visitors' tolerance of spicy food; in a cool, elegant setting that recreates an authentic spice market; spices, etc. Can be purchased to take home.

The Whole Earth
> *93/3 Soi Lang Suan, Ploenchit Rd.* Thai menu.

Tokugawa Japanese Restaurant
> *Ambassador Hotel.* Authentic setting.

U Fu Lao
> *442/1-3 Rama IV Rd.* Cantonese Chinese; good.

Vietnam Restaurant
> *82-84 Silom Rd.* You guessed it!

Bangkok is an exceptionally sophisticated dining city and can boast many fine international-style restaurants. There are fine French, German, Italian, Hungarian, Swiss and Scandinavian establishments as well as several grill rooms featuring beef from the U.S. and succulent lamb from New Zealand. And because the Gulf of Siam is just a few hours distant, fresh seafood is a daily treat whether grilled under the stars or consumed in air-conditioned comfort. You can also dine by candlelight while cruising along the Chao Phraya River or eat in a splendid Thai teak pavilion while classical dancers and musicians entertain you. Because of the climate, most restaurants do not require coat and tie for the men but certainly do expect all their patrons to be properly dressed. If dining inside, ladies will want to carry a shawl or sweater in case blasts of cool air are aimed directly at their table.

European and American Restaurants

Alleycat
116 Silom Rd. English and inexpensive; steak and kidney pie, pork pie, etc. Open from 11 a.m. daily.

Amigo's Grill
Ambassador Hotel. Spanish decor and menu; a total contrast to the world outside.

Bank Vault
Royal Orchid Hotel. Grill room so named because new hotel stands on site of former Hong Kong and Shanghai bank.

Bobby's Arms
Soi Charuwan. Popular English-style pub.

La Brasserie
Regent Hotel. This is the Regent's bistro, with a dining room and indoor fountain/courtyard seating areas; service is superb, food is excellent (Continental, Chinese, you name it) and remarkably reasonably priced; one of Bangkok's best values.

Castillion
Dusit Thani Hotel. French cuisine despite its name.

Cedar
54 Soi Lang Suan, Ploenchit Rd. Lebanese dishes.

Charly's
66 North Sathorn Rd. Restored villa with fondue restaurant featuring Swiss favorites and an international grill room for steaks; extensive and attractive grounds.

Le Cristal
Regent Hotel. The finest European dining in Thailand may not be an exaggeration; a charming blend of the Continent and Thai styles, with service Regent is renowned for throughout Asia.

Fireplace Grill
Le Meridien President. Charming and intimate; downstairs; continental menu.

Fondue House
28 Soi Somkhit, Ploenchit Rd. Beef fondue and other Swiss dishes in pleasant setting.

Gazebo Terrace

Royal Orchid Hotel. Mediterranean and seafood specialties on an edge of Chao Phraya River.

George and Dragon

Soi 23 Sukhumvit. Another English-style pub.

Giorgio's

Royal Orchid Sheraton. Grills alfresco on riverside terrace.

Indra Grill

Indra Regent Hotel. Steaks from the U.S. and continental dishes grilled Turkish-style.

Italian Pavilion

19 Soi 4 Sukhumvit Rd. Italian specialties.

Kanit

Soi Charuwan. Spanish decor and menu.

Le Gourmet Grill

Montien Hotel. Pressed duckling and other French creations; award-winning chef Michel Binaux.

Le Petit Moulin

2/33 Soi 22 Sukhumvit. More French cuisine.

Lord Jim Restaurant

Oriental Hotel. Very popular seafood spot.

Molo Kai

35 Soi Pipat 2 Convent Rd. Steaks and lobster French style.

Nana Fondue

6/2-3 Soi 3 Sukhumvit Rd. Fondues the French way.

Norden

5 Soi 20 Sukhumvit Rd. Scandinavian smorgasbord daily.

Normandie Grill

Oriental Hotel. The best in town for French food and atmosphere; nice views; tres elegant.

Pornphet Seafood

2662 New Petchaburi Rd. Phuket lobster and other sumptuous fruits of the sea.

Riverside Terrace

Oriental Hotel. Casual ambience by the Chao Phraya; family barbecue dinner on Tuesday, Thursday and Sunday; Thai buffets on Monday and Friday evening; romantic.

Ro De Orm

440/2 Suriwong Rd. Danish open sandwiches and other Scandinavian specialties.

Avenue One

Siam Inter-Continental Hotel. Excellent grill room with French haute cuisine; established reputation.

Tara

Siam Square Soi 9. American steak house.

The Bachelors

593 Sukumvit Rd. Lobsters as you like them!

Tramps

95/4-5 Rajdamri Rd. Seafood and imported meats.

Trattoria Da Roberto

Patpong II. Italian cuisine.

Zur Taverne

1/11 Soi 3, Sukhumvit. German dishes and pizza.

NIGHTLIFE IN BANGKOK

Few other metropolises today offer the variety, profligacy and nonstop activity that one can find at any moment of the day in Bangkok. Those who indulge in this sort of thing say that only one's quest for passion and the size of one's wallet are deterrents to the experiences available.

However, those wishing to indulge in such pleasures are forced to profit from their own research. But, if you just wish to browse and gawk and not commit yourself, head straight for **The Bookseller Company** at *81 Patpong Rd.*—a terrific excuse for getting a good book or magazine (in any language) and checking the wildness out at Patpong at the same time.

Other nighttime activities include Thai-style boxing, which can be at either **Rajdamnern** or **Lumpini** stadiums at 6 p.m. (also 1 p.m. on weekends). As in all boxing, this sport is not for the timid but can be interesting because of the ritual that precedes each bout, the music and the manner in which the barefooted combatants attack each other. This is not simply a match of gloves but of fists, elbows, knees, bare feet and body rushes while the crowd roars and jeers. On-the-spot gambling is also a major activity at these matches.

At least one evening in Bangkok should be spent at a typical Thai dinner, planned with your Western palate in mind and accompanied by classical dances and songs, a bit of sword fighting and some fairy tales. There are many excellent opportunities available: the **Sukhothai Restaurant** at the Dusit Thani Hotel, the **Thai Night buffet** and dancing under the stars at the Siam Intercontinental Hotel, the **Salanorasingh Restaurant**, *20 Sukhumvit Soi 6 (opposite Rajah Hotel)*, **Riverside Terrace** on Monday and Friday at the Oriental Hotel, **Maneeya Lotus** in *Ploenchit Rd.* and the **Thai-Mon Twilight cultural tour** of Koh Kred. This begins at 3 p.m. and lasts five hours, featuring a riverboat cruise, dinner, sightseeing and classical show. A **candle-light dinner** cruise is also available aboard the *Oriental Queen*, on a charter basis. Check with the **Oriental Hotel** for details.

There are many legitimate **nightclubs** and **discos** in Bangkok, especially among the better hotels, that are worth visiting for a little diversion and local music:

Bubbles
> *Dusit Thani Hotel.* Disco open from 9:30 p.m. to midnight.

Casablanca
> *Montien Hotel.* Upbeat nightclub; live music from 9 p.m.

Cat's Eye
> *President of Bangkok.* Musical groups nightly.

Juliana's of London
> *Bangkok Hilton.* Features one of the "in" groups in town.

The Club
> *Ambassador Hotel.* Live nightclub from 8 p.m.-1 a.m.

The Den
> *Indra Regent Hotel.* Imported musical groups from 9 p.m. nightly.

Tiara
> *Dusit Thani Hotel.* Supper club with panoramic view of capital; international entertainment and house band for dancing. Open from 7 p.m. to midnight weekdays, until 1 a.m. on weekends/ holidays.

Tropicana
> *Rama Tower.* Disco from 8 p.m. nightly.

SHOPPING IN BANGKOK

Absolutely the most sensible way to survive the "elements" of Bangkok—traffic noises and fumes, enervating heat and humidity—is to plan plenty of time for browsing through the many colorful shops full of Thai silks and cottons, semiprecious and precious stones for jewelry, bronze ware, celadon and delightful handicrafts. Shopping in Bangkok is truly a feast for one's eyes and the prices are generally bargains of the first rate. Check the cost of a Thai silk gown or complete place-settings for 12 in bronze flatware at any North American department store, then shop around in Bangkok and realize savings of up to 400%.

The Tourism Authority of Thailand suggests that you avoid *touts* (strangers who approach you with a "deal") and sidewalk vendors—unless you just wish to practice the well-known Asian art of bargaining. It is wise always to demand a receipt for any goods purchased as well as a certificate of guarantee for jewelry and gems. Antiques and genuine works of art should only be considered in the most reliable of shops and export documents are often necessary upon departure. As mentioned before, Buddha images are forbidden to leave the county under any circumstances and ignorance of the law still constitutes a crime.

Most of the TAT-member shops will also arrange for shipping and insurance, but remember to safeguard receipts in case of loss or theft. For major complaints, TAT suggests that you write to them directly and someone in the Tourist Service Improvement Division will investigate the problem and keep you informed of any progress in the matter.

Thai Silk

The American Jim Thompson is irrevocably tied to the present success of the Thai silk industry, for he is generally credited with reviving this ancient art after World War II and with promoting its value and variety in the best fashion houses and boudoirs around the world. Thompson was a 40-year-old former O.S.S. agent in Bangkok at the end of the war. He fell in love with Thailand and considered it home until his mysterious disappearance in the Malaysian jungle in 1968. (The biographer William Warren believes Thompson simply got lost deep in the underbrush, walked away from the search party and finally succumbed). An architect by training, Thompson started the Thai Silk Company with a few weavers and gradually upgraded the quality of the material by using color-fast dyes and broader looms to meet the specifications of decorators and designers in Europe and the U.S.

Making silk has always been a home industry for the Thai people and lovely maidens were expected to rear their own silk worms, produce the yarn and weave all the fabric for their family life. By tradition, every maiden would create a masterpiece once in her lifetime—a wedding costume. Today's Thai silk is one of the most sumptuous fabrics available, with colors and patterns that knock your eyes out. Choosing some dress lengths from among a variety of bolts is like being in an ice cream emporium—there are too many tempting flavors. True Thai silk is made in 40-inch widths and can be used for evening gowns, dresses and suits, men's shirts, any kind of accessory for both sexes and home furnishings. Good Thai silk is 100% pure, heavier and more expensive than lesser quality (or silk and synthetic mixtures) and must be properly cared for with professional dry cleaning and pressing. However, it is worth the expense and will last a lifetime if treated with kindness.

Her Majesty Queen Sirikit rarely appears publicly without wearing some type of Thai silk fabric and she is especially fond of **Mut-Mee**, which is a particular tie-dye process that is said to date from prehistoric times. Mut-Mee silk is peculiar to the northeastern part of Thailand; the designs on the material are usually taken from nature. Most popular are animal designs, trees and flowers, waves and watermelon. Even King Bhumibol is interested in supporting the making of this unique material and has suggested that a national attire of Mut-Mee silk would be far more comfortable for men in this tropical climate. Already, Mut-Mee silk shirts are replacing formal wear for men in the evening.

There are many excellent shops selling Thai silk throughout Bangkok. **Jim Thompson's Thai Silk Company** on Surawong Rd. is one of the best, although when I've been there the clerks have been particularly snotty. Try **Star of Siam** on Ratchadamri Rd. for a more gracious experience. And if you prefer lesser quality silk and a synthetic mix, there are material shops around every corner and 24-hour tailors to boot. Many of the beautiful costumes worn by hotel and restaurant staff are a synthetic mix and nothing is lost in the process. Thai cottons are also wonderful and inexpensive, with equally vibrant colors and patterns and very cool for both men and women in this heat and humidity.

Handicrafts

The Thais are imaginative carvers, beaters, molders and painters and there are plenty of interesting handicrafts to buy as gifts and souvenirs: carvings of teak, lacquerware, macrame jute plant hangers, celadon bowls and antique animal reproductions, papier-mâché mobiles, prints of temple rubbings, stuffed cotton animals and exquisite dolls, pounded silver items and nielloware. One of the most popular items is the 100-and-some piece set of bronze flatware, manufactured now with a nontarnish finish, that services up to a dozen diners and several courses. Other bronze items include candlesticks, bowls, ashtrays, punch bowl sets, large and small knick-knacks. Teak and rattan furniture are also plentiful, but one never knows how it all will wear in another climate.

There are numerous handicraft shops in Bangkok but perhaps one of the most interesting is the **Silom Village Trade Center**, which offers exhibitions of silk weaving and printing, silversmithing, celadon pottery, bronzeware, lacquerware, umbrella making, teakwood carving and more. There are also some very touristy, but nonetheless colorful, shows of classical dance, swordfighting and boxing as well as three different eating places.

Jewelry

Semiprecious and precious stones are wonderful buys in Bangkok, especially if you know your gems and their relative value in the marketplace today. Both mounted and loose stones of diamonds, rubies, emeralds, topaz, sapphires, garnets, moonstones, zircons and cat's eyes are on display wherever you cast your eyes. One of the most popular items available is the princess ring, set with a series of jeweled tiers graduating to a single stone at the peak. Another is the nine-stone ring, a narrow gold band set with a diamond, ruby, emerald, topaz, garnet, sapphire, moonstone, zircon and cat's eye, in that order. However, unless you plan to spend more than a few hundred dollars on some pleasing bauble, be very, very careful. Even top jewelers have a difficult time determining the authentic from the fake, today. Make large purchases from a reputable store and insist upon a Certificate of Authenticity. No matter how attractive or tempting a piece of jewelry might be, keep in mind that it's practically impossible to demand a refund from 12,000 miles away in the Western Hemisphere.

Hotel Shops and Arcades

Bangkok's top hotels all have large shopping arcades for browsing and price comparison (remember the high rents they must be paying). There are also plenty of shops in the Patpong-Surawongse-Silom area (near the Montien, Sheraton, Dusit Thani hotels) as well as a **central department store** and a large Thai handicrafts shop on Oriental Avenue. Guests at the Oriental Hotel are next door to many fashionable boutiques, Thai handicrafts and jewelers in the **Oriental Plaza** shopping center. **Siam Centre** is next to the Siam Intercontinental, with a variety of shops selling women's fashions and jewelry as well as two foreign exchange facilities. Guests at the Erawan and Regent of Bangkok are close to the **Rajprasong Shopping Centre** as well as the two-story **Star of Siam** and other fine stores. And arcade fanciers will find that the **Indra Hotel** has the largest variety of shops in town.

Markets

No shopping spree in Bangkok is complete, however, without a tour of the markets that offer a whole new world of exotica as well as plenty of local color! Every Friday evening, hundreds of sellers begin setting up their wares in the Chatuchak Park by the northern bus terminal. This is the **Weekend Market**, which swings from Saturday morning until dusk on Sunday and is especially appealing to those who love a carnival atmosphere. Everything possible is available here, from dyed mice (live) to hot chiles. Plan to spend a few hours wandering among the stalls, but watch your handbags and camera cases because—well, nobody's perfect and pickpockets love crowded places.

There are also two thieves' markets in town, one full of antiques and porcelain (**Verng Nakorn Kasem**) situated between New and Yawaraj roads near the Sang Burapa shopping complex. The other (**Hlung Ga-Suang**) is east of the Pramane Ground on Atsadang Rd. (along Klong Lawd) and offers everything but antiques. Both are open daily. Spices and saris can be found in the Indian district on Pahurat Rd. and the Chinese district on Sampeng Lane is crowded, noisy and full of intrigue.

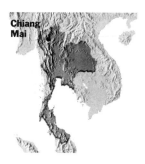

Chiang Mai

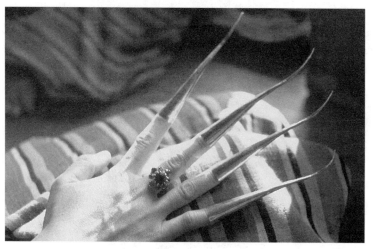

An outrageous manicure in Chiang Mai

CHIANG MAI IN A CAPSULE

Cultural capital of the north...City of Roses...500 miles northwest of Bangkok...reachable by plane, train, or bus daily...known for beautiful women and charming people...once an independent state...founded by King Mengrai in A.D. 1298 in fertile flatland of Ping River. 1000 feet above sea level...uncrowded and unhurried...Buddhism reached highest peak here around 1450...more than 100 ancient temples still exist within 1 square city mile...population around 200,000. Lovely mountain vistas...colorful hilltribes...local crafts and cottage industries...dry and cool climate...a popular hill station during the winter months...especially with royal family...the favored city with most travelers.

After most travelers have had their fill of Bangkok—which is either after two hours or two months—they head for the northern city of Chiang Mai for a breath of fresh air—literally. Although vastly smaller than Bangkok, Chiang Mai is Thailand's second largest city. There are hundreds of wats in the area and the city is home to perhaps the most prolific handicrafts trade in the kingdom.

Chiang Mai is also the gateway to the northern hilltribes, although the villages in the surrounding highlands are so accustomed to seeing Western tourists, you're better advised to base yourself in the towns of Nan or Tak to experience cultures that have yet to be overly commercialized.

Chiang Mai offers a pace of life considerably slower than in Bangkok. It's a compact city that can be seen easily, as many of its attractions are all within walking distance of each other. Public transportation is good. Particularly cheap ways to get around include by tuk-tuk and the city's red minibuses.

WHAT TO SEE AND DO IN CHIANG MAI

Bhubing Palace

Winter home of royal family; about 5 km from Wat Prathat. Some 1300 meters high. Beautiful mountain views and flowers. Grounds open to public on weekends and holidays.

Chiang Mai National Museum
Near Wat Jed Yot; ancient statues of Buddha and a collection of old weapons. Open 9 a.m.-noon, 1-4 p.m., closed Mon. and Tues. Admission is 2 baht on weekends only.

Chiang Mai University
Opened 1965 and located about 5 km from town on approximately 500 acres. Visit Tribal Research Center on weekdays; also Arboretum and Zoo nearby.

Huay Kaew Falls
Near Chiang Mai Zoo; located only about 7 km from town. This is also a spot for picnics. Very popular.

Kruba Srivichai Monument
Near Huay Kaew Falls. The shrine honors venerable old monk who initiated the road up to the monastery on Suthep Mountain.

Meo Village

Located near Bhubing Palace near a hilltribe of interest. Reachable by jeep and foot. Extremely friendly people and children who are accustomed to Western visitors. They've got interesting handicrafts for sale.

Wat Chiang Man
Former residence of King Mengrai, founder of Chiang Mai, this was the first temple built. It dates from 1300. The elephant statues are Ceylonese-style. There are also 2 famous Buddha statues here.

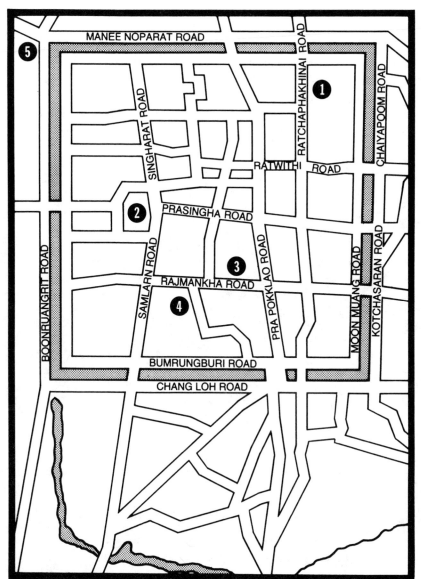

CHIANG MAI

Key

1) Wat Chiang Man
2) Wat Pra Singh
3) Wat Chedi Luang
4) Wat Meng Rai
5) Chiang Mai Orchid

Wat Jed Yod

Located near National Museum, the wat contains ashes of King Tilokaraj in the stupa. The king sent his architects to Burma to design this copy of Buddha Gaya in 1447. Chedi has 7 spires, but suffered damage during the Burmese invasion of 1566.

Wat Chedi Luang

Built in 1411; the large chedi was damaged by an earthquake in 1545 and never repaired. Emerald Buddha said to have resided here in the great pagoda for over 80 years. King Mengrai is said to have been killed by lightning on the grounds. *Indakin*, or the City Pillar, is near entrance of this Wat.

Wat Ku Tao

Built in 1613 in the shape of 5 gourds of various sizes; beautifully decorated with colored porcelain which is said to represent the 5 Lord Buddhas.

Wat Pra Singh

Built in 1345 as one of Chiang Mai's oldest and biggest temples. Built to house **Pra Singh**, the most venerated statue in the north. Important to Songkran Festival in mid-April.

Wat Prathat

Located on top of Suthep Mountain, this is the city's landmark. Reachable by 290 naga-lined steps; it's 3,520 feet above sea level and was built in 1383 by King Guena. A large chedi in the center of the temple contains part of holy relics of Lord Buddha. It's visited each year by Buddhist pilgrims from throughout the land. Tempting little stalls run by local Meo people run all the way up.

Wat Suan Dork

Built around 1383, it contains ashes of Chiang Mai's royal family. The 500-year old bronze image is said to be one of the largest and most beautiful in Thailand.

Chiang Mai Environs

★★★ *Doi Indhanon National Park*

About 100 km from Chiang Mai, this is Thailand's most famous park area with 1,005 square km of space in 3 provinces. Very impressive scenery and wildlife; includes the country's highest mountain. Visit also Vachiratarn and Siriphum waterfalls and Borijinda Cave—all great for picnics and for the most adventurous of travelers.

Hot Springs

About 165 km north of Chiang Mai; near Fang and in Ban Pa-in area. About 50 hot springs can be found in a 10-acre clearing in the forest. Three are bubbling continuously. Avoid it if you can't stand the smell of sulfurous gases.

Lamphun

Quaint small town some 26 km south of Chiang Mai; pleasant trip along a winding road lined with elegant trees. Two interesting temples and a silk brocade factory here.

Mae Klang Falls

Located along Chiang Mai-Hod Rd. about 70 km from the city. Huge waterfalls; a scenic spot for picnics.

Mae Sa Falls

About 25 km from city; known as the cascade because one part is broken into sections.

Mae Sa Mai

About 30 km from Chiang Mai; known for occasional sights of elephants at work in the forest. There's a daily demonstration from 9:30 a.m.-11 a.m. 40 baht admission fee.

Ob Luang

Famous gorge about 105 km from city; located on Chiang Mai-Mae Sarieng Rd. Great view of the deep valley; scenic mountains and teak forest.

Wat Chedi Liem

Located at Sarapee, about 15 km south of city. The name denotes squared-shape of chedi. It's a copy of chedi at Wat Ku Kut at Lamphun.

Wat Ku Kut

Lamphun, about 26 km from Chiang Mai. This was built during the reign of Queen Chammadhevi, legendary monarch. About 60 ancient Buddhas gaze upon you here.

Wat Phra Baht

Pasang, about 44 km from Chiang Mai. Legend says that Lord Buddha and His Disciples rested here and dried his robes on some stones, which now have mystical quality. In the monastery is Buddha's footprint, although this shrine is not considered as sacred as the Shrine of Holy Footprint near Saraburi, 136 km north of Bangkok. The village of Pasang is also famous for handwoven cottons and batiks.

Wat Prathat Chom Thong

About 58 km from city along Chiang Mai-Hod Rd. Located near Mae Klang Falls and Doi Indhanon National Park, this Burmese-style temple was built around 1451. It houses a notable collection of bronze Buddha statues.

Wat Prathat Haripoonchai

Located at Lamphun, some 26 km from Chiang Mai, this temple was built in 1157 along the banks of the Kuang River not far from Wat Ku Kut. A large chedi here houses the holy relic called Prathat **Haripoonchai**, considered one of the most sacred monuments in the north.

Chiang Rai

The Thais take their martial arts quite seriously.

Considered "upcountry" and linked to Bangkok (950 km to the south) and Chiang Mai by air and road. The city was founded by King Mengrai in 1262, whose statue stands along the road to Mae Chan. The 2 famous temples in Chiang Rai are **Wat Pra Singh** and Wat **Phra Keo**; the latter is said to be the original residence of the Emerald Buddha, which now sits in the temple of the same name on the royal palace grounds.

Hilltribes

Hilltribes are one of the great attractions of visiting the north of Thailand; there are about 7 tribes around the Chiang Mai area: Meo, Red and White Karen, Lisu, Lahu, Yao and Akha—sometimes outnumbering indigenous Thais in small villages. Chiang Rai province boasts its own large group: Akha, Yao, Blue and White Meo, Lisu, Lahu and Skaw. The Karen are the most nomadic and clusters range from the Burmese border down. Most of the tribes in Thailand appeared only within the last century. Most are Chinese/Burmese/

Laotian in origin. Many villages can be visited quite safely, especially if you carry small gifts of cigarettes and pens—and plenty of money to buy locally made handicrafts.

Golden Triangle

This is the notorious area where northern Thailand, Myanmar and Laos meet amid verdant mountains, dense jungle and hectares of opium fields that are as well guarded as a chili recipe in Texas. The Golden Triangle is known as the smuggling capital of the Far East— especially in the trade of opium. It's not always safe to visit here; bandits are prevalent and foreigners should be accompanied by armed protection. It's an adventure, especially from Chiang Saen to Chiang Rai in boats down the notorious Mekong River, flanked by jungle on both sides. You'll come upon the Laotian town of Ban Houei Sai; but none of this is for the faint-hearted.

In fact, the intense rivalries between battling war lords can make visiting this area very dangerous—and U.S. drug enforcement officials are beginning to admit that the war on drugs is lost in the Golden Triangle. It's estimated that nearly 60 percent of the world's heroin comes from the Myanmar section of the Golden Triangle, 75 percent of which finds its way to New York City. And with last year's opium harvest generally considered the region's best ever, there is even more competition between former Chinese Kuomintang guerrillas, dope-peddling anti-communist rebels in Laos and the communist party leaders and syndicate bosses of Myanmar.

INSIDER TIP

Khun Sa, a notorious heroin trafficker and self-styled "freedom fighter" from the region, reached a ceasefire with a rival drug lord Chao Yelaiin, an ethnic-Wa of Burma, last October. The "cooperation agreement," as it was called by the Bangkok Post, is expected to result in an upsurge in heroin trafficking in the region. Khun, who's wanted by the United States on narcotics smuggling charges, agreed to the settlement with his traditional rival as it became more apparent that the heroin factories in Shan state were becoming increasingly dependent on raw opium produced in Wa-controlled areas. The Myanmar government accuses Khun Sa and his "rebels" of massacring 122 villagers in Shan state in March of 1993... You may have heard in recent years that the Golden Triangle is but a shadow of its former self in terms of danger and notoriety. Although some areas can be visited that have traditionally been totally off-limits, a lot of blood is still spilt in these jungles.

Heavily-armed mule teams regularly traverse the lush jungles and hillsides transporting opium or refined white heroin powder, most of which is headed for Bangkok before reaching the outside world. Northern Thailand is considered to be mainly under the influence of a fanatical warlord named Khun Sa. His archrival is an ethnic-Wa Burmese named Chao Yelai. Don't mess with these guys. During the past three years, thousands of people have been killed in drug-related skirmishes. You (and your party) could be ambushed by these "bandits" at any time. Be careful.

TOURS

Bhubing Palace and Wat Prathat

3-1/2 hours, Fri., Sat. and government holidays only. 8:30 a.m. and 1:30 p.m. Visit the palace and the most famous temple in Chiang Mai; contains a holy relic of Lord Buddha; beautiful views.

Meo Hilltribe and Wat Prathat

3-1/2 hours, daily. 8:30 a.m. and 1:30 p.m. See colorful costumes and the most famous temple. Bhubing Palace is also toured on weekends.

Home Industries

3-1/2 hours, daily; 8:30 a.m. and 1:30 p.m. Visit local weaving factories at Sankampaeng; umbrella making in the village of Bor Sarng; Thai celadon kiln; teak carvings; laquerware and silverware.

City Tour

3-1/2 hours, daily; 8:30 a.m. and 1:30 p.m. Visit Wat Chiang Man, Wat Jedi Luang, Wat Pra Singh, Wat Suan Dork and Wat Jed Yod.

New Meo Hilltribe

3-1/2 hours daily; 8:30 a.m. and 1:30 p.m. Also stop at Mae Sa waterfalls and largest orchid farm in Chiang Mai.

White Karen Hilltribe and Pasang and Lamphun

3-1/2 hours daily; 8:30 a.m. and 1:30 p.m. Visit hilltribe village at Mae Tha and beautiful people at Pasang. See Wat Prathat Haripoonchai and Wat Jamathevi in Lamphun.

Red Karen Hilltribe

8-1/2 hours daily. Visit Red Karen Hilltribe village in Hod district. See Wat Prathat Chom Thong, then Mae Klang waterfall and the village where pottery is made.

Lamphun and Pasang

3-1/2 hours daily; 8:30 a.m. and 1:30 p.m. Visit historic town of Lamphun; see important Wat Prathat Haripoonchai, Wat Jamathevi—both are over 1000 years old. See Pasang village, known for beautiful girls and weavers.

Lisu Hilltribe

8-1/2 hours daily; visit also elephants at work in jungle; Lisu are tribe of Tibens and Burmese origin.

Mae Sa Waterfall and Orchid Farm

3-1/2 hours daily; 8:30 a.m. only. Northern area of Chiang Mai. A demonstration of elephants at work on timber; also beautiful Mae Sa waterfall and orchid farm.

Chiang Dao Shrine and Elephants

8-1/2 hours daily; visit demonstration of elephants at work in the jungle. Also Chiang Dao cave and shrine with Buddha images; Mae Sa waterfall.

Meo Tribal Village and Elephants

8-1/2 hours daily. Elephants in a jungle setting; Meo village and Mae Sa waterfall; also an orchid farm.

Mekong River and Elephants

11 hours daily. Elephants at work in northern jungle areas. Drive to Tha Ton landing on the Myanmar border. Take a boat trip on the Mekong River to see Lahu and Yao hilltribe villages.

Doi Indhanon National Park

8-1/2 hours daily. Visit Thailand's highest mountain for the most beautiful views in the land. Visit also Meo and Karen hilltribe villages, Mae Klang waterfalls and Wat Prathat Chom Thong, which was built in 1451.

Chiang Rai and Chiang Saen and Golden Triangle

12 hours daily. Full day by car from Chiang Mai to Mae Sai to see the Myanmar border and jade factory; and to Chiang Saen to see the Golden Triangle; visit Akha and Yao hilltribe villages.

Chiang Rai Tour

2 days. By car for Chiang Rai via Karen and Black Lahu and Meo hilltribe villages. Overnight in Chiang Rai. Visit Mae Sai to see the Myanmar border and jade factory. Also Akha and Yao hilltribe villages.

Mae Kok/Chiang Rai Tour

2 days. Visit Tha Ton landing and the elephants at work in the jungle. Take a boat trip along the Mekong River. Visit various hilltribe villages. A full day tour to Mae Sai and jade factory; see Akha and Yao hill-tribe villages—also Chiang Saen and the Golden Triangle.

Sukhotai and Si Satchanalai

2 days. Visit Thailand's first capital and oldest city; old town and museum and overnight in Swankaloke. After breakfast at hotel visit ancient town of Si-Satchanalai; rich in historic ruins and pottery made around 1300.

WHERE TO STAY IN CHIANG MAI

Amari Rincome
301 Huay Kaew Rd. ☎ *221130. FAX: 221915* • *158 rooms.* Quiet, established small hotel; open since 1969; same ownership and management as Nipa and Orchid Lodges in Pattaya; pleasant and casual atmosphere; a few minutes from city center. Thong Kwow restaurant in traditional setting. Lanna coffee shop overlooking swimming pool. Lobby lounge. Byblos discotheque. Large and small swimming pools. Conference facilities. Tennis court. ***Reservations: Utell.***

Chiang Inn
100 Chang Klan Rd. ☎ *235655. FAX: 274299* • *175 rooms.* Charming accommodation in the heart of town; walk around the corner to the Night Bazaar; northern Thailand decor. Romthong coffee shop. Hill Tribe grill. Lobby lounge. Mae Ping lounge. Wall nightclub. Convention facilities. Swimming pool. ***Reservations: Utell.***

Chiang Mai Hills Hotel ★★
18 Huay Kaew Rd. ☎ *210030* • *285 rooms.* Situated between city center and Doi Suthep monastery; 5-story building overlooking lovely grounds and ponds; pleasant setting. Orchid Room coffee shop. Chiang Doi Thai and Japanese restaurant in garden. Saturn discotheque. Swimming pool and health club. ***Reservations: Direct.***

Chiang Mai Orchid
100-102 Huay Kaew Rd. ☎ *222091. FAX: 221625* • *267 rooms.* A beautiful hotel; decor emphasizes the essence of Thai-Burmese design; lovely woods, carvings and weavings throughout; lobby is a Meo hill-tribe experience; hotel is a showcase for northern culture and crafts. Le Pavillon French restaurant. Kamogawa Japanese cuisine. 3-tiered Mae Rim coffee shop. Opium Den bar. Lobby bar. Warehouse disco. Convention facilities. Swimming pool and health club. Orchid Club with private lounge for executive clientele. Squash court.
Reservations: Utell.

Holiday Inn Green Hills
24 Chiang Mai Super Highway. Tambon Changpuerk. ☎ *220100. FAX: 221602* • *200 rooms.* Convenient to road leading to elephant camps. Four restaurants serving Western and Asian dishes. Business level. Business center. Meeting rooms. Pool. Tennis.
Reservations: Holiday Inn.

Novotel Suriwongse
110 Chang Klan Rd. ☎ *251051. FAX: 251024* • *168 rooms.* Restaurant, coffee shop. Swimming pool. Shops. Meeting rooms.
Reservations: Utell.

Royal Princess
112 Chang Klan Rd. ☎ *281033. FAX: 281044* • *198 rooms.* Nine-story high-rise in center of Chiang Mai; extensive renovations. Coffee shop.

Golden Lotus Chinese restaurant. Top floor cocktail lounge with panoramic view of city. Basement nightclub. Swimming pool.

Reservations: Utell.

SAMPLING LOCAL FARE IN CHIANG MAI

Thai food in Chiang Mai tends to be less fiery than the central and southern areas of the country and the restaurants are far more casual and quiet. A specialty of Chiang Mai is the Lanna Khantoke dinner, which features northern dishes along with songs and dances of the hilltribes. The setting is a lovely carved teakwood background and the whole evening lasts about three hours, for a set price of around $10 a person.

European and other Asian food can be enjoyed with great pleasure in Chiang Mai, although hardly with the same degree of variety as in Bangkok. However, there are some popular standbys worthy of a stop.

WHERE TO EAT IN CHIANG MAI

European Restaurants

The Chalet

71 Charoen Prathet Rd., near Diamond Hotel. European dishes in charming setting.

Hans Munchen

115/3 Loi Claw Rd., off Chang Klan Rd. A German/pub/restaurant; all dishes personally prepared by owner Franz.

Hill Tribe Grill

Chiang Inn Hotel. You could buy out the Night Bazaar for what a dinner costs here; intimate surroundings.

Le Pavillon

Hyatt Orchid Chiang Mai. French cuisine in superb setting; quite the best in town; expensive, too.

The Pub

Huay Kaew Rd., near Rincome Hotel. A fun native hut; managed by charming English fellow and Thai wife; tap beer and steak and kidney pie plus other worthy delectables; lunch and dinner, except Monday noon.

Thong Kwow

Rincome Hotel. European and Westernized Thai dishes in lovely, old-world setting; a beautiful, airy dining room.

Thai and Asian Restaurants

Baan Suan

51/3 Chiang Mai, San Kampaeng Rd. Authentic restaurant out near umbrella-making center; if you're in the area.

Bua Tong

Grand Palace Hotel. Good Chinese food.

Chiang Mai Coca
Huay Kaew Rd. More casual Chinese.

Golden Lotus
Chiang Mai Palace Hotel. Good Chinese buffet.

Hong Yok
Muangmai Hotel. Chinese cuisine.

Kamogawa
Hyatt Orchid Hotel. Japanese; but watch for tour groups.

Lanna Khantoke
Diamond Hotel. Most impressive restored house of wealthy Burmese teak trader of a century ago; local dishes and performances; a Meo boy sings in 7 languages.

Mrs. K
Garnet Chiang Mai Hills Hotel. She will make anything! Chinese, Japanese, Thai, or European.

Old Chiang Mai Khantoke
Chiang Mai Cultural Center, Wua Lai Rd. New cultural hall in traditional design; typical northern dishes with hilltribe entertainment; nightly from 7 p.m.-10 p.m.

Whole Earth Vegetarian
88 Sridonchai Rd. Just for something different.

NIGHTLIFE IN CHIANG MAI

Although Chiang Mai's nightlife is a lot tamer than Bangkok's, there are some good restaurants and bars, with most of the best ones located in the major hotels. The Night Bazaar (see "Shopping") is a great place to go after dinner to browse for bargains—and there are lots here!

Byblos Disco
Rincome Hotel. Lots of pillows; very chic.

Crystal Club
Suriwongse Hotel. A supper club; if you like that sort of thing.

Saturn
Garnet Chiang Mai Hills Hotel. Swinging disco.

The Wall Club
Chiang Inn. Very popular and fun.

The Warehouse Disco
Chiang Mai Orchid Hotel. The best in town.

SHOPPING IN CHIANG MAI

Shopping in this Rose of the North is yet another of its many cultural attractions, for the Chiang Mai area is undoubtedly one of the world's largest centers of cottage industries. These people are true artisans as they work at the craft of silk weaving, wood carving, silverware and pottery making. Temple bells, paper manufactured by ancient processes and hand-painted umbrellas are also produced here. At least one day should be spent on an organized tour, or in a hired car, visiting the many small industries that employ thousands of skilled laborers to manufacture charming and inexpensive items completely by hand. For less than $2 each, you can stock up on small lacquered boxes, temple bells and handmade umbrellas as gifts and souvenirs.

The Umbrella Village is located at Bo Sang, along the highway to Sankampaeng. It was founded in 1978 to consolidate the umbrella makers of the area, to preserve the intricate processes of this ancient craft and improve the living conditions of the artisans. Each small factory has a colorful display of new umbrellas drying in the sun, made of cotton, silk or sa-paper (Brossonetia papyrifera). The paper is also handmade from the bark of mulberry trees, which are abundant in the forest of northern Thailand. The frames are all handmade of bamboo and the covering material is waterproofed by the application of a paste that includes the juice of persimmons. The handpainted designs are both traditional and modern and custom orders are accepted. And if you feel the umbrellas are too cumbersome to carry home, shipping can be arranged, but it's a crime to pay more for postage than the handmade item.

Just south of the Umbrella Village and along the same Sankampaeng Road is **Sai Thong, House of Antiques**. The Lanna-style house is worthy of a stop, for it is one of the most stunningly carved structures in all of Thailand and a very interesting place to browse. **Thai silk** is another cottage industry along this road, but I would suggest making such purchases in Bangkok where the quality is more reliable.

Wua Lai Road near Chiang Mai Gate is famous for its **silverware** and **wood carving** home industries, but the lacquerware is really the most impressive here. Ornately painted trunks are the *piece de resistance* but the small black and gold boxes are sold for a song (less then $2) and make lovely gifts. Highway No. 108, about 5 km from town, is the center of pottery production and Highway No. 107 is well known for its celadon industry. At each small community, you can tour the facilities and watch the process before surveying the inevitable showroom.

However, some of the best shopping in Chiang Mai is located along Tha Phae and Witchayanon roads, right in the center of town. Here, you can find those delightful temple bells as well as other brass and bronze ornaments. Here, too, you can find a vast variety of **hilltribe clothing**, made to fit the Western frame. Dresses, jackets, shirts in black and red patterns are in all the shops and cost only a few dollars—with a little serious bargaining. Another amusing place to bargain and buy is along both sides of the steps up to Wat Phra That Doi Suthep, for along with the tourist items are mixed some unusual pieces brought in from Myanmar. There is also a fabulous covered Night Bazaar, situated near the Suriwong and Chiang Inn hotels, that features stalls and stalls of clothing and accessories. Great buys here with a little bargaining savvy! You'll find traditional inexpensive garments and crafts produced by the local hilltribes.

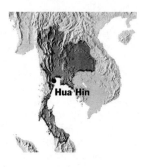

Hua Hin

HUA HIN IN A CAPSULE

Thailand's oldest beach resort; now making a bid as an alternative to the touristy Pattaya...first established in the 1920s...long popular with locals and visitors from surrounding countries...can now boast some deluxe accommodations suitable for the taste of North Americans...located on western shores of Gulf of Thailand...same latitude as Pattaya...and 105 miles south of Bangkok...sandy beaches...picturesque backdrop of green hills...lovely bay...a wonderful place for a relaxing family-type holiday.

The beach resort of Pattaya may be a little sleazy for some. Hua Hin is an excellent alternative. It's Thailand's oldest beach resort and has been a traditional retreat for the royal family. Some of its attractions include the palace **Klai Kangwon**, built by Rama VII in the 1920s. Also check out the **Railway Hotel** (an old seaside resort that has undergone massive renovations), as well as the railroad station itself.

WHERE TO STAY IN HUA HIN

Melia Hua Hin   ★ ★ ★ ★
33 /3 Naresdamri Rd. ☎ *511066. FAX: 511007 • 297 rooms.* All rooms with balconies and ocean views; restaurants, business services, swimming pool, helipad.   *Reservations: Utell.*

Royal Garden Resort   ★ ★ ★ ★
107/1 Phetkasem Beach Rd. ☎ *511881. FAX: 512422 • 220 rooms.* Lovely private beach; rooms and suites with views of Gulf of Siam; seafood/steak, barbecue, Italian restaurants. Bar, disco, entertainment. Swimming pool. Trips to nearby attractions.   *Reservations: Utell.*

Royal Garden Village   ★ ★ ★ ★
43/1 Phetkasem Beach Rd. ☎ *520250. FAX: 520259 • 162 rooms.* Thai-style village resort surrounded by gardens and lily ponds; deco-

rated with Thai art and antiques; Completely renovated in 1993; Thai, seafood and barbecue restaurants. Private beach, watersports, tennis, golf nearby.   *Reservations: Utell.*

Sofitel Central Hua Hin   ★★★★
1 Damnernkasem Rd. *512021. FAX: 511014 • 154 rooms and 64 Thai-style villas.*Good beach; nicely furnished rooms; activities for children; three restaurants, snack bar. Two swimming pools, children's pool, two tennis courts, two putting greens, windsurfing, 18-hole golf course nearby.

Reservations: Pullman-Sofitel Hotels ☎ *(800-221-4542).*

Pattaya

PATTAYA IN A CAPSULE

A sleepy fishing village until the late 1960s...now a sophisticated beach resort with over 5,000 hotel rooms...a paradise for swingers and water-sport fanciers. It's 3 hours-plus by air-conditioned bus from Bangkok–but book early in season and on weekends. This is strictly a recreation area with tennis, waterskiing, parasailing, snorkeling, scuba diving, sailing and fishing...walking the beach and ogling the bikini crowd. Food stalls and restaurants offer an endless variety of international cuisines...glamorous nightspots and discos for after dark...nonstop entertainment. There are plenty of bars and local companionship if you've forgotten your own.

How to turn a sleepy little fishing hamlet into the Gulf of Thailand's version of Acapulco. That's the book the developers of Pattaya must have read before they erected the "best little whorehouse in Thailand." Pattaya is a huge resort town now, packed with foreigners seeking sunshine, beaches and companionship.

It started back during the Vietnam War, when the area became known as a premier R&R spot for American GIs. Today, there are girls galore, as the city's legend as a non-stop, pleasure-packed utopia for single men lives on.

The tourists brought trash with them—tons of it. The water became polluted, the beaches rubbish-strewn. But there's been an effort in recent years to clean the resort up—and it's beginning to show.

Pattaya is also a haven for lovers of watersports. There are a few islands off the coast—**Koh Larn** (with accommodations), **Koh Lin**, **Kho Sak** and **Koh Pai**—that offer decent diving.

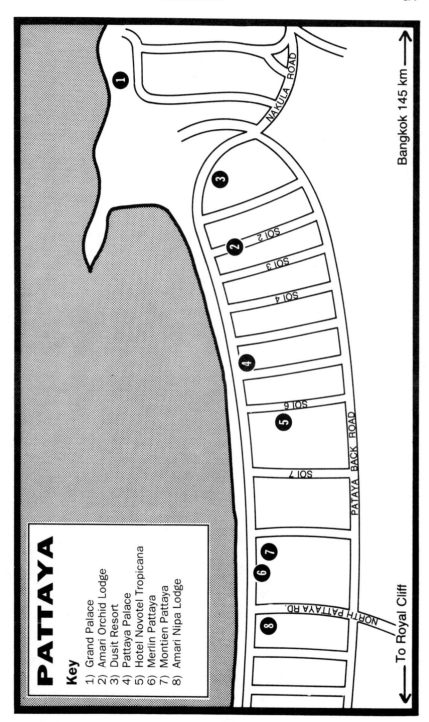

PATTAYA

Key

1) Grand Palace
2) Amari Orchid Lodge
3) Dusit Resort
4) Pattaya Palace
5) Hotel Novotel Tropicana
6) Merlin Pattaya
7) Montien Pattaya
8) Amari Nipa Lodge

NAKULA ROAD

Bangkok 145 km →

SOI 2

SOI 3

SOI 4

SOI 6

PATAYA BACK ROAD

SOI 7

NORTH PATTAYA RD.

← To Royal Cliff

WHERE TO STAY IN PATTAYA

Amari Nipa Lodge Resort

Pattaya Beach, Cholburi. ☎ *428321. FAX: 428097 • 150 rooms.* Low-rise built in 1965; one of the oldest resort hotels in the area; casual atmosphere; simple accommodations; interesting amenities; sister hotel of Amari Orchid Lodge and Chiang Mai's Amari Rincome Hotel. Oriental Den Asian specialties. Buccaneer Terrace charcoal grill/seafood restaurant. Hafen Stuble German food. Orient Express French restaurant (in 2 former Thai railway cars). Cou Cou Club. Video room. Orchid Terrace coffee shop. Swimming pool and snack bar. Friday night Thai-style barbecue party with dances and hilltribe fashion show. ***Reservations: Utell.***

Amari Orchid Resort

Pattaya Beach, Cholburi. ☎ *428161. FAX: 428165 • 236 rooms.* Casual, low-rise structure opened in 1963; sister of Nipa Lodge and Rincome Hotel in Chiang Mai; located in over 10 acres of tropical gardens. Crow's Nest coffee terrace. La Gritta Italian restaurant. Lobby bar. Byblos piano lounge. Garden bar. Orchid grill. Red Baron English/German specialties. Olympic-size swimming pool. ***Reservations: Utell.***

Dusit Resort

240/2 Pattaya Beach Rd. ☎ *425-6224. FAX: 428239 • 500 rooms.* Extensive recreational facilities; rooms and suites with private balconies; Western and Asian restaurants, outdoor lounge and sundeck cafe. Free-form swimming pools, watersports, tennis, squash, jogging track, putting green, fitness center. Large conference hall. ***Reservations: SRS, Utell.***

Grand Palace ★★★★

Corner Pattaya Beach, Cholburi. ☎ *428294. FAX: 428239 • 500 rooms (40 suites).* New Y-shaped structure at northern end of the beach; located on 15 acres of lovely gardens; great views; contains Thailand's largest convention facilities; modern lobby with open courtyard behind; plus rooms and suites; 30 duplex suites near pool, with own butler; the tops in personal comfort and privacy; an unbeatable resort hotel. Food market featuring stalls of different cuisines. Nouvelle cuisine dining room. Country & Western saloon. Jazz lounge. Chinese den. Thai music bistro. Discotheque/nightclub; 24-hour coffee shop; 2 swimming pools; 2 tennis courts; 2 private beaches for guests. Recreation center and children's playground. Health club. ***Reservations: Direct.***

Merlin Pattaya

Pattaya Beach, Cholburi. ☎ *428755. FAX: 421673 • 360 rooms;* also Y-shaped to maximize sea views. Built in 1975 as a Holiday Inn property; dark commercial lobby area; overly air-conditioned for my tastes; motel-mentality guest room decor; has own rock garden and sea frontage. La Veranda bar. Sontaya seafood restaurant. Sea Breeze cafe. Rhine Continental grillroom. La Concha lounge. Cookie Jar pastry shop. Surfside nightclub. Large swimming pool. Small putting green. 2 tennis courts. Children's playground.

Reservations: Specialty Tours *(800-421-3913).*

Montien Pattaya ★★★★

Pattaya Beach, Cholburi. *428155. FAX: 423155 • 320 rooms.* One of this resort's most attractive hotels; located in 9 acres of tropical gardens; all rooms have full sea view and balcony; beautifully decorated and recently refurbished; open-air public areas; centrally located; same ownership and management as Bangkok hotel. Veranda coffee shop. Hokkaido Japanese restaurant. Grillroom. Siam Room cocktail lounge/nightclub. Swimming pool and sundeck. 2 tennis courts. Private beach and watersports. Thai classical dancing programs. Massage service. *Reservations: Utell.*

Hotel Novotel Tropicana ★★

North Pattaya Beach, Cholburi. *418516. FAX: 423031 • 200 rooms.* Tropical garden atmosphere in 7 lush acres; plenty of seclusion in the midst of Pattaya's sweeping shoreline; low-rise structure with guest rooms recently upgraded; located between Merlin and Pattaya Palace high rises; relaxing, casual atmosphere; all rooms with balcony or terrace setting; cabana-style also available. South Seas cafe. Mai Kai grill. Boat bar. Seahorse disco. 2 swimming pools. Conference facilities. Polynesian nightclub. Tennis courts. Watersports.

Reservations: Utell.

Pattaya Palace ★★

Pattaya Beach, Cholburi. *423025. FAX: 428026 • 291 rooms (17 suites).* Built in 1970 as a Hyatt property; renovated in 1980; half of the guest rooms have sea views; large double-height lobby; spacious junior suites. Coffee shop. Marlin seafood restaurant. Captain's bar. Evergreen cocktail lounge. Kontiki nightclub. Buo Thong Chinese restaurant. Large swimming pool and terrace cafe. Children's playground. 6 tennis courts. Sauna and massage. Businessmen's club. Miniature putting green. *Reservations: Direct.*

Royal Cliff ★★★★

Pattaya Beach, Cholburi. ☎ *250421. FAX: 250511 • 957 rooms (128 suites).* Self-contained resort; on southern end of Pattaya; overlooks own mile-long stretch of private beach; reachable only by long flight of stairs or elevator; rather out of the way from the mainstream; so be prepared to stay awhile; taxi rides can be expensive! Royal Wing with 86 suites; its own swimming pool, another restaurant/bar and open-air dining terrace; hotel will arrange local fishing boats and equipment for guests. Terrace grill. Lobster Pot seafood restaurant. Piano bar. Coffee shop. Supper club. Sunset bar. 3 swimming pools.

Massage parlor. Beach bar. Meeting/conference rooms. 800-hotel personnel. 6 tennis courts. Bowling alley. Jogging track. Squash courts. Watersports. Golf course nearby.   ***Reservations: Utell.***

Royal Garden Resort Pattaya

218 Pattaya Beach Rd. ☎ *428126. FAX: 429926 • 300 rooms.* Rooms and suites have views of Pattaya Bay; large swimming pool; four-story shopping mall. Thai and international restaurants, Garden Cafe, poolside barbecue restaurant. Watersports, pool, private beach.

                                                   Reservations: Utell.

Siam Bayshore

Pattaya Beach, Cholburi. ☎ *428678. FAX: 251-1156 • 274 rooms.* Situated on 20 acres at southern end; beginning of the crescent beach; 14 low-rise buildings connected by covered walkways; lots of greenery and privacy; futuristic in feeling; many facilities, including professional tennis club on premises; all rooms with private balconies; also private beach club. Bali Hai seafood and Chinese restaurant. Midships coffee shop. Speakeasy lounge. Ocean Floor nightclub. The Greenery lounge. Bayshore Rotisserie. Meeting and conference facilities. 4 tennis courts. 2 swimming pools. Beach club.   ***Reservations: Utell.***

Siam Bayview   ★★★★

Pattaya Beach, Cholburi. ☎ *423871. FAX: 251-1156 • 300 rooms.* Developed by owners of Siam Bayshore; designed for upscale market; 3-story Bayside wing with 87 rooms; 12-story tower with plush rooms; all with private balcony; stylish, antique-decorated lobby; destined to become one of the resort's finest hostelries. Coffee shop. Specialty restaurant. Cocktail lounge. 2 swimming pools. Seafood restaurant. Nightclub and discotheque. Tennis courts.

                                                   Reservations: Utell.

SAMPLING LOCAL FARE IN PATTAYA

Pattaya is known for its unlimited charms of sun, sand and sex, where singles and swingers can commingle for the time of their lives. The beach and an exciting nightlife are the pulse of Pattaya. This is a place noted for its commercialization, resulting pollution and not an insignificant amount of prostitution, although family groups can enjoy the atmosphere of some of the better hotels. And after a full day in the sun, visitors can choose from French, German, Italian, Hungarian, Swiss, Japanese, Chinese, Indonesian, Indian, Arabic, Mexican and many Thai restaurants for a little repast. (Not to mention the bars, discos, nightclubs and massage parlors that would keep the devil himself hopping to and fro.) But, speaking of eating; the seafood is superb!

WHERE TO EAT IN PATTAYA

European Restaurants

Alt Heidelberg
273 Beach Rd. German specialties.

Alter Bier Garten

Soi 7, Pattaya Beach Rd. More beer and sauerbraten; also Thai dishes and fresh seafood.

Buccaneer Terrace

Nipa Lodge. Excellent grilled lobster and filets; known for Swiss and Continental menu.

Cartier's Restaurant

South Pattaya, opposite Beach Inn Hotel. Steaks cooked to order; and fresh seafood; combo dinners, too.

Chalet Swiss

South Pattaya. Fondues and other delicacies.

Chez Jean

Pattay Naklua Rd., opposite post office. Filet steaks are popular here.

Coral Reef

South Pattaya. Crab souffle; seafood royal; lobster au pernod.

Dolf Riks

South Pattaya Rd. Run by Indonesian-born Dutchman; hearty dishes plus Indonesian rijsttafel on Sun. and Wed.; classical music too.

Grill Room

Royal Cliff Beach Hotel. U.S. steaks and local seafood; expensive and very dressy.

Hafen Stuble

Nipa Lodge. More Deutschland dishes.

Haus Munchen

Next to Merlin Pattaya. Roasted and suckling pigs.

Hideaway Grill Room

South Pattaya. Escargots; duck in orange sauce; New Zealand lamb.

John's Hungarian Inn

South Pattaya. Spicy Hungarian dishes and fresh fish.

La Gritta

Orchid Lodge. Rock lobster; seafood; pizza.

Maris Stella Grill

Wongse Amatya. Charming grill room in low-rise hotel complex.

Milano

South Pattaya. One of many popular pizza and spaghetti places.

Rhine Grillroom

Merlin Pattaya. More German and Continental specialties in former Baron's Grill.

Rotisserie Grill Room

Siam Bayshore Hotel. Very elegant and expensive.

Seafood Restaurant

South Pattaya. All combinations of fresh fruits from the sea.

Suthep Kitchen

Pattaya Beach Rd. Excellent lobster and prawns; veal also a specialty.

Trade Winds

Pattaya Beach Rd. English food prepared with a Scottish touch.

Viking Restaurant

South Pattaya. Seafood in the Scandinavian manner.

Thai and Asian Restaurants

Al Shahab (Moti Mahal)

South Pattaya. Indian, Pakistani, Arabic, Iranian and Thai food; take your choice.

Balihai

Siam Bayshore Hotel. Peking duck, bird's nest soup and other Chinese specialties.

Cafe India

183/9 Soi Chaiyasit, South Pattaya. Moslem and Arab dishes; branch of Bangkok restaurant.

Chalam

South Pattaya. Fried fish with chili sauces, Chinese noodles.

Cliff Top Seafood Pavilion

Asia Pattaya Hotel. Seafood in many excellent guises; spectacular view.

Dee's Pattaya

Next to Palm Garden Hotel. Thai and Chinese at reasonable prices.

Hokkaido

Montien Pattaya Hotel. Japanese dishes in a teahouse atmosphere; elegant and soothing.

Latif Restaurant

109/15 M 10, South Pattaya. Tandoor cooking and Indian kabobs.

Layla

South Pattaya. Arab and Moslem dishes.

Nang Nual Restaurant

South Pattaya. Seafood grills and other Thai food.

Palm Kitchen

Near Palm Lodge. Thai-style seafood and steaks.

Sontaya

Merlin Pattaya Hotel. Excellent seafood restaurant with Thai dishes.

Tai Hee Restaurant

South Pattaya. Hot fish-tail soup and other Chinese delicacies.

Talay Tong
>   *Ocean View Hotel.* Chinese/Thai restaurant.

Thai Garden
>   *South Pattaya.* Seafood and Chinese/Thai dishes.

The Oriental Den
>   *Nipa Lodge.* Seafood and Chinese-style barbecues.

Villa Restaurant
>   *South Pattaya.* Chinese restaurant.

Yamato
>   *Soi Yamato.* Japanese.

NIGHTLIFE IN PATTAYA

The action in Pattaya is non-stop, as a cacophony of rock & roll blares from the southside discos and bars until well into the early morning.

Alcazar Cabaret
>   *78/14 Pattaya 2nd Rd.* Two shows every evening; with 35-member transvestite troupe.

Annabella
>   *Wongse Amatya Hotel.* Pop-rock band; disco.

Byblos
>   *Orchid Lodge.* Disco music and lights.

Cou Cou Club
>   *Nipa Lodge.* Disco music and lights.

Grace
>   *South Pattaya.* Disco music; girls.

Kontiki
>   *Pattaya Palace Hotel.* Disco and pop music.

Mai Kai Supper Club
>   *Tropicana Hotel.* Dinner and dancing.

Neptune Nightclub
>   *Asia Pattaya Hotel.* Disco and rock group.

Ocean Floor
>   *Siam Bayshore Hotel.* Rock and pop group.

Simon Club
>   *South Pattaya.* Disco music and lights.

Supper Club
>   *Royal Cliff Beach Hotel.* Dinner and dancing; floor show Tue. and Fri.

Surf Side
>   *Merlin Pattaya Hotel.* Pop and rock group.

Tahiti
> *Sea View Hotel.* Disco/rock/soul group.

The Marine Disco
> *South Pattaya.* Disco and girls.

The Wall Club
> *Chiang Inn Hotel.* Disco music and lights.

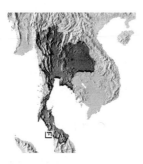

Phuket

A view of the Amanpuri Hotel in Phuket. Despite being overly commercialized, Phuket has retained a great deal of charm.

PHUKET IN A CAPSULE

360-square-mile island off west coast of Isthmus of Kra; which separates Gulf of Thailand and Andaman Sea...equidistant from Myanmar and Malaysian borders...one of most beautiful places in all of Thailand. Economy based on tin and rubber...plus natural beauty that local officials are preserving...no high-rises...local temples and waterfalls for visiting...popular spot.

Phuket is Thailand's largest island and is connected to the mainland by the Sarasin Causeway. It's the only island in the kingdom that is a self-contained province. It's a beautiful, mountainous island, with coral reefs beneath the clear Andaman Sea. The island, virtually unknown to tourists a couple of decades ago, has blossomed into a world-class destination. Yet you can still find your very own stretch of white sand beach.

Patong is the island's most popular beach area and a little reminiscent of Pattaya with its massage parlors and the like, but only a little.

Phuket Town is the provincial capital and worth a stop, if nothing else, for its shops.

Koh Phi Phi is a spectacular little island that makes for a great getaway from the over-commercialism of nearby Phuket.

WHERE TO STAY IN PHUKET

Amanpuri   ★★★★★

P.O. Box 196, Surin Beach, Phuket. ☎ *324333. FAX: 322200 • 42 luxury bungalows.* Developed by the same people who operate the Aman resorts in Bali. This is the most expensive and, many say, the most beautiful hotel in Thailand; huge bungalows with sea views; restaurants serving Italian and Thai food. Swimming pool, beach, tennis, squash, sailing and fishing.   ***Reservations: Prima Reservations.***

Amari Coral Beach Hotel   ★★★★

104 Moo4, Patong Beach, Kathu District, Phuket 83120. ☎ *340106. FAX: 340115 • 203 rooms.* All rooms air-conditioned; facing sea in secluded setting; excellent location; a member of Siam Lodge Hotels. Giant swimming pool. Chao Lay coffee shop and terrace. Rimtalay specialty/seafood restaurant. Conference rooms. Health center. Music lounge. Video films. Tennis. Squash. Badminton. Jogging trails. Nature walks. Water sports.   ***Reservations: Utell.***

Club Mediterranee   ★★★★

Kata Beach. ☎ *214830 • 90-acre resort village.* Two-story accommodations for 600 people curved along a protected stretch of white sand. Center of village; resembles Thai palace; all rooms double occupancy with individual sleeping areas separated by sliding doors; all have balconies overlooking sea. Nightclub. Huge sundeck. Windsurfing. Swimming pool. Theater/dance floor complex. Several open-air dining pavilions. Arts and crafts workshop. Boutique. Annex seafood restaurant up on hilltop perch. 7 tennis courts. 4 squash courts. Tai Chi and other martial arts. Deep-sea fishing (extra charge). Archery. Volleyball. Picnics to offshore islands. Miniclub and conference center. Boat trips. One-week programs at village and 15-day Siamese Smiles excursions. Open to everyone on a membership basis.
Reservations: Club Med.

Dusit Laguna Resort   ★★★★

390 Srisoontorn Rd. ☎ *311320. FAX: 311174 • 232 rooms.* Pretty white sand beach. Restaurants including Thai, Italian and other dining spots. Pub, lounge. Watersports, fishing, boating, swimming pool, private beach, tennis courts, jogging track, putting green. Meeting rooms. Shopping arcade.   ***Reservations: Utell.***

Holiday Inn
Patong Beach. ☎ *340608. FAX: 340435 • 280 rooms.* Riviera Restaurant, Thai restaurant, pizzeria, coffee shop. Golf driving range, pool, tennis, deepsea fishing, watersports, diving center. Shopping center. Meeting rooms.   ***Reservations: Holiday Inn.***

Meridien Phuket
P.O. Box 277, Phuket. ☎ *340485. FAX: 340479 • 460 rooms.* One of several luxury hotels contributing a European flair to the cosmopolitan beach life in Phuket; new property with excellent credentials. Four restaurants, tennis/ squash courts, fitness center and two swimming pools.   ***Reservations: Meridien Hotels.***

Patong Beach Hotel
Phuket P.O. Box 25, Phuket. ☎ *321304. FAX: 32154 • 103 rooms.* Located right on Patong Beach. Dining room, bar. Swimming pool. Tennis. Shops. Video lounge.   ***Reservations: Utell.***

Phuket Island Resort
73/2 Rasda Rd., Phuket. ☎ *381010. FAX: 381018 • 194 rooms.* All rooms and bungalows with views from hillock. Golf. Tennis. Swimming. Beach club. 2 restaurants. Outdoor dining terraces. 2 bars. Shop. Games center. Deep-sea fishing and underwater sports.
                                                   Reservations: Utell.

Phuket Yacht Club Hotel and Beach Resort
Nai Harn Beach. ☎ *381156. FAX: 381164 • 108 rooms and suites.* Managed by the Mandarin Oriental Group; exclusive resort club; hosts prestigious regattas; rooms and suites all have patios and large sundecks; luxurious in-room amenities. Five restaurants and lounges. Outdoor swimming pool, fitness center, two tennis courts, yacht charters. Babysitting service. Car rental. Conference rooms. Tour desk.
                                   Reservations: Mandarin Oriental/LHW.

Sheraton Grande Laguna Beach Resort
Bang Tao Bay. ☎ *324101. FAX: 324108 • 292 rooms.* All rooms with balconies and views of ocean, lagoon, pool and/or garden. Accommodations for the handicapped; 51 two-bedroom villa apartments and duplexes. Nine restaurants and bar-lounges, including Thai, Chinese and Italian/Continental dining spots. Swimming pool with swim-up bar, outdoor Jacuzzis, watersports, fitness center, two tennis courts, 18-hole golf course. Entertainment center. Meeting rooms.
                                                   Reservations: Sheraton.

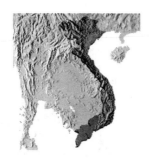

VIETNAM

Nha Trang's huge white Buddha was built in 1963.

VIETNAM IN A CAPSULE

One of the most physically beautiful countries in the world...with a people to match...70 million of them...of the 1/2 million Americans who fought here during the Vietnam War, 58,000 died here and 2,238 are still MIA...the subsequent international economic embargo of Vietnam crippled the country...it has perhaps the lowest standard of living in the world...certainly in SE Asia...however, the new relation between the U.S. and Vietnam has spawned a surge in tourism...lifting of the embargo is now allowing American businesses to begin opening offices in Vietnam...there are more than 3200 km of coastline...more than the state of California...the U.S. dollar is accepted throughout most of the country.

Two decades after U.S. troops pulled out of Vietnam, Americans are returning to this still-battle-scarred country, only this time, they're coming as tourists. It started with the U.S. government's removal of restrictions against travel to Vietnam in 1992 and was accelerated by President Clinton's lifting of the trade embargo in February, 1994. Several tour operators now offer group and individual tour packages to Vietnam. As diplomatic relations between the U.S. and Vietnam go forward and as soon as a U.S. embassy is established, travel into and out of Vietnam should become easier.

Tours from the U.S. usually fly into Bangkok or Hong Kong, convenient gateways for air connections into Vietnam. Although operators say most of their inquiries are for tours that combine Vietnam with Cambodia and Laos, you probably won't see many all-Indochina tours advertised until Cambodia's on-again/off-again political problems are resolved. You will, however, be able to choose from a fairly good selection of tour packages that combine Vietnam with other Asian destinations, including China. (There are good flight connections from Nanking, China into Vietnam.)

Americans who have already gone to Vietnam say they're amazed by the friendliness the people show toward U.S. visitors, given the recent history of the two countries. They're also surprised to find that just about everything is priced in U.S. dollars, rather than in Vietnamese currency, the dong (about 10,000 dong equals US$1). Even the departure tax of $6 is paid in U.S. currency. At press time American Express was negotiating an agreement that will permit use of its credit cards in Vietnam. (Call your local American Express office before you go.)

Despite poverty and a third-world infrastructure, Vietnam—and particularly Ho Chi Minh City (which most people here still refer to as Saigon; in fact, the central part of the city is still referred to as Saigon)—still retains its jaunty air. Rickshaws (called cyclos in Vietnam) buzz around town; street vendors hawk everything from lacquerware to old tires and city boulevards are graced by beautiful, newly restored colonial-era mansions built by the French.

The average hotel leaves something to be desired, although those frequented by tourists are usually comfortable, if not luxurious. However, there are currently about 10 or 12 hotels in construction in Ho Chi Minh City (which will be located in Saigon, Cu Chi, which saw heavy action during the Vietnam War, and Cholon, the city's Chinatown). Among these is the 260-room Omni Saigon Hotel and the 600-room New World Hotel, both scheduled to open

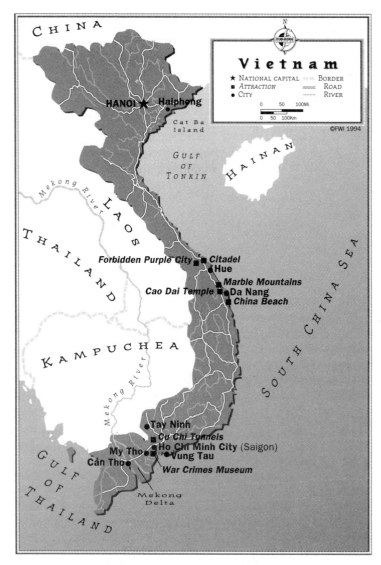

in Ho Chi Minh City in early 1994 (Hong Kong-based New World is also building a hotel in Phnom Penh, Cambodia). Also, Club Med plans to build a vacation village sometime soon in Vietnam, but is first testing the waters by including the country in the 1994 schedules of its cruise vessel, Club Med 2.

Of the hotels already in operation in Ho Chi Minh City, the most luxurious—and the most curious—is the floating Hotel Saigon. Operated by Australia's Southern Pacific Hotel Corporation, the boat-hotel was once a fixture on the Great Barrier Reef. It has about

200 air-conditioned rooms with all the modern amenities, including hairdryers in the bathrooms and a swimming pool on the mainland. Other good hotels in Ho Chi Minh City where tourists are accommodated include the century-old, but newly refurbished Continental Hotel, a favorite of W. Somerset Maugham, and the Century Saigon, which is operated by a Hong Kong firm and occupies the site of the former Oscar Hotel. In Hanoi, the capital, the lovely former Metropole Hotel has gotten a new lease on life, thanks to Pullman/Sofitel, which restored this *grande dame* of the French colonial era. The Hotel Pullman Metropole has a superb French restaurant and a swimming pool.

INSIDER TIP

The discovery of new species continues. Apparently Dr. John MacKinnon, British-born ecologist, has discovered a fascinating new mammal species that resembles a goat, but is more closely related to the cow. DNA samples taken from the horns of the beast, believed habitating an area near Vietnam's 350-square-mile Vu Quang Nature Reserve, about 175 miles southwest of Hanoi near the border with Laos, have shown that the animal is nothing like scientists have ever seen. This is indeed the discovery of a large mammal previously unknown to science. The last time something happened of this magnitude was the 1937 discovery of the kouprey, a now nearly extinct species of wild cattle, in the forests of Cambodia. The new creature is called Pseudoryx nghetinhensis, meaning the false oryx of Nghe tinh (the former name of the province where it was found). The villagers call the animal a spindlehorn. It's believed that until people began populating the region around 1950, the Pseudoryx had no natural enemies. The animal is horned and thought to weigh in excess of 200 lbs. It most likely sports a brown coat with black-and-white markings and a scent gland used to stake its territory. MacKinnon argues that its existence suggests that cows may have come from the forests, and not from grassy plains and savannahs, as is most commonly believed. A spindlehorn has yet to be captured for study. But don't hold your breath. Scientists say that perhaps 300 of the creatures exist.

Vietnam's flora and fauna are something to behold, although the forests have been extensively denuded in the last century. But compared to other regions of Southeast Asia, Vietnam is Eden. The forests contain as many as 12,000 species of plants. Just more than half of them have been identified. More than 250 species of mammals roam the topography; 770 bird species traverse its skies. Nearly 200 species of reptile slither about, hundreds of species of fish swim in its lakes and coastal waters and 80 species of amphibians do both. The discoveries of new species continue, but, in sad contrast, hundreds more are expected to soon become extinct. Among those threatened are the tapir (which some believe is already extinct), the Javan rhino and the kouprey. The Sumatran rhino has not been seen in Vietnam for years.

History of Vietnam

As Americans, we're all too aware of the recent history of Vietnam. For the last 30 years, its past has been entwined with our own. As Vietnam crippled the U.S. spiritually, we ravaged Vietnam economically. As Vietnam reshaped our own awareness of the world by repelling and finally bursting the bubble of the infallibility of American intervention abroad, we regrouped as a nation, only to witness the crumbling of an impotent strain of Southeast Asian Marxism. Nearly 60,000 young Americans paid for this social rebirth—both America's and Vietnam's—with their lives, along with perhaps hundreds of thousands of Vietnamese.

Of course, Vietnamese history predates this conflict by centuries, if not milleniums. And, perhaps not surprisingly, much of the country's culturally rich history has been marred by conflicts.

The early Ly Dynasty seemed to be at war with everyone, and at the same time. There were the Chinese. And there were the Chams. And the Khmers. The list goes on. However, the ancient Vietnamese were a resilient lot. They pushed south toward the Gulf of Thailand and virtually annihilated the retreating Chams.

The Tran Dynasty ruled Vietnam in 1225 and faced its most potent threat from the north. The 300,000-plus Mongol soldiers of Kublai Khan attacked the nation and were repelled. But the dynasty would eventually crumble by 1400, when the Chinese again attempted to gain control. After a largely successful 20-year effort to eradicate Vietnamese culture, Le Loi emerged as the new leader of a free Vietnam. He was phenomenally wealthy and used his riches to help the poor, which made him extraordinarily popular. His family rule included the annexing of Laos and basically ended in 1524, but not until after a significant amount of reforms had been initiated, including civil rights for women. But it was also a time when China culturally dominated Vietnam.

The Split Between North & South

Soon after Le's demise, conflict again interceded. Vietnam was split between north and south, under the rule of two factions, the Nguyen and the Trinh. Fortified by Portuguese arms, the Nguyen lords prevailed and eventually conquered all of what is present-day Cambodia.

Various factions continued to battle each other and they intermittently ruled Vietnam. Finally, a rebellion in 1771 spread to the south and Nguyen Lu became king of the south, while Nguyen Nhac became king of the central part of the country and Nguyen Hue became king in the north. The Chinese, again seeking to take advantage of the internal turmoil in Vietnam, attacked in the north, but were defeated in 1789.

Nguyen Anh, an exiled prince, managed to gain the support of French traders in India and, with the help of French mercenaries, captured Vietnam in 1802. The Nguyen Dynasty lasted until 1945, at least on paper. But the Vietnamese, on the whole, began rejecting Western influences in the 19th century, in particular those transplanted via religious missionaries. Many of theses missionaries' converts were executed by the Vietnamese, prompting the French to capture and control three southern provinces in 1862.

After a French merchant was killed in 1872 by pirates, French retaliation sent the north into anarchy. The emperor, Tu Doc, sought Chinese, English, as well as American assistance in repelling the French, to no avail. Soon, the French were in control of all of what is known today as Indochina. The Indochinese Union was formed in 1887.

The French are generally thought to have controlled the region poorly. There were heavy taxes. Bandits prospered. The opium trade flourished. A growing sense of Vietnamese nationalism then helped fuel the emergence of the Communist Party, led by Ho Chi Minh. After World War II had severely exhausted France's colonial resources and influence, the communists began emerging as the strongest political party in Vietnam. Incidentally, this group, which became known as the Viet Minh during WWII, were supported by both the Chinese and the Americans when they fought the Japanese.

The Japanese overthrew the French government in Vietnam in 1945. During their short reign, an estimated 10 million people starved to death due to Japanese requisitions of rice that year.

After the atomic bombs had been dropped on Japan by the Americans later that year, the Viet Minh assumed full control of the north. Other non-communist groups wrestled for power in the south. The Democratic Republic of Vietnam was formed in Hanoi on September 2, 1945.

Return of the French

Because of further Chinese incursions in the north and a volatile situation in the south (which incidentally the British sought to control with both French and Japanese support), the north was forced to bargain with the French to purge Vietnam of the pesky Chinese. French rule of Vietnam was the price Ho Chi Minh had to pay.

But less than a year later, Vietnamese opposition to the French had risen again. With France foundering in Indochina on American aid, Vietnam again became independent, but still divided north and south. The government in South Vietnam, bolstered by Western support, lost support among the Buddhists as it sought to implement pro-Catholic policies. Protesters hit the streets and a U.S. backed coup in 1963 installed the first of a number of puppet military regimes.

The War in Vietnam

Meanwhile, minds in the north were thinking unification. The Viet Cong was formed in 1960 to force the withdrawal of all foreign troops on Vietnamese soil. In 1964, North Vietnamese troops were making forays into the south. The rickety regime in Saigon was becoming weaker through mass desertions and disillusioned peasants.

The Americans, who had actually had troops inside Vietnam as early as 1955, made a full-scale military commitment to the preservation of the South Vietnamese government.

The turning point in the war came with the Tet (Chinese New Year) Offensive of 1968. Saigon was attacked by the Viet Cong. Mass devastation took place in the countryside. In one three-week period, more than 165,000 civilians were killed in the fighting.

Growing resistance to the war by Americans helped form the American policy of "Vietnamization," which marked the first efforts toward sending American troops home. But shortly afterwards, the U.S. began its massive carpet bombing of Cambodia. The public outcry in the U.S., combined with the phenomenal and unexpected perseverence and resiliency of the communist troops, ultimately forced the U.S. to negotiate with Hanoi. The withdrawal of all U.S. troops from Vietnam was ceded for Hanoi's recognition of the South's independence. But in 1975, North Vietnamese troops rolled into Saigon after a massive offensive and Saigon fell.

Post-War Vietnam

The country then began the painful process of socialization. Hundreds of thousands of Vietnamese fled their country for the U.S. and Europe. Cut off from the West economically, Vietnam suffered greatly.

In 1977, Vietnam entered the United Nations. At the end of the following year, they invaded Cambodia and disposed of Pol Pot's murderous Khmer Rouge regime in January of 1979, installing a pro-Hanoi government. The Vietnamese government began withdrawing their troops from Cambodia in 1989 and agreed in October, 1991 to the Paris Peace Agreement that paved the way to the first free elections in Cambodia (Cambodia).

There are still many scars from 30 years of warfare. Over 650,000 Vietnamese have died; 4,000 bridges and 50,000 miles of road must be rebuilt. The country has a per capita income of below $200 and Vietnam is considered to be the most promising new area of investment for the world's corporations. After all, there is little place else for Vietnam to go but up. The U.S. ASEAN Council expects $2.6 billion U.S. dollars to flow within the next two years.

PLANNING AHEAD

VIETNAM TOURIST

VT, Vietnam's official tourist information office, doesn't maintain an office in the U.S., but you can obtain informative brochures from the U.S. representative, (Ms.) Hont Nguyen, *200 Waterside Plaza, New York, NY 10010* (☎ *212-685-8001*).

VISAS

Tour operators obtain visas for travelers, but as the processing period can take as long as a month (mainly because they have to be issued outside the U.S., at least until diplomatic relations between the two countries are fully established) don't wait until the last minute to book.

The best way to get a visa, as it is with all of the restricted countries in the region, is to get to Bangkok first. There you can pick up a visa in just a few days for around U.S.$60-90, depending on the travel agent. SHOP AROUND! One of the increasingly popular ways of getting to Vietnam is through Cambodia. Again, arrange for your Vietnamese visa in Bangkok, not Phnom Penh. If you do it this way, you can expect to pay as little as U.S.$40 for the single-entry tourist visa. Making Vietnamese visa arrangements in Cambodia is both expensive and time consuming, as it is in Vientiane. In Bangkok, you'll need to get two passport-type photos.

INOCULATIONS

Arrival within six days after leaving or transiting a yellow fever zone requires an inoculation. But you should have all the proper vaccinations for coming to Vietnam. Disease is rife here.

ENTRY BY AIR

Entry by air is by regularly scheduled flights into Hanoi and Ho Chi Minh City. Both cities are served by a variety of airlines, including Thai, Cathay Pacific, JAL, Korean Air, Garuda Indonesia, Philippine Airlines, MAS, Air France and others depending on your departure point. United Airlines has announced plans to establish a Vietnam route but company officials could not confirm a start date or flight schedule at press time. Continental and Northwest are also negotiating Vietnam service.

There's also, of course, the infamous Vietnam Airlines, which has been likened by more than a few travelers to a fleet of coffins with wings.

There have been reports by Westerners of having to bribe Vietnamese immigration officials both in Hanoi and Ho Chi Minh City after arrival, even with all documentation in order. It can be expensive—upwards of U.S.$100.

INSIDER TIP

Vietnam Airlines ("Hang Khong" in Vietnamese and nicknamed "Hang On Vietnam" by those who have survived a VA flight) and its ancient fleet of Soviet-built Tupolev and Antonov aircraft, has had a miserable reputation over the years, both for service and safety. In the past, the advice had always been to avoid VA whenever possible. However, the airline is beginning to realize that most travelers' first goal when flying is getting to their destinations alive, the second being that their luggage arrives sometime within a year or two later. VA seems to be answering the call. The airline has purchased a new fleet of French-built airbuses for use on international routes. And the Vietnamese start-up of Pacific Airlines may give VA a run for its money and kick-start some good old-fashioned competition into the friendly Marxist skies. The attention to safety at VA seems to be improving, but don't expect filet mignon and headphones to catch "Jurassic Park" just yet.

ENTRY BY LAND

From Cambodia, the border crossing at Moc Bai is currently open to Westerners, who usually are on a bus from Phnom Penh to Ho Chi Minh City. There have been reports of Westerners being detained by Vietnamese border guards trying to solicit bribes. Be cool.

The border between Vietnam and Laos is currently closed to Westerners and the Chinese border to the north is marginally open to foreigners.

ENTRY BY SEA

In 1994, seven cruise vessels, *Song of Flower, Ocean Pearl, Aurora I, Seabourn Pride, Marco Polo, ClubMed 2* and *Sea Goddess II* will call in Vietnam. The demand for cruises in 1994 will determine if more ships make Vietnam a part of their itinerary for 1995.

OFFICIAL LANGUAGE

The official language is Vietnamese, which is a combination of Chinese, Tai and Mon-Khmer. English is spoken by the many Vietnamese who worked with Americans during the Vietnam War. There's been a renewed interest in English since the country began opening itself to tourism in 1989.

CURRENCY

The official currency in Vietnam is the **dong**, although U.S. dollars seemed to be accepted everywhere. Banknotes come in the denominations of 200d, 500d, 1000d, 2000d, 5000d and 10,000d. The largest bill, 10,000 dong, is about $5 U.S. Most travelers today are using the dollars over the dong and many upscale hotels require payment in dollars. Carry a good amount of U.S. money in small denominations. You may be using dollars entirely while you're in Vietnam.

INSIDER TIP

Under U.S. Treasury restrictions, American travelers may spend up to US$200 per day in Vietnam (transportation and communication excluded) to purchase items related to travel. A $100 value limit is set on merchandise Americans bring back from the country, but this may increase since the lifting of the embargo. This doesn't include maps, books and other educational material. But receipts are required. Vietnamese officials stringently restrict the exporting of antiques.

TIPPING

Tipping is becoming increasingly expected in Vietnam, although it certainly isn't required. Some establishments add a 10% surcharge. Keeping some duty-free booze and foreign cigarettes on you is always a good idea. Marlboros and 555s are the best bets for the butts, Johnnie Walker Red Label whiskey for the booze.

BUSINESS HOURS

Most businesses open between 7 and 8 in the morning, shut down for a couple of hours around 11-12 noon, and open again until 4 or 5. Government offices are generally open a half-day on Saturday. Museums are generally closed Mondays.

TELEPHONE, TELEX AND FAX

These services are actually quite good, especially in Ho Chi Minh City. But they are outrageously expensive! So beware. Should really be used for emergencies only. The influx of foreign business into both Hanoi and Ho Chi Minh City should soon bring these costs down. Telexes aren't of much use any longer as the West has mostly discarded them in favor of the Fax. Want to Fax the U.S. from Vietnam? Expect to pay around U.S.$10-12 per page!

WHAT TO WEAR

Vietnam has a sticky, tropical climate. Light cotton clothing is a must, particularly in the south. In the north (especially the mountainous north), it can become quite cool on winter evenings. A sweater or wrap would be appropriate. Jackets and ties for doing business only.

LOCAL TIME

Vietnam is seven hours ahead of Greenwich mean time. It's in the same time zone as Bangkok and Phnom Penh.

NEWSPAPERS AND MAGAZINES

English-language periodicals in Vietnam include *Vietnam Weekly* and *Vietnam Economic News*, both geared toward foreign business travelers. Best bet in Ho Chi Minh City is the *Bangkok Post* for newspapers and *Time* or *Newsweek* for magazines. *Vietnam Today*, available in the U.S. and internationally, is a magazine providing up-to-date information for the business community. ☎ *415-333-3800* in the U.S. *FAX 415-333-6888.*

ELECTRICAL CURRENT

Since Vietnam's infrastructure is still rudimentary and power outages occur without warning, be sure to bring a flashlight. The electric current is 220V/50 cycles in most places. Take along adapter plugs and a converter.

CLIMATE

Dress comfortably and pack clothes that are easy to launder and a comfy pair of soft-soled shoes. Bring plenty of film. The climate in Ho Chi Minh City, and elsewhere in the south, is hottest (in the 80s and 90sF.) and most humid in March and April, with the dry season running from November to April and the rainy season from May to October.

In Hanoi, and elsewhere in the north, although the seasons occur at about the same time, temperatures are cooler and there is less rain, except in coastal areas during the summer.

LOCAL TRANSPORTATION

Buses are one of the best ways to get around because they're so cheap and they get to so many places within the country. And they're even better if you've got a lot of time—because they take a lot of time. Oh, yeah—they break down a lot, too. There are more runs during the night now that curfew restrictions have been relaxed.

Cars are a better way to get around than buses but are usually quite expensive, at least 30 cents a km on top of a day charge. And you can't rent them yourself yet, at least to drive. Alas, yours will have to come with a driver. It's better that way anyhow. There's right-side-drive in Vietnam and, although the cops are tough, one of the most common infractions is driving on the left. There are a lot of companies that hire out cars and drivers in Ho Chi Minh City.

You can rent a **moped** without a special license in Vietnam, or hire a moped driver. You can even now rent a **motorcycle** in Ho Chi Minh City for about U.S.$10 per day. You will need an international drivers license with a motorcycle certificate.

Trains are also a great way of getting around, at least along the coast. They're slower than the buses, but are a helluva lot more comfy if you shell out enough dollars (you'll be required to pay in dollars) for anything more than a hard seat. The only problem is that the government slaps a surcharge on rail travel that makes it virtually as expensive as flying the same route (at least between Ho Chi Minh City and Hanoi).

Hitchhiking is a piece of cake in Vietnam and not nearly as risky as in Cambodia, but expect to pay for your ride.

Cyclos are also a cheap way to get around, especially the cities. And they're everywhere that tourists hang out.

TOUR OPERATORS

(Note: Local numbers are for information; toll-free numbers are for reservations). In the U.S., you can contact:

Absolute Asia
155 W. 68 St., Suite 525
New York, NY 10023
☎ *212-595-5782; 800-736-8187*

EastQuest
Beekman St., #607
New York, NY 10038
☎ *212-406-2224; 800-638-3449*

IPI/InterPacific Tours International
111 E. 15th St.
New York, NY 10003
☎ *212-953-6010; 800-221-3594*

Here Today, There Tomorrow
1901 Pennsylvania Ave., N.W., #204
Washington, D.C. 20006
☎ *202-296-6373; 800-368-5965*

Sino-American Tours
37 Bowery
New York, N.Y. 10002
☎ *212-966-5866; 800-221-7982*

Abercrombie & Kent International
1520 Kensington Rd.
Oak Brook, IL 60521-2106
☎ *708-954-2944; 800-323-7308*

Or in Bangkok, Thailand, you can contact:

Exotissimo Travel
21/17 Sukhumvit Soi 4, Bangkok 10110
☎ *253-5240/1, 255-2747; FAX: 254-7683.*

Lam Son International Ltd.
23/1 Sukhumvit Soi 4, Bangkok 10110
☎ *255-6692/3/4/5;*
FAX: 255-8859

Red Carpet Service & Tour
459 New Rama 6 Rd., Phayathai, Bangkok 10400
☎ *215-9951, 215-3331;*
FAX: (662) 215-3331

Viet Tour Holidays
1717 Lard Prao Rd., Samsennok, Huay-Kwang, Bangkok 10310
☎ *511-3272; FAX: 511-3357*

Vikamla Tours
Room 401 Nana Condo, 23/11 Sukhumvit Soi 4, Bangkok 10110
☎ *252-2340, 255-8859*

FESTIVALS AND HOLIDAYS

Like the rest of Southeast Asia, Vietnam enjoys its holidays and festivals.

January 1	New Year's Day	*Public Holiday*
February (moveable)	Tet (Traditional New Year)	*This is the big celebration of the year. It's the time that people forget their grievances; they pay off debts, kiss and make up—that sort of thing. Interestingly enough, Tet also marks everyone's birthday. The Vietnamese don't celebrate individual birthdays. On Tet, everyone's a full year older! The celebration is marked with a tremendous amount of eating. It's believed that the first full week of the year determines how the rest of it will go.*
February 3	Founding of the Communist Party Day	*Public holiday.*
March (moveable)	Hai Ba Trung Day	*Marks the revolt the Trung sisters led against the Chinese in A.D. 41.*
April 30	Liberation Day of South Vietnam	*Public Holiday. Marks the toppling of the Saigon government in 1975.*
April (moveable)	Thanh Minh, Holiday of the Dead	*Feast of the Pure Light. Vietnamese walk outdoors to contact spirits of the dead. Shrines and tombs are cleaned.*
May 1	May Day	*Public holiday.*
May 19	Birthday of Ho Chi Minh	*Public holiday.*
May 28	Celebration of the birth, death and enlightenment of Buddha	*Public holiday.*
August (moveable)	Wandering Souls Day	*After Tet, this is the second most important festival. By praying for the dead, their sins can be absolved. They can leave hell hungry and naked to their loved ones. Celebrations in temples and homes. Money is burned.*
September 2	National Day	*Public holiday.*
September 3	President Ho's Anniversary	*Public holiday.*
September (moveable)	Mid-Autumn Festival	*A children's holiday that features parades.*
November (moveable)	Confucius' Birthday	

Ho Chi
Minh City

Ho Chi Minh City

HO CHI MINH CITY IN A CAPSULE

Formerly known as Saigon...still called Saigon by most...renamed after the Americans left in 1975...but central district is still called Saigon... population of 4 million...once called Paris of the East because of its French colonial architecture and sidewalk cafes...much more open than conservative Hanoi to the north...free enterprise abounds on the streets...city is 70 km from the South China Sea...Vietnam's economic reforms are most evident in Ho Chi Minh City...tourism here is booming...compared with other SE Asian cities, there is very little crime.

This is a city that has been called no fewer than seven names through the years and the latest one, Ho Chi Minh City, is about as embraced by its population as the Marxism that tagged it. People who live here call it Saigon and people who don't live here call it Saigon. In fact, so many people still call the city Saigon, the government allows the central district to be officially called Saigon. And in that spirit, *we'll* call it Saigon—except in the headings.

Like its neighbor to the west, Phnom Penh in Cambodia (although for different reasons), Saigon swelled with refugees from the countryside during the height of the Vietnam War as North Vietnamese forces were toppling the South and closing in on the capital. After the fall of Saigon, the city actually started to resemble Hanoi for a while—with its glum-faced citizenry looking over their shoulders for someone to tout, but instead catching the narrow gaze of the secret police. But all that's changed and it's Happy Days Again in some respects for Saigonites, who are starting to come out of the woodwork to service the burgeoning number of Western tourists who have descended upon the city in relative swarms in recent years.

There is no doubt that bustling Saigon is the industrial, business and—many argue—the cultural heart of Vietnam. There are thriving markets and discos and eateries. The ethnic Chinese of Cholon (Hoa) are again exerting their economic might. Before the fall of Saigon, the Hoa controlled more than three quarters of the industry of South Vietnam and nearly half the banks. After 1975, they were persecuted as opportunists by the Vietnamese—but now they're accepted, even encouraged to invest by the government. In fact, Hanoi sees Hoa prosperity as integral in its efforts at moving toward a free market system. Of course, the move toward free enterprise has its inevitable victims. It's estimated that hundreds of thousands of Vietnamese in Saigon alone are unemployed.

In terms of lifestyle, Saigon is like the Southern California of Vietnam. And, if you're real lucky (or unlucky, depending upon your viewpoint) you might catch a glimpse of a young Saigonite skateboarding along a rutted sidewalk boogying to an American rock anthem blasting in his headset.

The people of Saigon are remarkably friendly to Americans, considering the horrific experiences most had to endure just a short generation ago. In fact, once it's gleaned you're not a Russian, you're still likely to be followed down the street by a posse of curious children.

WHAT TO SEE AND DO IN HO CHI MINH CITY

Places that are must-see in the city generally include the Reunification Palace, formerly the Presidential Palace; the War Museum, which is filled with photographs and memorabilia, including exhibits that depict the horrors of the Vietnam War; the Historical Museum, containing some noteworthy archaeological artifacts and a beautiful bronze Buddha that dates from about the 5th century A.D., and the Cu Chi tunnels, which were originally built during Vietnam's battle for independence from the French. The tunnels were greatly enlarged during the war with the U.S. to accommodate the Viet Cong, and contain living quarters, kitchens and surgical areas for the wounded.

Botanical Gardens

At the end of Le Duan Blvd., there were once thousands of species of beautiful orchids and other flowers here, although the war did a lot to dilapidate the place. It's still worth a visit though, if for nothing other than the small zoo on the grounds.

Central Market

Here's where you'll feel the economic pulse of the "new" Vietnam. This is Saigon's Ben Thanh and its definitely a must-see if you're going to hit the market scene—there are maybe 40 or so sprinkled about Saigon. Here you'll find an incredible array of imported goods, including the usual assault of Japanese electronic goods. VCRs are becoming popular—as are the peripherals that come along with them, namely Hong Kong skin flicks.

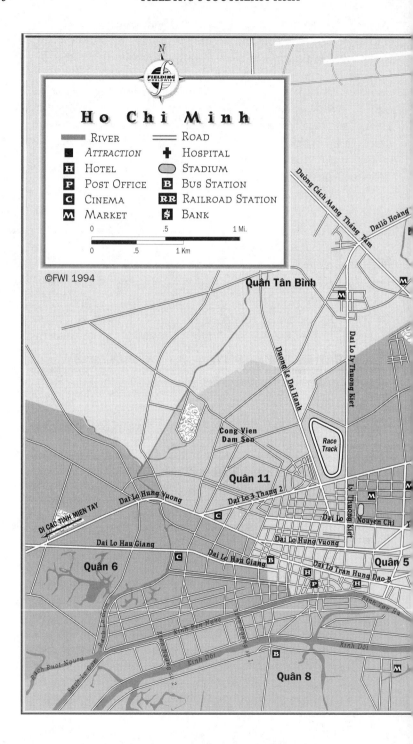

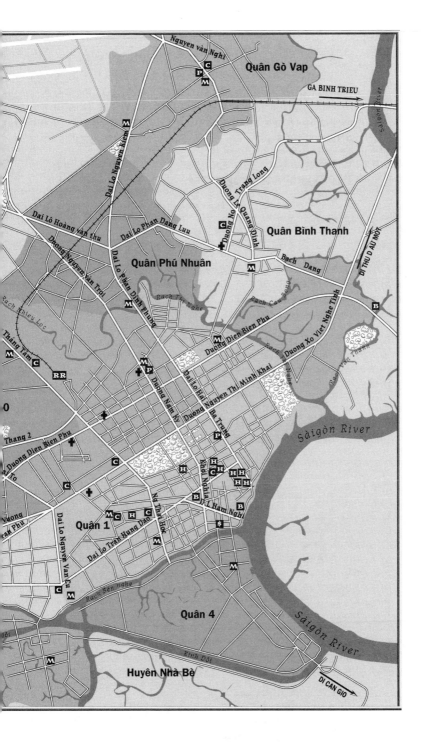

Cholon

Talk about the economic pulse of the new Vietnam. This is Saigon's Chinatown, where nearly 400,000 ethnic Chinese are helping to breathe new fire into the Vietnamese economy. There are also the pagodas here. The beautiful **Thien Hau Temple** was built in 1825 and is dedicated to the cult of Thien Hau, the goddess of the sea and protector of fishermen. The **Quan Am Pagoda**, built in 1816, has some incredible ceramic illustrations of traditional legends. The **Phuoc An Hoi Quan Pagoda** may be the most elaborately decorated in the city. There's also **Cha Tam Church**, where South Vietnamese President Ngo Dinh Diem fled during his escape in 1963, and the Taoist shrine **Khanh Van Nam Vien Pagoda.** Also check out the produce market of **Binh Tay**.

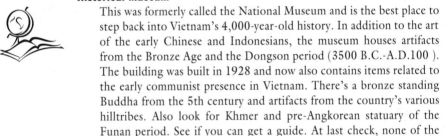

Historical Museum

This was formerly called the National Museum and is the best place to step back into Vietnam's 4,000-year-old history. In addition to the art of the early Chinese and Indonesians, the museum houses artifacts from the Bronze Age and the Dongson period (3500 B.C.-A.D.100). The building was built in 1928 and now also contains items related to the early communist presence in Vietnam. There's a bronze standing Buddha from the 5th century and artifacts from the country's various hilltribes. Also look for Khmer and pre-Angkorean statuary of the Funan period. See if you can get a guide. At last check, none of the labeling was in English. Open 8-11:30 a.m. and 1-4 p.m. Tues.-Fri. Small admission fee.

Notre Dame Cathedral

Built in 1883 and designed by the French architect Bouvard, this Catholic church (near Tu Do Street) is constructed of granite and red brick. It's quite a magnificent sight in contrast with its surroundings. Tu Do Street was the old red-light district in Saigon.

Reunification Hall (Presidential Palace)

This is the modern administrative center, located to the southeast of Xo Viet Nghe Tinh Street, where, in a famous photograph, an NVA tank slammed through the gates in April 1975, which symbolically marked the U.S. defeat in the war. The President and the entire South Vietnam cabinet were in the palace at the time and were arrested shortly afterwards. You can tour the former palace in a group. Open 7:30-10:30 a.m. and 1-4:30 p.m. Mon.-Sun. There is an admission charge.

The Rex Hotel

Located at the intersection of Nguyen Hué and Le Loi Blvds.This was the famous hangout of American officers during the war. It has regained some of its previous glory and now features a number of almost luxurious amenities (at least by Vietnam standards). There's a beauty parlor and an on-site tailor. There are also some respectable business services, such as photocopiers and a fax machine. The place is always packed, so if you're planning a stay, reserve early. The bar's a good place for expensive drinks.

War Crimes Museum

On Vo Van Tan Street near the intersection of Le Qui Don Street. This may be the most popular attraction in Saigon. Built on the site of the former Information Service Office of Saigon University, the museum exhibits a slew of photos depicting events of the Vietnam War in general and alleged and real American atrocites in particular. Many of the shots are absolutely gruesome. Some of the events covered here are the My Lai massacre and the effects of Napalm, Agent Orange and phosperous bombs on the Vietnamese people. Particulary nauseating are the jars of deformed human fetuses. Outside the museum is a collection of war material, U.S. choppers and tanks.

Vinh Nghiem Pagoda

This is one of the largest pagodas in Saigon. It was built in 1967 in the modern Japanese style. It's an impressive sight; at seven stories, it's one of the largest pagodas in Vietnam.

Xa Loi Pagoda

Located near the War Crimes Museum, this temple was built in 1956 and features a multi-story tower which houses a sacred relic of the Lord Buddha. There's a huge bronze-guilded Buddha in the main sanctuary. The pagoda was the site where monks self-immolated themselves in opposition to President Ngo Dinh Diem in the mid 1960s.

Ho Chi Minh City Environs

★ *Cu Chi Tunnels*

This is a vast network of more than 200 km of underground tunnels in Tay Ninh, a little under 40 km northwest of Saigon. These tunnels were constructed and used by the Viet Cong to conduct operations, sometimes within the perimeters of U.S. military bases, and hide from the enemy. These are thoroughly fascinating subterranean vestibules, where the VC lived, slept and ate. There are underground hospitals, kitchens and communications centers. There are living areas, sleeping quarters and munitions storage centers. There are even "street" signs under the earth to help guide errant guerrillas and newcomers. When operational, these tunnels amazingly stretched all the way from Saigon to the Cambodian border. What you'll crawl through today are actually widened versions of the originals. Getting access to tunnel areas other than the touristed ones is problematic. You may even get a chance to fire an AK-47 or an M-16 for a U.S. buck a bullet. Full automatic can be pricey.

My Tho

In the Mekong Delta, about 70 km southwest of Saigon, this is the capital of Dinh Tuong Province. This fertile area is home to several interesting temples—including **Vinh Trang Pagoda** and **My Thoo Church**. There's also a bustling central market. This area is often included on tours outside of Saigon.

Vung Tau Beach

This is a popular beach resort a couple of hours south of Saigon at the mouth of the Saigon River. The front and back beaches are the choice of Vietnamese surf frollickers, while secluded Pineapple Beach features villas and a large statue of Christ overlooking the South China Sea. There are several decent temples here, including the largest one in Vietnam: Niet Bau Tinh Xa.

Tay Ninh

Usually combined with a visit to the Cu Chi tunnels, Tay Ninh is a town about 100 km northwest of Saigon. This is the capital of the Tay Ninh Provonce, which borders the Cambodian border. Back in the 1970s, Cambodian Khmer Rouge guerrillas, in their campaign of terror against anyone Vietnamese, attacked villages in the province frequently and relentlessly. These attacks were part of the reasons the Vietnamese Army invaded Cambodia in late 1978. A few weeks later, in January 1979, Pol Pot's Phnom Penh government collapsed and the Khmer Rouge fled into western Cambodia. Tay Ninh is primarily known for the indigenous religion of Caodaism and the **Cao Dai Great Temple**. Set inside a complex of schools and other buildings and built between 1933 and 1955, the temple is distinctive for the European influences in its Oriental architecture. It's one of the most intriguing temples in Vietnam, if not all of Southeast Asia. Tay Ninh Province was also the strategic end of the Ho Chi Minh trail during the Vietnam War.

WHERE TO STAY IN HO CHI MINH CITY

Bat Dat Hotel

238-244 Tran Hung Dao B Blvd. ☎ *555-817* • *117 rooms*. Recommended by the backpack set. Cheap rooms with air con.; cheaper still with fan; Chinese restaurant. Inexpensive.   ***Reservations: Direct.***

Caravelle Hotel

17 Lam Son Square. ☎ *293-2704. FAX: 84-8-299-746* • *115 rooms*. Very, very French, to a fault. Once owned by the Catholic Church. Recently renovated; 9th floor restaurant; gift shop; gym; sauna; tailor in-house; massage; excellent location. Moderate.

                                         Reservations: Direct.

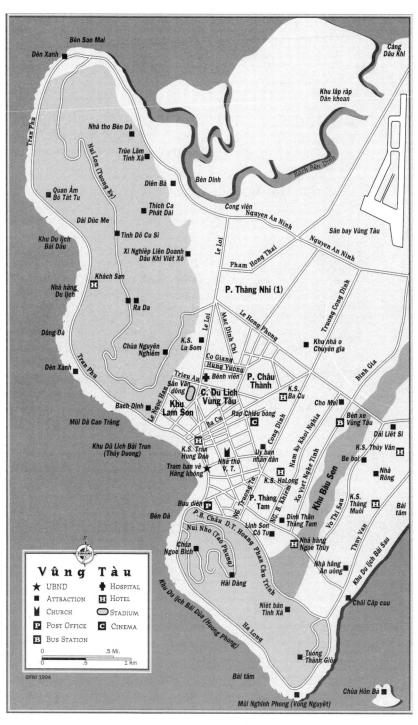

Bến Sao Mai

Đèn Xanh

Trần Phú

Cảng Dầu Khí

Khu lắp ráp Dàn khoan

Nhà thờ Bến Dà

Trúc Lâm Tịnh Xá

Diên Bà

Bến Dình

Núi Lơn (Tương Kỳ)

Rạch Bến Dình

Quan Âm Bồ Tát Tu

Thích Ca Phát Dài

Cong viên Nguyen An Ninh

Sân bay Vũng Tàu

Dài Dức Me

Nguyen An Ninh

Khu Du lịch Bãi Dầu

Tịnh Dộ Cu Sĩ

Lê Lợi

Xí Nghiệp Liên Doanh Dầu Khi Viêt Xô

Pham Hong Thai

Nhà hàng Du lịch

Khách Sạn

P. Thàng Nhi (1)

Truong Cong Dinh

Ra Da

Lê Lợi

Lê Hong Phong

Khu nhà ơ Chuyên gia

Bình Gia

Dông Dà

Chùa Nguyên Nghiêm

K.S. Lu Som

Mạc Dinh Chi

Đèn Xanh

Trần Phú

Co Giang

Hùng Vương

P. Châu Thành

K.S. Ba Cu

Cho Moi

Bạch Dinh

Triêu Âu

Bénh viên

Sân Văn dông

Lê Ngọc Hân

C. Du Lich Vùng Tàu

Khu Lam Son

Ba Cu

Rạp Chiêu bông

C

Cong Dinh

Bến xe Vũng Tàu

B

Dài Liệt Sĩ

Mũi Dà Cao Tràng

Khu Dũ Lịch Bãi Trun (Thùy Duong)

K.S. Trần Hung Dao

H

Nam Ký Khơi Nghĩa

Nhà thờ V. T.

Uy ban nhan dân

K.S. Thùy Vân

H

Be boi

Nhà Rồng

Trạm bán vé Hàng không

Ng. Truong To

K.S. HaLong

Xo Viet Nghe Tinh

K.S. Thàng Muoi

H

Bãi tâm

Buu diên

P

P. Thàng Tam

Bến Dà

P.B. Châu

D.T. Hoàng

Núi Nhỏ (Tao Phụng)

Linh Son Cô Tu

Dình Thàn Thàng Tam

Vo Thi Sau

Khu Bầu Sen

Phan Chu Trinh

Nhà hàng Ngoc Thủy

Thuy Van

Khu Du Lịch Bãi Sau

Chùa Ngoc Bich

Nhà hàng An uông

Hải Dàng

Chòi Câp cuu

Khu Du lịch Bãi Dùa (Huong Phong)

Niêt bàn Tịnh Xá

Ha Long

Vûng Tàu

★ UBND

■ ATTRACTION

Ⱶ CHURCH

P POST OFFICE

B BUS STATION

Ⱶ HOSPITAL

H HOTEL

◯ STADIUM

C CINEMA

0   .5 Mi.

0   .5   1 Km

©FWI 1994

Tuong Thành Gio

Bãi tâm

Chùa Hòn Bà

Mũi Nghinh Phong (Vọng Nguyêt)

Chains First Hotel

Khach San De Nhat. ☎ *441-199. FAX: 84-8-444-282* • *132 rooms.* Near the airport; tennis courts; business services; airport shuttle; gift shop; coffee shop; 3 restaurants; sauna; air con.; refrigerator. Has separate area with rooms with fans. Moderate to inexpensive.

Reservations: Direct.

Cholon Hotel

Su Van Hanh Street. ☎ *357-058* • Popular with visiting Taiwanese; clean rooms; restaurant. Inexpensive. *Reservations: Direct*

Continental Hotel

132 Dong Khoi Street. ☎ *296-042. FAX: 84-8-290-936* • *87 rooms.* This was the setting of Graham Greene's novel *The Quiet American.* Large rooms with air con.; Bamboo Bar; expensive Italian restaurant; good service. Moderate to expensive. *Reservations: Direct.*

Dong Khoi Hotel

12 Ngo Duc Ke Street. ☎ *294-046* • *34 rooms.* Old French colonial building. Air con. suites with high ceilings. Friendly proprietors; good security. Inexpensive. *Reservations: Direct.*

Huong Sen Hotel

66-70 Dong Khoi Street. ☎ *290-259. FAX: 84-8-299-744* • *50 rooms.* Air con.; telephone; TV; hot water; refrigerator. Moderate.

Reservations: Direct.

Majestic Hotel

1 Dong Khoi Street. ☎ *295-515. FAX: 84-8-291-470* • *100 plus rooms.* Once the city's best hotel, a fire ravaged it. Now passable. Some of the rooms have a river view; 2 restaurants; postal and some business services. Moderate. *Reservations: Direct.*

Mondial Hotel

109 Dong Khoi Street. ☎ *296-291. FAX: 84-8-293-324* • *40 rooms.* Some rooms with balconies; bar and lounge; French restaurant with European cuisine. Moderate. *Reservations: Direct.*

Norfolk Hotel

117 Le Thanh. ☎ *295-368. FAX: 84-8-293-415* • *45 rooms.* Located in central Saigon. Usually booked solid. Australian owners/ managers. Attached bathroom; air con.; well-furnished; elegant lobby; hot water; color TV with Star satellite network; wetbar; business center with secretarial services; fax; meeting facilities; restaurant; bar; rooftop BBQ. Moderate. *Reservations: Direct*

Orchid Hotel

29A Don Dat Street. ☎ *231-809. FAX: 84-8-231-811* • *30 rooms.* Air con. rooms; bathroom; telephones; refrigerators; bar; restaurant; coffee shop. Moderate. *Reservations: Direct.*

Palace Hotel

56-64 Nguyen Hue Blvd. ☎ *297-284. FAX: 84-8-299-872* • Rooms have bathrooms and hot water; swimming pool; bar; restaurant; great location. Moderate.   ***Reservations: Direct***

Regent Hotel

700 Tran Hung Dao Blvd. ☎ *353-548. FAX: 84-8-357-094* • Also called the Hotel 700. Located in Cholon. Joint Vietnam/Thai venture. Moderate.   ***Reservations: Direct.***

Rex Hotel

14 Nguyen Hue Blvd. ☎ *296-042. FAX: 84-8-291-269* • *120-plus rooms.* A favorite of American officers during the war. Enjoying a new life with the opening of tourist and business frontiers in the city. Air con.; color TV; refrigerators with wet bars; 3 restaurants; IDD telephones; hot water; cassette players; large statuary and topiary; art gallery; dance area; business center; cinema; tailor in-house; large gift shop; tennis court; swimming pool. Expensive. ***Reservations: Direct.***

Riverside Hotel

19 Ton Duc Thang Street. ☎ *224-038. FAX: 84-8-298-070* • *34 rooms.* Rooms have TV; telephone; refrigerator; self-contained bathrooms; business center; bar; restaurant. Moderate.   ***Reservations: Direct.***

Saigon Floating Hotel   ★ ★ ★ ★ ★

Saigon River at Hero Square on the edge of the central city. ☎ *290-783. FAX: 84-8-290784* • *200 rooms.* Towed from Australia's Great Barrier Reef in 1989. The best hotel in Saigon. Floats on the Saigon River; swimming pool; tennis court; ice machines; 24-hour room service; 2 restaurants; business center; fitness center; saunas; conference room; disco; 2 bars; cafe; meeting rooms for up to 200 people; gift shop. Rooms have color TV; radio; refrigerator/wet bar; valet service; laundry service; IDD calling. Expensive.   ***Reservations: Direct.***

WHERE TO EAT IN SAIGON

Probably the heartiest places to eat in Saigon are at the hundreds of street stalls on the streets. For the most part they're safe, excellent and extremely inexpensive—with prices usually less than a dollar. But if you want more ambience, there are a number of decent establishments in town. The best, and also the most expensive, are found at the better hotels. Here's a look at some of the eateries around Saigon.

1

131 Dong Khoi Street. ☎ *225-837* • A hangout for expats, backpackers and hipsters.

Chez Guido

Continental Hotel • Expensive Italian cuisine; good portions.

Givral Cafe

169 Dong Khoi Street • Like the Brodard, mostly expats and journalists, but better food.

La Bibliotheque
84 Nguyen Du • Very good Vietnamese fare and excellent beef.

Marina Cafe
Saigon Floating Hotel • Great lunchtime buffet; the prices aren't too bad. Menu features U.S. steak (with the embargo, the meat must have been cowjacked) and seafood. Probably the best Western food in-country.

Maxim's
13 Dong Khoi Street. ☎ *299-820* • Live music, decent food, high prices.

Nha Hang 5 Me Linh
Near the statue of Tran Hung Dao • Great Vietnamese fare. Even Cobra!

Naha Hang 51 Nguyen Hue
51 Nguyen Hue Blvd. • Ditto.

Nhon Bashi Japanese Restaurant
On the ground floor of the Rex Hotel • Run-of-the-mill Japanese fare but expensive.

Oriental Court
Saigon Floating Hotel • Good Asian cuisine for Western palates.

Palace Hotel
15th floor restaurant • The best view of Saigon in town.

Sinh Cafe
6 Pham Ngu Lao Street • A good mingling place for travelers.

Veranda
Saigon Floating Hotel • International cuisine.

Hanoi

HANOI IN A CAPSULE

Hanoi is the capital of the Socialist Republic of Vietnam...it's a city of lakes and parks...about 70 km inland from the Gulf of Tonkin...it sits on the bank of the Red River...the streets are tree-lined...trees are uplifting the pavement...it's been a major settlement since A.D. 1010....it became capital of North Vietnam after the Geneva Agreement of 1954...it's not nearly as kinetic and energetic as Saigon...it is inferior in both tourism and infrastructure...because it's more dreary than its sister to the south, it's probably the best place to launch your tour of Vietnam...was heavily bombed during the Vietnam War...Like Ho Chi Minh City, Hanoi has had more than a half-dozen names over the years.

Although not as popular with tourists as Ho Chi Minh City and certainly lacking the hustle and bustle of its sister to the south, there's still plenty to see and do in the capital. Some of the sights include the Fine Arts Museum, which houses traditional Vietnamese art as well as European-influenced works; the Water Puppet Theater, Vietnam's humorous version of Punch and Judy; Ho Chi Minh's mausoleum (the Vietnamese hero's body reposes in a glass coffin); the Ho Chi Minh Museum, which opened in 1990 in honor of the 100th anniversary of Ho's birth; and the Hanoi Hilton, the prison where U.S. soldiers were kept (and which may soon be torn down to make way for an actual hotel).

Hanoi was founded in A.D. 1010 at the beginning of the Lu Dynasty; it is the oldest capital city in Southeast Asia. The city was racked by constant bombing from U.S. Air Force B-52 bombers from 1966 to 1972. The center of Hanoi itself doesn't reveal a lot of scars, but the outlying areas do. The French colonial buildings of the capital are in desperate need of renovation—at the very least a coat of paint. But like the big city in the south, Hanoi's people are extremely friendly and seem to bear few ill feelings toward Westerners,

Americans in particular. In fact, you can almost call this city of more than 3 million charming.

Whereas movement of Westerners in the city was once strictly controlled, tourists today move about Hanoi freely. Bicycles can be hired, and even sights off the beaten track are within easy reach of the traveler.

WHAT TO SEE AND DO IN HANOI

Army Museum

If you want to see tanks and planes and grenades and shells, this is the place. Better to see this museum before checking out the War Crimes Museum in Saigon. It's not as shocking and sobering. However, here you'll find the wreckage of B-52s and American fighter jets, such as F1-11s—if this kind of stuff fascinates you.

Ho Chi Minh Mausoleum and Museum   ★

Somehow you're not surprised when your guide tells you that this mausoleum was modeled after the Lenin tomb in Moscow. The structure itself is a huge imposing building polygonal in shape. It's no doubt the best-maintained building in all of Hanoi. The inner chamber is where the embalmed body of Ho rests; guards surround it. The old man's an eery-looking sight and his impact on all of our lives this half of the century is felt through the glass. From the mausoleum, you can tour **Ho's house** near the Communist Party guesthouse—which was the former **presidential palace** and residence of the former French governors of Indochina. When the North's quest for independence finally came to fruition in 1954, Ho refused to live in the palace, opting instead for the meager electrician's house on the palace grounds; he claimed the palace belonged to the people. Open 7:30-11:30 a.m. Tues.-Thurs. and Sat.-Sun.

Hanoi Hilton

This is the morbidly humorous name given to the grisly, foreboding Hanoi prison structure that housed U.S. POWs during the Vietnam War. Prisoners were tortured here up until at least 1969. Some were held 7 years or longer. This is a dark sight. Off of Hai Ba Trung Street.

National Arts Museum

Vietnamese sculpture is exhibited in this small museum located next to the Van Mieu, Vietnam's first university. The museum also features bronze drums and modern Vietnamese painting. Open 8-12 and 1-4 p.m. Tues.-Sun.

National History Museum   ★

This is actually a great place to visit, especially after seeing all the other sights and coming to the conclusion that the Vietnamese must love to yawn. This is Vietnam's leading museum and the center for cultural and historical research. Granted it's tough to know exactly what you're looking at if you don't read Vietnamese or don't have a guide, but the exhibits here are impressive. It's all designed so you can walk though the different periods of Vietnamese history. There are some beautiful bronze Dongson drums and funeral urns, Nguyen Dynasty pieces, models of ancient cities, weapons from the Tay Son revolt and much more. If you're lucky, you may even get a private tour from one of the museum's curators. Open 8-12 and 1-4 p.m. Tues.-Sun. There is an admission fee.

Old Hanoi

Check out the old quarter of Hanoi, a maze of narrow back alleys with shops selling antiques, flowers and handicrafts.

Quan Su Pagoda

Built in the late 1930s, this pagoda is on a site that once served as the quarters for visiting Buddhist VIPs. Some of the Buddha sculptures inside the temple are exquisite. This place is usually packed with way-farers.

Temple of Literature (Van Mieu Pagoda)

This is the biggest temple attraction in Hanoi. It was founded in 1070 during the reign of Ly Thanh Tong. It is dedicated to Confucious and purportedly modeled after a temple in Shantung, China. There are courtyards, a big bronze bell and multi-storied roofs in the complex. The courtyards feature beautifully carved stelae.

Hanoi Environs

★ *Cat Ba*

Sixty km east of Haiphong can be found some of the best beaches in Vietnam, or that's what Hanoi officials would have you believe. Cat Ba Island has largely been declared a protected region and features tropical forests, mangrove swamps, towering dolomite hills, waterfalls, lakes, caves and, of course, gorgeous beaches. There's also a thriving animal population, including the Francois monkey.

Haiphong

Haiphong, with a population of more than 1 million, is the second largest city in the north and Vietnam's major port. For the most part, much of the area surrounding the city is actually an eyesore—a gray urban sprawl pockmarked with factories and bombed-out buildings, despite massive rebuilding in the city. The Americans pounded Haiphong during the Vietnam War and the Vietnamese purportedly downed more than 300 U.S. aircraft from the city's antiaircraft batteries. Today, there's a resort and even Vietnam's first casino. The hotels, though, are generally overpriced. Surprisingly, much of the old French colonial architecture survived the bombardment, mostly in the downtown area around the **theatre square**. A couple of kilometers south of the city center is the **Du Hang Pagoda**, said to have been built in the 1600s. Also check out the numerous street markets near Cau Dat Street.

★ *Ha Long Bay*

Ha Long Bay, 20 km past Haiphong, is targeted for tourism, but it's anyone's guess what form it will take and when it will take form. Nonetheless, the area has some rather breathtaking scenery, including beautiful limestone formations, sheer edifice cliffs, huge rock arches, peaceful coves and seemingly thousands of islets.

INSIDER TIP

It seems like Ha Long Bay is pretty close to the capital–after all, how long could it take to go a hundred miles? A long darn time. It's a trip that can easily take 6 hours or more–one way. The trip includes both a river and harbor crossing by ferry. So be warned; it's no day trip. If you're traveling alone you might be required to travel with a guide. As an American, you may be refused access to some areas, such as Pleiku, the former U.S. air base down south.

WHERE TO STAY IN HANOI

Bin Minh Hotel

    27 Ly Thai To Street. ☎ *266-441. FAX: 84-4-257-725* • *43 rooms.* Air con.; telephones; hot water. Good location. Moderate.

                                          Reservations: Direct.

Bong Sen Hotel

    34 Hang Bun Street. ☎ *254-017* • *26 rooms.* New hotel (1991) with air con. rooms; TV; refrigerator; attached bathrooms. Moderate.

                                          Reservations: Direct.

Boss Hotel

    60 Nguyen Du Street. ☎ *252-690. FAX: 84-4-257-634* • *15 rooms.* Air con.; TV; telephone; refrigerators; hot water. Moderate.

                                          Reservations: Direct.

Dan Chu Hotel

    29 Trang Tien Street. ☎ *253-323* • A 100-year-old building and it shows. Friendly service. Air con.; telephone; TV; dining room; lounge bar. Moderate.   *Reservations: Direct.*

Dong Loi

    94 Ly Thuong Kiet Street. ☎ *255-721* • *35 rooms.* Recently renovated. Basic accommodations. Restaurant. Inexpensive.

                                          Reservations: Direct.

Friendship Hotel

    23 Quan Thanh Street. ☎ *253-182* • Singles and doubles. Bar; gift-shop. Moderate.   *Reservations: Direct.*

Hong Ha Hotel

78 Yen Phu Street. ☎ *253-688* • *30 rooms.* North of the railway bridge. Air con.; telephones; TV; hot water; refrigerators. Not a bad deal. Inexpensive. ***Reservations: Direct.***

Pullman Metropole

15 Ngo Quyen Street. ☎ *266-919. FAX: 84-4-266-920* • *109 rooms (16 suites).* Totally renovated. The best hotel in Hanoi. All the rooms have air con.; attached bathrooms; IDD telephones; satellite TV; private safe deposit boxes; bar; restaurant with French and Asian cuisine; airport shuttle. Expensive. ***Reservations:*** ☎ *(800) 221-4542 in the U.S.*

Rose Hotel

20 Phan Boi Chau Street. ☎ *254-438. FAX: 84-4-254-437* • Near the railway station. Singles and doubles. Moderate. ***Reservations: Direct.***

Tay Ho International Hotel

Quang An, Tu Liem. ☎ *232-379. FAX: 84-4-232-390* • *118 rooms.* Nice digs but a bad location. Out in the boonies. Restaurant; bar; swimming pool; air con.; telephones; car rental; massage; TV; refrigerators. Moderate. ***Reservations: Direct.***

Thang Long Hotel

Giang Vo. ☎ *252-270* • Drab 10-story structure near Giang Vo, with service to match. Air con.; TV; 2 restaurants; shop; bar. Inexpensive. ***Reservations: Direct.***

Trang Tien Hotel

35 Trang Tien Street • Basic guesthouse fare, but popular with the backpacker set. Restaurant downstairs. A good place to trade trail stories. Inexpensive. ***Reservations: Direct.***

WHERE TO EAT IN HANOI

A Restaurant

Thang Long Hotel • One of two of perhaps the most creatively named eateries in Tomorrowland. Basic Vietnamese fare. The place seats hundreds. **B Restaurant** is a lot smaller and has a menu in English. Hooray.

Bodega Cafe

57 Trang Tien Street • For good pastries.

Dan Chu Hotel Restaurant

Where else? • Cheery atmosphere, average food. Menus in 3 languages.

Darling Cafe

33 Hang Quat Street • Decent Western food, cheap. Popular with backpackers.

Hoa Binh Hotel Restaurant

Hoa Binh Hotel • This is good, cheap, food.

Piano Restaurant

Hang Vai Street • Features some imported wines and beers; good shrimp and crab; live music.

Restaurant 202

202 Nha Hang Street • This may be the best restaurant in Hanoi. Both Vietnamese and Western food, but specializes in the latter.

Rose Restaurant

15 Tran Quoe Tian Street. ☎ *254-400* • This place is usually quite crowded. Both Asian and Western cuisine.

Sophia Restaurant

6 Hang Bai Street. ☎ *255-069* • There's a cafe downstairs and restaurant upstairs. Average.

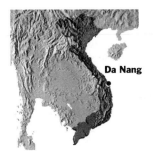

Da Nang

DA NANG IN A CAPSULE

Third largest city in Vietnam...and the principal port in the central part of the country...a repository of traditional art objects and architecture from the Cham dynasty, which dates from the 2nd century A.D. ...it was here that the French originally landed to begin their "excursion" into Vietnam...a century later, the first U.S. combat troops arrived to begin their Vietnam "excursion"...Da Nang fell to the Viet Cong in March 1975...it signified South Vietnam's defeat in the war...this is an ancient city with a rich cultural history...situated on a peninsula where the Han River flows into the South China Sea...today it's a thriving beach town and worth a couple of days' visit.

WHAT TO SEE AND DO IN DA NANG

Cham Museum ★★

Located where Tran Phu and Le Dinh Duong Streets meet. This houses probably the best collection of Cham art to be found anywhere. There are more than 300 artifacts in the museum, many dating to the 7th century. The buildings were constructed in 1915 and feature open, airy rooms, each containing a particular period or genre of work. There are beautiful sculptures reflecting the 1,000-year Cham period. The museum was founded the École Française d'Extrême Orient in 1915 and expanded in 1935. Check out the magnificent sandstone carvings. Indonesian and Malay influences are seen in the work before the 10th century, while Khmer influences become more apparent in the work after that date. Worth a few visits. Open 8-11 and 1-5 p.m. every day. There is an admission fee.

Cao Dai Temple

This is an interesting church on Haiphong Street. It's the second largest in Vietnam, next to the one at the sect's base in Tay Ninh. Prayers are held four times a day.

Da Nang Cathedral

Located on Tran Phu Street, this church serves Da Nang's Catholic community. Built in 1923 by the French, it's worth a peek for its single-spire, pink sandstone architecture.

Ho Chi Minh Museum

Here you can see various weaponry of the Vietnam War. There's also a replica of Ho's Hanoi house on display. Open 7-11 and 1-4:30 p.m. Tues-Sun.

Beaches

One of the best parts of any Da Nang visit is the beaches and there are some good ones in the Da Nang area. **China Beach** was an R&R area during the war and was made popular by the U.S. TV series of the same name. There's a hotel and a number of restaurants in the area. There's also **Nam O Beach**, about 15 km northwest of the city. It's a good place to see the locals' fishing boats. **My Khe Beach** is a little more than 5 km from Da Nang and one of the better beaches in the area. But watch out for the undertow. **Thanh Binh Beach** is often packed with locals and can be dirty.

Marble Mountains

These are the beautiful limestone peaks that rise above Da Nang. Because of their relative ruggedness and strategic location overlooking Da Nang, they were a favorite spot of the Viet Cong during the War. The VC could snipe at American troops below virtually uncontested. **Thuy Son** is a village in the mountains that sells local handicrafts. The **Tam Thai Pagoda** has also been carved into the mountains.

INSIDER TIP

If you do much traveling into the interior from Da Nang, remember that roads are often washed out between May and October, which is the wet monsoon season in Vietnam. Medical facilities are next to nonexistent; and doctors will, in many instances, demand cash on the spot or they may not take care of you.

WHERE TO STAY IN DA NANG

Pacific Hotel

92 Phan Chu Trinh Street. ☎ *221-37* • *48 rooms.* Basic accomodations; TV; refrigerators; restaurant. Inexpensive.   ***Reservations: Direct.***

Phuong Dong Hotel

93 Phan Chau Trinh Street. ☎ *212-66. FAX: 84-51-22854* • Air con.; TV; refrigerators; hot water. Inexpensive.   ***Reservations: Direct.***

Hai Au Hotel

177 Tran Phu Street. ☎ *227-22. FAX: 84-51-228-54* • *40 rooms.* Air con.; telephones; hot water; restaurant; bar; sauna; massage. Moderate.   ***Reservations: Direct.***

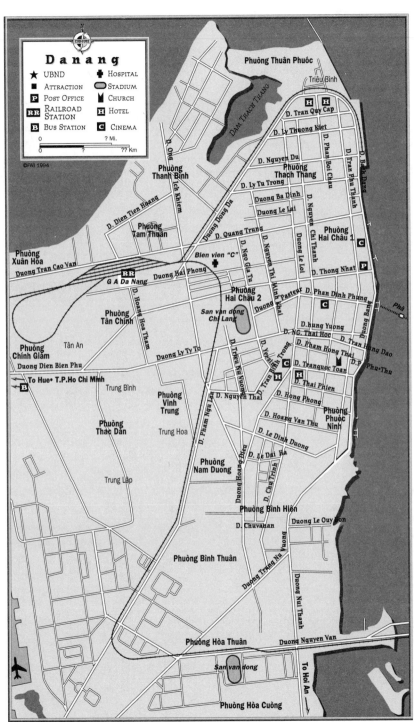

Danang

- ★ UBND
- ■ Attraction
- P Post Office
- RR Railroad Station
- B Bus Station
- ✚ Hospital
- Stadium
- Church
- H Hotel
- C Cinema

0   ? Mi.
0   ?   ?? Km

©FWI 1994

Phuòng Thuân Phuóc
Triêu Bình
ĐAM TRACH THANG
D. Tran Quy Cap
D. Ly Thuong Kiet
D. Nguyen Du
Phuòng Thach Thang
D. Ly Tu Trong
Duong Ba Dinh
Duong Le Lai
Phuòng Thanh Bình
D. Ong
Ich Khiem
D. Dien Tien Hoang
Phuòng Tam Thuân
Duong Dong Da
D. Quang Trung
Phuòng Xuân Hoa
Duong Tran Cao Van
RR
G A Da Nang
Duong Hai Phong
Phuòng Tân Chinh
D. Hoang Hoa Tham
Phuòng Chinh Giâm
Tân An
Duong Dien Bien Phu
To Hue• T.P.Ho Chi Minh
B
Trung Bình
Phuòng Vinh Trung
Trung Hoa
Phuòng Thac Dan
Trung Lâp
D. Pham Ngu Lao
Duong Ly Ty Tp
D. Trieu Na Vuong
D. Nguyen Thai
Phuòng Nam Duong
Duong Hoang Dieu
D. Le Dai Ha
D. Chu Trinh
Phuòng Bình Hiên
D. Chuvanan
Phuòng Bình Thuân
Duong Trang Na Vuong
Duong Nui Thanh
Phuòng Hòa Thuân
San van dong
Phuòng Hòa Cuông
D. Phan Boi Chau
D. Tran Phu Thanh
D. Bah Dang
Phuòng Hai Châu 1
C
D. Nguyen Chi Thanh
Duong Le Loi
Bien vien "C"
D. Ngo Gia Tu
D. Nguyen Thi Minh Khai
Phuòng Hai Châu 2
Duong Pasteur
San van dong Chi Lang
D. Yen Bai
D. Tran Bình Trong
C
H
D. Nguyen Thai
D. Hong Phong
D. Hoang Van Thu
D. Le Dinh Duong
D. Thong Nhat
P
D. Phan Dinh Phung
C
D.hung Yuong
D. NG. Thai Hoc
D. Pham Hong Thai
D. Tranquoc Toan
H
D. Thai Phien
Phuòng Phuóc Ninh
D. Tran Hung Dao
D.P. Phu•Thu
Phà
H H
Duong Le Quy Don
Duong Nguyen Van
To Hoi An

Huu Nghi

7 Dong Da Street. ☎ *225-63* • Air con.. Inexpensive.

Reservations: Direct.

Marble Mountain Hotel

7 Dong Da Street. ☎ *232-58* • Air con.; refrigerators; room service. Inexpensive. *Reservations: Direct.*

WHERE TO EAT IN DA NANG

Kim Dinh Restaurant

7 Bach Dang Street • This stretches out over the Han River. Good food, good views.

Restuarant 72

72 Tran Phu Street • Good shrimp spring rolls.

Tranh Lieh Restaurant

42 Bach Dang Street • Extensive menu.

Tu Do Restaurant

Tran Phu Street • Perhaps the best restaurant in Da Nang. Prices to match.

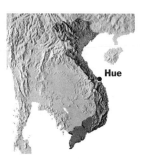

Hue

Hue was the capital of Vietnam during the Nguyen Dynasty (1802–1945).

HUE IN A CAPSULE

Hue served as the capital of Vietnam for more than 140 years...it houses ancient temples, imperial buildings and French-style edifices...was established in the 17th century...invaded by the French in 1833 and by the Japanese in 1945...was hammered by U.S. forces during the Tet offensive...many historical monuments were destroyed during this military action...but a great many remain.

WHAT TO SEE AND DO IN HUE

Citadel

This is a large, moated and walled area that has a perimeter of some 10 km. It was begun in 1804 by Emperor Gia Long. The Citadel used to enclose the entire city. Its 7m high walls were originally built of earth but it was decided in the 1820s to cover them with bricks. This laborious process took thousands of workers and years to complete. Even today, it is used as a military fortress. The most famous gate is the **Ngo Mon Gate**.

Forbidden Purple City

The imperial family and its entourage were the only individuals permitted to use this royal palace. There were 60 buildings situated in 20 courtyards. "Feminine" affairs happened in the west area of the complex, while the men did their manly things in the east area. Fighting during the Tet offensive ruined the complex.

Imperial City

This is in the Citadel and was built in the early 19th century and modeled after the Forbidden City in Peking. There are numerous palaces and temples within these walls, as well as towers, a library and a museum. There are also areas for religious ceremonies. The South Gate is the main entrance.

Khai Dinh Tomb

The last monument of the Nguyen dynasty was constructed between 1920 and 1931. It sits magnificently on the slopes of Chau E Mountain. It has a long staircase flanked by dragons. There are ceiling murals and ceramic frescoes.

Minh Mang Tomb

Built in 1840 by King Minh Mang and known for its magnificent architecture, military statuaries and elaborate decorations. It's perhaps the most beautiful of Hue's pagodas and tombs. You can get to this location, about 12 km south of Hue by tour boat or car.

Thien Mu Pagoda

A bizzare sight. Yes, it's a pagoda. But your curiosity is more peaked by something else. It's an old Astin. Yeah, a British car. It was the same car that brought the Buddhist monk Thich Quang Duc to Saigon. There he became the subject of Malcom Browne's famous photo. It shows the monk immolating himself in 1963. A copy of the photo is pasted on the windshield. Weird.

Tu Doc Tomb

This was once the Royal Palace of Tu Doc, who ruled Hue more than 100 years ago. There are pavilions in a tranquil setting of forested hills and lakes.

WHERE TO STAY IN HUE

Ben Nghe Guest House

4 Ben Nghe Street. ☎ *3687* • Attached bath; hot water. Rave reviews from backpackers. Inexpensive. ***Reservations: Direct.***

Hue City Tourism Villas

11, 16, 18 Ly Thuong Kiet Street and 5 Le Loi Street. ☎ *(11) 3753; (16) 3679; (18) 3964; (5) 3945* • These 4 properties get mixed reviews from travelers. Basic accommodations; fans; hot water. Inexpensive.

Reservations: Direct.

Hue Hotel

49 Le Loi Street. ☎ *3390. FAX: 84-54-3399* • *150 rooms.* Largest and the newest hotel in Hue. Air con.; tennis courts; 2 restaurants; disco; karaoke; swimming pool; post office; gift shop; TV; telephones; refrigerators; barbers; hairdressers; massage; hot water; all the amenities. Moderate—but for what it buys, it's cheap!*Reservations: Direct.*

Huong Giang Hotel

51 Le Loi Street. ☎ *3958. FAX: 84-54-3424* • *42 rooms.* 2 restaurants; cafe; gift shop; sauna; massage; car and bike rentals; air con.; refrigerators; attached bathrooms; hot water. Great deal. Often full. Moderate. *Resrvations: Direct.*

Kinh Do Hotel

Vo Thi Sau Street. ☎ *3036* • Rooms in 3 price ranges. Restaurant; bar; sauna; massage; dancing. Inexpensive to moderate.

Reservations: Direct.

Thuan Hoa Hotel

Nguyen Tri Phuonf Street. ☎ *2553* • Basic accommodations if a bit overpriced. Moderate. *Reservations: Direct.*

WHERE TO EAT IN HUE

Huong Giang Restaurant

51 Le Loi Street • Vietnamese and European cuisine.

Ngu Binh Restaurant

7 Ly Thuong Kiet Street • Food is average. Great place to meet new friends.

Song Huong Floating Restaurant

North of the Trang Tien Bridge on the bank of the Perfume River • Great Vietnamese fare at low prices.

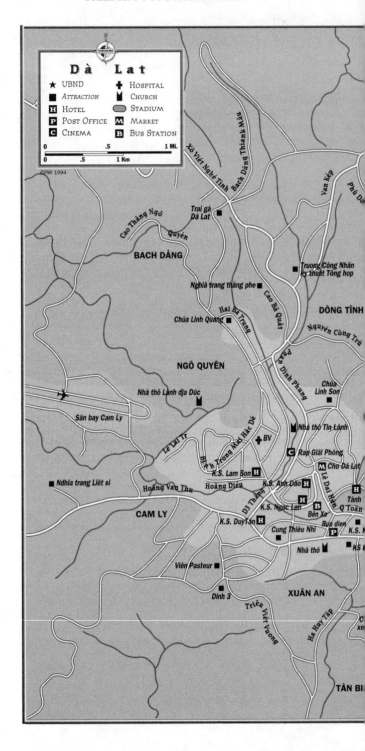

Dà Lat

★ UBND
■ ATTRACTION
H HOTEL
P POST OFFICE
C CINEMA
✝ HOSPITAL
M CHURCH
STADIUM
M MARKET
B BUS STATION

0   .5   1 Mi.
0   .5   1 Km
©FWI 1994

Xô Viết Nghê Tính
Bach Dáng Thành Mâu
Van Kép
Phà Dó

Cao Thâng Ngô
Quyén
Trai gà Dà Lat ■
BACH DÁNG
Truong Công Nhân ky thuât Tông hop ■
Nghĩa trang tháng phe ■
Cao Bá Quát
DÔNG TÍNH
Hai Bà Trưng
Chùa Linh Quang ■
Nguyên Công Trú
NGÔ QUYÊN
Phan Dinh Phung
Chùa Linh Son ■
Nhà thô Lành dịa Dùc ■
Sân bay Cam Ly
Le Lai Tr
Nhà thô Tin Lành M
✝ BV
Bình Trong Mai Hâc Dê
C Rap Giải Phòng
■ Ndhia trang Liêt si
K.S. Lam Son H
M Cho Dà Lat
Hoàng Diêu
K.S. Anh Dáo H
Lê Dai Hành
H Tành
Hoàng Vau Thu
D3 Tháng
K.S. Ngóc Lan
B Q Toàn
Bên Xe
CAM LY
K.S. DuyTân H
Cung Thiêu Nhi
Bưu diên
P K.S.
Nhà thô M
KS
Viên Pasteur ■
Dinh 3 ■
XUÂN AN
Triêu Viêt Vuong
Ha Huy Tâp
xe
TÂN BI

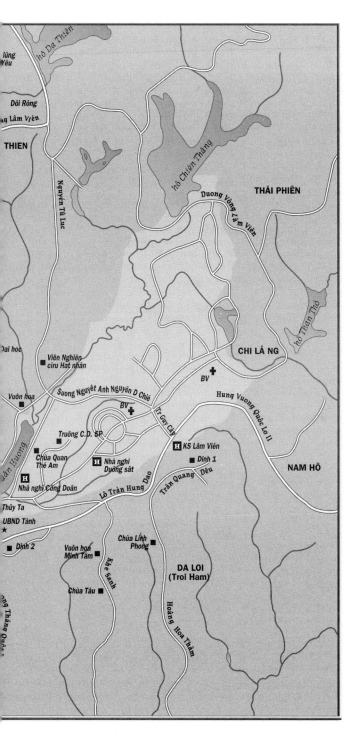

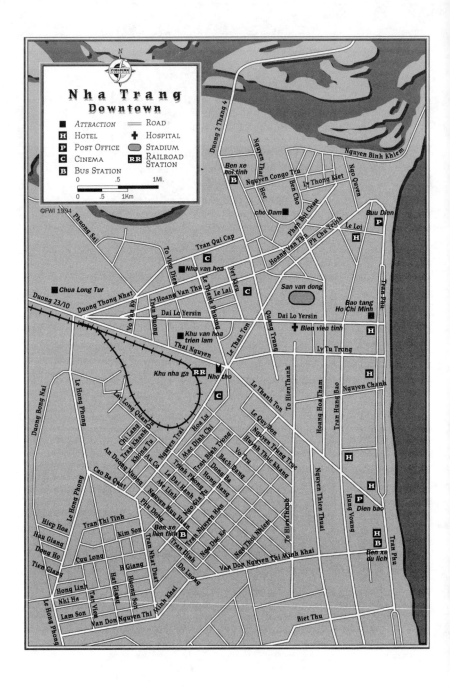

INDEX

Where in the World
is USA TODAY?

EVERYWHERE...

In over 90 countries around the globe,
USA TODAY's International Edition
brings world travelers all the news from home,
along with special features for Americans abroad.
Look for us whenever you travel in Europe,
the Middle East, Asia and the Pacific.
Because wherever you go – there we are.

Get the latest travel & entertainment information faxed instantly to you for just $4.95*

The new Fielding's fax-on-demand service.

Now get up-to-the-minute reviews of the best dining, lodging, local attractions, or entertainment just before your next trip. Choose from 31 U.S. and international destinations and each has five different category guides.

Take the guesswork out of last-minute travel planning with reliable city guides sent to any fax machine or address you choose. Select just the information you want to be sent to your hotel, your home, your office or even your next destination.

All category guides include money-saving "best buy" recommendations, consensus star-ratings that save time, and cost comparisons for value shopping.

Fielding's Cityfax™ now combines the immediacy of daily newspaper listings and reviews with the wit and perspective of a Fielding Travel Guide in an easy-to-use, constantly updated format.

Order a minimum of two or all five category guides of the destination of your choice, 24 hours a day, seven days a week. All you need is a phone, a fax machine, and a credit card.

5 different category guides for each destination

❶ Restaurants

❷ Hotels & Resorts

❸ Local Attractions

❹ Events & Diversions

❺ Music, Dance & Theater

Choose from 31 destinations

1 Atlanta	18 New York City
2 Baltimore	19 Orlando
3 Boston	20 Philadelphia
4 Chicago	21 Phoenix
5 Dallas	22 San Diego
6 Denver	23 San Francisco
7 Detroit	24 San Jose/Oakland
8 Hawaii	25 Santa Fe
9 Houston	26 Seattle
10 Kansas City	27 St. Louis
11 Las Vegas	28 Tampa/St.Pete
12 L.A.: Downtown	29 Washington DC
13 L.A.: Orange County	
14 L.A.: The Valleys	INTERNATIONAL
15 L.A.: Westside	30 London
16 Miami	31 Paris
17 New Orleans	

Order each category guide faxed to you for $4.95, or order all five guides delivered by U.S. Priority Mail for just $12.95 (plus $3.50 shipping and handling), a savings of $8.30!

Fielding's Cityfax™

CALL: 800-635-9777 FROM ANYWHERE IN THE U.S.
OUTSIDE THE U.S. CALL: 852-172-75-552
HONG KONG CALLERS DIAL: 173-675-552

Introducing first hand, "fresh off the boat" reviews for cruise fanatics.

Order Fielding's new quarterly newsletter to get in-depth reviews and information on cruises and ship holidays. The only newsletter with candid opinions and expert ratings of: concept, ship, cruise, experience, service, cabins, food, staff, who sails, itineraries and more. Only $24 per year.

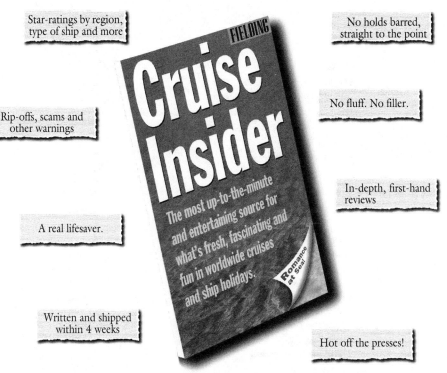

Star-ratings by region, type of ship and more

No holds barred, straight to the point

Rip-offs, scams and other warnings

No fluff. No filler.

In-depth, first-hand reviews

A real lifesaver.

Written and shipped within 4 weeks

Hot off the presses!

Fielding's "Cruise Insider" Newsletter is a 50-plus page quarterly publication, available at an annual subscription rate of only $24.00, limited to the first 12,000 subscribers.

Call 1-800-FW2-GUIDE to reserve your subscription today.

(VISA, MasterCard and American Express accepted.)

Order Your Fielding Travel Guides Today

BOOKS	$ EA.
Amazon	$16.95
Australia	$12.95
Bahamas	$12.95
Belgium	$16.95
Bermuda	$12.95
Borneo	$16.95
Brazil	$16.95
Britain	$16.95
Budget Europe	$16.95
Caribbean	$18.95
Europe	$16.95
Far East	$19.95
France	$16.95
Hawaii	$15.95
Holland	$15.95
Italy	$16.95
Kenya's Best Hotels, Lodges & Homestays	$16.95
London Agenda	$12.95
Los Angeles Agenda	$12.95
Malaysia and Singapore	$16.95
Mexico	$16.95
New York Agenda	$12.95
New Zealand	$12.95
Paris Agenda	$12.95
Portugal	$16.95
Scandinavia	$16.95
Seychelles	$12.95
Southeast Asia	$16.95
Spain	$16.95
The World's Great Voyages	$16.95
The World's Most Dangerous Places	$19.95
The World's Most Romantic Places	$16.95
Vacation Places Rated	$19.95
Vietnam	$16.95
Worldwide Cruises	$17.95

To order by phone call toll-free 1-800-FW-2-GUIDE

(VISA, MasterCard and American Express accepted.)

To order by mail send your check or money order,
including $2.00 per book for shipping and handling (sorry, no COD's) to:
Fielding Worldwide, Inc. 308 S. Catalina Avenue, Redondo Beach, CA 90277 U.S.A.

**Get 10% off your order by saying "Fielding Discount"
or send in this page with your order**

Favorite People, Places & Experiences

ADDRESS:	NOTES:

Name

Address

Telephone

Name

Address

Telephone

Name

Address

Telephone

Name

Address

Telephone

Name

Address

Telephone

Name

Address

Telephone

Name

Address

Telephone

Favorite People, Places & Experiences

ADDRESS:	NOTES:

Name

Address

Telephone

Name

Address

Telephone

Name

Address

Telephone

Name

Address

Telephone

Name

Address

Telephone

Name

Address

Telephone

Name

Address

Telephone

Favorite People, Places & Experiences

ADDRESS:	NOTES:

Name

Address

Telephone

Name

Address

Telephone

Name

Address

Telephone

Name

Address

Telephone

Name

Address

Telephone

Name

Address

Telephone

Name

Address

Telephone

Favorite People, Places & Experiences

ADDRESS:	NOTES:

Name

Address

Telephone

Name

Address

Telephone

Name

Address

Telephone

Name

Address

Telephone

Name

Address

Telephone

Name

Address

Telephone

Name

Address

Telephone

Favorite People, Places & Experiences

ADDRESS:	NOTES:

Name

Address

Telephone

Name

Address

Telephone

Name

Address

Telephone

Name

Address

Telephone

Name

Address

Telephone

Name

Address

Telephone

Name

Address

Telephone

Favorite People, Places & Experiences

ADDRESS: **NOTES:**

Name

Address

Telephone

Name

Address

Telephone

Name

Address

Telephone

Name

Address

Telephone

Name

Address

Telephone

Name

Address

Telephone

Name

Address

Telephone

Favorite People, Places & Experiences

ADDRESS:	NOTES:
Name	
Address	
Telephone	
Name	
Address	
Telephone	
Name	
Address	
Telephone	
Name	
Address	
Telephone	
Name	
Address	
Telephone	
Name	
Address	
Telephone	
Name	
Address	
Telephone	

Favorite People, Places & Experiences

ADDRESS:	NOTES:

Name

Address

Telephone

Name

Address

Telephone

Name

Address

Telephone

Name

Address

Telephone

Name

Address

Telephone

Name

Address

Telephone

Name

Address

Telephone

Favorite People, Places & Experiences

ADDRESS:	NOTES:

Name

Address

Telephone

Name

Address

Telephone

Name

Address

Telephone

Name

Address

Telephone

Name

Address

Telephone

Name

Address

Telephone

Name

Address

Telephone

Favorite People, Places & Experiences

ADDRESS:	NOTES:

Name

Address

Telephone

Name

Address

Telephone

Name

Address

Telephone

Name

Address

Telephone

Name

Address

Telephone

Name

Address

Telephone

Name

Address

Telephone

Favorite People, Places & Experiences

ADDRESS:	NOTES:

Name

Address

Telephone

Name

Address

Telephone

Name

Address

Telephone

Name

Address

Telephone

Name

Address

Telephone

Name

Address

Telephone

Name

Address

Telephone

Favorite People, Places & Experiences

ADDRESS:	NOTES:

Name

Address

Telephone

Name

Address

Telephone

Name

Address

Telephone

Name

Address

Telephone

Name

Address

Telephone

Name

Address

Telephone

Name

Address

Telephone